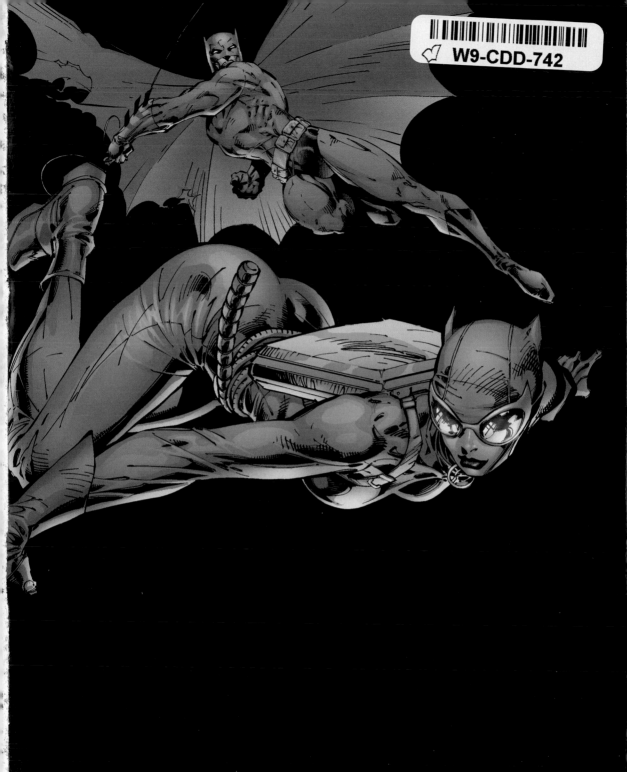

# BATMAN
# HUSH

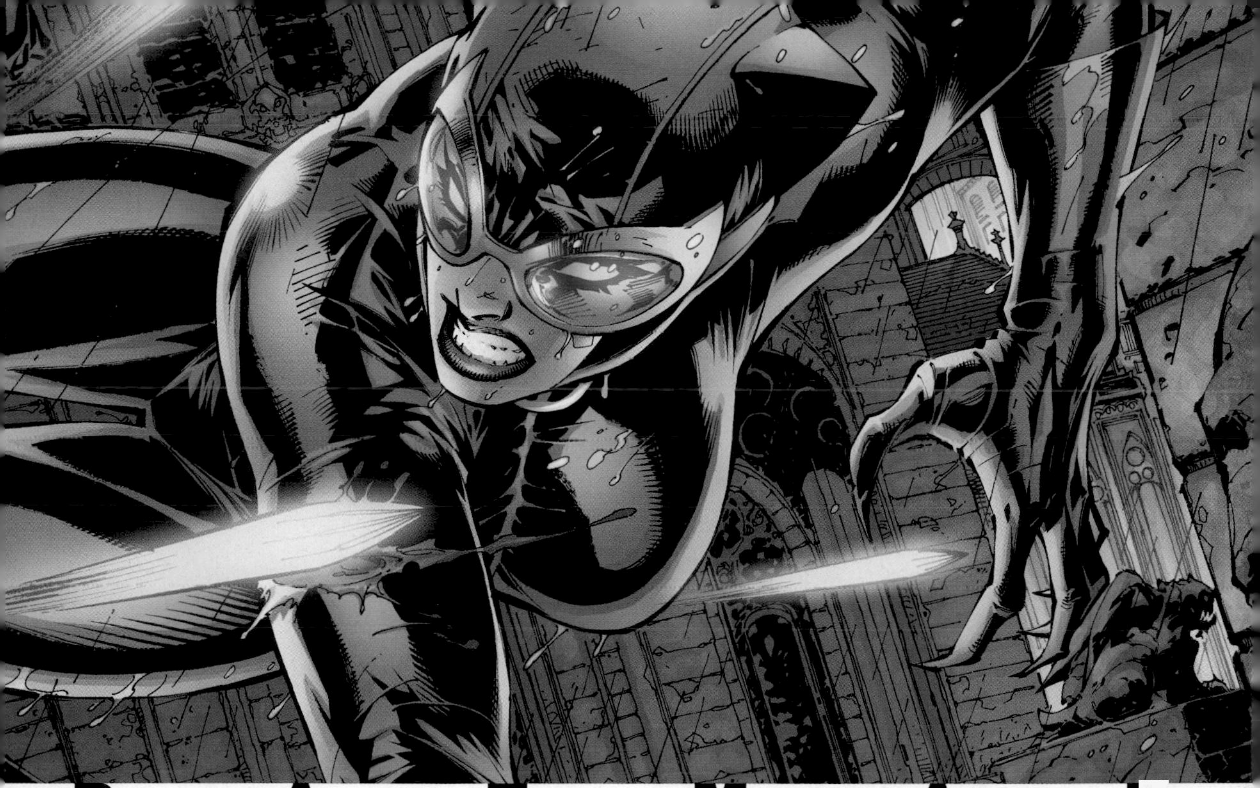

# BATMAN

# HUSH


**Jeph Loeb**
**Writer**

**Jim Lee**
**Penciller**

**Scott Williams**
**Inker**

**Richard Starkings**
**Letterer**

**Alex Sinclair**
**Colorist**

**Jim Lee & Scott Williams**
**Original series covers**


**BATMAN created by Bob Kane**

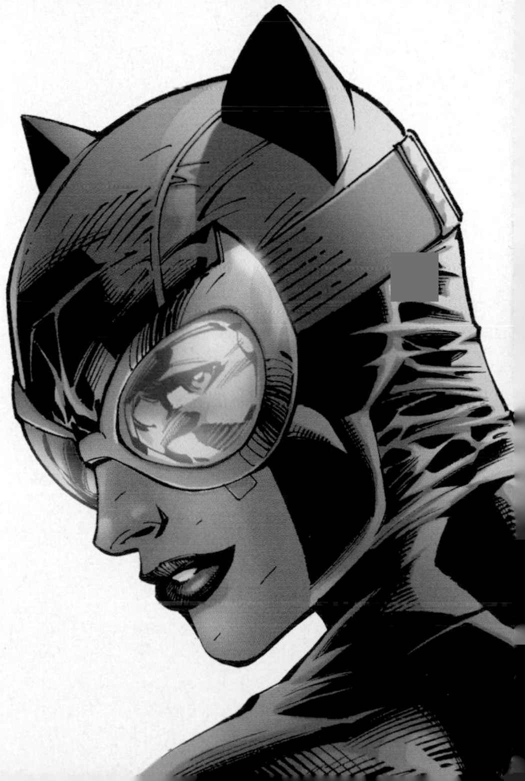

Bob Schreck  Editor-Original Series
Michael Wright  Associate Editor-Original Series
Morgan Dontanville  Assistant Editor-Original Series
Sean Mackiewicz  Editor
Robbin Brosterman  Design Director – Books

Bob Harras  Senior VP – Editor-in-Chief, DC Comics

Diane Nelson  President
Dan DiDio and Jim Lee  Co-Publishers
Geoff Johns  Chief Creative Officer
John Rood  Executive VP – Sales, Marketing and Business Development
Amy Genkins  Senior VP – Business and Legal Affairs
Nairi Gardiner  Senior VP – Finance
Jeff Boison  VP – Publishing Planning
Mark Chiarello  VP – Art Direction and Design
John Cunningham  VP – Marketing
Terri Cunningham  VP – Editorial Administration
Alison Gill  Senior VP – Manufacturing and Operations
Hank Kanalz  Senior VP – Vertigo and Integrated Publishing
Jay Kogan  VP – Business and Legal Affairs, Publishing
Jack Mahan  VP – Business Affairs, Talent
Nick Napolitano  VP – Manufacturing Administration
Sue Pohja  VP – Book Sales
Courtney Simmons  Senior VP – Publicity
Bob Wayne  Senior VP – Sales

Cover illustration by Jim Lee and
Scott Williams.
Cover color by Alex Sinclair.

BATMAN: HUSH
Published by DC Comics. Cover, text and compilation Copyright © 2009 DC Comics.
All Rights Reserved. Originally published in single magazine form in BATMAN 608-619, Wizard 0.
Copyright © 2002, 2003 DC Comics. All Rights Reserved. All characters, their distinctive likenesses and
related elements featured in this publication are trademarks of DC Comics. The stories, characters
and incidents featured in this publication are entirely fictional. DC Comics does not read
or accept unsolicited submissions of ideas, stories or artwork.

DC Comics, 1700 Broadway, New York, NY 10019.
A Warner Bros. Entertainment Company.
Printed by RR Donnelley, Salem, VA, USA. 3/31/14. Tenth Printing.
ISBN: 978-1-4012-2317-5

   Library of Congress Cataloging-in-Publication Data

Loeb, Jeph.
  Batman : hush / Jeph Loeb, Jim Lee, Scott Williams.
    p. cm.
  "Originally published in single magazine form in Batman 608-619, Wizard 0."
  ISBN 978-1-4012-2317-5
  1. Graphic novels. I. Lee, Jim, 1964- II. Williams, Scott. III. Title. IV. Title: Hush.
  PN6728.B36L637 2012
  741.5'973–dc23
                      2012024473

SUSTAINABLE
FORESTRY
INITIATIVE
Certified Chain of Custody
At Least 20% Certified Forest Content
www.sfiprogram.org
SFI-01042
APPLIES TO TEXT STOCK ONLY

When I was a little boy my family would get together in my father's den every Wednesday and Thursday night at 7:30 p.m. to watch a new television show called *Batman*. Twice a week, Adam West and Burt Ward would BIFF! BAM! and POW! with some of Hollywood's most notables playing The Joker, The Riddler, etc. While I'd like to lay claim to remembering best Julie Newmar's sleek cat outfit as my strongest memory, it only ranks a close second. My most vivid memory was actually of my father's backside blocking the television. You see, *Batman* had a very distinct message at the bottom of the screen below the logo: IN COLOR. My father had purchased a brand-new RCA color television and spent most of the show getting up and adjusting the reds and greens (it was a very colorful show) in order to get it, as he would say, "Just right." It didn't matter that the rest of us couldn't actually tell the difference each time he got up and twisted some knob; for my Dad there was a world of difference.

What does all this have to do with HUSH? Glad you asked. On a bright and sunny California afternoon, in the parking lot of the Warner Bros. studio, I met with Mark Chiarello (DC's Editorial Art Director), who had traveled out from the not so bright or sunny New York City to see if I would be interested in writing BATMAN on a monthly basis. Mark had the good (mis)fortune of being my editor on BATMAN: DARK VICTORY, the follow-up to my other Batman opus BATMAN: THE LONG HALLOWEEN, and despite having lived through that experience still wanted to gauge my interest.

# JUST RIGHT

INTRODUCTION BY JEPH LOEB

Before I answered, I asked (as I always do) the most important question any comic-book writer can ask before he takes an assignment. I don't care if you grew up reading every issue of *The Adventures of Pow Wow Jones* and this is your only chance to prove to the world that you and Pow Wow were made for each other, you have to ask:

"Who's going to draw it?"

Because, my friends, no matter how good a comic-book story is, it is still a visual medium. We don't write short stories, or novels, or poetry for that matter. We write stories that someone has to draw. And if you find yourself stuck with the unlucky reality of having someone draw your story that doesn't suit what you've got in your head, it's a little like trying to listen to a song you wrote for a piano played on a tuba. It's your song all right, it just doesn't sound ... well... "Just right."

I had a pretty good ace in the hole when I asked. I had only worked on Batman with Tim Sale, who is something of a master illustrator and has made me look better than I am on more than a few occasions. Mark knew Tim was busy. Who could Chiarello possibly come up with who was going to match my ace?

"Jim Lee."

The guy who, at a very young age, sold more copies of a single comic book than anyone else in history. (A record he still holds today — at about 8 million.)

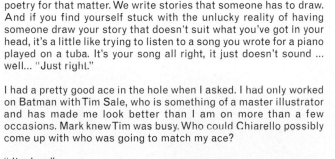

I gulped. If I had the Ace of Hearts, Mark threw down the Ace of Diamonds. Now, we can sit here until tomorrow morning and argue who was better — Michelangelo or da Vinci, but let's save the time and accept that they are both great artists. Different but, no question about it, brilliant. That's how I feel about Tim and Jim.

So, I did what any writer would do without asking how much the job paid. I said "Yes."

Now I had a bigger problem. What story was I going to tell? The greatest challenge a comic-book writer faces is making sure that the story suits the artist's strengths. (Don't forget about that tuba!). Tim and I had only told stories that took place in the mythical "Year One." This is where Batman is starting out and has no Robin or Nightwing or Oracle as part of his cadre. He makes mistakes because he's learning his detective craft, and he has an uneasy alliance with the Gotham City police force.

Jim and I were going to be working in the "Present Day" continuity of Batman. The Dark Knight's at the top of his game now, having inspired a Robin or three, Nightwing, two Batgirls, and an Oracle. Kind of like the dozens of artists who followed Jim's spectacular rocket to comic-book stardom. Gotham City is now his to protect, and he does a damn fine job of it. Kind of like the comic-book industry as a whole, and the contribution Jim has made to it as both a creator and a publisher. The trick is, when you're that good, you need a bigger challenge. Kind of like... Jim.

Where Tim works well in the shadows and ink, Jim demands that you see it all. The magic is in the details. What glorious details! Backgrounds and Batmobiles and babes! Catwoman! Poison Ivy! And... a certain Man of Steel!

I'll let you in on a little secret. No, it's not who or what is the mysterious person in the bandages who seems to have something to do with Batman's plight. This is better. Jim doesn't do his wizardry alone. Nope. He has help.

Scott Williams has inked Jim for longer than either of them likes to admit. If Jim ever needed another arm, it's Scott. Jim's pencils are good, mind you, but Scott has a way of making them glimmer. Scott is more than an inker — he's a partner and advisor. When I've asked if something looks "Just right," we've often deferred to Scott.

He just knows, um... righter.

That only gets us to the black and white of it all. Jim's handpicked colorist is Alex Sinclair. The result is the spectacular vibrancy of color you'll see throughout these chapters. If comics have made a single gigantic leap in the last sixty-odd years, it's in the area of color. Look inside and see what Alex has created!

In fairness to Jim, I can't do anything with my story without help as well. My advisor and "partner in words" is Richard Starkings, who, along with Wes Abbott, has lettered these chapters with such style that even the offbeat notes sound like sweet harmony. As you read the story, take a moment to look at the words themselves. That's Richard's gift.

None of this is possible without the amazing Bat-editorial staff, led by Morgan Dontanville and the Keeper of The Cave, Bob Schreck.

Hopefully, when you've read this collection you'll sit back and relax and say to yourself, "Yep, they got it just right."

— Jeph Loeb
New Year's Day, 2003
Los Angeles, California

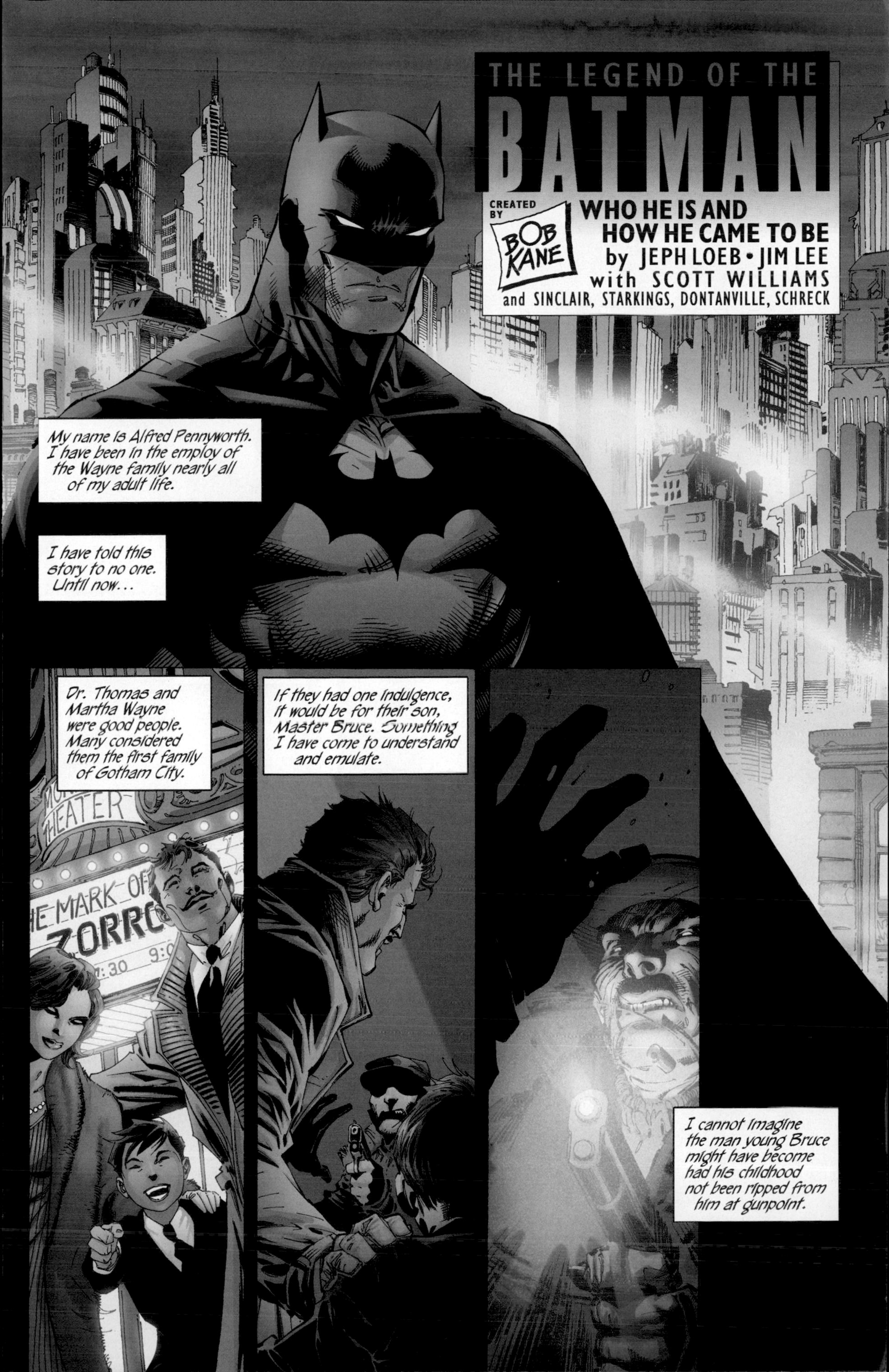
THE LEGEND OF THE
BATMAN
CREATED BY BOB KANE
WHO HE IS AND HOW HE CAME TO BE
by JEPH LOEB • JIM LEE
with SCOTT WILLIAMS
and SINCLAIR, STARKINGS, DONTANVILLE, SCHRECK
My name is Alfred Pennyworth. I have been in the employ of the Wayne family nearly all of my adult life.
I have told this story to no one. Until now...
Dr. Thomas and Martha Wayne were good people. Many considered them the first family of Gotham City.
THEATER
THE MARK OF ZORRO
7:30 9:0
If they had one indulgence, it would be for their son, Master Bruce. Something I have come to understand and emulate.
I cannot imagine the man young Bruce might have become had his childhood not been ripped from him at gunpoint.

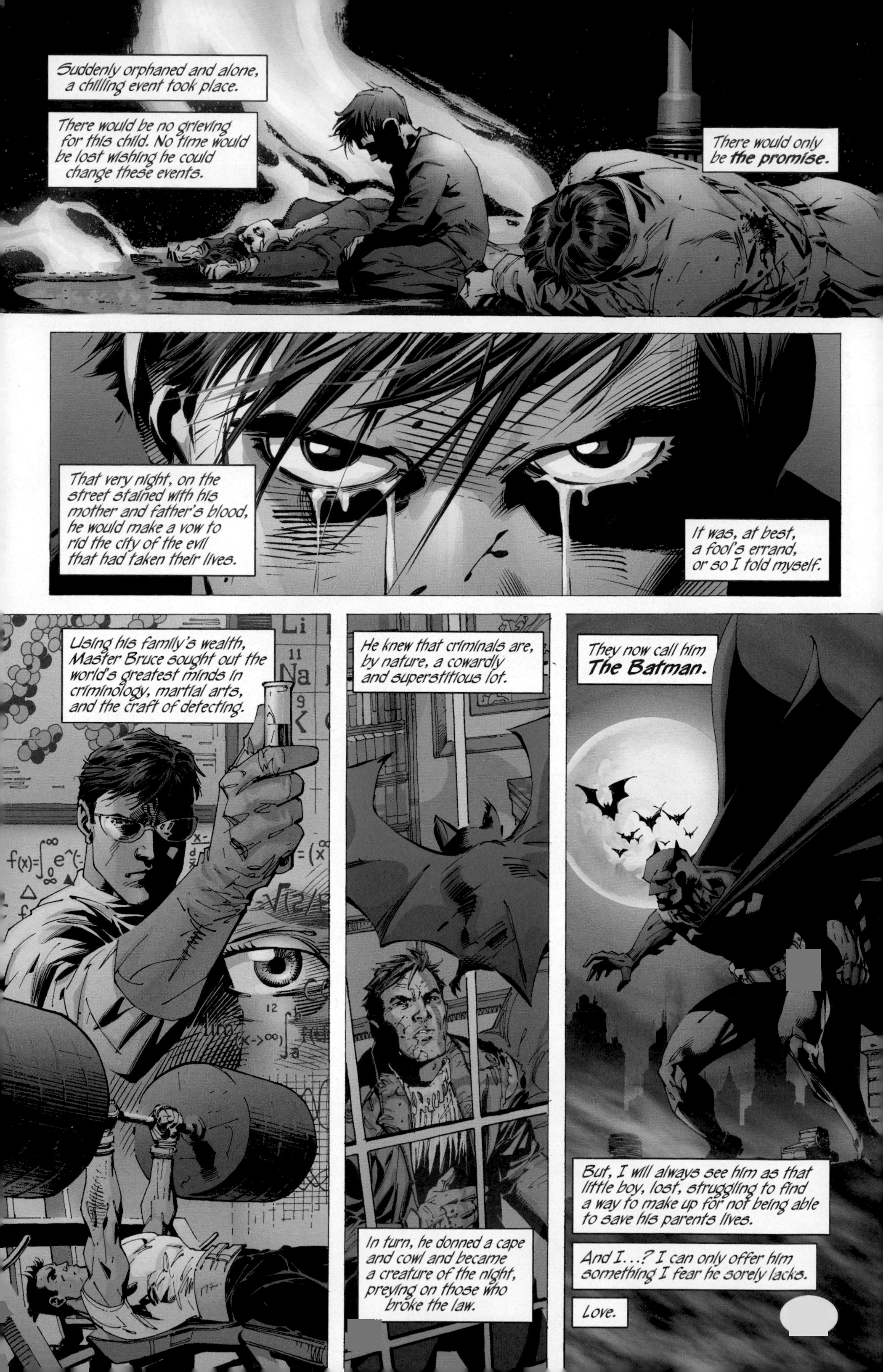

Suddenly orphaned and alone, a chilling event took place.
There would be no grieving for this child. No time would be lost wishing he could change these events.
There would only be **the promise.**
That very night, on the street stained with his mother and father's blood, he would make a vow to rid the city of the evil that had taken their lives.
It was, at best, a fool's errand, or so I told myself.
Using his family's wealth, Master Bruce sought out the world's greatest minds in criminology, martial arts, and the craft of detecting.
He knew that criminals are, by nature, a cowardly and superstitious lot.
In turn, he donned a cape and cowl and became a creature of the night, preying on those who broke the law.
They now call him **The Batman.**
But, I will always see him as that little boy, lost, struggling to find a way to make up for not being able to save his parents lives.
And I...? I can only offer him something I fear he sorely lacks.
Love.

BATMAN 608

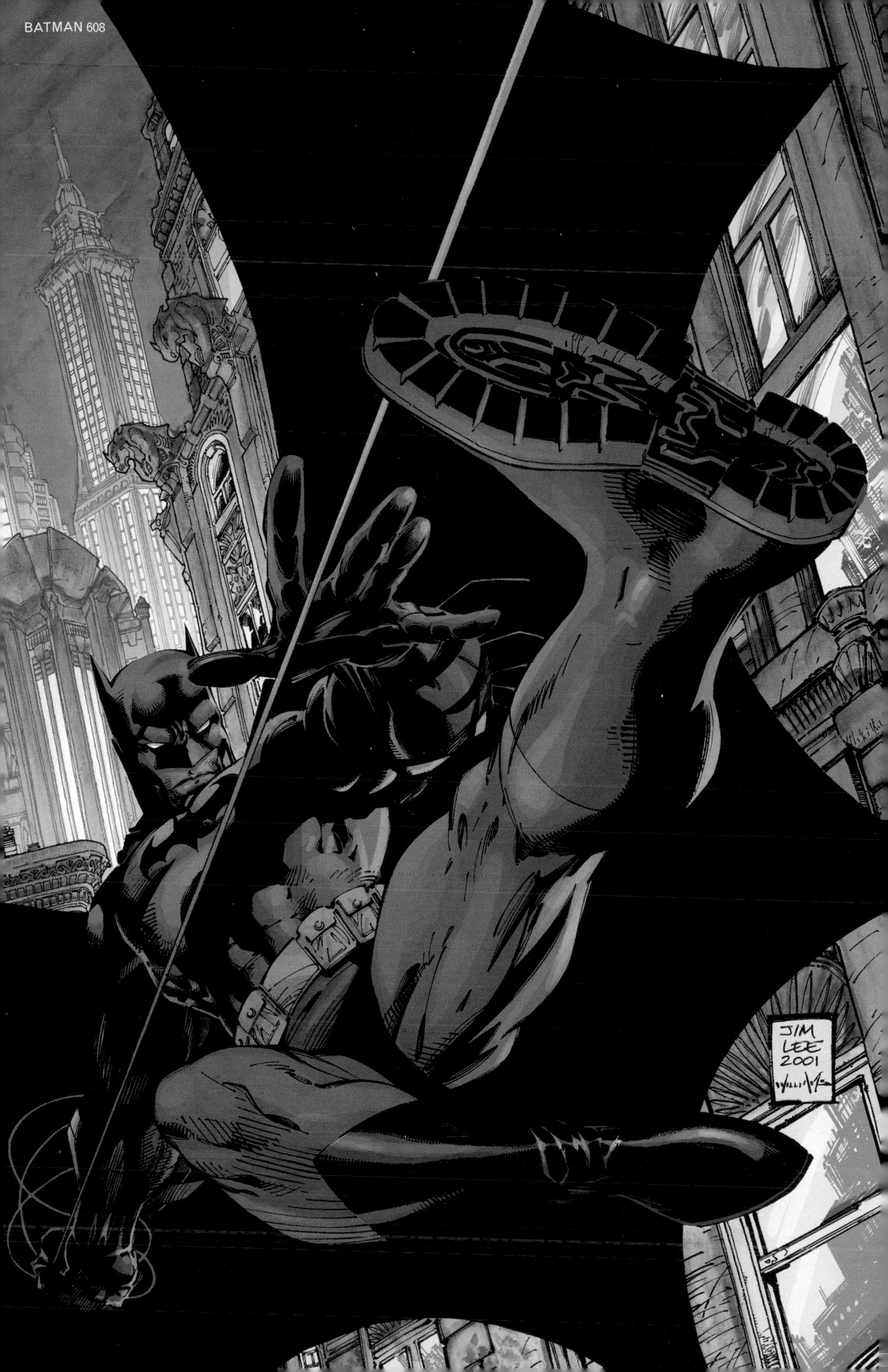
JIM
LEE
2001

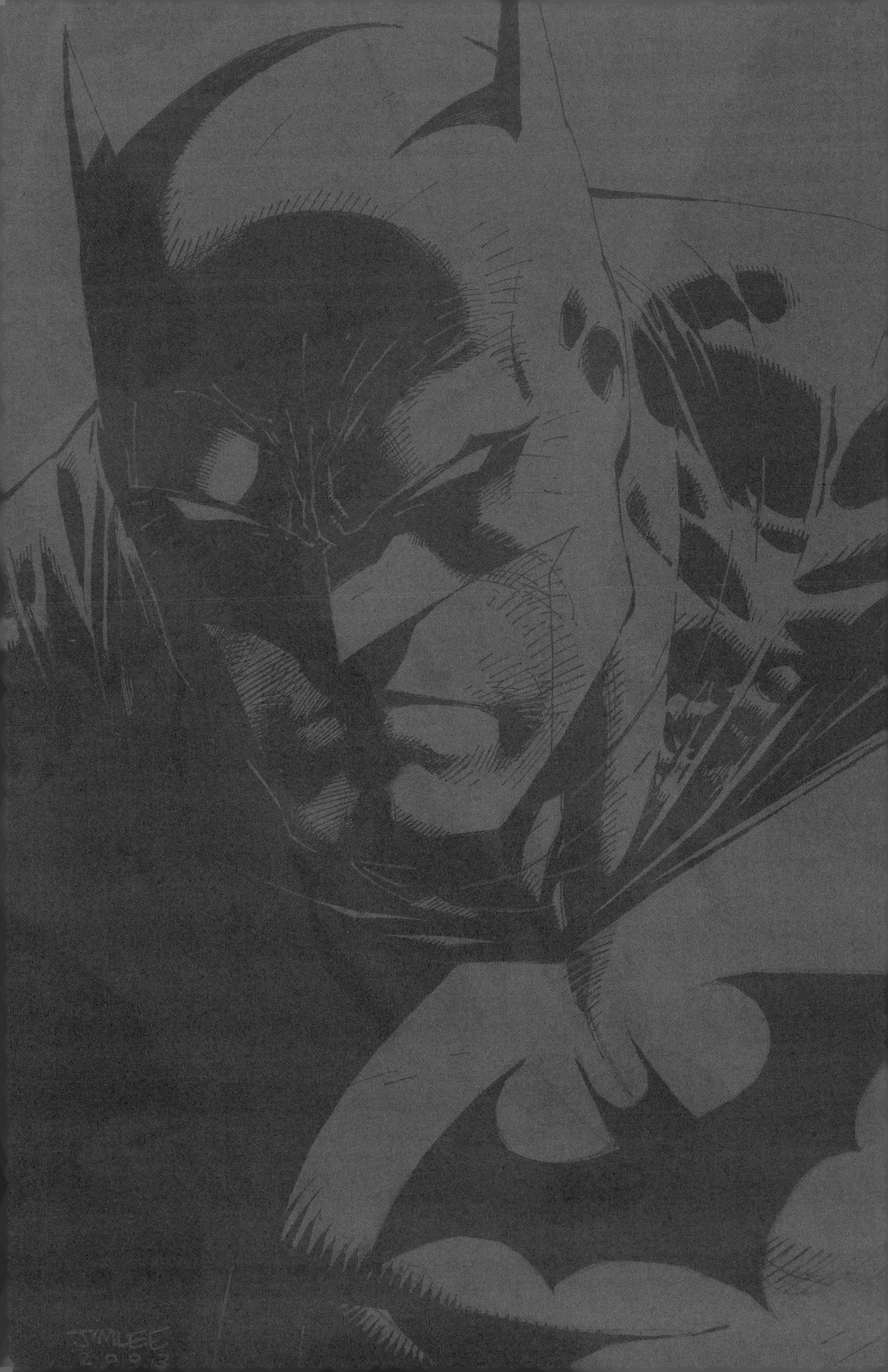

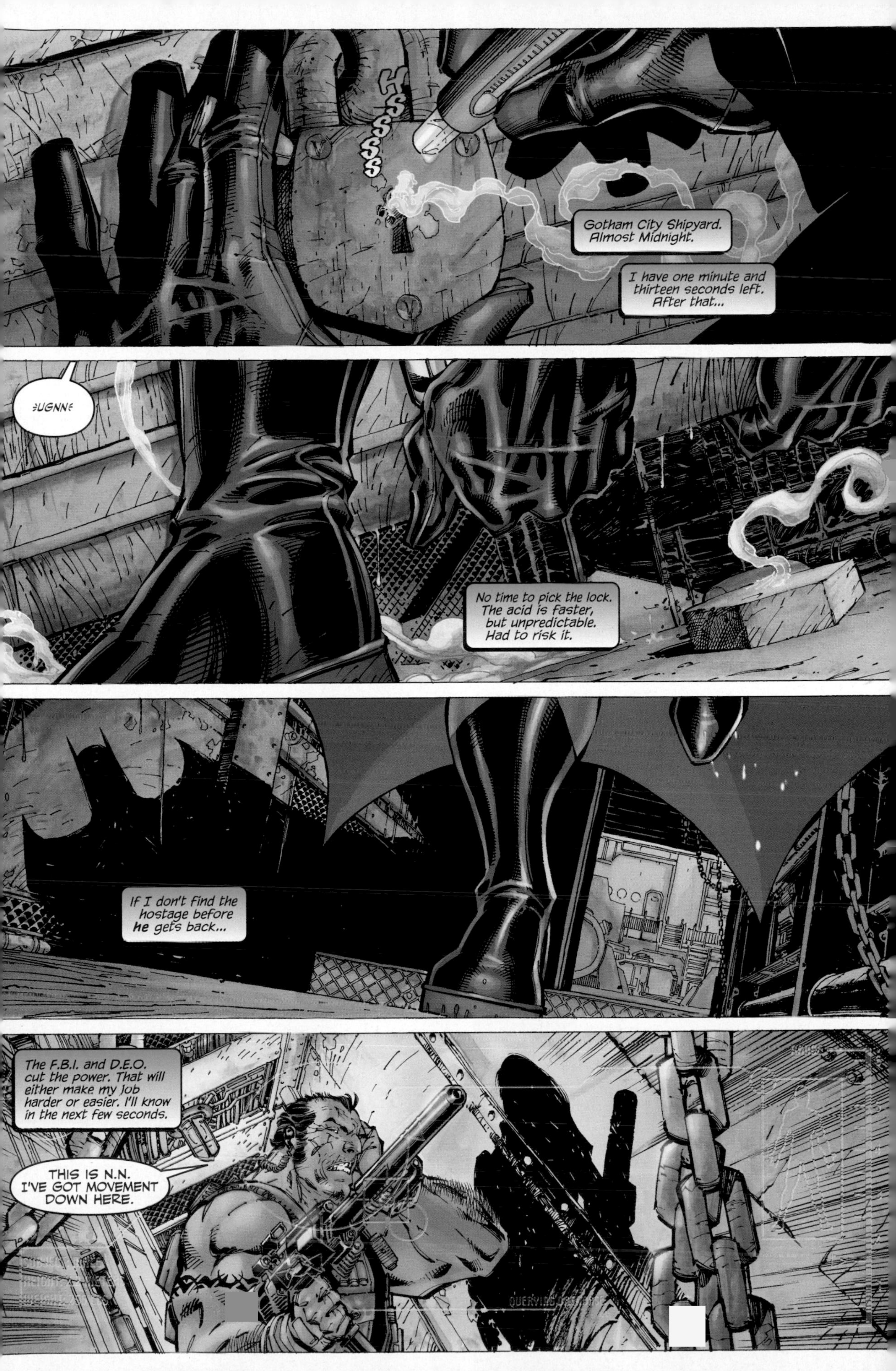
HSSSSS
Gotham City Shipyard. Almost Midnight.
I have one minute and thirteen seconds left. After that...
UGNN
No time to pick the lock. The acid is faster, but unpredictable. Had to risk it.
If I don't find the hostage before he gets back...
The F.B.I. and D.E.O. cut the power. That will either make my job harder or easier. I'll know in the next few seconds.
THIS IS N.N. I'VE GOT MOVEMENT DOWN HERE.

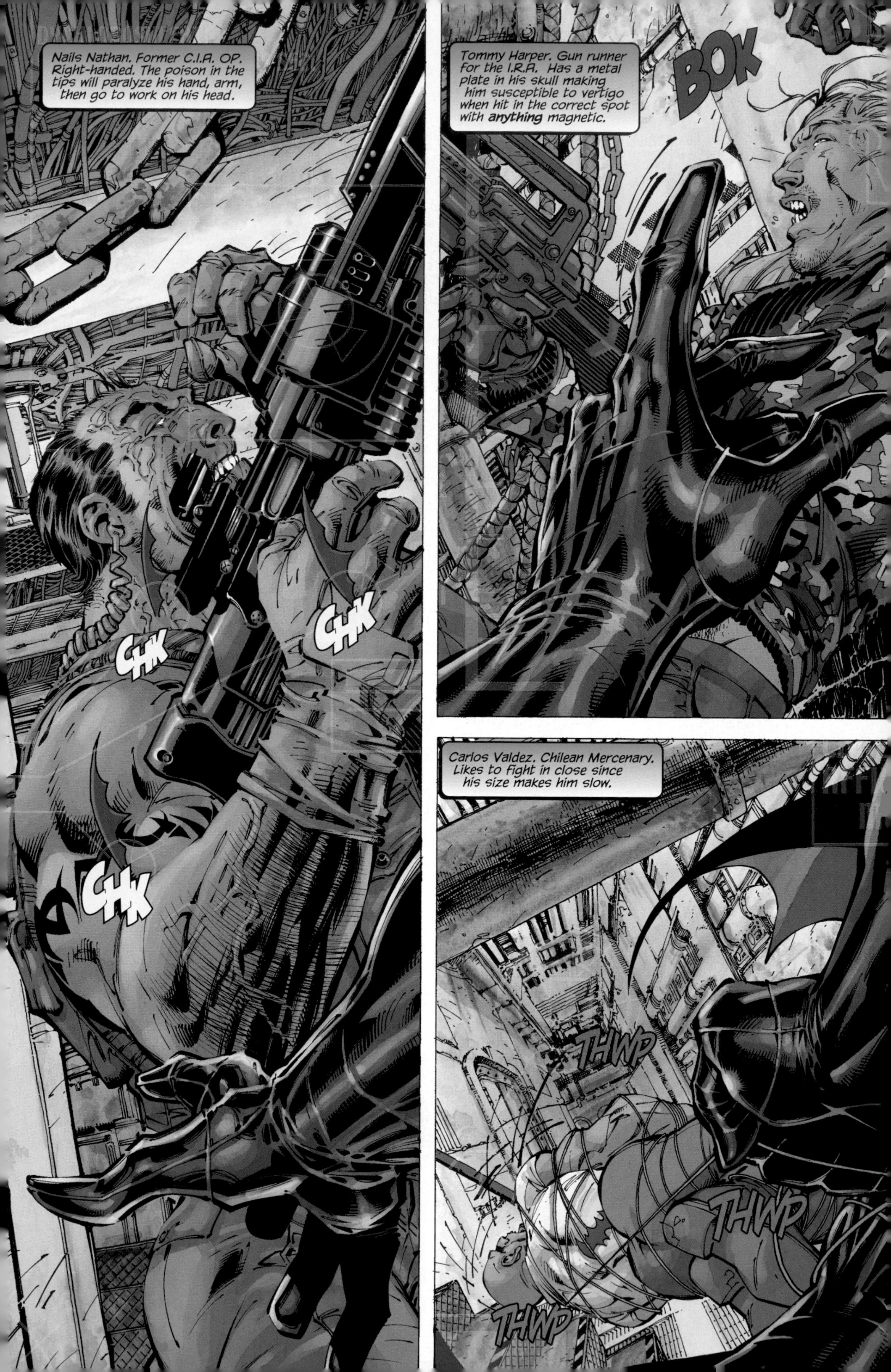
Nails Nathan. Former C.I.A. OP. Right-handed. The poison in the tips will paralyze his hand, arm, then go to work on his head.
CHK
CHK
CHK
Tommy Harper. Gun runner for the I.R.A. Has a metal plate in his skull making him susceptible to vertigo when hit in the correct spot with **anything** magnetic.
BOK
Carlos Valdez. Chilean Mercenary. Likes to fight in close since his size makes him slow.
THWP
THWP
THWP

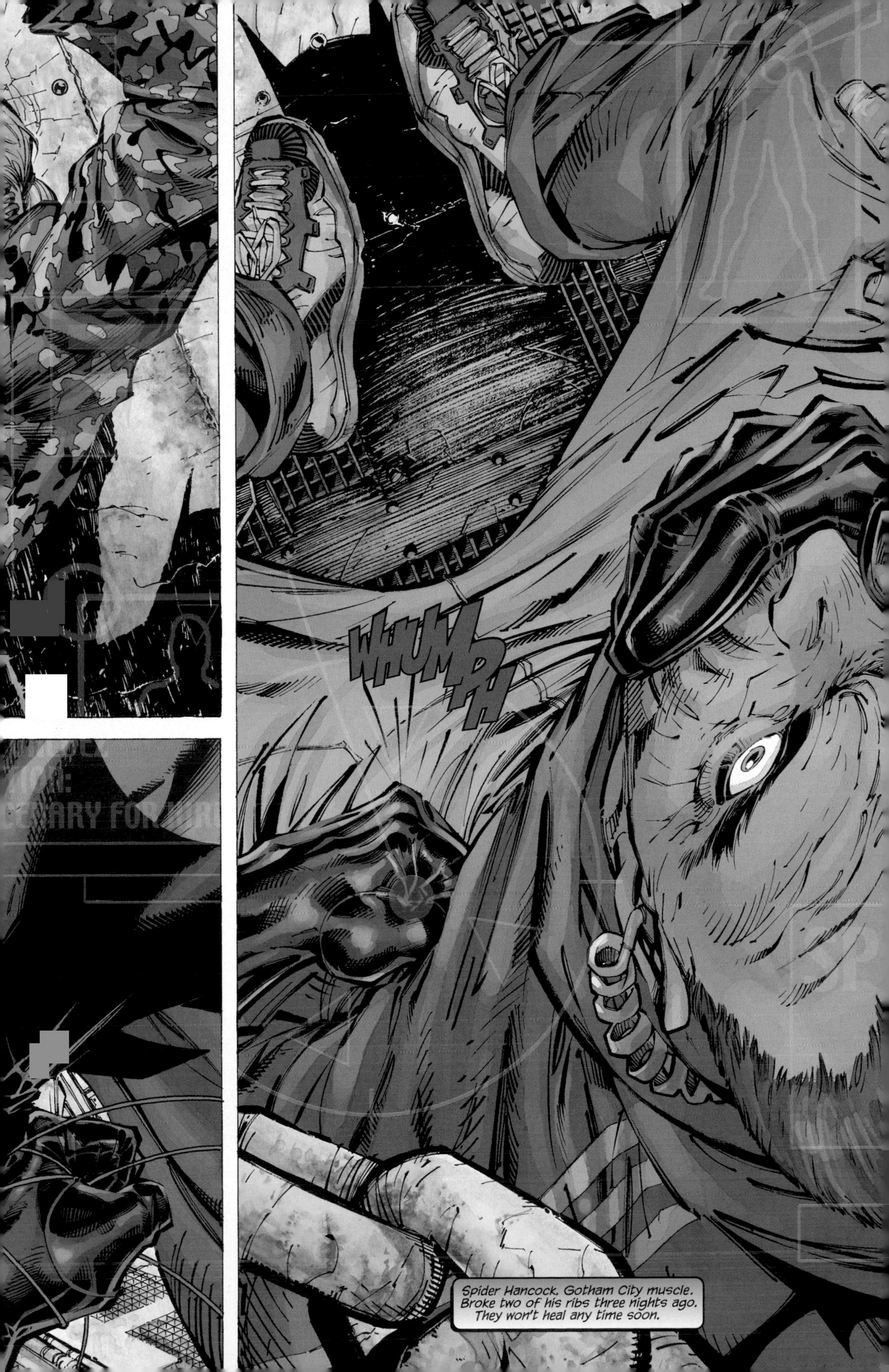
WHUMPH
Spider Hancock, Gotham City muscle. Broke two of his ribs three nights ago. They won't heal any time soon.

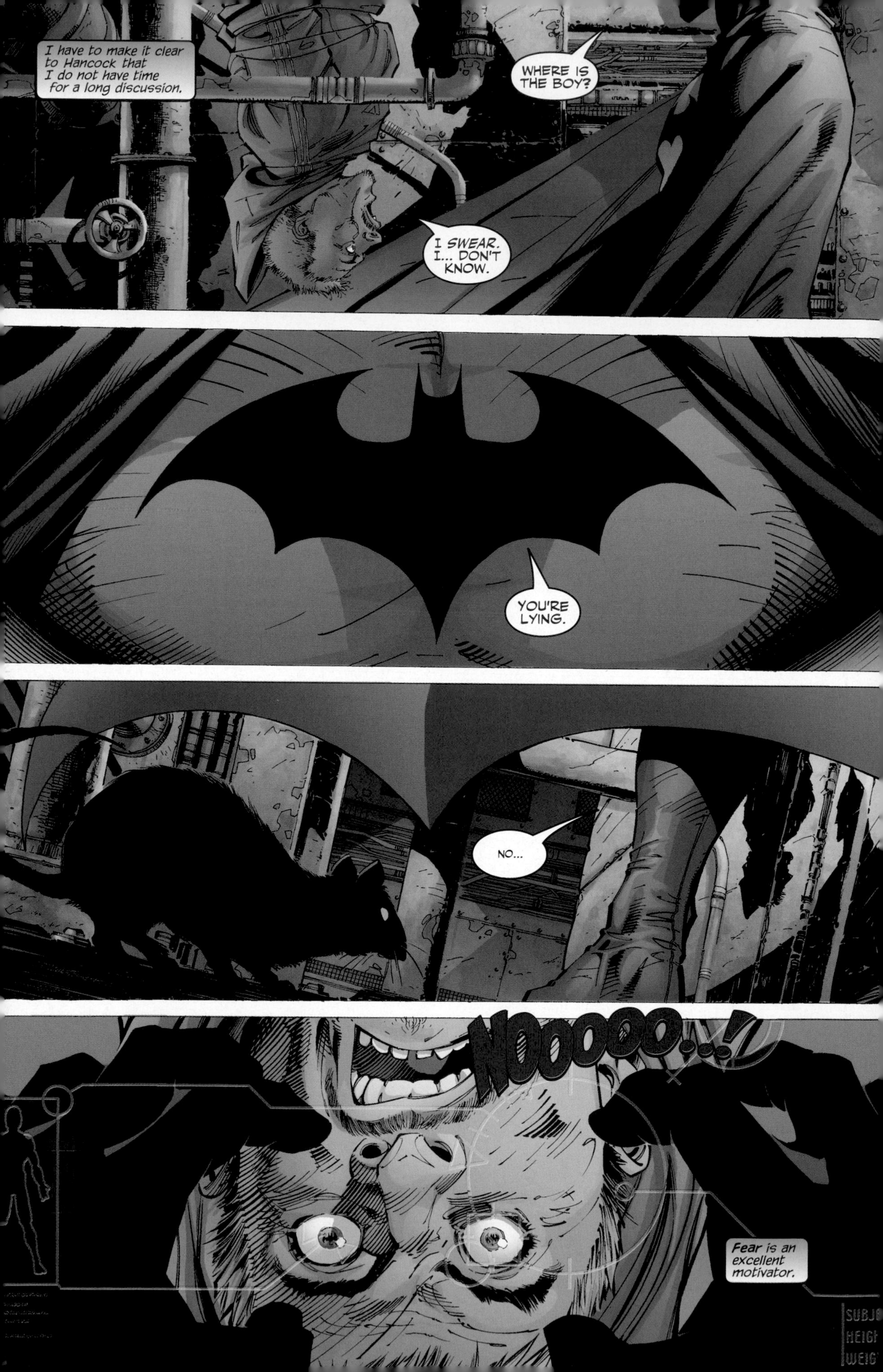

I have to make it clear to Hancock that I do not have time for a long discussion.
WHERE IS THE BOY?
I SWEAR. I... DON'T KNOW.
YOU'RE LYING.
NO...
NOOOOO...!
Fear is an excellent motivator.

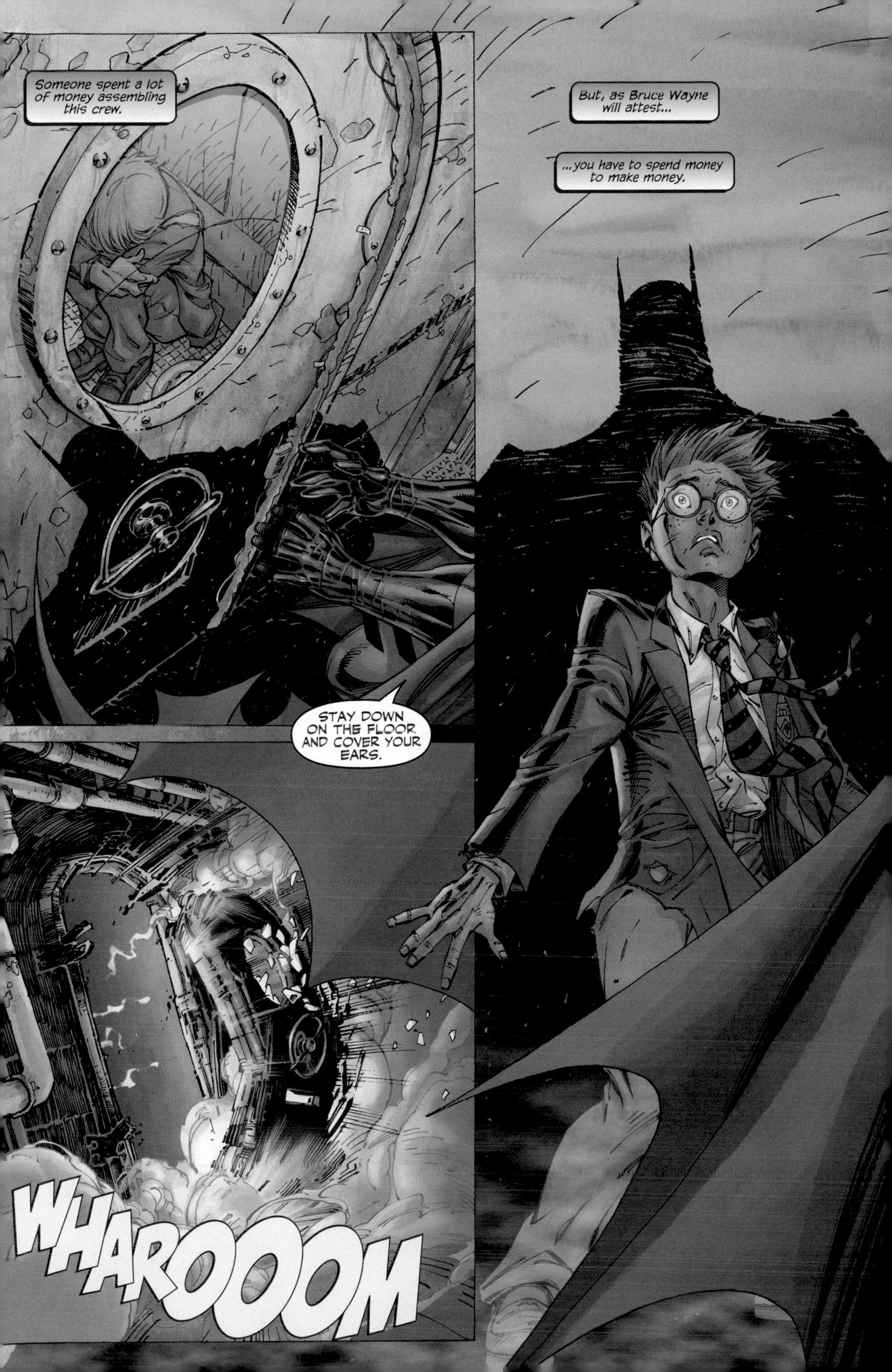
Someone spent a lot of money assembling this crew.
STAY DOWN ON THE FLOOR AND COVER YOUR EARS.
WHAROOOM
But, as Bruce Wayne will attest...
...you have to spend money to make money.

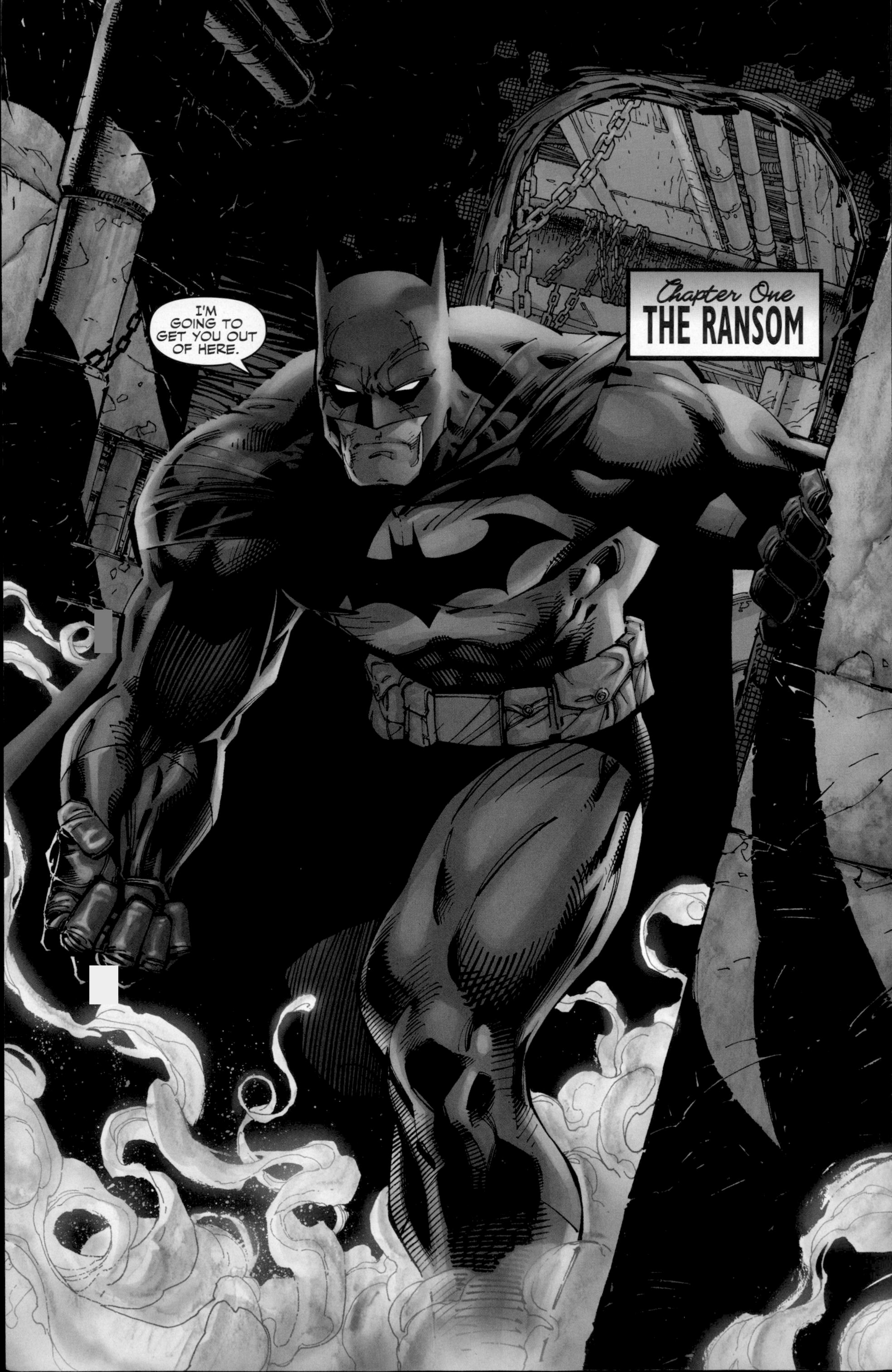
Chapter One
THE RANSOM
I'M GOING TO GET YOU OUT OF HERE.

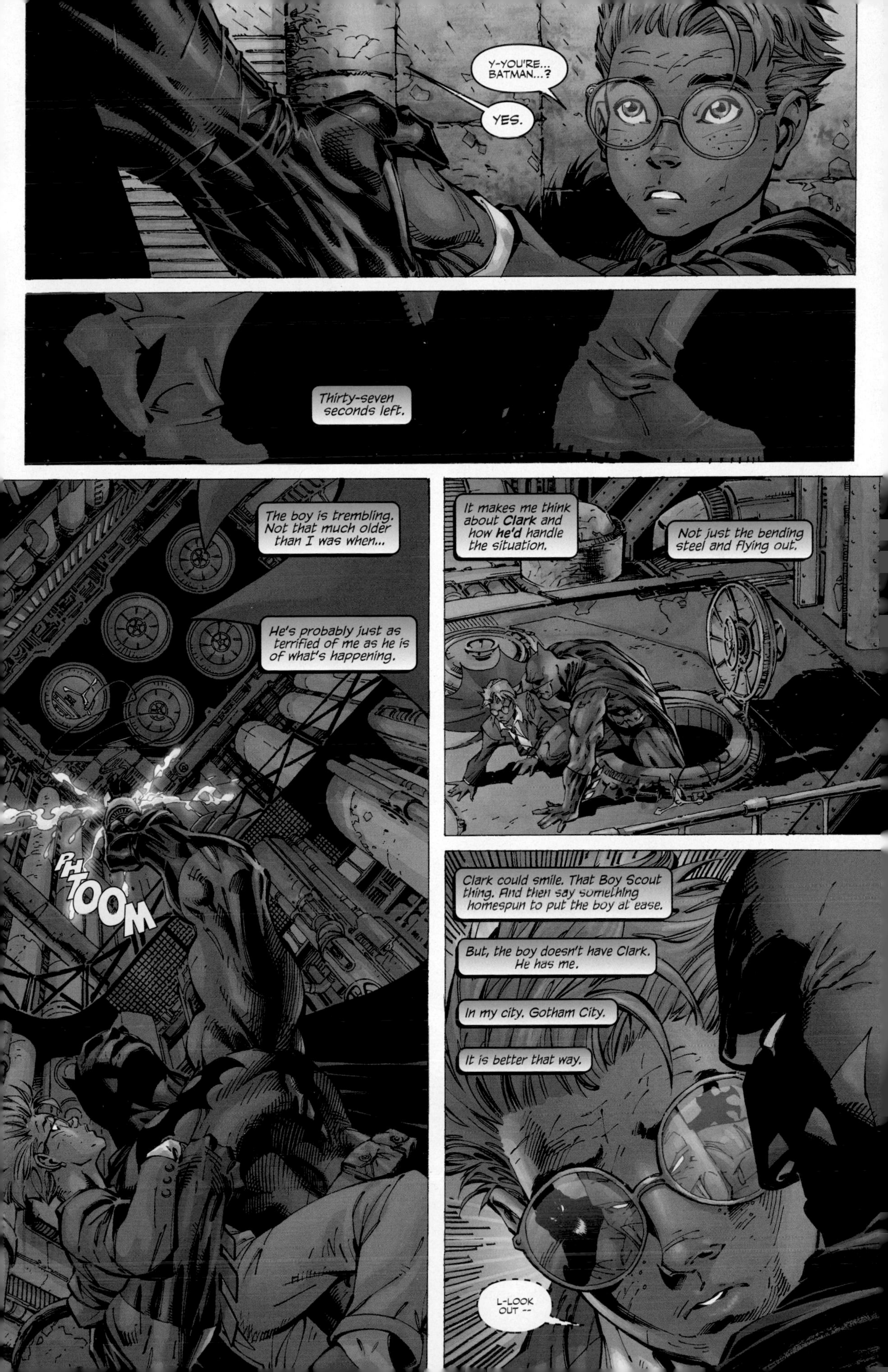
Y-YOU'RE... BATMAN...?
YES.
Thirty-seven seconds left.
The boy is trembling. Not that much older than I was when...
He's probably just as terrified of me as he is of what's happening.
PHTOOM
It makes me think about **Clark** and how **he'd** handle the situation.
Not just the bending steel and flying out.
Clark could smile. That Boy Scout thing. And then say something homespun to put the boy at ease.
But, the boy doesn't have Clark. He has me.
In my city. Gotham City.
It is better that way.
L-LOOK OUT --

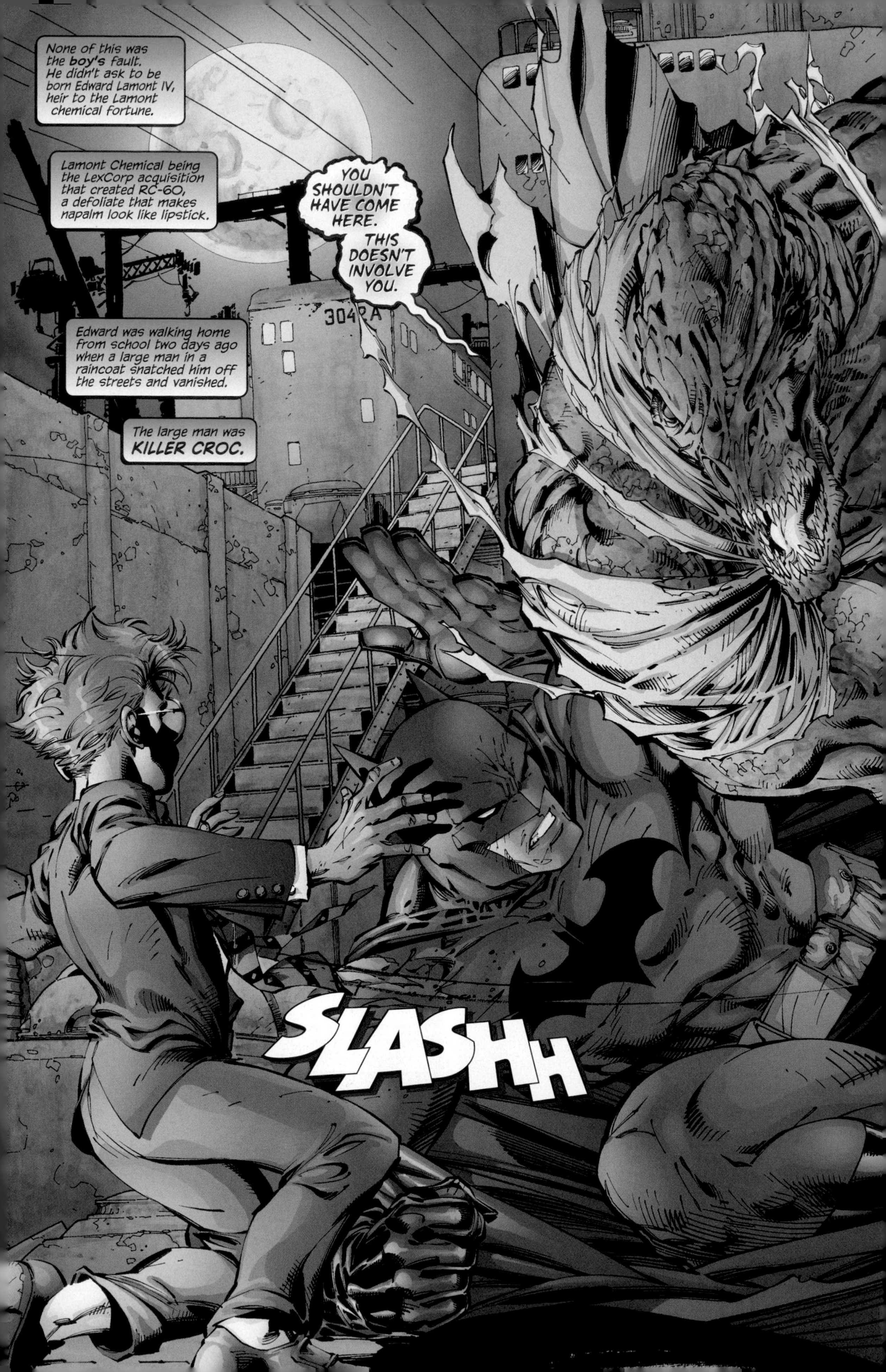
None of this was the boy's fault. He didn't ask to be born Edward Lamont IV, heir to the Lamont chemical fortune.
Lamont Chemical being the LexCorp acquisition that created RC-60, a defoliate that makes napalm look like lipstick.
YOU SHOULDN'T HAVE COME HERE.
THIS DOESN'T INVOLVE YOU.
Edward was walking home from school two days ago when a large man in a raincoat snatched him off the streets and vanished.
The large man was KILLER CROC.
SLASHH

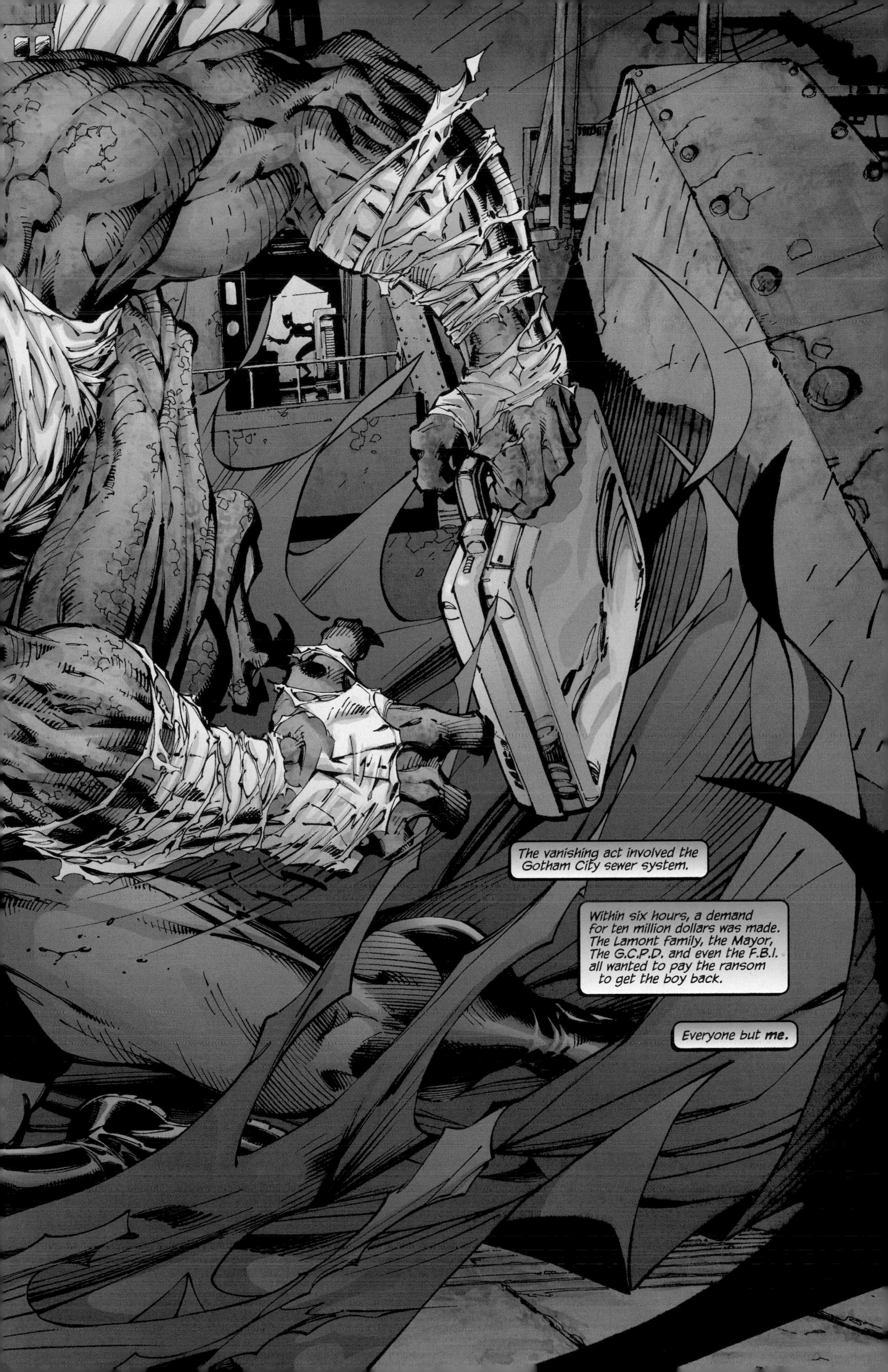
The vanishing act involved the Gotham City sewer system.
Within six hours, a demand for ten million dollars was made. The Lamont family, the Mayor, The G.C.P.D. and even the F.B.I. all wanted to pay the ransom to get the boy back.
Everyone but **me.**

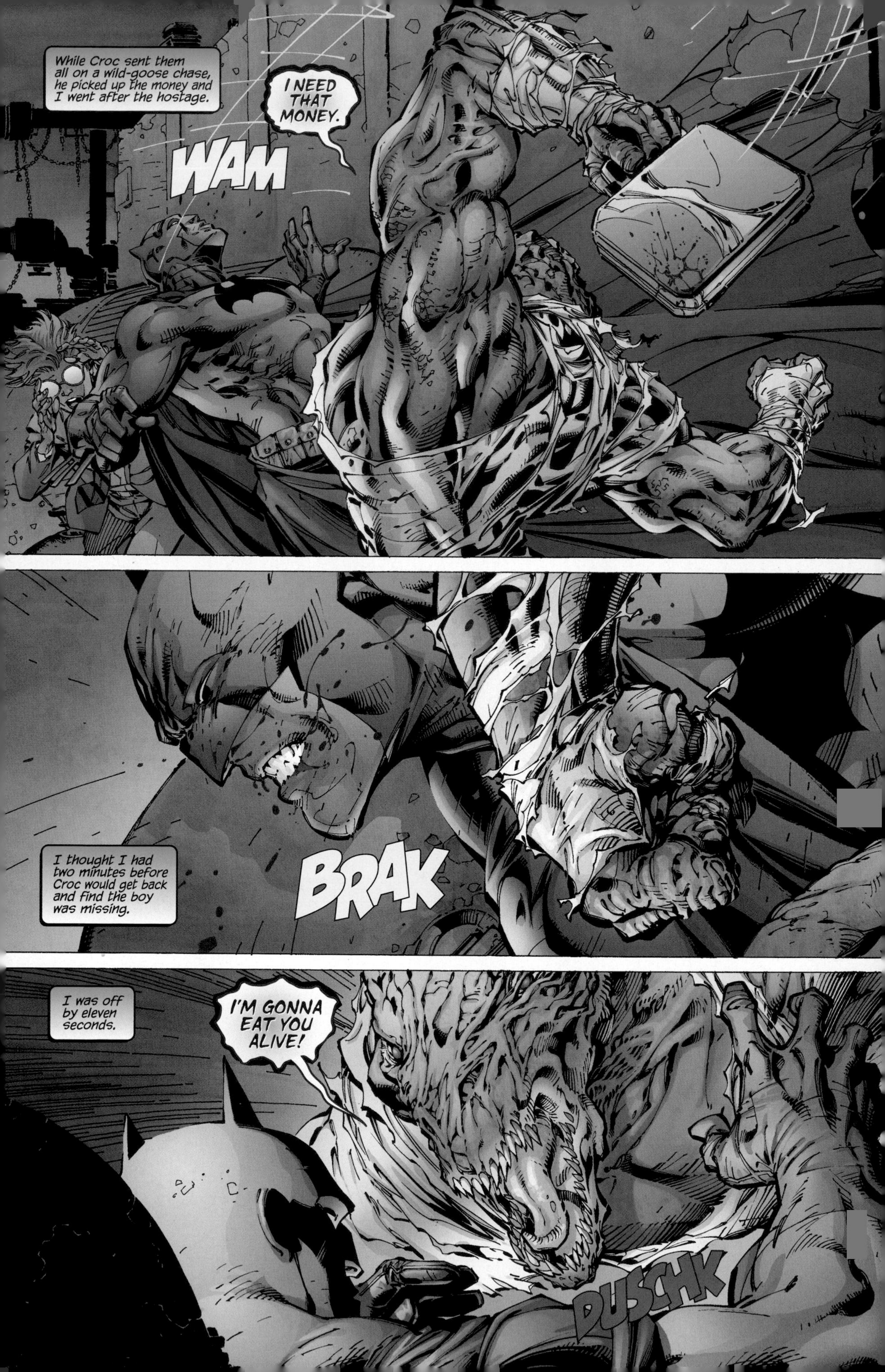
While Croc sent them all on a wild-goose chase, he picked up the money and I went after the hostage.
I NEED THAT MONEY.
WAM
I thought I had two minutes before Croc would get back and find the boy was missing.
BRAK
I was off by eleven seconds.
I'M GONNA EAT YOU ALIVE!
DUSCHK

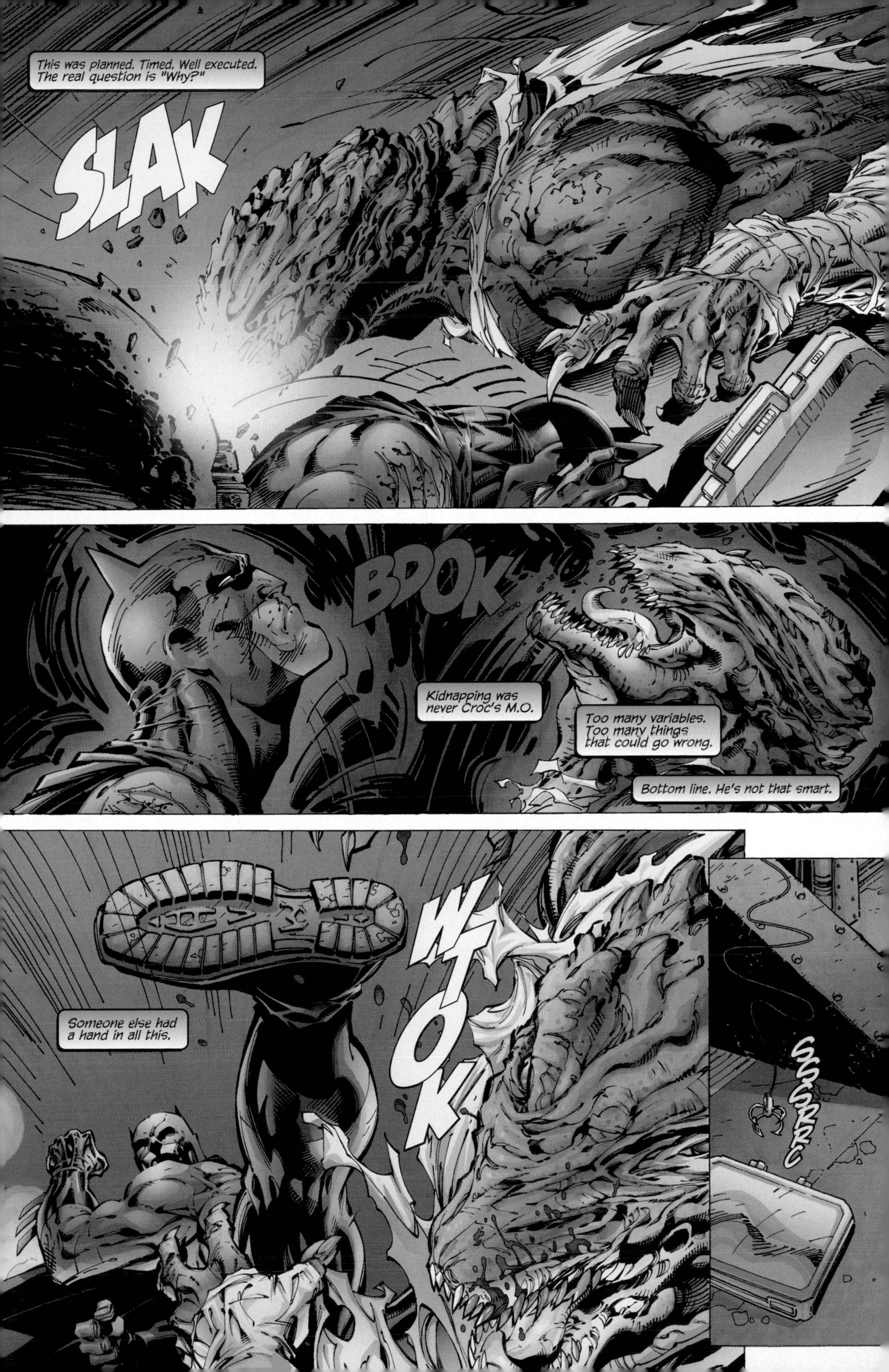
This was planned. Timed. Well executed. The real question is "Why?"
SLAK
BDOK
Kidnapping was never Croc's M.O.
Too many variables. Too many things that could go wrong.
Bottom line. He's not that smart.
Someone else had a hand in all this.
WTOK

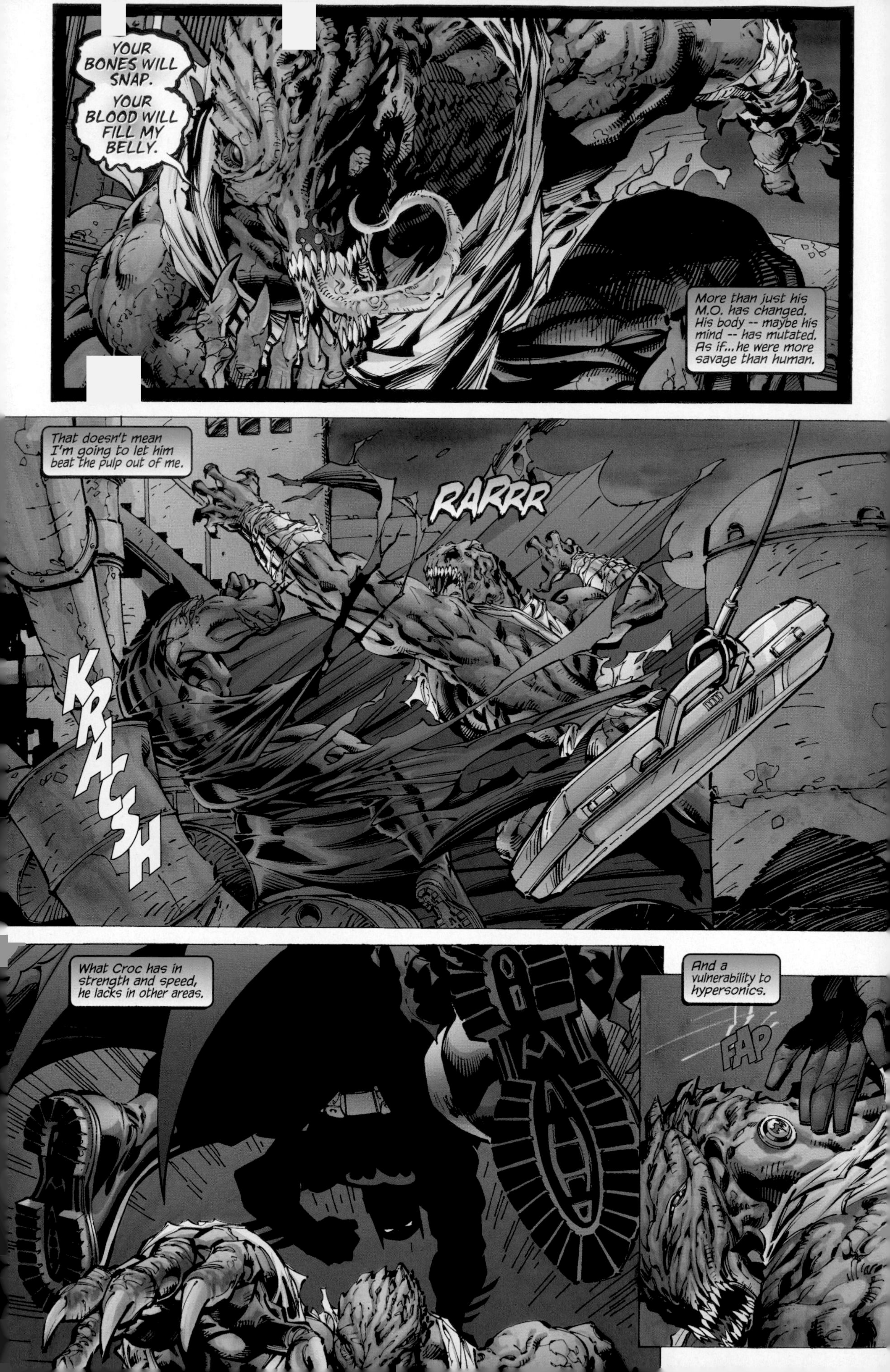
YOUR BONES WILL SNAP.
YOUR BLOOD WILL FILL MY BELLY.
More than just his M.O. has changed. His body -- maybe his mind -- has mutated. As if...he were more savage than human.
That doesn't mean I'm going to let him beat the pulp out of me.
RARRR
KRACSH
What Croc has in strength and speed, he lacks in other areas.
And a vulnerability to hypersonics.
FAP

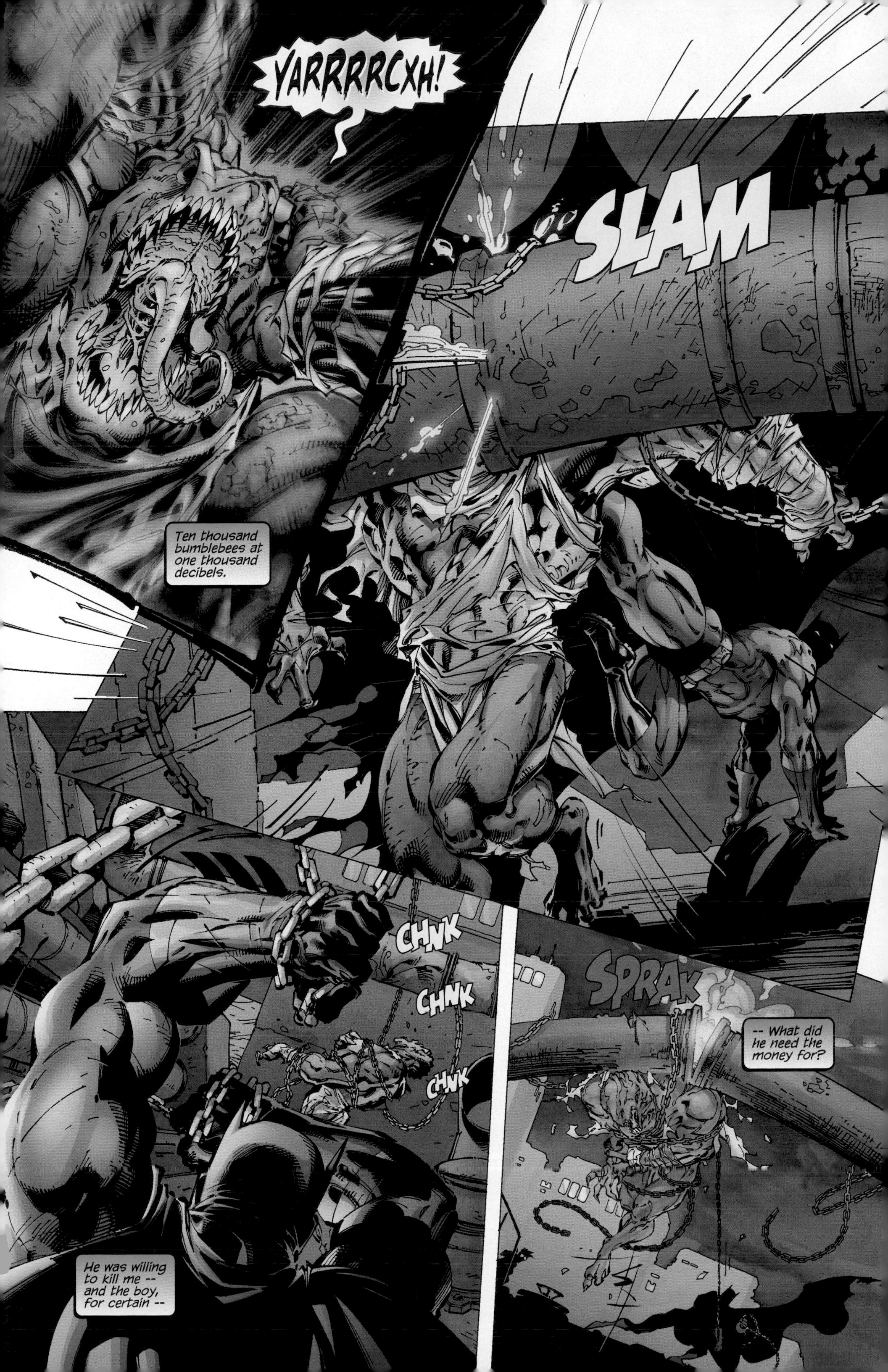
YARRRRCXH!
SLAM
Ten thousand bumblebees at one thousand decibels.
CHNK
CHNK
CHNK
SPRAK
-- What did he need the money for?
He was willing to kill me -- and the boy, for certain --

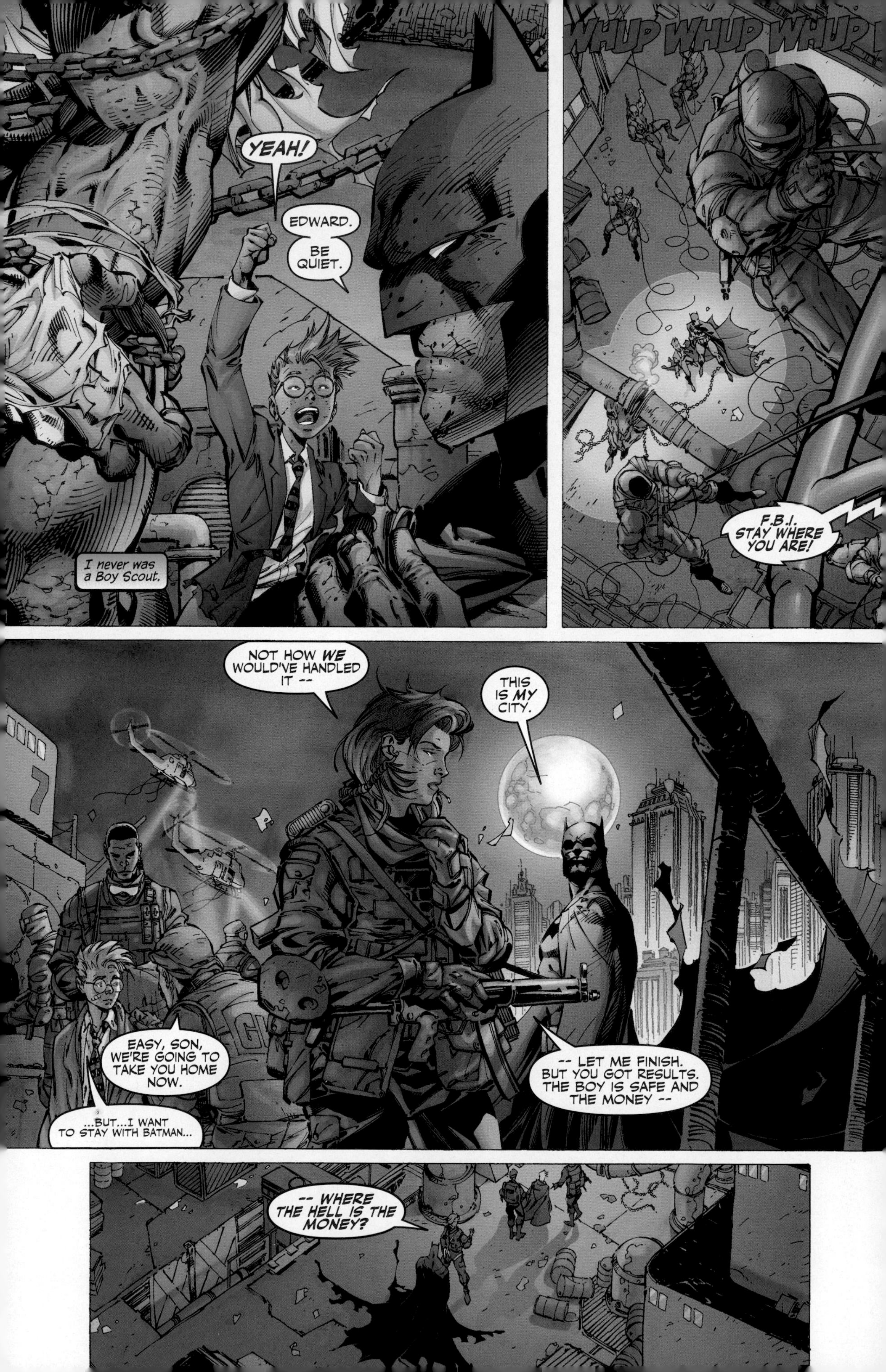
YEAH!
EDWARD.
BE QUIET.
I never was a Boy Scout.
WHUP WHUP WHUP
F.B.I. STAY WHERE YOU ARE!
NOT HOW WE WOULD'VE HANDLED IT --
THIS IS MY CITY.
EASY, SON, WE'RE GOING TO TAKE YOU HOME NOW.
...BUT...I WANT TO STAY WITH BATMAN...
-- LET ME FINISH. BUT YOU GOT RESULTS. THE BOY IS SAFE AND THE MONEY --
-- WHERE THE HELL IS THE MONEY?

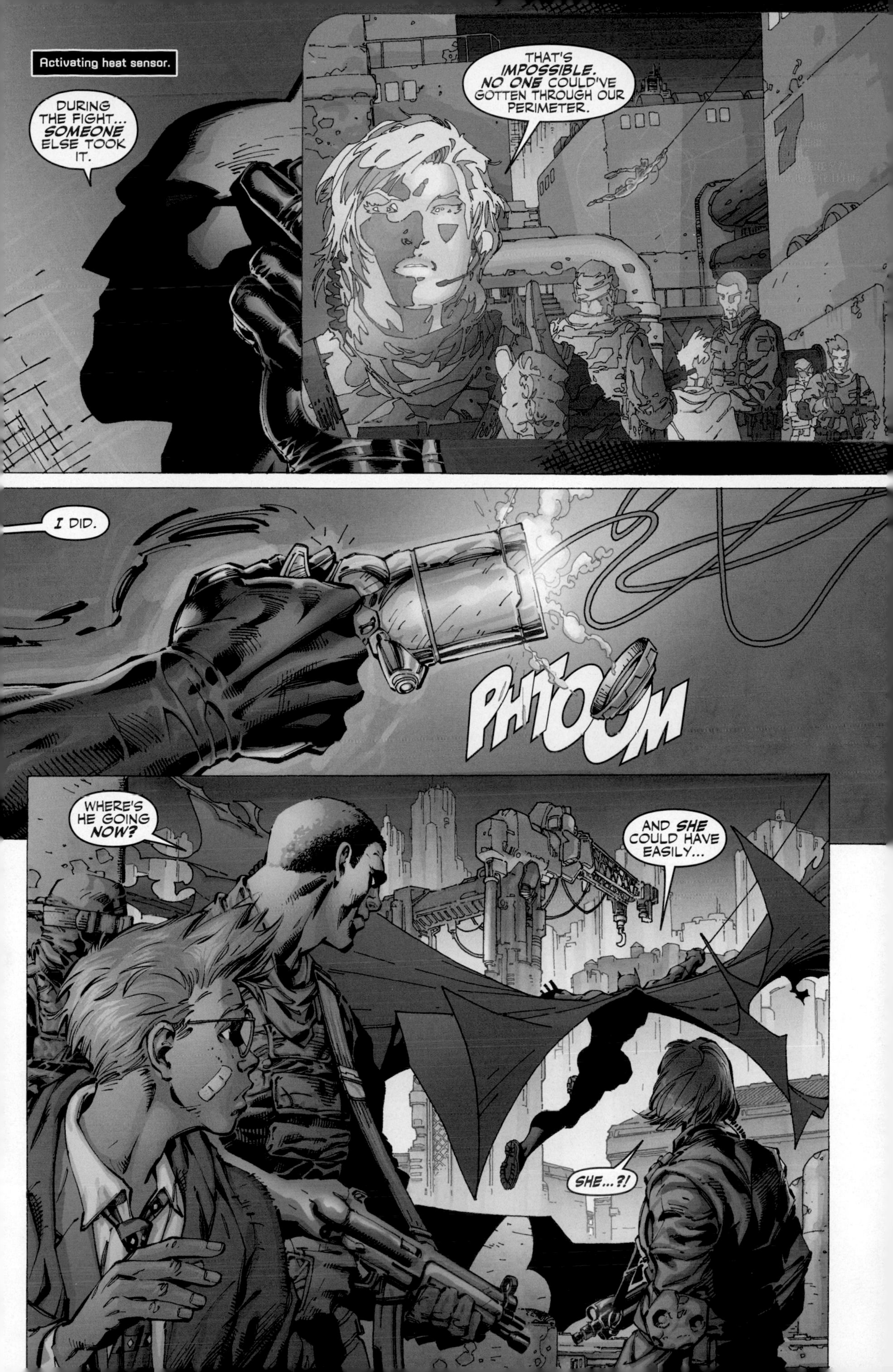

Activating heat sensor.
DURING THE FIGHT... SOMEONE ELSE TOOK IT.
THAT'S IMPOSSIBLE. NO ONE COULD'VE GOTTEN THROUGH OUR PERIMETER.
I DID.
PHTOOM
WHERE'S HE GOING NOW?
AND SHE COULD HAVE EASILY...
SHE...?!

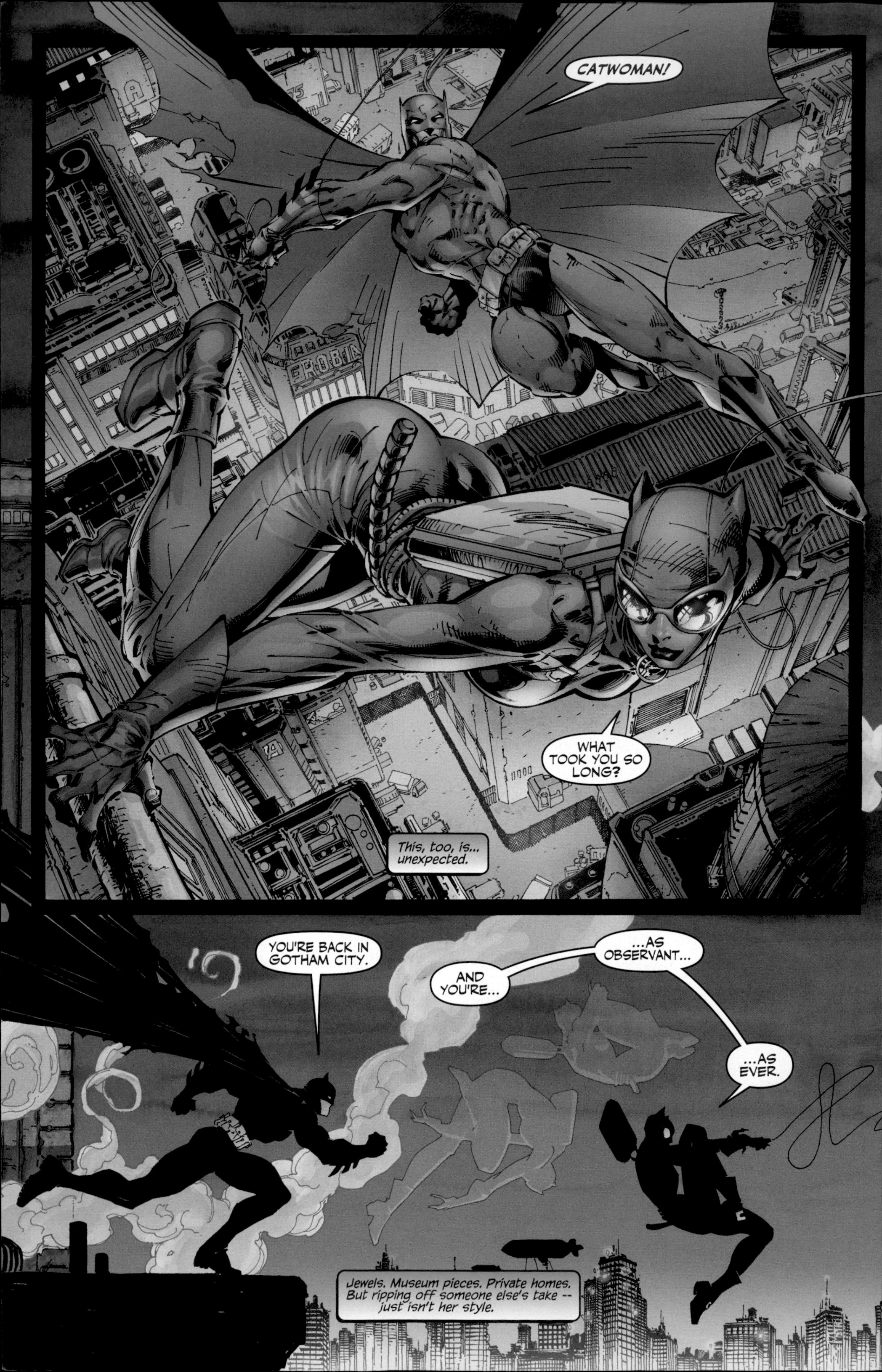

CATWOMAN!
WHAT TOOK YOU SO LONG?
This, too, is... unexpected.
YOU'RE BACK IN GOTHAM CITY.
AND YOU'RE...
...AS OBSERVANT...
...AS EVER.
Jewels. Museum pieces. Private homes. But ripping off someone else's take -- just isn't her style.

I have known Catwoman... *Selina Kyle* for years.

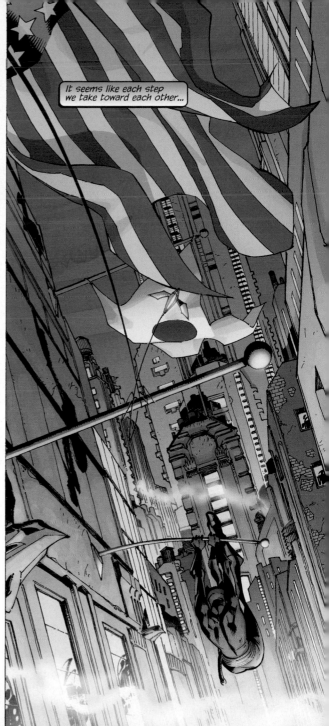

It seems like each step we take toward each other...

...we only get further apart.

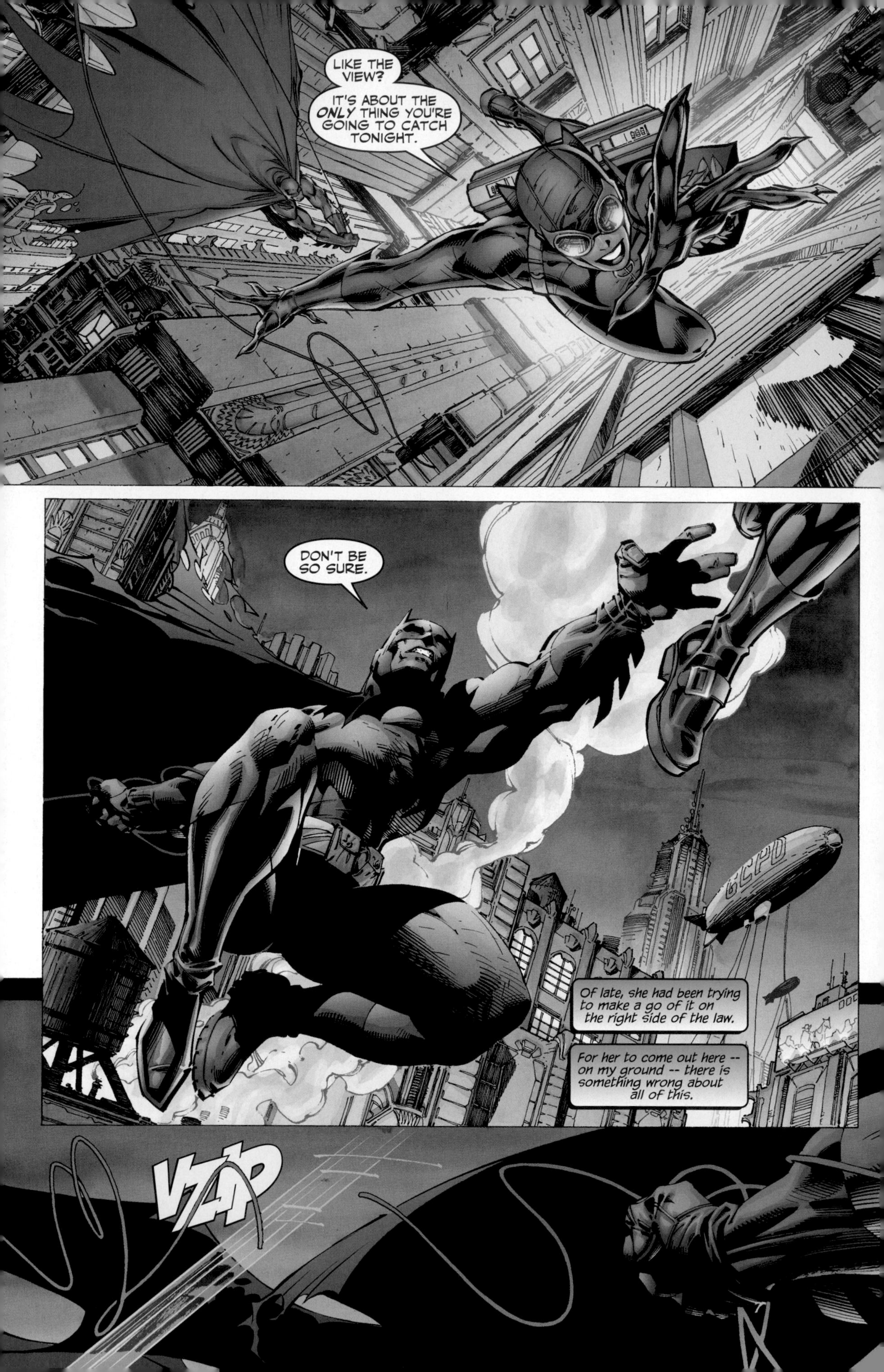
LIKE THE VIEW?
IT'S ABOUT THE ONLY THING YOU'RE GOING TO CATCH TONIGHT.
DON'T BE SO SURE.
GCPD
Of late, she had been trying to make a go of it on the right side of the law.
For her to come out here -- on my ground -- there is something wrong about all of this.
VZIP

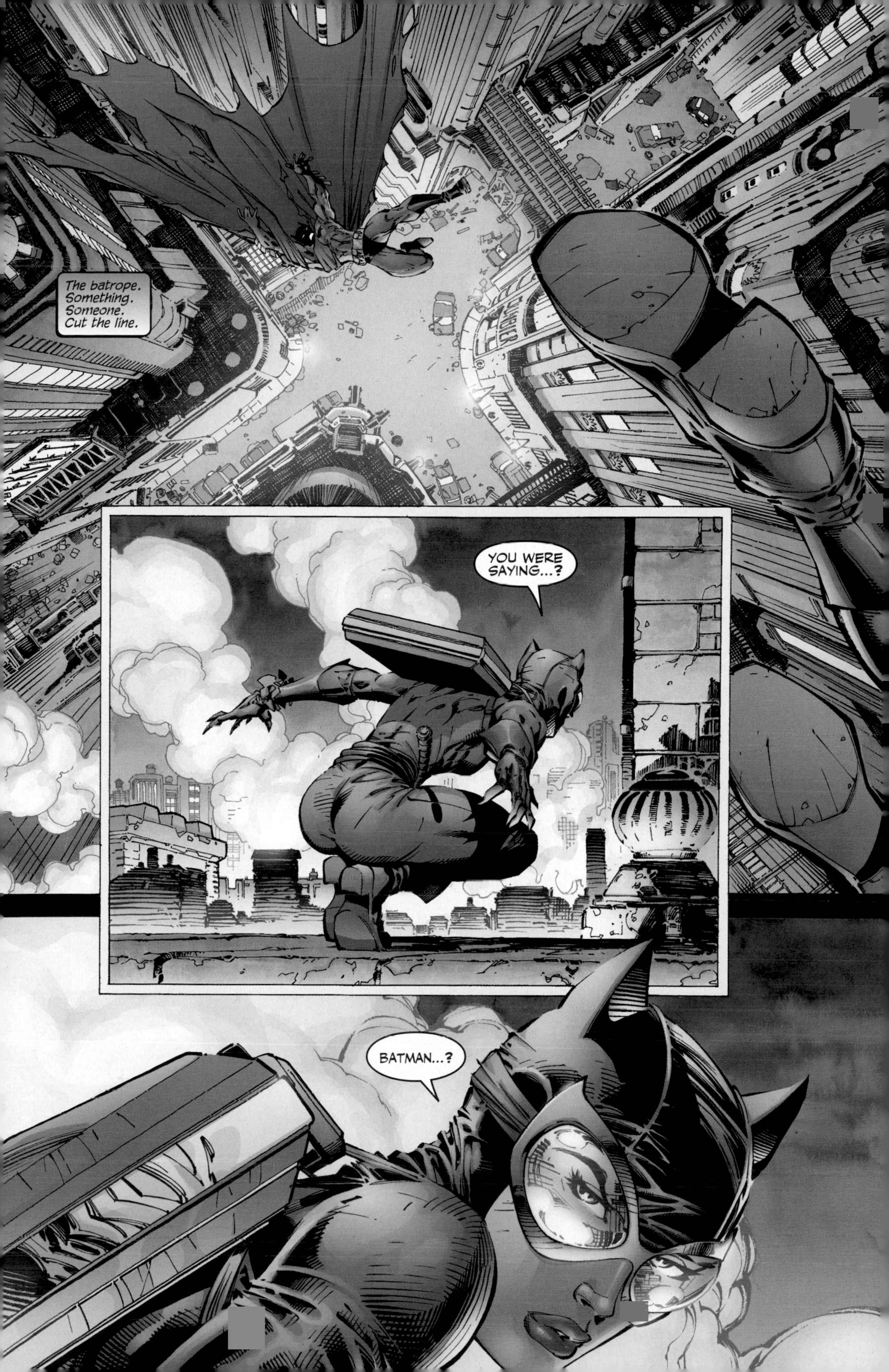
The batrope.
Something.
Someone.
Cut the line.
YOU WERE SAYING...?
BATMAN...?

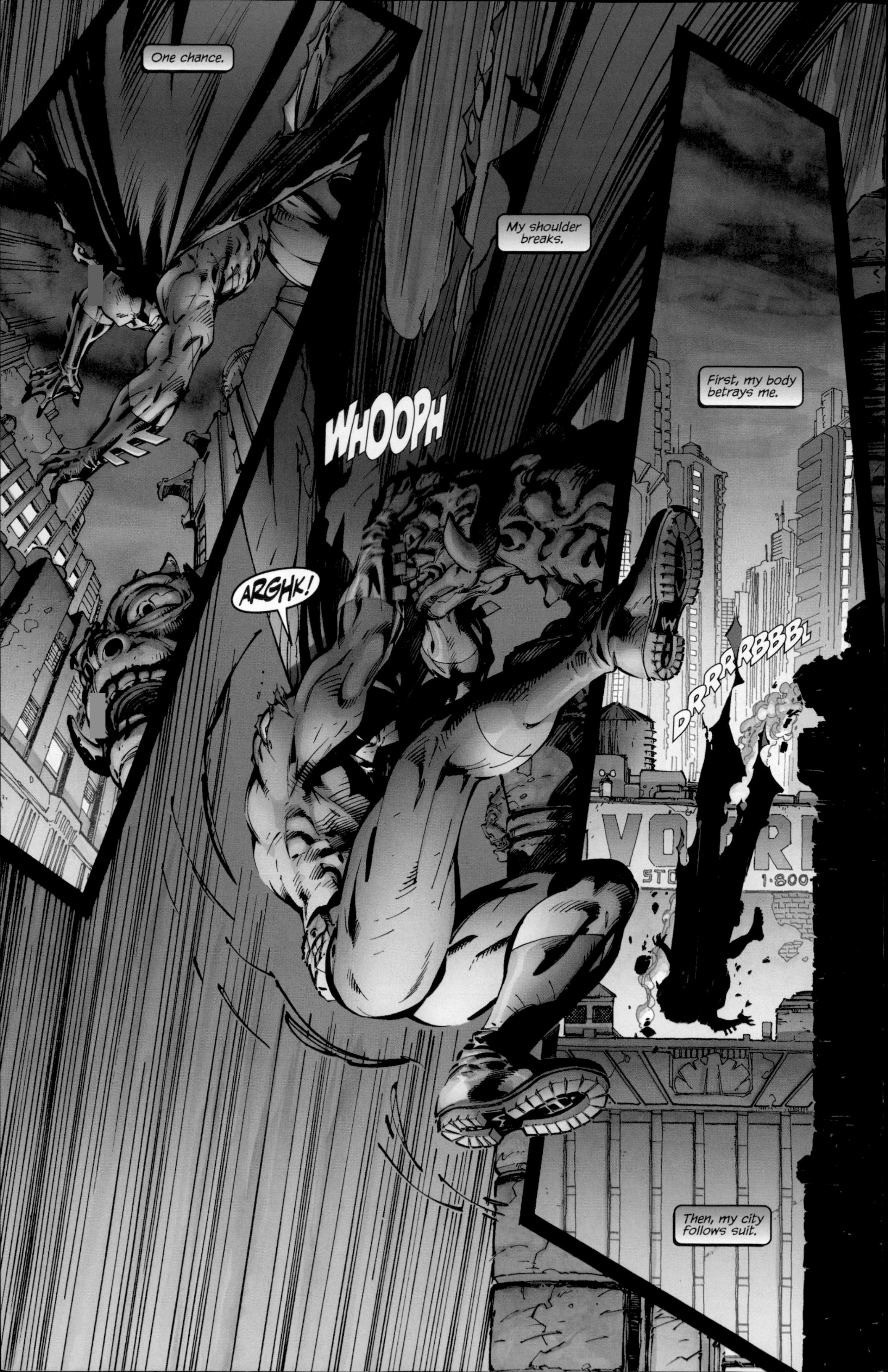
One chance.
My shoulder breaks.
WHOOPH
ARGHK!
First, my body betrays me.
DRRRRBBBL
Then, my city follows suit.

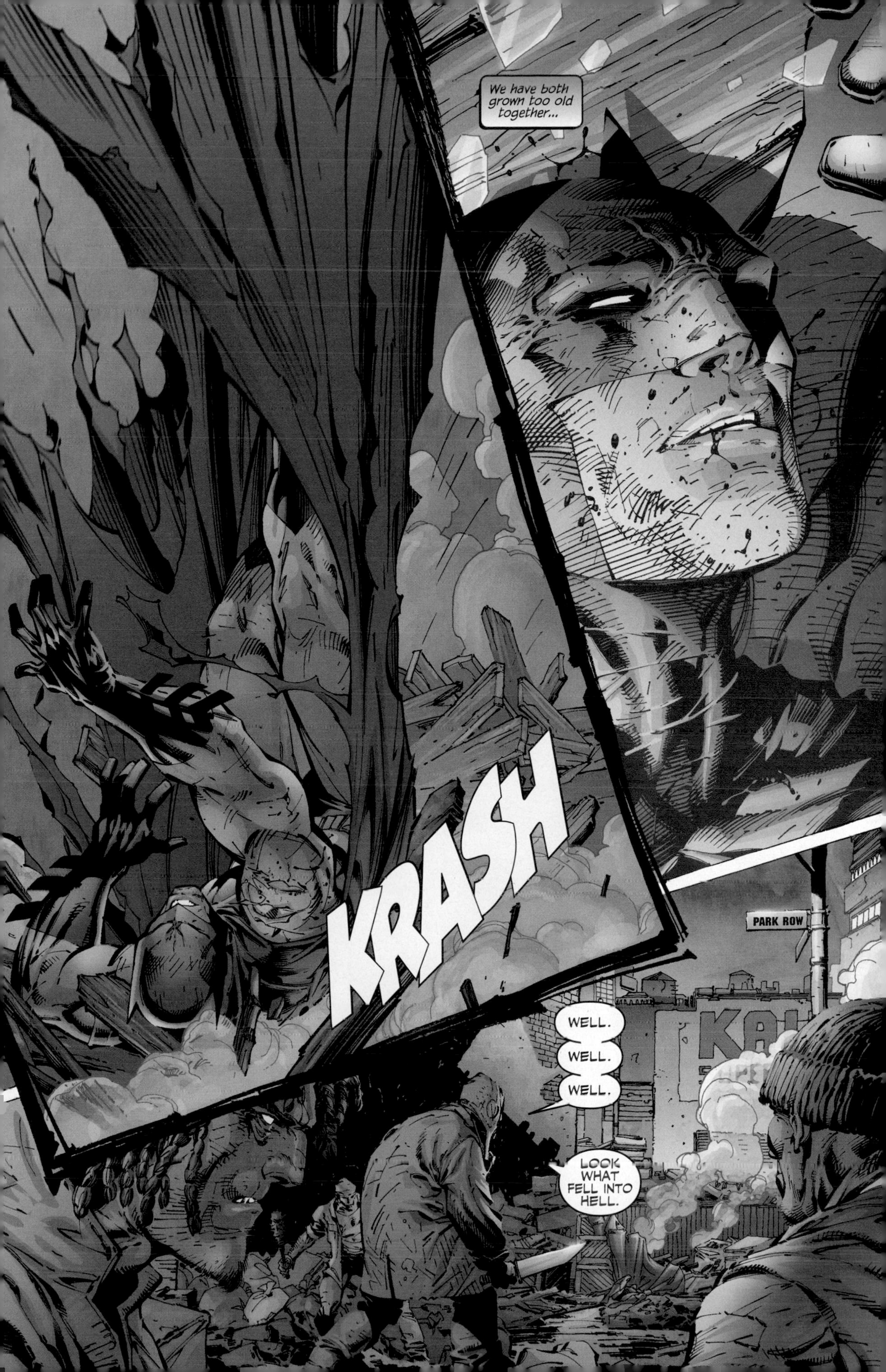
We have both grown too old together...
KRASH
PARK ROW
WELL.
WELL.
WELL.
LOOK WHAT FELL INTO HELL.

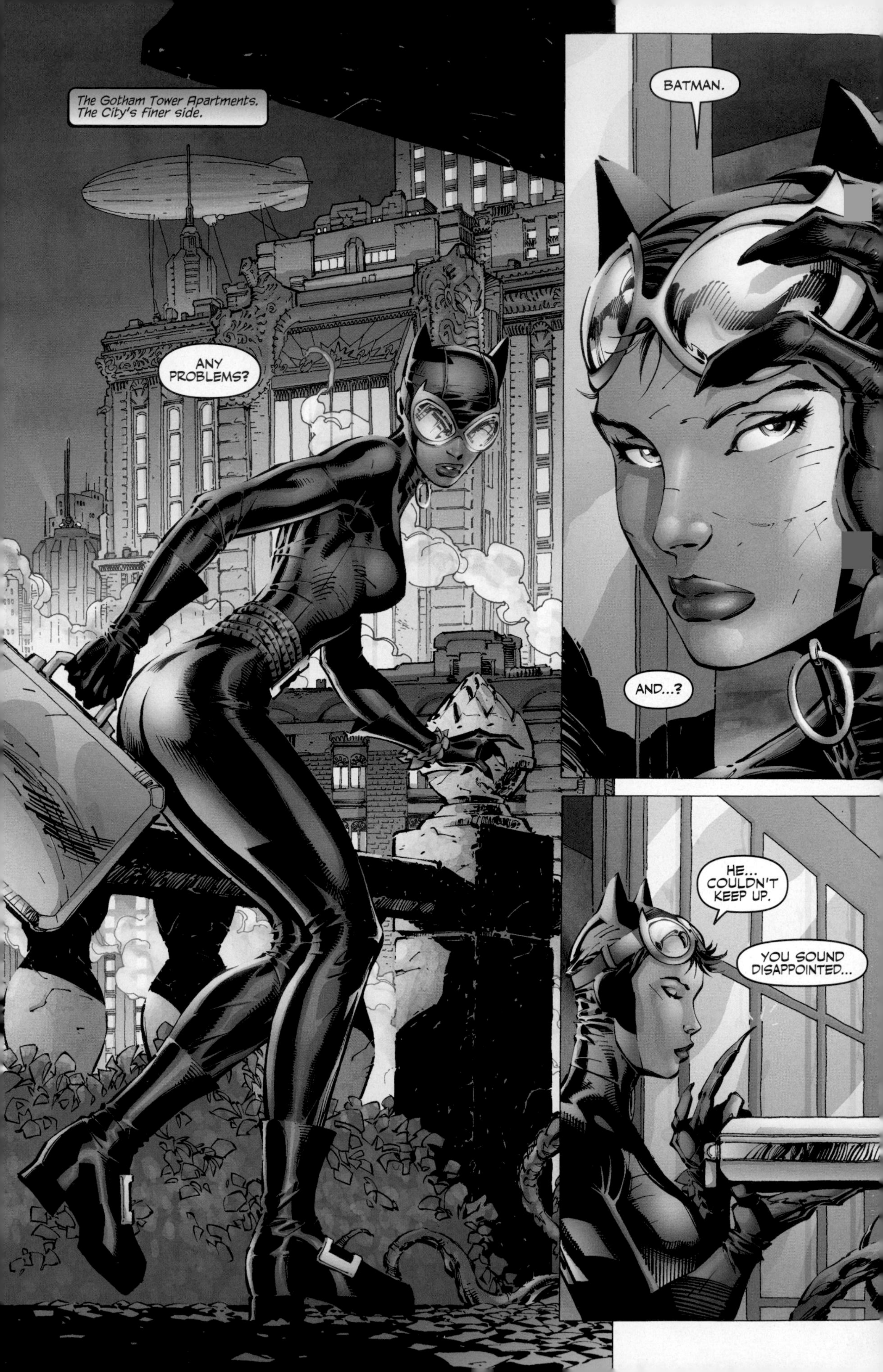
The Gotham Tower Apartments.
The City's finer side.
ANY PROBLEMS?
BATMAN.
AND...?
HE... COULDN'T KEEP UP.
YOU SOUND DISAPPOINTED...

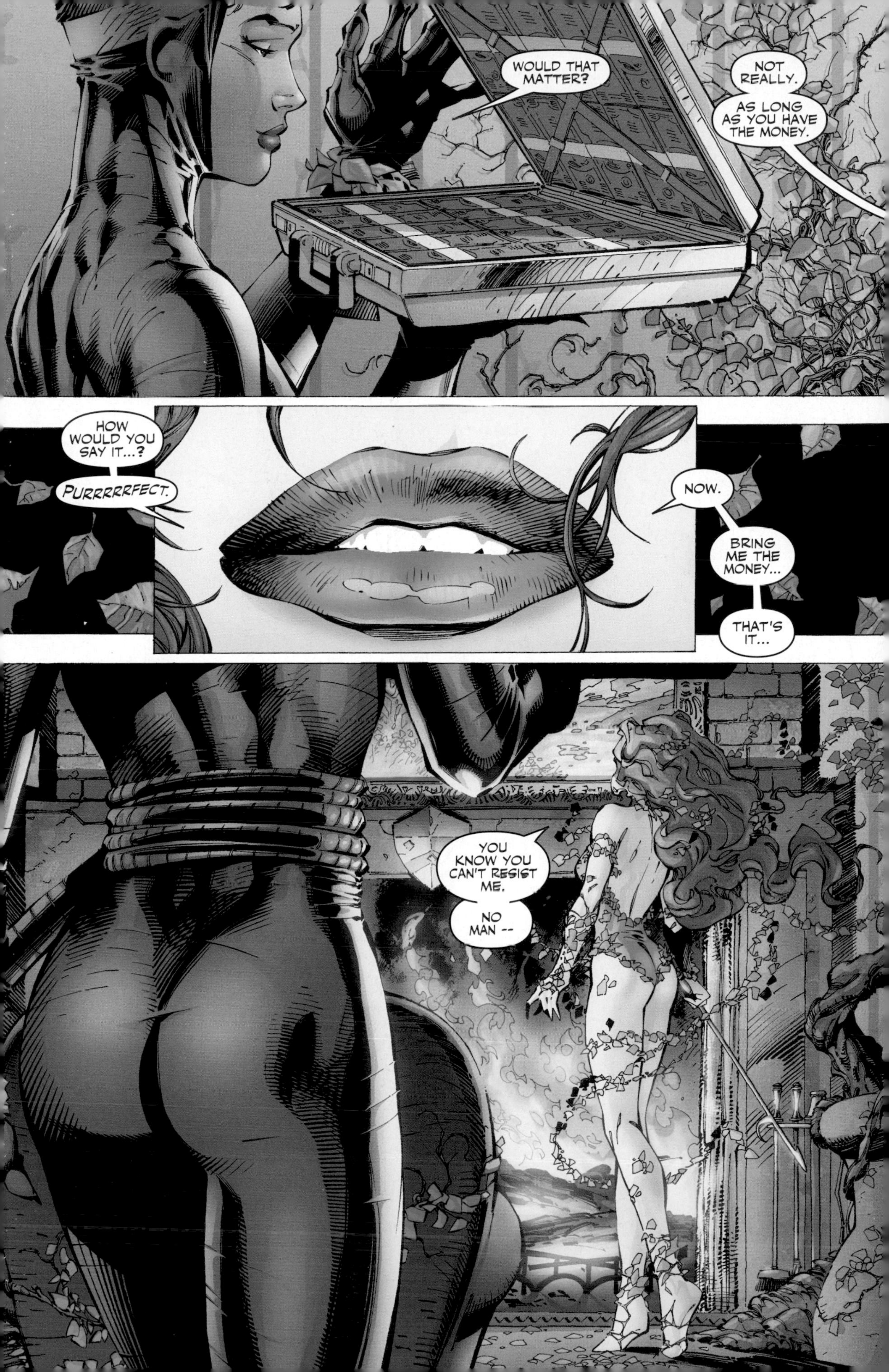
WOULD THAT MATTER?
NOT REALLY.
AS LONG AS YOU HAVE THE MONEY.
HOW WOULD YOU SAY IT...?
PURRRRRFECT.
NOW.
BRING ME THE MONEY...
THAT'S IT...
YOU KNOW YOU CAN'T RESIST ME.
NO MAN --

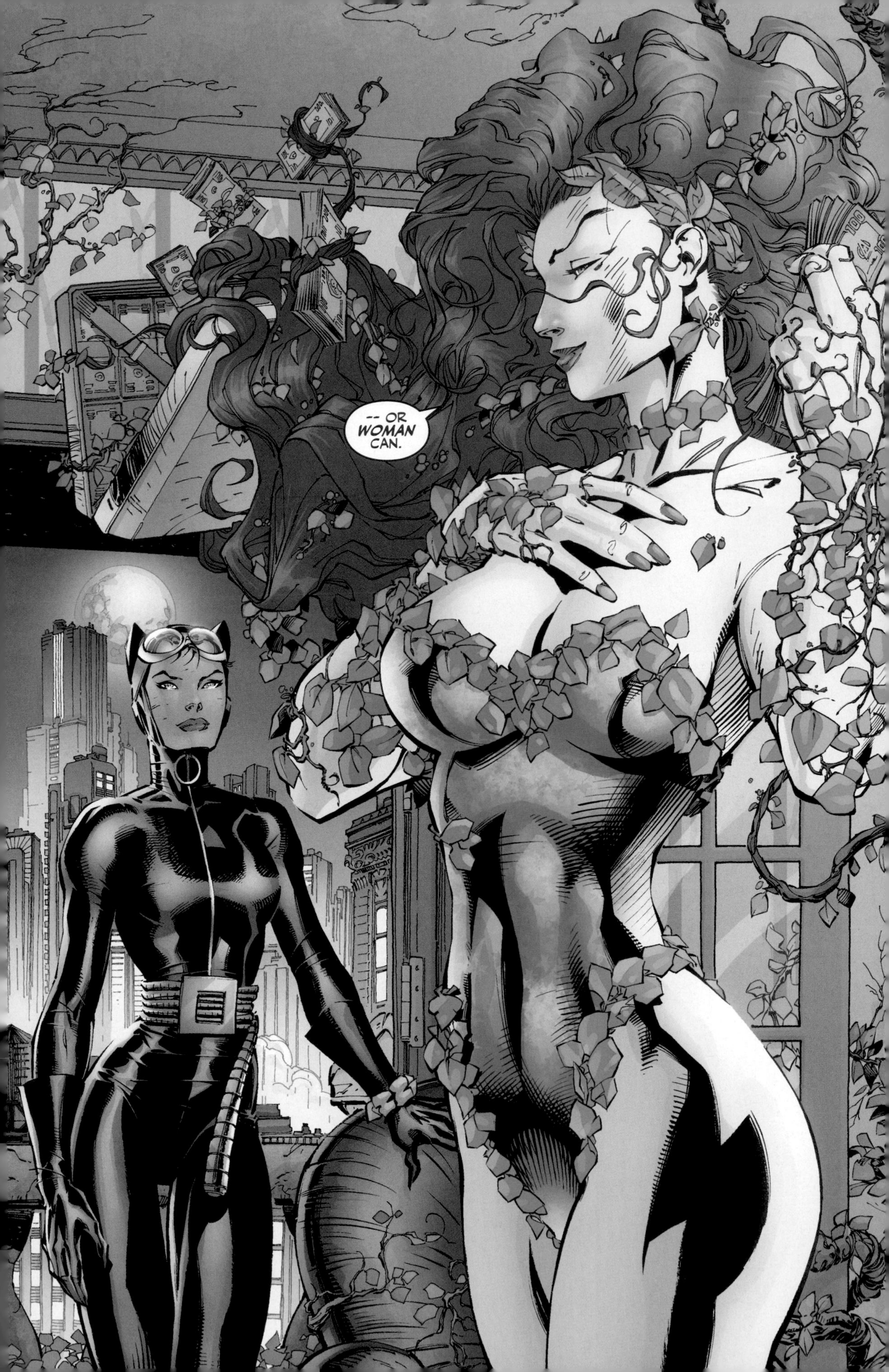
-- OR WOMAN CAN.

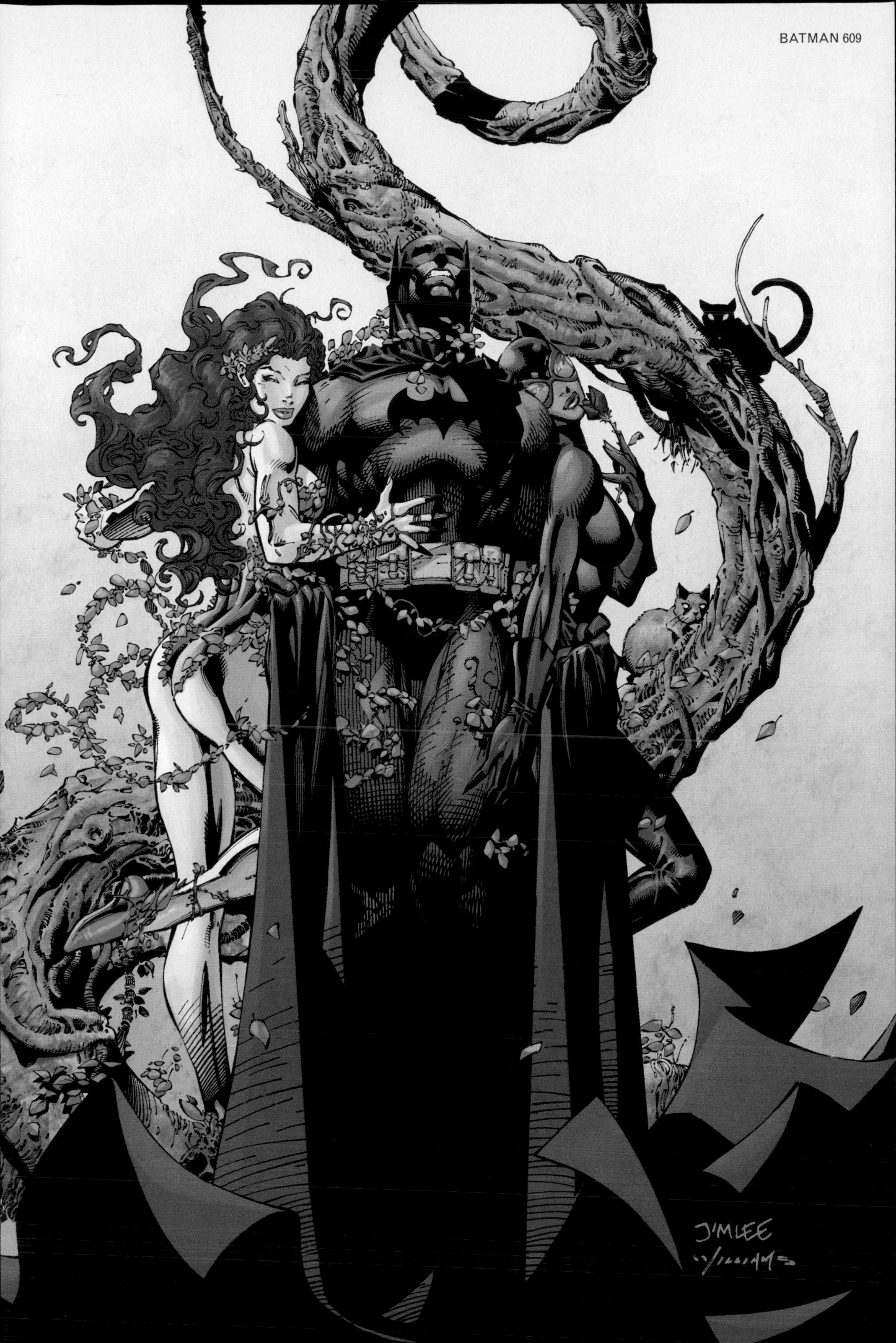
JIM LEE

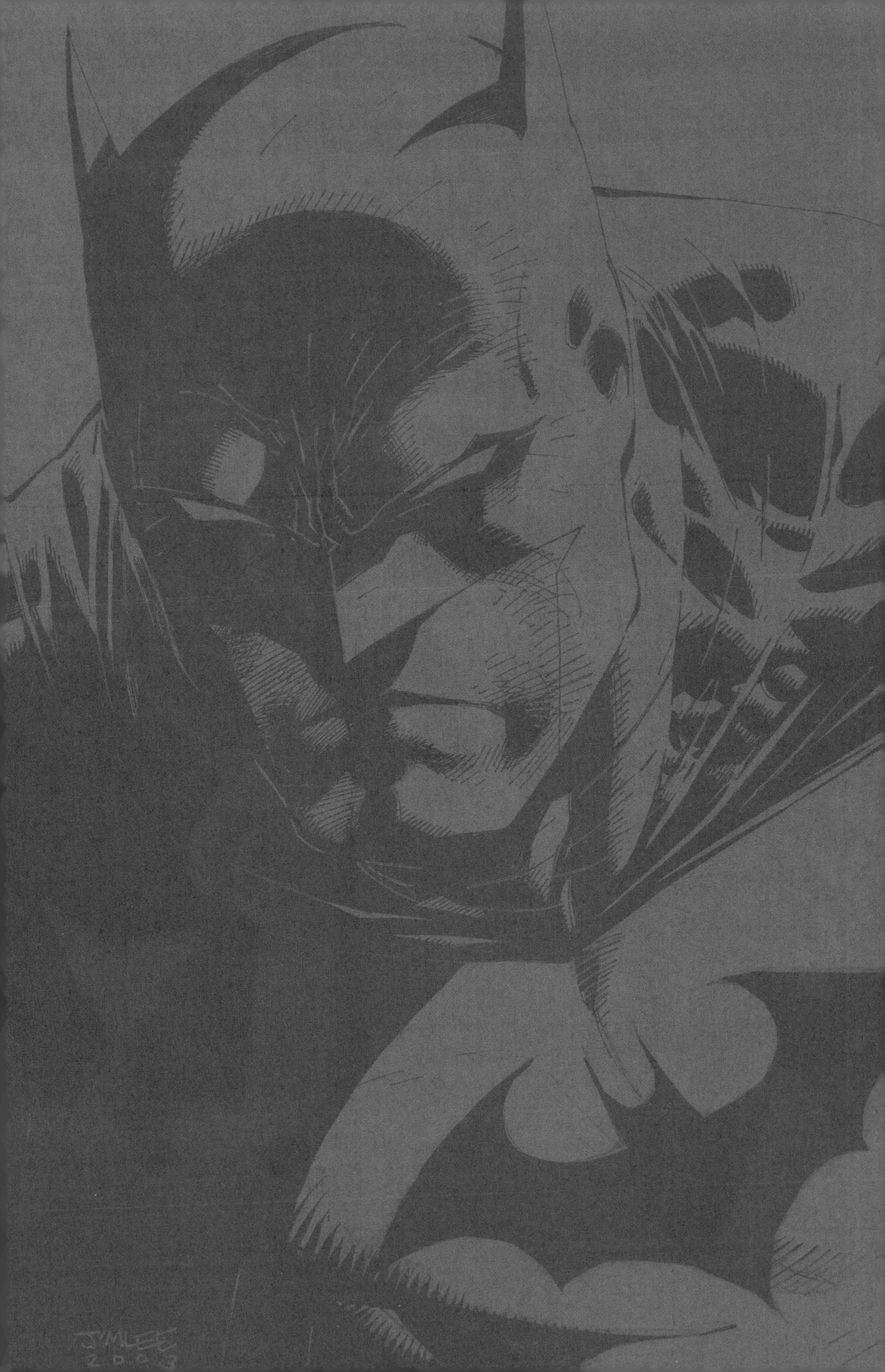

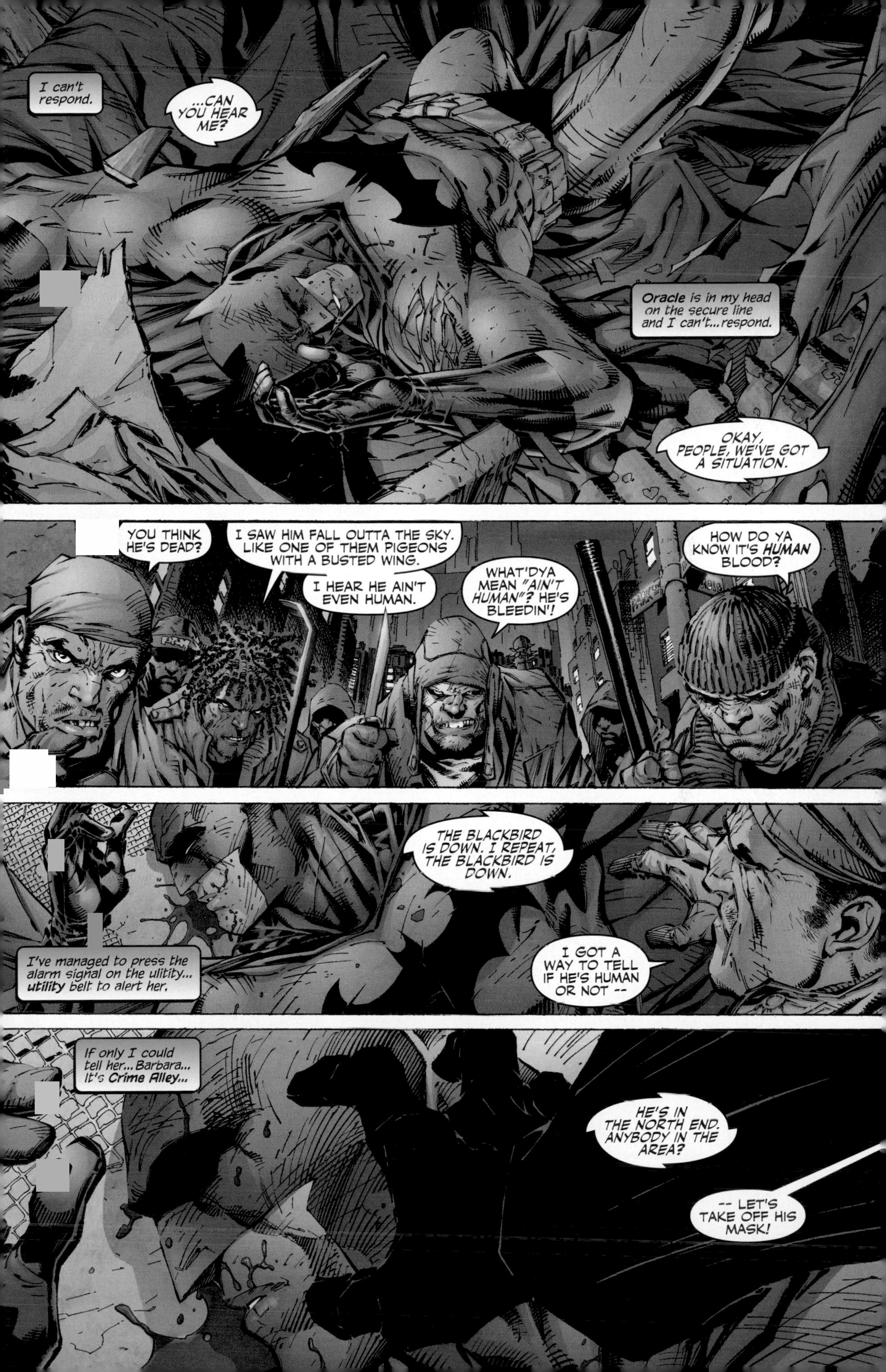

I can't respond.
...CAN YOU HEAR ME?
Oracle is in my head on the secure line and I can't...respond.
OKAY, PEOPLE, WE'VE GOT A SITUATION.
YOU THINK HE'S DEAD?
I SAW HIM FALL OUTTA THE SKY. LIKE ONE OF THEM PIGEONS WITH A BUSTED WING.
I HEAR HE AIN'T EVEN HUMAN.
WHAT'DYA MEAN "AIN'T HUMAN"? HE'S BLEEDIN'!
HOW DO YA KNOW IT'S HUMAN BLOOD?
THE BLACKBIRD IS DOWN. I REPEAT, THE BLACKBIRD IS DOWN.
I've managed to press the alarm signal on the ulitity... utility belt to alert her.
I GOT A WAY TO TELL IF HE'S HUMAN OR NOT --
If only I could tell her... Barbara... It's Crime Alley...
HE'S IN THE NORTH END. ANYBODY IN THE AREA?
-- LET'S TAKE OFF HIS MASK!

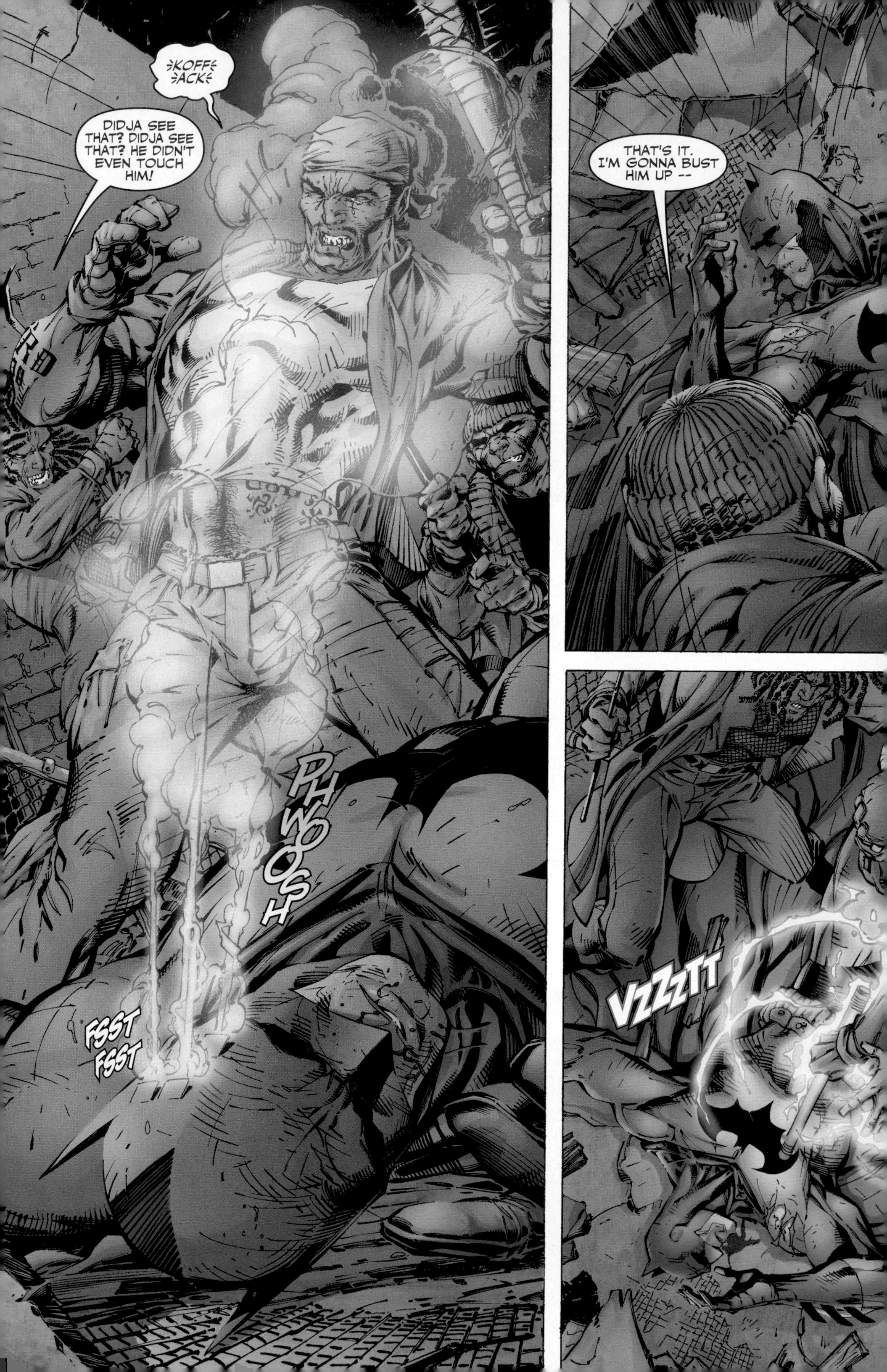

KOFF ACK
DIDJA SEE THAT? DIDJA SEE THAT? HE DIDN'T EVEN TOUCH HIM!
PHWOOSH
FSST FSST
THAT'S IT. I'M GONNA BUST HIM UP --
VZZZZTT

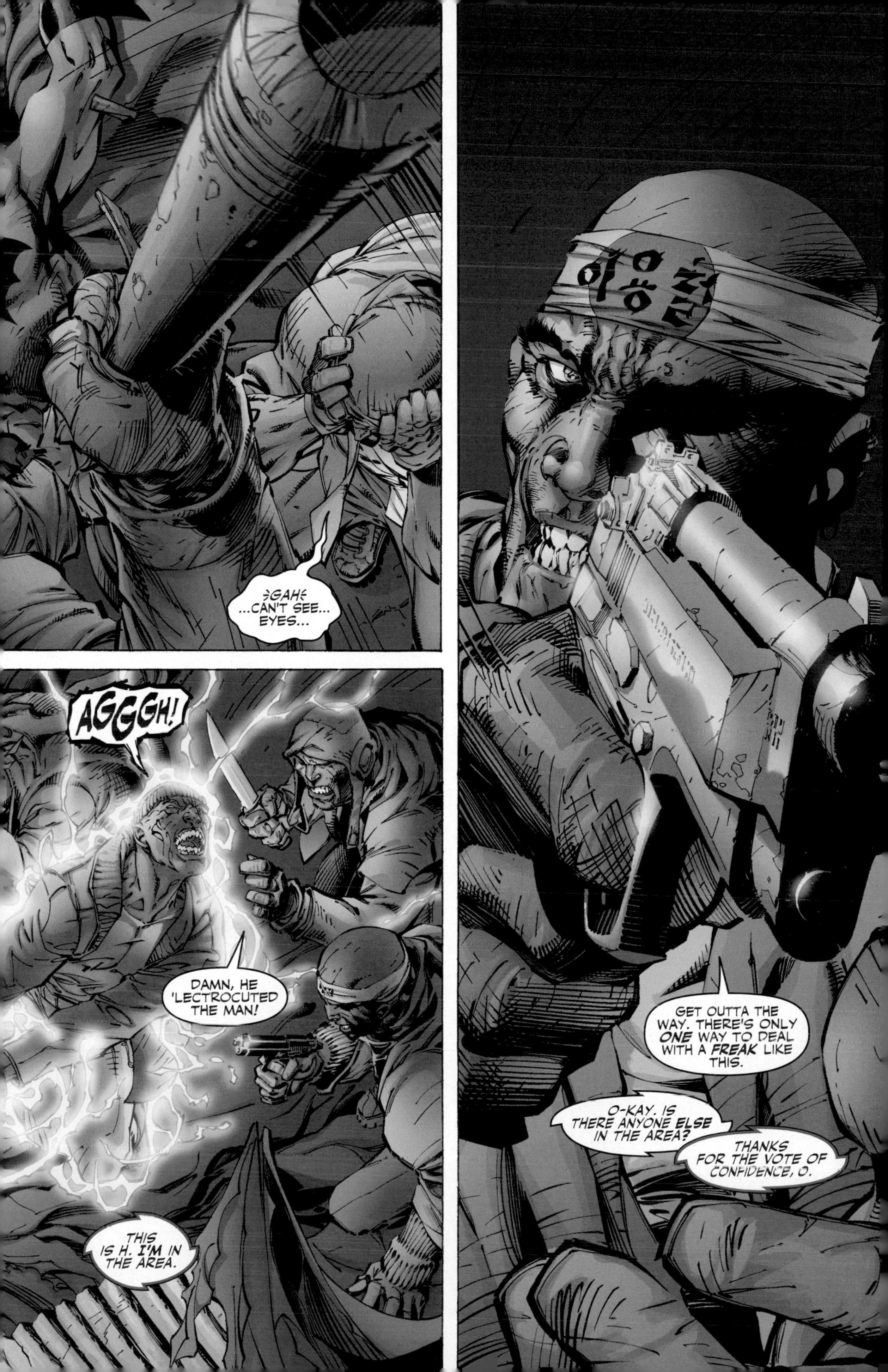

GAH
...CAN'T SEE... EYES...
AGGGH!
DAMN, HE 'LECTROCUTED THE MAN!
THIS IS H. I'M IN THE AREA.
GET OUTTA THE WAY. THERE'S ONLY ONE WAY TO DEAL WITH A FREAK LIKE THIS.
O-KAY. IS THERE ANYONE ELSE IN THE AREA?
THANKS FOR THE VOTE OF CONFIDENCE, O.

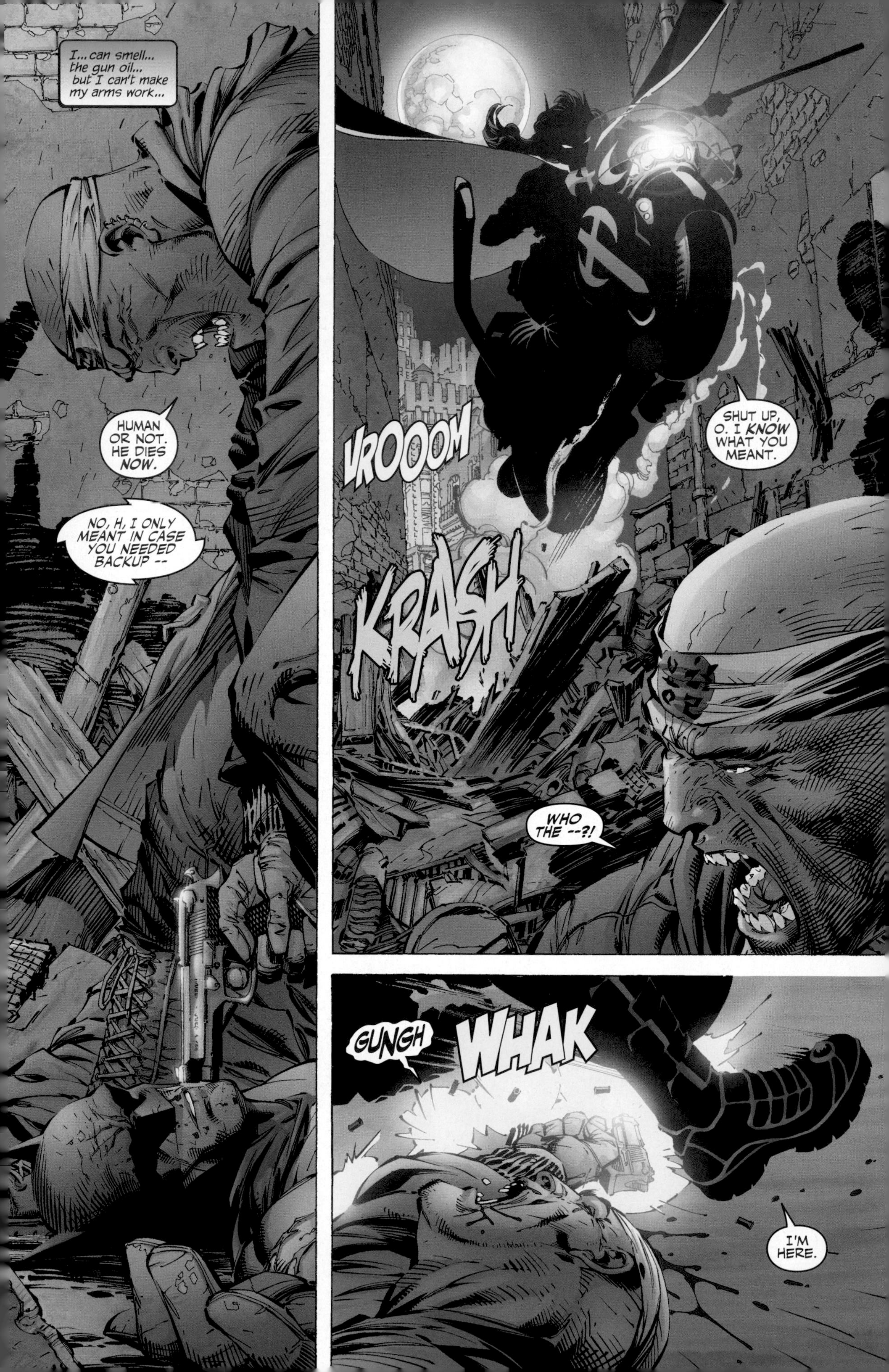

I... can smell... the gun oil... but I can't make my arms work...
HUMAN OR NOT. HE DIES NOW.
NO, H, I ONLY MEANT IN CASE YOU NEEDED BACKUP --
VROOOM
SHUT UP, O. I KNOW WHAT YOU MEANT.
KRASH
WHO THE --?!
GUNGH
WHAK
I'M HERE.

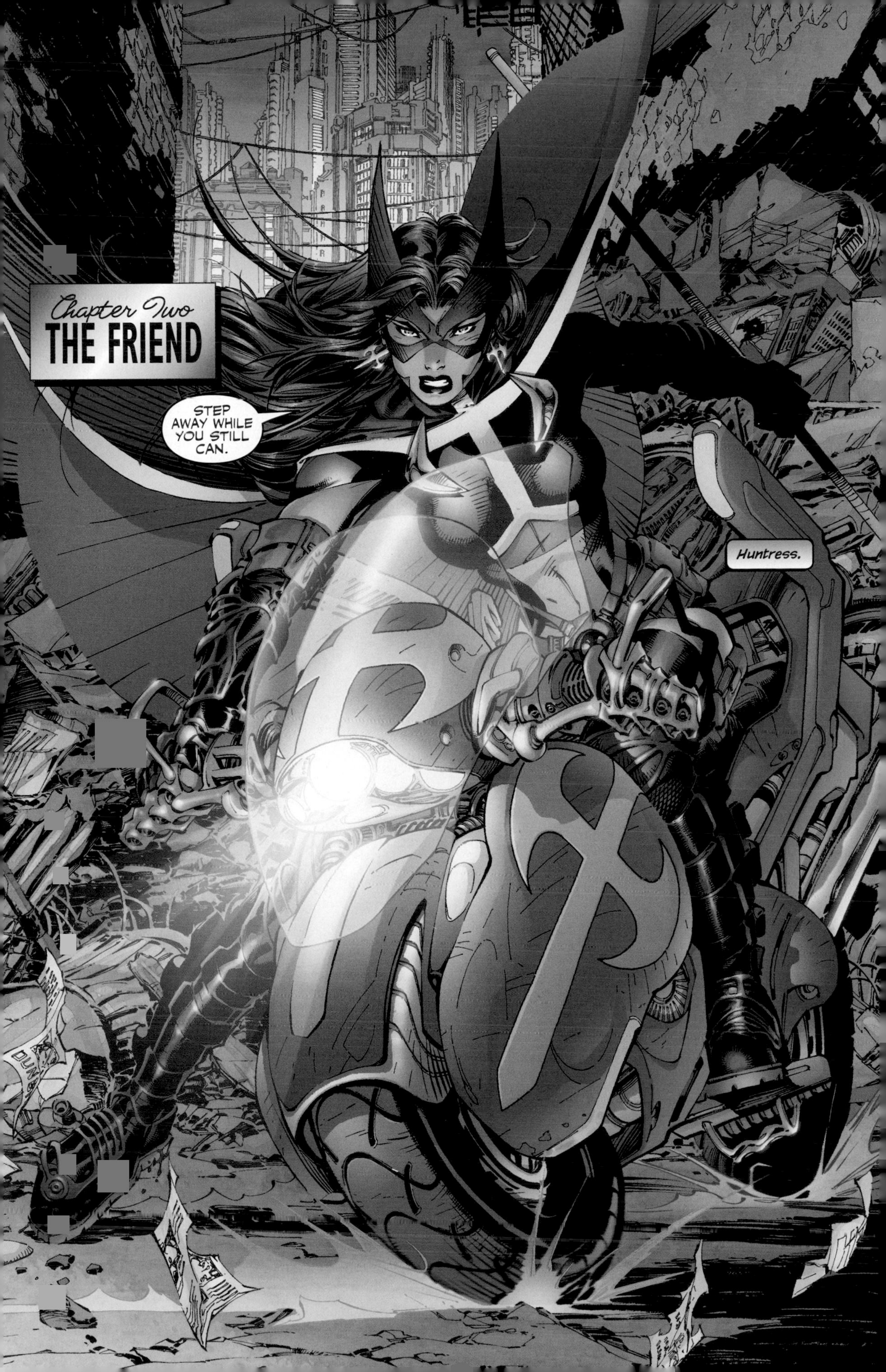
Chapter Two
THE FRIEND
STEP AWAY WHILE YOU STILL CAN.
Huntress.

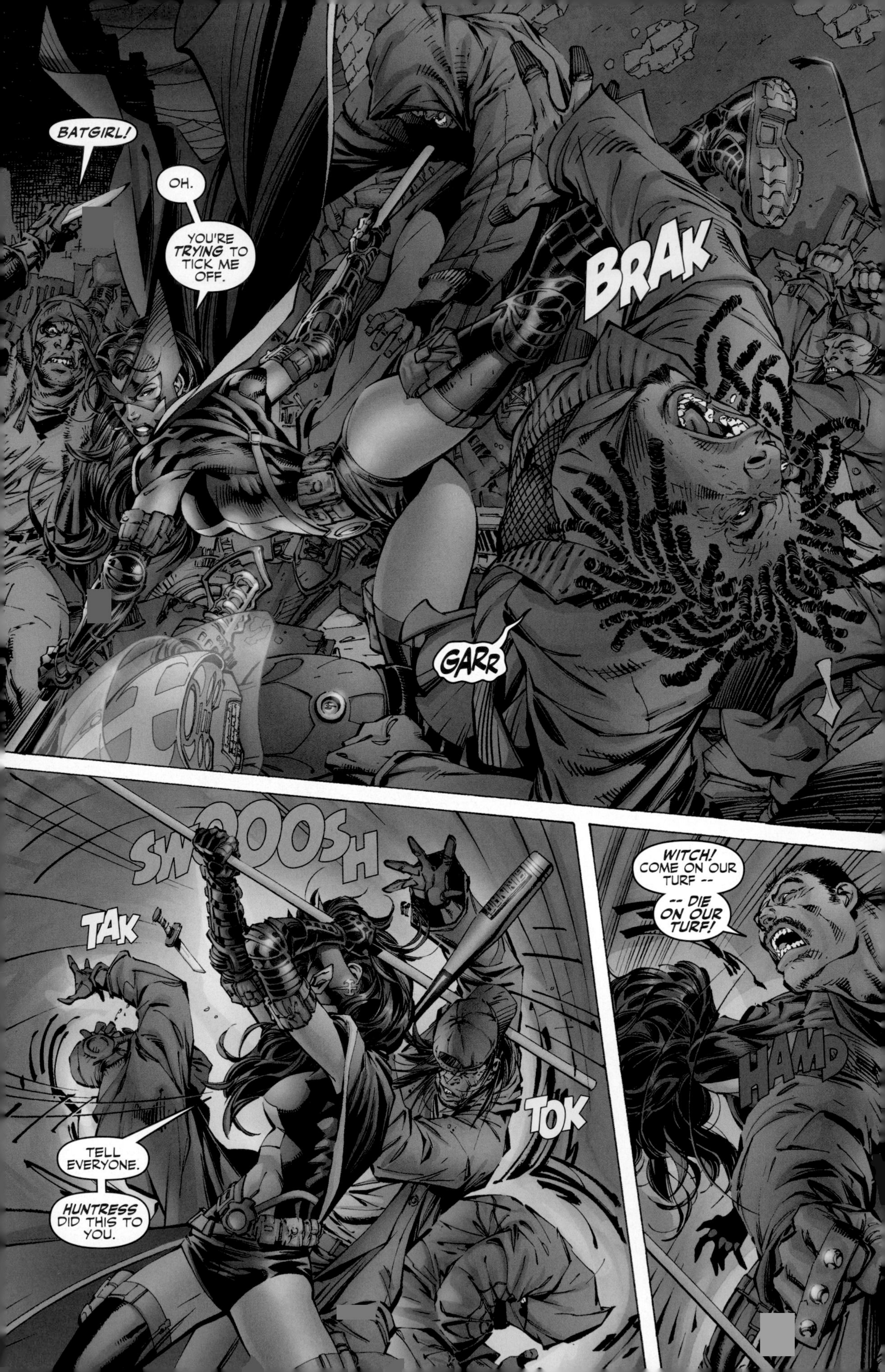
BATGIRL!
OH.
YOU'RE TRYING TO TICK ME OFF.
BRAK
GARR
SWOOOSH
TAK
TOK
TELL EVERYONE.
HUNTRESS DID THIS TO YOU.
WITCH! COME ON OUR TURF --
-- DIE ON OUR TURF!
HAMD

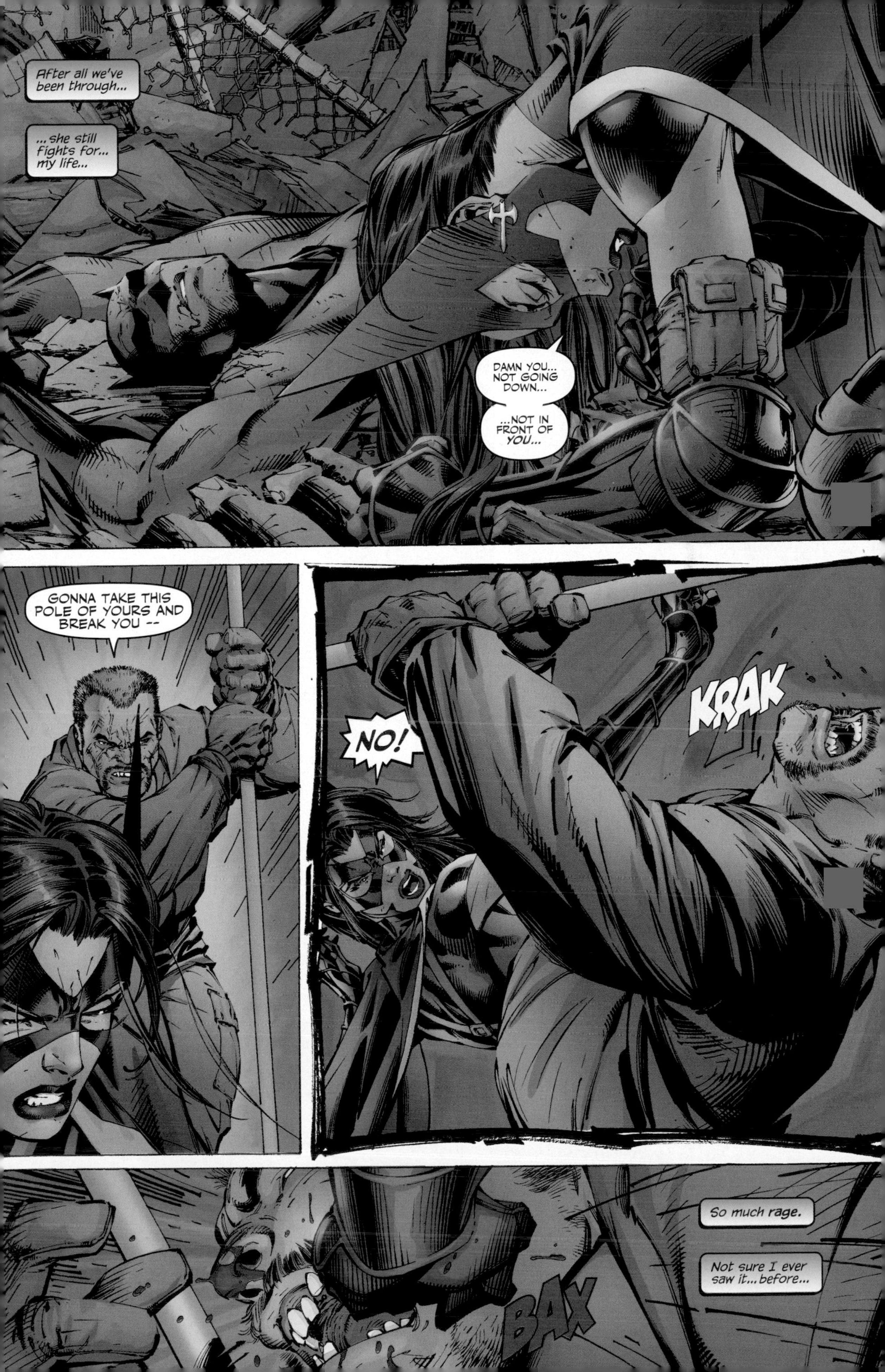
After all we've been through...
...she still fights for... my life...
DAMN YOU... NOT GOING DOWN...
...NOT IN FRONT OF YOU...
GONNA TAKE THIS POLE OF YOURS AND BREAK YOU --
NO!
KRAK
So much rage.
Not sure I ever saw it... before...
BAX

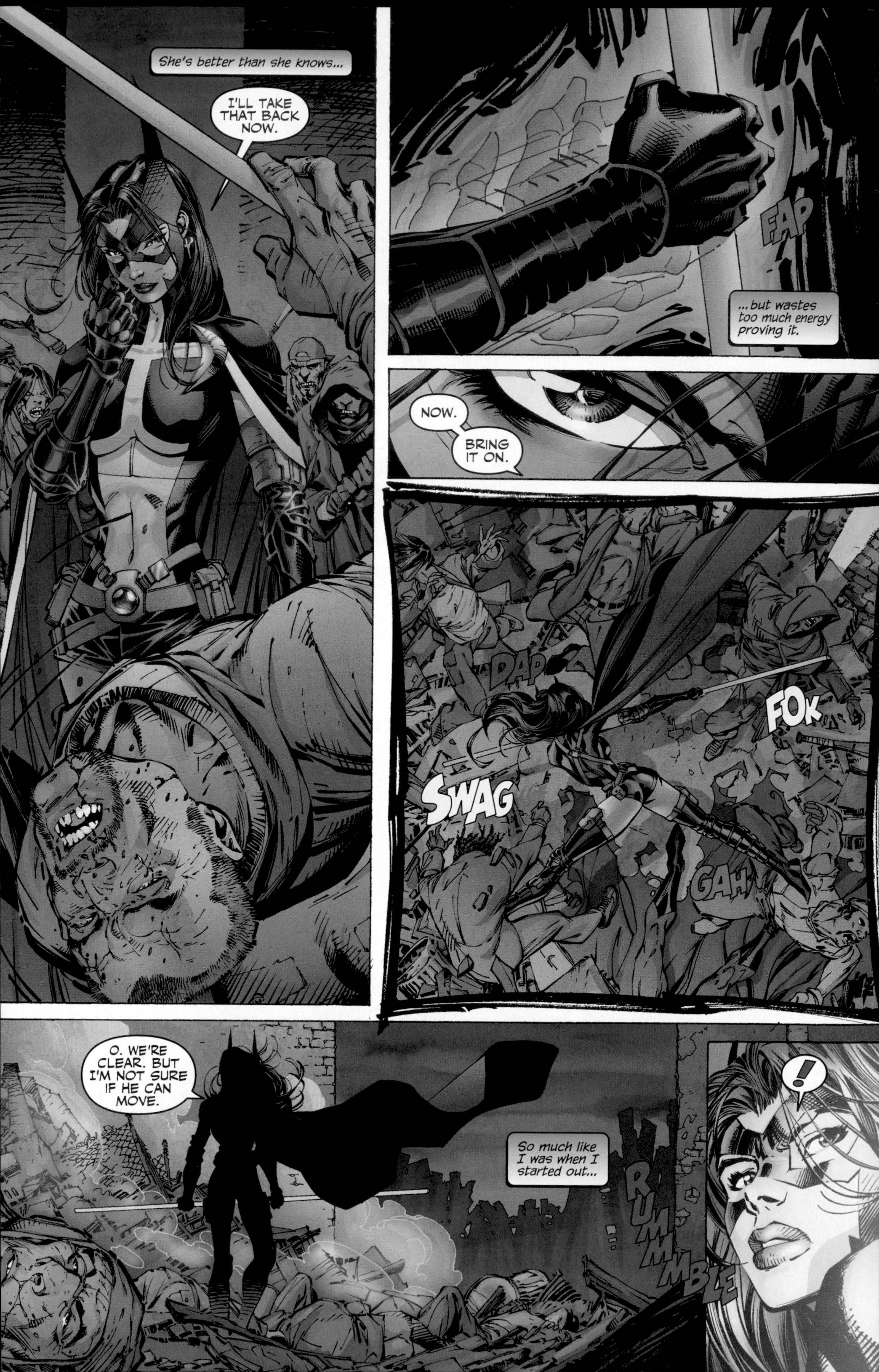

She's better than she knows...
I'LL TAKE THAT BACK NOW.
FAP
...but wastes too much energy proving it.
NOW.
BRING IT ON.
DAP
FOK
SWAG
GAH
O. WE'RE CLEAR. BUT I'M NOT SURE IF HE CAN MOVE.
So much like I was when I started out...
RUMMBLE
!

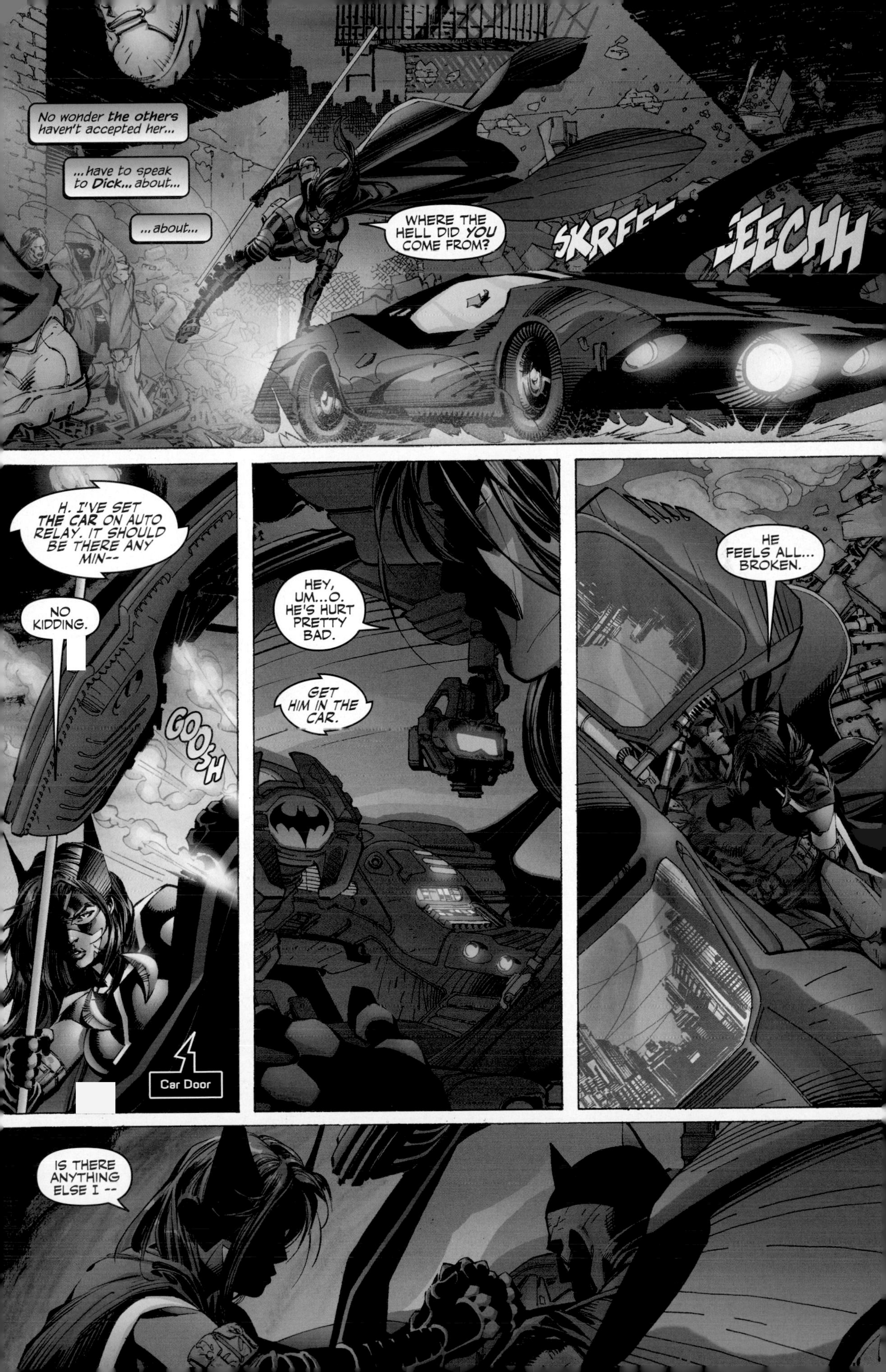
No wonder the others haven't accepted her...
...have to speak to Dick... about...
...about...
WHERE THE HELL DID YOU COME FROM?
SKREE--
-EECHH
H. I'VE SET THE CAR ON AUTO RELAY. IT SHOULD BE THERE ANY MIN--
NO KIDDING.
GOO'SH
Car Door
HEY, UM...O. HE'S HURT PRETTY BAD.
GET HIM IN THE CAR.
HE FEELS ALL... BROKEN.
IS THERE ANYTHING ELSE I --

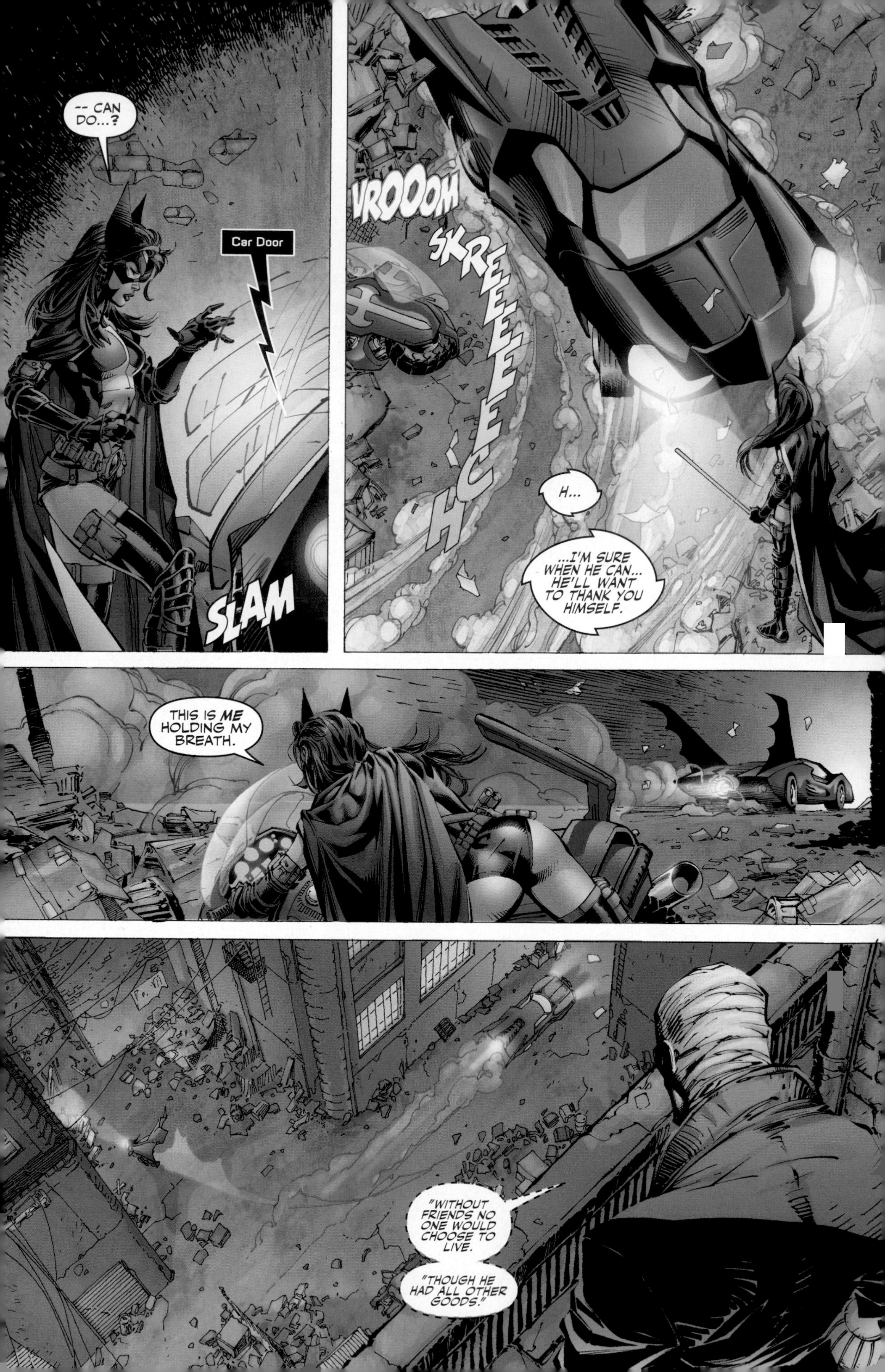

-- CAN DO...?
Car Door
SLAM
VROOOM
SKREEEEEEECH
H...
...I'M SURE WHEN HE CAN... HE'LL WANT TO THANK YOU HIMSELF.
THIS IS ME HOLDING MY BREATH.
"WITHOUT FRIENDS NO ONE WOULD CHOOSE TO LIVE.
"THOUGH HE HAD ALL OTHER GOODS."

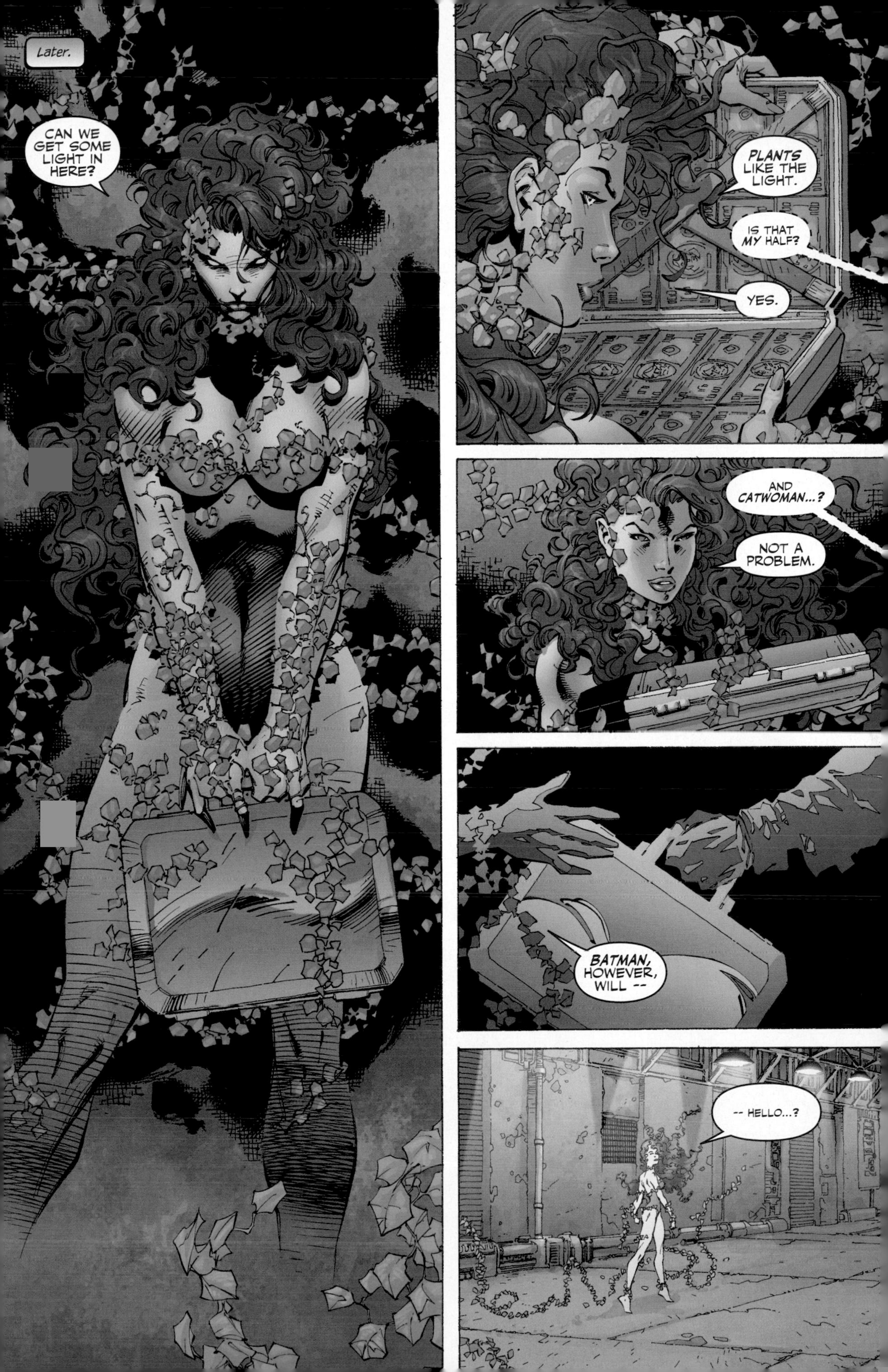
Later.
CAN WE GET SOME LIGHT IN HERE?
PLANTS LIKE THE LIGHT.
IS THAT MY HALF?
YES.
AND CATWOMAN...?
NOT A PROBLEM.
BATMAN, HOWEVER, WILL --
-- HELLO...?

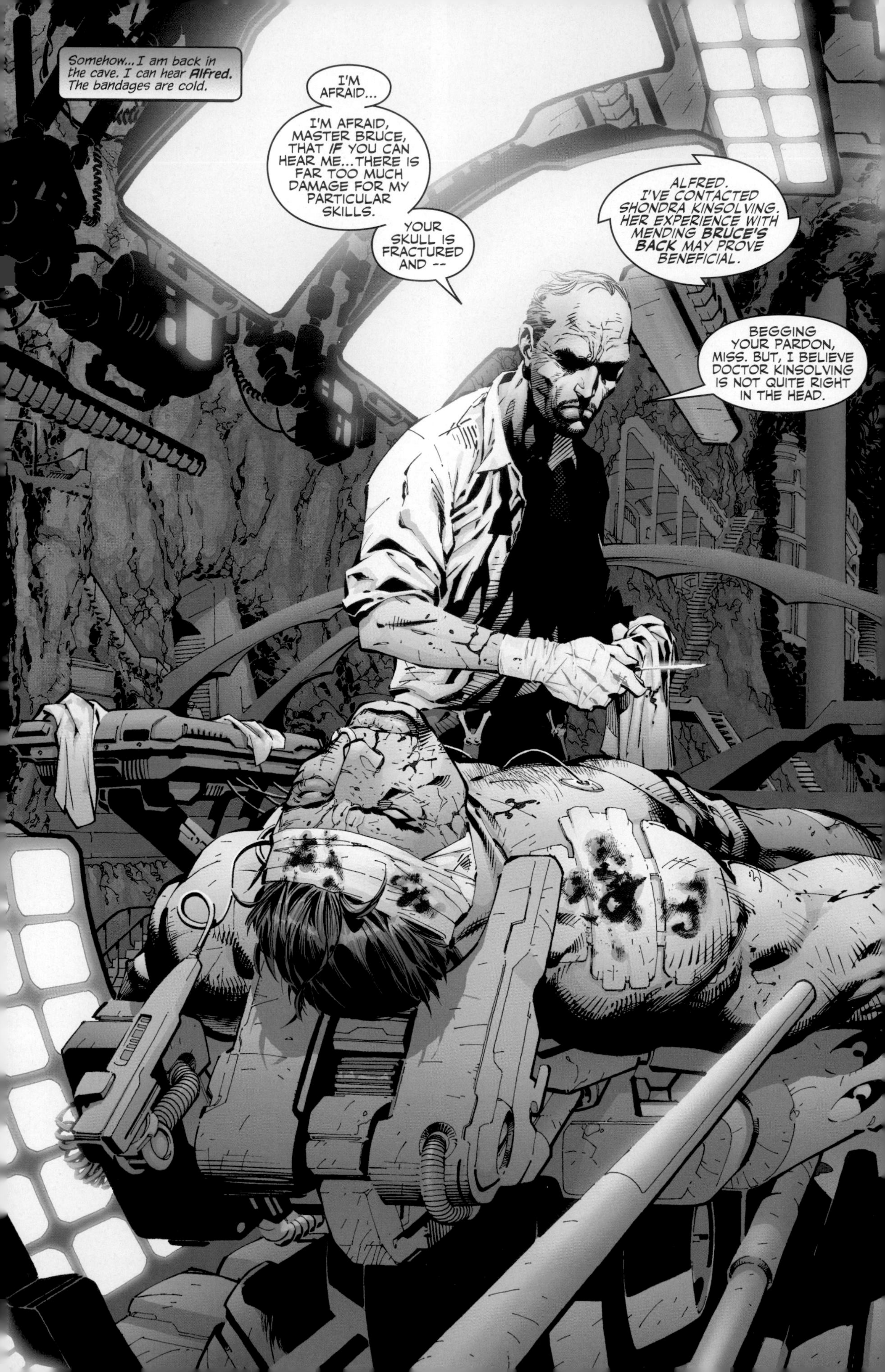
Somehow... I am back in the cave. I can hear Alfred. The bandages are cold.
I'M AFRAID...
I'M AFRAID, MASTER BRUCE, THAT IF YOU CAN HEAR ME...THERE IS FAR TOO MUCH DAMAGE FOR MY PARTICULAR SKILLS.
YOUR SKULL IS FRACTURED AND --
ALFRED. I'VE CONTACTED SHONDRA KINSOLVING. HER EXPERIENCE WITH MENDING BRUCE'S BACK MAY PROVE BENEFICIAL.
BEGGING YOUR PARDON, MISS. BUT, I BELIEVE DOCTOR KINSOLVING IS NOT QUITE RIGHT IN THE HEAD.

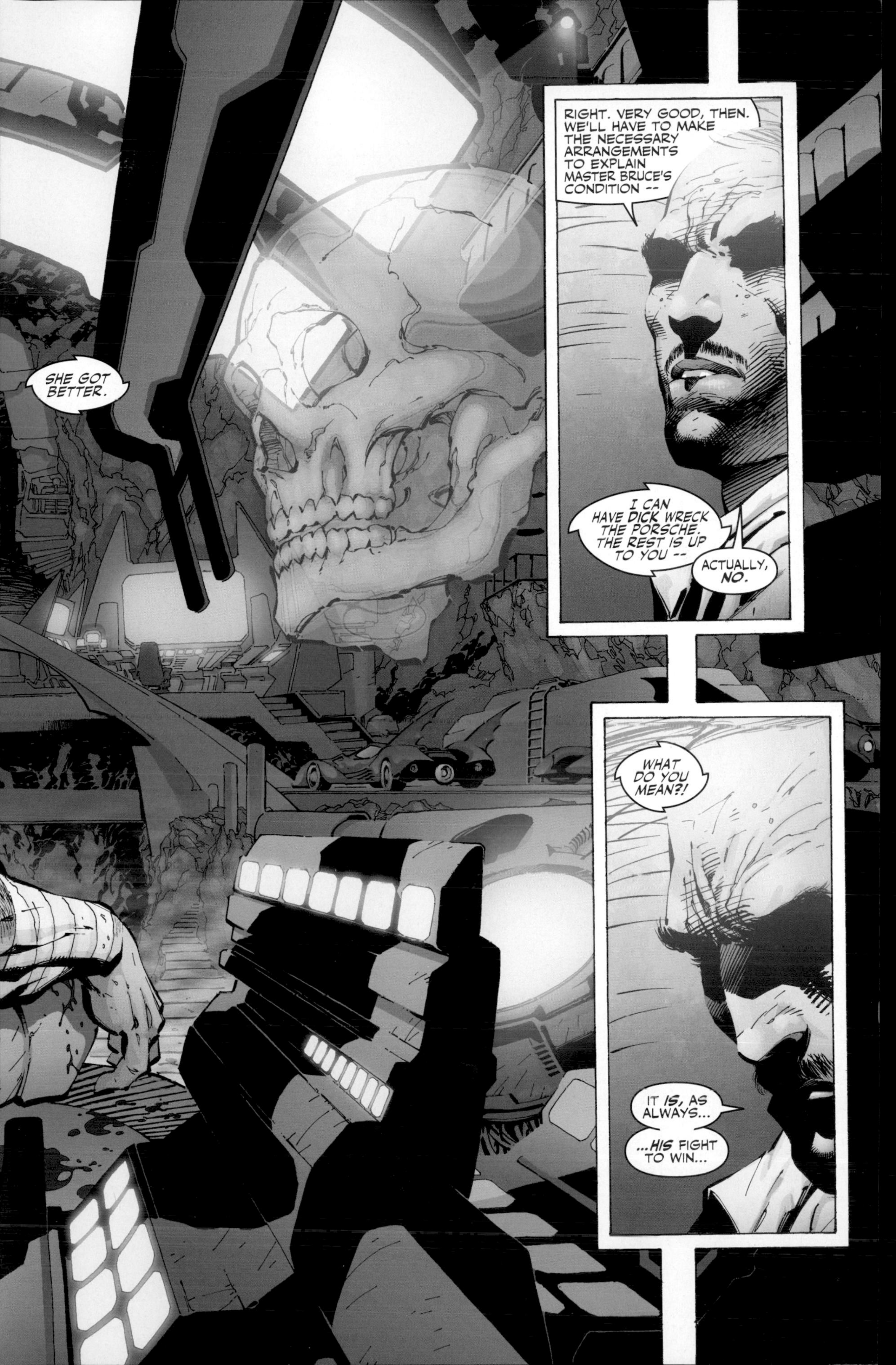
SHE GOT BETTER.
RIGHT. VERY GOOD, THEN. WE'LL HAVE TO MAKE THE NECESSARY ARRANGEMENTS TO EXPLAIN MASTER BRUCE'S CONDITION --
I CAN HAVE DICK WRECK THE PORSCHE. THE REST IS UP TO YOU --
ACTUALLY, NO.
WHAT DO YOU MEAN?!
IT IS, AS ALWAYS...
...HIS FIGHT TO WIN...

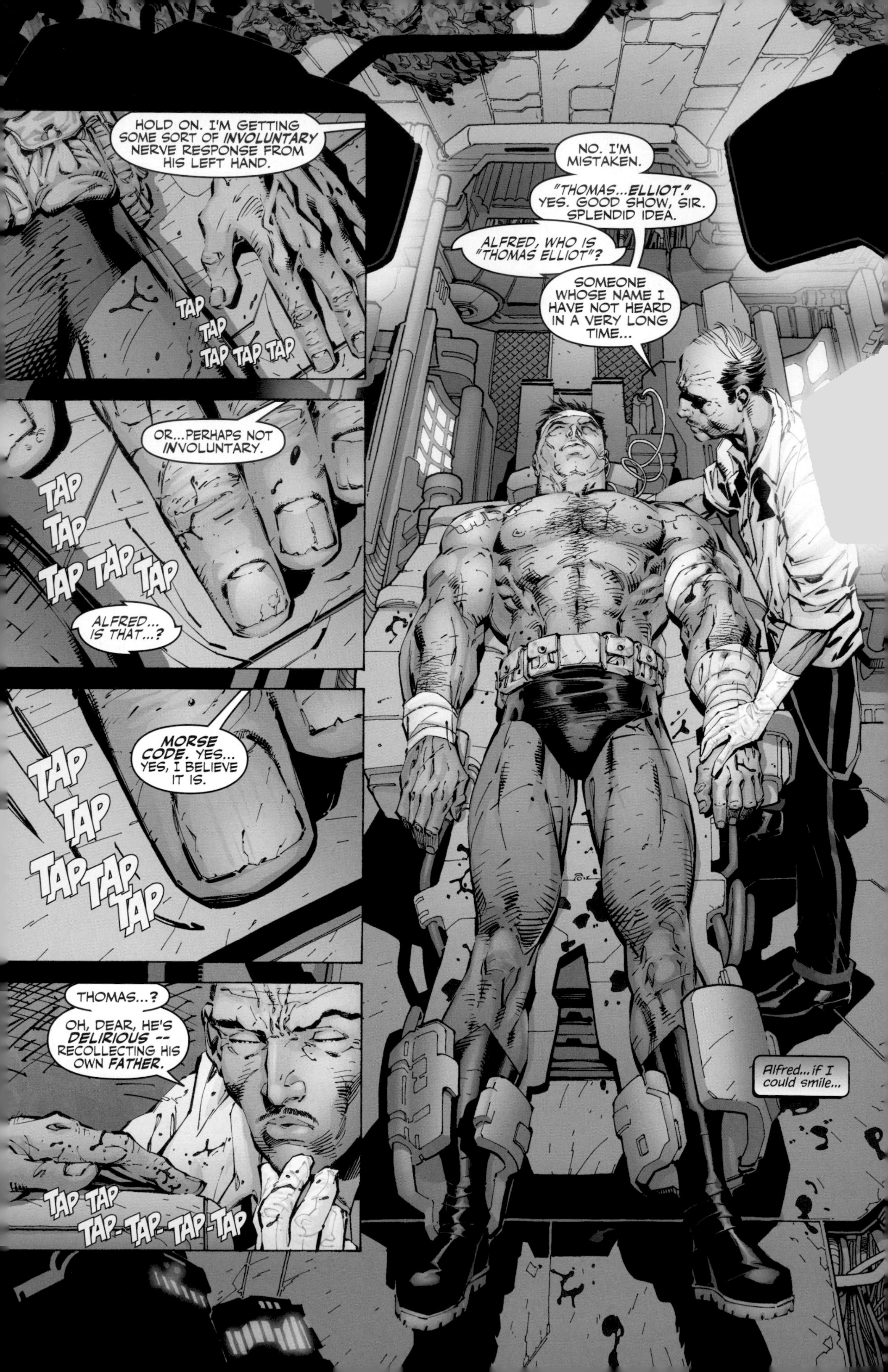
HOLD ON. I'M GETTING SOME SORT OF *INVOLUNTARY* NERVE RESPONSE FROM HIS LEFT HAND.
TAP TAP TAP TAP TAP
OR...PERHAPS NOT *IN*VOLUNTARY.
TAP TAP TAP TAP TAP
ALFRED... IS THAT...?
*MORSE CODE*. YES... YES, I BELIEVE IT IS.
TAP TAP TAP TAP TAP
THOMAS...?
OH, DEAR, HE'S *DELIRIOUS* -- RECOLLECTING HIS OWN *FATHER*.
TAP TAP TAP-TAP-TAP-TAP
NO. I'M MISTAKEN.
"THOMAS...*ELLIOT*." YES. GOOD SHOW, SIR. SPLENDID IDEA.
ALFRED, WHO IS "THOMAS ELLIOT"?
SOMEONE WHOSE NAME I HAVE NOT HEARD IN A VERY LONG TIME...
*Alfred...if I could smile...*

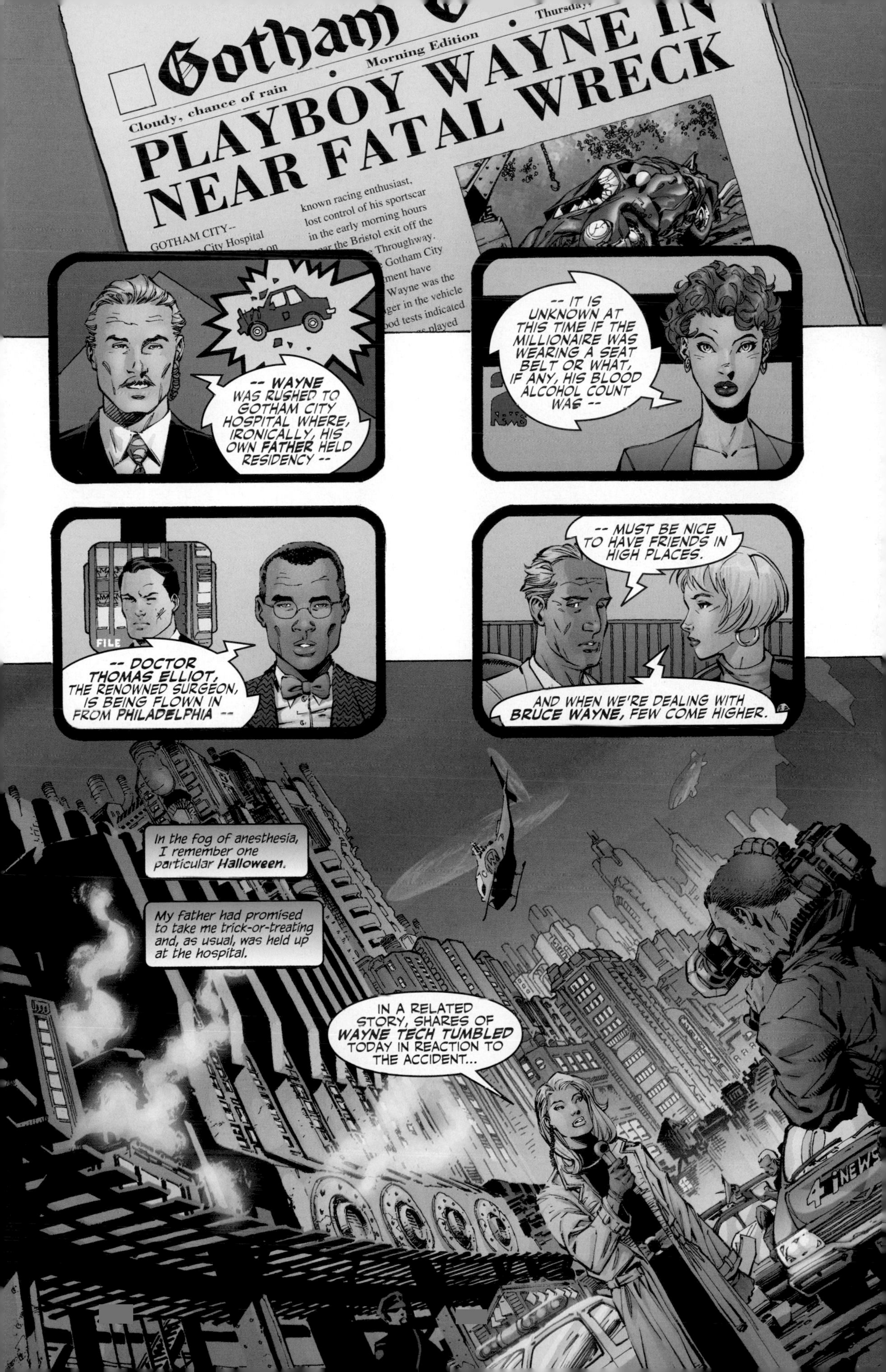
Gotham
Thursday,
Morning Edition
Cloudy, chance of rain
PLAYBOY WAYNE IN
NEAR FATAL WRECK
GOTHAM CITY--
City Hospital
known racing enthusiast,
lost control of his sportscar
in the early morning hours
near the Bristol exit off the
Throughway.
Gotham City
have
Wayne was the
in the vehicle
tests indicated
played
-- WAYNE WAS RUSHED TO GOTHAM CITY HOSPITAL WHERE, IRONICALLY, HIS OWN FATHER HELD RESIDENCY --
-- IT IS UNKNOWN AT THIS TIME IF THE MILLIONAIRE WAS WEARING A SEAT BELT OR WHAT, IF ANY, HIS BLOOD ALCOHOL COUNT WAS --
FILE
-- DOCTOR THOMAS ELLIOT, THE RENOWNED SURGEON, IS BEING FLOWN IN FROM PHILADELPHIA --
-- MUST BE NICE TO HAVE FRIENDS IN HIGH PLACES.
AND WHEN WE'RE DEALING WITH BRUCE WAYNE, FEW COME HIGHER.
In the fog of anesthesia, I remember one particular Halloween.
My father had promised to take me trick-or-treating and, as usual, was held up at the hospital.
IN A RELATED STORY, SHARES OF WAYNE TECH TUMBLED TODAY IN REACTION TO THE ACCIDENT...
4 NEWS

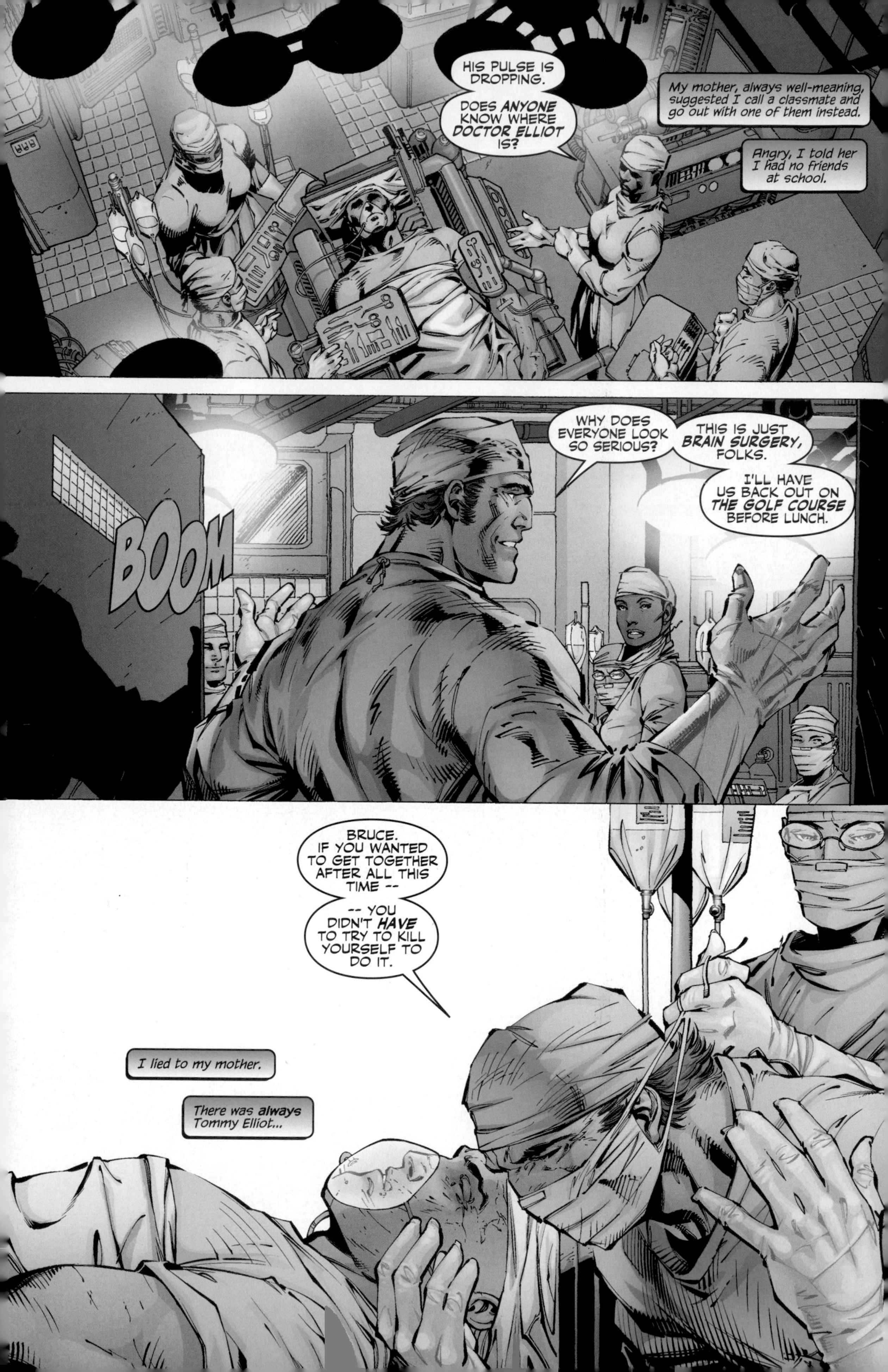

HIS PULSE IS DROPPING.
DOES ANYONE KNOW WHERE DOCTOR ELLIOT IS?
My mother, always well-meaning, suggested I call a classmate and go out with one of them instead.
Angry, I told her I had no friends at school.
BOOM
WHY DOES EVERYONE LOOK SO SERIOUS?
THIS IS JUST BRAIN SURGERY, FOLKS.
I'LL HAVE US BACK OUT ON THE GOLF COURSE BEFORE LUNCH.
BRUCE. IF YOU WANTED TO GET TOGETHER AFTER ALL THIS TIME --
-- YOU DIDN'T HAVE TO TRY TO KILL YOURSELF TO DO IT.
I lied to my mother.
There was always Tommy Elliot...

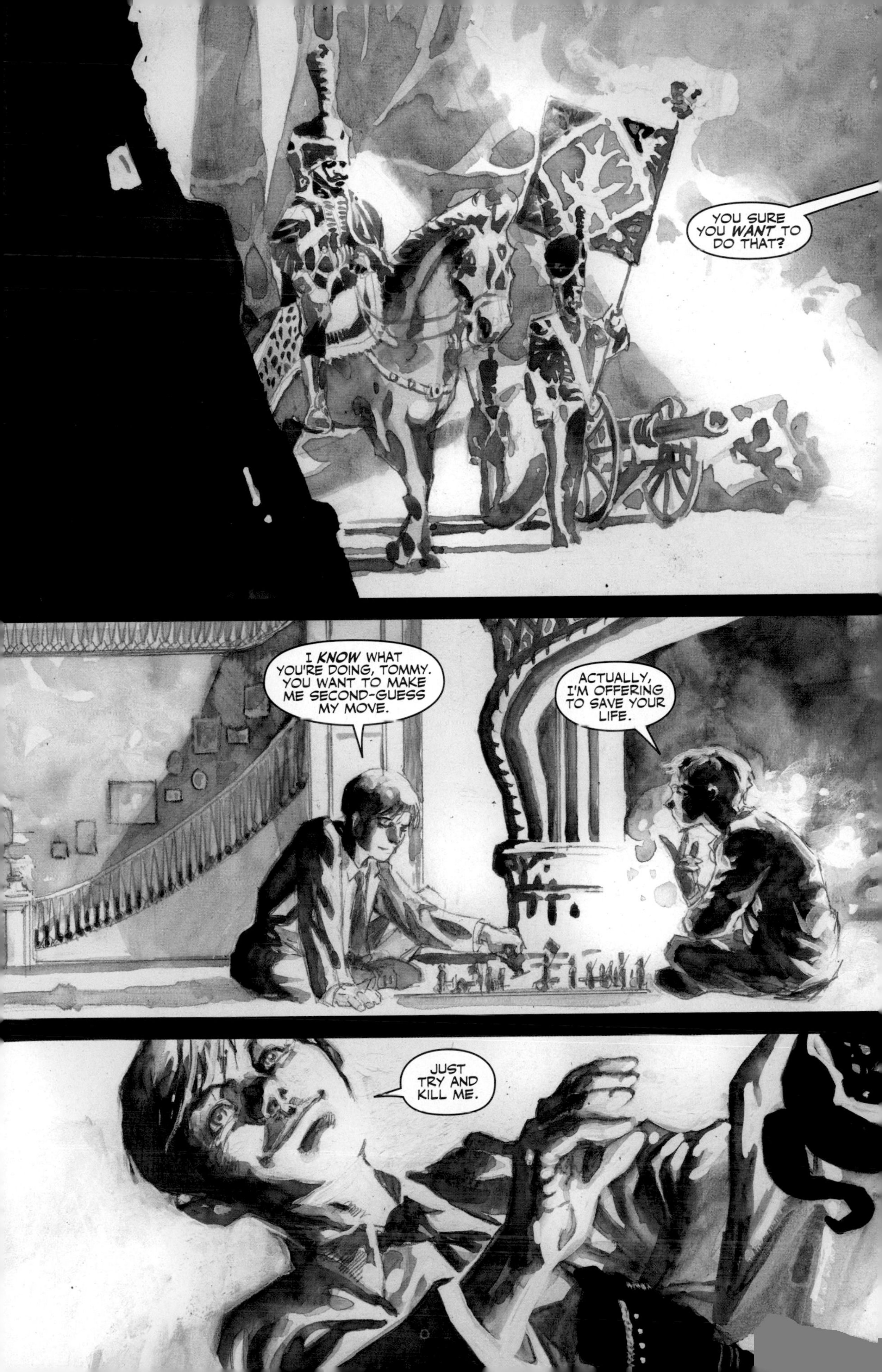
YOU SURE YOU *WANT* TO DO THAT?
I *KNOW* WHAT YOU'RE DOING, TOMMY. YOU WANT TO MAKE ME SECOND-GUESS MY MOVE.
ACTUALLY, I'M OFFERING TO SAVE YOUR LIFE.
JUST TRY AND KILL ME.

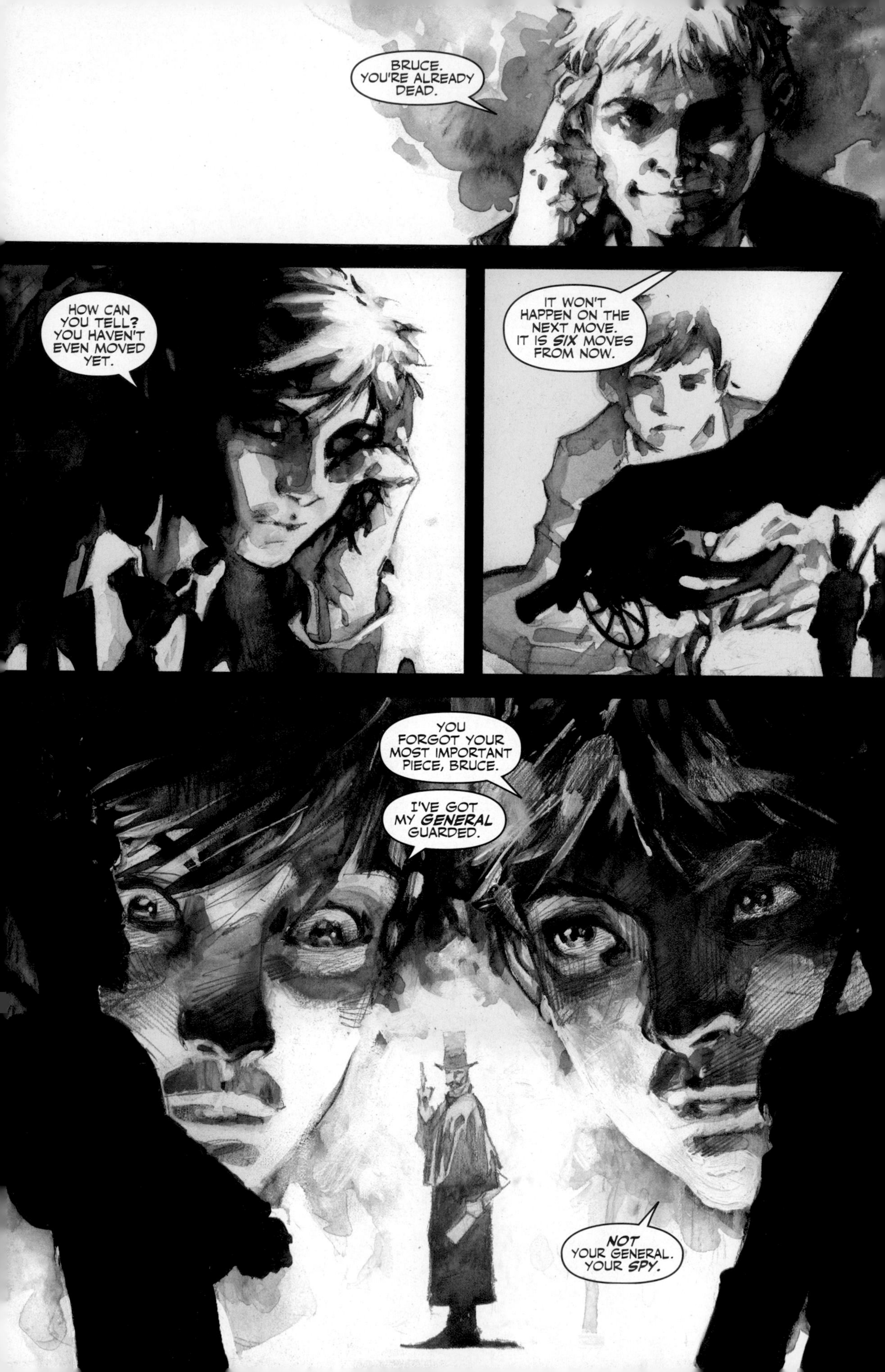
BRUCE. YOU'RE ALREADY DEAD.
HOW CAN YOU TELL? YOU HAVEN'T EVEN MOVED YET.
IT WON'T HAPPEN ON THE NEXT MOVE. IT IS SIX MOVES FROM NOW.
YOU FORGOT YOUR MOST IMPORTANT PIECE, BRUCE.
I'VE GOT MY GENERAL GUARDED.
NOT YOUR GENERAL. YOUR SPY.

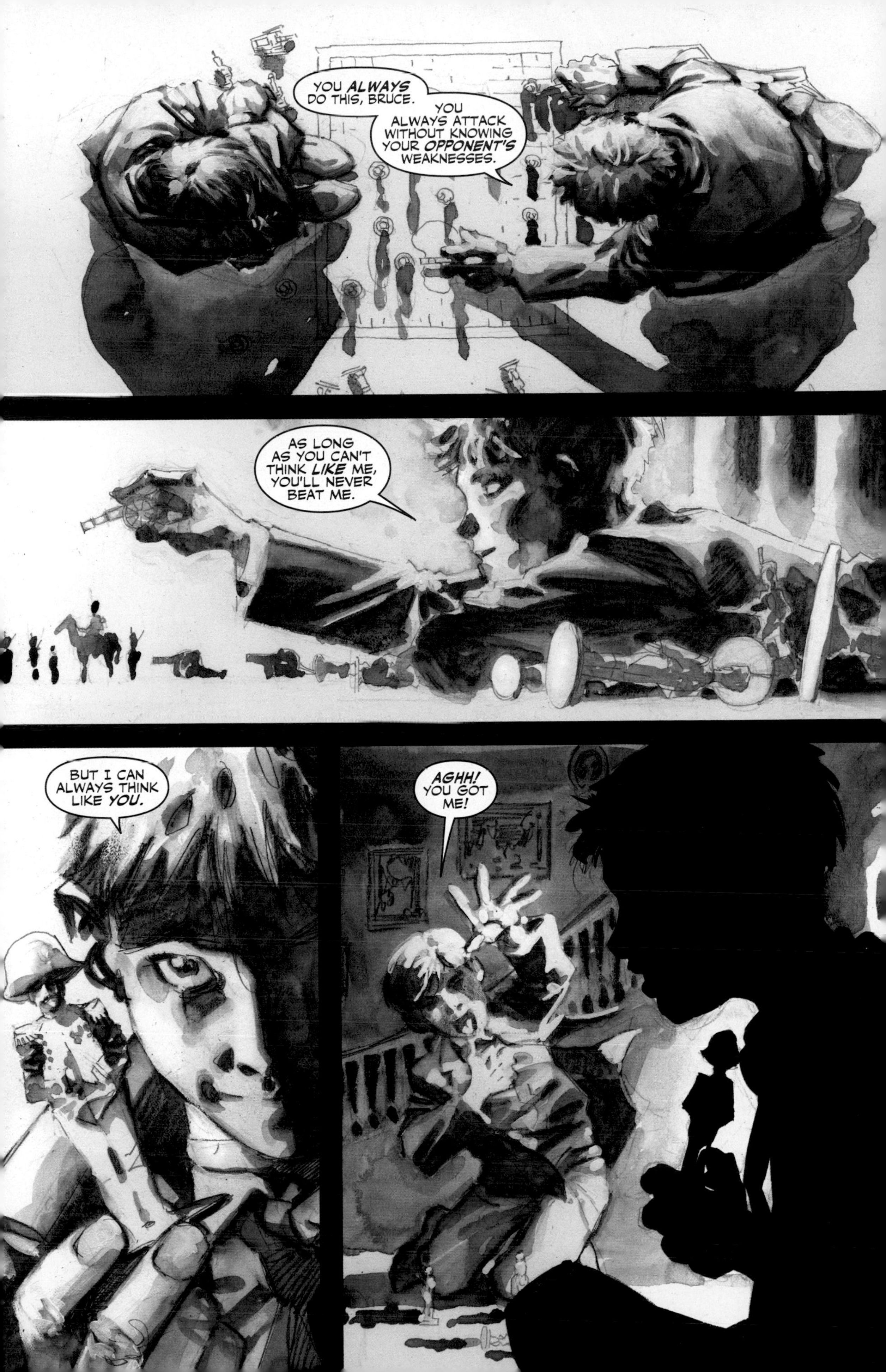
YOU ALWAYS DO THIS, BRUCE.
YOU ALWAYS ATTACK WITHOUT KNOWING YOUR OPPONENT'S WEAKNESSES.
AS LONG AS YOU CAN'T THINK LIKE ME, YOU'LL NEVER BEAT ME.
BUT I CAN ALWAYS THINK LIKE YOU.
AGHH! YOU GOT ME!

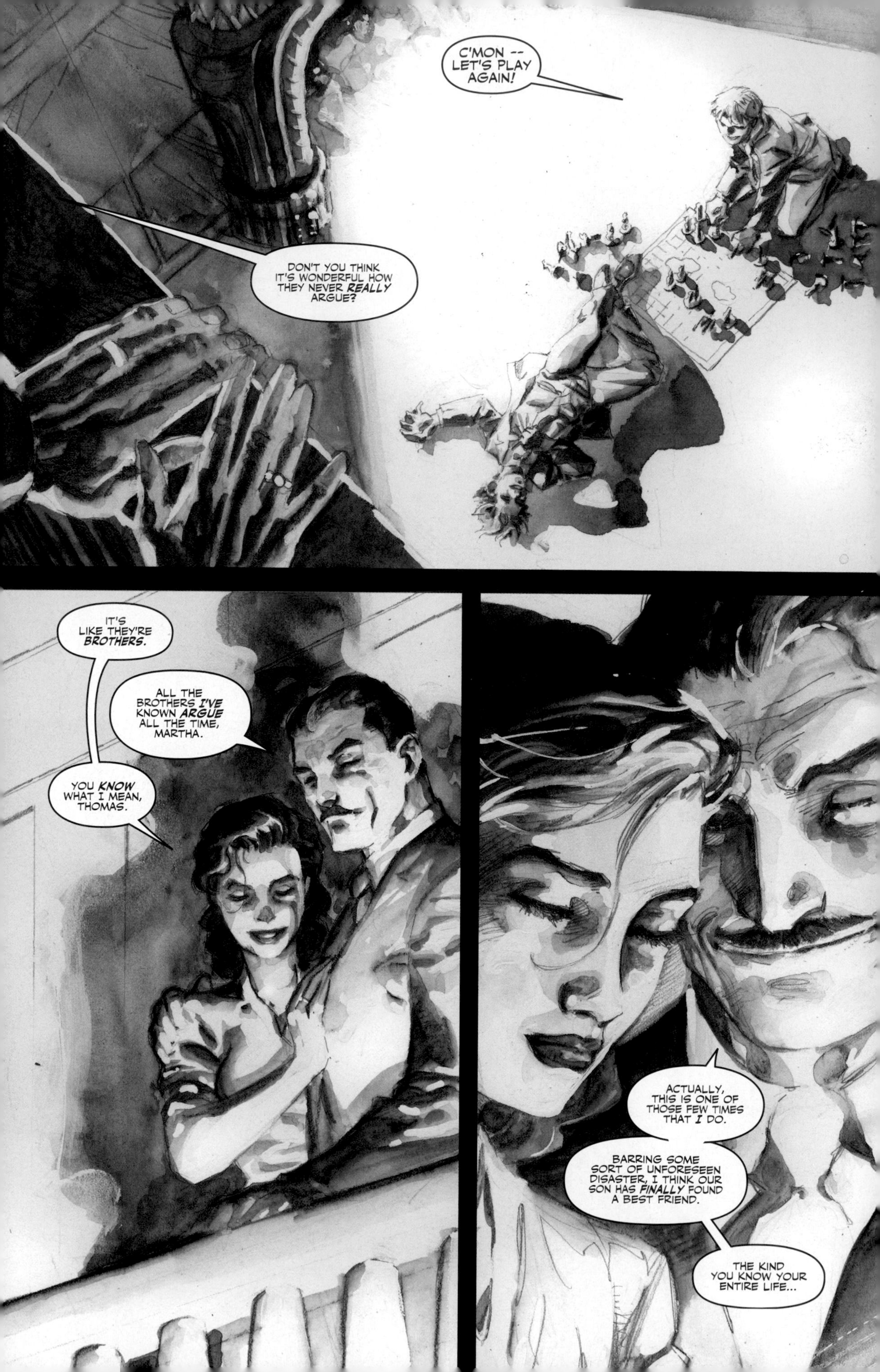

C'MON -- LET'S PLAY AGAIN!
DON'T YOU THINK IT'S WONDERFUL HOW THEY NEVER REALLY ARGUE?
IT'S LIKE THEY'RE BROTHERS.
ALL THE BROTHERS I'VE KNOWN ARGUE ALL THE TIME, MARTHA.
YOU KNOW WHAT I MEAN, THOMAS.
ACTUALLY, THIS IS ONE OF THOSE FEW TIMES THAT I DO.
BARRING SOME SORT OF UNFORESEEN DISASTER, I THINK OUR SON HAS FINALLY FOUND A BEST FRIEND.
THE KIND YOU KNOW YOUR ENTIRE LIFE...

DOCTOR. I THINK YOU CAN HANDLE IT FROM HERE. WHY DON'T YOU CLOSE?

WELL, I DON'T KNOW IF MISTER WAYNE WILL EVER PLAY *THE VIOLIN* AGAIN --

HAHAHAHA HA HA

HAHAHA HA HA

-- BUT I THINK IT'S SAFE TO SAY THAT...

PLANET
★★★ Friday, November 29, 2002

WAYNE OUT OF DANGER

is Lane

by Jimmy Olsen

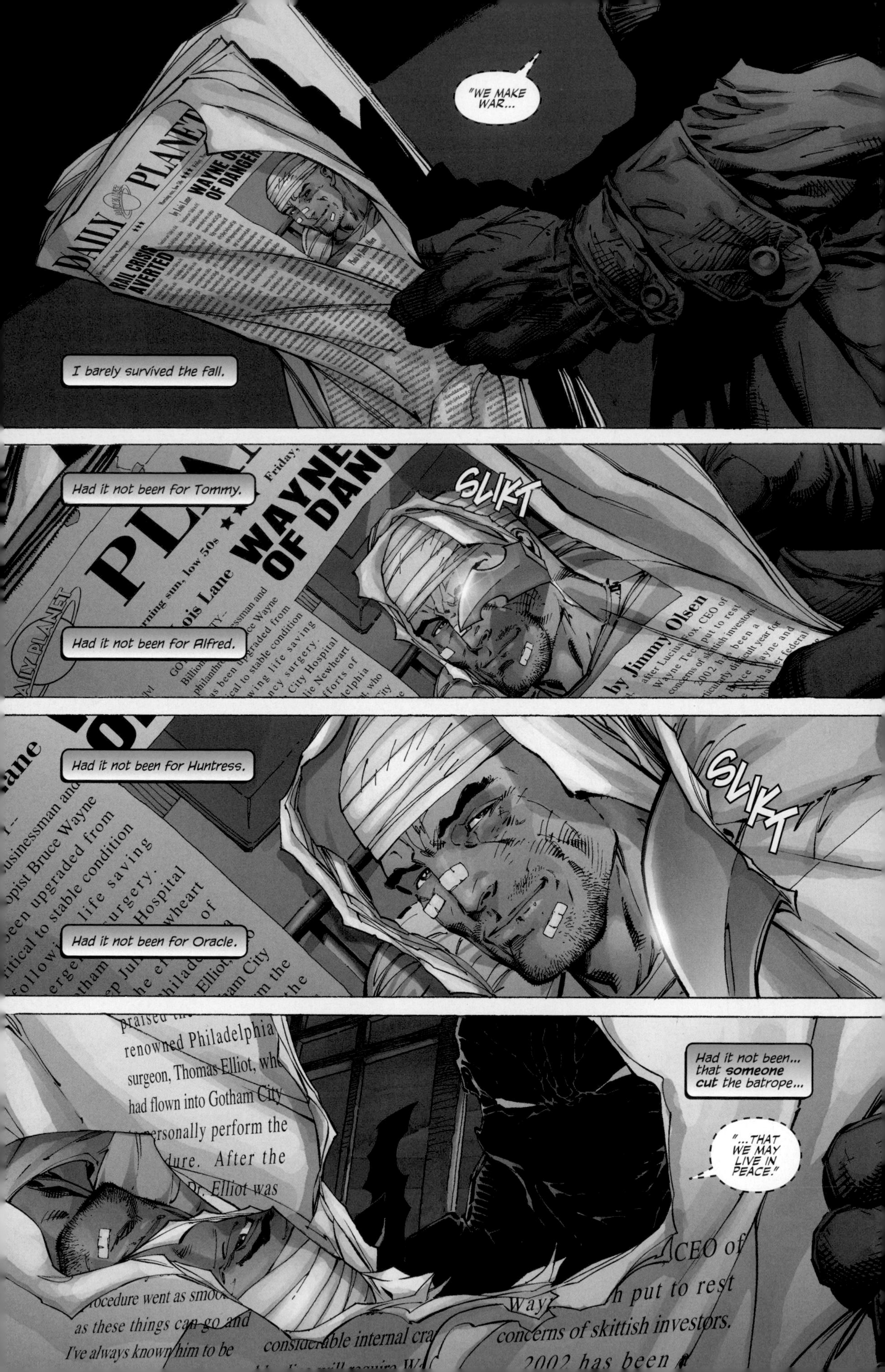
"WE MAKE WAR...
I barely survived the fall.
Had it not been for Tommy.
SLIKT
Had it not been for Alfred.
Had it not been for Huntress.
SLIKT
Had it not been for Oracle.
Had it not been... that **someone** **cut** the batrope...
"...THAT WE MAY LIVE IN PEACE."

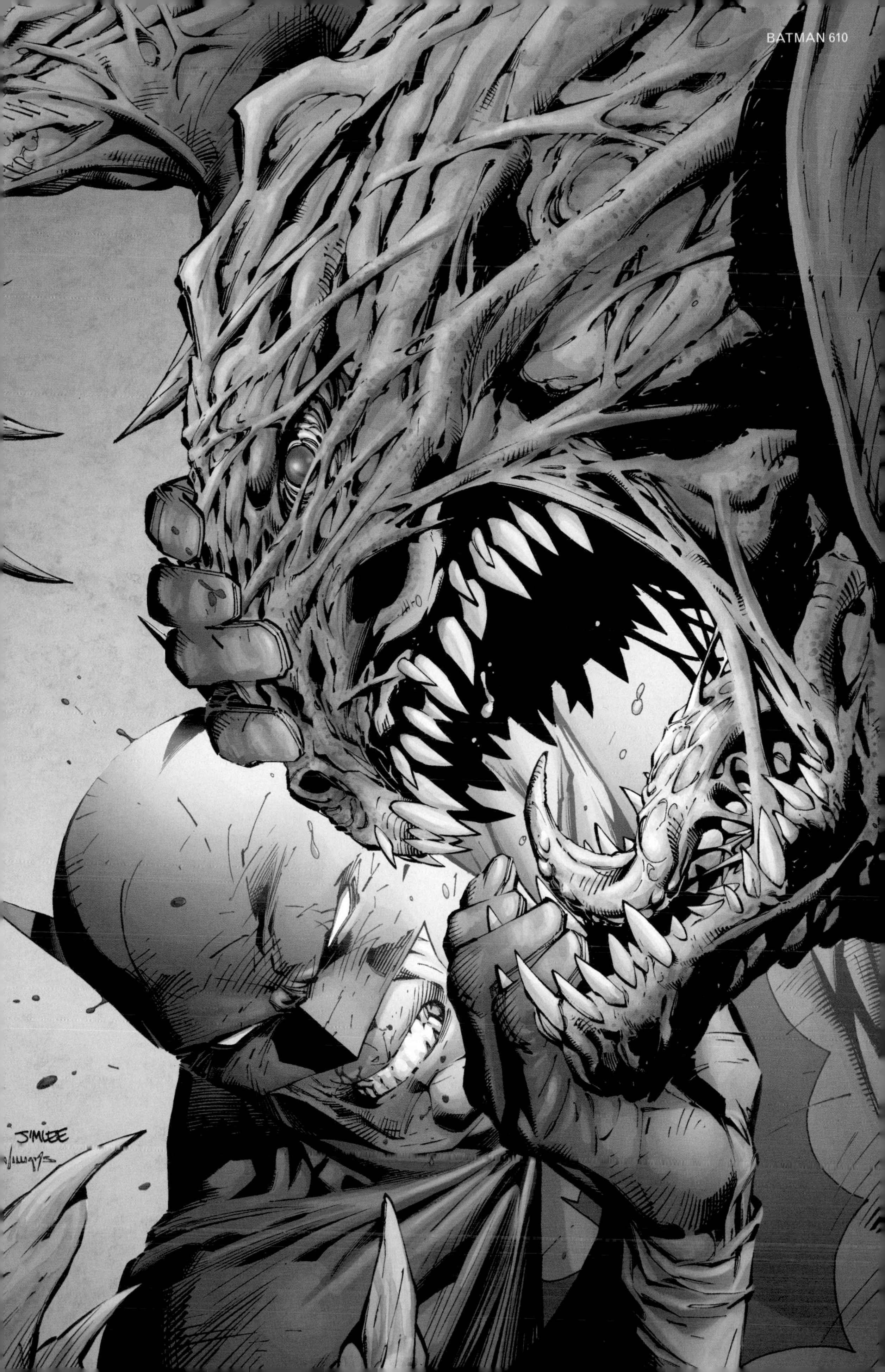
JIMLEE

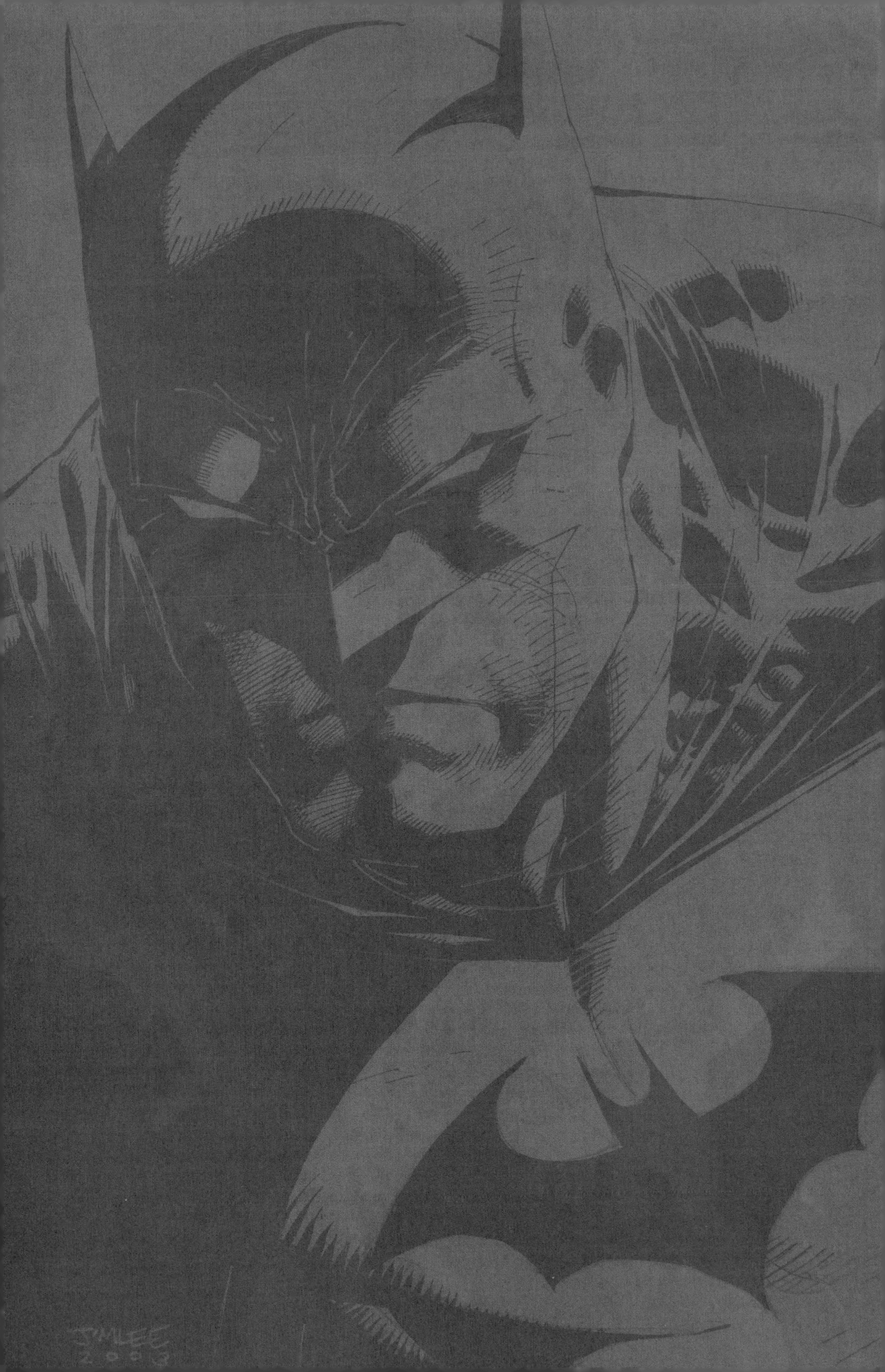
JIMLEE

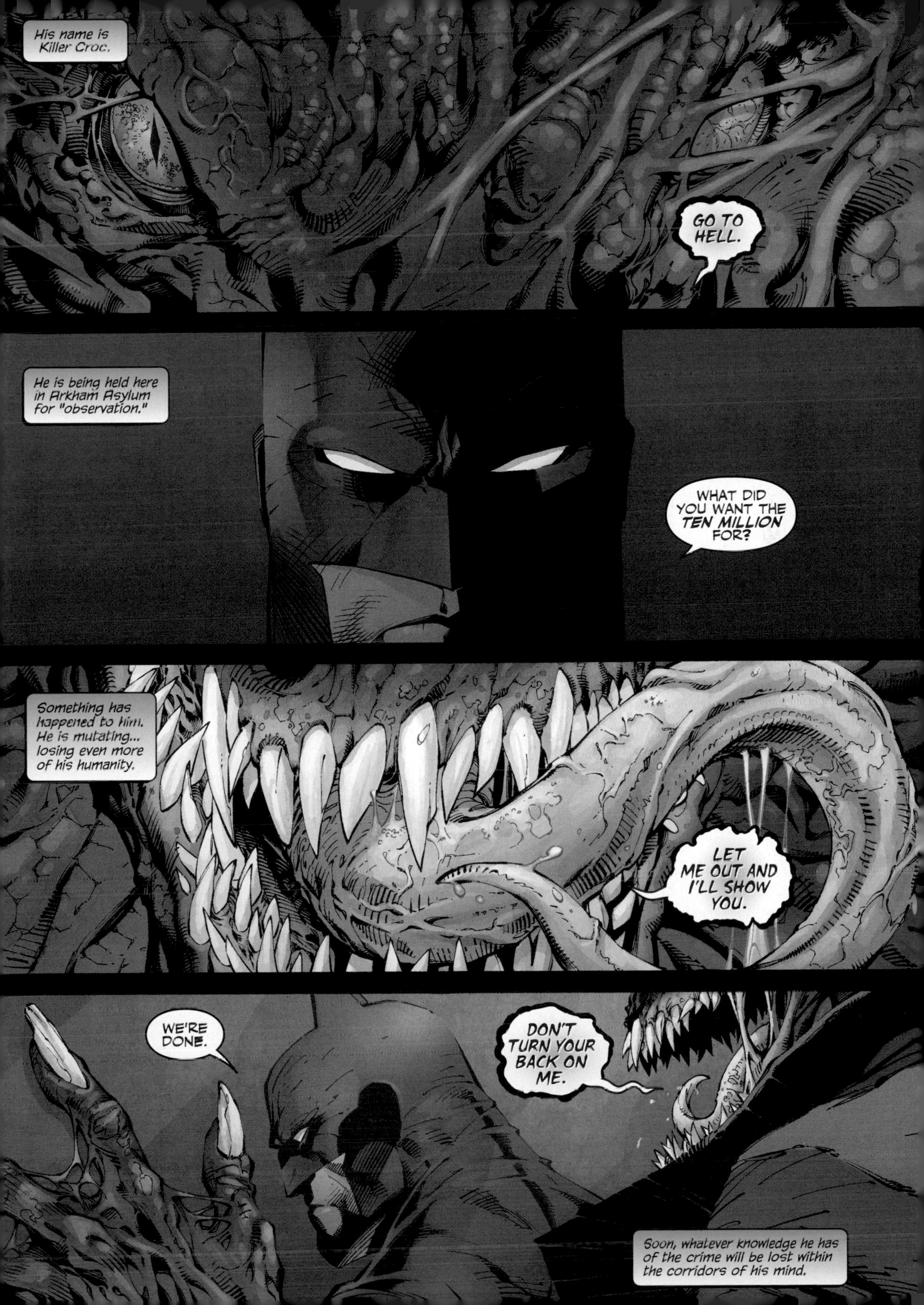
His name is Killer Croc.
GO TO HELL.
He is being held here in Arkham Asylum for "observation."
WHAT DID YOU WANT THE TEN MILLION FOR?
Something has happened to him. He is mutating... losing even more of his humanity.
LET ME OUT AND I'LL SHOW YOU.
WE'RE DONE.
DON'T TURN YOUR BACK ON ME.
Soon, whatever knowledge he has of the crime will be lost within the corridors of his mind.

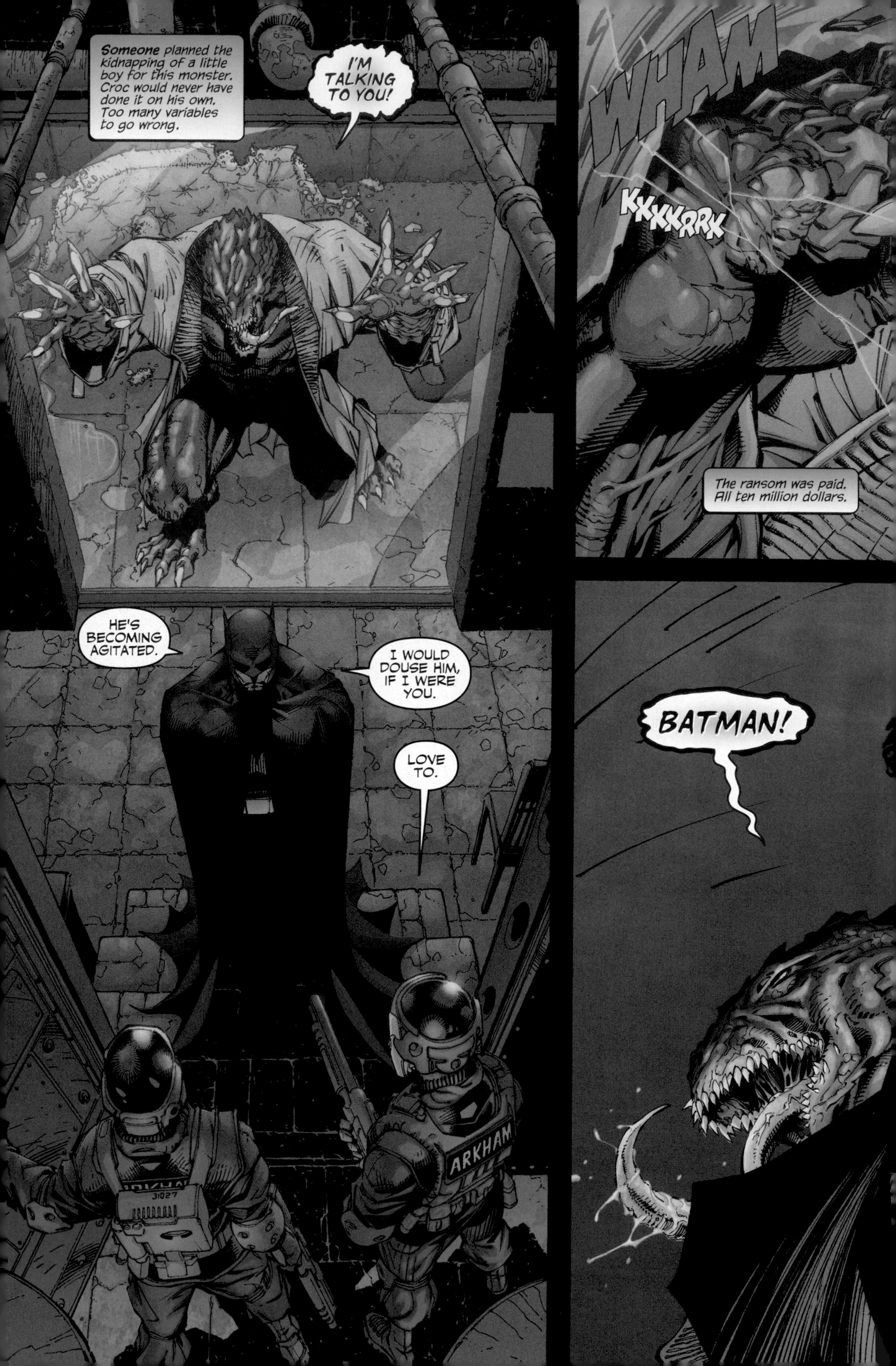
Someone planned the kidnapping of a little boy for this monster. Croc would never have done it on his own. Too many variables to go wrong.
I'M TALKING TO YOU!
WHAM
KXXXRRK
The ransom was paid. All ten million dollars.
HE'S BECOMING AGITATED.
I WOULD DOUSE HIM, IF I WERE YOU.
LOVE TO.
ARKHAM
BATMAN!

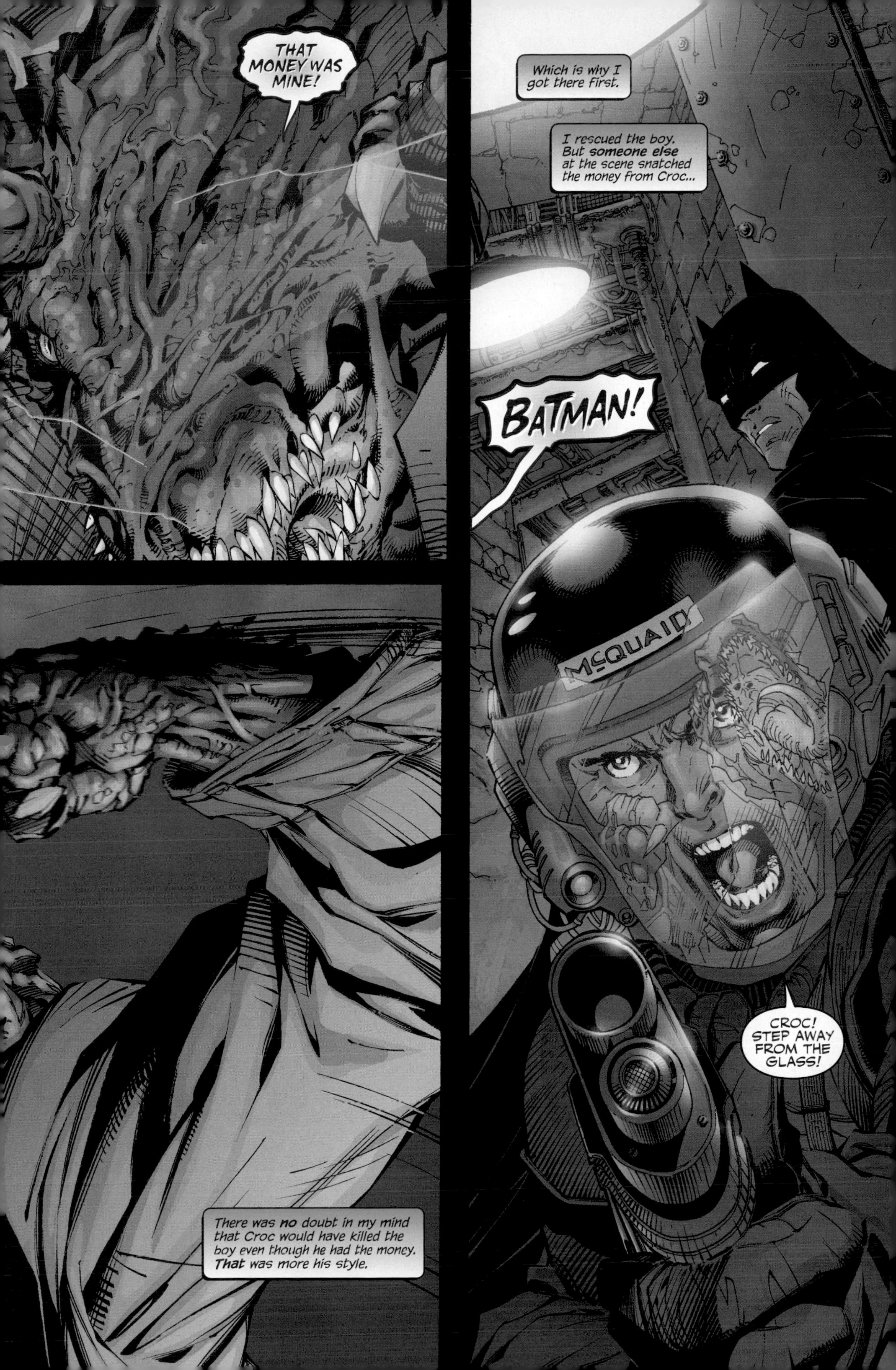
THAT MONEY WAS MINE!
Which is why I got there first.
I rescued the boy. But **someone else** at the scene snatched the money from Croc...
There was **no** doubt in my mind that Croc would have killed the boy even though he had the money. ***That*** was more his style.
BATMAN!
McQUAID
CROC! STEP AWAY FROM THE GLASS!

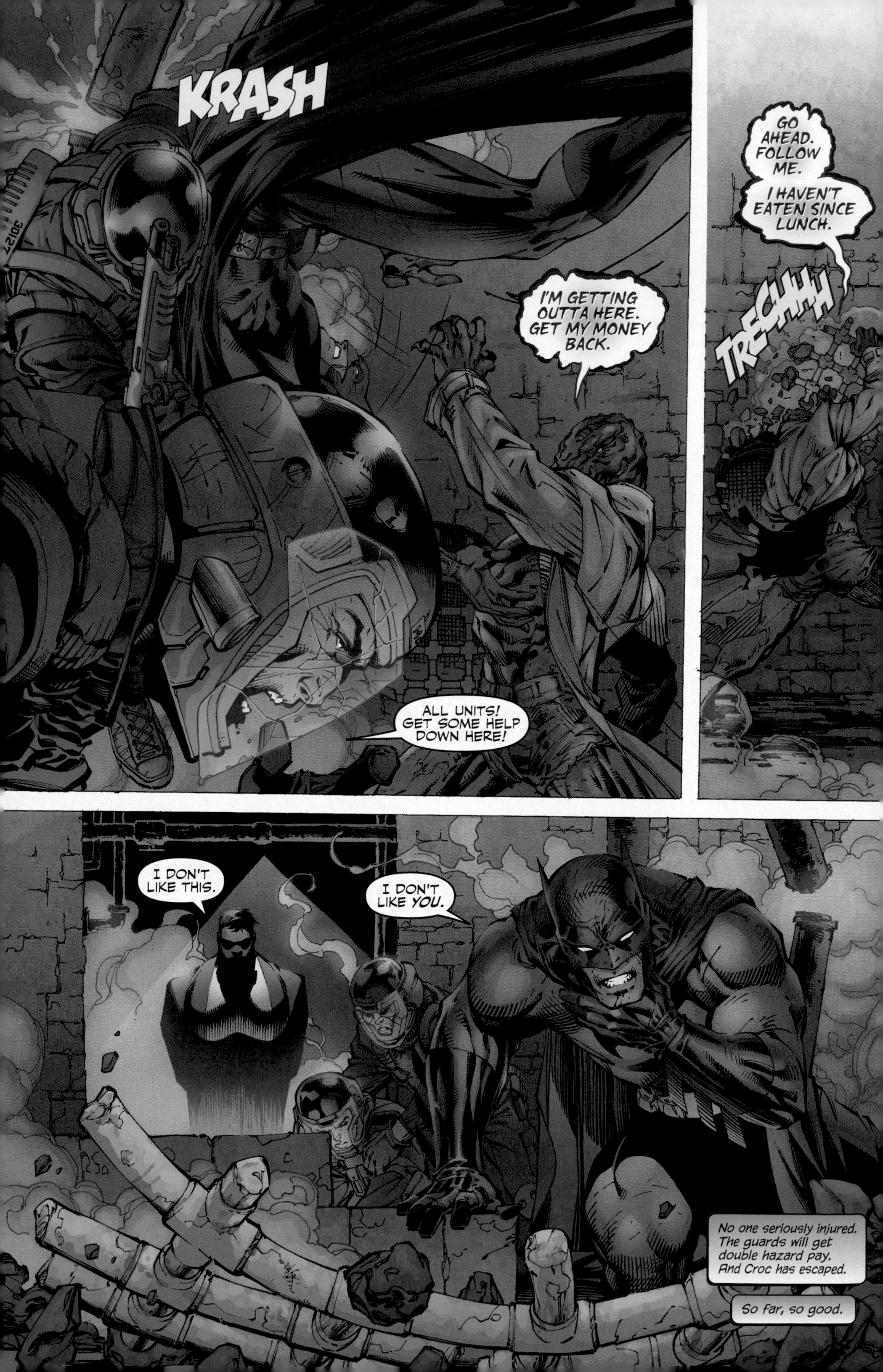
KRASH
I'M GETTING OUTTA HERE. GET MY MONEY BACK.
ALL UNITS! GET SOME HELP DOWN HERE!
GO AHEAD. FOLLOW ME.
I HAVEN'T EATEN SINCE LUNCH.
TRESHHH
I DON'T LIKE THIS.
I DON'T LIKE *YOU*.
*No one seriously injured. The guards will get double hazard pay. And Croc has escaped.*
*So far, so good.*

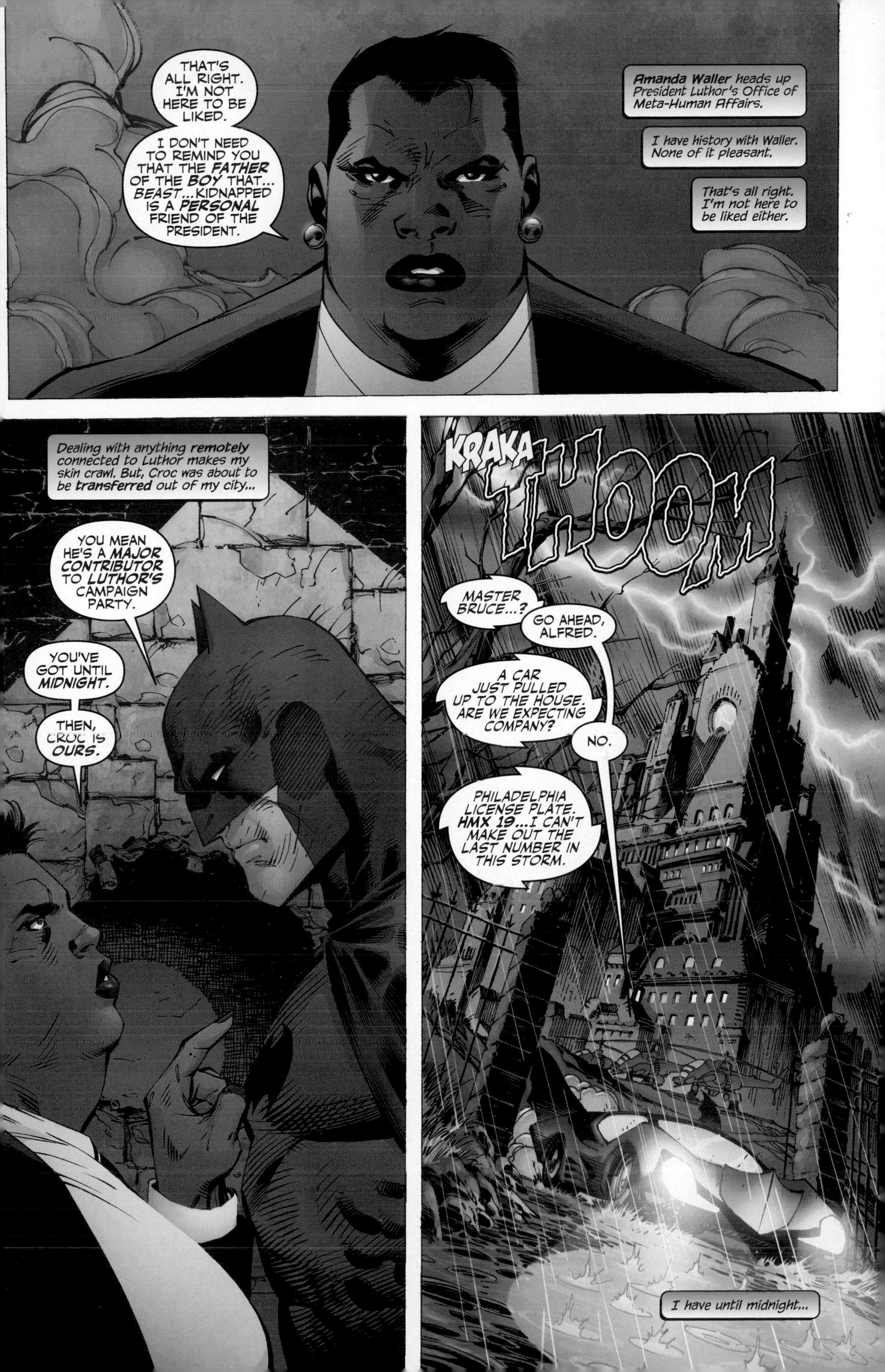
THAT'S ALL RIGHT. I'M NOT HERE TO BE LIKED.
I DON'T NEED TO REMIND YOU THAT THE FATHER OF THE BOY THAT... BEAST...KIDNAPPED IS A PERSONAL FRIEND OF THE PRESIDENT.
Amanda Waller heads up President Luthor's Office of Meta-Human Affairs.
I have history with Waller. None of it pleasant.
That's all right. I'm not here to be liked either.
Dealing with anything remotely connected to Luthor makes my skin crawl. But, Croc was about to be transferred out of my city...
YOU MEAN HE'S A MAJOR CONTRIBUTOR TO LUTHOR'S CAMPAIGN PARTY.
YOU'VE GOT UNTIL MIDNIGHT.
THEN, CROC IS OURS.
KRAKA THOOM
MASTER BRUCE...?
GO AHEAD, ALFRED.
A CAR JUST PULLED UP TO THE HOUSE. ARE WE EXPECTING COMPANY?
NO.
PHILADELPHIA LICENSE PLATE. HMX 19...I CAN'T MAKE OUT THE LAST NUMBER IN THIS STORM.
I have until midnight...

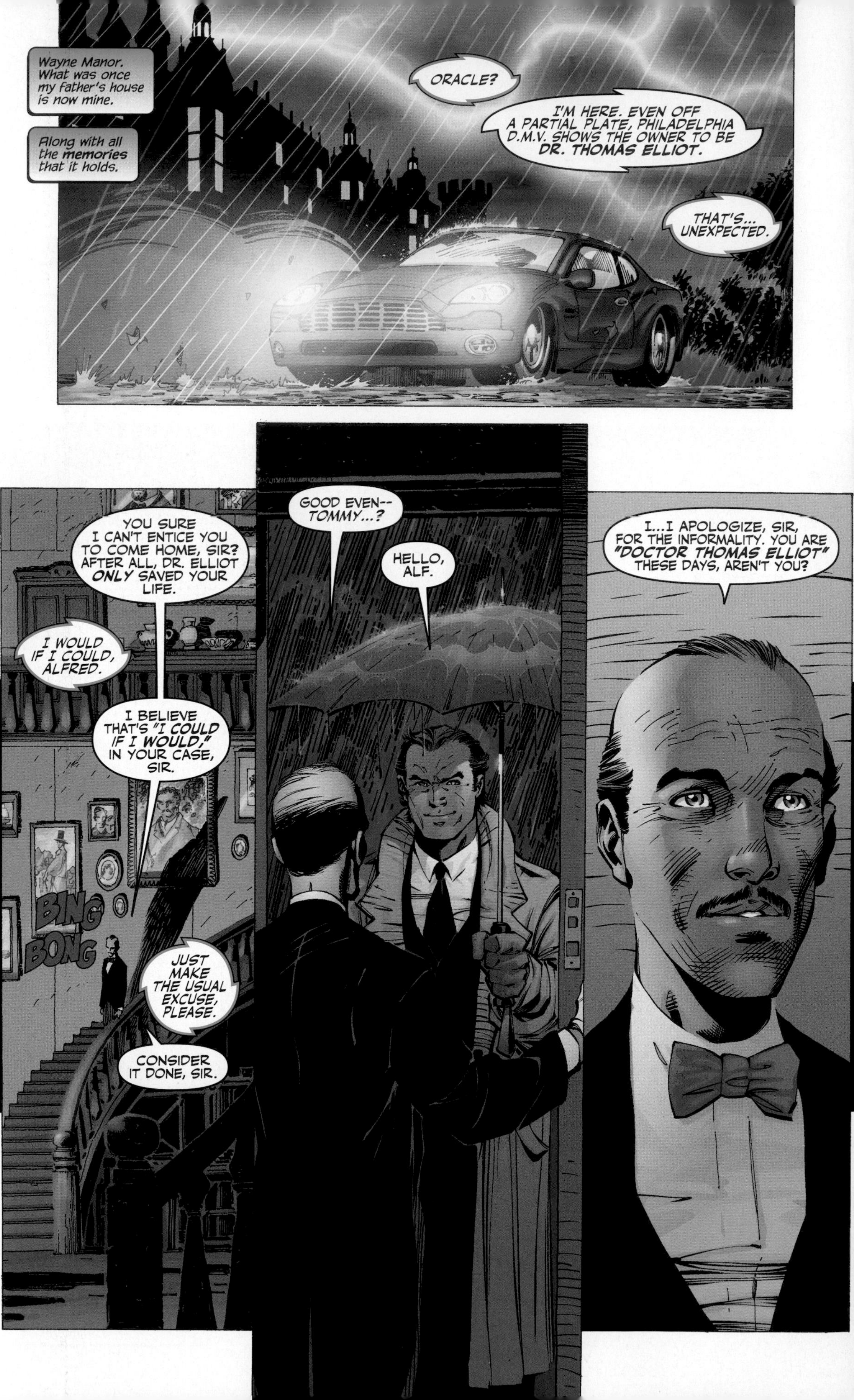
Wayne Manor. What was once my father's house is now mine.
Along with all the memories that it holds.
ORACLE?
I'M HERE. EVEN OFF A PARTIAL PLATE, PHILADELPHIA D.M.V. SHOWS THE OWNER TO BE DR. THOMAS ELLIOT.
THAT'S... UNEXPECTED.
YOU SURE I CAN'T ENTICE YOU TO COME HOME, SIR? AFTER ALL, DR. ELLIOT ONLY SAVED YOUR LIFE.
I WOULD IF I COULD, ALFRED.
I BELIEVE THAT'S "I COULD IF I WOULD," IN YOUR CASE, SIR.
BING BONG
JUST MAKE THE USUAL EXCUSE, PLEASE.
CONSIDER IT DONE, SIR.
GOOD EVEN-- TOMMY...?
HELLO, ALF.
I...I APOLOGIZE, SIR, FOR THE INFORMALITY. YOU ARE "DOCTOR THOMAS ELLIOT" THESE DAYS, AREN'T YOU?

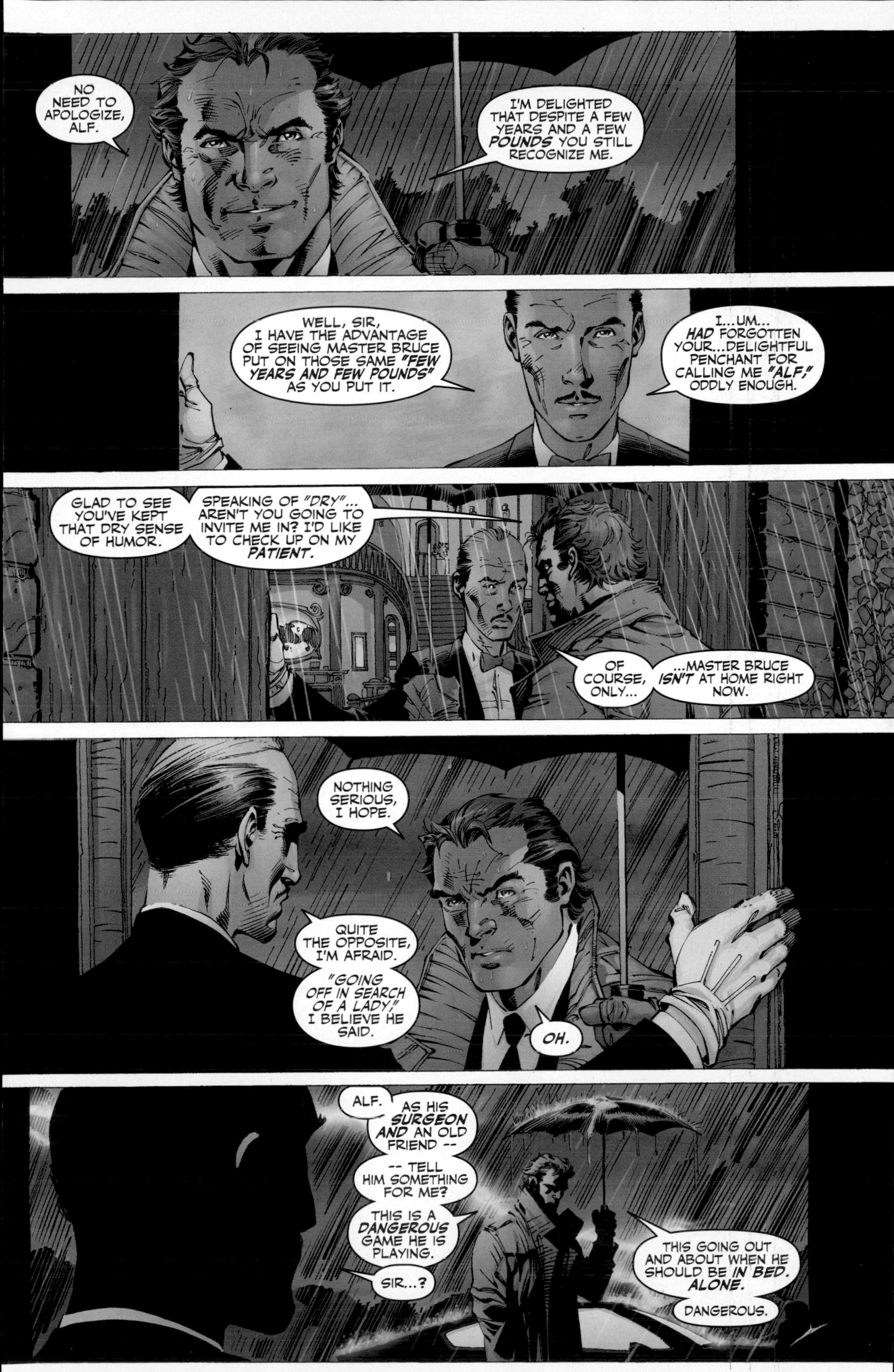
NO NEED TO APOLOGIZE, ALF.
I'M DELIGHTED THAT DESPITE A FEW YEARS AND A FEW POUNDS YOU STILL RECOGNIZE ME.
WELL, SIR, I HAVE THE ADVANTAGE OF SEEING MASTER BRUCE PUT ON THOSE SAME "FEW YEARS AND FEW POUNDS" AS YOU PUT IT.
I...UM... HAD FORGOTTEN YOUR...DELIGHTFUL PENCHANT FOR CALLING ME "ALF," ODDLY ENOUGH.
GLAD TO SEE YOU'VE KEPT THAT DRY SENSE OF HUMOR.
SPEAKING OF "DRY"... AREN'T YOU GOING TO INVITE ME IN? I'D LIKE TO CHECK UP ON MY PATIENT.
OF COURSE, ONLY...
...MASTER BRUCE ISN'T AT HOME RIGHT NOW.
NOTHING SERIOUS, I HOPE.
QUITE THE OPPOSITE, I'M AFRAID.
"GOING OFF IN SEARCH OF A LADY," I BELIEVE HE SAID.
OH.
ALF.
AS HIS SURGEON AND AN OLD FRIEND --
-- TELL HIM SOMETHING FOR ME?
THIS IS A DANGEROUS GAME HE IS PLAYING.
SIR...?
THIS GOING OUT AND ABOUT WHEN HE SHOULD BE IN BED. ALONE.
DANGEROUS.

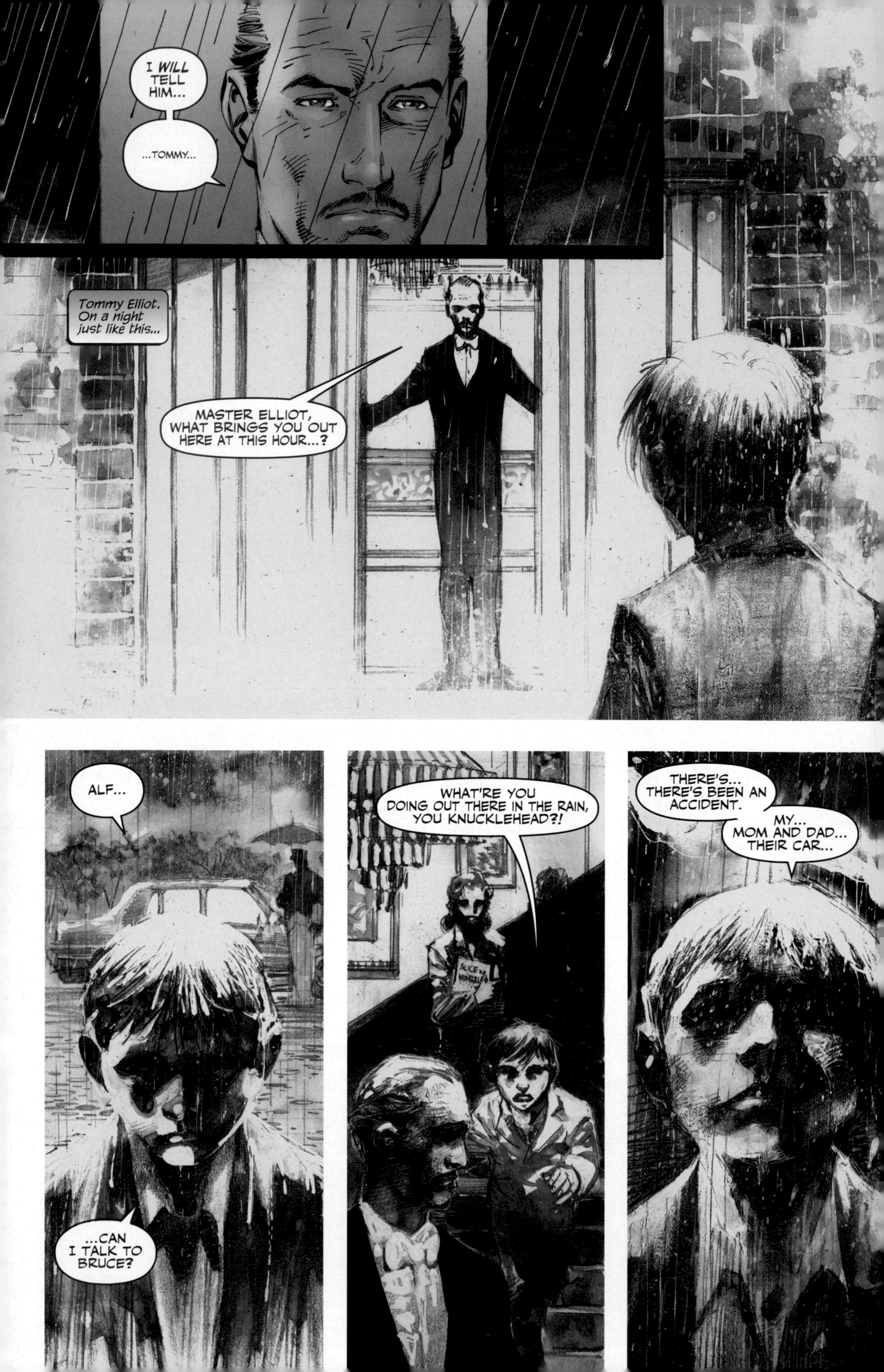
I *WILL* TELL HIM...
...TOMMY...
*Tommy Elliot. On a night just like this...*
MASTER ELLIOT, WHAT BRINGS YOU OUT HERE AT THIS HOUR...?
ALF...
...CAN I TALK TO BRUCE?
WHAT'RE YOU DOING OUT THERE IN THE RAIN, YOU KNUCKLEHEAD?!
THERE'S... THERE'S BEEN AN ACCIDENT.
MY... MOM AND DAD... THEIR CAR...

Gotham City Hospital. My father was Head of Trauma Surgery back then.

Hospitals are awful places at night.

Especially for children...

MY DAD IS IN THERE, TOMMY. NOTHING BAD IS GOING TO HAPPEN.

I *TRIED* TO WARN MISTER ELLIOT.

NIGHT LIKE THIS, THE ROADS GET SLIPPERY.

I SHOULD HAVE BEEN DRIVING THEM -- BUT HE *INSISTED* ON GOING OUT ALONE WITH THE MISSUS.

YOU MUSTN'T BLAME YOURSELF, *CLARENCE. ACCIDENTS* WILL HAPPEN.

AND GIVEN THE SITUATION, THEY COULD NOT BE IN BETTER HANDS.

YOU SWEAR...?

STICK A NEEDLE IN MY EYE.

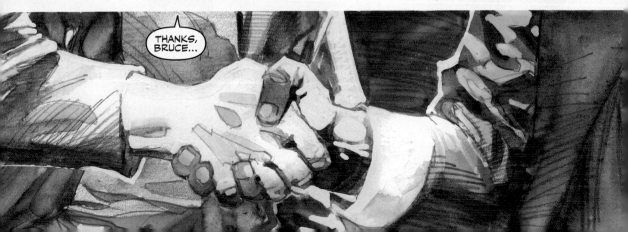

THANKS, BRUCE...

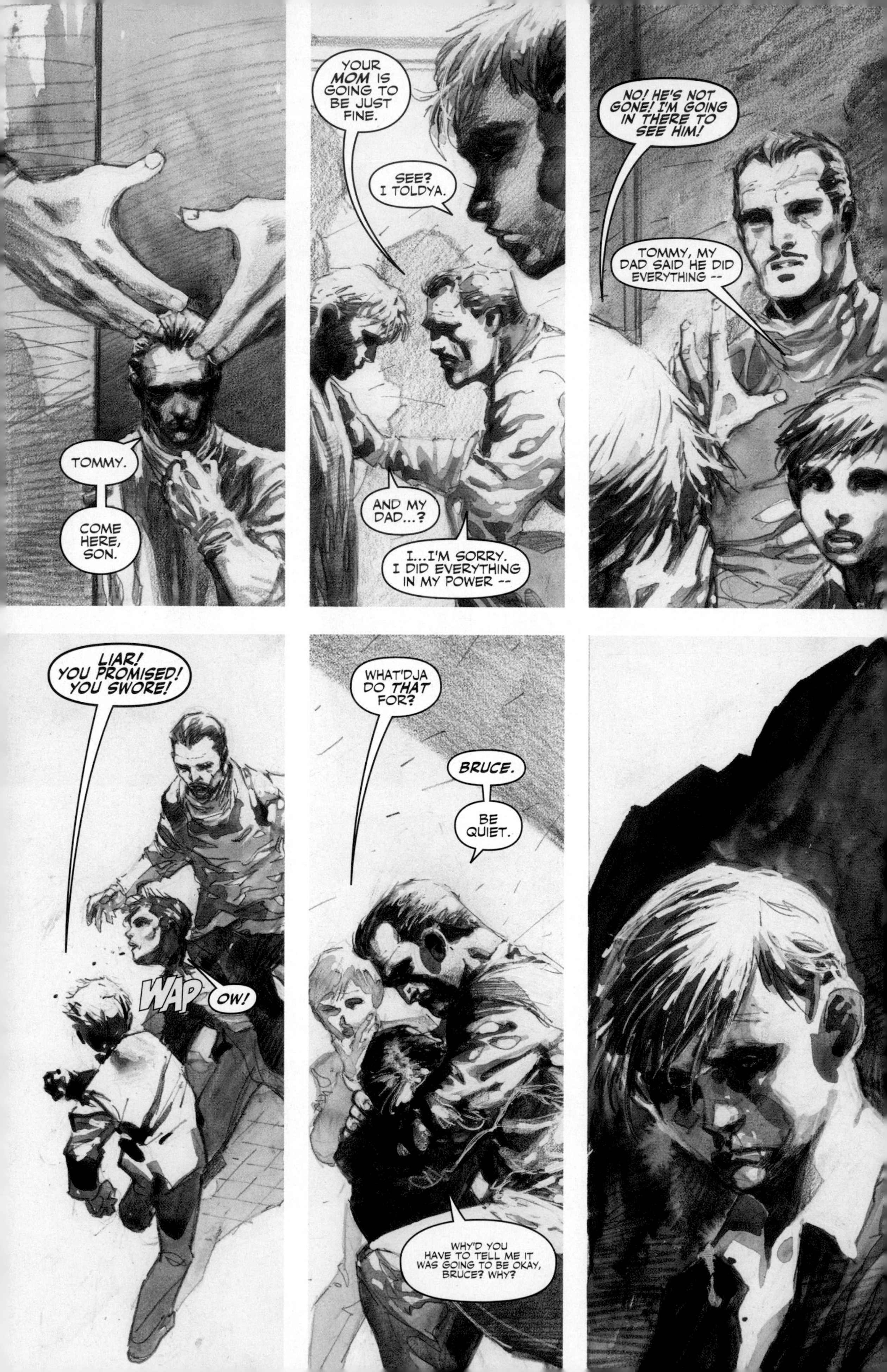
TOMMY.
COME HERE, SON.
YOUR *MOM* IS GOING TO BE JUST FINE.
SEE? I TOLDYA.
AND MY DAD...?
I...I'M SORRY. I DID EVERYTHING IN MY POWER --
NO! HE'S NOT GONE! I'M GOING IN THERE TO SEE HIM!
TOMMY, MY DAD SAID HE DID EVERYTHING --
LIAR! YOU PROMISED! YOU SWORE!
WAP
OW!
WHAT'DJA DO *THAT* FOR?
*BRUCE.*
BE QUIET.
WHY'D YOU HAVE TO TELL ME IT WAS GOING TO BE OKAY, BRUCE? WHY?

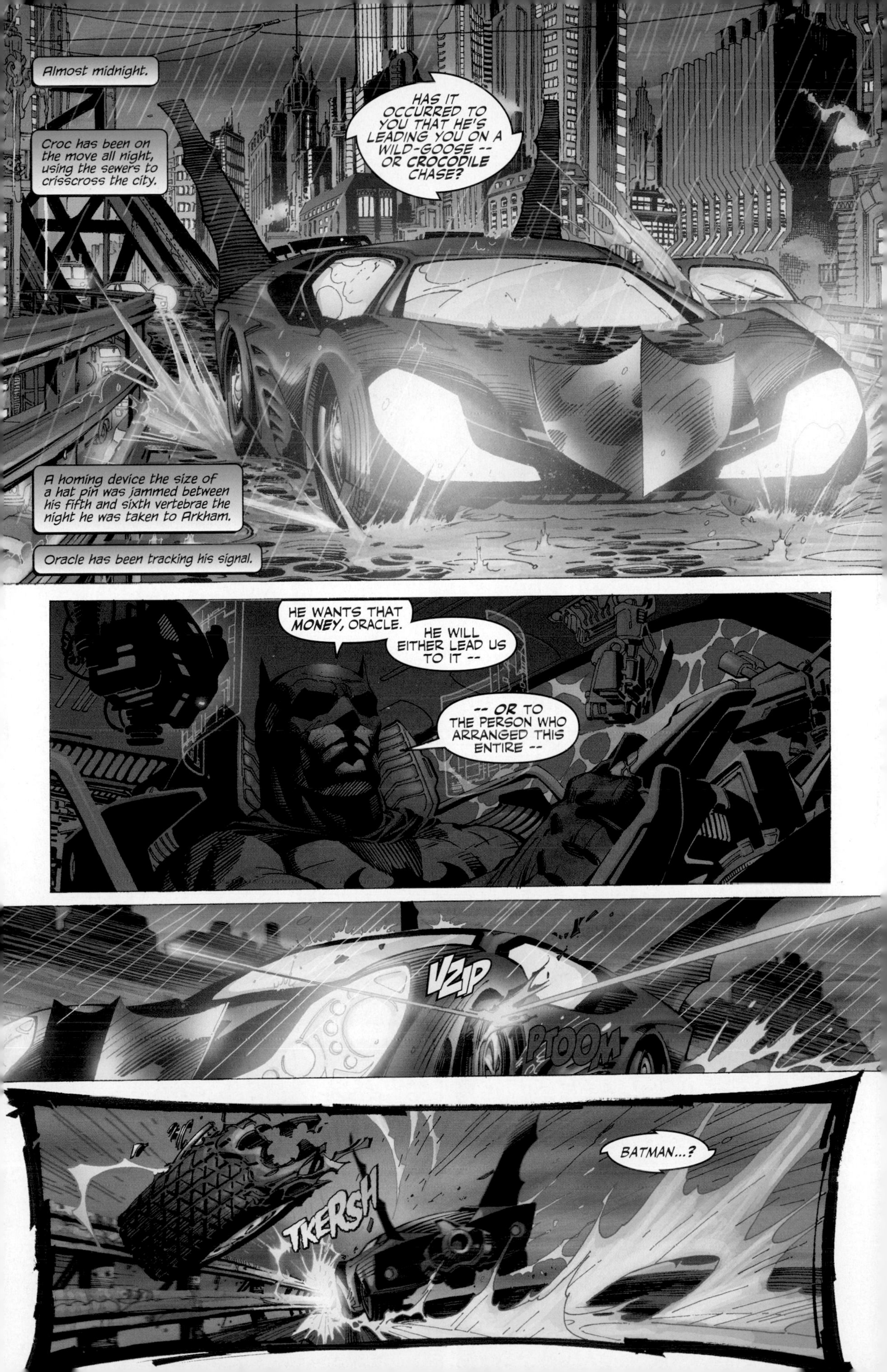
Almost midnight.
Croc has been on the move all night, using the sewers to crisscross the city.
HAS IT OCCURRED TO YOU THAT HE'S LEADING YOU ON A WILD-GOOSE -- OR CROCODILE CHASE?
A homing device the size of a hat pin was jammed between his fifth and sixth vertebrae the night he was taken to Arkham.
Oracle has been tracking his signal.
HE WANTS THAT MONEY, ORACLE.
HE WILL EITHER LEAD US TO IT --
-- OR TO THE PERSON WHO ARRANGED THIS ENTIRE --
VZIP
PTOOM
BATMAN...?
TKERSH

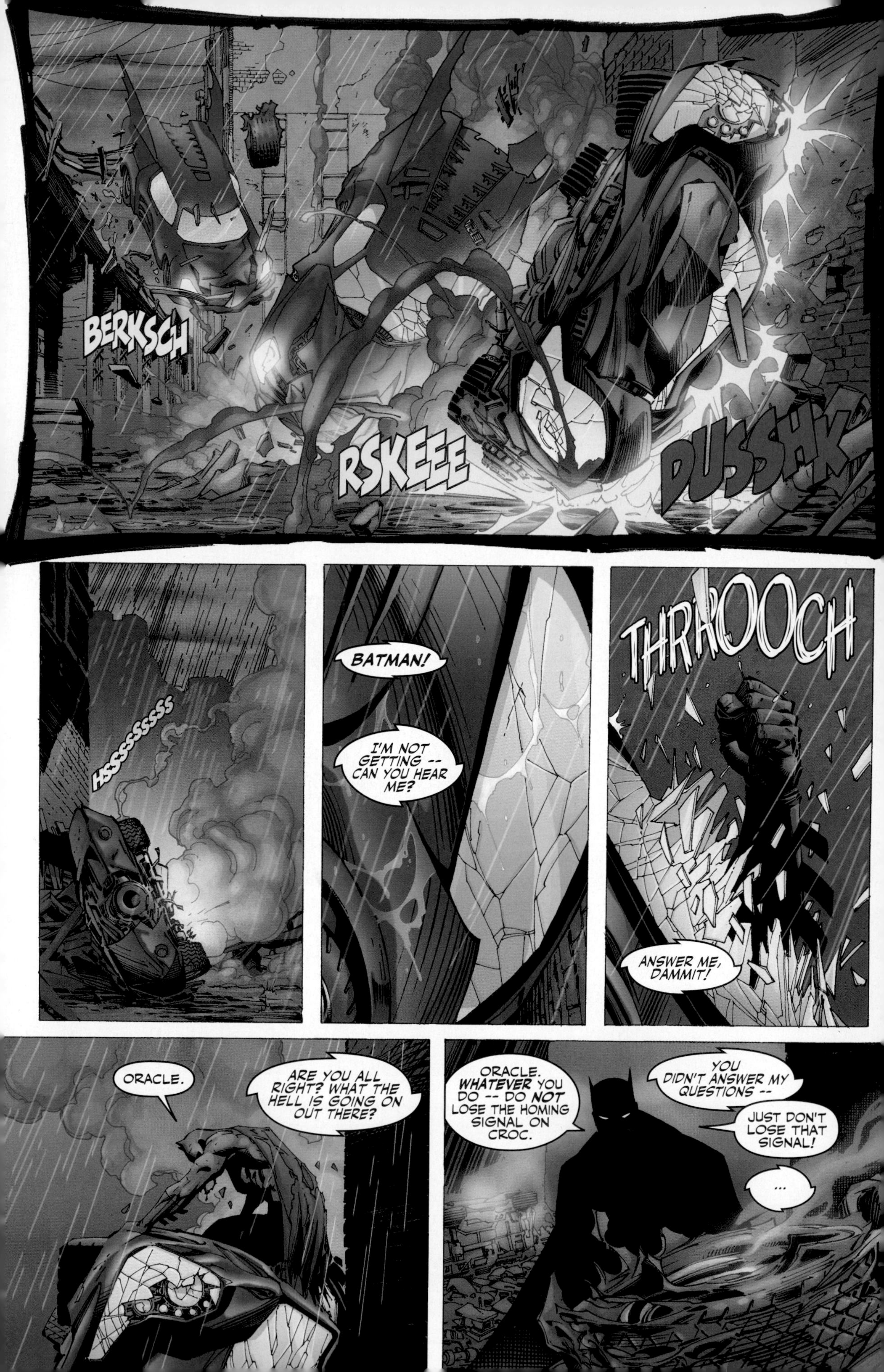

BERKSCH
RSKEEE
DUSSHK
HSSSSSSSSS
BATMAN!
I'M NOT GETTING -- CAN YOU HEAR ME?
THRROOCH
ANSWER ME, DAMMIT!
ORACLE.
ARE YOU ALL RIGHT? WHAT THE HELL IS GOING ON OUT THERE?
ORACLE. WHATEVER YOU DO -- DO NOT LOSE THE HOMING SIGNAL ON CROC.
YOU DIDN'T ANSWER MY QUESTIONS --
JUST DON'T LOSE THAT SIGNAL!
...

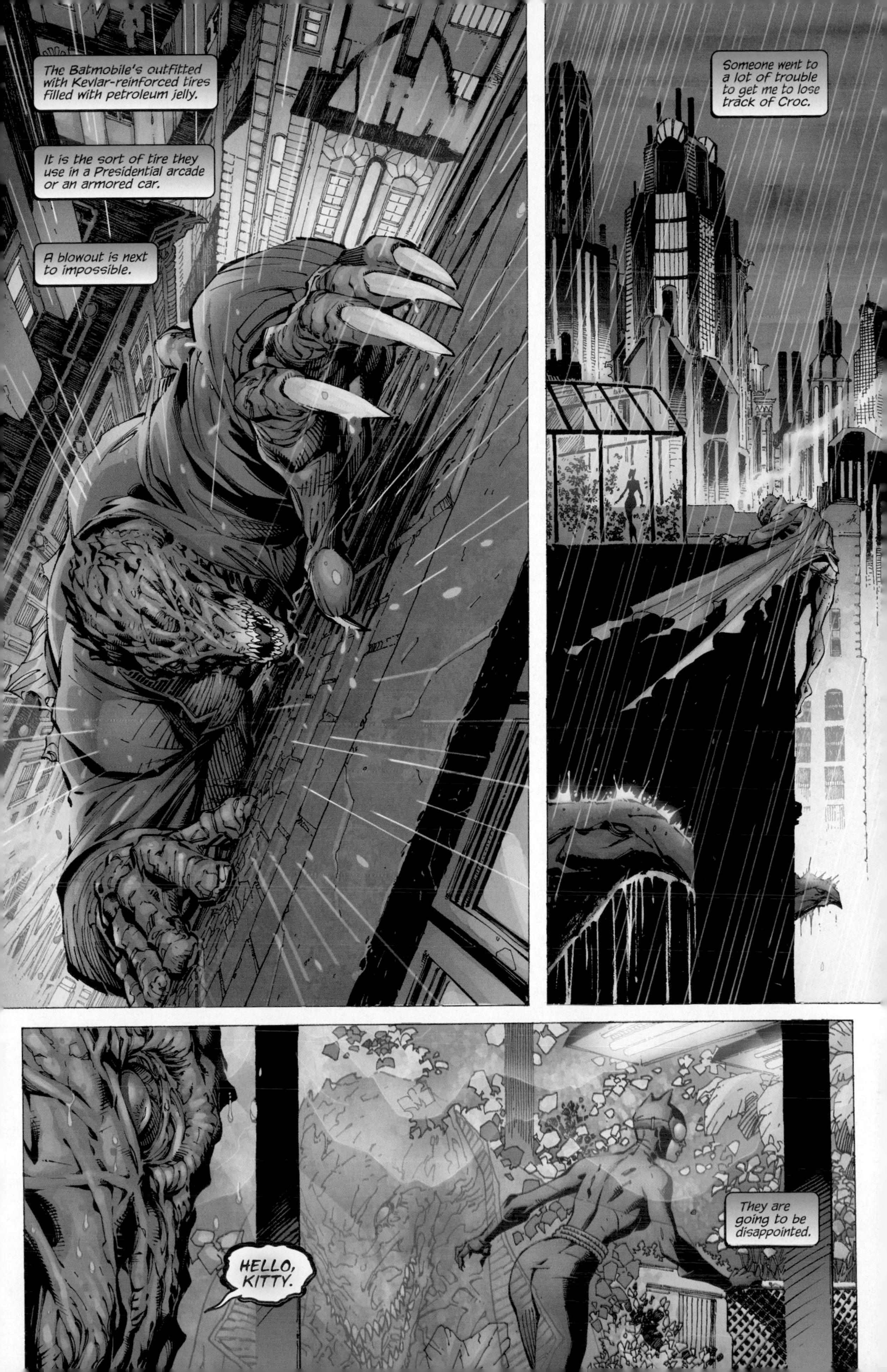

The Batmobile's outfitted with Kevlar-reinforced tires filled with petroleum jelly.
It is the sort of tire they use in a Presidential arcade or an armored car.
A blowout is next to impossible.
Someone went to a lot of trouble to get me to lose track of Croc.
HELLO, KITTY.
They are going to be disappointed.

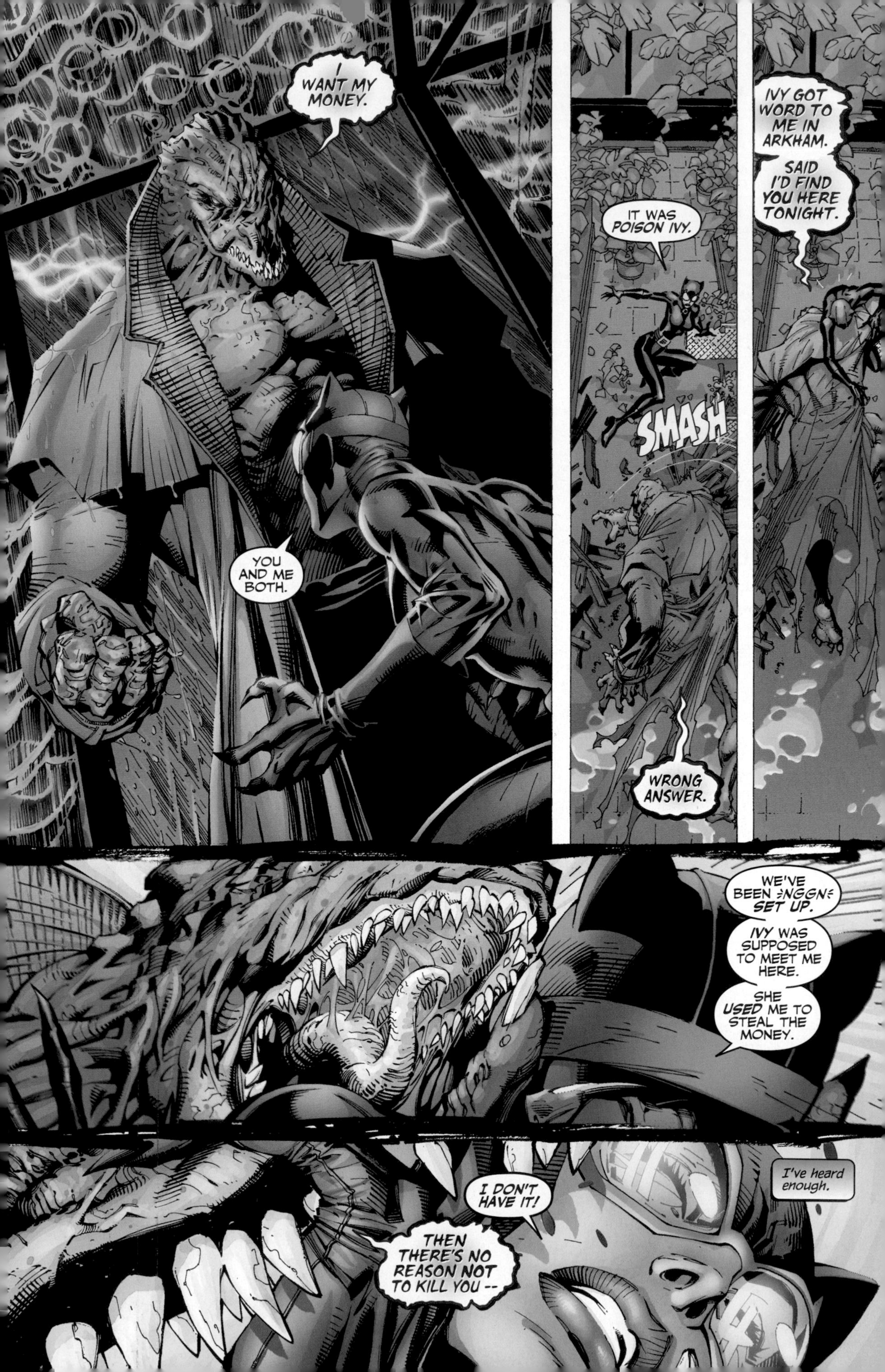
I WANT MY MONEY.
YOU AND ME BOTH.
IT WAS POISON IVY.
SMASH
WRONG ANSWER.
IVY GOT WORD TO ME IN ARKHAM.
SAID I'D FIND YOU HERE TONIGHT.
WE'VE BEEN -NGGN- SET UP.
IVY WAS SUPPOSED TO MEET ME HERE.
SHE USED ME TO STEAL THE MONEY.
I DON'T HAVE IT!
THEN THERE'S NO REASON NOT TO KILL YOU --
I've heard enough.

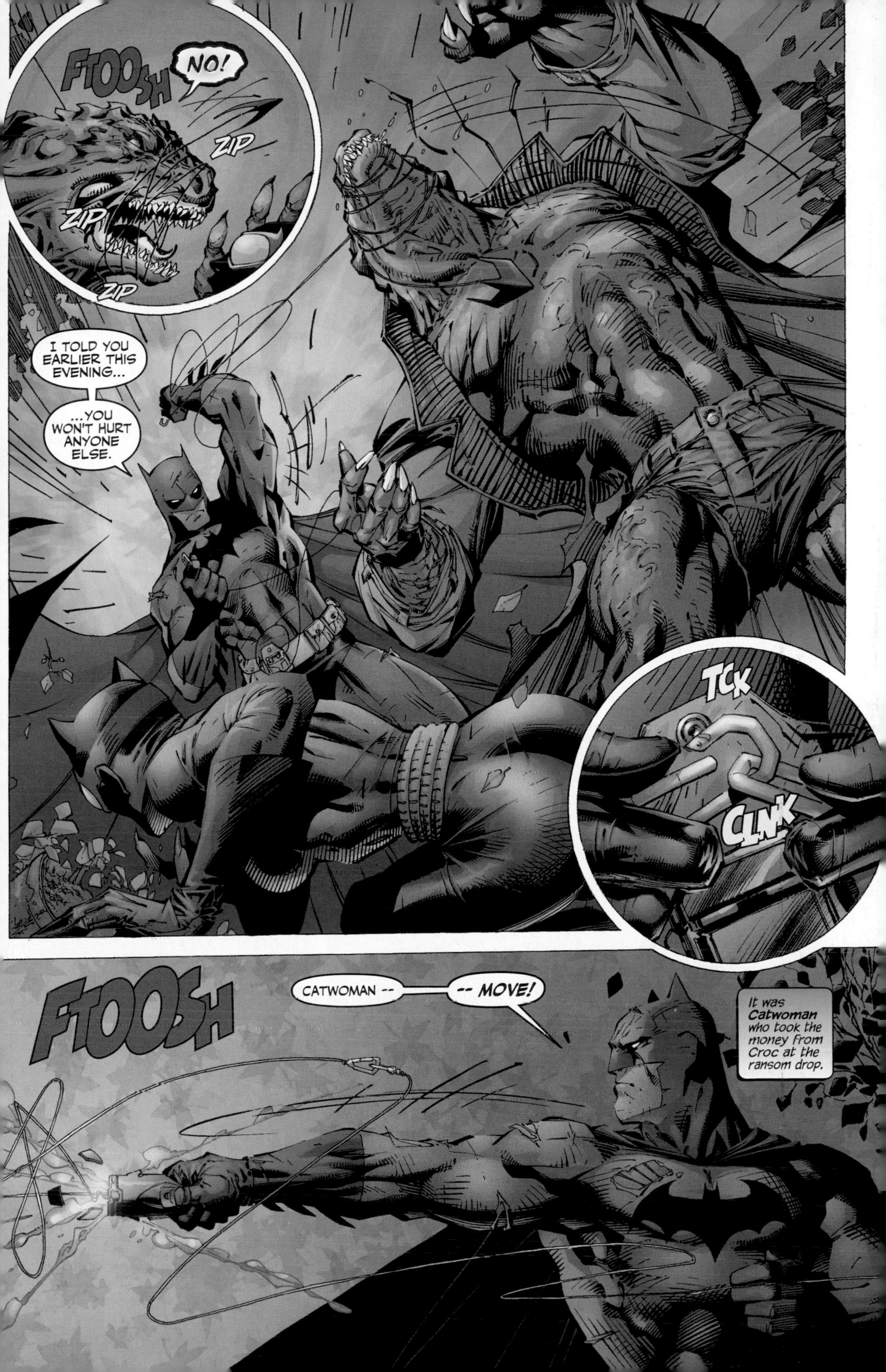
FTOOSH
NO!
ZIP
ZIP
ZIP
I TOLD YOU EARLIER THIS EVENING...
...YOU WON'T HURT ANYONE ELSE.
TCK
CLNK
FTOOSH
CATWOMAN --
-- MOVE!
It was Catwoman who took the money from Croc at the ransom drop.

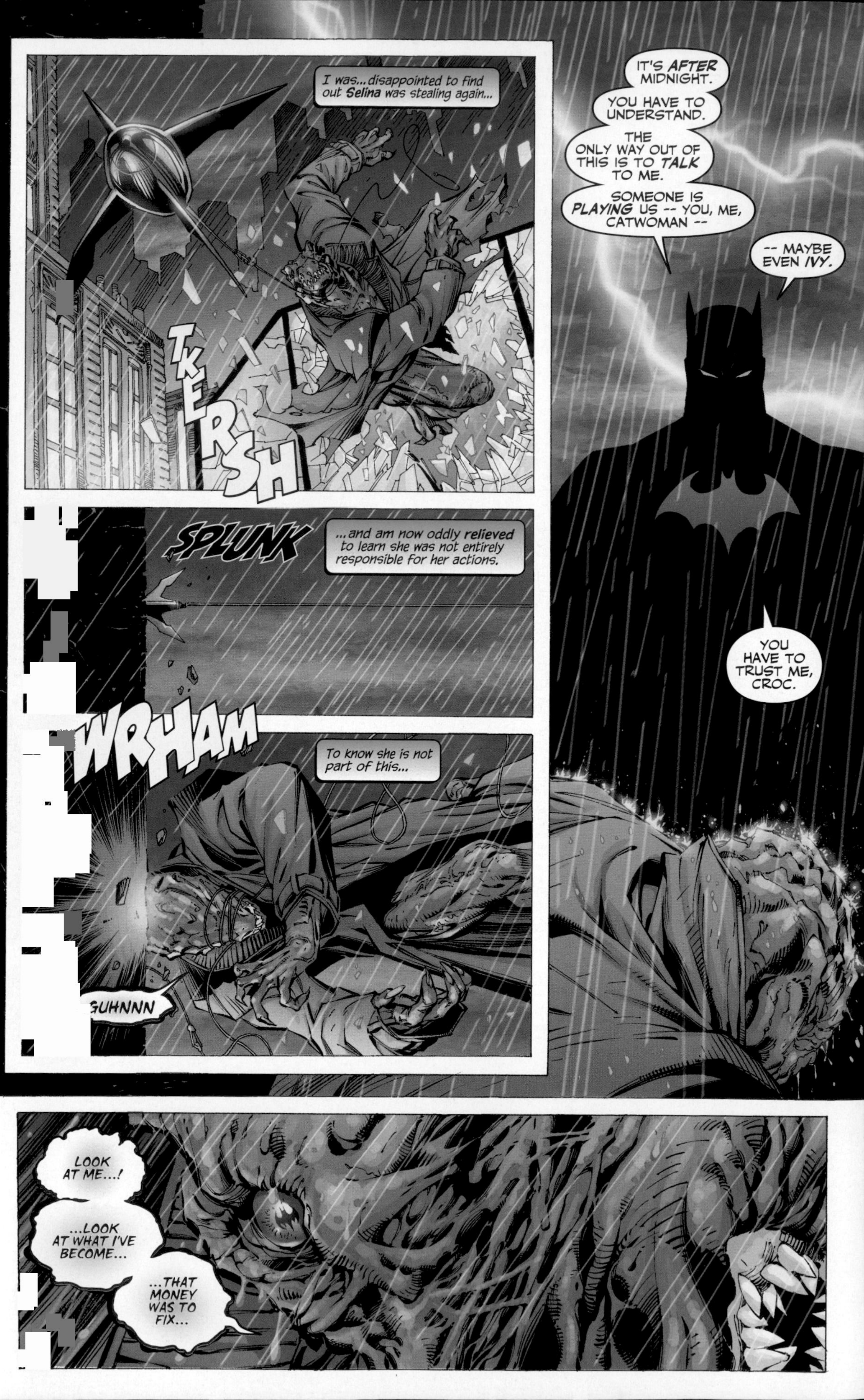

I was...disappointed to find out Selina was stealing again...
TKERSH
...and am now oddly relieved to learn she was not entirely responsible for her actions.
SPLUNK
WRHAM
To know she is not part of this...
GUHNNN
IT'S AFTER MIDNIGHT.
YOU HAVE TO UNDERSTAND.
THE ONLY WAY OUT OF THIS IS TO TALK TO ME.
SOMEONE IS PLAYING US -- YOU, ME, CATWOMAN --
-- MAYBE EVEN IVY.
YOU HAVE TO TRUST ME, CROC.
LOOK AT ME...!
...LOOK AT WHAT I'VE BECOME...
...THAT MONEY WAS TO FIX...

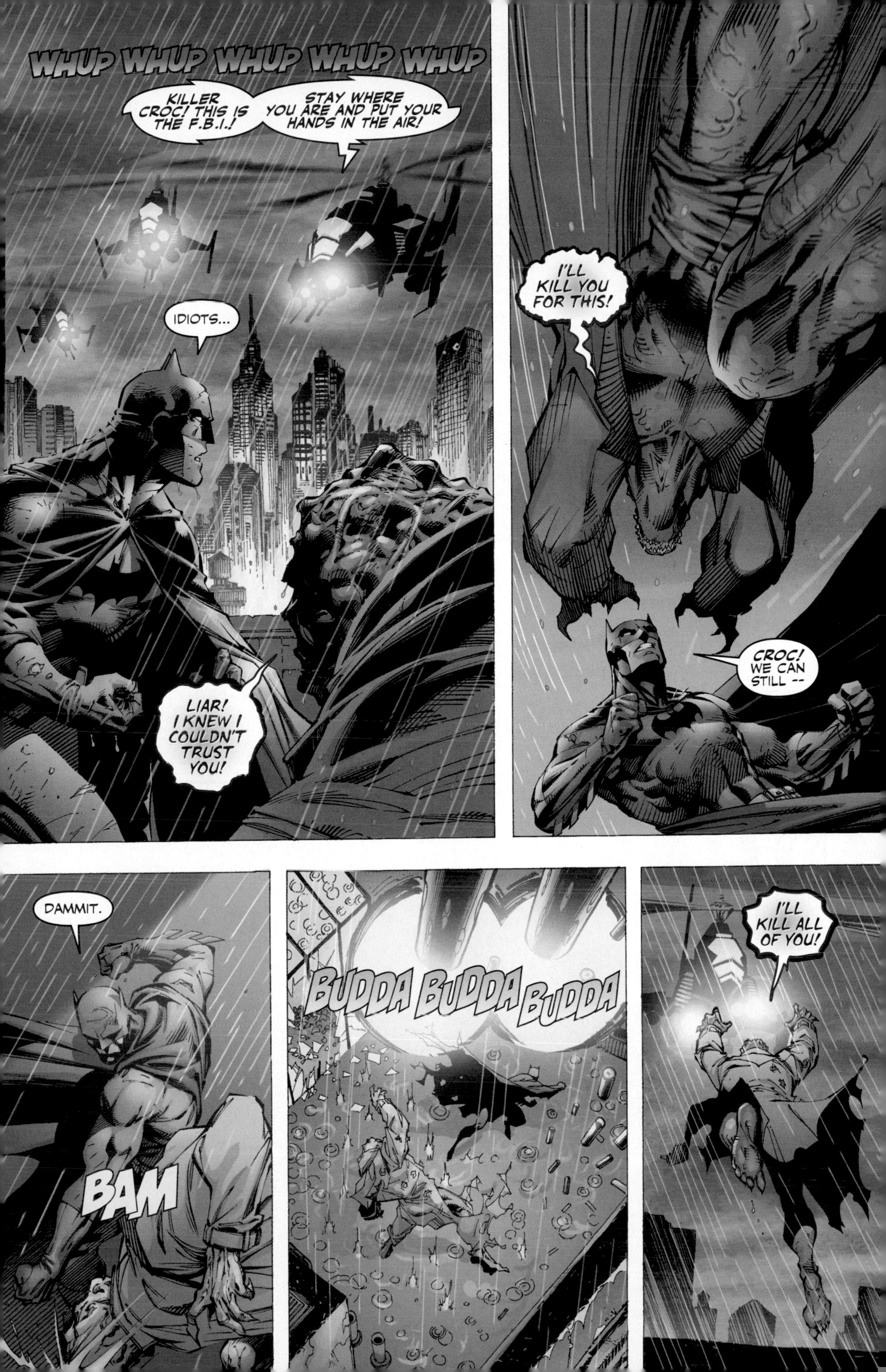
WHUP WHUP WHUP WHUP WHUP
KILLER CROC! THIS IS THE F.B.I.!
STAY WHERE YOU ARE AND PUT YOUR HANDS IN THE AIR!
IDIOTS...
LIAR! I KNEW I COULDN'T TRUST YOU!
I'LL KILL YOU FOR THIS!
CROC! WE CAN STILL --
DAMMIT.
BAM
BUDDA BUDDA BUDDA
I'LL KILL ALL OF YOU!

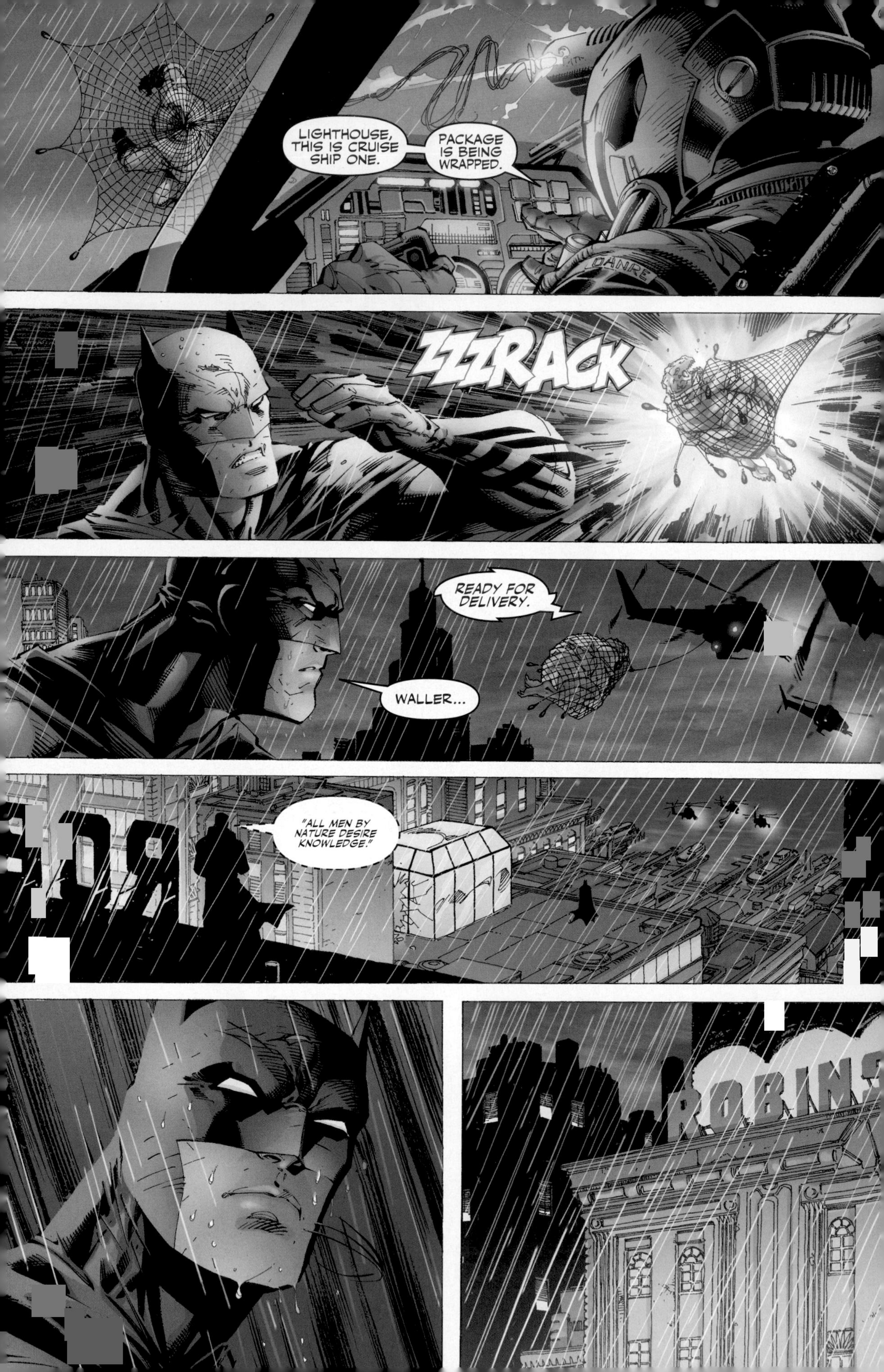
LIGHTHOUSE, THIS IS CRUISE SHIP ONE.
PACKAGE IS BEING WRAPPED.
DANRE
ZZZRACK
READY FOR DELIVERY.
WALLER...
"ALL MEN BY NATURE DESIRE KNOWLEDGE."
ROBINS

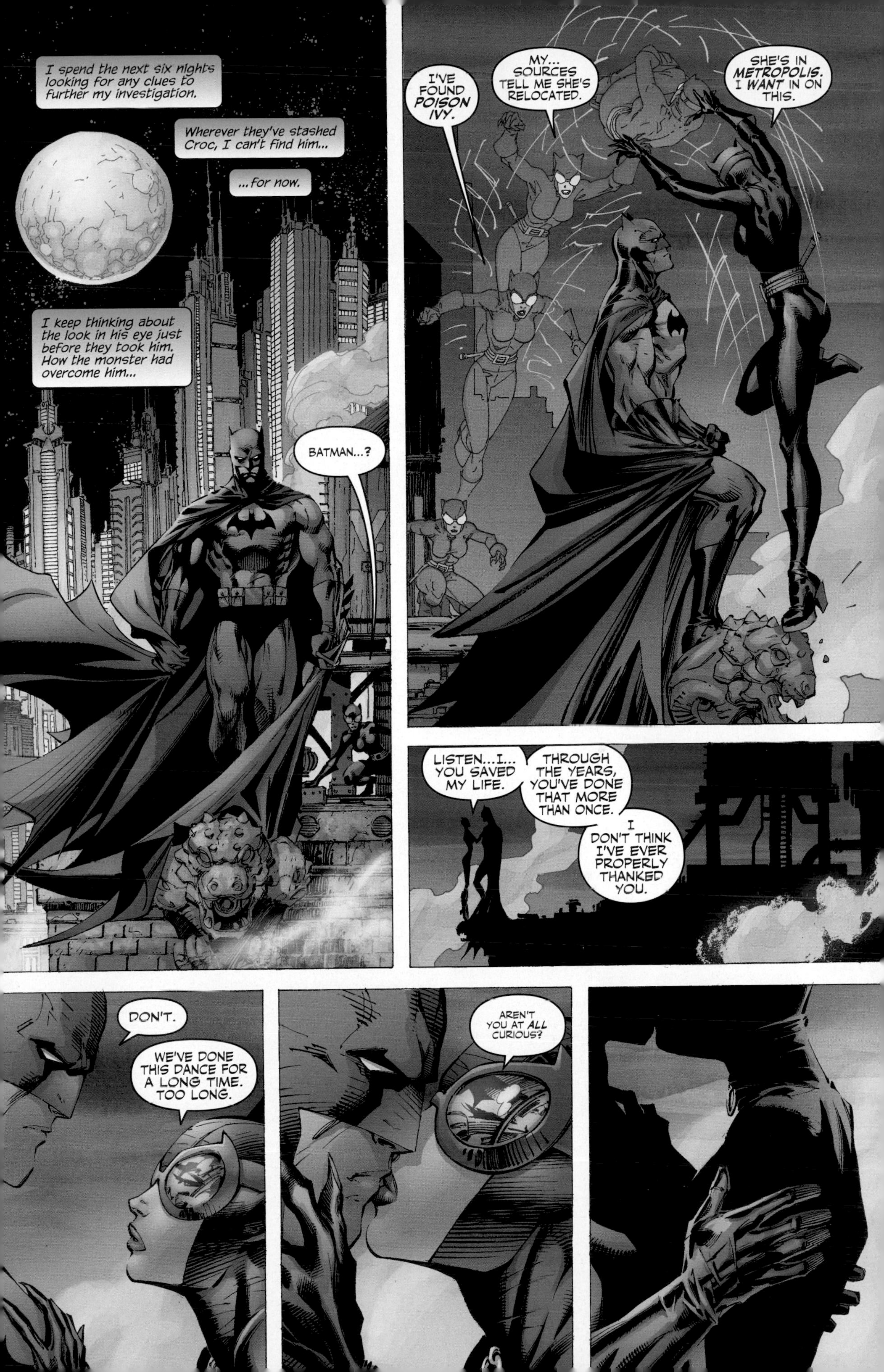

I spend the next six nights looking for any clues to further my investigation.
Wherever they've stashed Croc, I can't find him...
...for now.
I keep thinking about the look in his eye just before they took him. How the monster had overcome him...
BATMAN...?
I'VE FOUND POISON IVY.
MY... SOURCES TELL ME SHE'S RELOCATED.
SHE'S IN METROPOLIS. I WANT IN ON THIS.
LISTEN...I... YOU SAVED MY LIFE.
THROUGH THE YEARS, YOU'VE DONE THAT MORE THAN ONCE.
I DON'T THINK I'VE EVER PROPERLY THANKED YOU.
DON'T.
WE'VE DONE THIS DANCE FOR A LONG TIME. TOO LONG.
AREN'T YOU AT ALL CURIOUS?

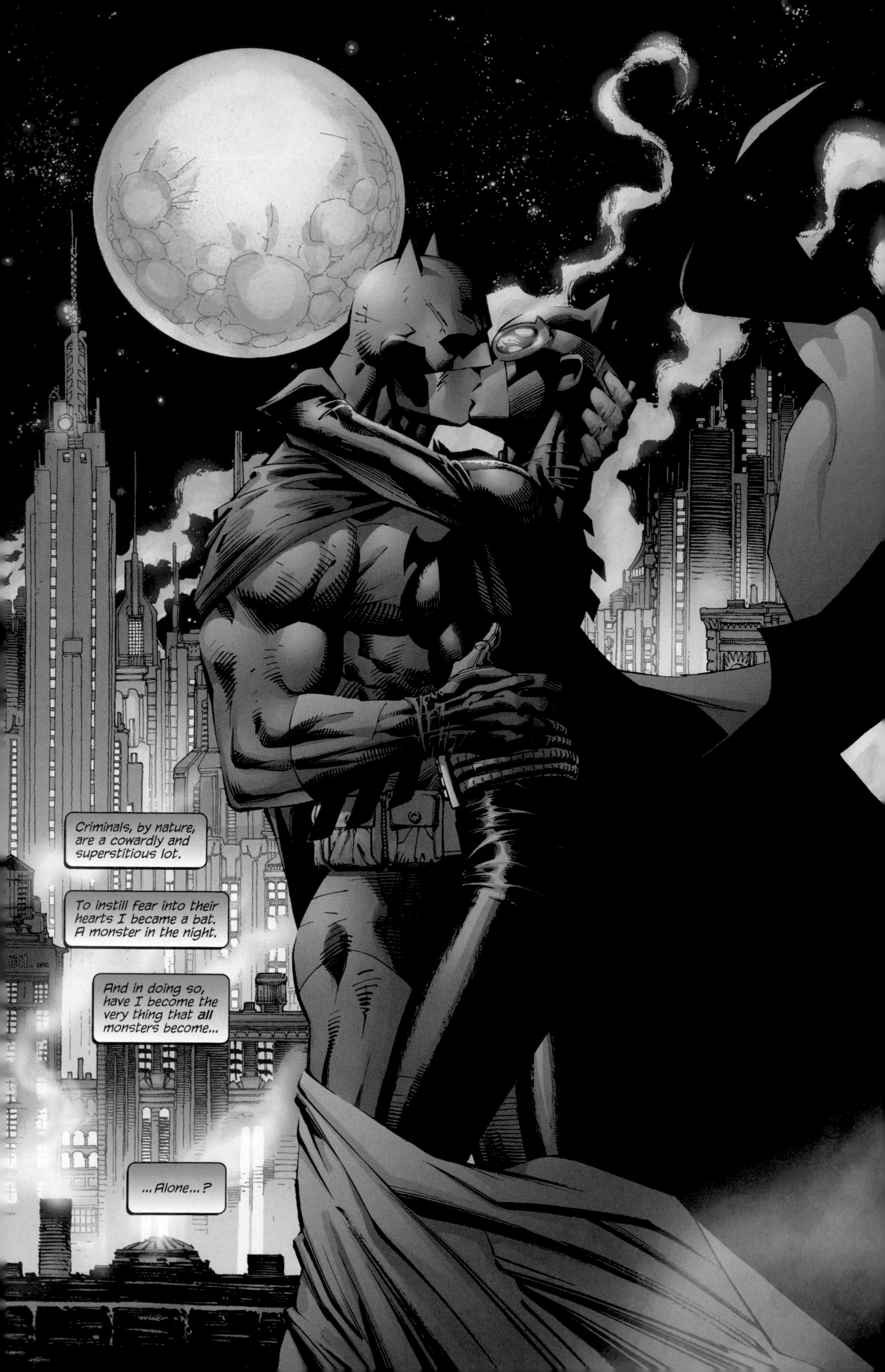
Criminals, by nature, are a cowardly and superstitious lot.
To instill fear into their hearts I became a bat. A monster in the night.
And in doing so, have I become the very thing that all monsters become...
...Alone...?

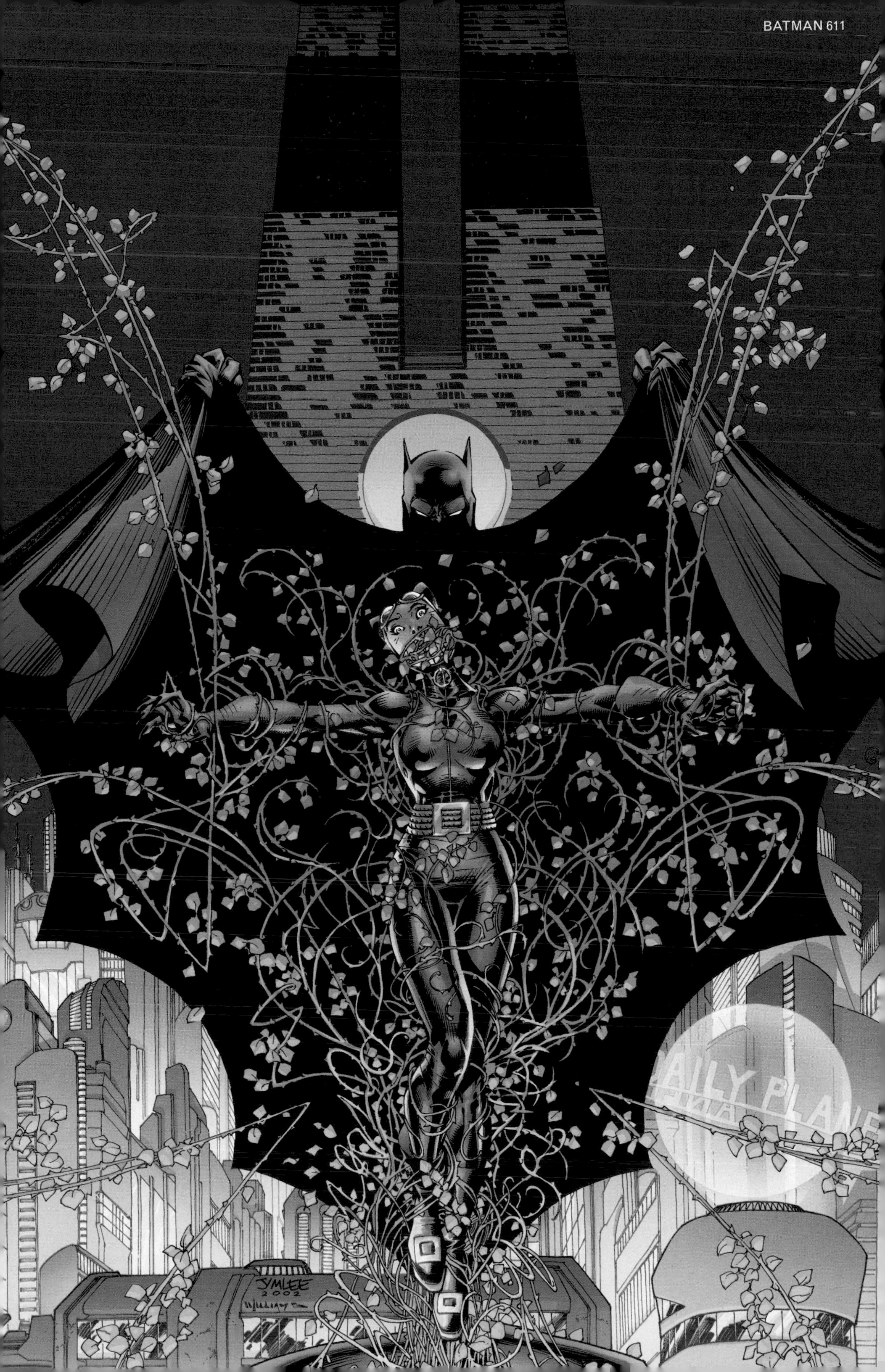

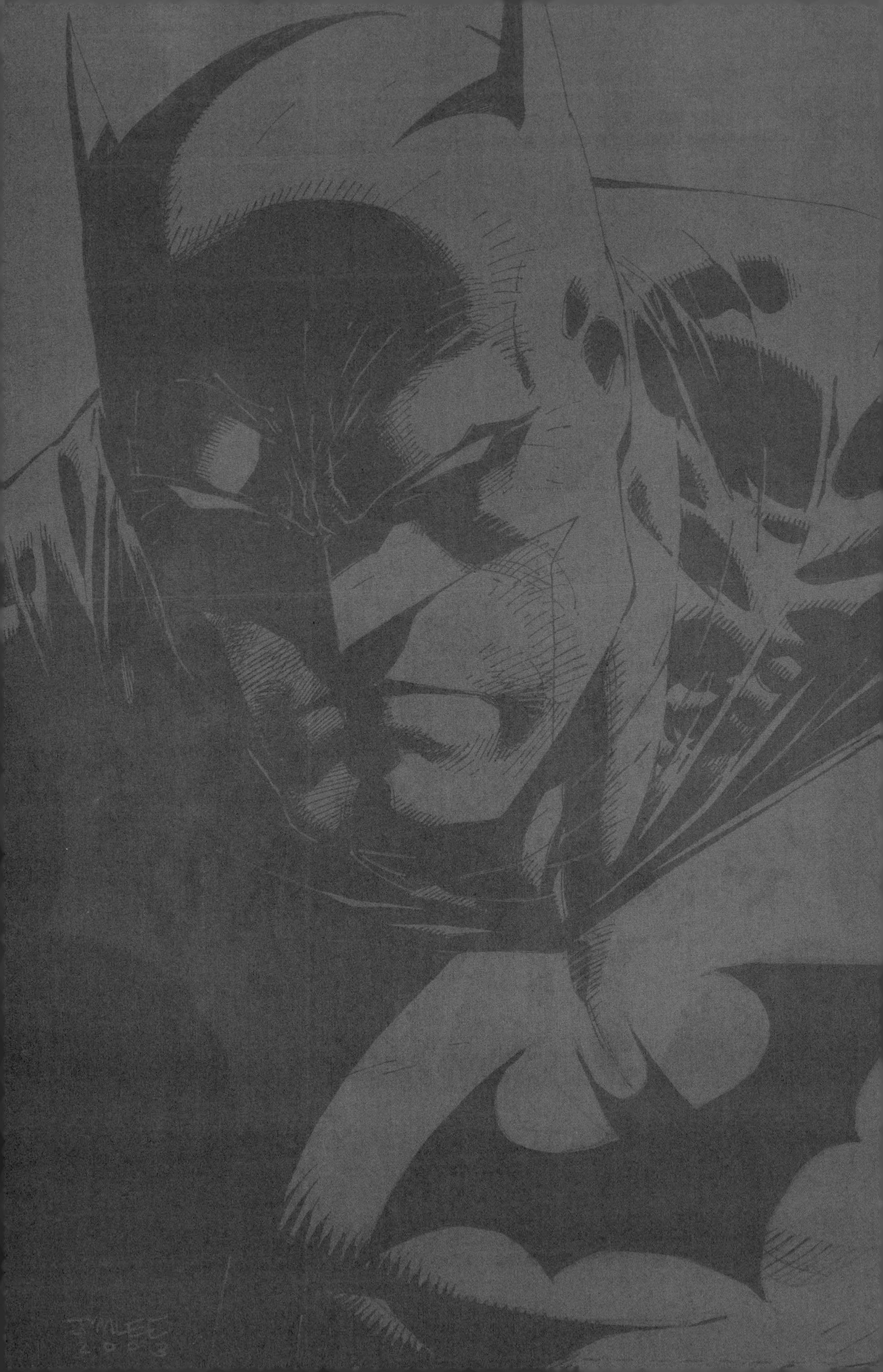

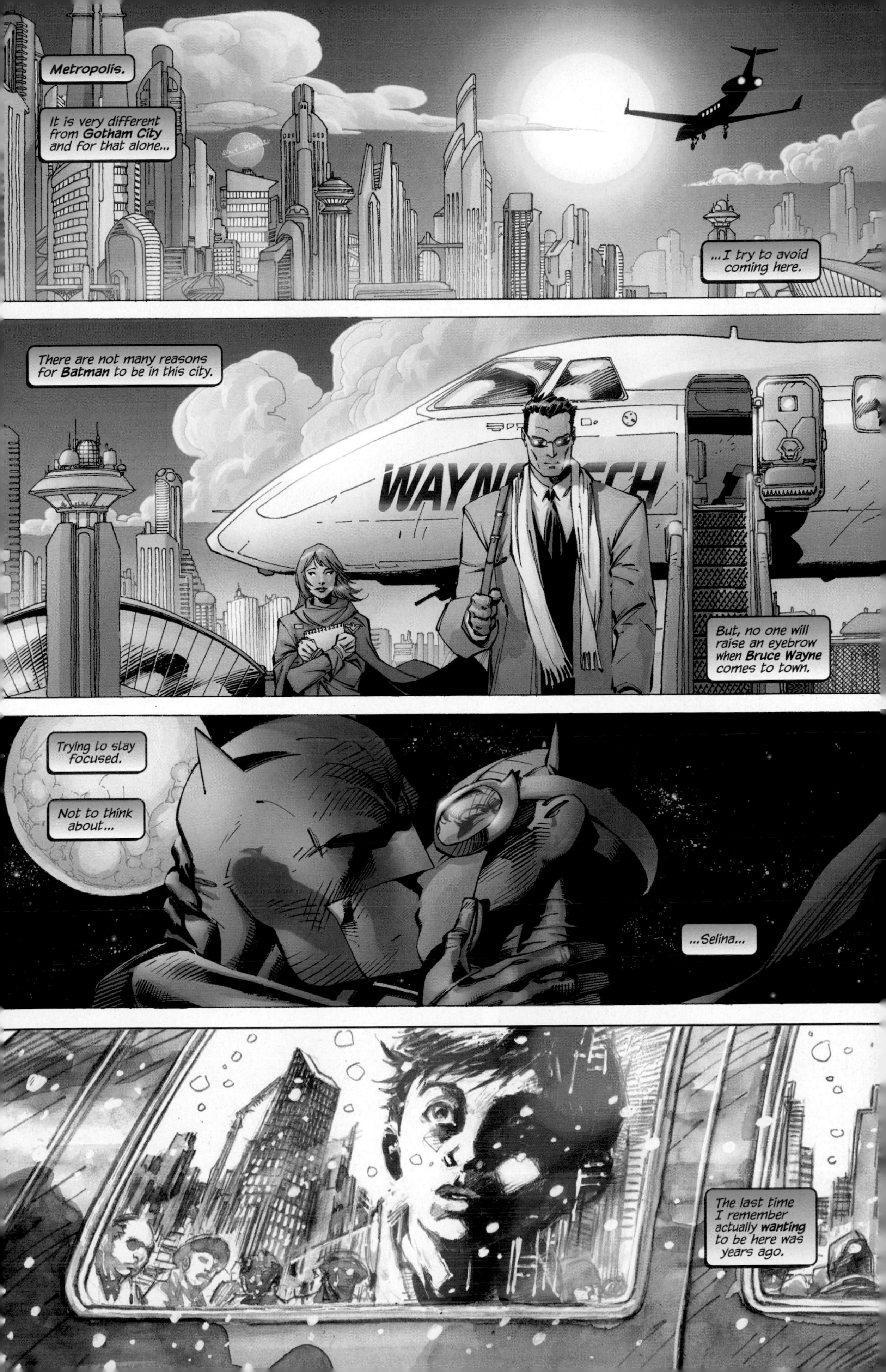

Metropolis.
It is very different from Gotham City and for that alone...
...I try to avoid coming here.
There are not many reasons for Batman to be in this city.
But, no one will raise an eyebrow when Bruce Wayne comes to town.
Trying to stay focused.
Not to think about...
...Selina...
The last time I remember actually wanting to be here was years ago.

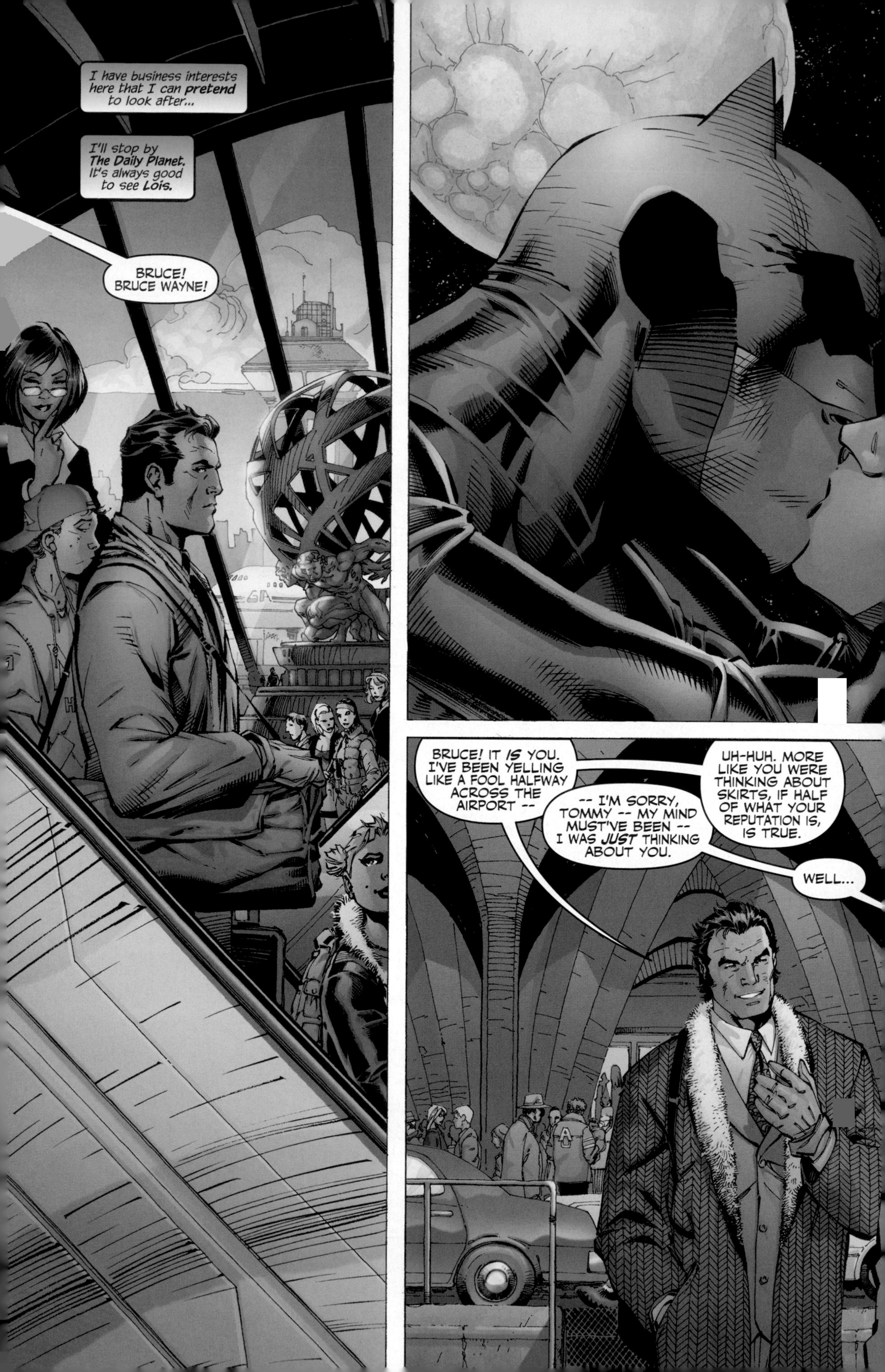

I have business interests here that I can **pretend** to look after...
I'll stop by **The Daily Planet.** It's always good to see **Lois.**
BRUCE! BRUCE WAYNE!
BRUCE! IT *IS* YOU. I'VE BEEN YELLING LIKE A FOOL HALFWAY ACROSS THE AIRPORT --
-- I'M SORRY, TOMMY -- MY MIND MUST'VE BEEN -- I WAS *JUST* THINKING ABOUT YOU.
UH-HUH. MORE LIKE YOU WERE THINKING ABOUT SKIRTS, IF HALF OF WHAT YOUR REPUTATION IS, IS TRUE.
WELL...

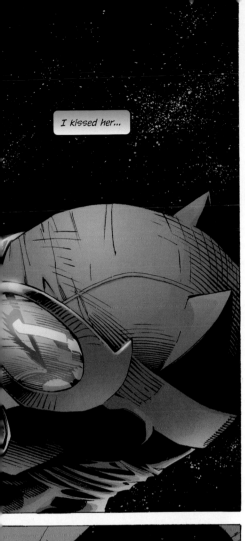

I kissed her...

Tommy...*Doctor Thomas Elliot*. The surgeon who saved my life and my childhood friend.

My *father* had a medical convention to attend. My *mother* thought we'd spend some time together.

My father brought *Alfred*. I brought *Tommy*.

YOU BOYS STAY *RIGHT HERE* WHILE ALFRED AND I GO REGISTER. *RIGHT* HERE, DO YOU UNDERSTAND?

YOU GOT IT, DOC.

YES, SIR.

Tommy spoke to my father in a way that no one else dared. But, that was Tommy...

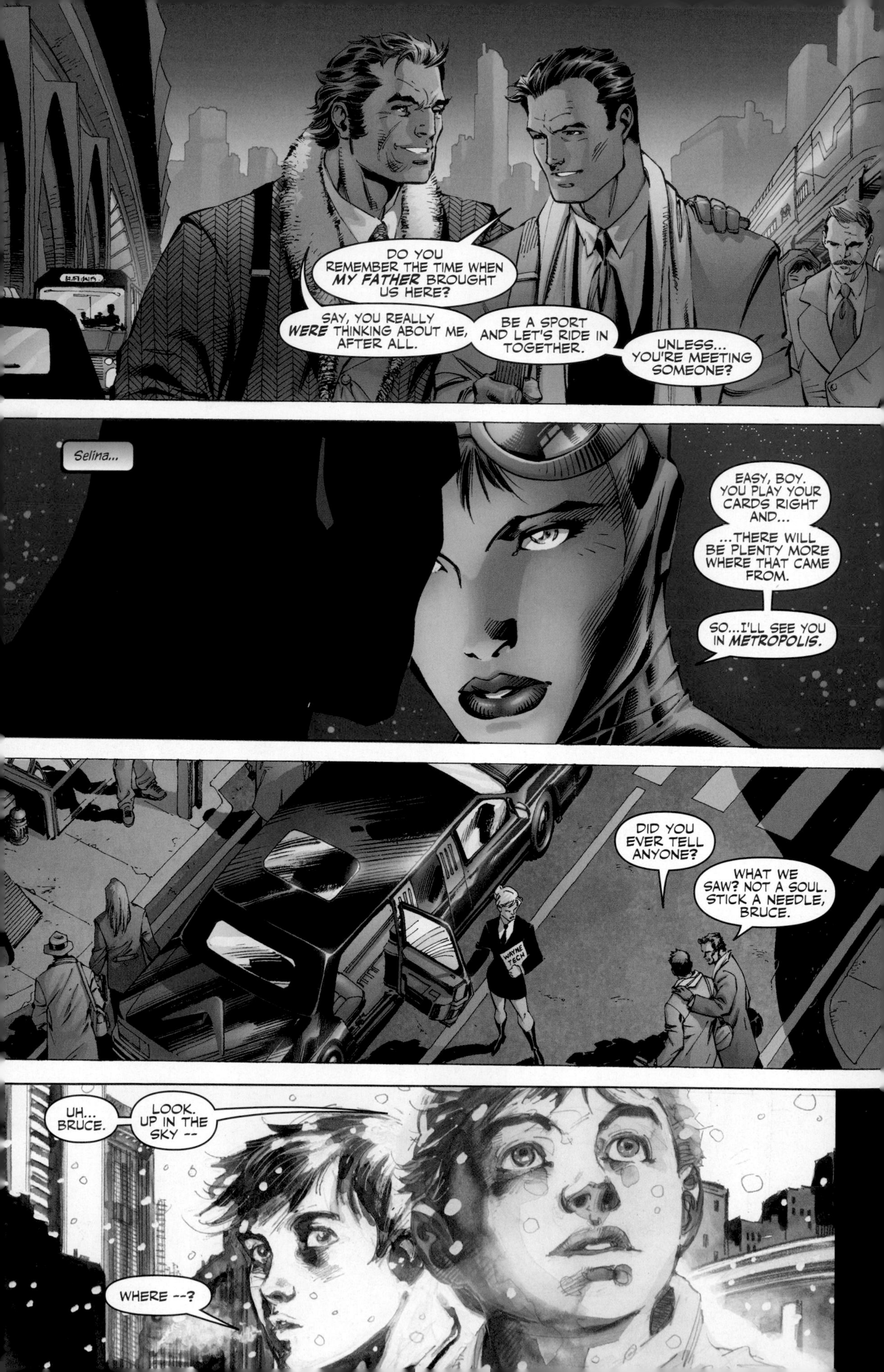
DO YOU REMEMBER THE TIME WHEN MY FATHER BROUGHT US HERE?
SAY, YOU REALLY WERE THINKING ABOUT ME, AFTER ALL.
BE A SPORT AND LET'S RIDE IN TOGETHER.
UNLESS... YOU'RE MEETING SOMEONE?
Selina...
EASY, BOY. YOU PLAY YOUR CARDS RIGHT AND...
...THERE WILL BE PLENTY MORE WHERE THAT CAME FROM.
SO...I'LL SEE YOU IN METROPOLIS.
DID YOU EVER TELL ANYONE?
WHAT WE SAW? NOT A SOUL. STICK A NEEDLE, BRUCE.
WAYNE TECH
UH... BRUCE.
LOOK. UP IN THE SKY --
WHERE --?

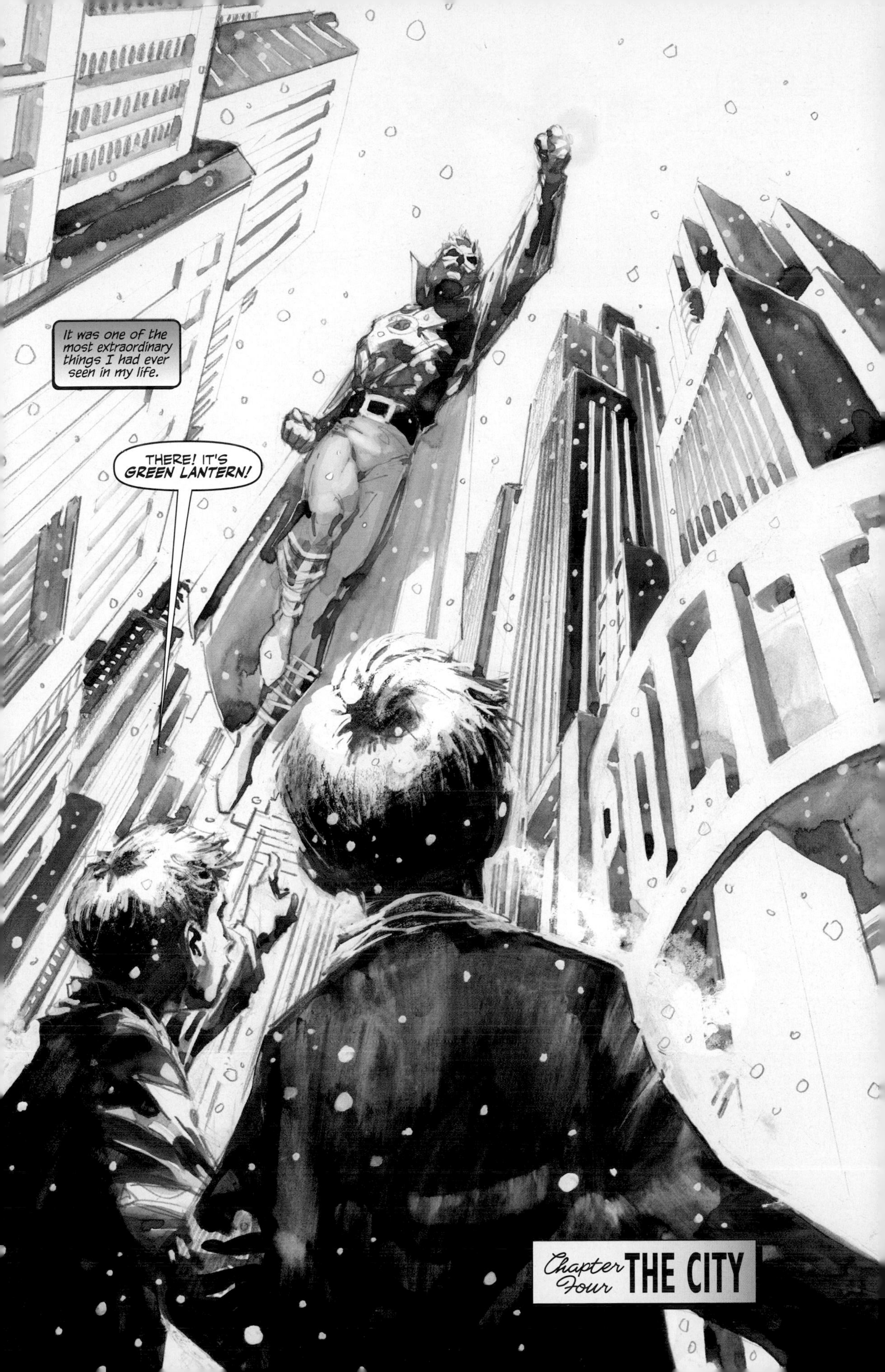
It was one of the most extraordinary things I had ever seen in my life.
THERE! IT'S GREEN LANTERN!
Chapter Four THE CITY

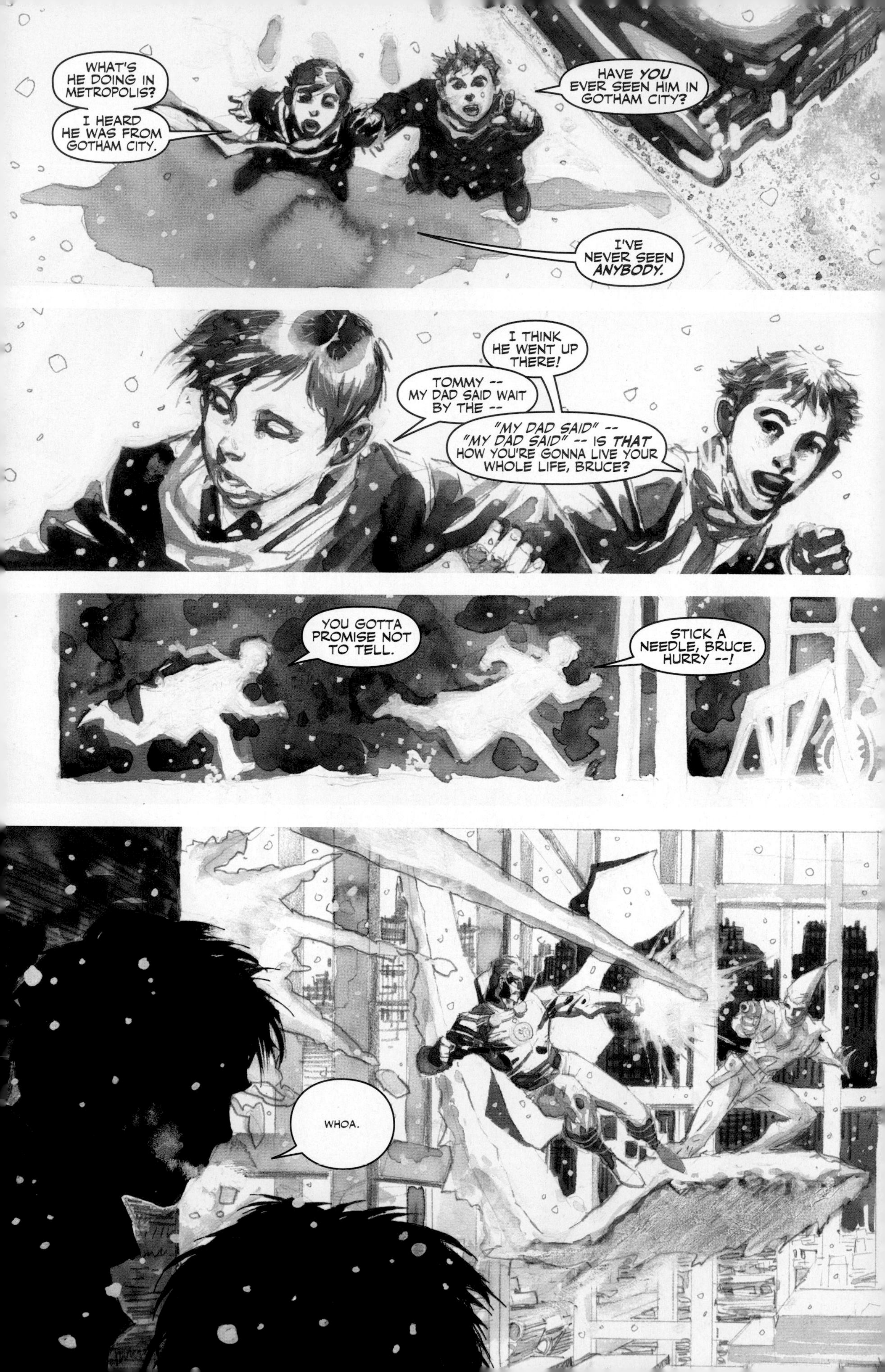
WHAT'S HE DOING IN METROPOLIS?
I HEARD HE WAS FROM GOTHAM CITY.
HAVE *YOU* EVER SEEN HIM IN GOTHAM CITY?
I'VE NEVER SEEN *ANYBODY.*
I THINK HE WENT UP THERE!
TOMMY -- MY DAD SAID WAIT BY THE --
*"MY DAD SAID" -- "MY DAD SAID"* -- IS *THAT* HOW YOU'RE GONNA LIVE YOUR WHOLE LIFE, BRUCE?
YOU GOTTA PROMISE NOT TO TELL.
STICK A NEEDLE, BRUCE. HURRY --!
WHOA.

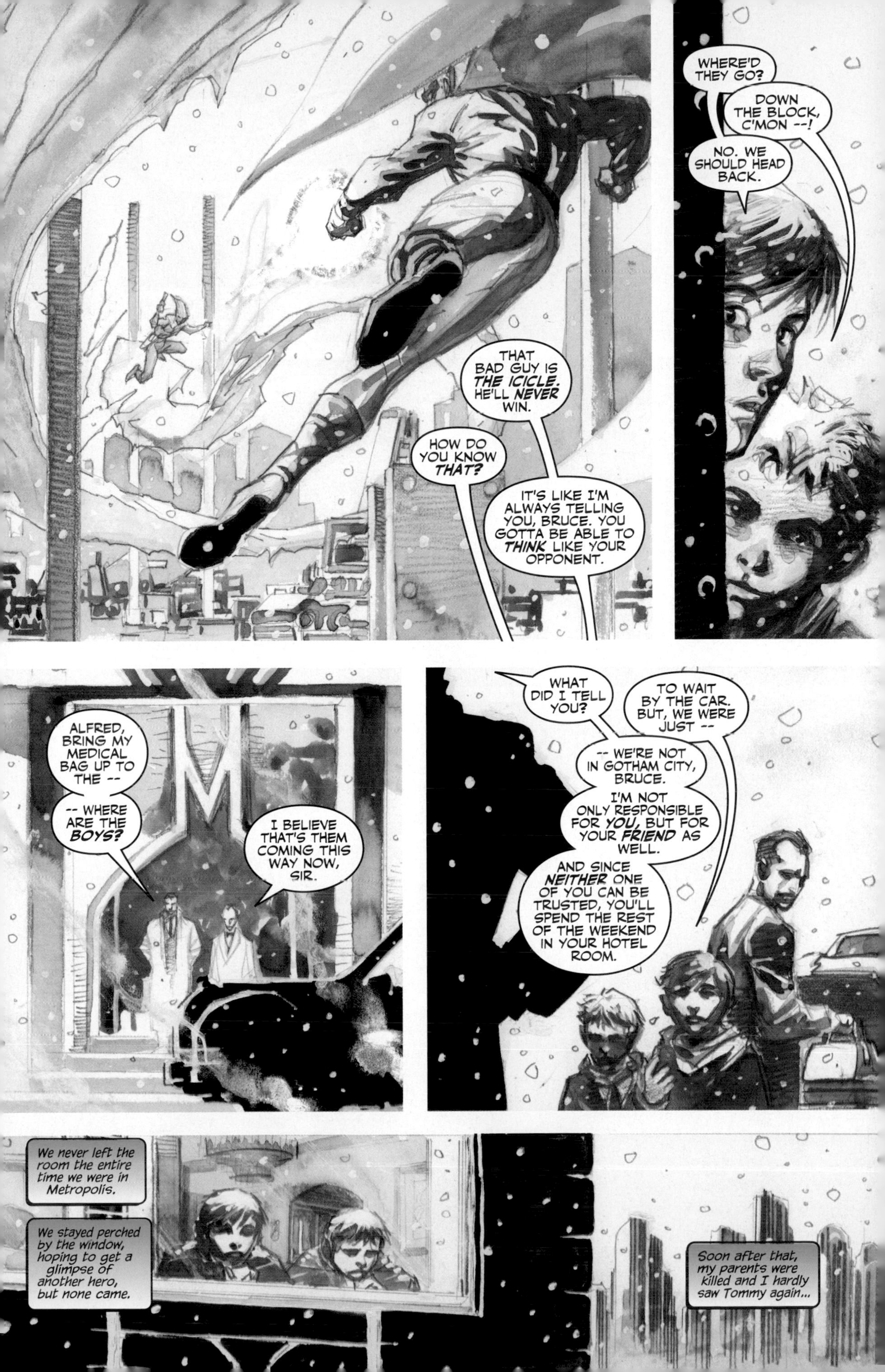
WHERE'D THEY GO?
DOWN THE BLOCK, C'MON --!
NO. WE SHOULD HEAD BACK.
THAT BAD GUY IS THE ICICLE. HE'LL NEVER WIN.
HOW DO YOU KNOW THAT?
IT'S LIKE I'M ALWAYS TELLING YOU, BRUCE. YOU GOTTA BE ABLE TO THINK LIKE YOUR OPPONENT.
ALFRED, BRING MY MEDICAL BAG UP TO THE --
-- WHERE ARE THE BOYS?
I BELIEVE THAT'S THEM COMING THIS WAY NOW, SIR.
WHAT DID I TELL YOU?
TO WAIT BY THE CAR. BUT, WE WERE JUST --
-- WE'RE NOT IN GOTHAM CITY, BRUCE.
I'M NOT ONLY RESPONSIBLE FOR YOU, BUT FOR YOUR FRIEND AS WELL.
AND SINCE NEITHER ONE OF YOU CAN BE TRUSTED, YOU'LL SPEND THE REST OF THE WEEKEND IN YOUR HOTEL ROOM.
We never left the room the entire time we were in Metropolis.
We stayed perched by the window, hoping to get a glimpse of another hero, but none came.
Soon after that, my parents were killed and I hardly saw Tommy again...

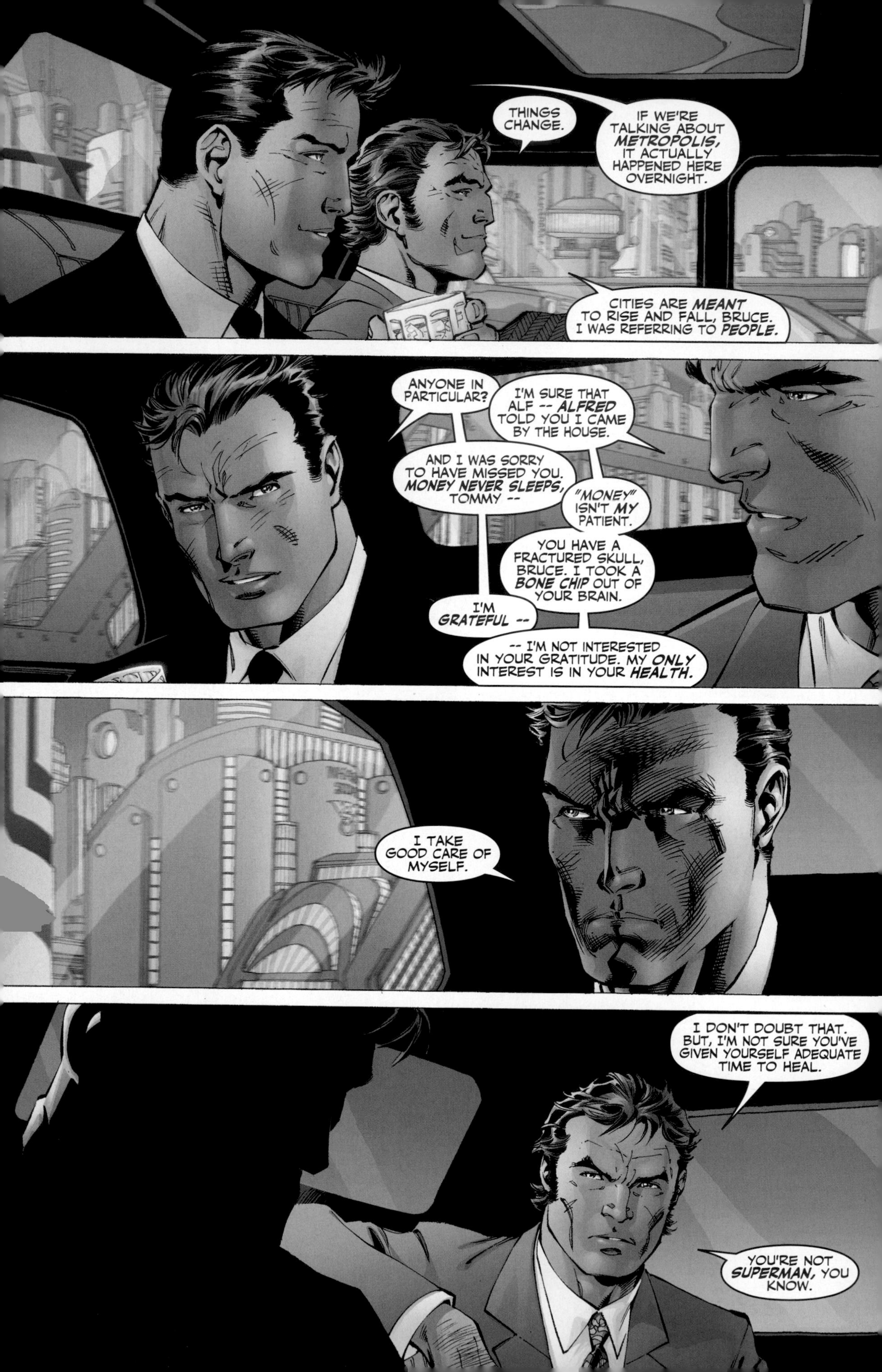
THINGS CHANGE.
IF WE'RE TALKING ABOUT METROPOLIS, IT ACTUALLY HAPPENED HERE OVERNIGHT.
CITIES ARE MEANT TO RISE AND FALL, BRUCE. I WAS REFERRING TO PEOPLE.
ANYONE IN PARTICULAR?
I'M SURE THAT ALF -- ALFRED TOLD YOU I CAME BY THE HOUSE.
AND I WAS SORRY TO HAVE MISSED YOU. MONEY NEVER SLEEPS, TOMMY --
"MONEY" ISN'T MY PATIENT.
YOU HAVE A FRACTURED SKULL, BRUCE. I TOOK A BONE CHIP OUT OF YOUR BRAIN.
I'M GRATEFUL --
-- I'M NOT INTERESTED IN YOUR GRATITUDE. MY ONLY INTEREST IS IN YOUR HEALTH.
I TAKE GOOD CARE OF MYSELF.
I DON'T DOUBT THAT. BUT, I'M NOT SURE YOU'VE GIVEN YOURSELF ADEQUATE TIME TO HEAL.
YOU'RE NOT SUPERMAN, YOU KNOW.

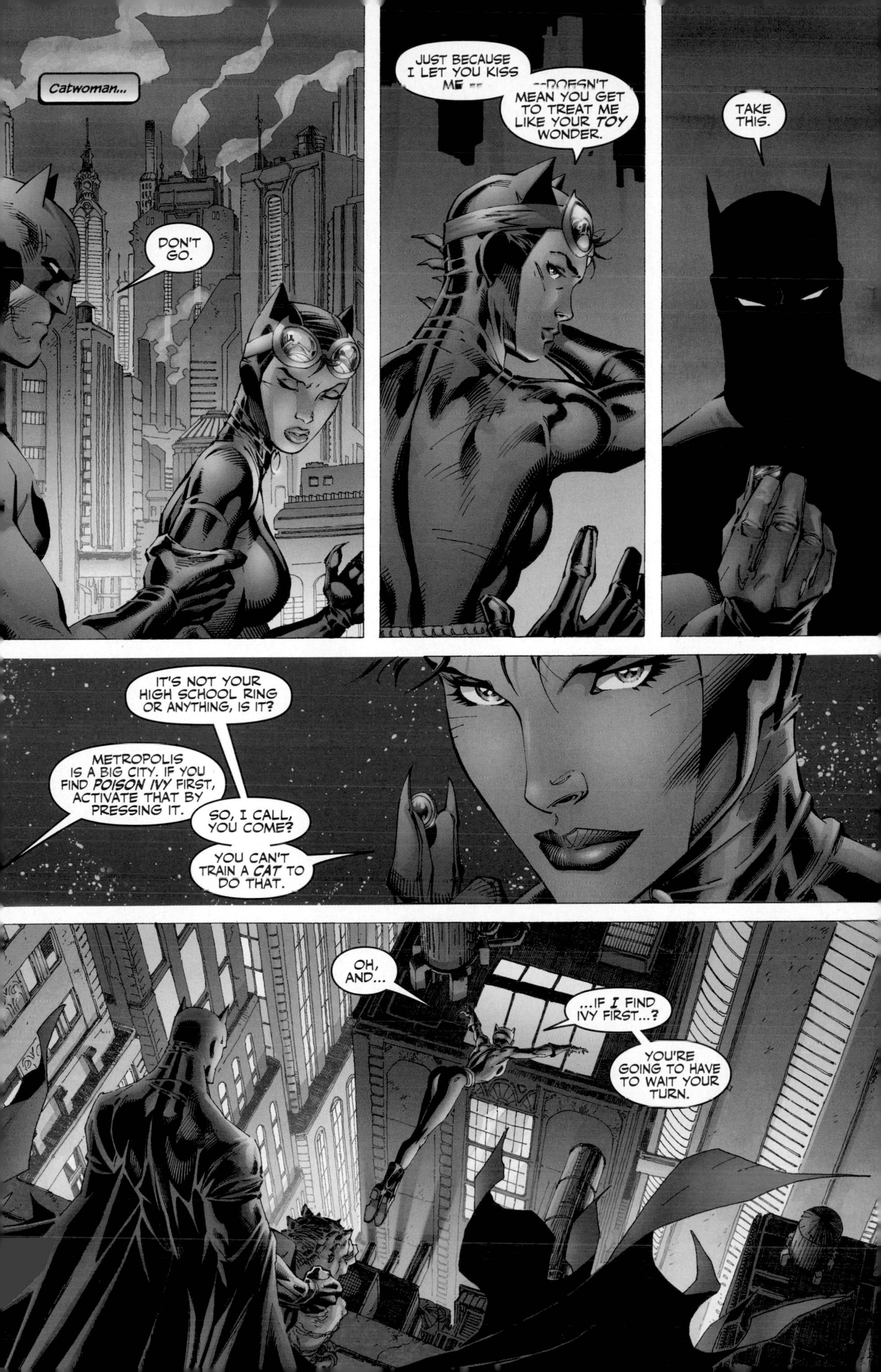
Catwoman...
DON'T GO.
JUST BECAUSE I LET YOU KISS ME--
--DOESN'T MEAN YOU GET TO TREAT ME LIKE YOUR TOY WONDER.
TAKE THIS.
IT'S NOT YOUR HIGH SCHOOL RING OR ANYTHING, IS IT?
METROPOLIS IS A BIG CITY. IF YOU FIND POISON IVY FIRST, ACTIVATE THAT BY PRESSING IT.
SO, I CALL, YOU COME?
YOU CAN'T TRAIN A CAT TO DO THAT.
OH, AND...
...IF I FIND IVY FIRST...?
YOU'RE GOING TO HAVE TO WAIT YOUR TURN.

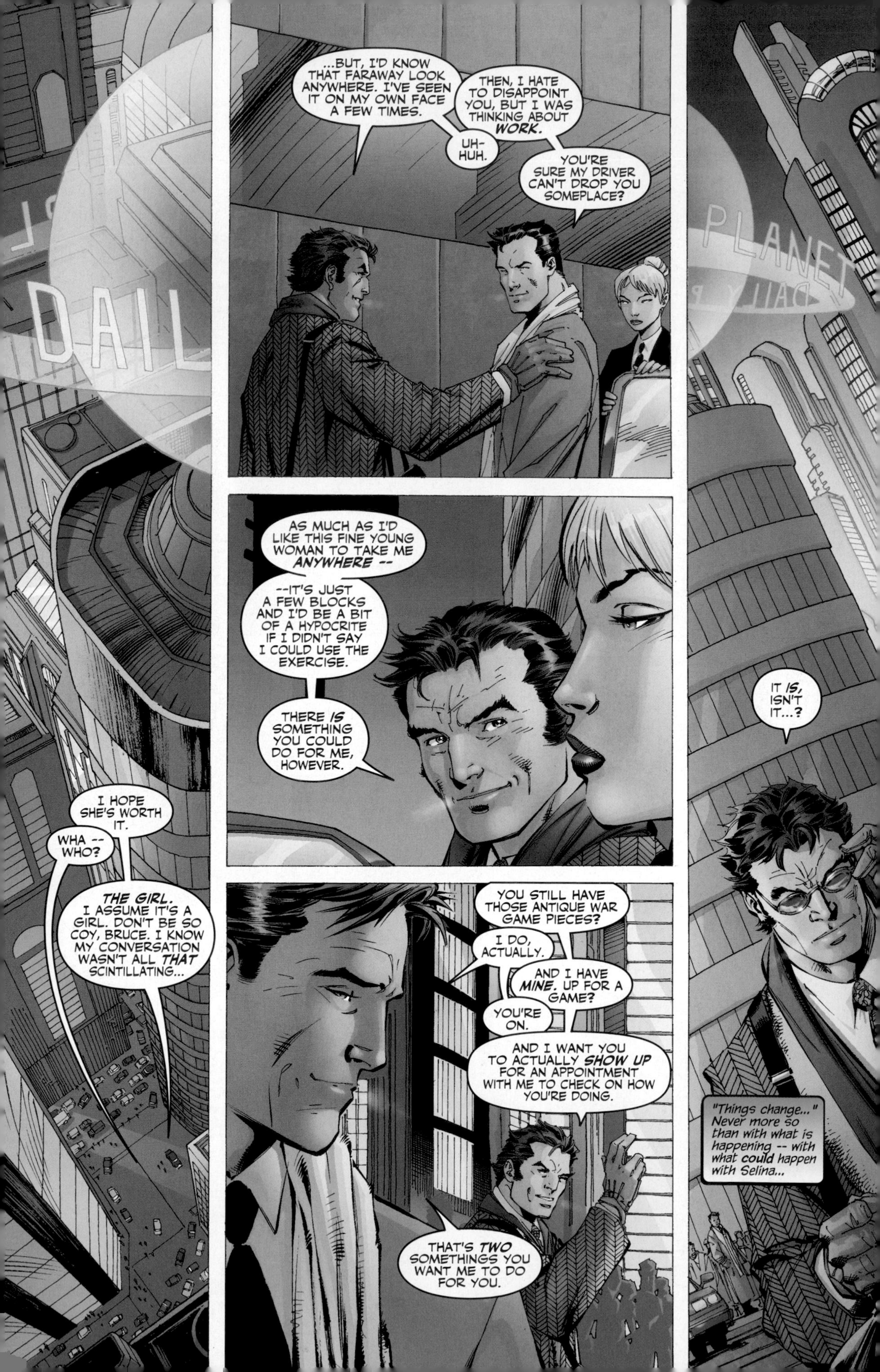
DAIL
...BUT, I'D KNOW THAT FARAWAY LOOK ANYWHERE. I'VE SEEN IT ON MY OWN FACE A FEW TIMES.
UH-HUH.
THEN, I HATE TO DISAPPOINT YOU, BUT I WAS THINKING ABOUT *WORK*.
YOU'RE SURE MY DRIVER CAN'T DROP YOU SOMEPLACE?
PLANET
AS MUCH AS I'D LIKE THIS FINE YOUNG WOMAN TO TAKE ME *ANYWHERE* --
--IT'S JUST A FEW BLOCKS AND I'D BE A BIT OF A HYPOCRITE IF I DIDN'T SAY I COULD USE THE EXERCISE.
THERE *IS* SOMETHING YOU COULD DO FOR ME, HOWEVER.
YOU STILL HAVE THOSE ANTIQUE WAR GAME PIECES?
I DO, ACTUALLY.
AND I HAVE *MINE*. UP FOR A GAME?
YOU'RE ON.
AND I WANT YOU TO ACTUALLY *SHOW UP* FOR AN APPOINTMENT WITH ME TO CHECK ON HOW YOU'RE DOING.
THAT'S *TWO* SOMETHINGS YOU WANT ME TO DO FOR YOU.
I HOPE SHE'S WORTH IT.
WHA -- WHO?
*THE GIRL.* I ASSUME IT'S A GIRL. DON'T BE SO COY, BRUCE. I KNOW MY CONVERSATION WASN'T ALL *THAT* SCINTILLATING...
IT *IS*, ISN'T IT...?
"Things change..." Never more so than with what is happening -- with what **could** happen with Selina...

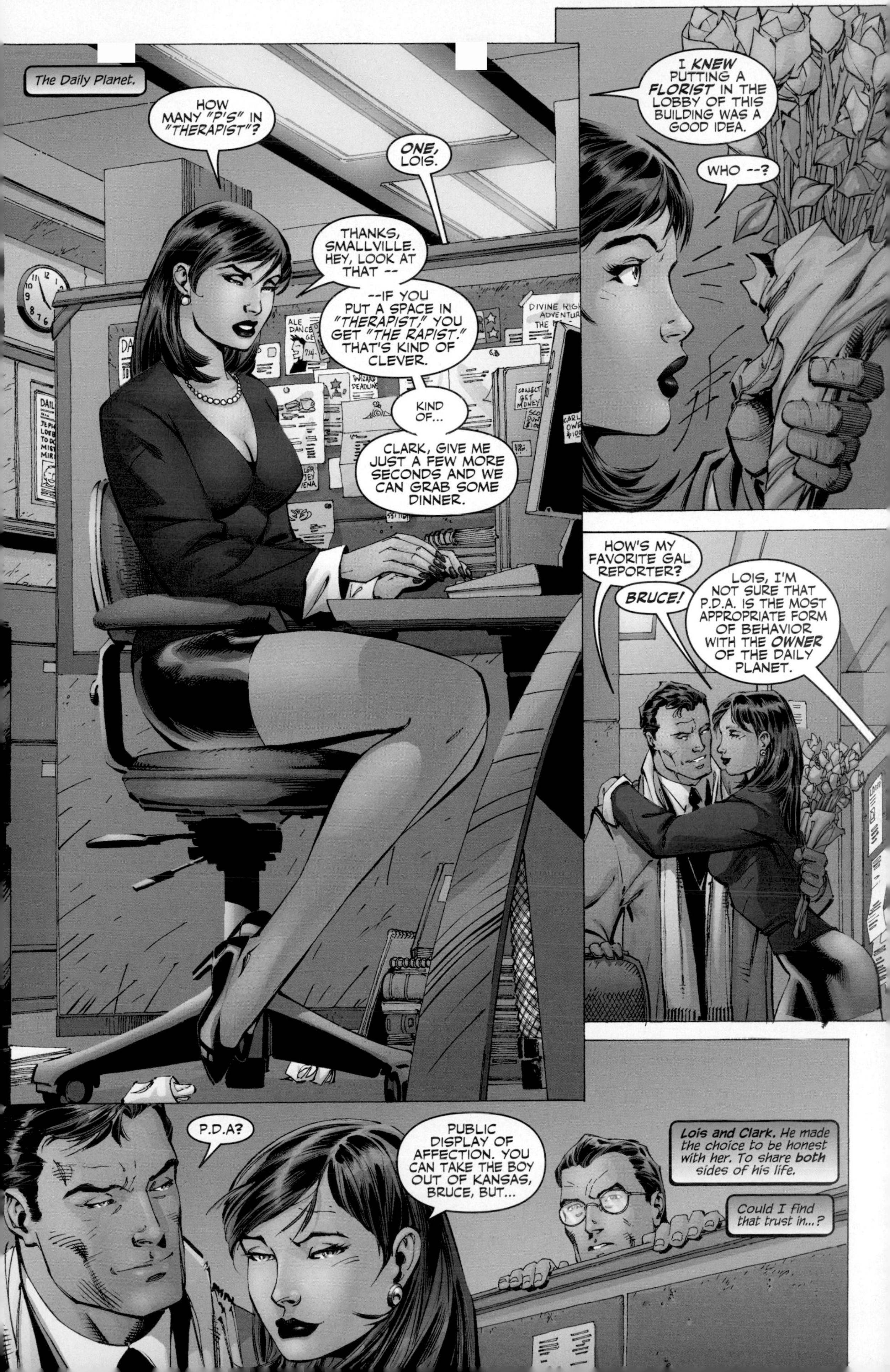
The Daily Planet.
HOW MANY "P'S" IN "THERAPIST"?
ONE, LOIS.
THANKS, SMALLVILLE. HEY, LOOK AT THAT --
--IF YOU PUT A SPACE IN "THERAPIST," YOU GET "THE RAPIST." THAT'S KIND OF CLEVER.
KIND OF...
CLARK, GIVE ME JUST A FEW MORE SECONDS AND WE CAN GRAB SOME DINNER.
I KNEW PUTTING A FLORIST IN THE LOBBY OF THIS BUILDING WAS A GOOD IDEA.
WHO --?
HOW'S MY FAVORITE GAL REPORTER?
BRUCE!
LOIS, I'M NOT SURE THAT P.D.A. IS THE MOST APPROPRIATE FORM OF BEHAVIOR WITH THE OWNER OF THE DAILY PLANET.
P.D.A?
PUBLIC DISPLAY OF AFFECTION. YOU CAN TAKE THE BOY OUT OF KANSAS, BRUCE, BUT...
Lois and Clark. He made the choice to be honest with her. To share both sides of his life.
Could I find that trust in...?

MIND IF I LOG ONTO YOUR COMPUTER, LOIS?

STOCK TIP.

ANYTHING YOU NEED, BRUCE.

CLARK, DINNER IS...

...GOING TO HAVE TO WAIT. I UNDERSTAND.

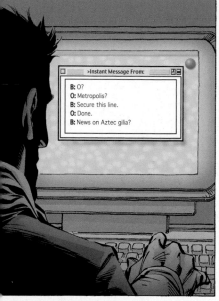

>Instant Message From:

**B:** O?
**O:** Metropolis?
**B:** Secure this line.
**O:** Done.
**B:** News on Aztec gilia?

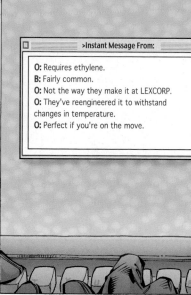

>Instant Message From:

**O:** Requires ethylene.
**B:** Fairly common.
**O:** Not the way they make it at LEXCORP.
**O:** They've reengineered it to withstand changes in temperature.
**O:** Perfect if you're on the move.

>Instant Message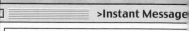

**O:** Before you ask, it'll take time.
**O:** L.C. not the easiest to hack into.
**B:** Don't. I have another door.
**B:** gtg.

IF I HAD READ ALL THAT, WOULD I HAVE BEEN JEALOUS OR RICH?

NEITHER. YOU'D HAVE BEEN BORED TO TEARS.

NO, SERIOUSLY, BRUCE, OTHER THAN MY SPARKLING PERSONALITY, WHAT BRINGS YOU TO --?

BRUCE!

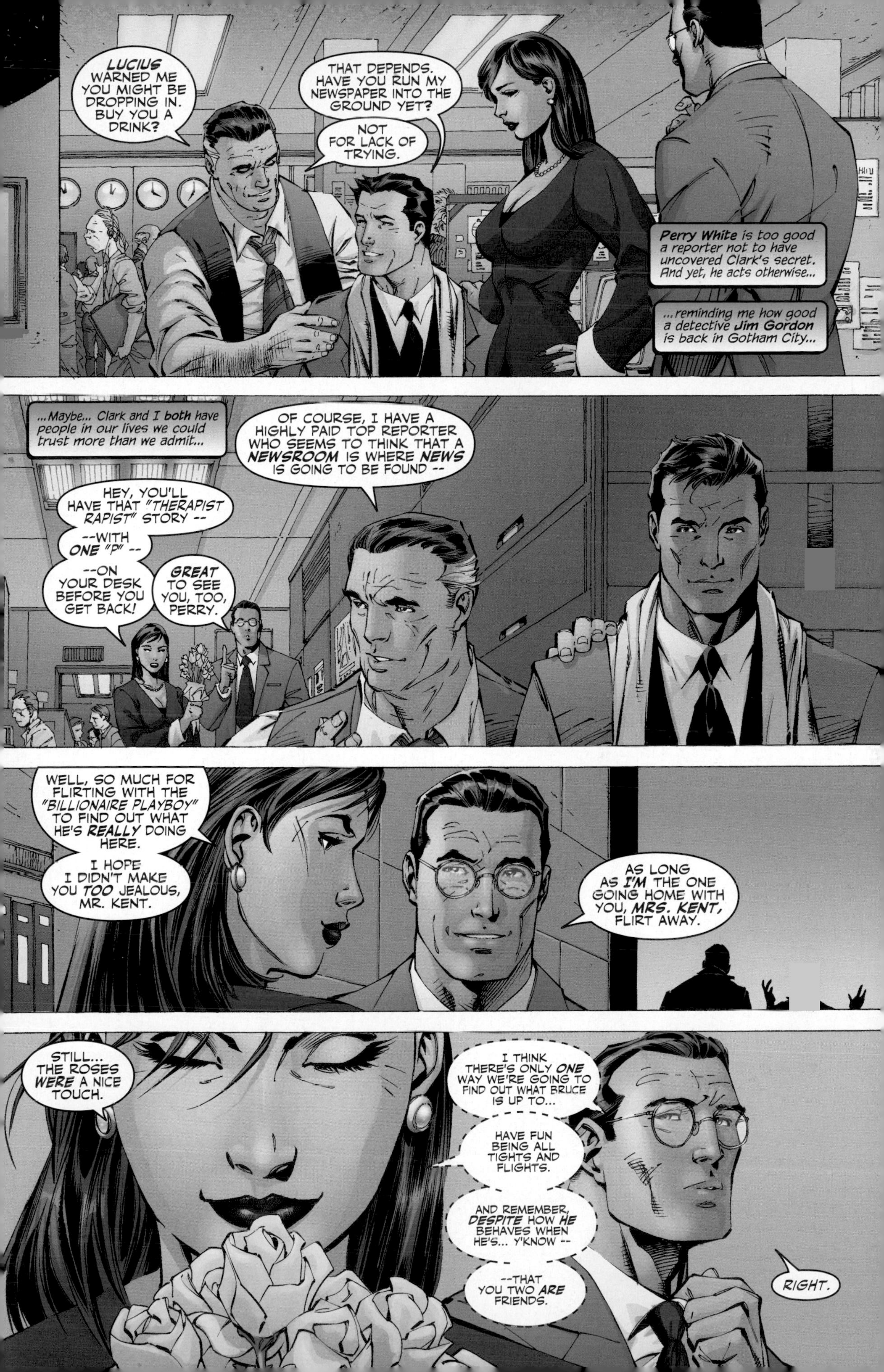
LUCIUS WARNED ME YOU MIGHT BE DROPPING IN. BUY YOU A DRINK?
THAT DEPENDS. HAVE YOU RUN MY NEWSPAPER INTO THE GROUND YET?
NOT FOR LACK OF TRYING.
Perry White is too good a reporter not to have uncovered Clark's secret. And yet, he acts otherwise...
...reminding me how good a detective Jim Gordon is back in Gotham City...
...Maybe... Clark and I both have people in our lives we could trust more than we admit...
OF COURSE, I HAVE A HIGHLY PAID TOP REPORTER WHO SEEMS TO THINK THAT A NEWSROOM IS WHERE NEWS IS GOING TO BE FOUND --
HEY, YOU'LL HAVE THAT "THERAPIST RAPIST" STORY --
--WITH ONE "P" --
--ON YOUR DESK BEFORE YOU GET BACK!
GREAT TO SEE YOU, TOO, PERRY.
WELL, SO MUCH FOR FLIRTING WITH THE "BILLIONAIRE PLAYBOY" TO FIND OUT WHAT HE'S REALLY DOING HERE.
I HOPE I DIDN'T MAKE YOU TOO JEALOUS, MR. KENT.
AS LONG AS I'M THE ONE GOING HOME WITH YOU, MRS. KENT, FLIRT AWAY.
STILL... THE ROSES WERE A NICE TOUCH.
I THINK THERE'S ONLY ONE WAY WE'RE GOING TO FIND OUT WHAT BRUCE IS UP TO...
HAVE FUN BEING ALL TIGHTS AND FLIGHTS.
AND REMEMBER, DESPITE HOW HE BEHAVES WHEN HE'S... Y'KNOW --
--THAT YOU TWO ARE FRIENDS.
RIGHT.

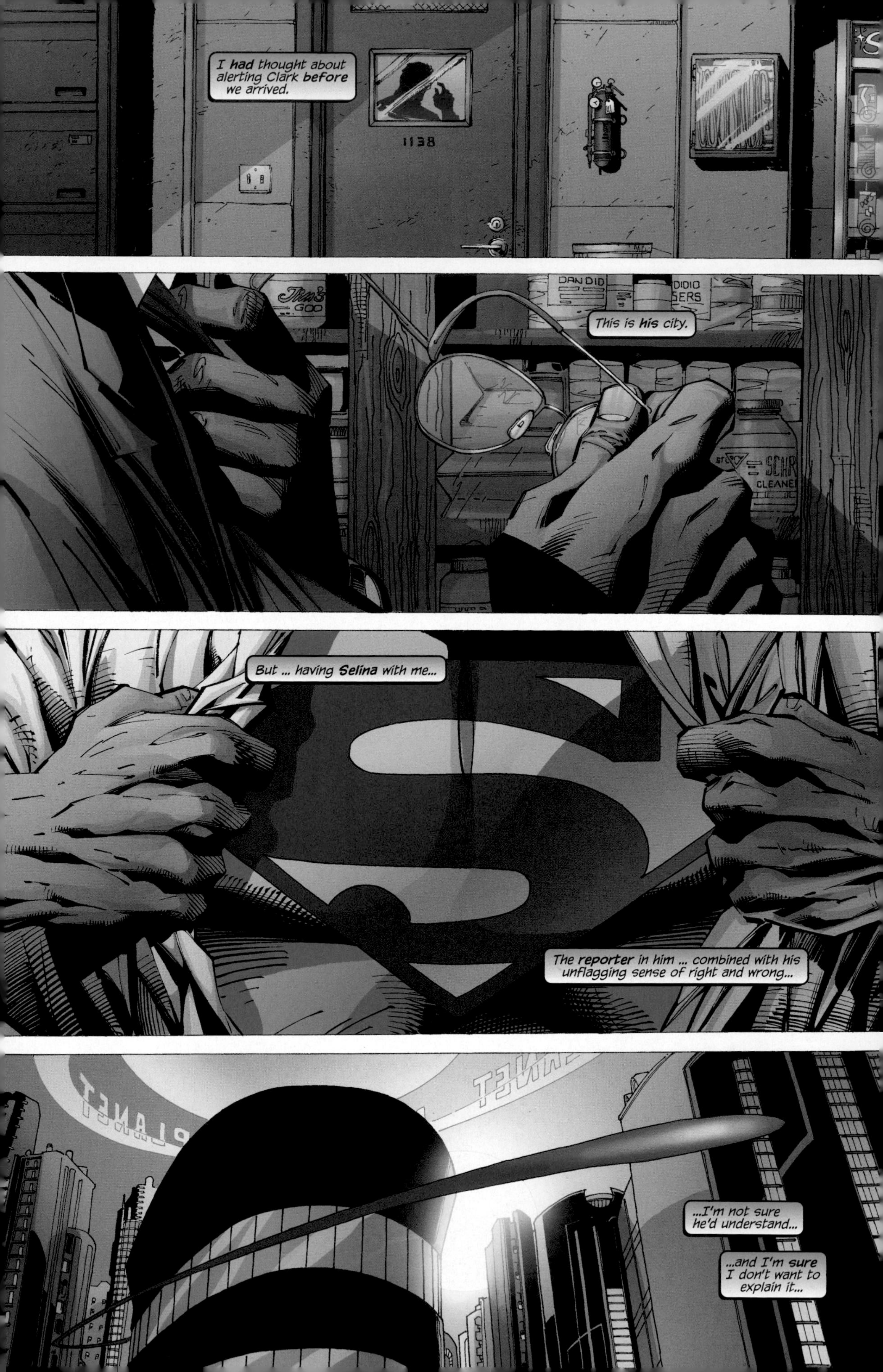
I had thought about alerting Clark before we arrived.
1138
DAN DID
This is his city.
But ... having Selina with me...
The reporter in him ... combined with his unflagging sense of right and wrong...
...I'm not sure he'd understand...
...and I'm sure I don't want to explain it...

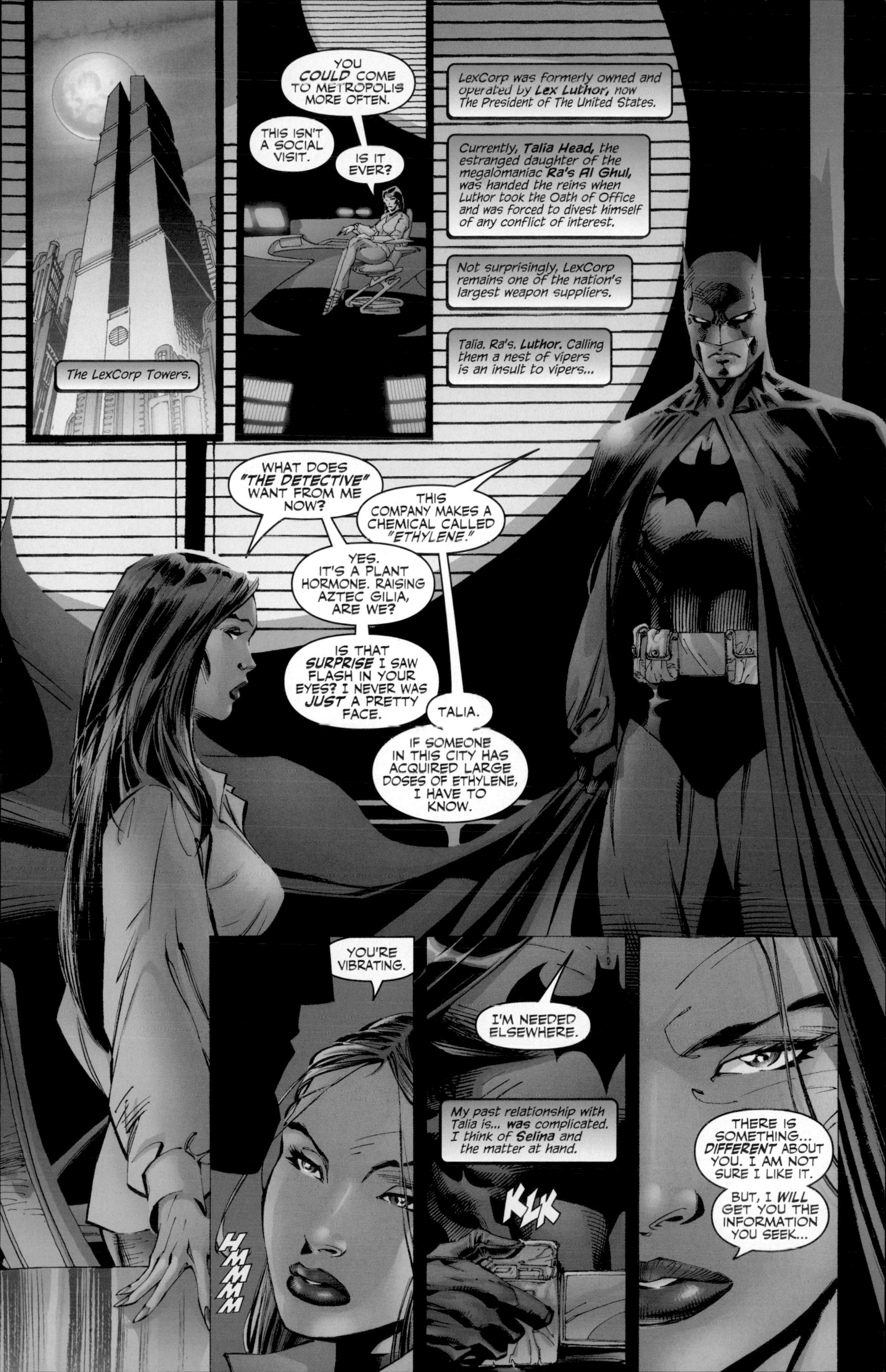

The LexCorp Towers.
YOU COULD COME TO METROPOLIS MORE OFTEN.
THIS ISN'T A SOCIAL VISIT.
IS IT EVER?
LexCorp was formerly owned and operated by Lex Luthor, now The President of The United States.
Currently, Talia Head, the estranged daughter of the megalomaniac Ra's Al Ghul, was handed the reins when Luthor took the Oath of Office and was forced to divest himself of any conflict of interest.
Not surprisingly, LexCorp remains one of the nation's largest weapon suppliers.
Talia. Ra's. Luthor. Calling them a nest of vipers is an insult to vipers...
WHAT DOES "THE DETECTIVE" WANT FROM ME NOW?
THIS COMPANY MAKES A CHEMICAL CALLED "ETHYLENE."
YES. IT'S A PLANT HORMONE. RAISING AZTEC GILIA, ARE WE?
IS THAT SURPRISE I SAW FLASH IN YOUR EYES? I NEVER WAS JUST A PRETTY FACE.
TALIA.
IF SOMEONE IN THIS CITY HAS ACQUIRED LARGE DOSES OF ETHYLENE, I HAVE TO KNOW.
YOU'RE VIBRATING.
HMMMM
I'M NEEDED ELSEWHERE.
My past relationship with Talia is... was complicated. I think of Selina and the matter at hand.
KLK
THERE IS SOMETHING... DIFFERENT ABOUT YOU. I AM NOT SURE I LIKE IT.
BUT, I WILL GET YOU THE INFORMATION YOU SEEK...

DOES IT *EVER* GET DARK IN THIS CITY?

EVEN AT NIGHT, IT'S LIT UP LIKE IT'S IMPORTANT OR SOMETHING.

YOUR *"PAGER/HOMING-DEVICE THING"* WORKS.

OBVIOUSLY.

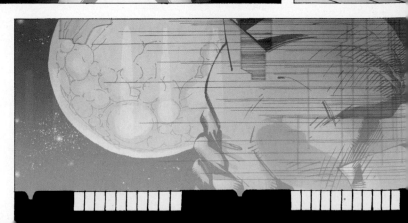

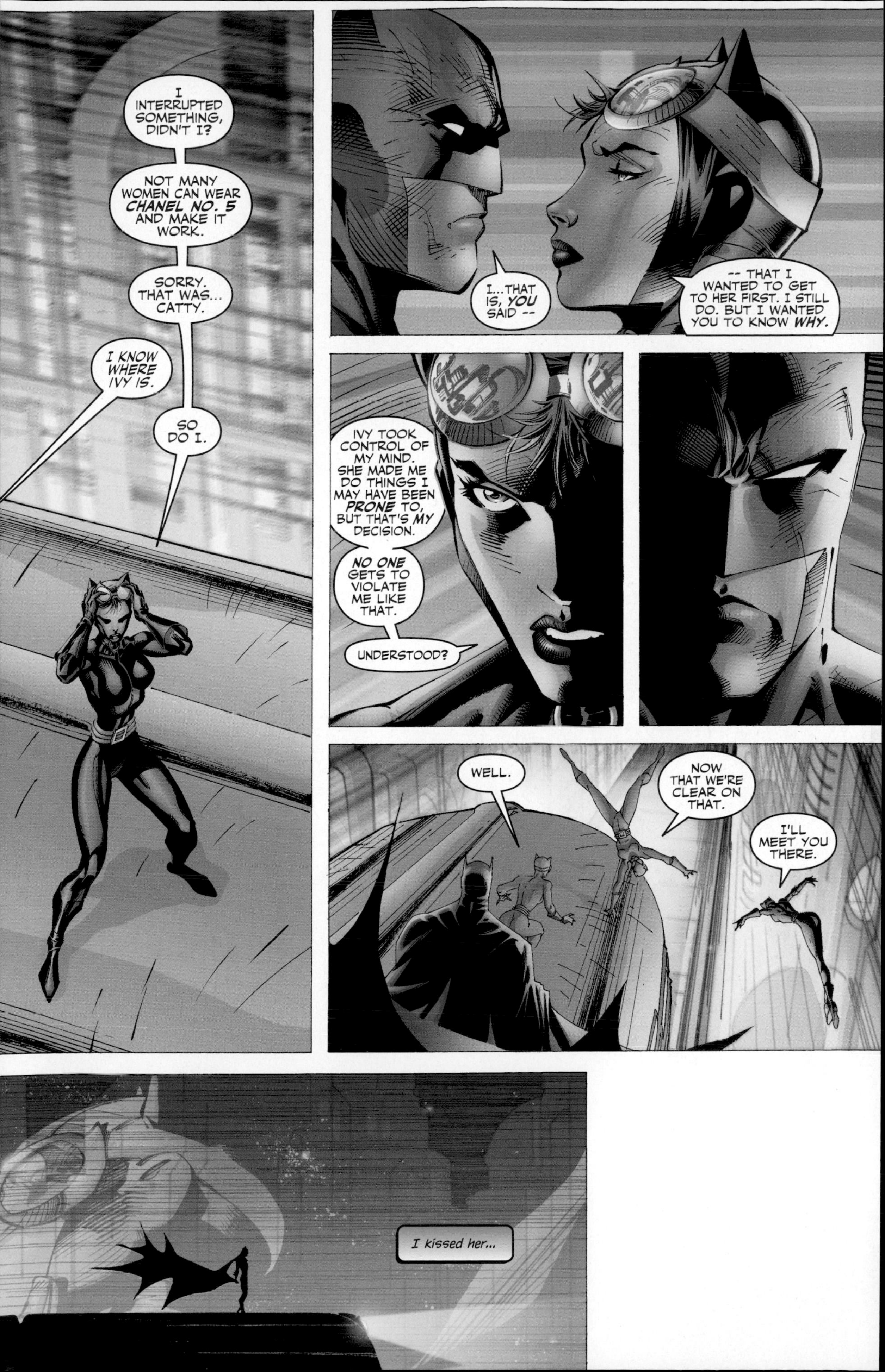
I INTERRUPTED SOMETHING, DIDN'T I?
NOT MANY WOMEN CAN WEAR CHANEL NO. 5 AND MAKE IT WORK.
SORRY. THAT WAS... CATTY.
I KNOW WHERE IVY IS.
SO DO I.
I...THAT IS, YOU SAID --
-- THAT I WANTED TO GET TO HER FIRST. I STILL DO. BUT I WANTED YOU TO KNOW WHY.
IVY TOOK CONTROL OF MY MIND. SHE MADE ME DO THINGS I MAY HAVE BEEN PRONE TO, BUT THAT'S MY DECISION.
NO ONE GETS TO VIOLATE ME LIKE THAT.
UNDERSTOOD?
WELL.
NOW THAT WE'RE CLEAR ON THAT.
I'LL MEET YOU THERE.
I kissed her...

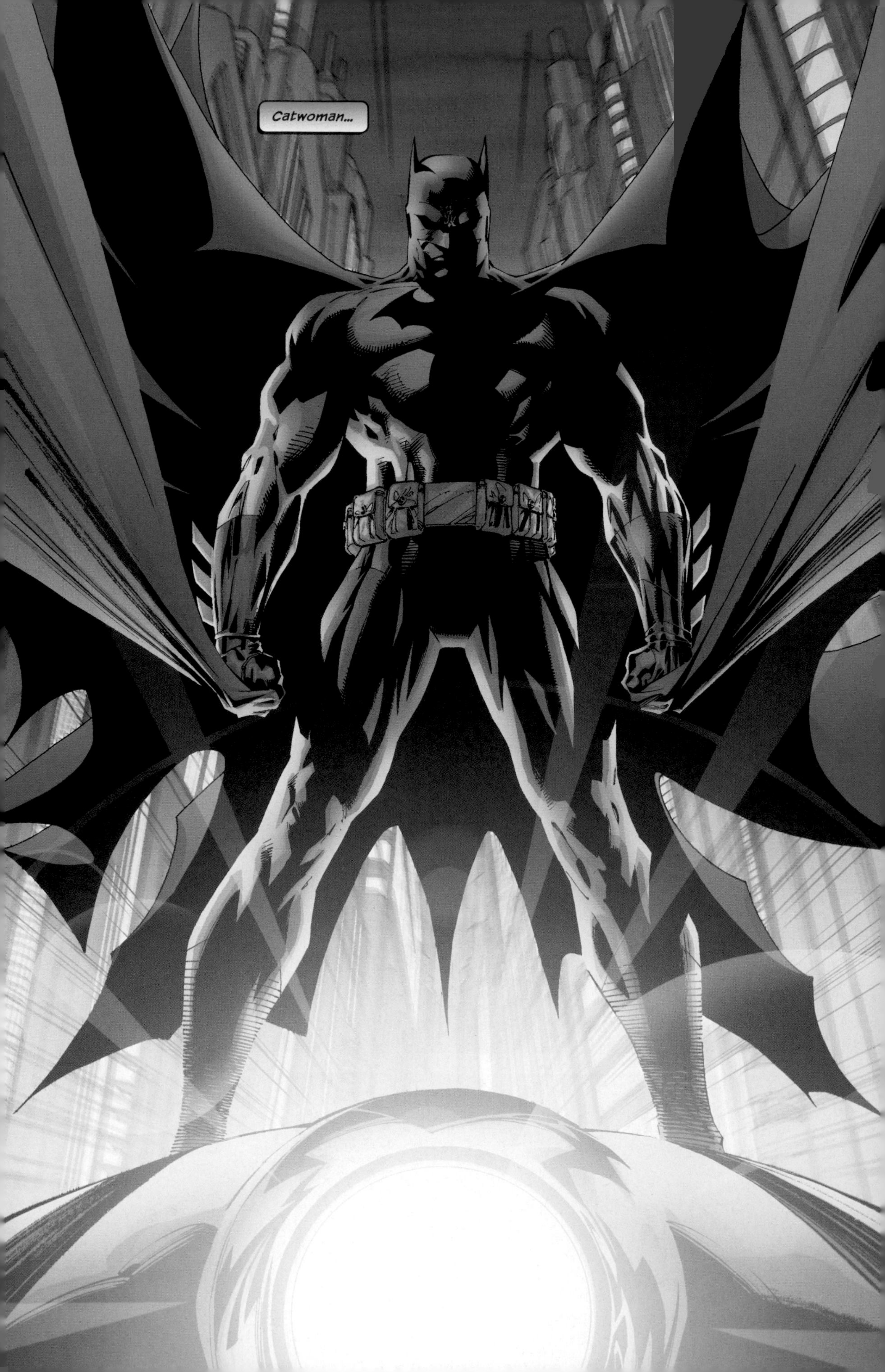
Catwoman...

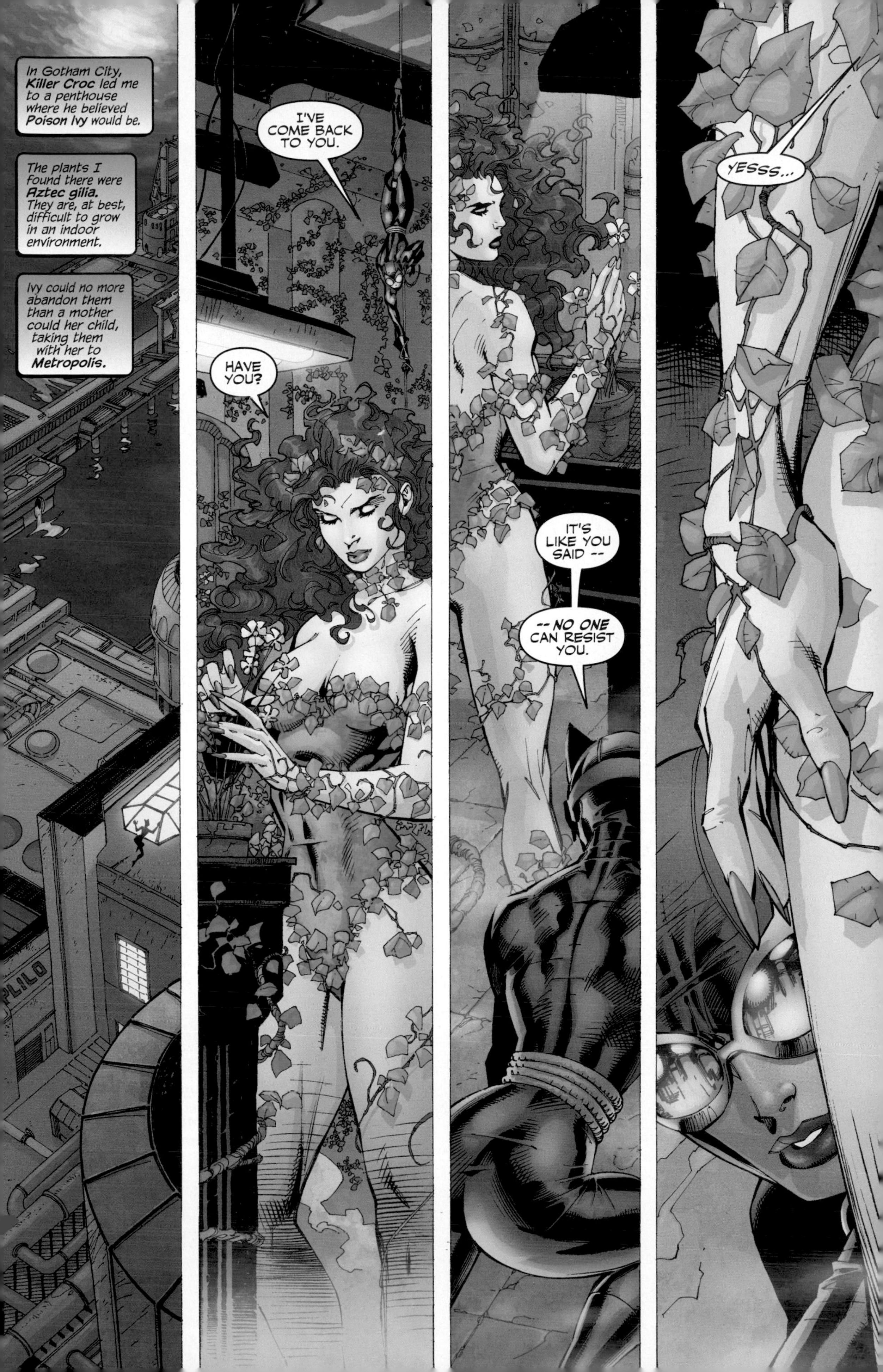

In Gotham City, Killer Croc led me to a penthouse where he believed Poison Ivy would be.
The plants I found there were Aztec gilia. They are, at best, difficult to grow in an indoor environment.
Ivy could no more abandon them than a mother could her child, taking them with her to Metropolis.
I'VE COME BACK TO YOU.
HAVE YOU?
IT'S LIKE YOU SAID --
-- NO ONE CAN RESIST YOU.
YESSS...

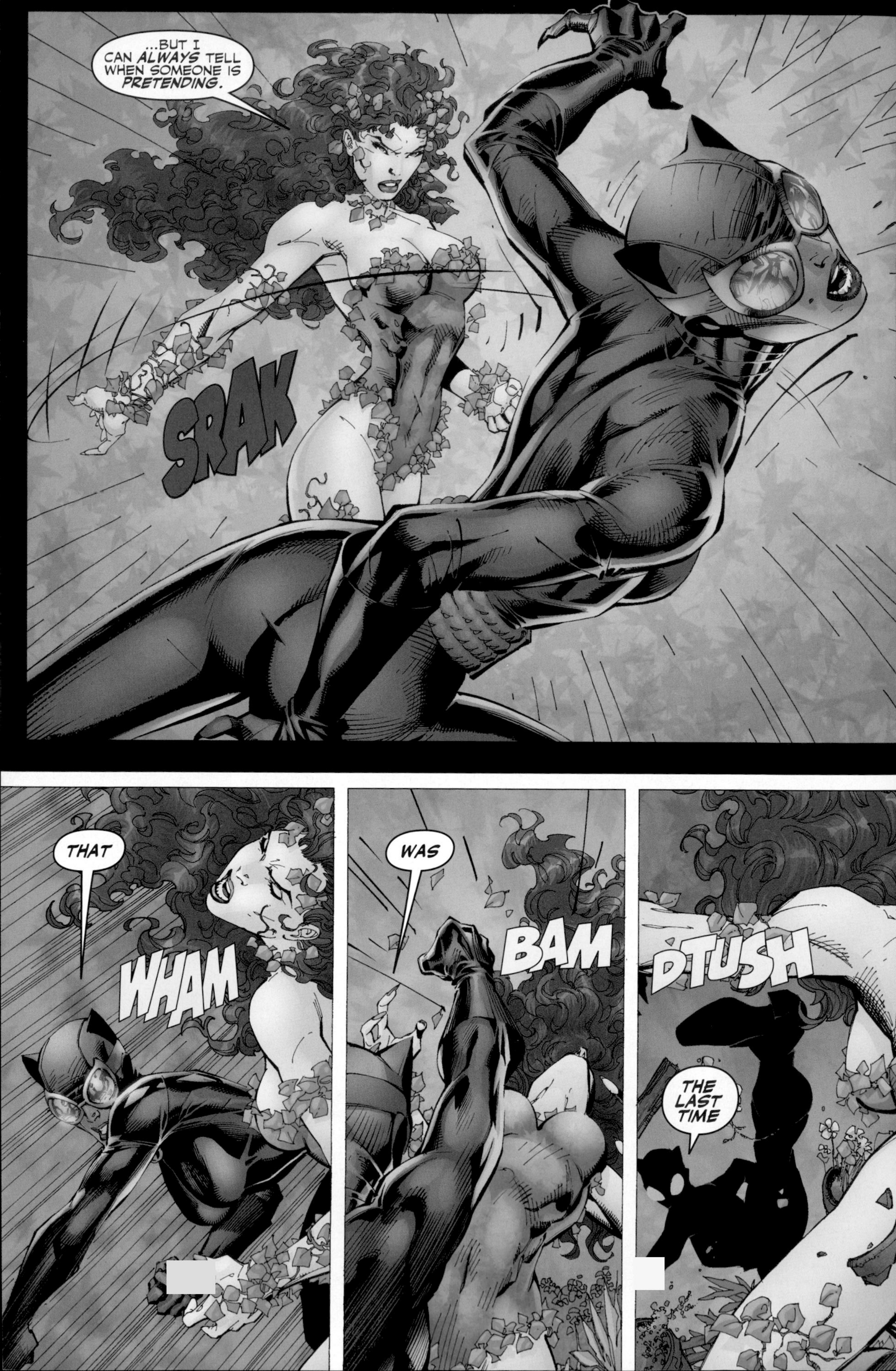
...BUT I CAN ALWAYS TELL WHEN SOMEONE IS PRETENDING.
SRAK
THAT
WHAM
WAS
BAM
DTUSH
THE LAST TIME

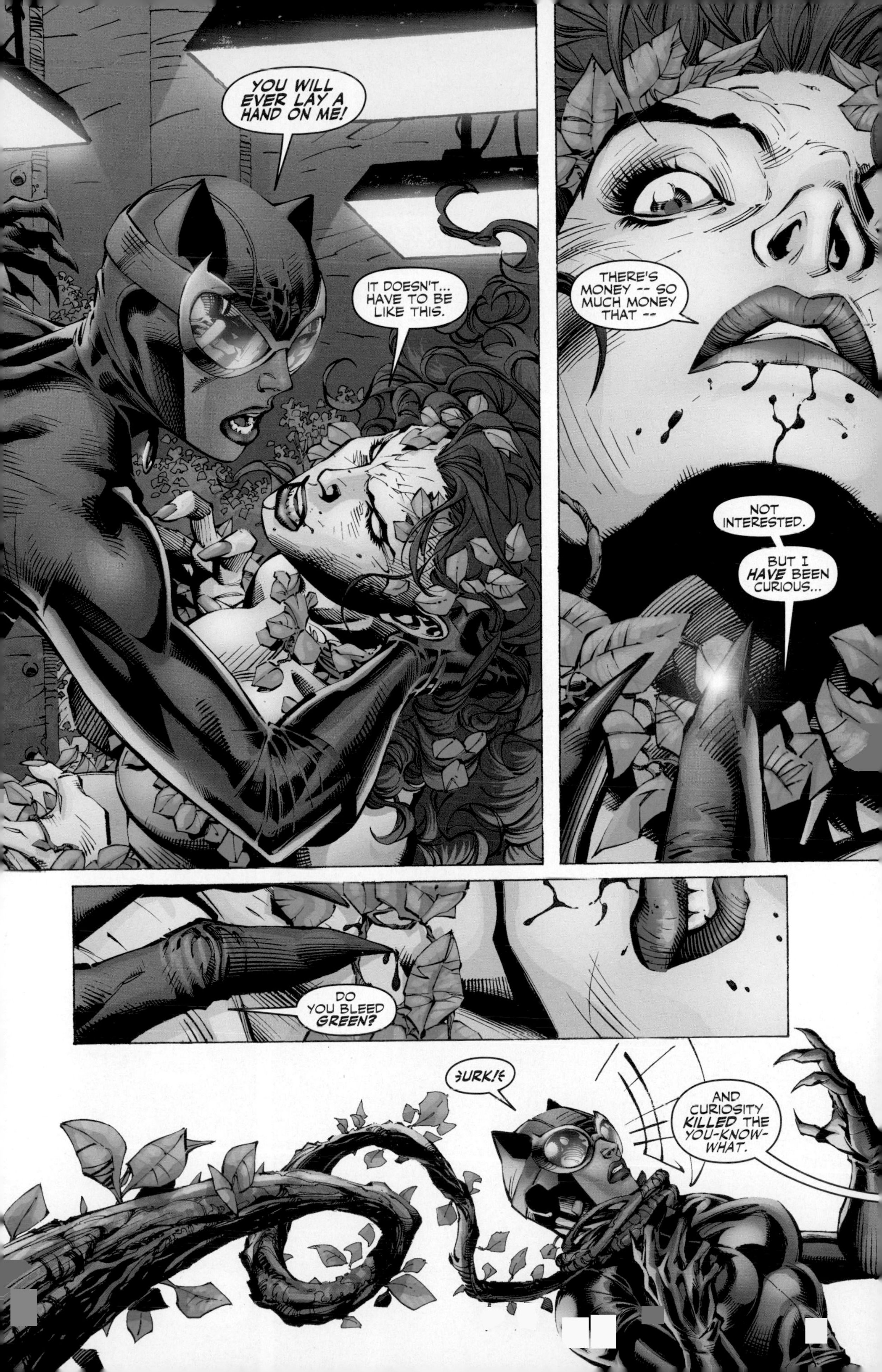
YOU WILL EVER LAY A HAND ON ME!
IT DOESN'T... HAVE TO BE LIKE THIS.
THERE'S MONEY -- SO MUCH MONEY THAT --
NOT INTERESTED.
BUT I *HAVE* BEEN CURIOUS...
DO YOU BLEED *GREEN?*
URK!
AND CURIOSITY *KILLED* THE YOU-KNOW-WHAT.

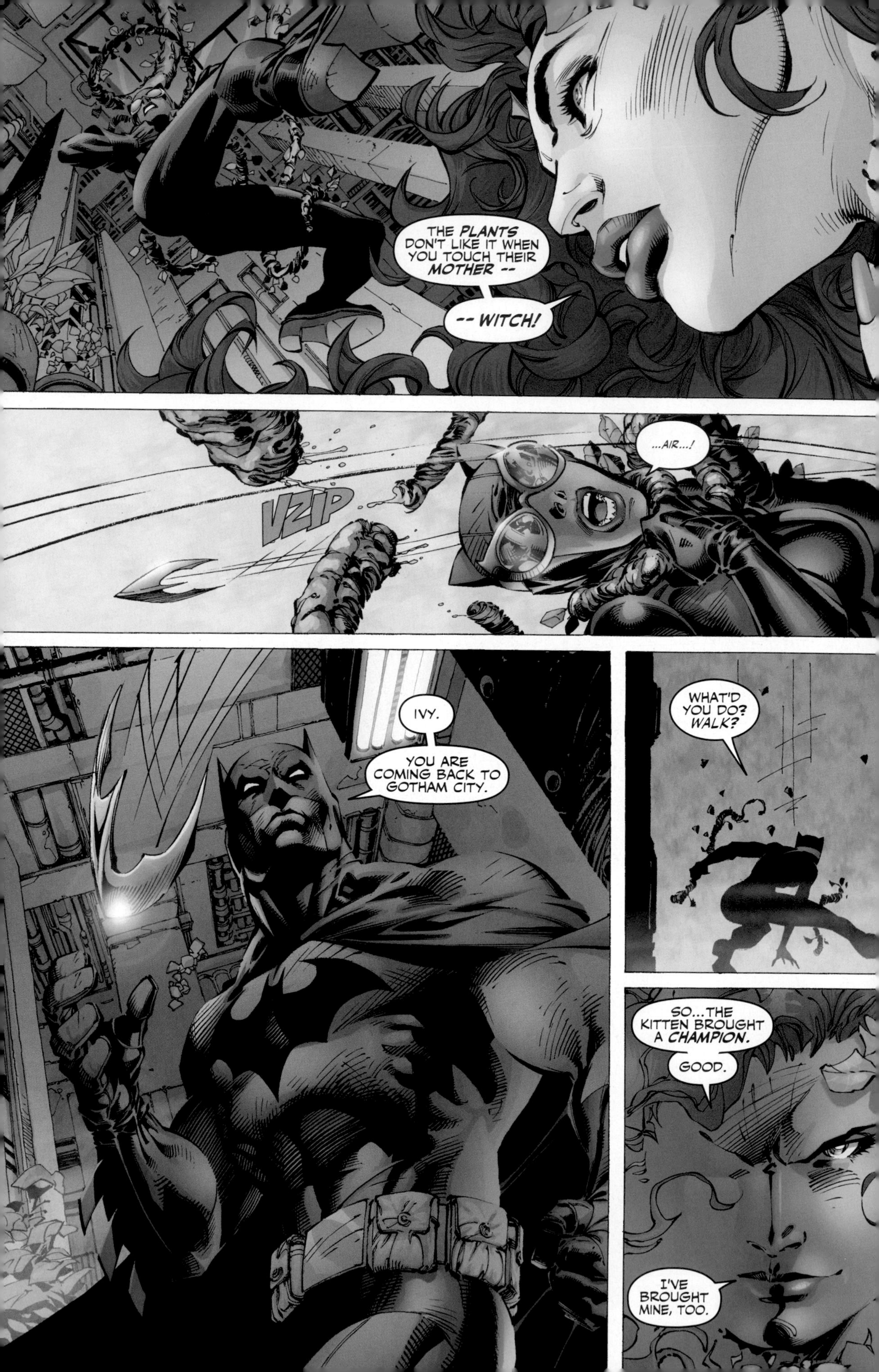
THE PLANTS DON'T LIKE IT WHEN YOU TOUCH THEIR MOTHER --
-- WITCH!
...AIR...!
VZIP
IVY.
YOU ARE COMING BACK TO GOTHAM CITY.
WHAT'D YOU DO? WALK?
SO...THE KITTEN BROUGHT A CHAMPION.
GOOD.
I'VE BROUGHT MINE, TOO.

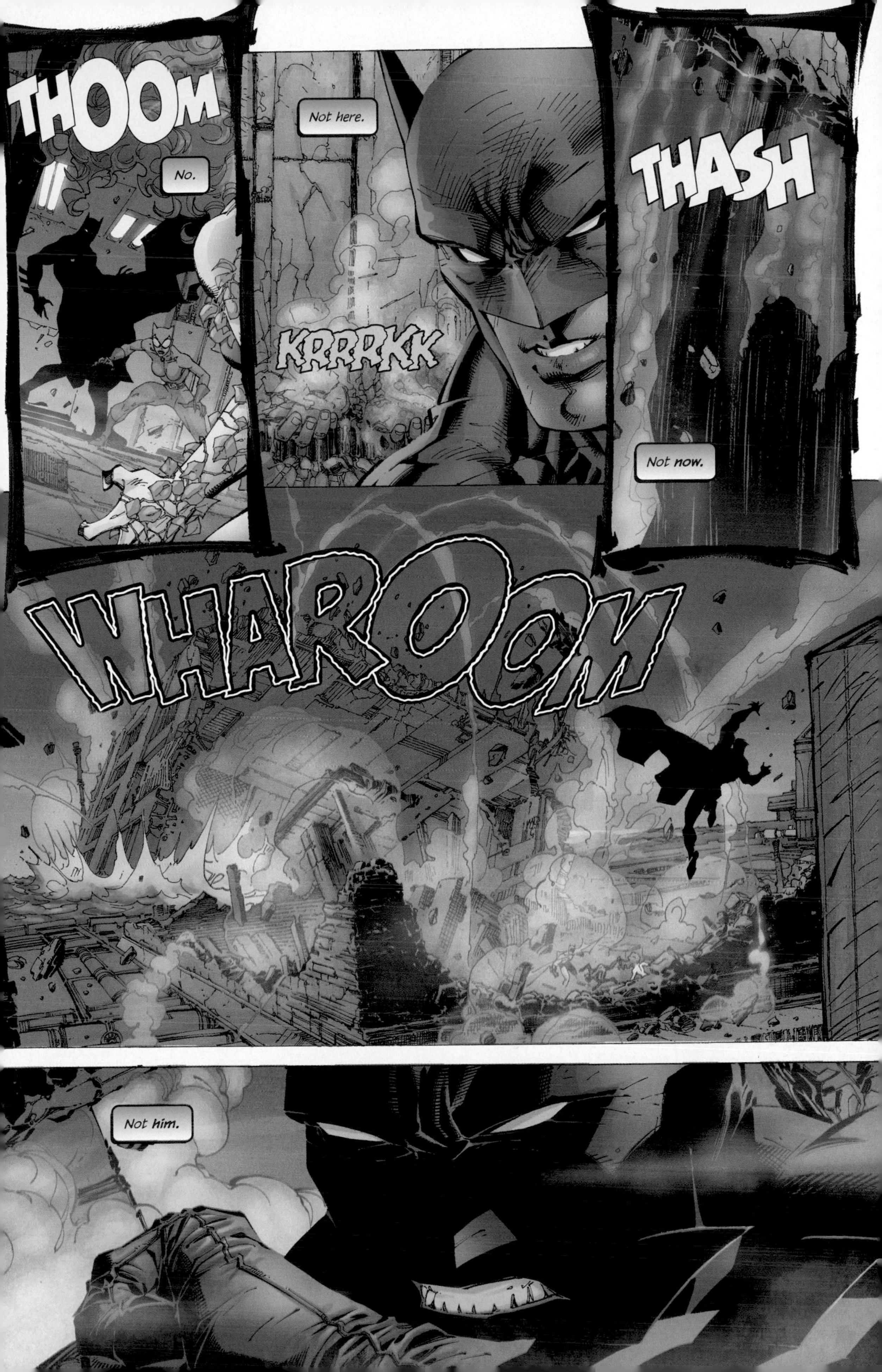
THOOM
No.
Not here.
KRRRKK
THASH
Not now.
WHAROOM
Not him.

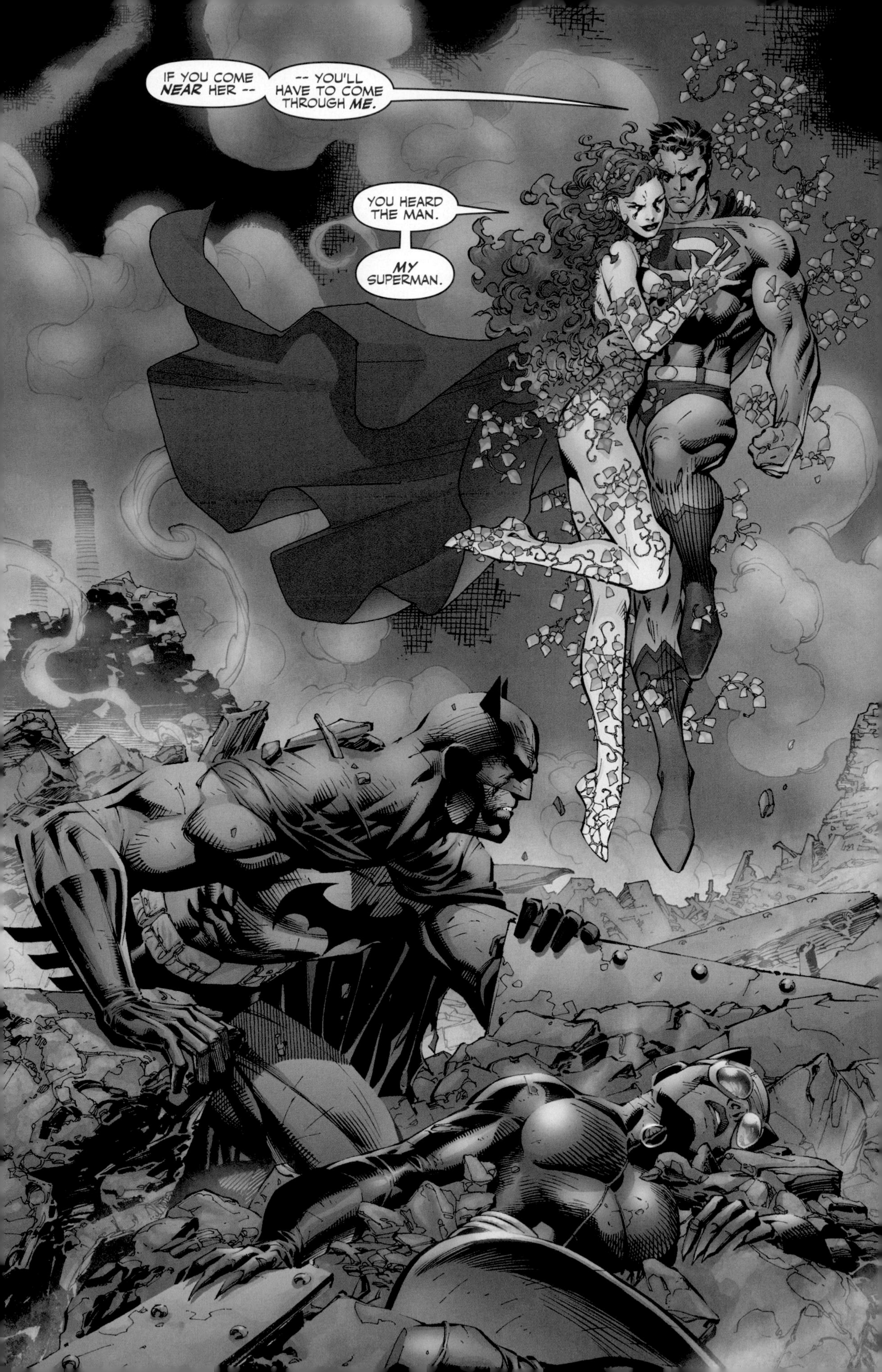
IF YOU COME NEAR HER --
-- YOU'LL HAVE TO COME THROUGH ME.
YOU HEARD THE MAN.
MY SUPERMAN.

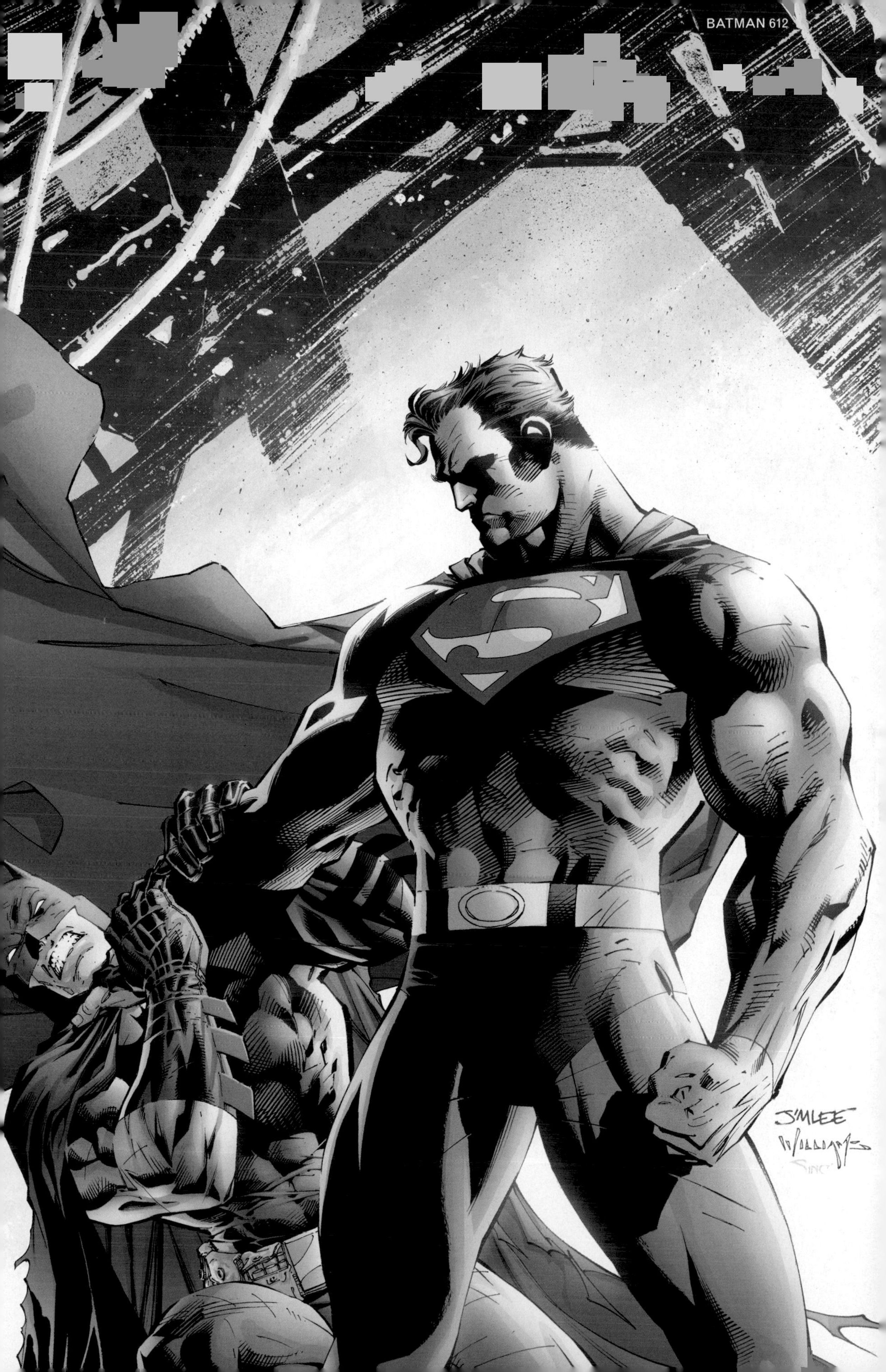
BATMAN 612

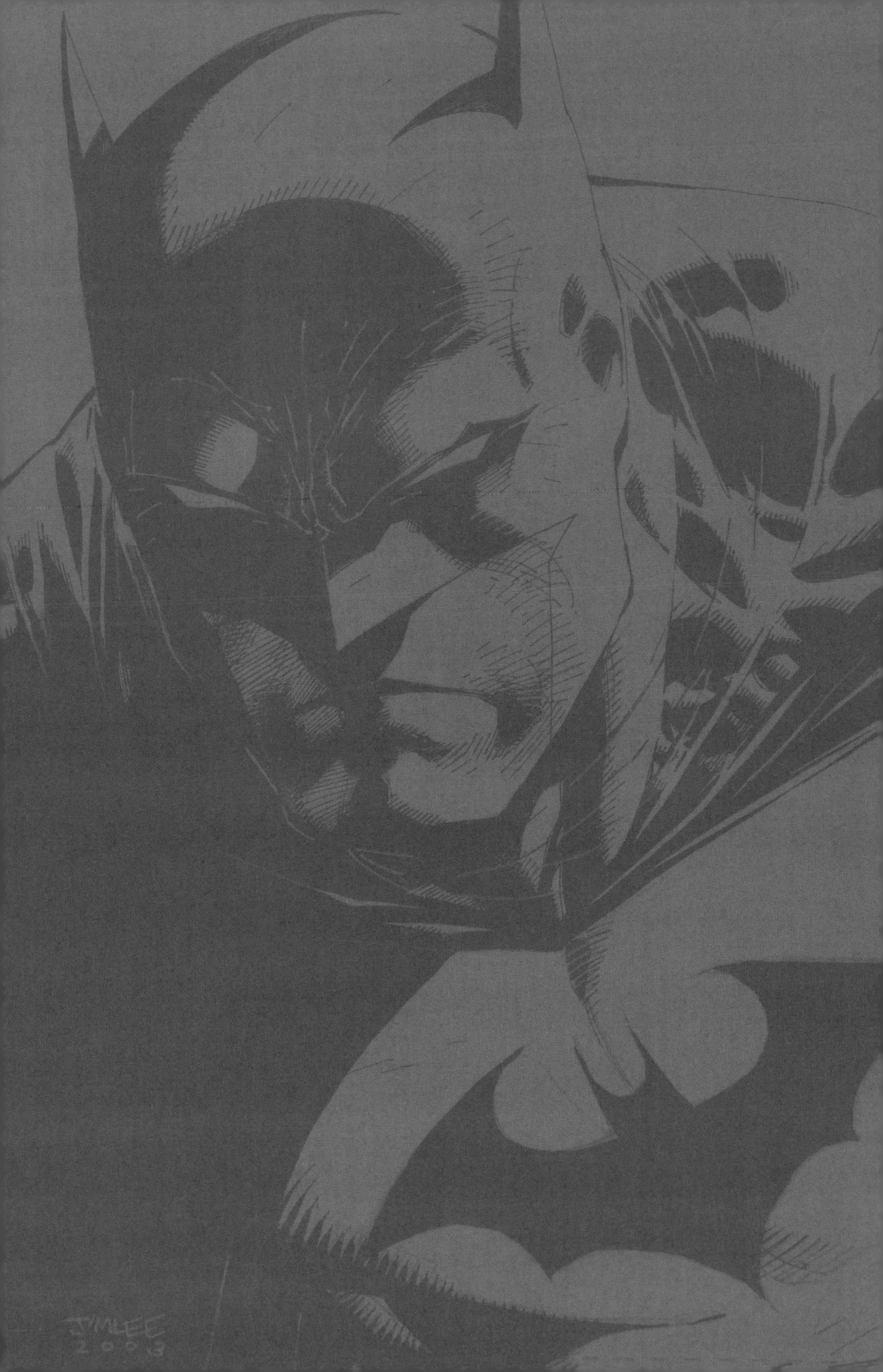
JIM LEE
2003

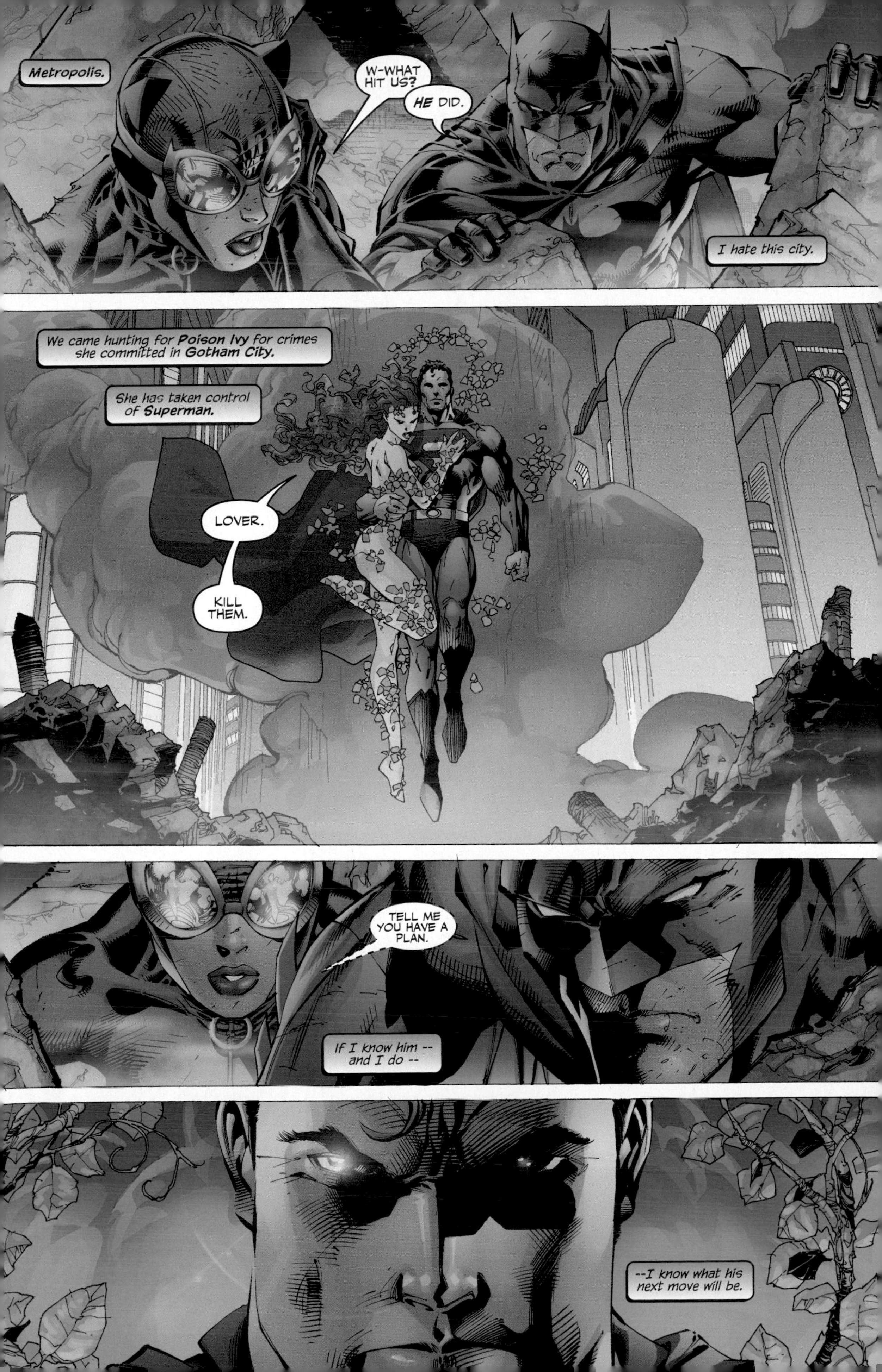

Metropolis.
W-WHAT HIT US?
HE DID.
I hate this city.
We came hunting for Poison Ivy for crimes she committed in Gotham City.
She has taken control of Superman.
LOVER.
KILL THEM.
TELL ME YOU HAVE A PLAN.
If I know him -- and I do --
--I know what his next move will be.

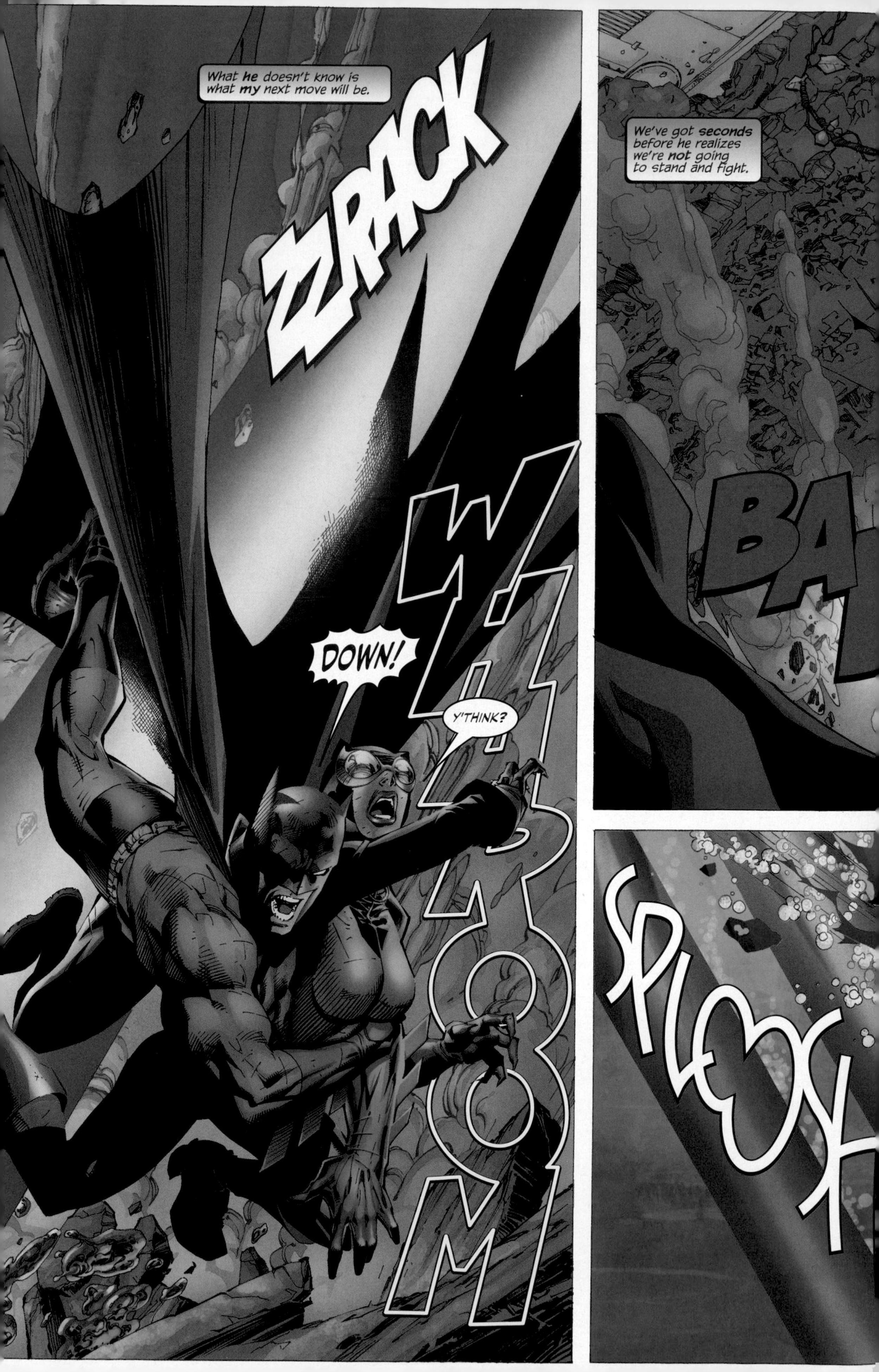

What he doesn't know is what my next move will be.
ZZRACK
DOWN!
Y'THINK?
WHOOM
We've got seconds before he realizes we're not going to stand and fight.
BA
SPLOOSH

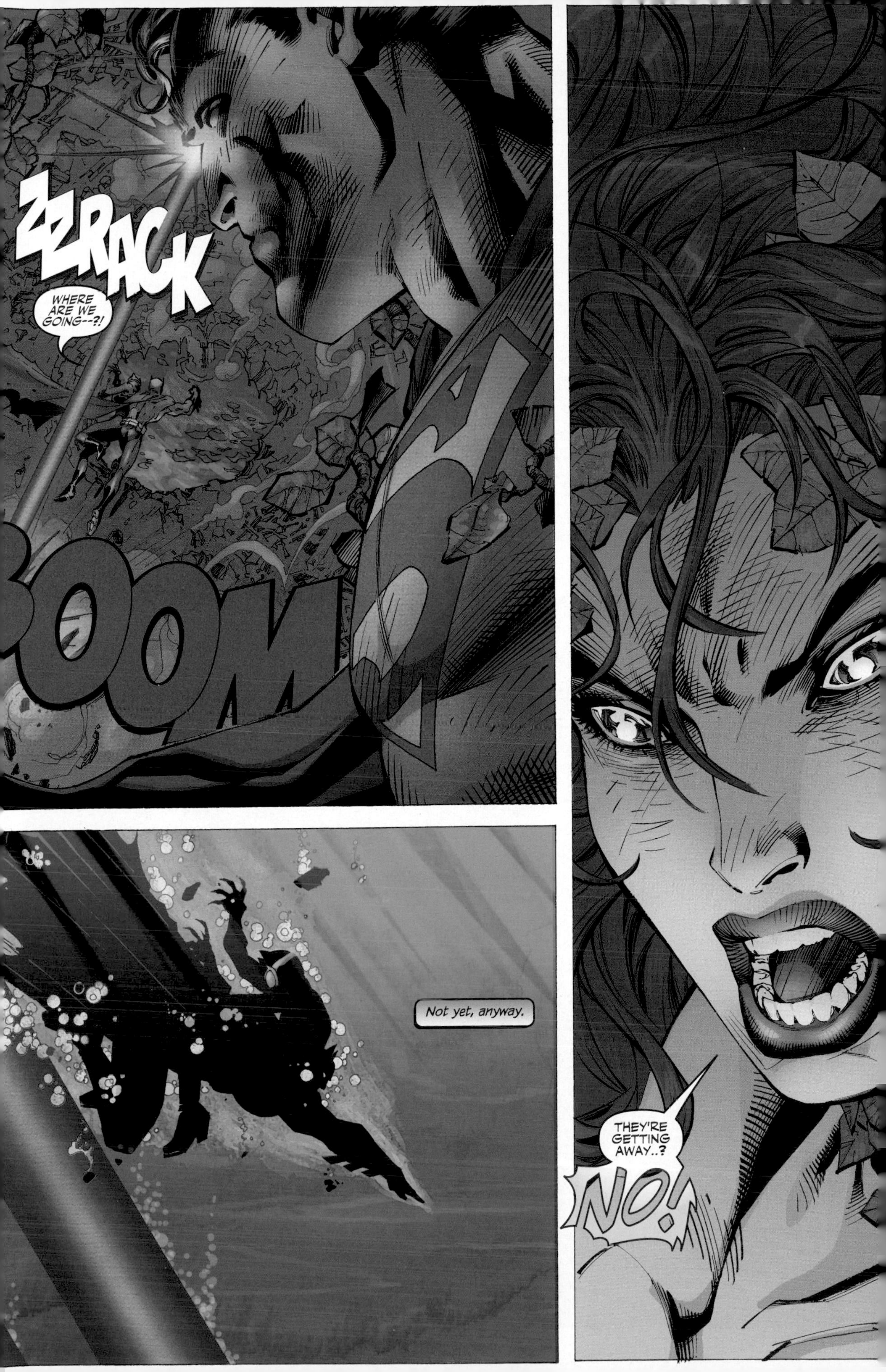
ZZRACK
WHERE ARE WE GOING--?!
BOOM
Not yet, anyway.
THEY'RE GETTING AWAY..?
NO!

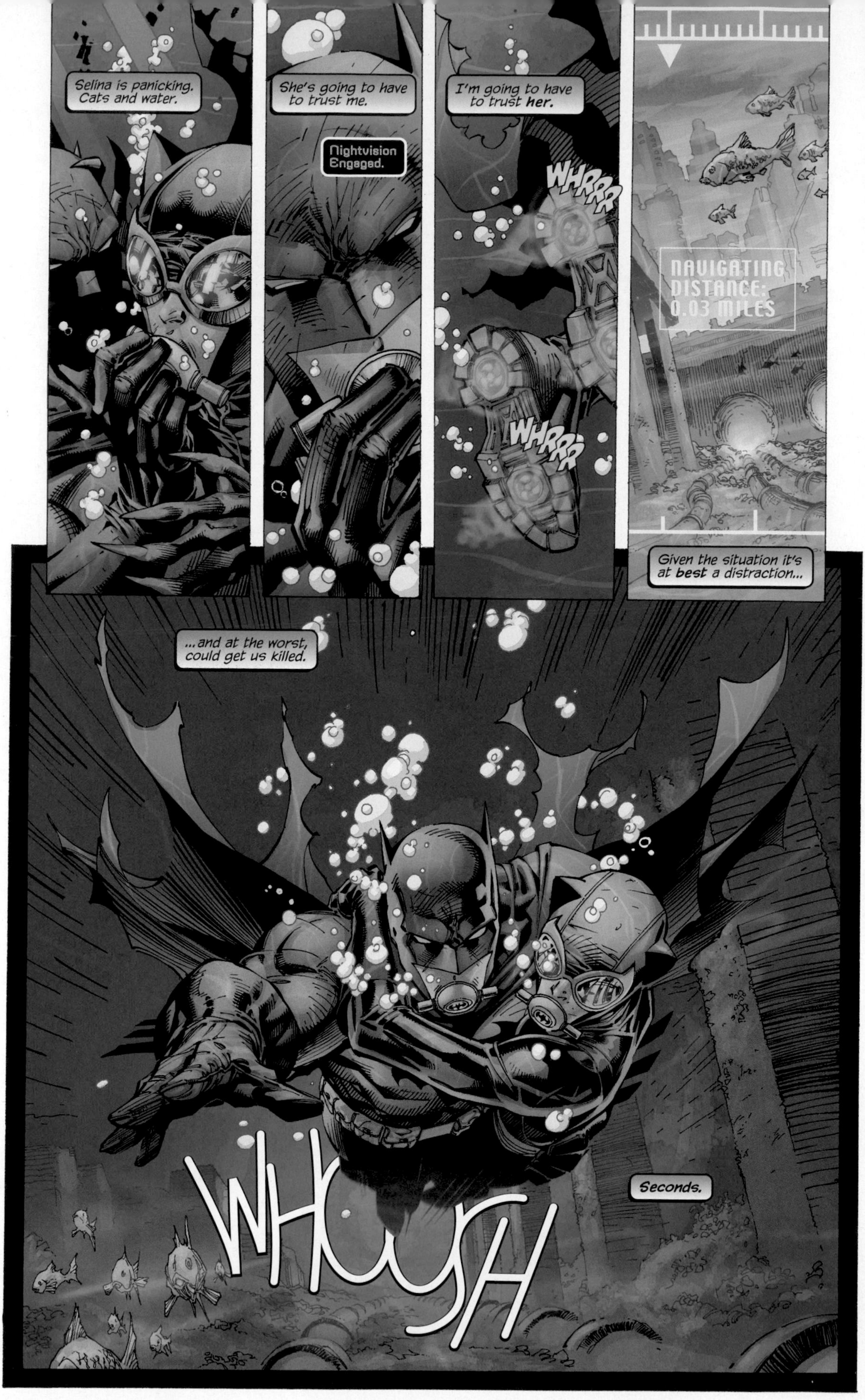
Selina is panicking. Cats and water.
She's going to have to trust me.
Nightvision Engaged.
I'm going to have to trust her.
WHRRR
WHRRR
NAVIGATING DISTANCE: 0.03 MILES
Given the situation it's at best a distraction...
...and at the worst, could get us killed.
WHOOSH
Seconds.

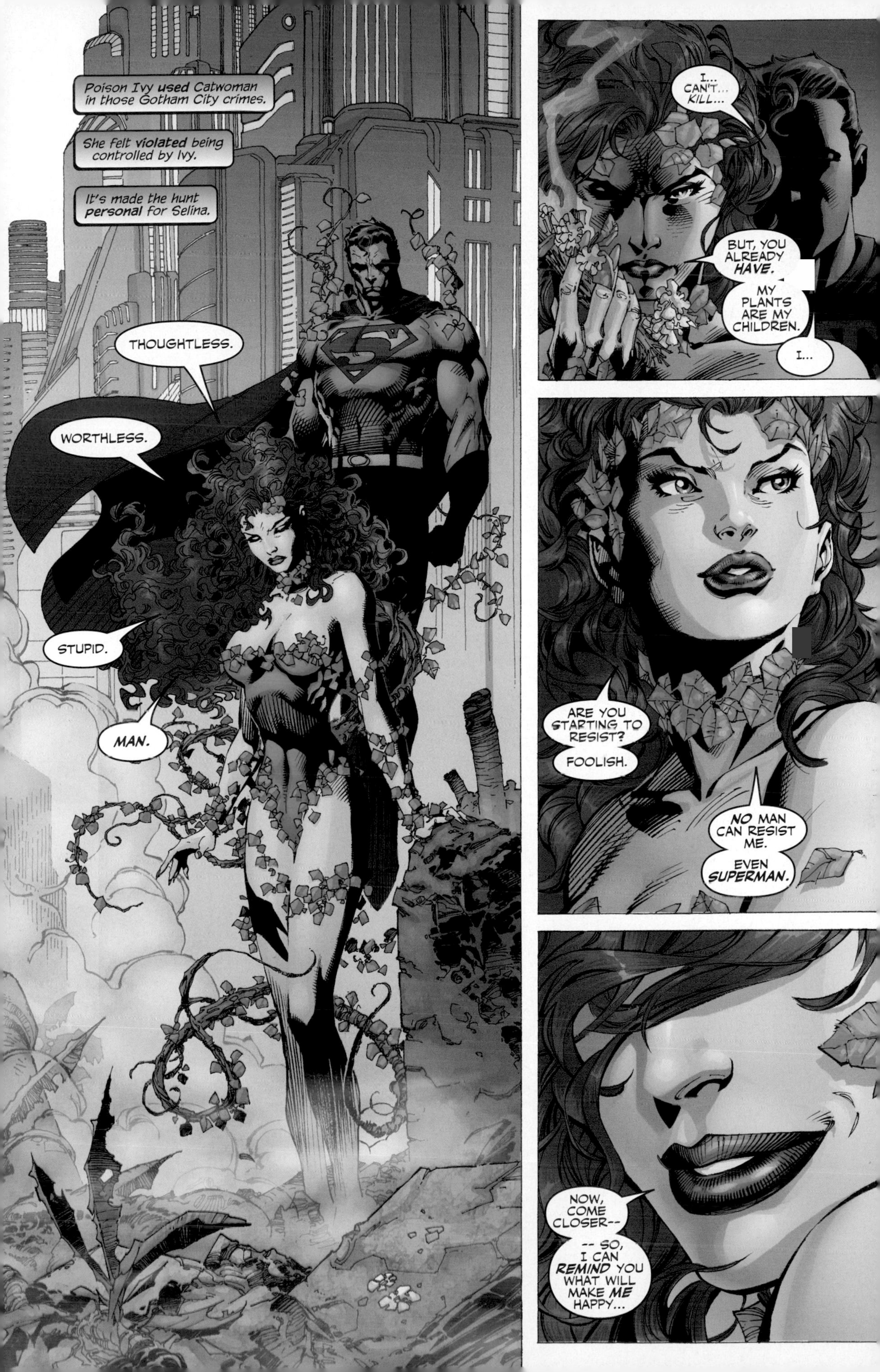
Poison Ivy used Catwoman in those Gotham City crimes.
She felt violated being controlled by Ivy.
It's made the hunt personal for Selina.
THOUGHTLESS.
WORTHLESS.
STUPID.
MAN.
I... CAN'T... KILL...
BUT, YOU ALREADY HAVE.
MY PLANTS ARE MY CHILDREN.
I...
ARE YOU STARTING TO RESIST?
FOOLISH.
NO MAN CAN RESIST ME.
EVEN SUPERMAN.
NOW, COME CLOSER--
-- SO, I CAN REMIND YOU WHAT WILL MAKE ME HAPPY...

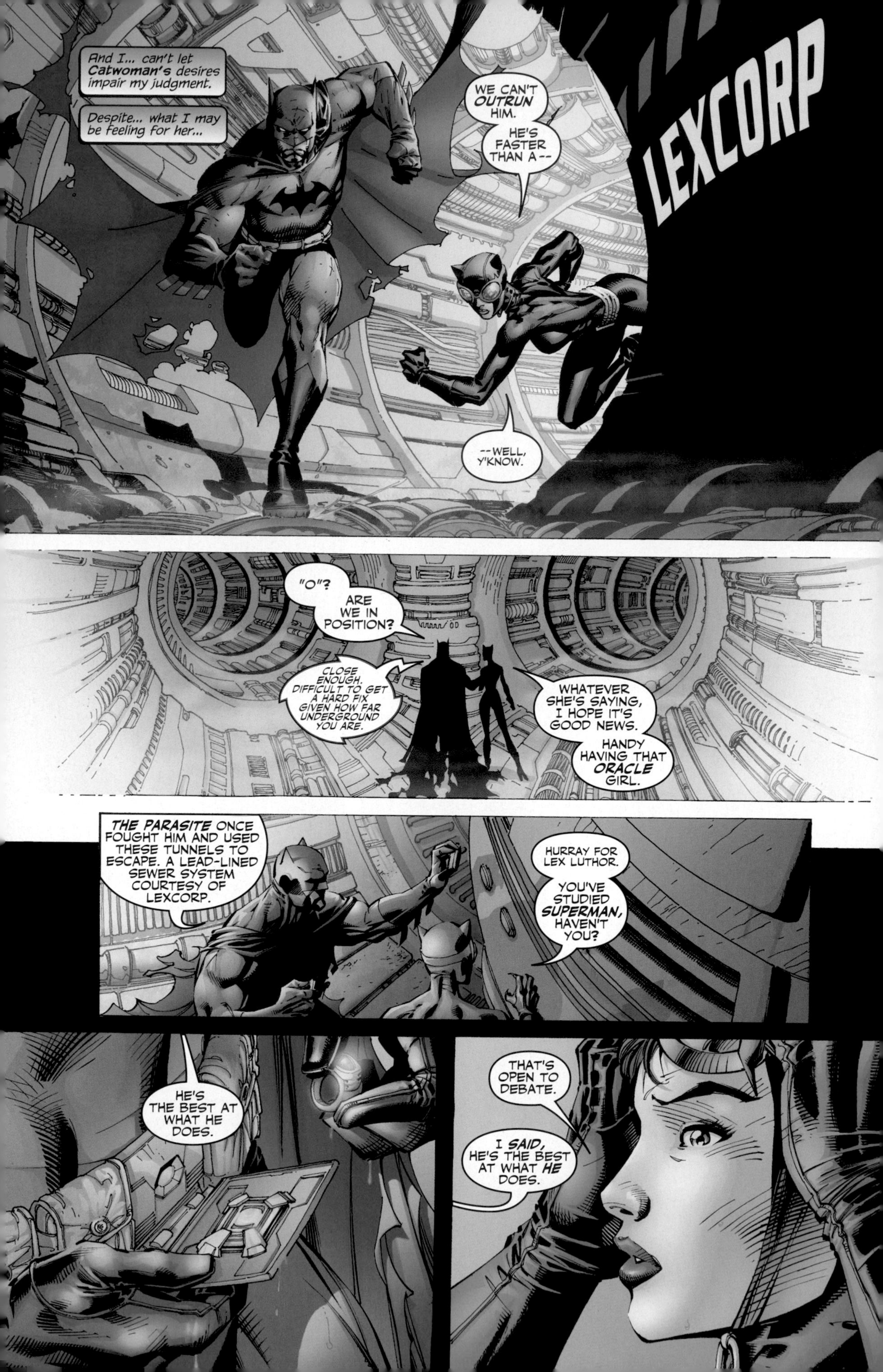
And I... can't let Catwoman's desires impair my judgment.
Despite... what I may be feeling for her...
WE CAN'T OUTRUN HIM.
HE'S FASTER THAN A--
LEXCORP
--WELL, Y'KNOW.
"O"? ARE WE IN POSITION?
CLOSE ENOUGH. DIFFICULT TO GET A HARD FIX GIVEN HOW FAR UNDERGROUND YOU ARE.
WHATEVER SHE'S SAYING, I HOPE IT'S GOOD NEWS.
HANDY HAVING THAT ORACLE GIRL.
THE PARASITE ONCE FOUGHT HIM AND USED THESE TUNNELS TO ESCAPE. A LEAD-LINED SEWER SYSTEM COURTESY OF LEXCORP.
HURRAY FOR LEX LUTHOR.
YOU'VE STUDIED SUPERMAN, HAVEN'T YOU?
HE'S THE BEST AT WHAT HE DOES.
THAT'S OPEN TO DEBATE.
I SAID, HE'S THE BEST AT WHAT HE DOES.

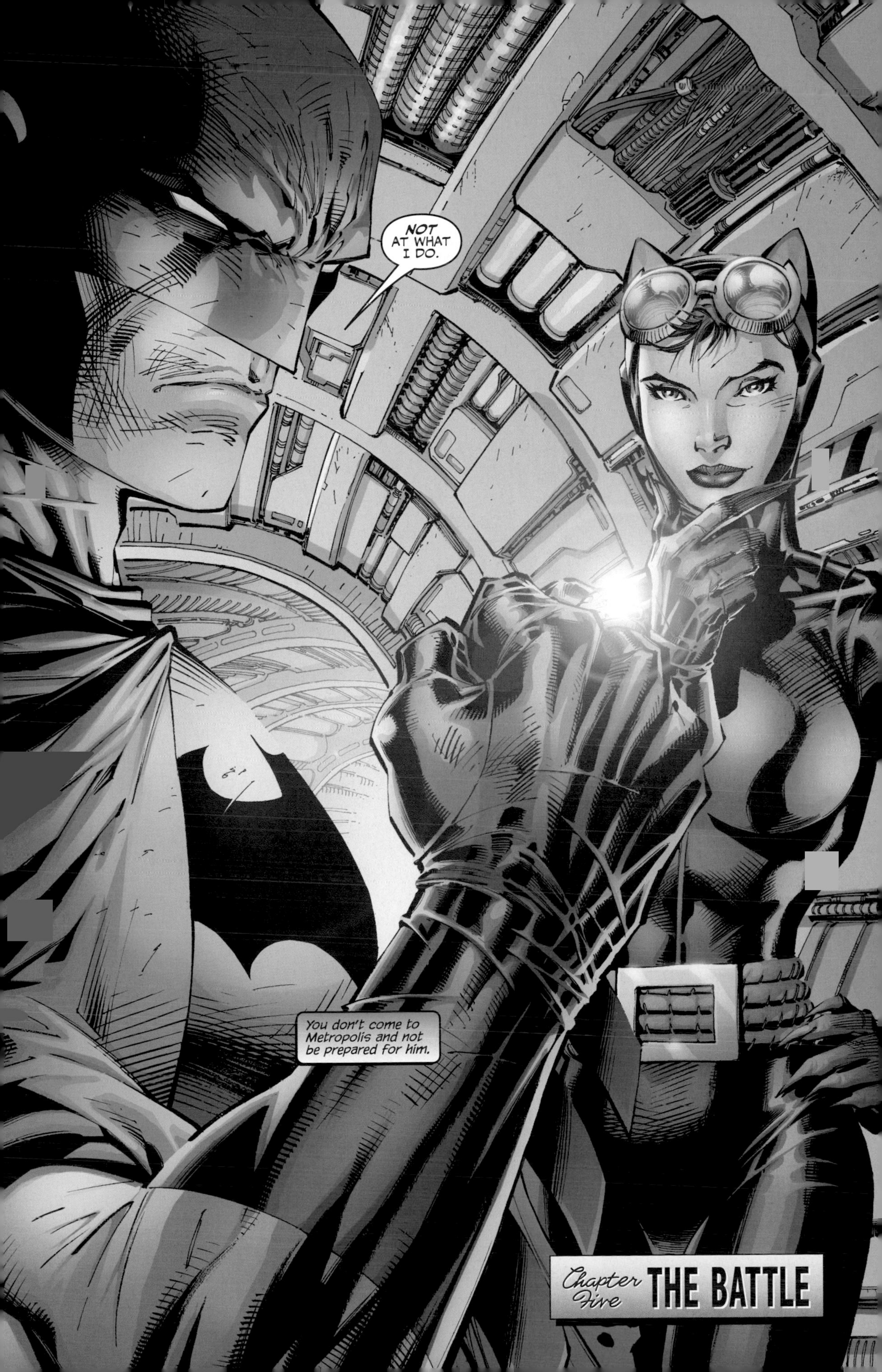
NOT AT WHAT I DO.
You don't come to Metropolis and not be prepared for him.
Chapter Five THE BATTLE

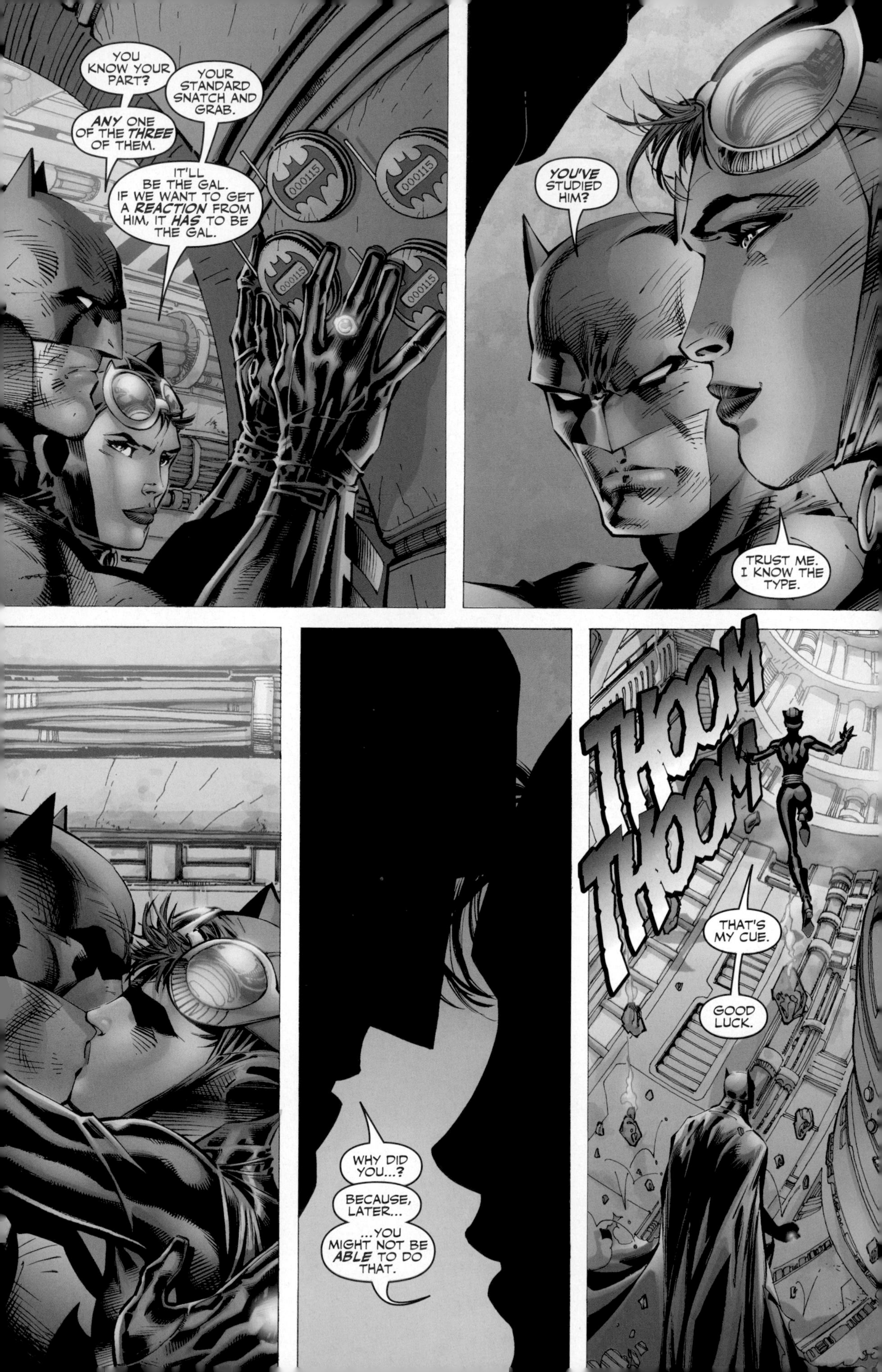

YOU KNOW YOUR PART?
YOUR STANDARD SNATCH AND GRAB.
ANY ONE OF THE THREE OF THEM.
IT'LL BE THE GAL. IF WE WANT TO GET A REACTION FROM HIM, IT HAS TO BE THE GAL.
YOU'VE STUDIED HIM?
TRUST ME. I KNOW THE TYPE.
WHY DID YOU...?
BECAUSE, LATER...
...YOU MIGHT NOT BE ABLE TO DO THAT.
THOOM
THOOM
THAT'S MY CUE.
GOOD LUCK.

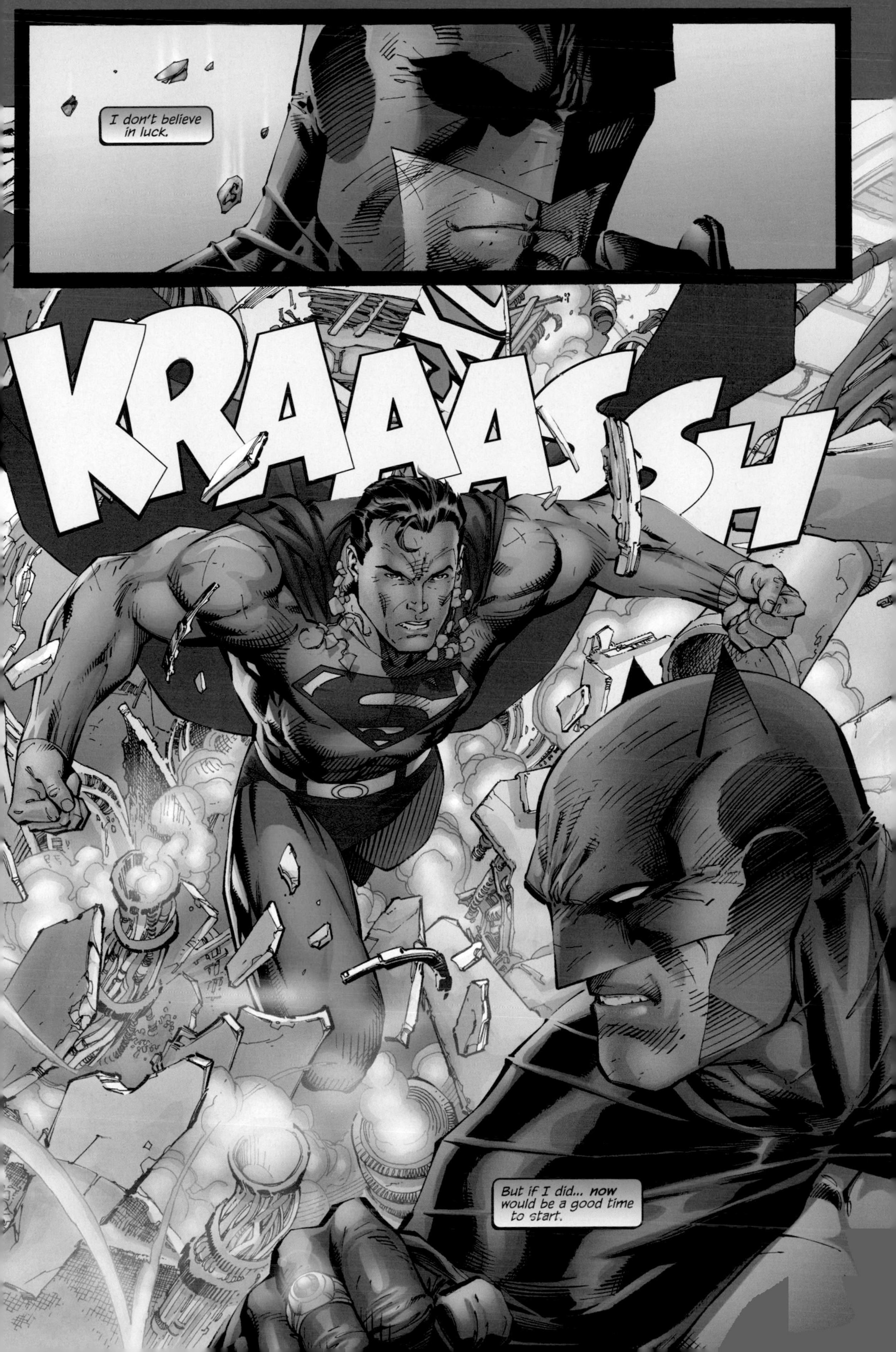
I don't believe in luck.
KRAAASH
But if I did... now would be a good time to start.

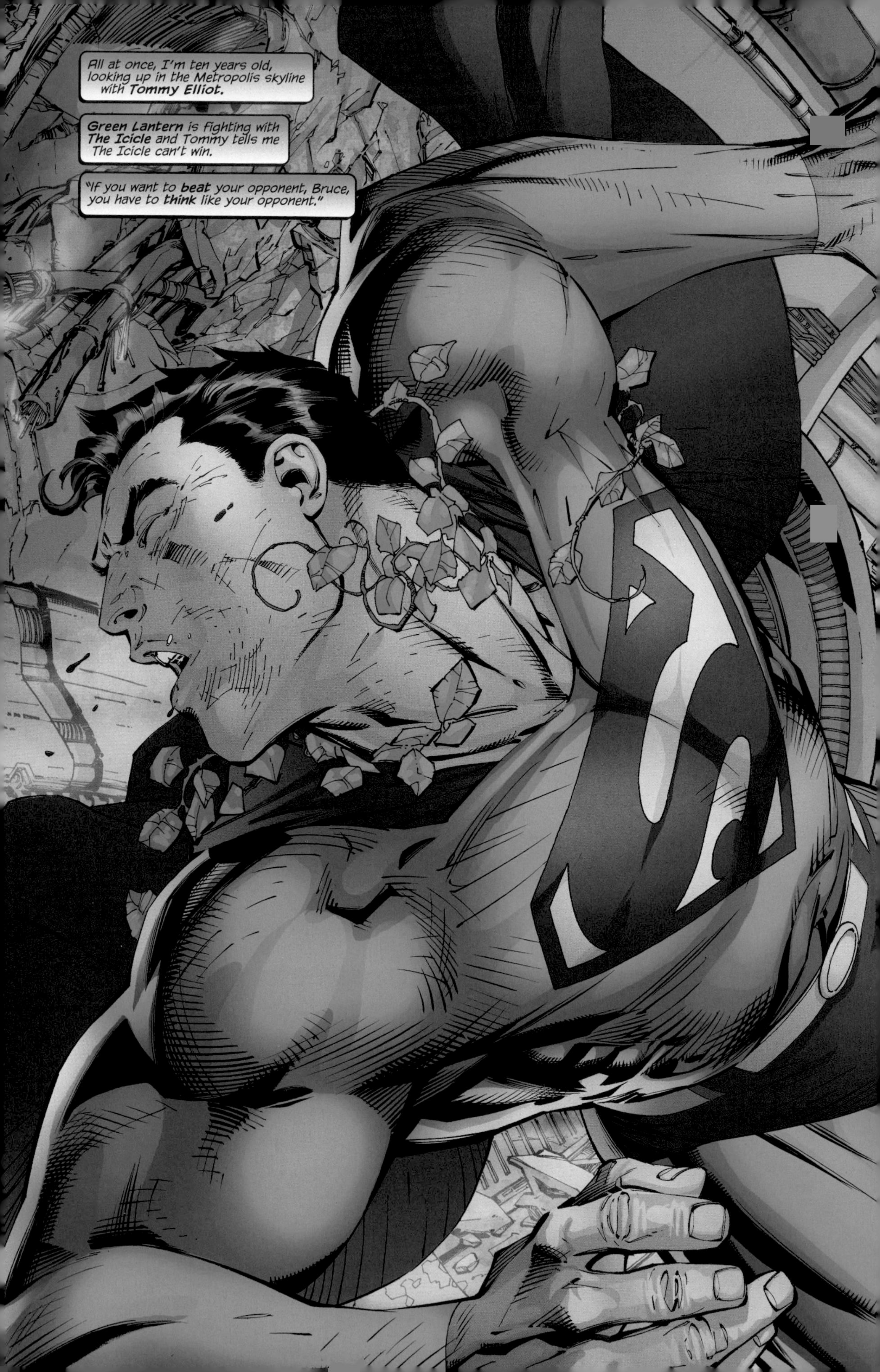
All at once, I'm ten years old, looking up in the Metropolis skyline with Tommy Elliot.
Green Lantern is fighting with The Icicle and Tommy tells me The Icicle can't win.
"If you want to beat your opponent, Bruce, you have to think like your opponent."

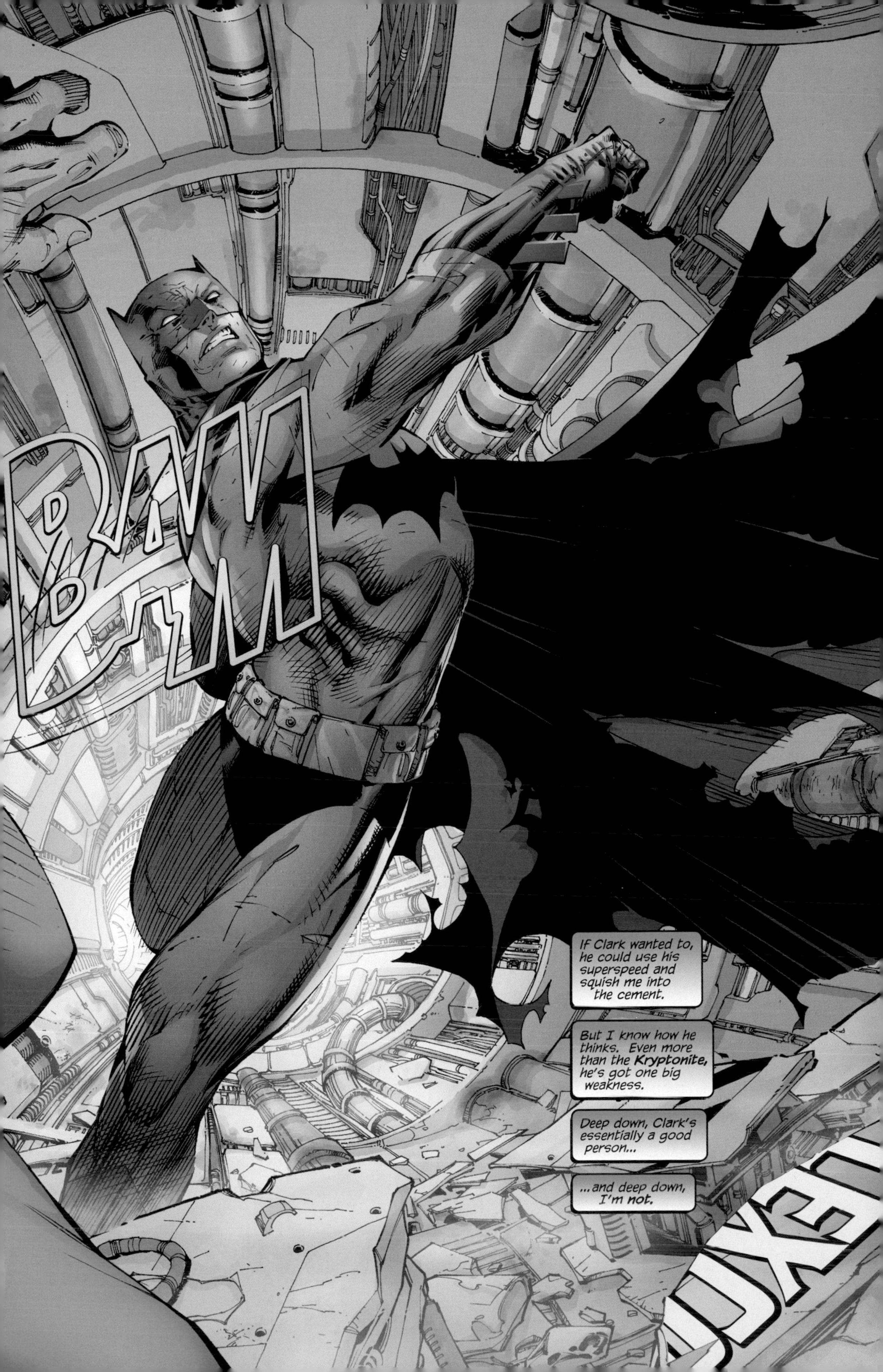
BAM
BAM
If Clark wanted to, he could use his superspeed and squish me into the cement.
But I know how he thinks. Even more than the **Kryptonite**, he's got one big weakness.
Deep down, Clark's essentially a good person...
...and deep down, I'm **not.**

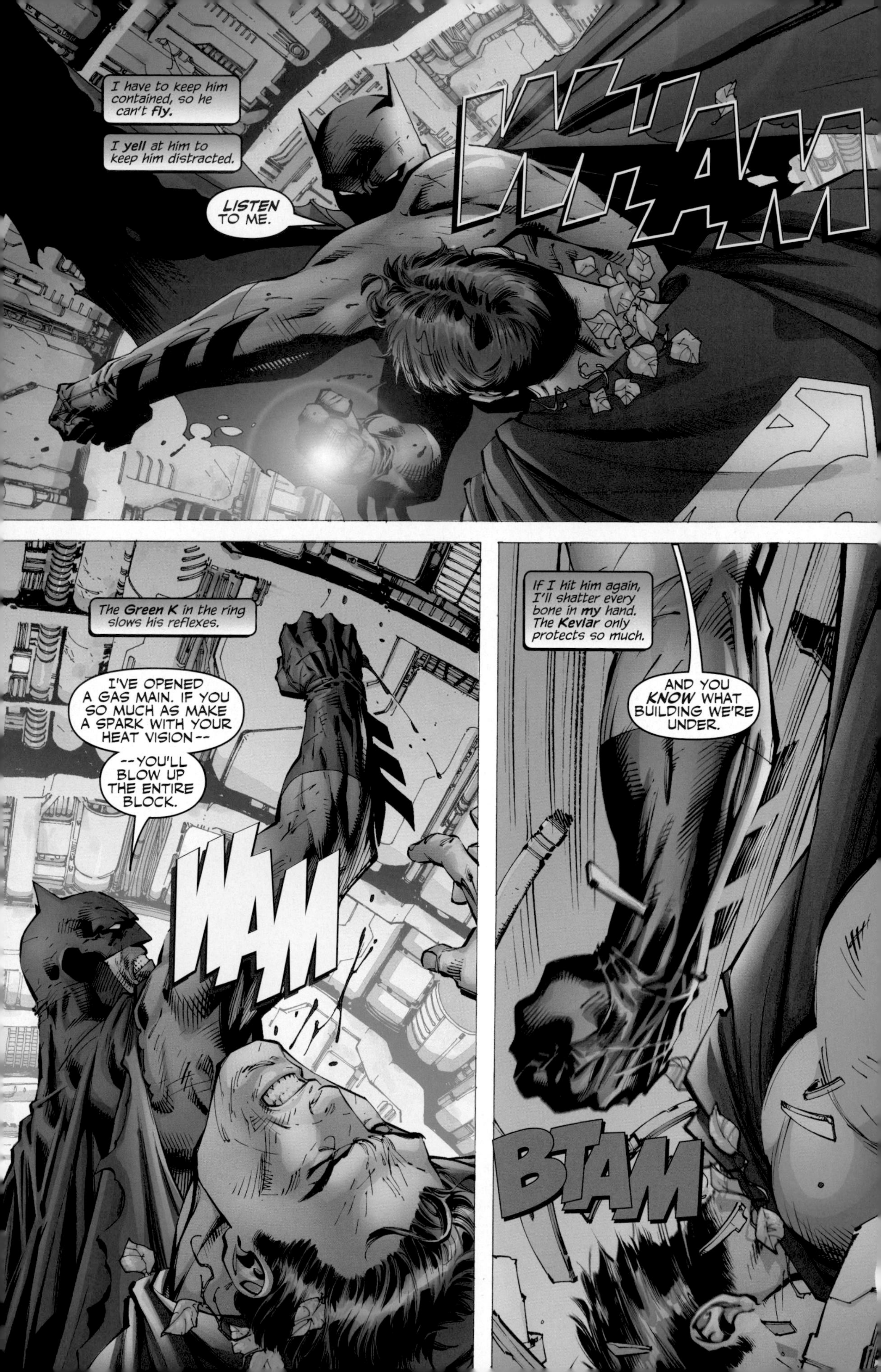

I have to keep him contained, so he can't **fly.**
I **yell** at him to keep him distracted.
LISTEN TO ME.
WHAM
The **Green K** in the ring slows his reflexes.
I'VE OPENED A GAS MAIN. IF YOU SO MUCH AS MAKE A SPARK WITH YOUR HEAT VISION--
--YOU'LL BLOW UP THE ENTIRE BLOCK.
WAM
If I hit him again, I'll shatter every bone in **my** hand. The **Kevlar** only protects so much.
AND YOU ***KNOW*** WHAT BUILDING WE'RE UNDER.
BTAM

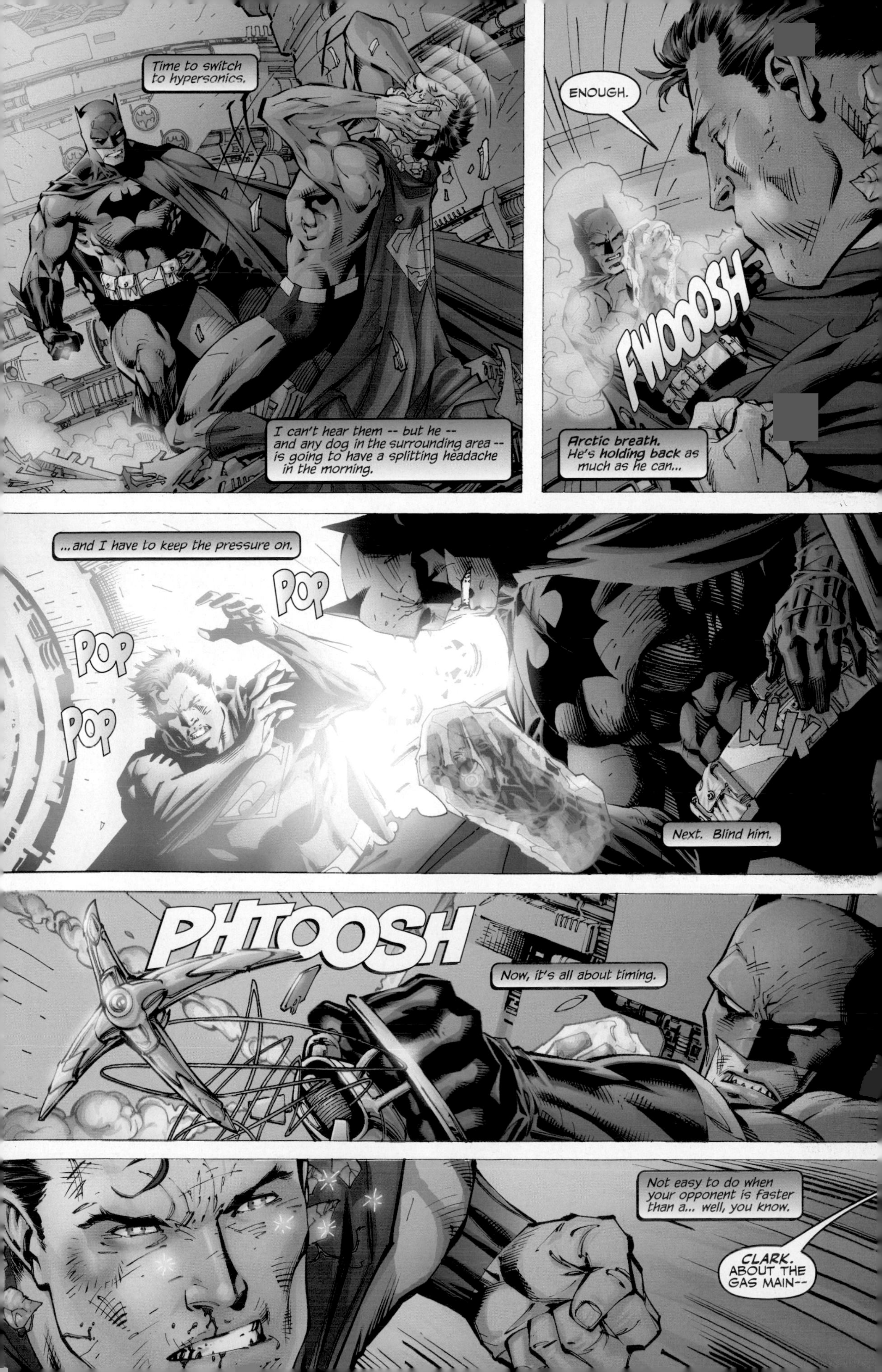

Time to switch to hypersonics.
I can't hear them -- but he -- and any dog in the surrounding area -- is going to have a splitting headache in the morning.
ENOUGH.
FWOOOSH
Arctic breath. He's holding back as much as he can...
...and I have to keep the pressure on.
POP
POP
POP
KLIK
Next. Blind him.
PHTOOSH
Now, it's all about timing.
Not easy to do when your opponent is faster than a... well, you know.
CLARK. ABOUT THE GAS MAIN--

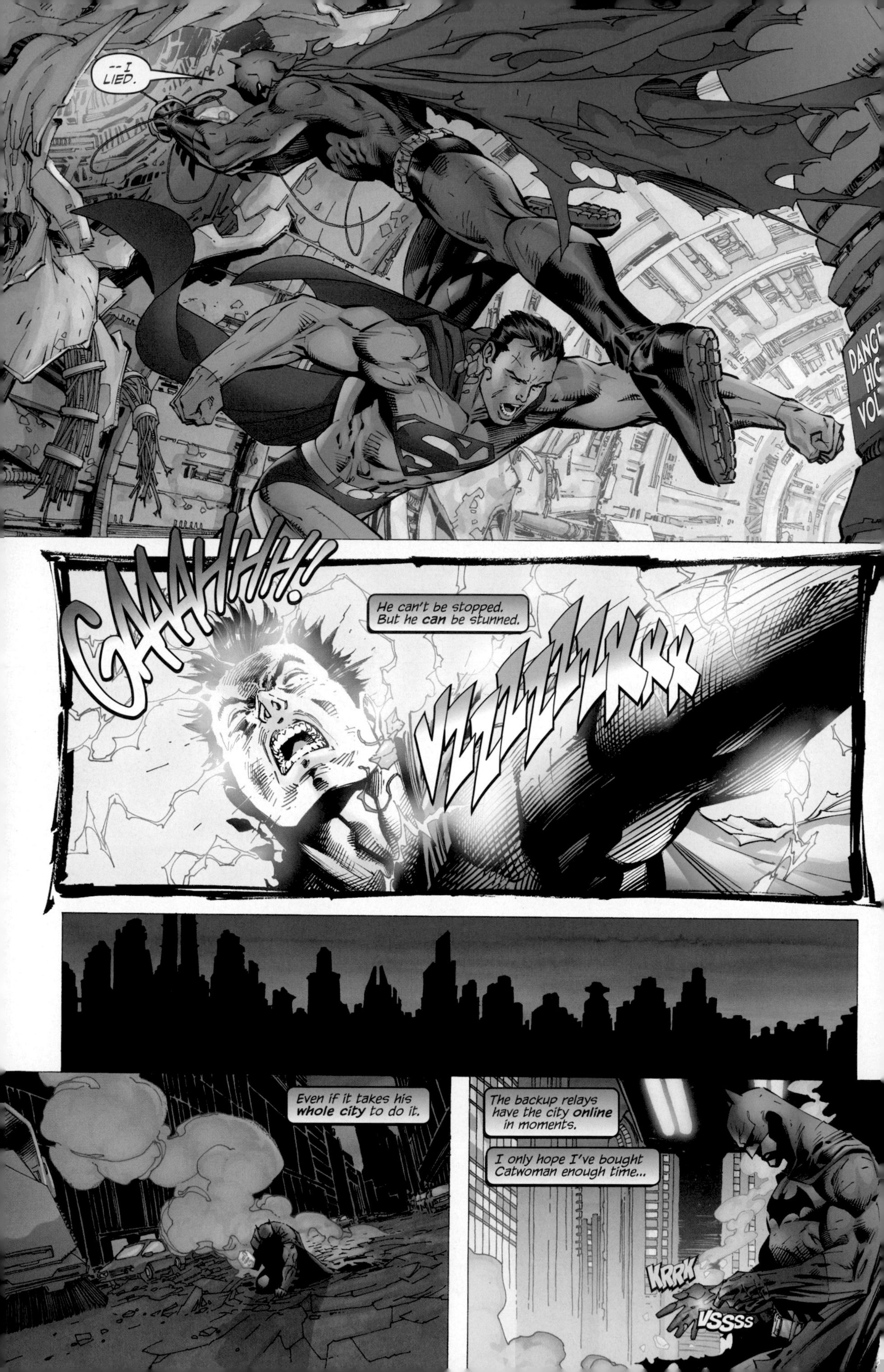
--I LIED.
DANG
HIG
VOL
GAAHHH!
He can't be stopped. But he can be stunned.
VZZZZZKXX
Even if it takes his whole city to do it.
The backup relays have the city online in moments.
I only hope I've bought Catwoman enough time...
KRRK
VSSSS

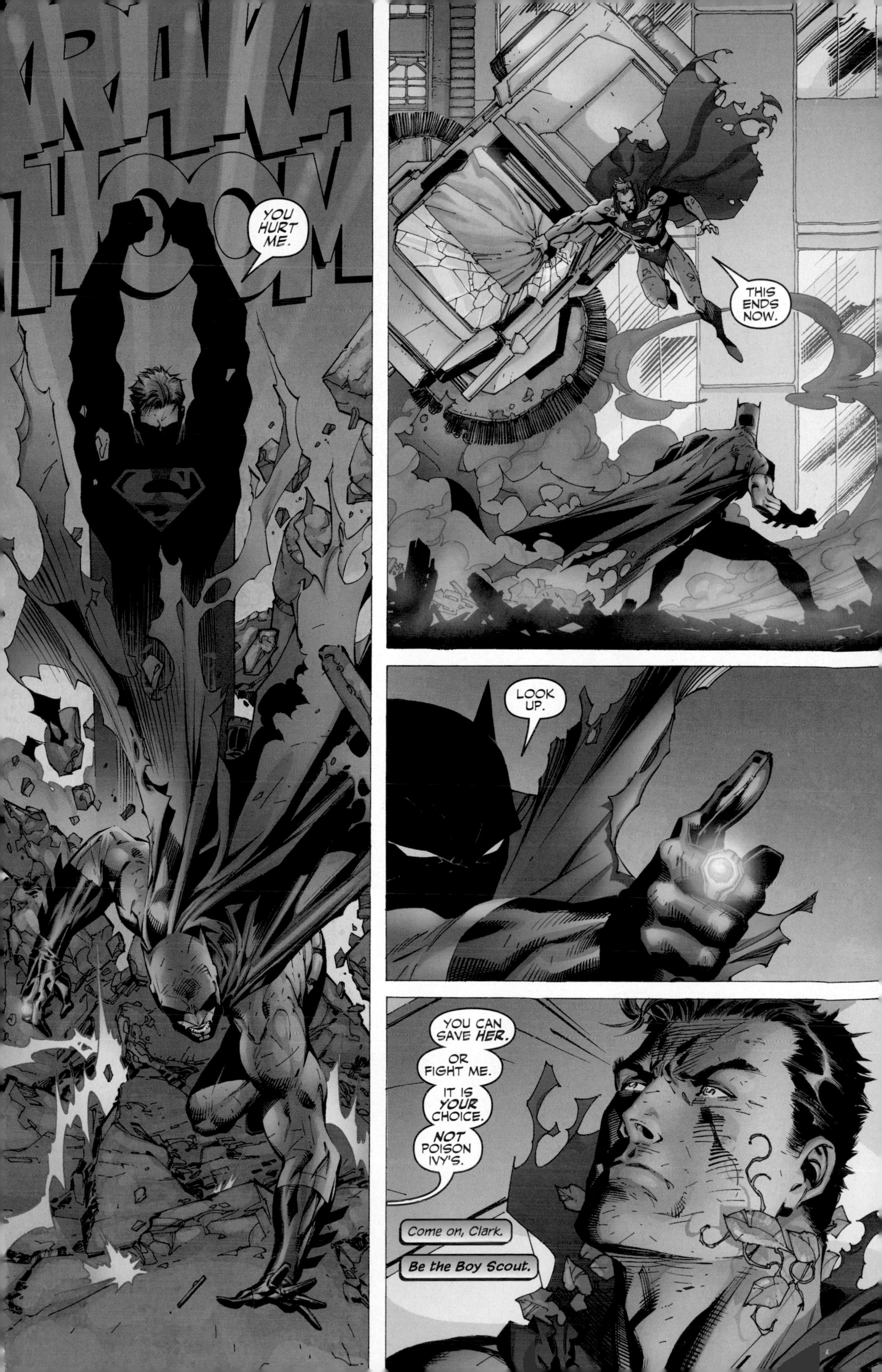
KRAKA
THOOM
YOU HURT ME.
THIS ENDS NOW.
LOOK UP.
YOU CAN SAVE *HER.*
OR FIGHT ME.
IT IS *YOUR* CHOICE.
*NOT* POISON IVY'S.
Come on, Clark.
Be the Boy Scout.

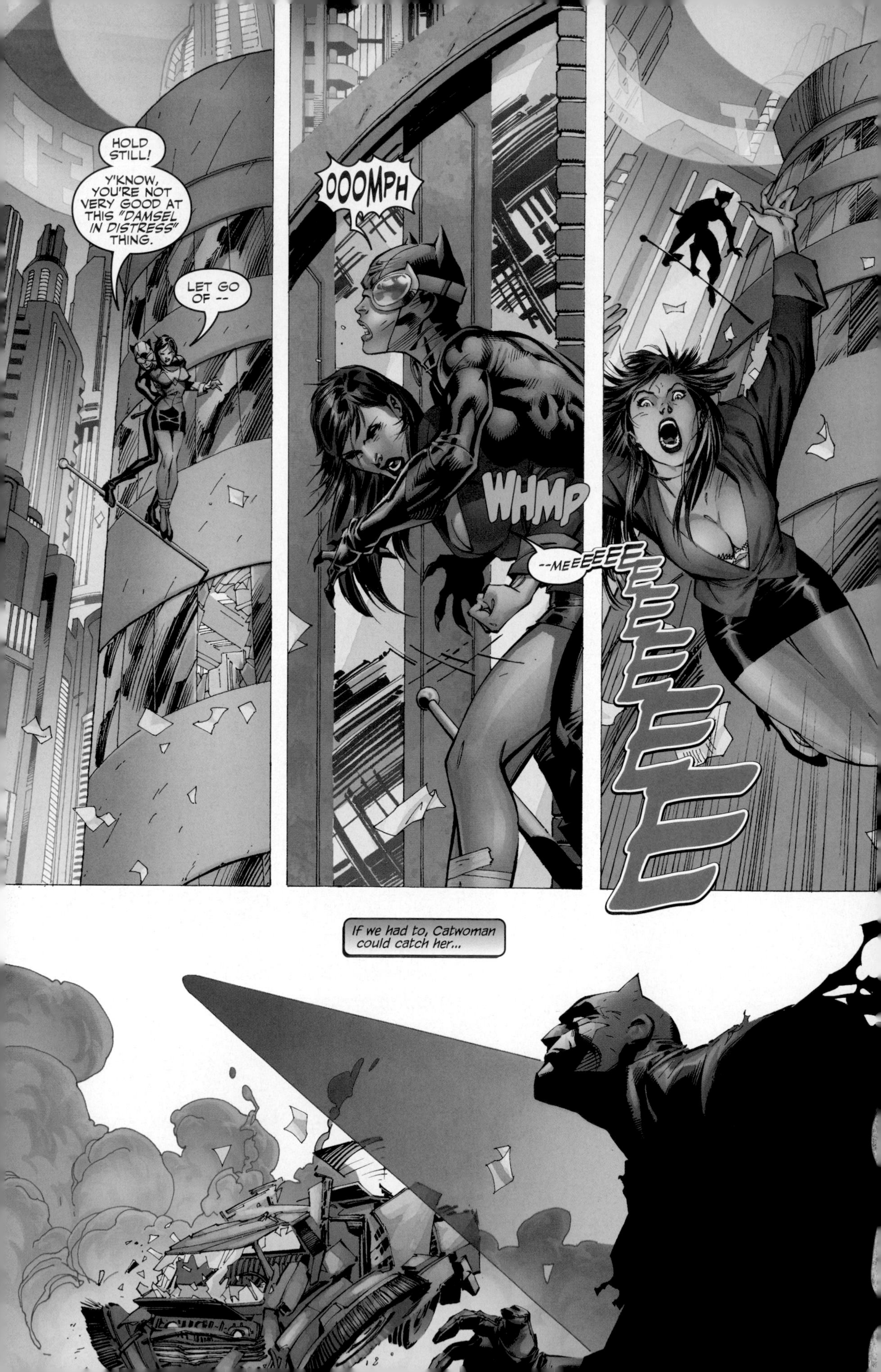
HOLD STILL!
Y'KNOW, YOU'RE NOT VERY GOOD AT THIS "DAMSEL IN DISTRESS" THING.
LET GO OF --
OOOMPH
WHMP
--MEEEEEEEEEEEEEEEE
If we had to, Catwoman could catch her...

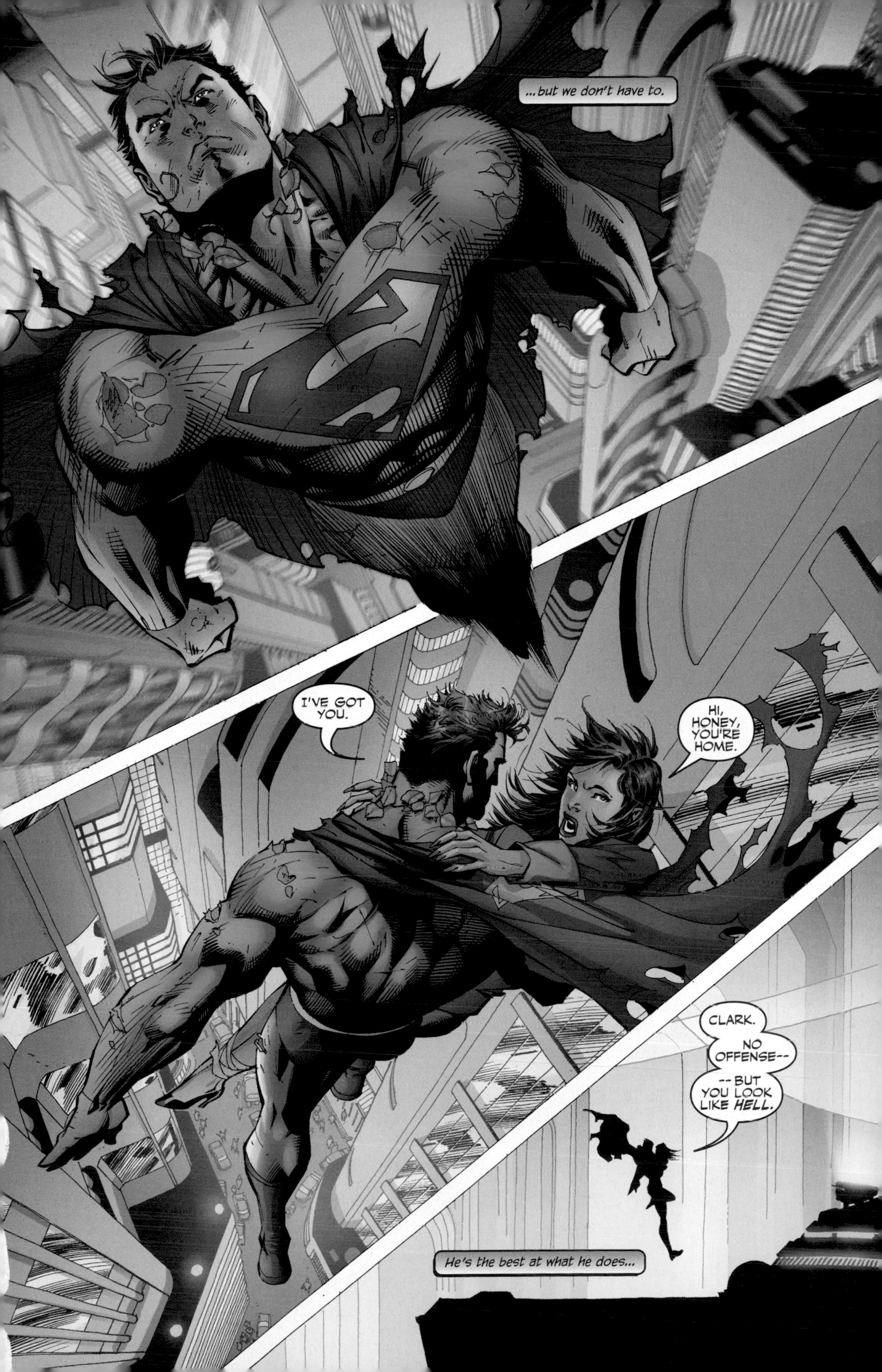
...but we don't have to.
I'VE GOT YOU.
HI, HONEY, YOU'RE HOME.
CLARK.
NO OFFENSE--
--BUT YOU LOOK LIKE *HELL*.
He's the best at what he does...

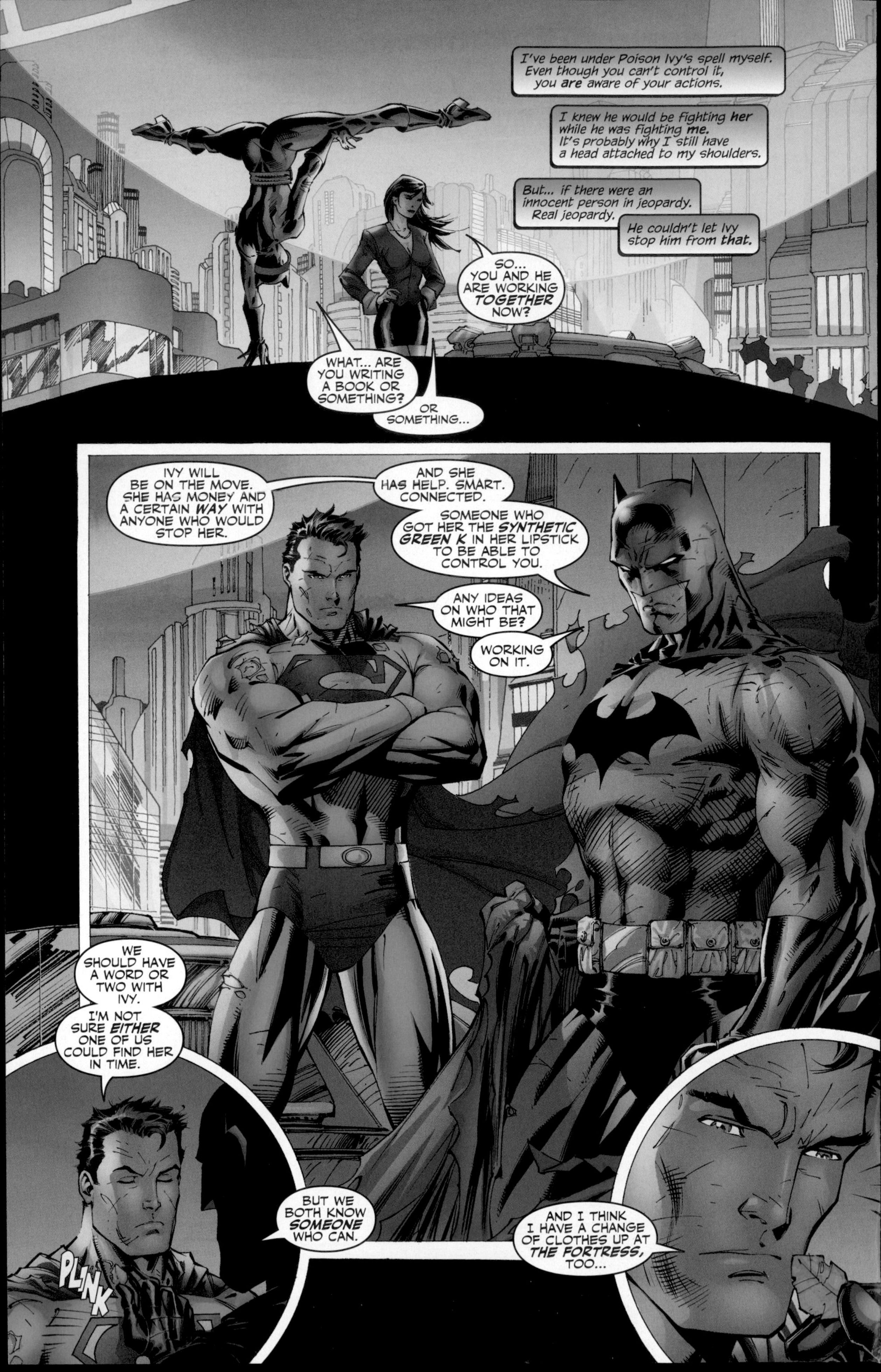
I've been under Poison Ivy's spell myself. Even though you can't control it, you are aware of your actions.
I knew he would be fighting her while he was fighting me. It's probably why I still have a head attached to my shoulders.
But... if there were an innocent person in jeopardy. Real jeopardy.
He couldn't let Ivy stop him from that.
SO... YOU AND HE ARE WORKING TOGETHER NOW?
WHAT... ARE YOU WRITING A BOOK OR SOMETHING?
OR SOMETHING...
IVY WILL BE ON THE MOVE. SHE HAS MONEY AND A CERTAIN WAY WITH ANYONE WHO WOULD STOP HER.
AND SHE HAS HELP. SMART. CONNECTED.
SOMEONE WHO GOT HER THE SYNTHETIC GREEN K IN HER LIPSTICK TO BE ABLE TO CONTROL YOU.
ANY IDEAS ON WHO THAT MIGHT BE?
WORKING ON IT.
WE SHOULD HAVE A WORD OR TWO WITH IVY.
I'M NOT SURE EITHER ONE OF US COULD FIND HER IN TIME.
BUT WE BOTH KNOW SOMEONE WHO CAN.
AND I THINK I HAVE A CHANGE OF CLOTHES UP AT THE FORTRESS, TOO...
PLINK

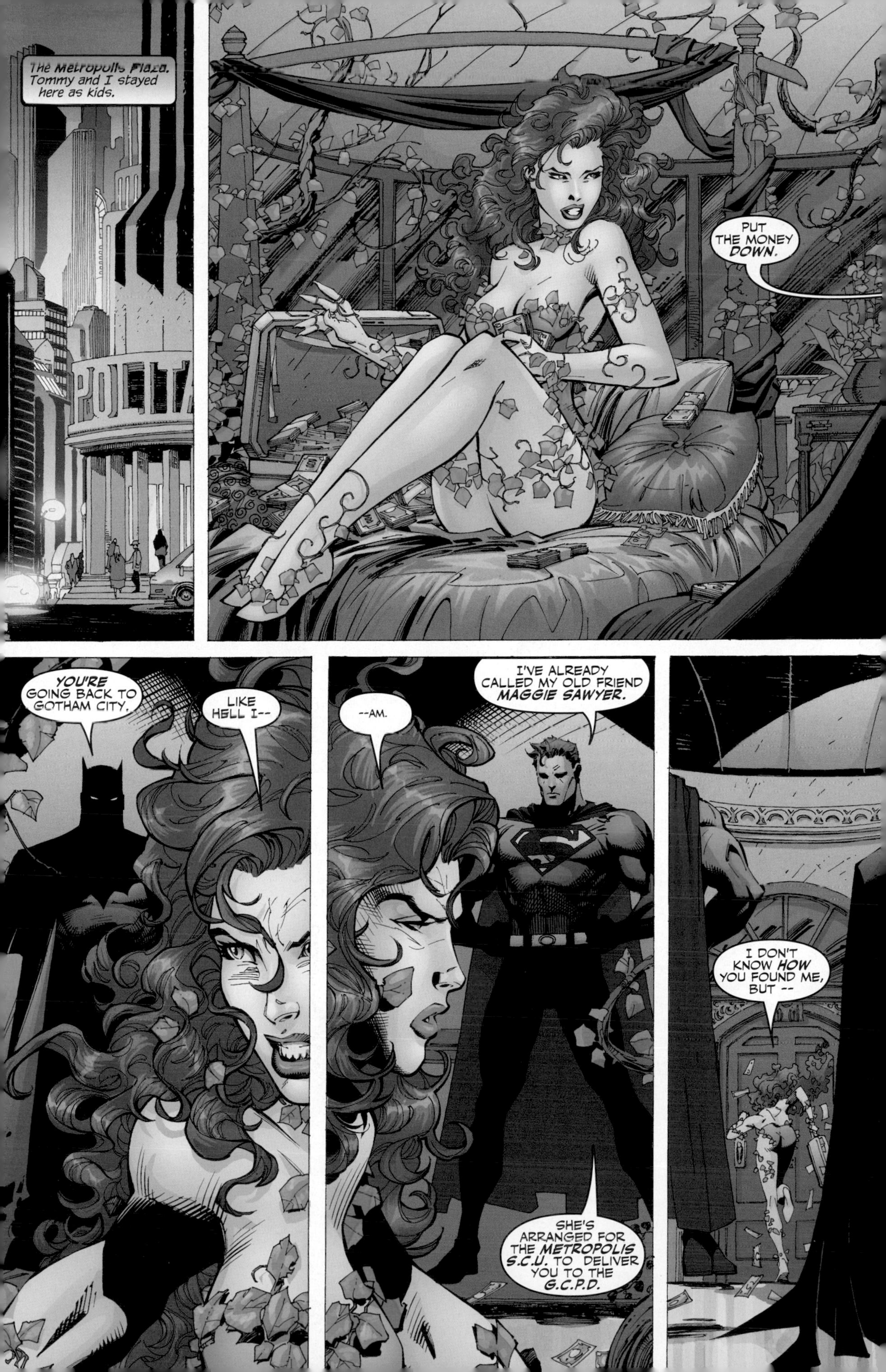
The Metropolis Plaza. Tommy and I stayed here as kids.
PUT THE MONEY DOWN.
YOU'RE GOING BACK TO GOTHAM CITY.
LIKE HELL I--
--AM.
I'VE ALREADY CALLED MY OLD FRIEND MAGGIE SAWYER.
SHE'S ARRANGED FOR THE METROPOLIS S.C.U. TO DELIVER YOU TO THE G.C.P.D.
I DON'T KNOW HOW YOU FOUND ME, BUT --

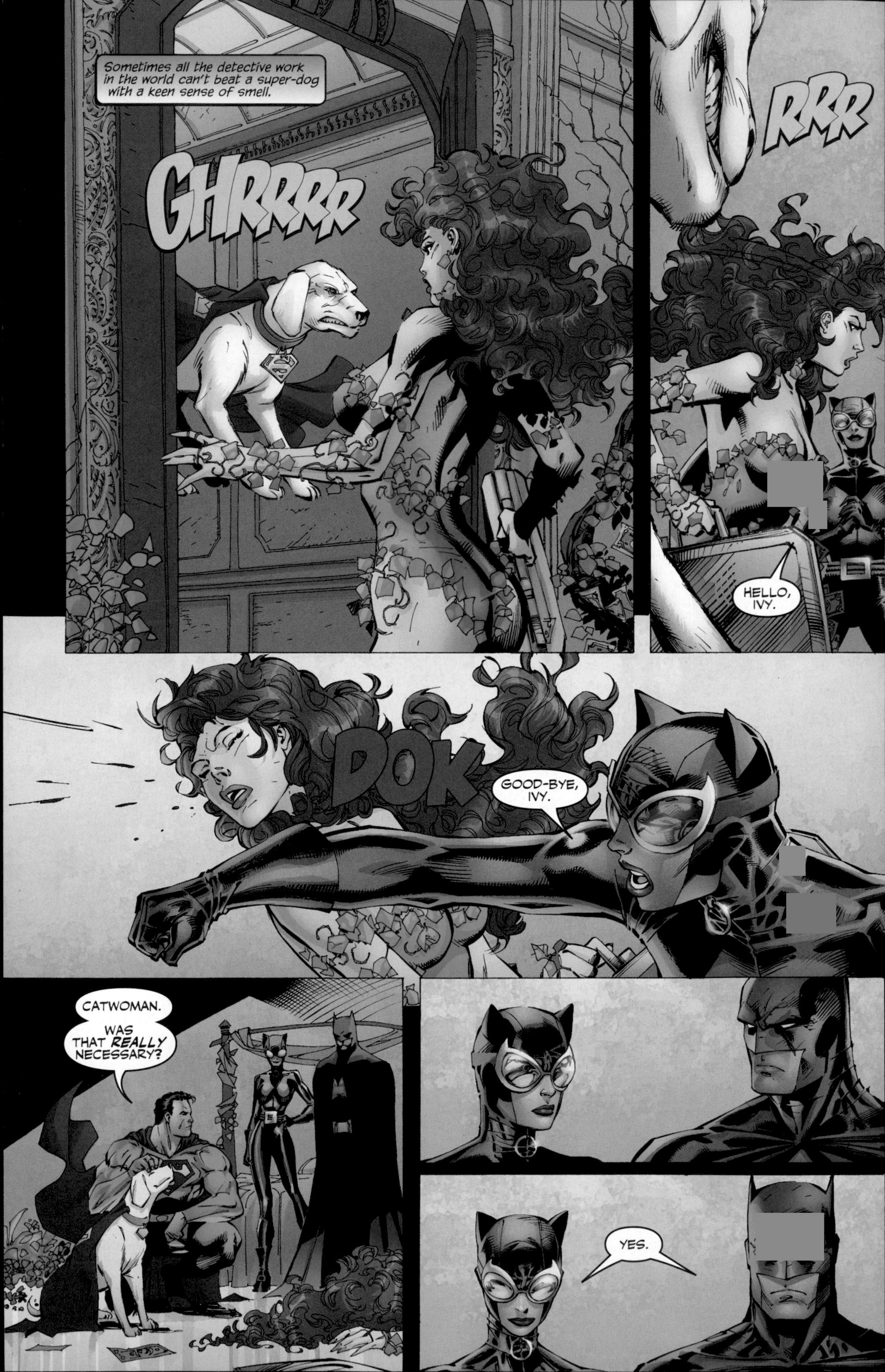
Sometimes all the detective work in the world can't beat a super-dog with a keen sense of smell.
GHRRRR
RRR
HELLO, IVY.
DOK
GOOD-BYE, IVY.
CATWOMAN. WAS THAT REALLY NECESSARY?
YES.

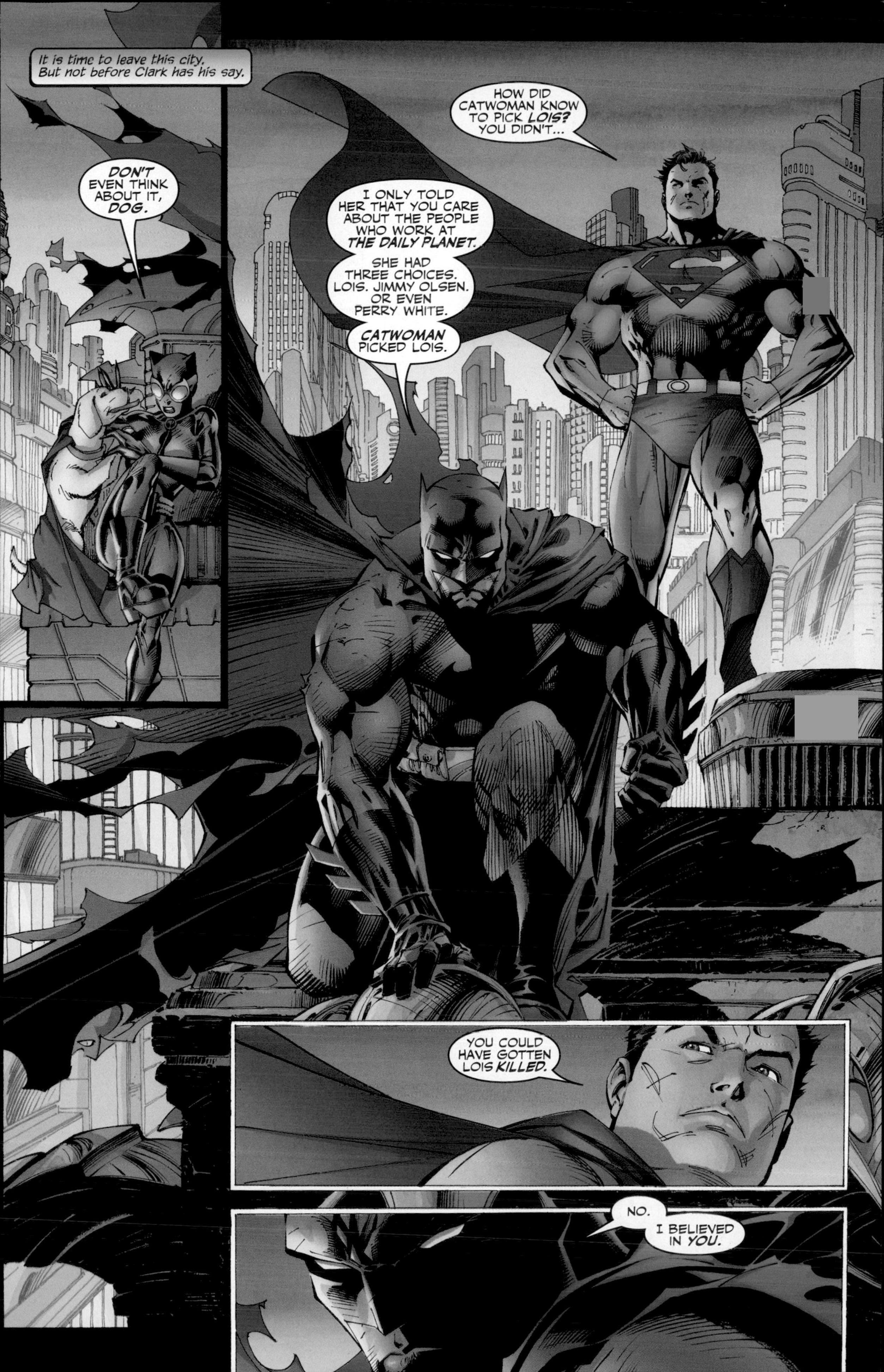
It is time to leave this city. But not before Clark has his say.
HOW DID CATWOMAN KNOW TO PICK LOIS? YOU DIDN'T...
DON'T EVEN THINK ABOUT IT, DOG.
I ONLY TOLD HER THAT YOU CARE ABOUT THE PEOPLE WHO WORK AT THE DAILY PLANET.
SHE HAD THREE CHOICES. LOIS. JIMMY OLSEN. OR EVEN PERRY WHITE.
CATWOMAN PICKED LOIS.
YOU COULD HAVE GOTTEN LOIS KILLED.
NO.
I BELIEVED IN YOU.

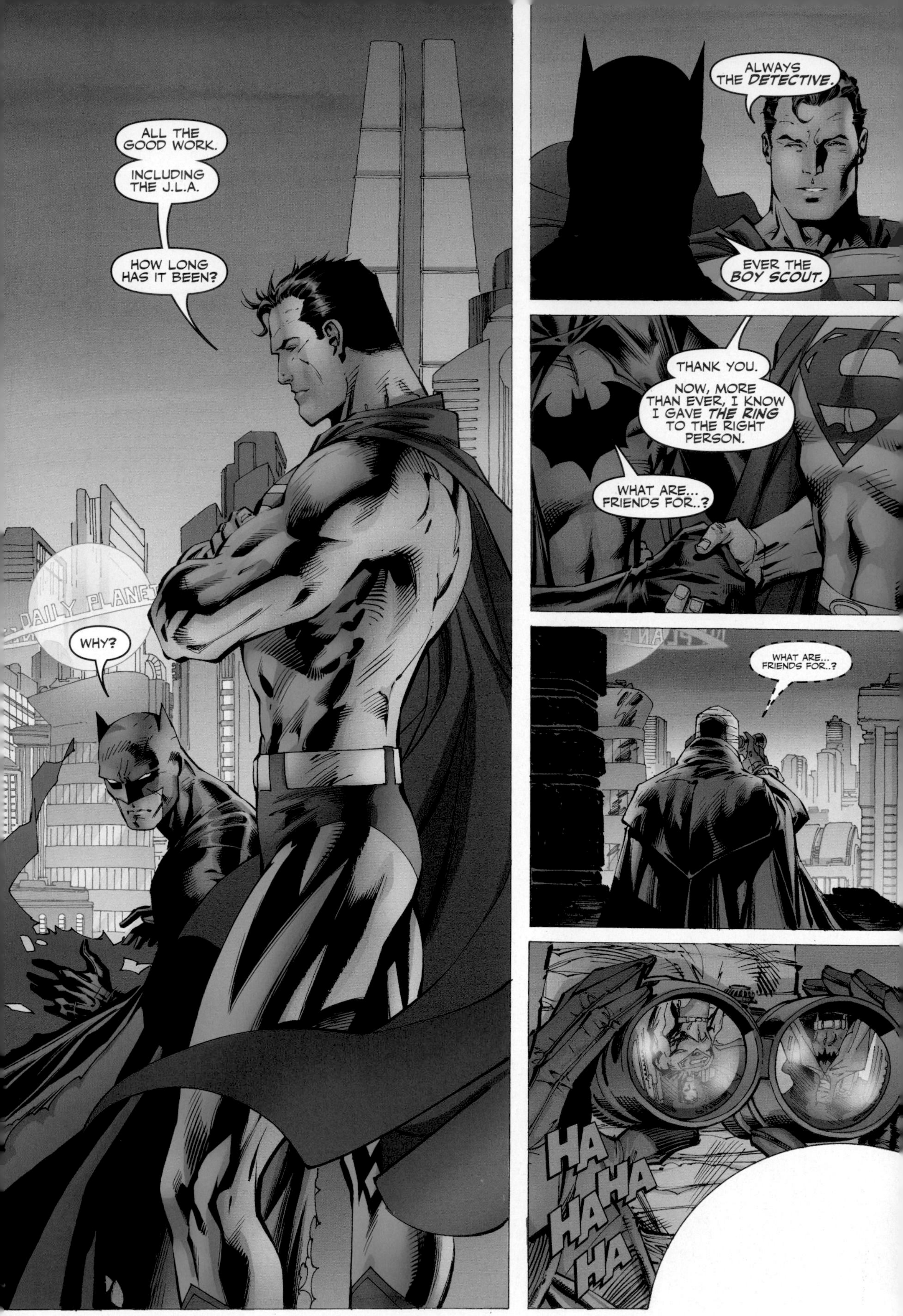
ALL THE GOOD WORK.
INCLUDING THE J.L.A.
HOW LONG HAS IT BEEN?
DAILY PLANET
WHY?
ALWAYS THE DETECTIVE.
EVER THE BOY SCOUT.
THANK YOU.
NOW, MORE THAN EVER, I KNOW I GAVE THE RING TO THE RIGHT PERSON.
WHAT ARE... FRIENDS FOR..?
WHAT ARE... FRIENDS FOR..?
HA HA HA HA HA HA

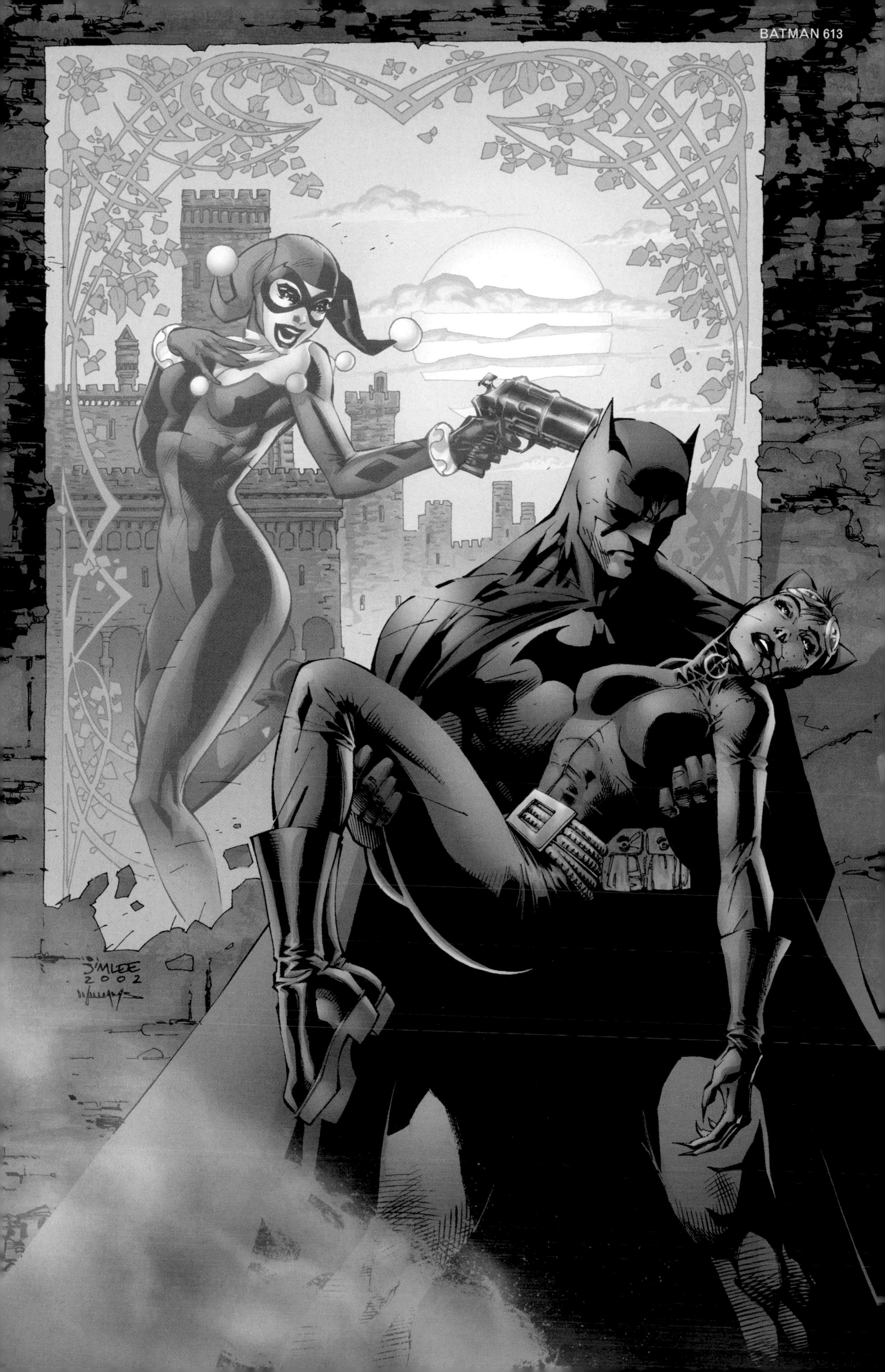
JIMLEE
2002

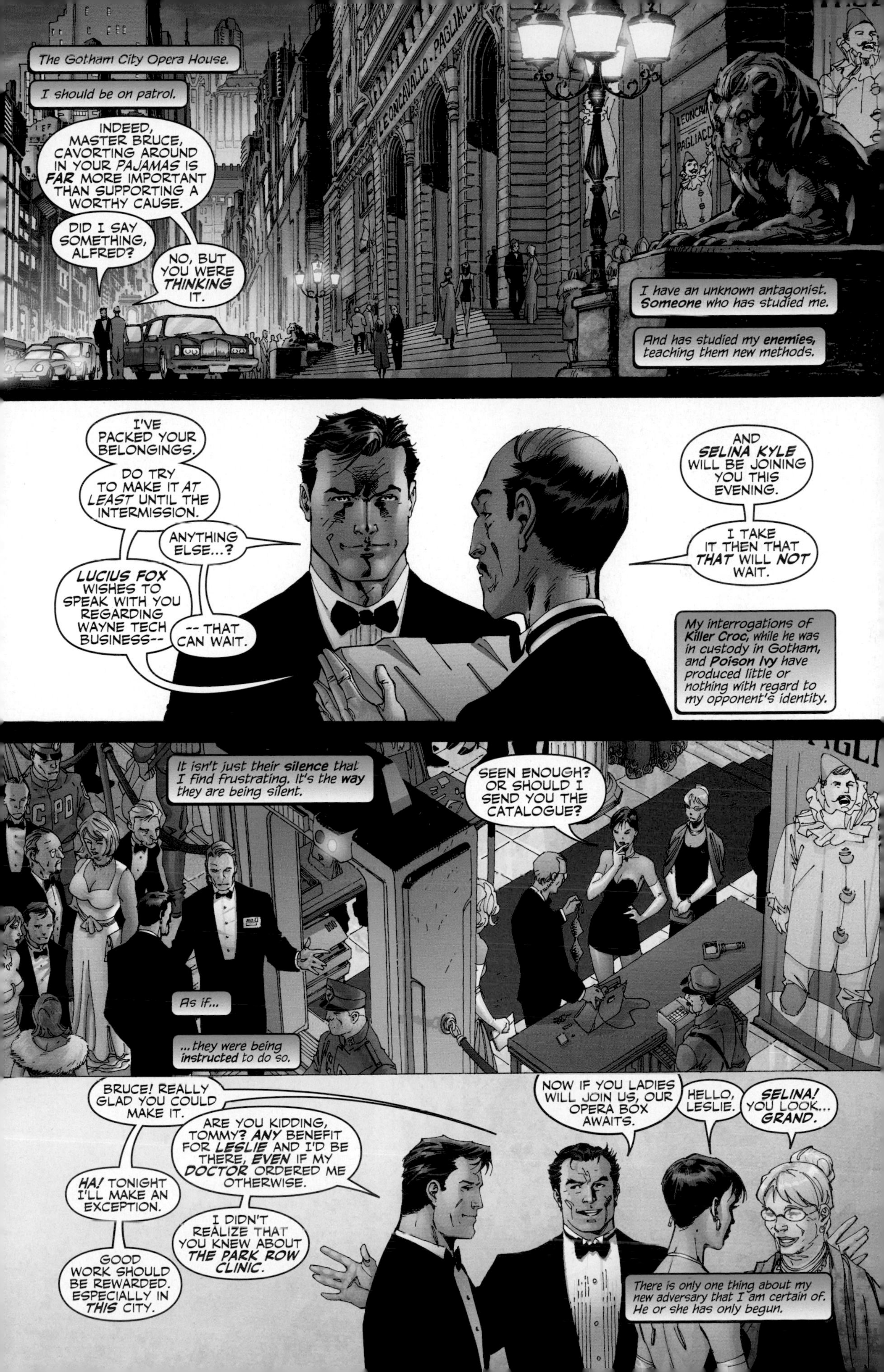
The Gotham City Opera House.
I should be on patrol.
INDEED, MASTER BRUCE, CAVORTING AROUND IN YOUR PAJAMAS IS FAR MORE IMPORTANT THAN SUPPORTING A WORTHY CAUSE.
DID I SAY SOMETHING, ALFRED?
NO, BUT YOU WERE THINKING IT.
LEONCAVALLO · PAGLIACCI
I have an unknown antagonist. Someone who has studied me.
And has studied my enemies, teaching them new methods.
I'VE PACKED YOUR BELONGINGS.
DO TRY TO MAKE IT AT LEAST UNTIL THE INTERMISSION.
ANYTHING ELSE...?
LUCIUS FOX WISHES TO SPEAK WITH YOU REGARDING WAYNE TECH BUSINESS--
-- THAT CAN WAIT.
AND SELINA KYLE WILL BE JOINING YOU THIS EVENING.
I TAKE IT THEN THAT THAT WILL NOT WAIT.
My interrogations of Killer Croc, while he was in custody in Gotham, and Poison Ivy have produced little or nothing with regard to my opponent's identity.
It isn't just their silence that I find frustrating. It's the way they are being silent.
SEEN ENOUGH? OR SHOULD I SEND YOU THE CATALOGUE?
As if...
...they were being instructed to do so.
BRUCE! REALLY GLAD YOU COULD MAKE IT.
ARE YOU KIDDING, TOMMY? ANY BENEFIT FOR LESLIE AND I'D BE THERE, EVEN IF MY DOCTOR ORDERED ME OTHERWISE.
HA! TONIGHT I'LL MAKE AN EXCEPTION.
I DIDN'T REALIZE THAT YOU KNEW ABOUT THE PARK ROW CLINIC.
GOOD WORK SHOULD BE REWARDED. ESPECIALLY IN THIS CITY.
NOW IF YOU LADIES WILL JOIN US, OUR OPERA BOX AWAITS.
HELLO, LESLIE.
SELINA! YOU LOOK... GRAND.
There is only one thing about my new adversary that I am certain of. He or she has only begun.

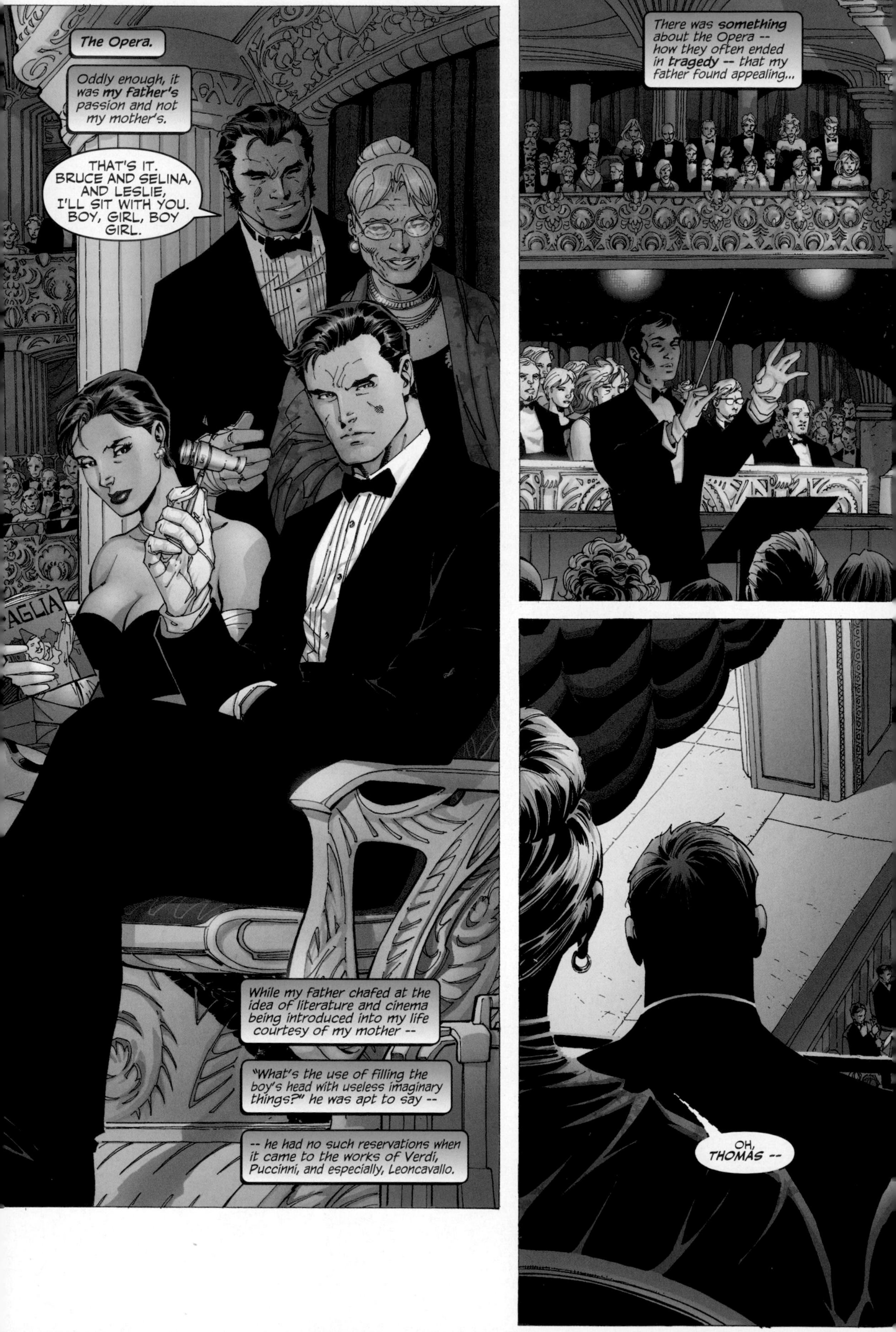

The Opera.
Oddly enough, it was my father's passion and not my mother's.
THAT'S IT. BRUCE AND SELINA, AND LESLIE, I'LL SIT WITH YOU. BOY, GIRL, BOY GIRL.
AGLIA
While my father chafed at the idea of literature and cinema being introduced into my life courtesy of my mother --
"What's the use of filling the boy's head with useless imaginary things?" he was apt to say --
-- he had no such reservations when it came to the works of Verdi, Puccinni, and especially, Leoncavallo.
There was something about the Opera -- how they often ended in tragedy -- that my father found appealing...
OH, THOMAS --

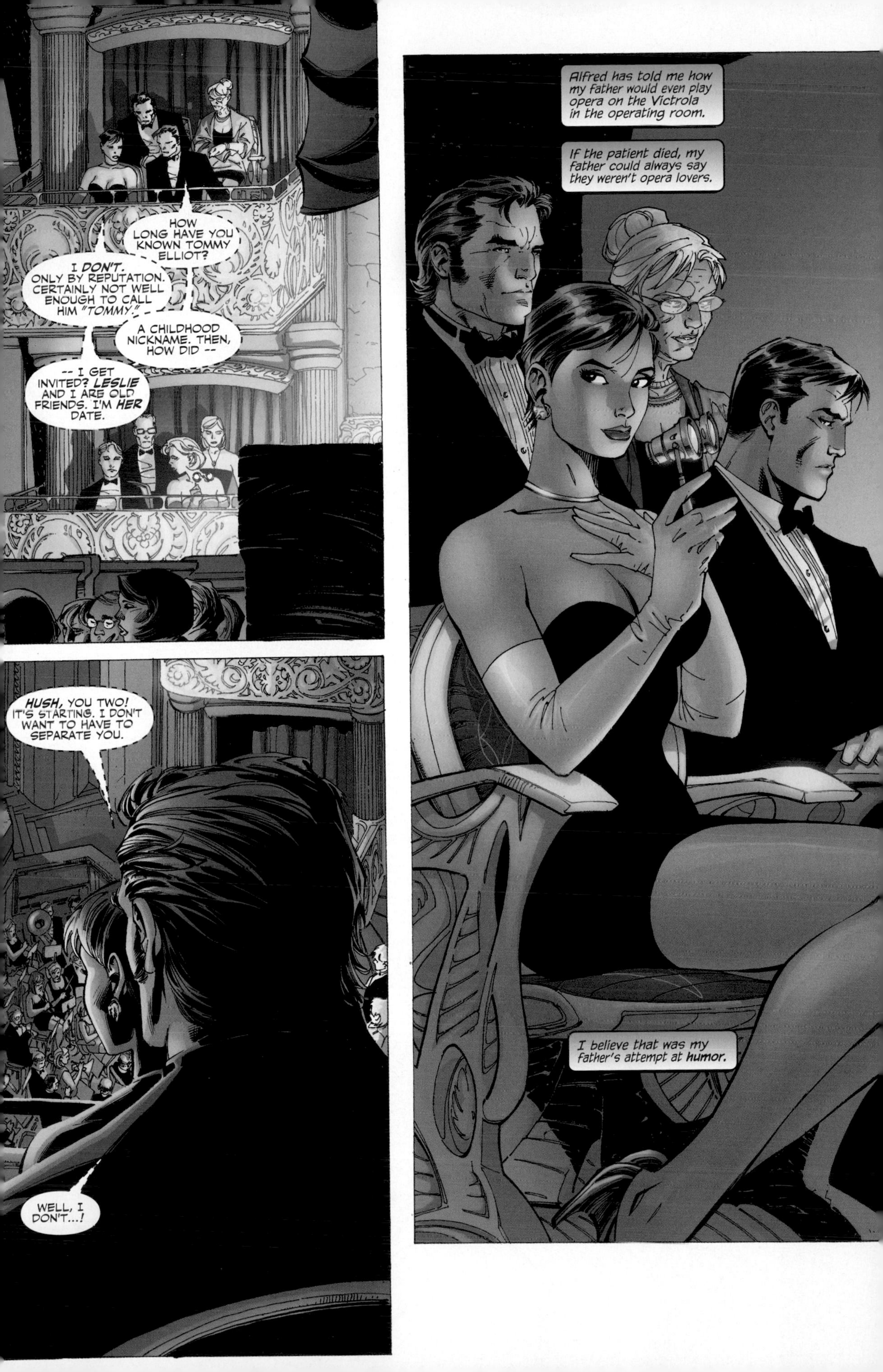
HOW LONG HAVE YOU KNOWN TOMMY ELLIOT?
I DON'T. ONLY BY REPUTATION. CERTAINLY NOT WELL ENOUGH TO CALL HIM "TOMMY."
A CHILDHOOD NICKNAME. THEN, HOW DID --
-- I GET INVITED? LESLIE AND I ARE OLD FRIENDS. I'M HER DATE.
HUSH, YOU TWO! IT'S STARTING. I DON'T WANT TO HAVE TO SEPARATE YOU.
WELL, I DON'T...!
Alfred has told me how my father would even play opera on the Victrola in the operating room.
If the patient died, my father could always say they weren't opera lovers.
I believe that was my father's attempt at humor.

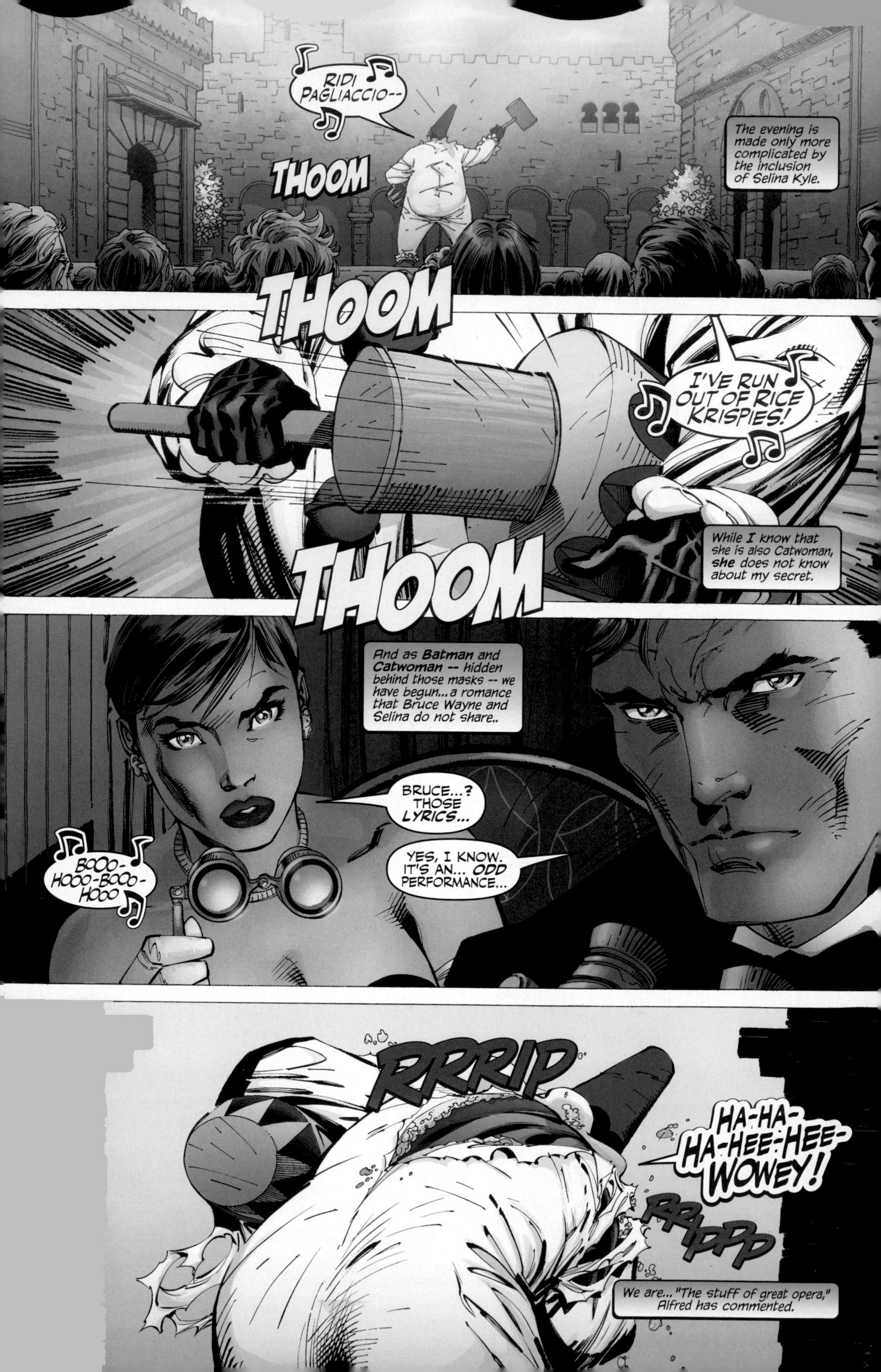

RIDI PAGLIACCIO--
THOOM
The evening is made only more complicated by the inclusion of Selina Kyle.
THOOM
I'VE RUN OUT OF RICE KRISPIES!
THOOM
While I know that she is also Catwoman, she does not know about my secret.
And as Batman and Catwoman -- hidden behind those masks -- we have begun...a romance that Bruce Wayne and Selina do not share..
BRUCE...? THOSE LYRICS...
BOOO-HOOO-BOOO-HOOO
YES, I KNOW. IT'S AN... ODD PERFORMANCE...
RRRIP
HA-HA-HA-HEE-HEE-WOWEY!
RRRIPPP
We are... "The stuff of great opera," Alfred has commented.

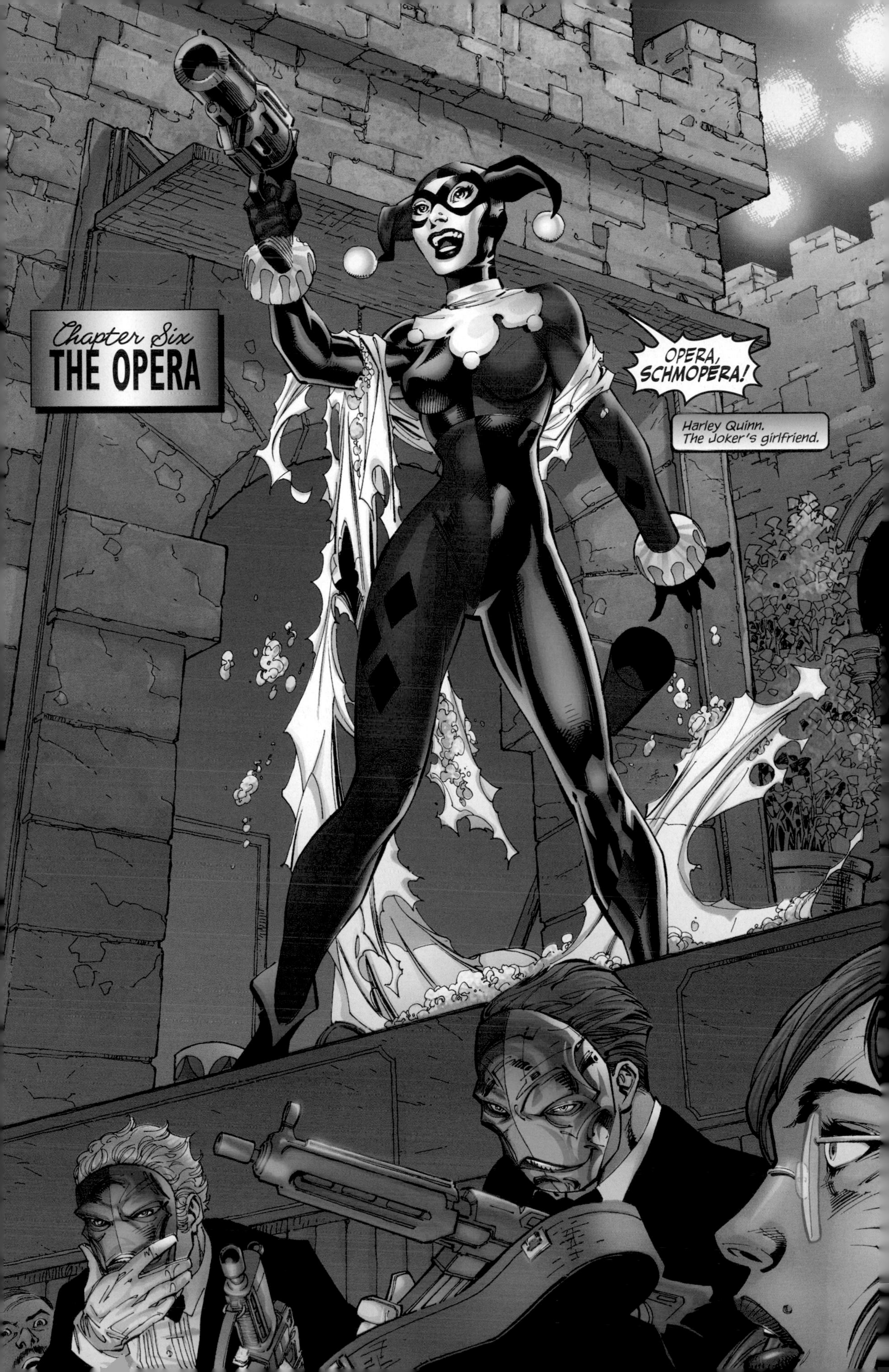

Chapter Six
THE OPERA
OPERA, SCHMOPERA!
Harley Quinn. The Joker's girlfriend.

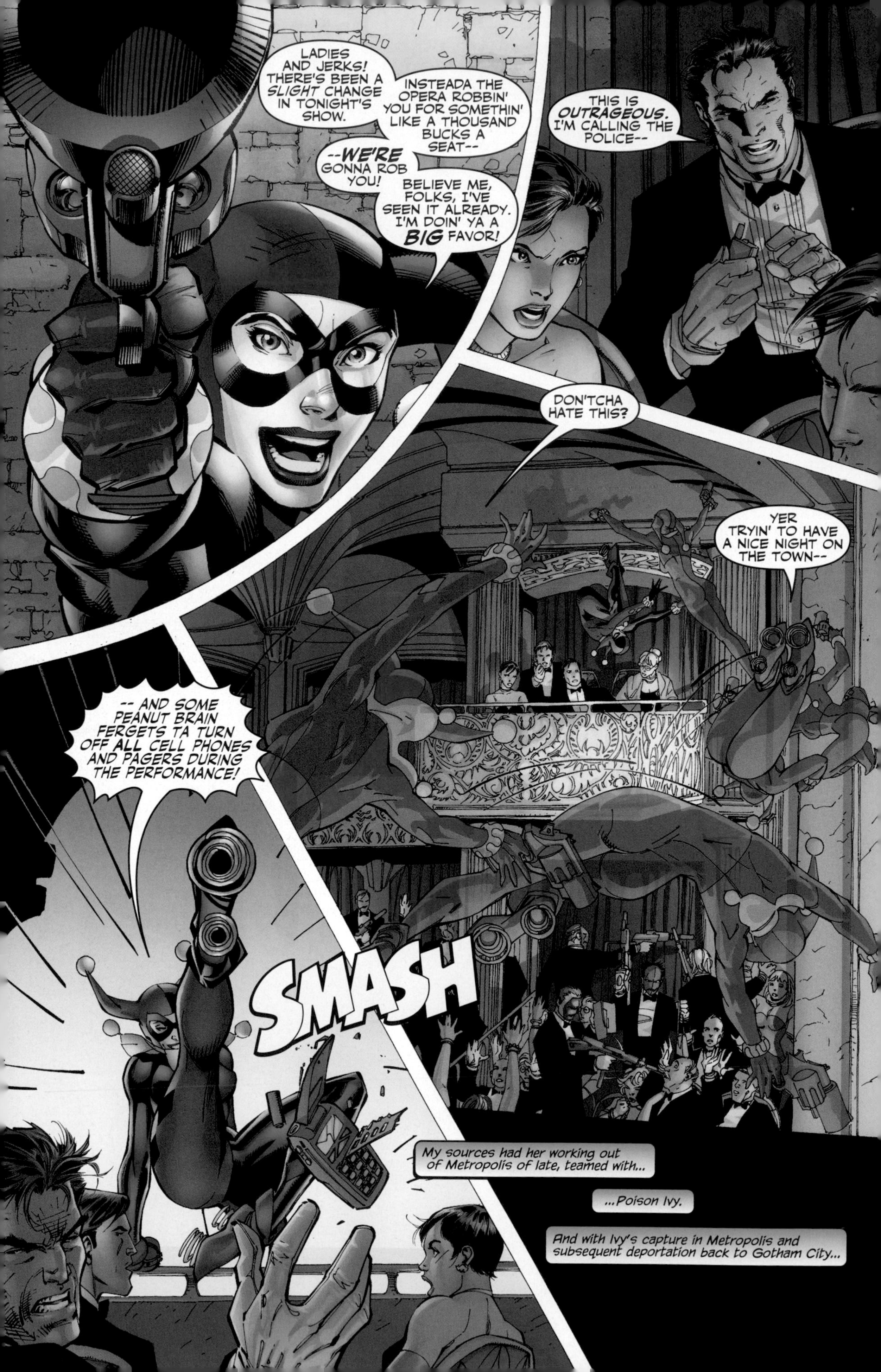
LADIES AND JERKS! THERE'S BEEN A SLIGHT CHANGE IN TONIGHT'S SHOW.
INSTEADA THE OPERA ROBBIN' YOU FOR SOMETHIN' LIKE A THOUSAND BUCKS A SEAT--
--WE'RE GONNA ROB YOU!
BELIEVE ME, FOLKS, I'VE SEEN IT ALREADY. I'M DOIN' YA A BIG FAVOR!
THIS IS OUTRAGEOUS. I'M CALLING THE POLICE--
DON'TCHA HATE THIS?
YER TRYIN' TO HAVE A NICE NIGHT ON THE TOWN--
-- AND SOME PEANUT BRAIN FERGETS TA TURN OFF ALL CELL PHONES AND PAGERS DURING THE PERFORMANCE!
SMASH
My sources had her working out of Metropolis of late, teamed with...
...Poison Ivy.
And with Ivy's capture in Metropolis and subsequent deportation back to Gotham City...

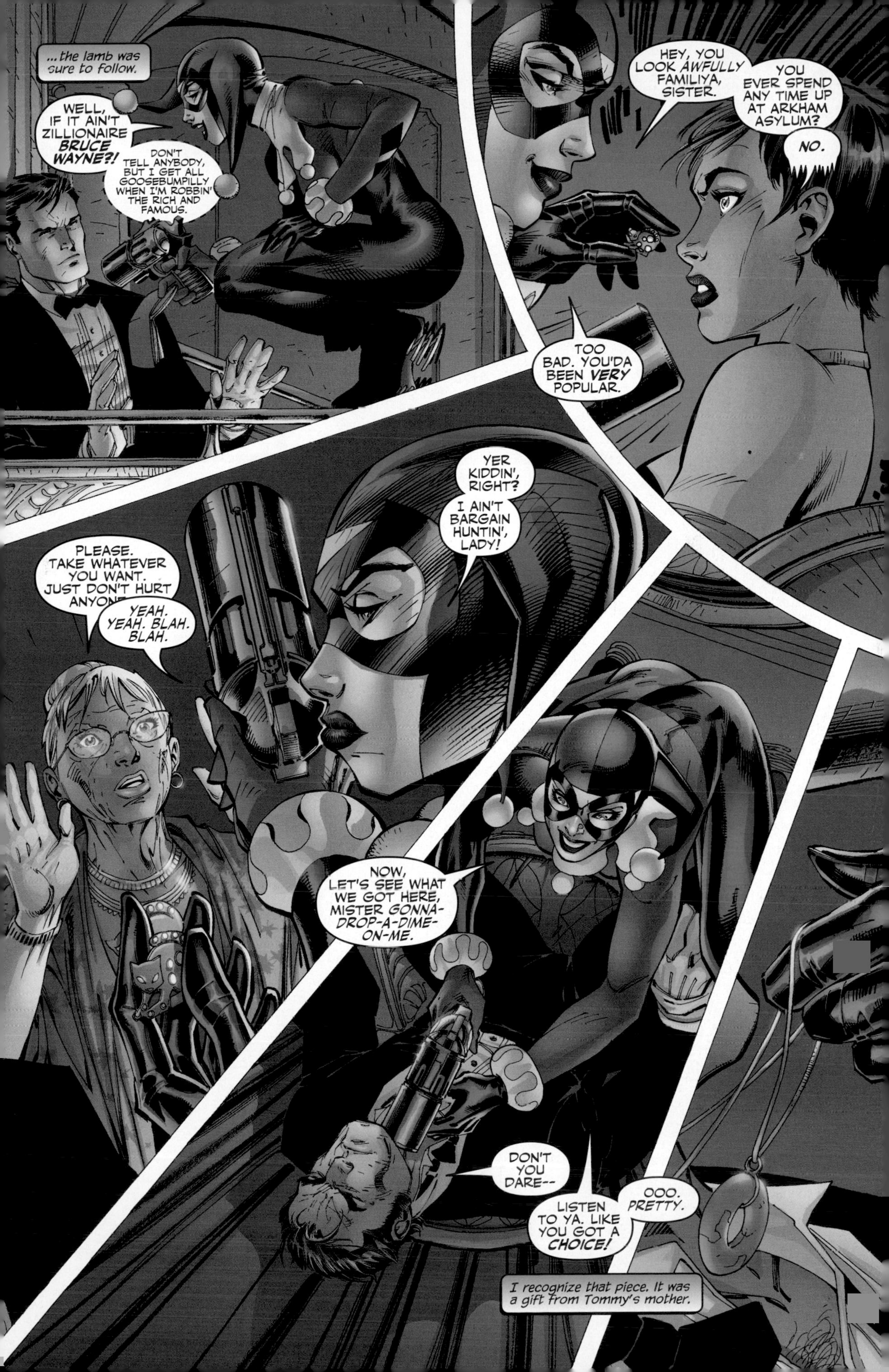
...the lamb was sure to follow.
WELL, IF IT AIN'T ZILLIONAIRE ***BRUCE WAYNE?!***
DON'T TELL ANYBODY, BUT I GET ALL GOOSEBUMPILLY WHEN I'M ROBBIN' THE RICH AND FAMOUS.
HEY, YOU LOOK *AWFULLY* FAMILIYA, SISTER.
YOU EVER SPEND ANY TIME UP AT ARKHAM ASYLUM?
***NO.***
TOO BAD. YOU'DA BEEN ***VERY*** POPULAR.
PLEASE. TAKE WHATEVER YOU WANT. JUST DON'T HURT ANYON
*YEAH. YEAH. BLAH. BLAH.*
YER KIDDIN', RIGHT?
I AIN'T BARGAIN HUNTIN', LADY!
NOW, LET'S SEE WHAT WE GOT HERE, MISTER *GONNA-DROP-A-DIME-ON-ME.*
DON'T YOU DARE--
LISTEN TO YA. LIKE YOU GOT A ***CHOICE!***
OOO. *PRETTY.*
*I recognize that piece. It was a gift from Tommy's mother.*

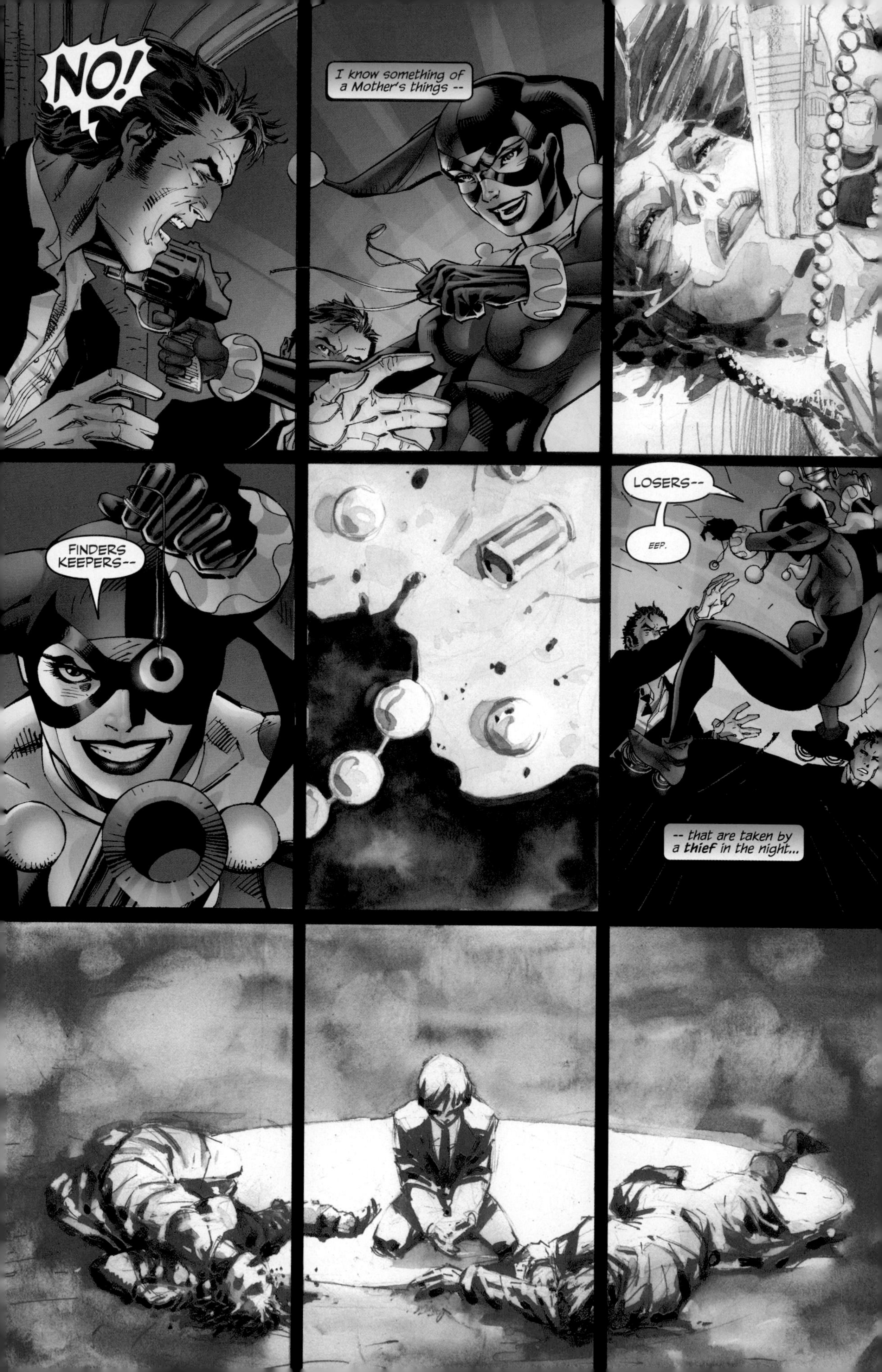
NO!
I know something of a Mother's things --
FINDERS KEEPERS--
LOSERS--
EEP.
-- that are taken by a thief in the night...

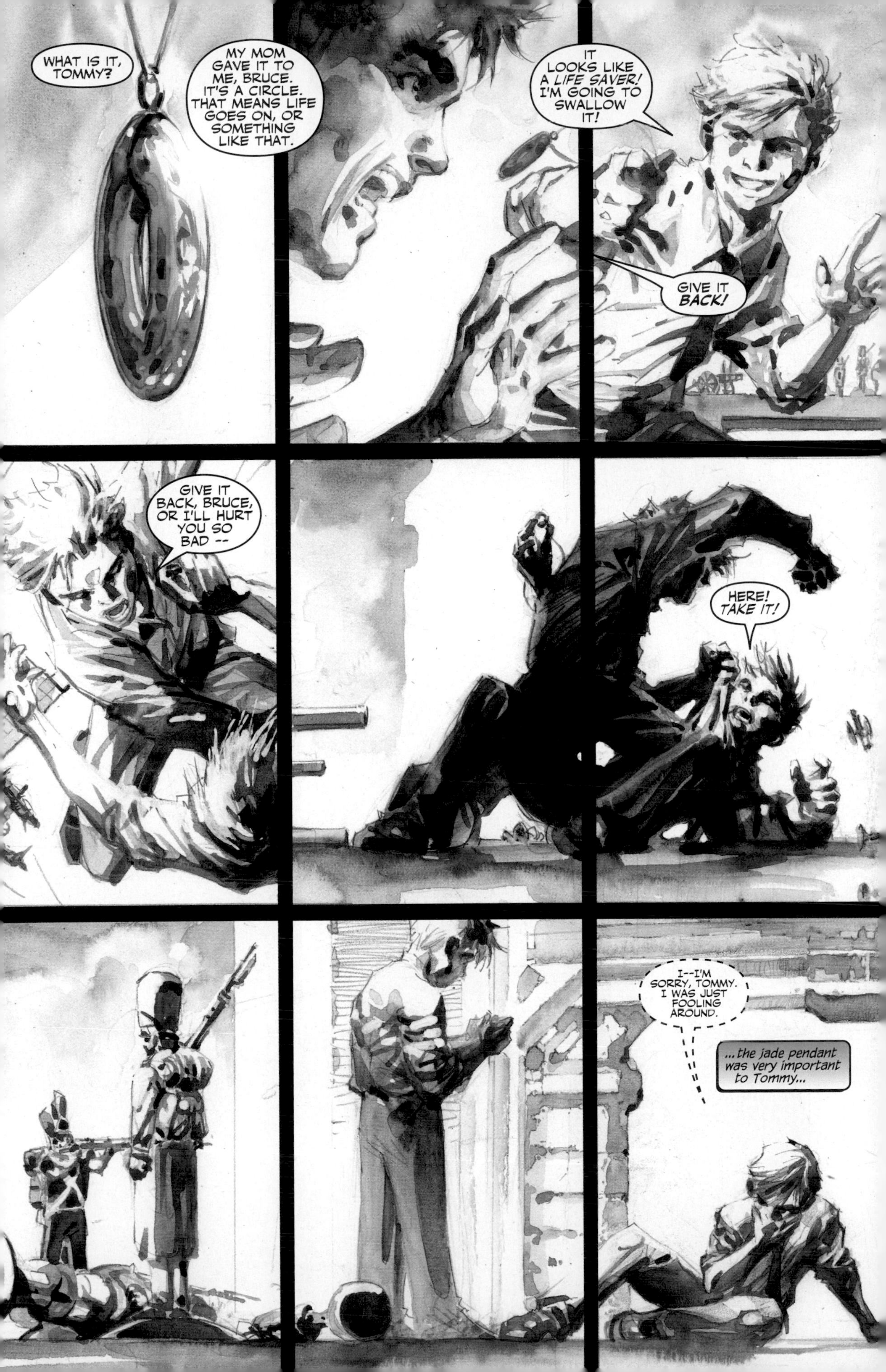
WHAT IS IT, TOMMY?
MY MOM GAVE IT TO ME, BRUCE. IT'S A CIRCLE. THAT MEANS LIFE GOES ON, OR SOMETHING LIKE THAT.
IT LOOKS LIKE A *LIFE SAVER!* I'M GOING TO SWALLOW IT!
GIVE IT *BACK!*
GIVE IT BACK, BRUCE, OR I'LL HURT YOU SO BAD --
HERE! *TAKE IT!*
I--I'M SORRY, TOMMY. I WAS JUST FOOLING AROUND.
...the jade pendant was very important to Tommy...

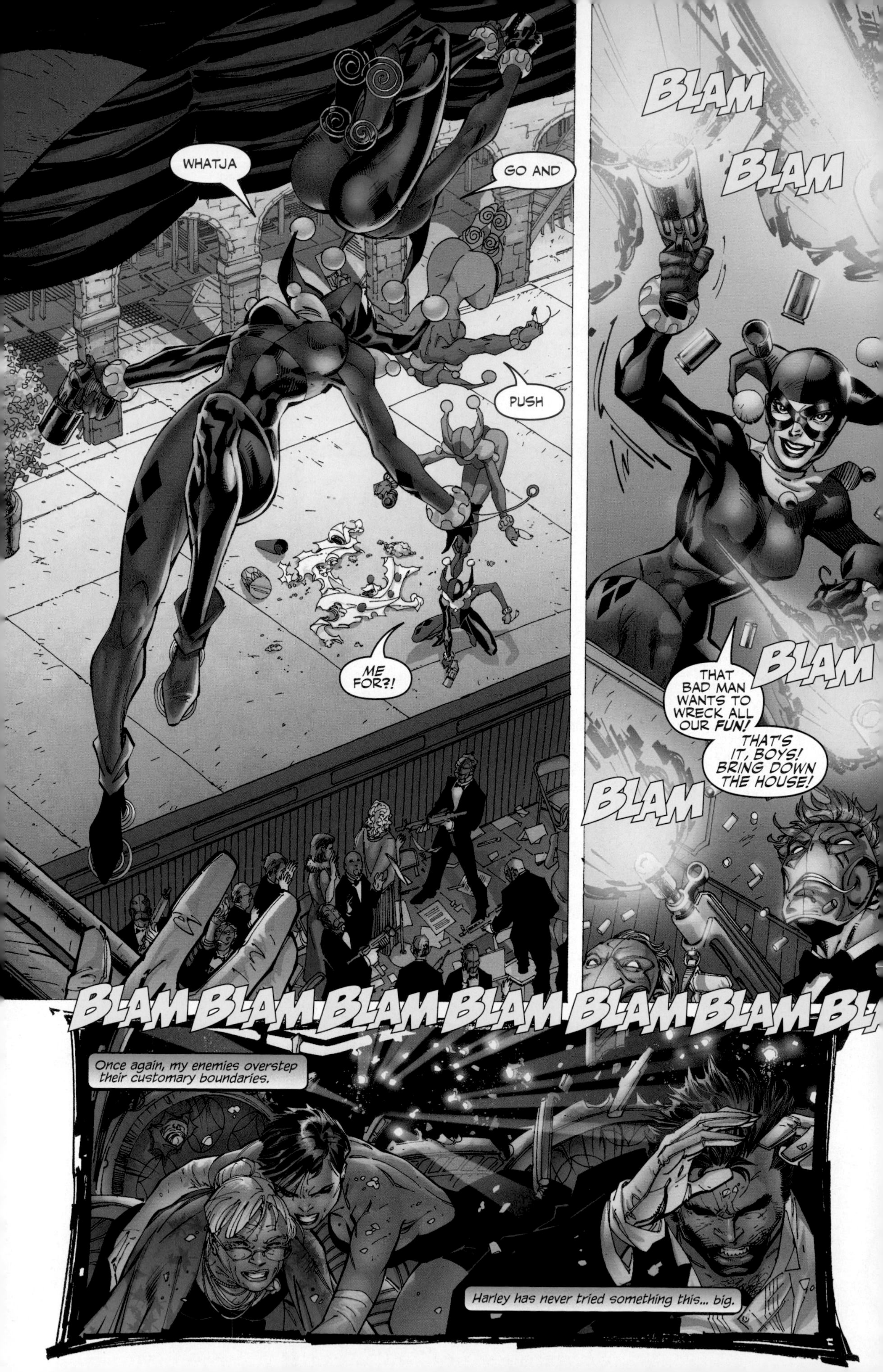
WHATJA
GO AND
PUSH
ME FOR?!
BLAM
BLAM
BLAM
THAT BAD MAN WANTS TO WRECK ALL OUR FUN!
THAT'S IT, BOYS! BRING DOWN THE HOUSE!
BLAM
BLAM BLAM BLAM BLAM BLAM BLAM BL
Once again, my enemies overstep their customary boundaries.
Harley has never tried something this... big.

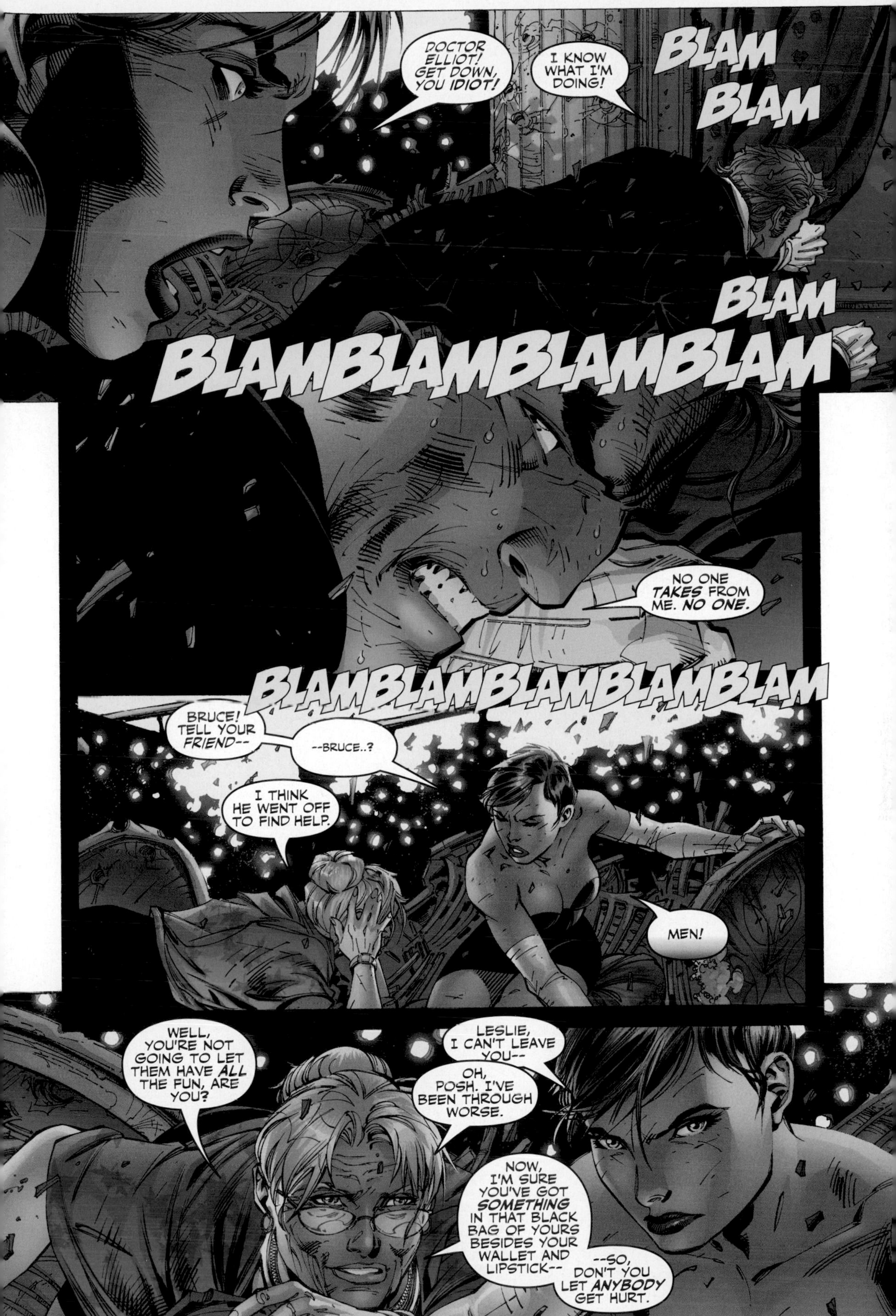

DOCTOR ELLIOT! GET DOWN, YOU *IDIOT*!
I KNOW WHAT I'M DOING!
BLAM
BLAM
BLAM
BLAMBLAMBLAMBLAM
NO ONE *TAKES* FROM ME. *NO ONE*.
BLAMBLAMBLAMBLAMBLAM
BRUCE! TELL YOUR *FRIEND*--
--BRUCE..?
I THINK HE WENT OFF TO FIND HELP.
MEN!
WELL, YOU'RE NOT GOING TO LET THEM HAVE *ALL* THE FUN, ARE YOU?
LESLIE, I CAN'T LEAVE YOU--
OH, POSH. I'VE BEEN THROUGH WORSE.
NOW, I'M SURE YOU'VE GOT *SOMETHING* IN THAT BLACK BAG OF YOURS BESIDES YOUR WALLET AND LIPSTICK--
--SO, DON'T YOU LET *ANYBODY* GET HURT.

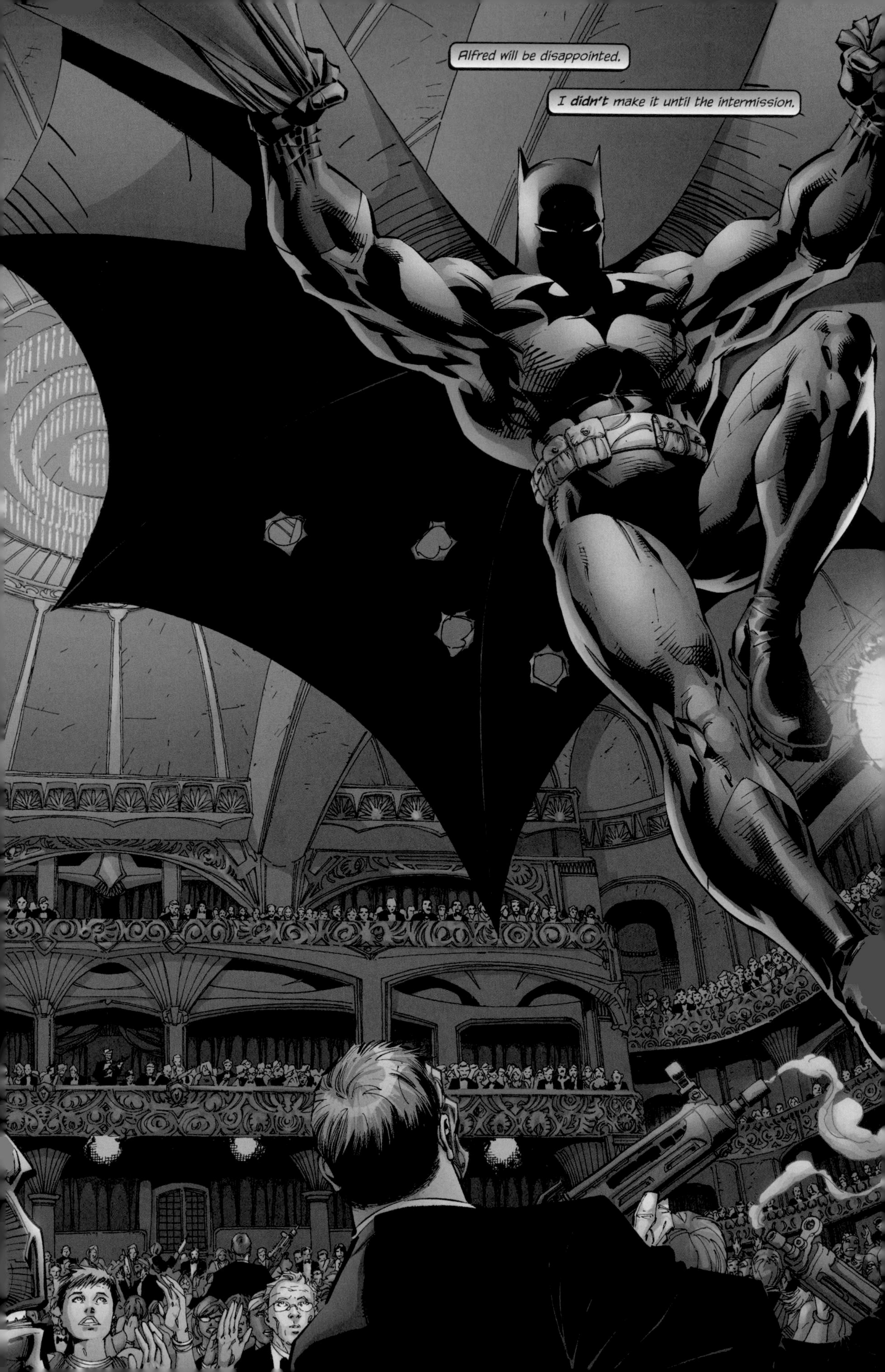
Alfred will be disappointed.
I didn't make it until the intermission.

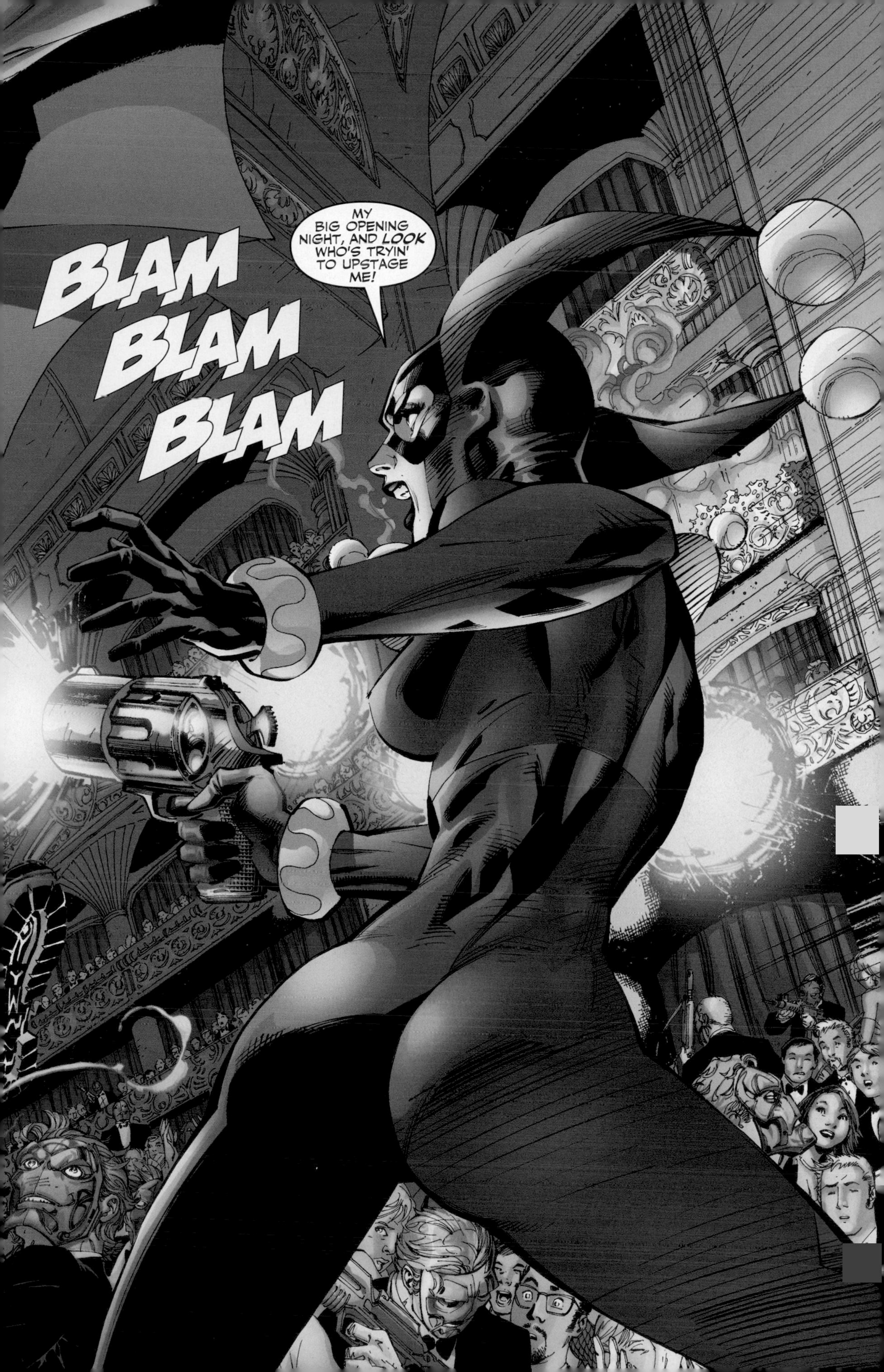

BLAM
BLAM
BLAM
MY BIG OPENING NIGHT, AND LOOK WHO'S TRYIN' TO UPSTAGE ME!

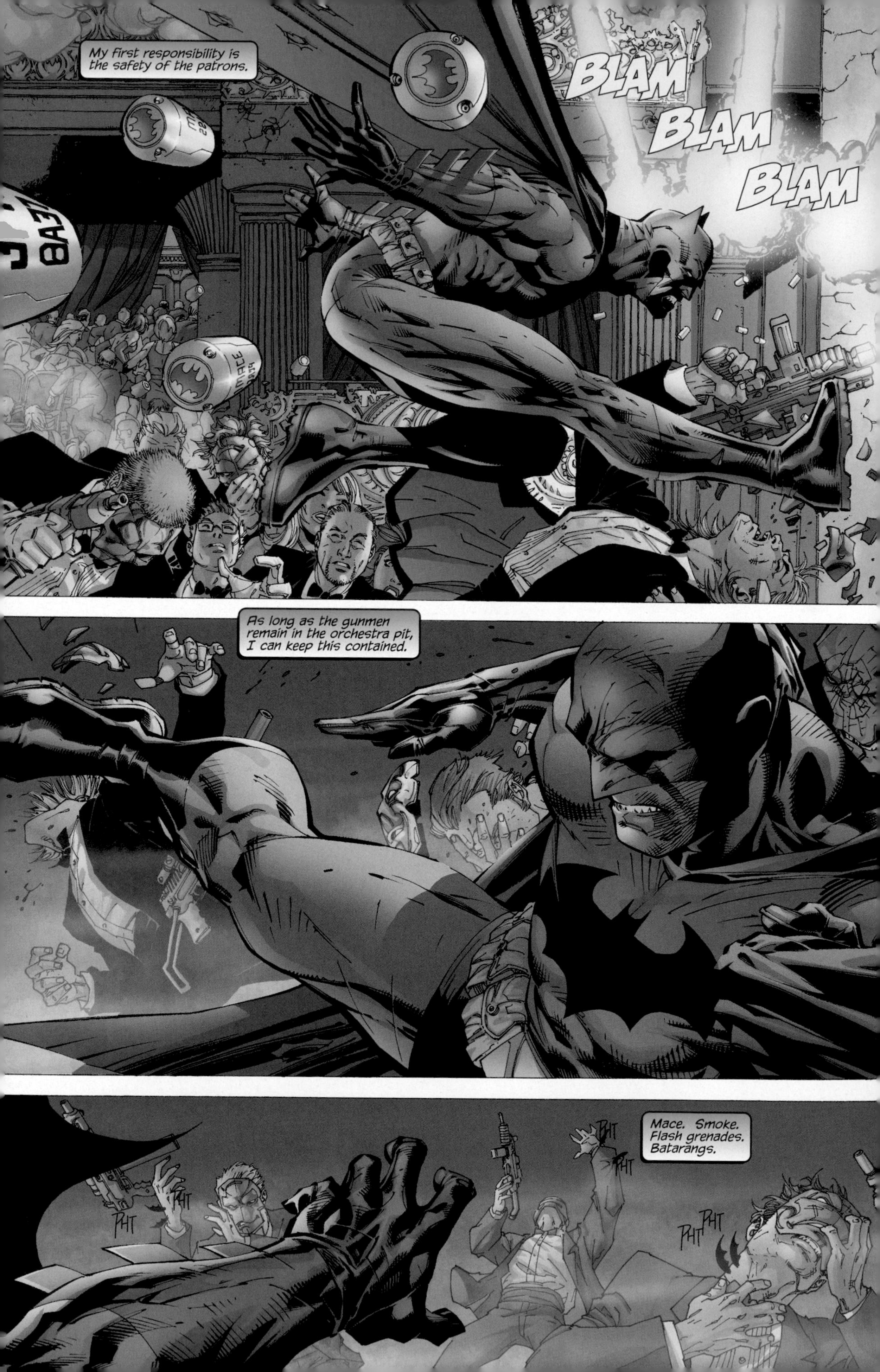
My first responsibility is the safety of the patrons.
BLAM
BLAM
BLAM
As long as the gunmen remain in the orchestra pit, I can keep this contained.
Mace. Smoke. Flash grenades. Batarangs.
PHT
PHT
PHT
PHT
PHT
PHT

BLAMBLAMBLAM

TSK. TSK. TSK. MISTER B.

YOU REALLY *ONLY* KNOW HOW TO STICK TO THE *SCRIPT*, HUH?

Script? In the past, Harley has been, at best, delusional. But... could this entire robbery be scripted? And for whom?

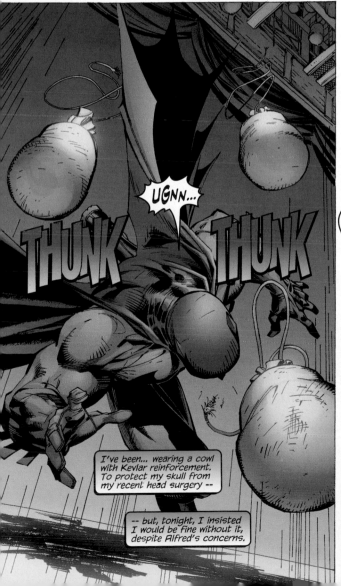

UGNN...

THUNK  THUNK

I've been... wearing a cowl with Kevlar reinforcement. To protect my skull from my recent head surgery --

-- but, tonight, I insisted I would be fine without it, despite Alfred's concerns.

A LITTLE WORK ON YOUR *IMPROV* MIGHT DO YA SOME GOOD!

Thought I was stronger. I needed to be stronger. And my enemy takes advantage of my hubris.

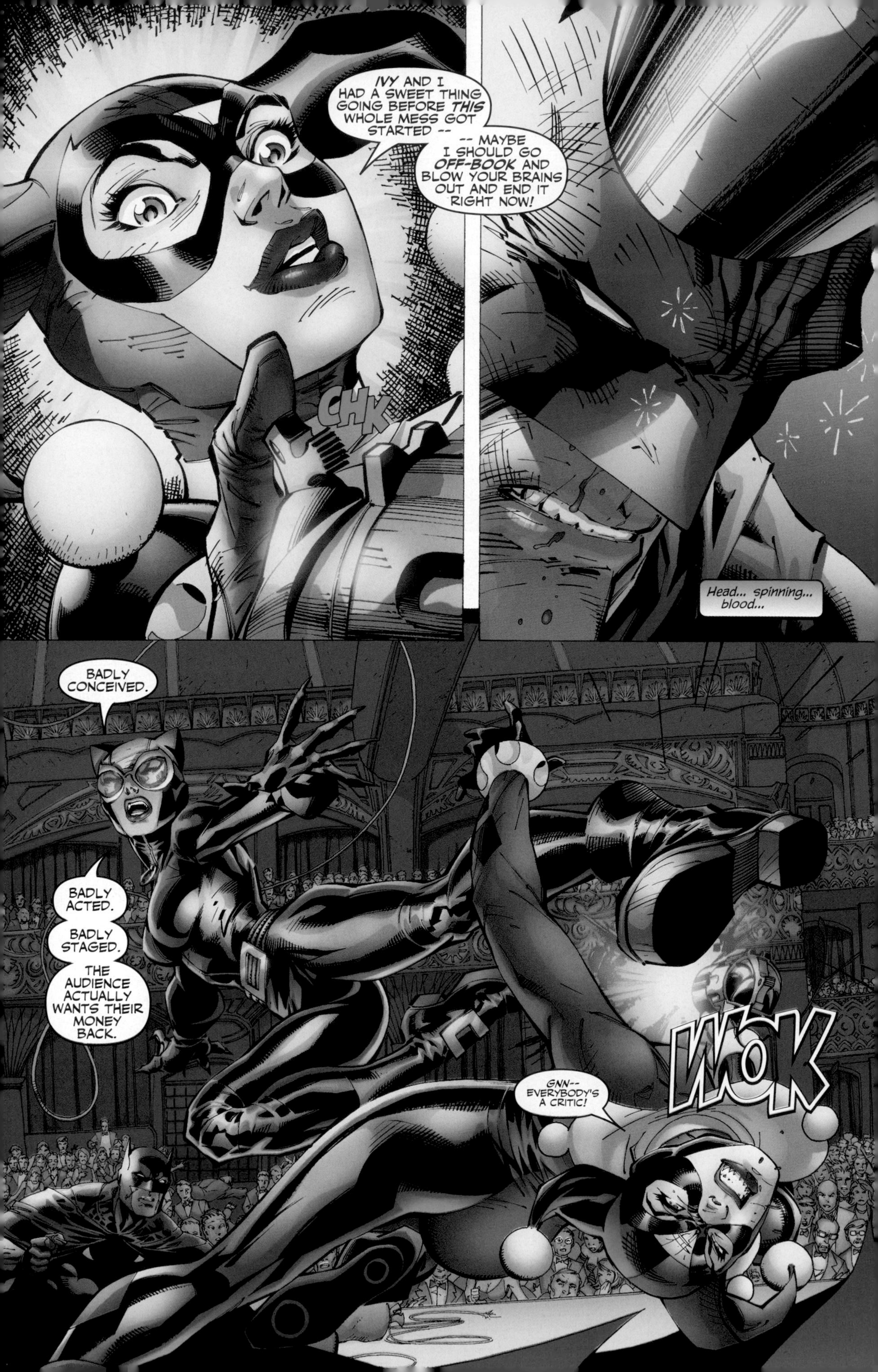
IVY AND I HAD A SWEET THING GOING BEFORE THIS WHOLE MESS GOT STARTED --
-- MAYBE I SHOULD GO OFF-BOOK AND BLOW YOUR BRAINS OUT AND END IT RIGHT NOW!
CHK
Head... spinning... blood...
BADLY CONCEIVED.
BADLY ACTED.
BADLY STAGED.
THE AUDIENCE ACTUALLY WANTS THEIR MONEY BACK.
WOK
GNN-- EVERYBODY'S A CRITIC!

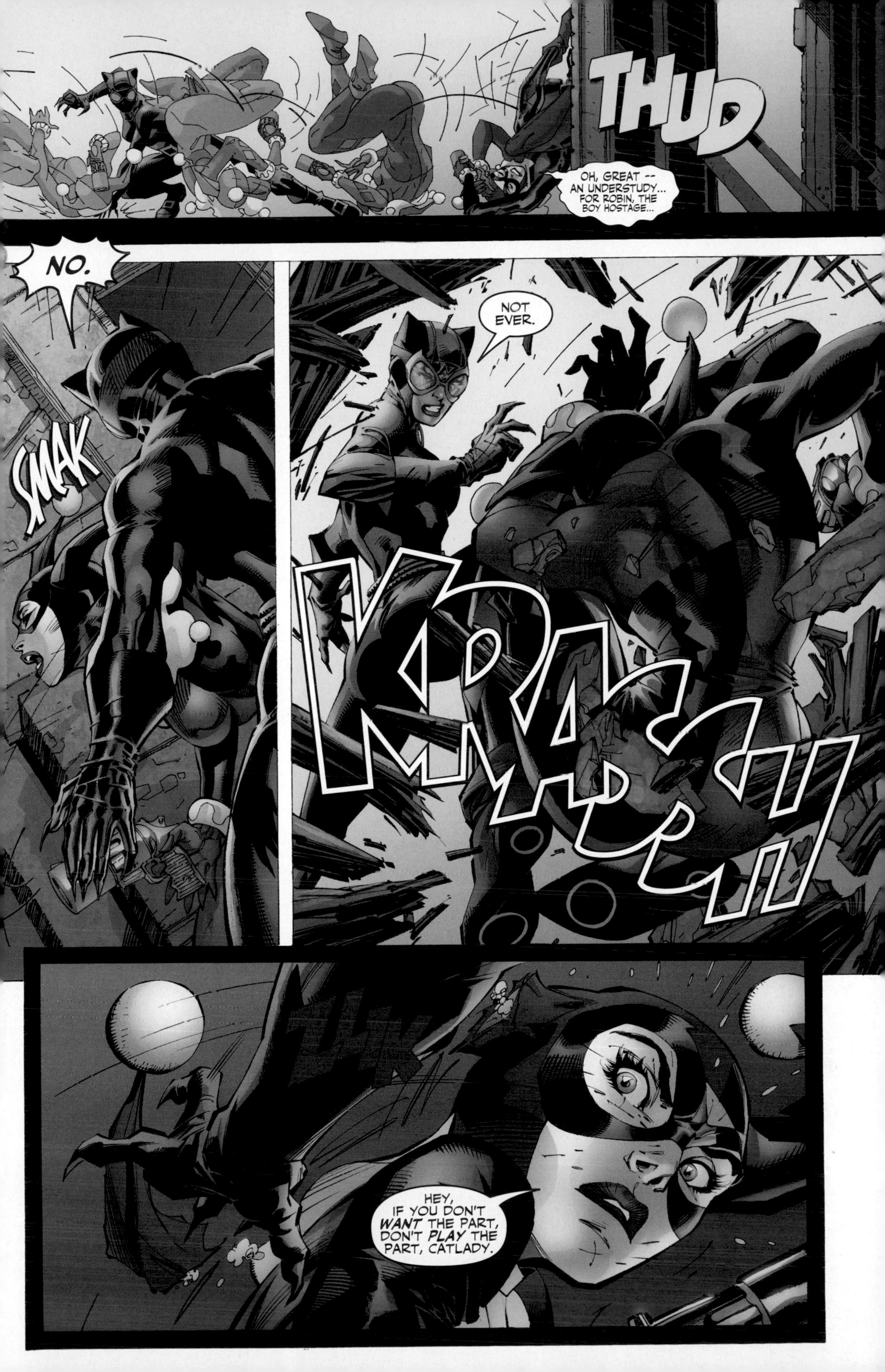
THUD
OH, GREAT -- AN UNDERSTUDY... FOR ROBIN, THE BOY HOSTAGE...
NO.
SMAK
NOT EVER.
KRAKSH
HEY, IF YOU DON'T WANT THE PART, DON'T PLAY THE PART, CATLADY.

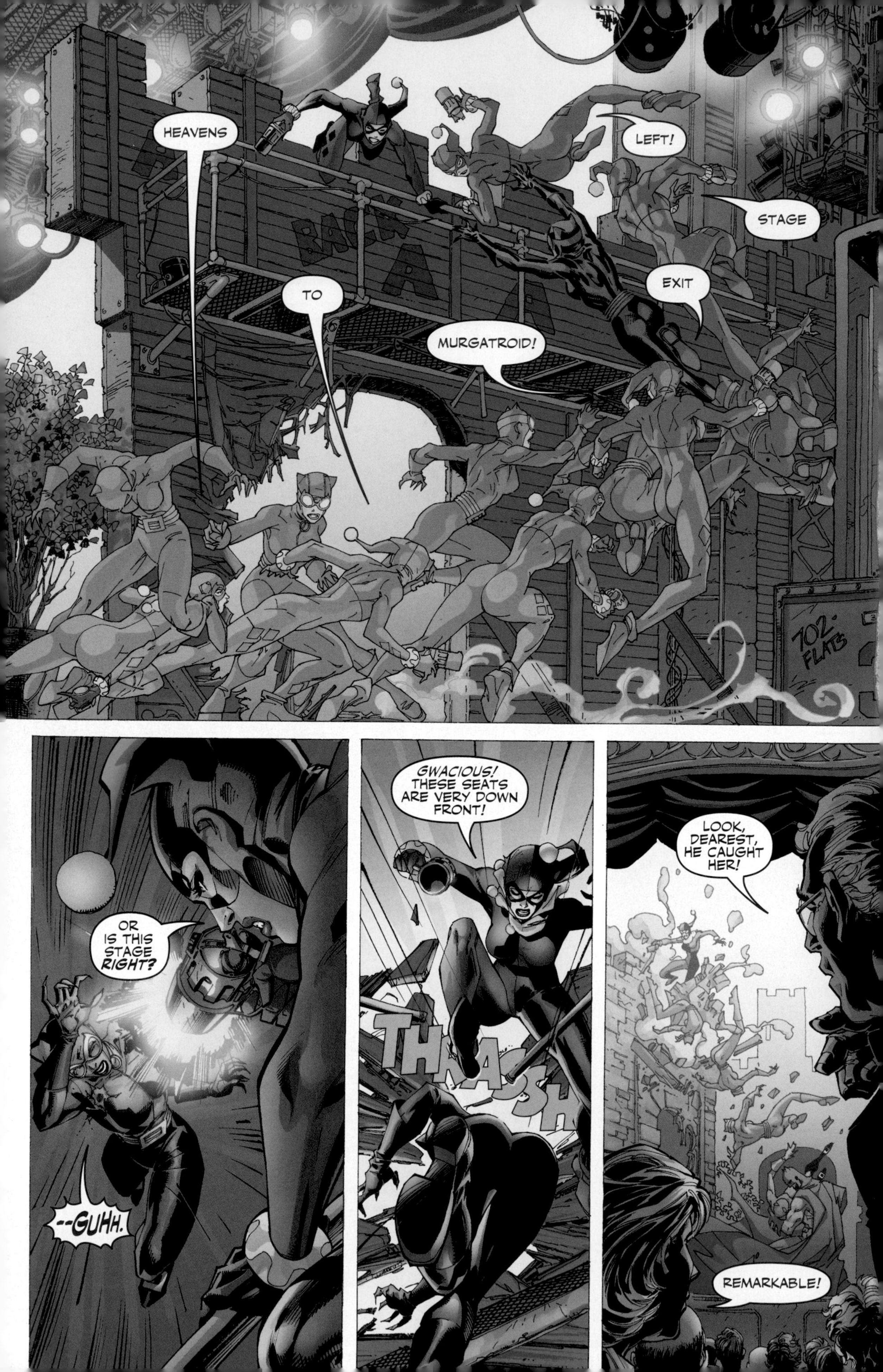
HEAVENS
TO
MURGATROID!
EXIT
STAGE
LEFT!
702-FLATS
OR IS THIS STAGE *RIGHT?*
--GUHH.
*GWACIOUS!* THESE SEATS ARE VERY DOWN FRONT!
THRASH
LOOK, DEAREST, HE CAUGHT HER!
REMARKABLE!

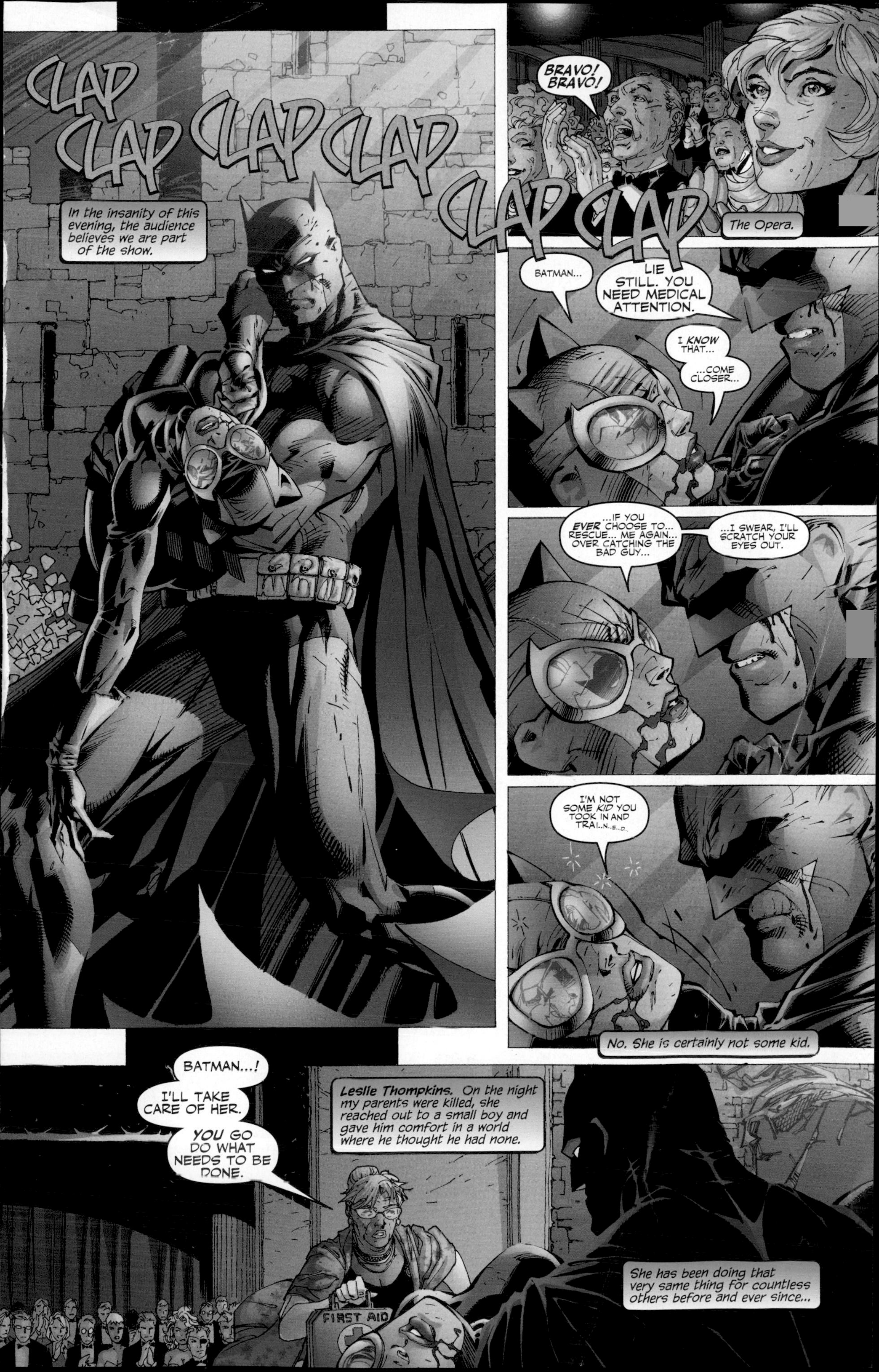
CLAP CLAP CLAP CLAP CLAP CLAP
In the insanity of this evening, the audience believes we are part of the show.
BRAVO! BRAVO!
The Opera.
BATMAN...
LIE STILL. YOU NEED MEDICAL ATTENTION.
I KNOW THAT...
...COME CLOSER...
...IF YOU EVER CHOOSE TO... RESCUE... ME AGAIN... OVER CATCHING THE BAD GUY...
...I SWEAR, I'LL SCRATCH YOUR EYES OUT.
I'M NOT SOME KID YOU TOOK IN AND TRAI..N..E..D
No. She is certainly not some kid.
BATMAN...!
I'LL TAKE CARE OF HER.
YOU GO DO WHAT NEEDS TO BE DONE.
Leslie Thompkins. On the night my parents were killed, she reached out to a small boy and gave him comfort in a world where he thought he had none.
FIRST AID
She has been doing that very same thing for countless others before and ever since...

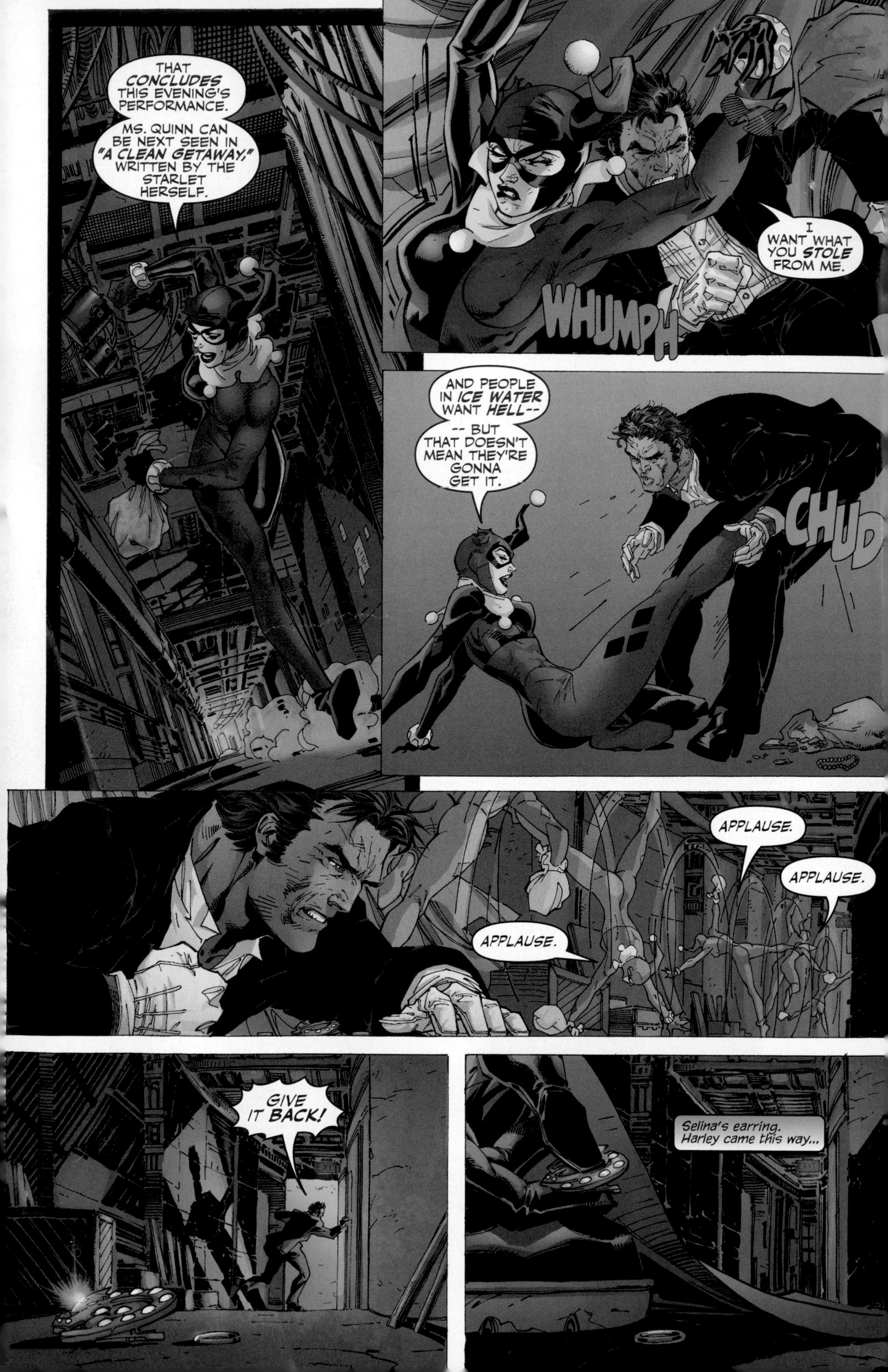

THAT CONCLUDES THIS EVENING'S PERFORMANCE.
MS. QUINN CAN BE NEXT SEEN IN "A CLEAN GETAWAY," WRITTEN BY THE STARLET HERSELF.
I WANT WHAT YOU STOLE FROM ME.
WHUMPH
AND PEOPLE IN ICE WATER WANT HELL--
-- BUT THAT DOESN'T MEAN THEY'RE GONNA GET IT.
CHUD
APPLAUSE.
APPLAUSE.
APPLAUSE.
GIVE IT BACK!
Selina's earring. Harley came this way...

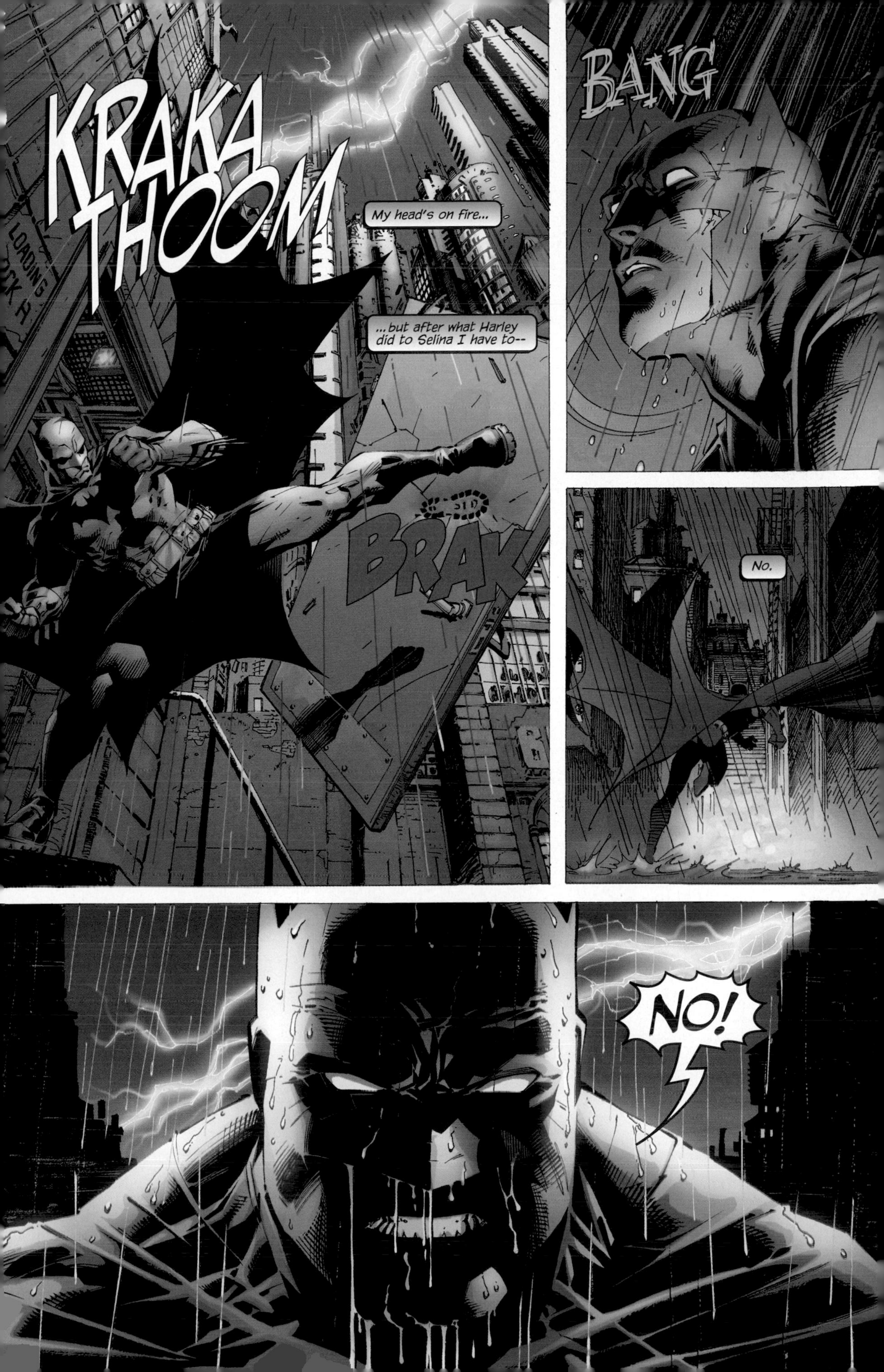
KRAKA THOOM
My head's on fire...
...but after what Harley did to Selina I have to--
BRAK
BANG
No.
NO!

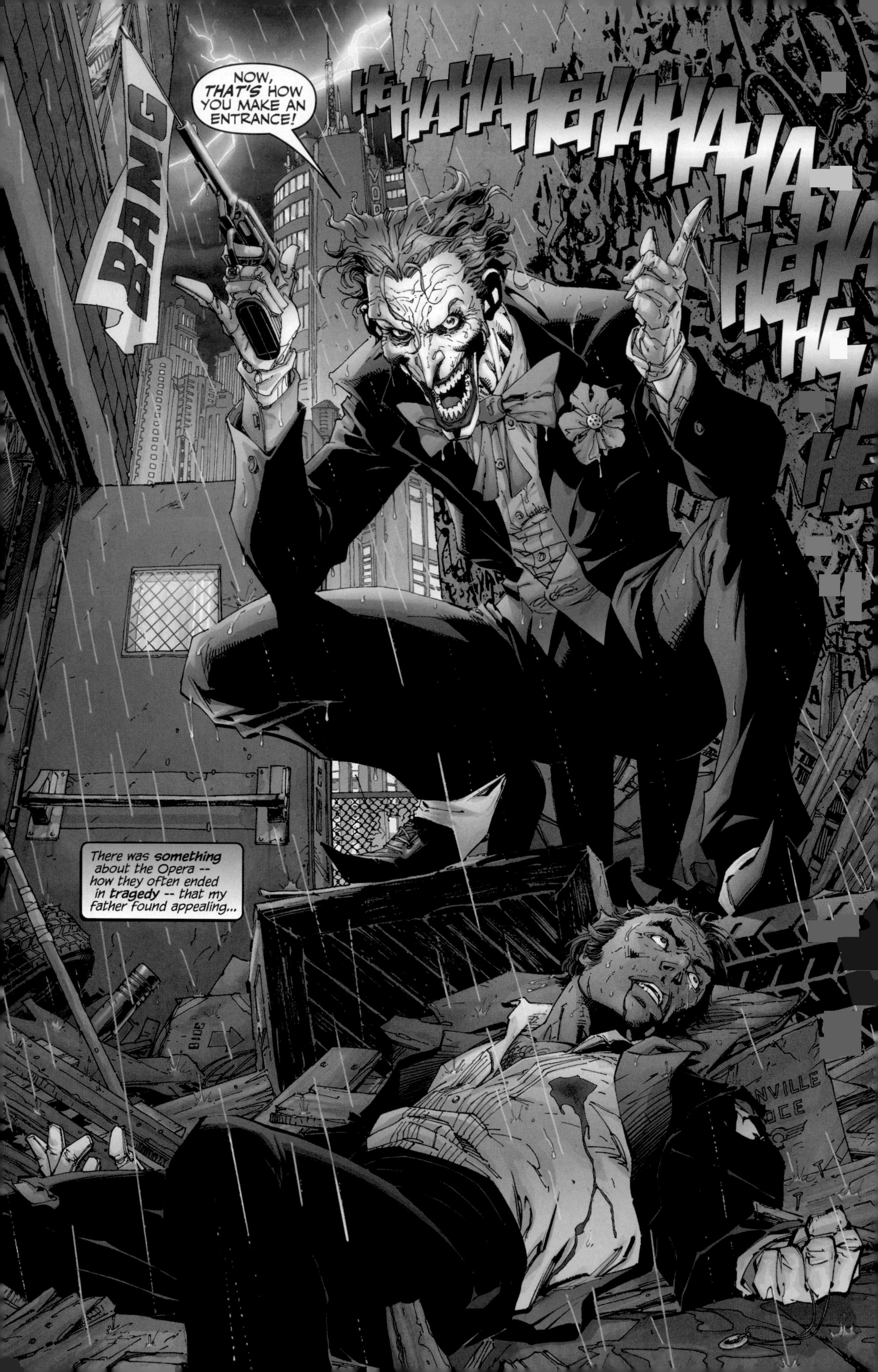
NOW, THAT'S HOW YOU MAKE AN ENTRANCE!
HEHAHAHEHAHAHAHA-HAHEHAHEHE
BANG
There was something about the Opera -- how they often ended in tragedy -- that my father found appealing...

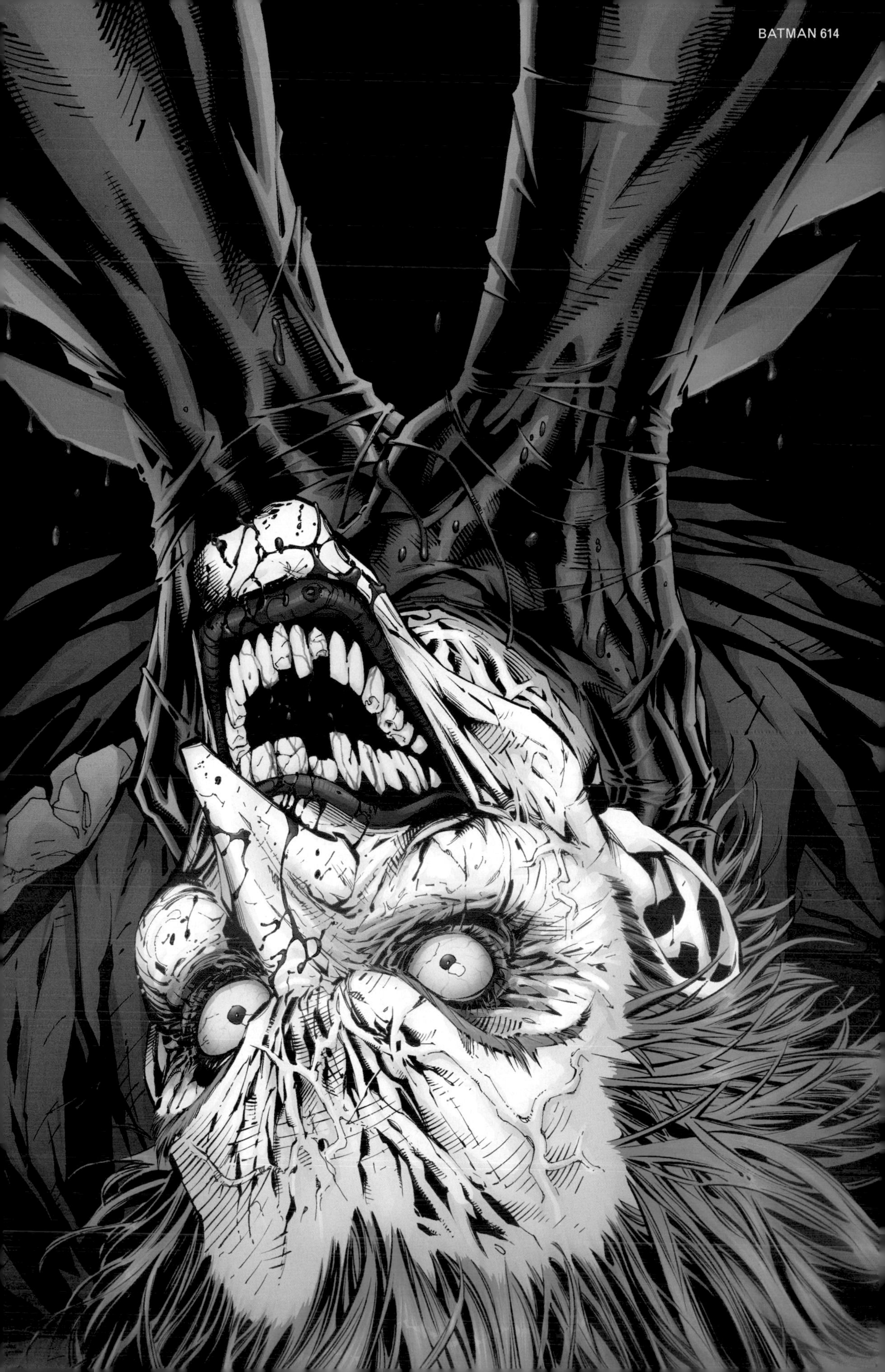

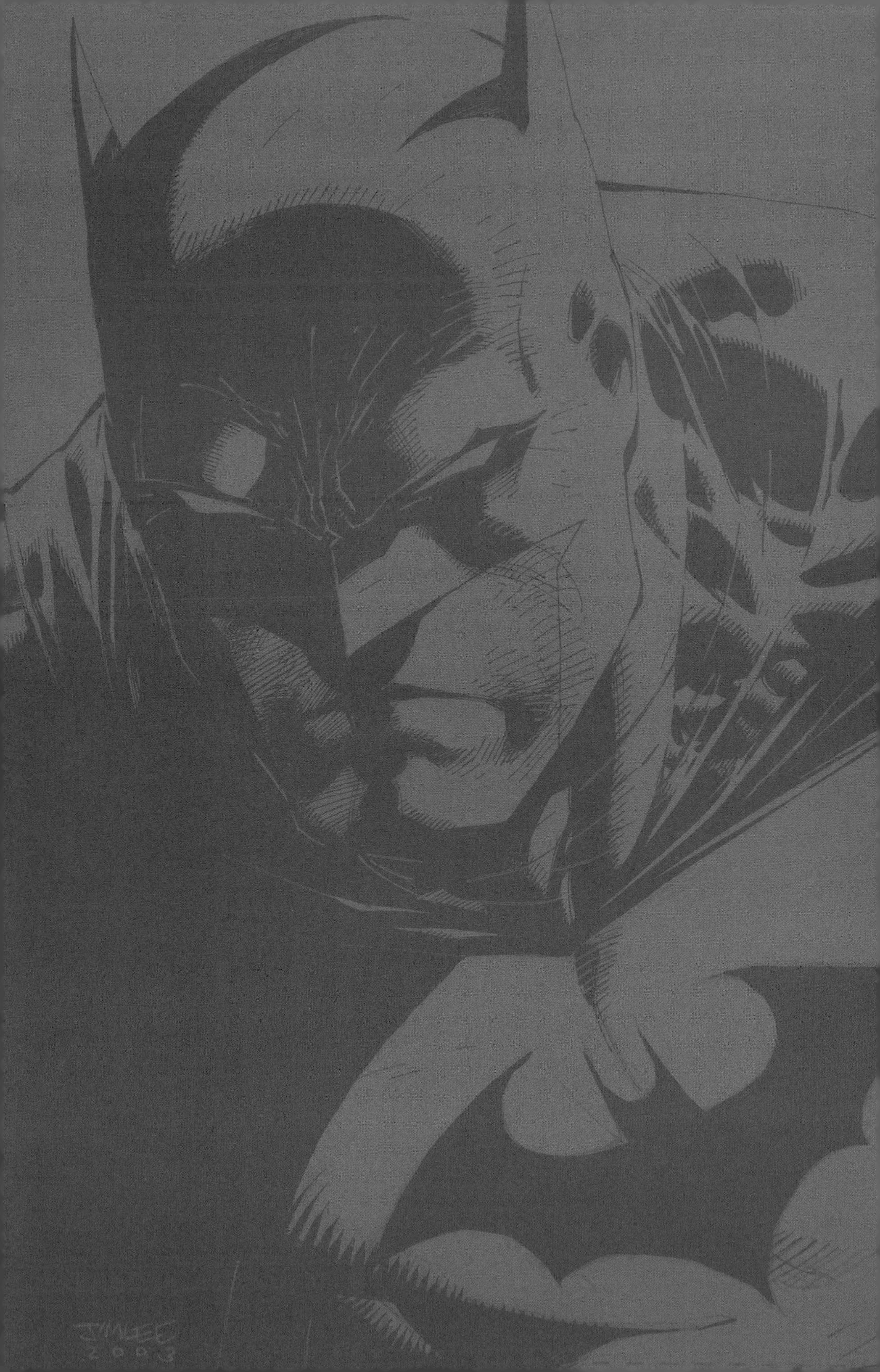

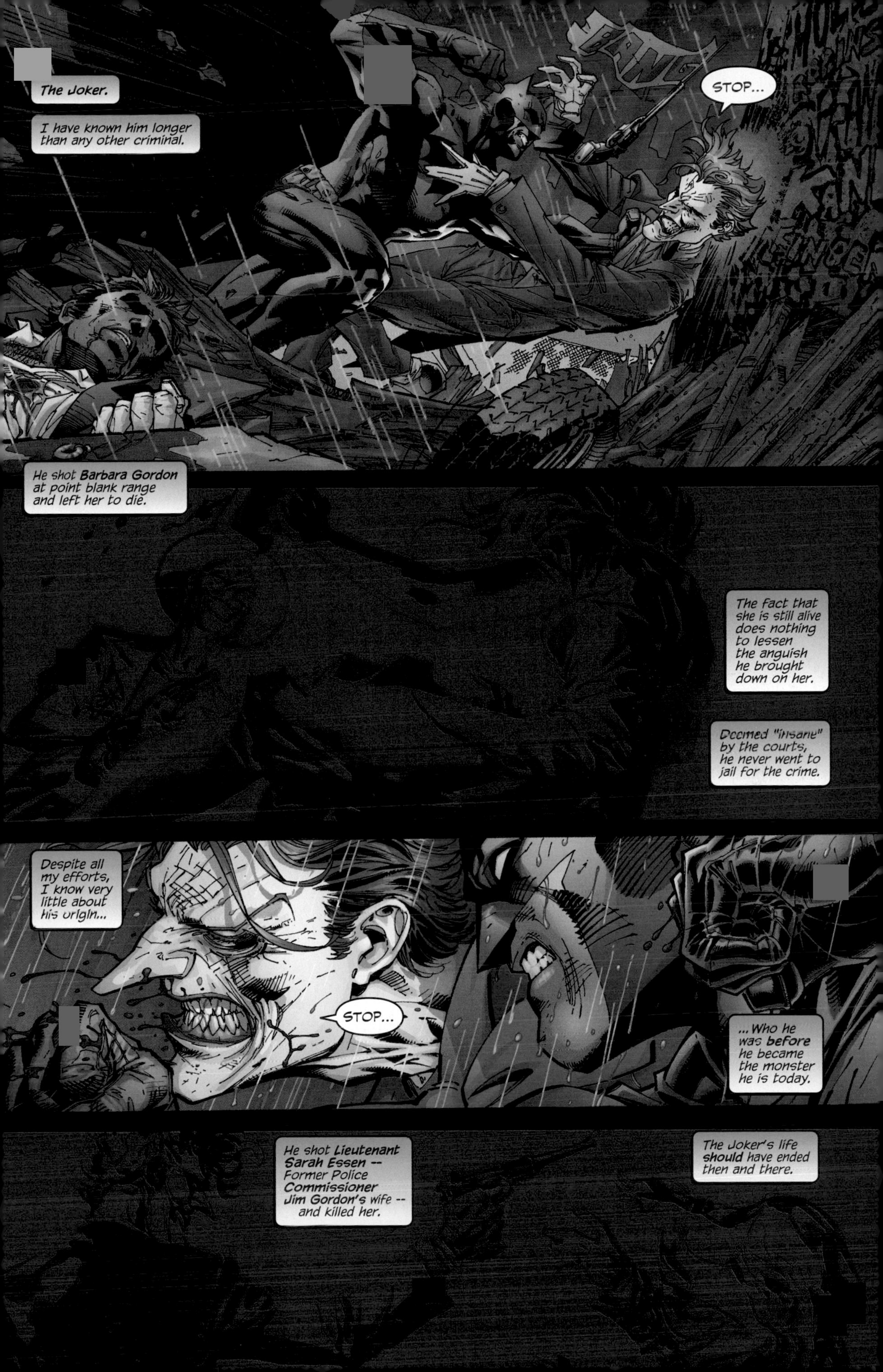

The Joker.
I have known him longer than any other criminal.
BANG
STOP...
He shot **Barbara Gordon** at point blank range and left her to die.
The fact that she is still alive does nothing to lessen the anguish he brought down on her.
Deemed "insane" by the courts, he never went to jail for the crime.
Despite all my efforts, I know very little about his origin...
STOP...
...Who he was **before** he became the monster he is today.
He shot **Lieutenant Sarah Essen** -- Former Police **Commissioner Jim Gordon's** wife -- and killed her.
The Joker's life **should** have ended then and there.

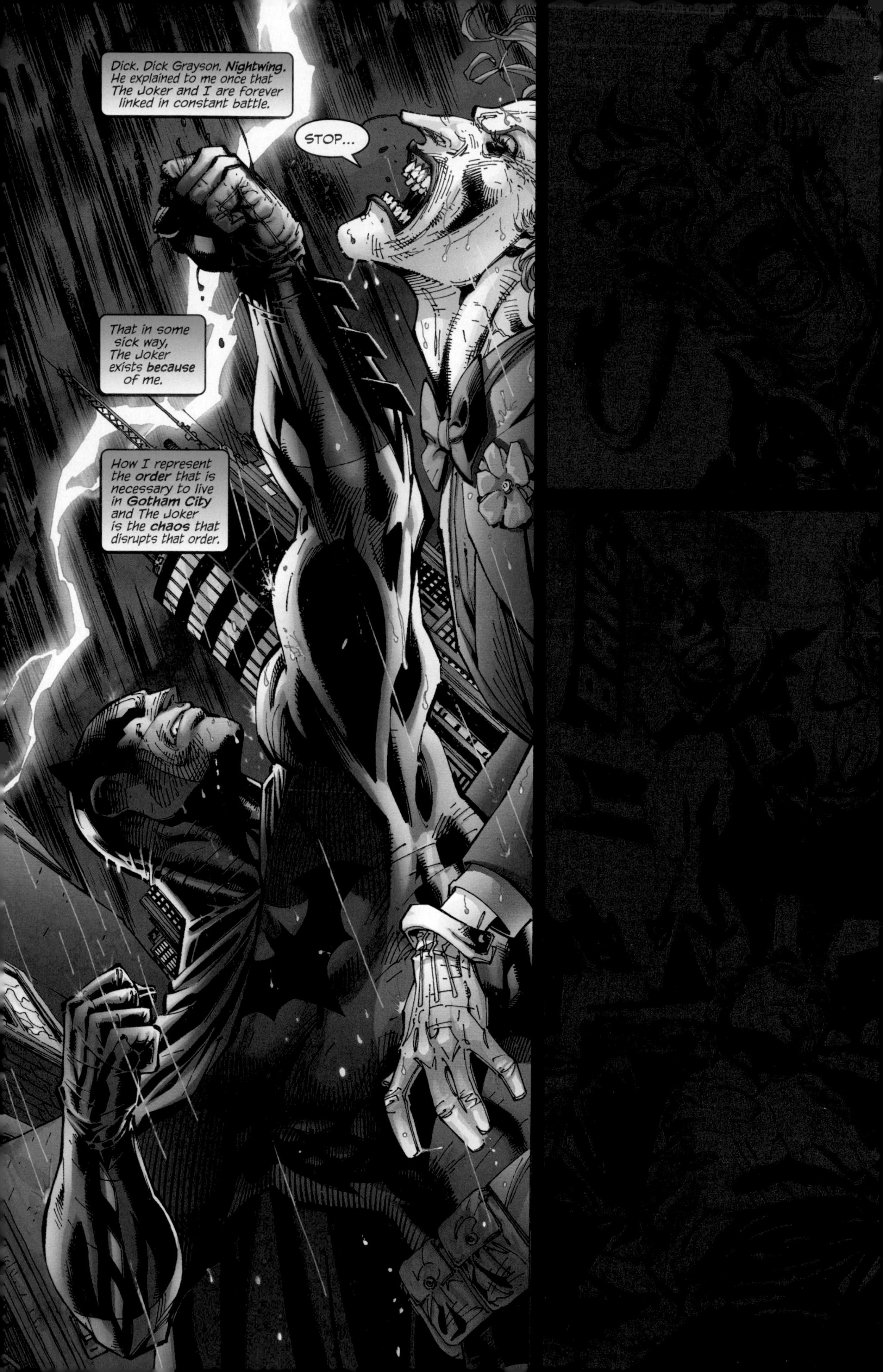

Dick. Dick Grayson. Nightwing. He explained to me once that The Joker and I are forever linked in constant battle.
STOP...
That in some sick way, The Joker exists because of me.
How I represent the order that is necessary to live in Gotham City and The Joker is the chaos that disrupts that order.

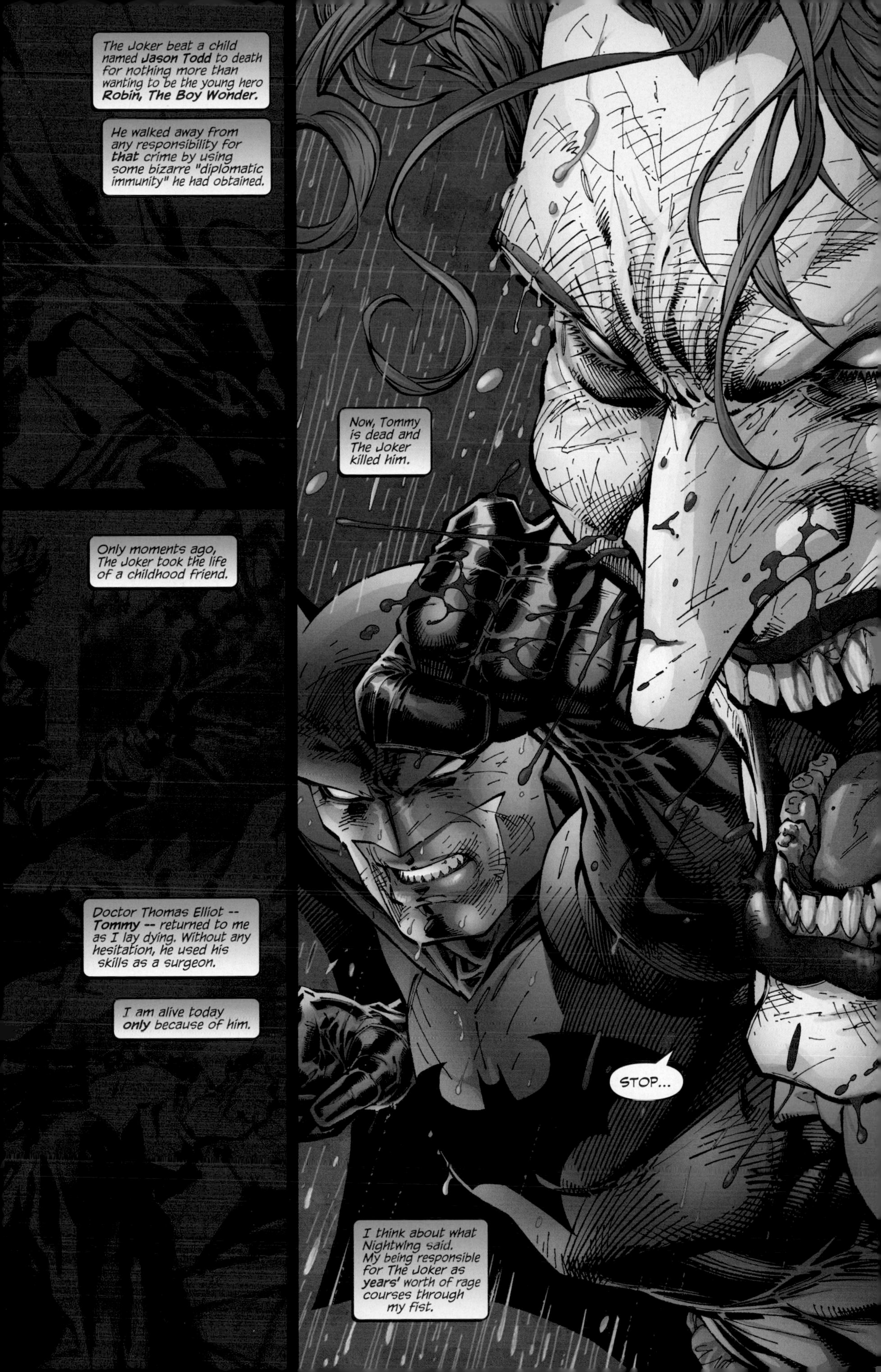

The Joker beat a child named **Jason Todd** to death for nothing more than wanting to be the young hero ***Robin, The Boy Wonder.***
He walked away from any responsibility for ***that*** crime by using some bizarre "diplomatic immunity" he had obtained.
Only moments ago, The Joker took the life of a childhood friend.
Doctor Thomas Elliot -- ***Tommy*** -- returned to me as I lay dying. Without any hesitation, he used his skills as a surgeon.
I am alive today ***only*** because of him.
Now, Tommy is dead and The Joker killed him.
STOP...
I think about what Nightwing said. My being responsible for The Joker as ***years'*** worth of rage courses through my fist.

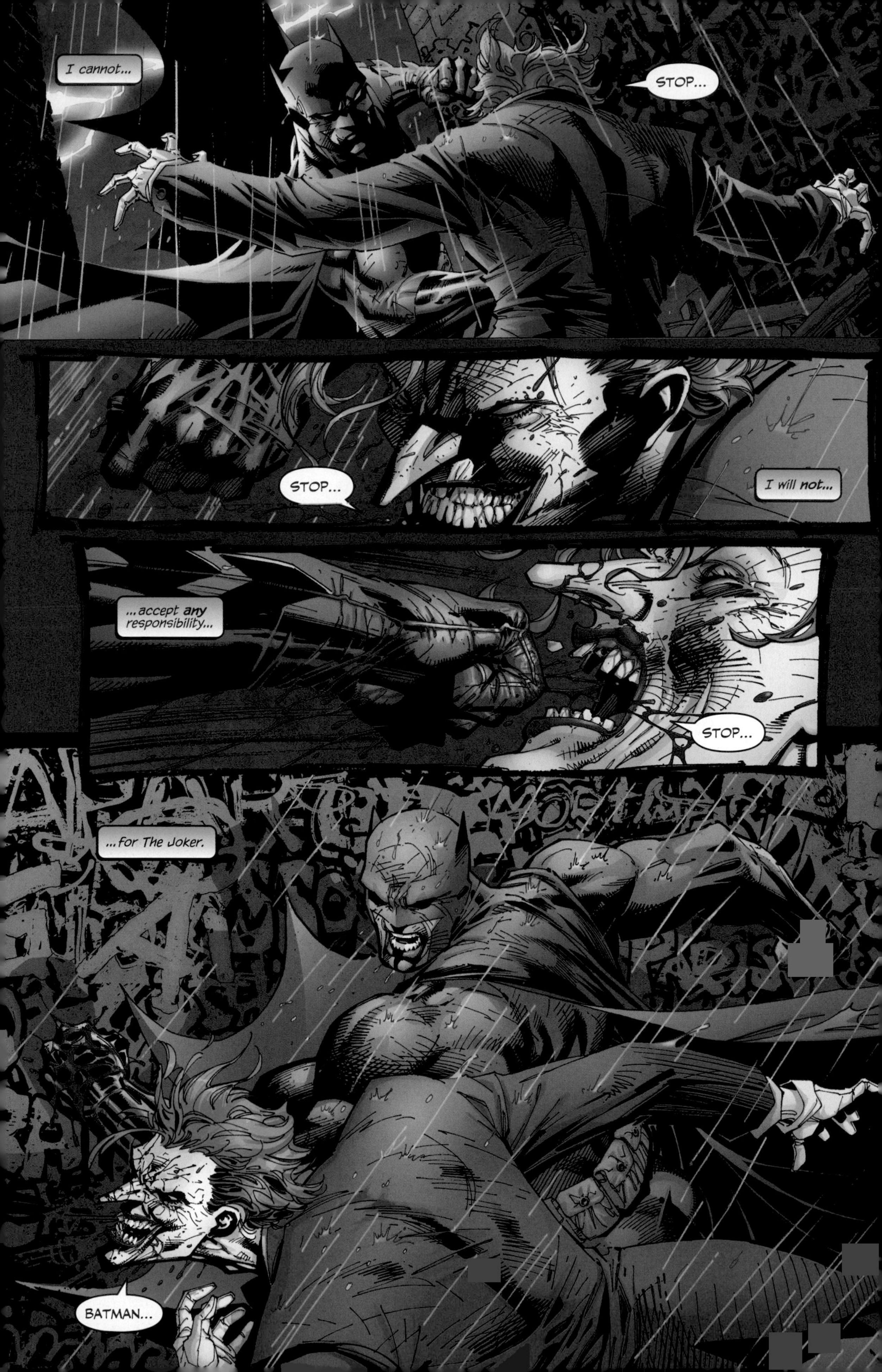

I cannot...
STOP...
STOP...
I will not...
...accept any responsibility...
STOP...
...for The Joker.
BATMAN...

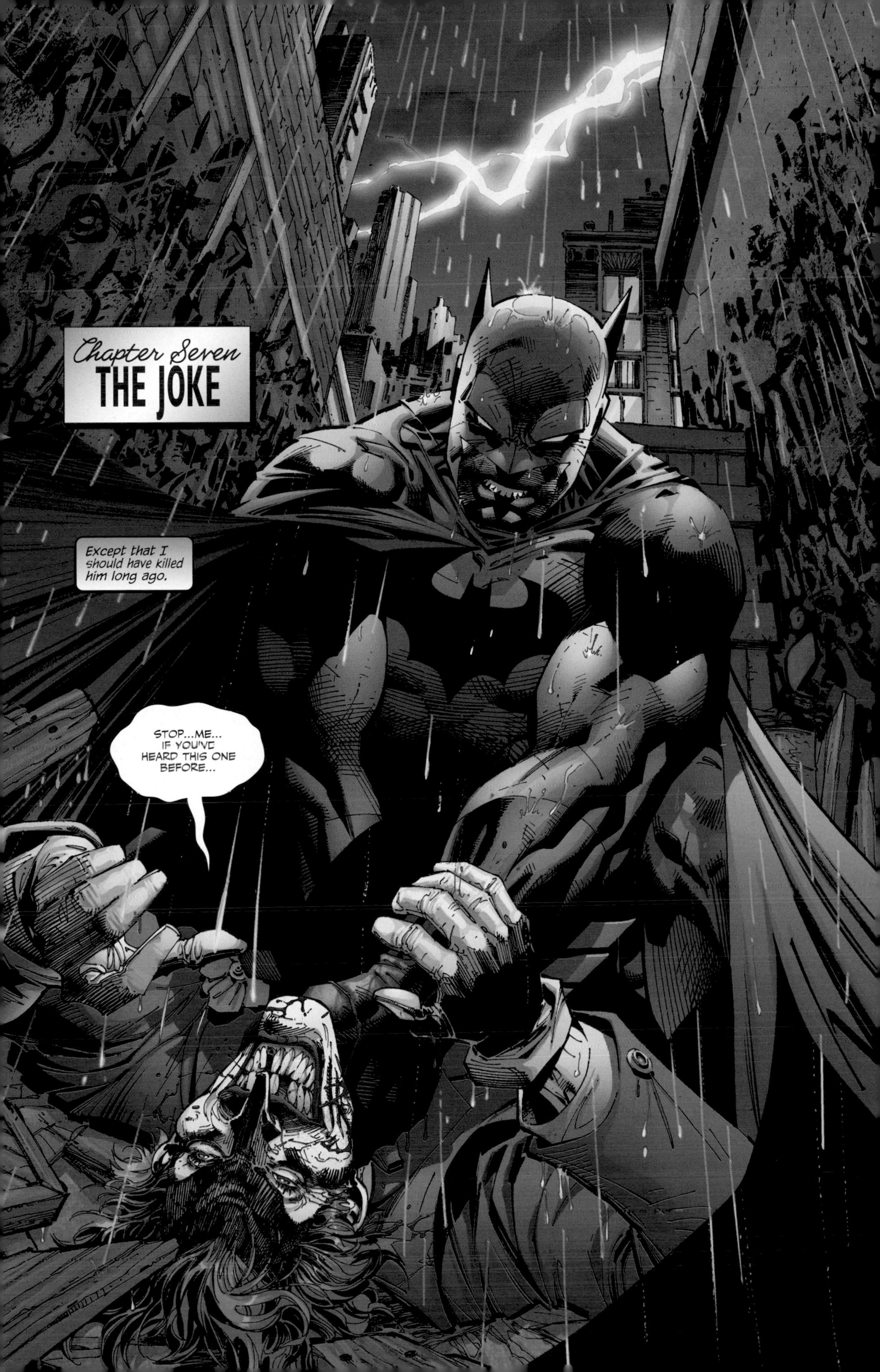
Chapter Seven
THE JOKE
Except that I should have killed him long ago.
STOP...ME... IF YOU'VE HEARD THIS ONE BEFORE...

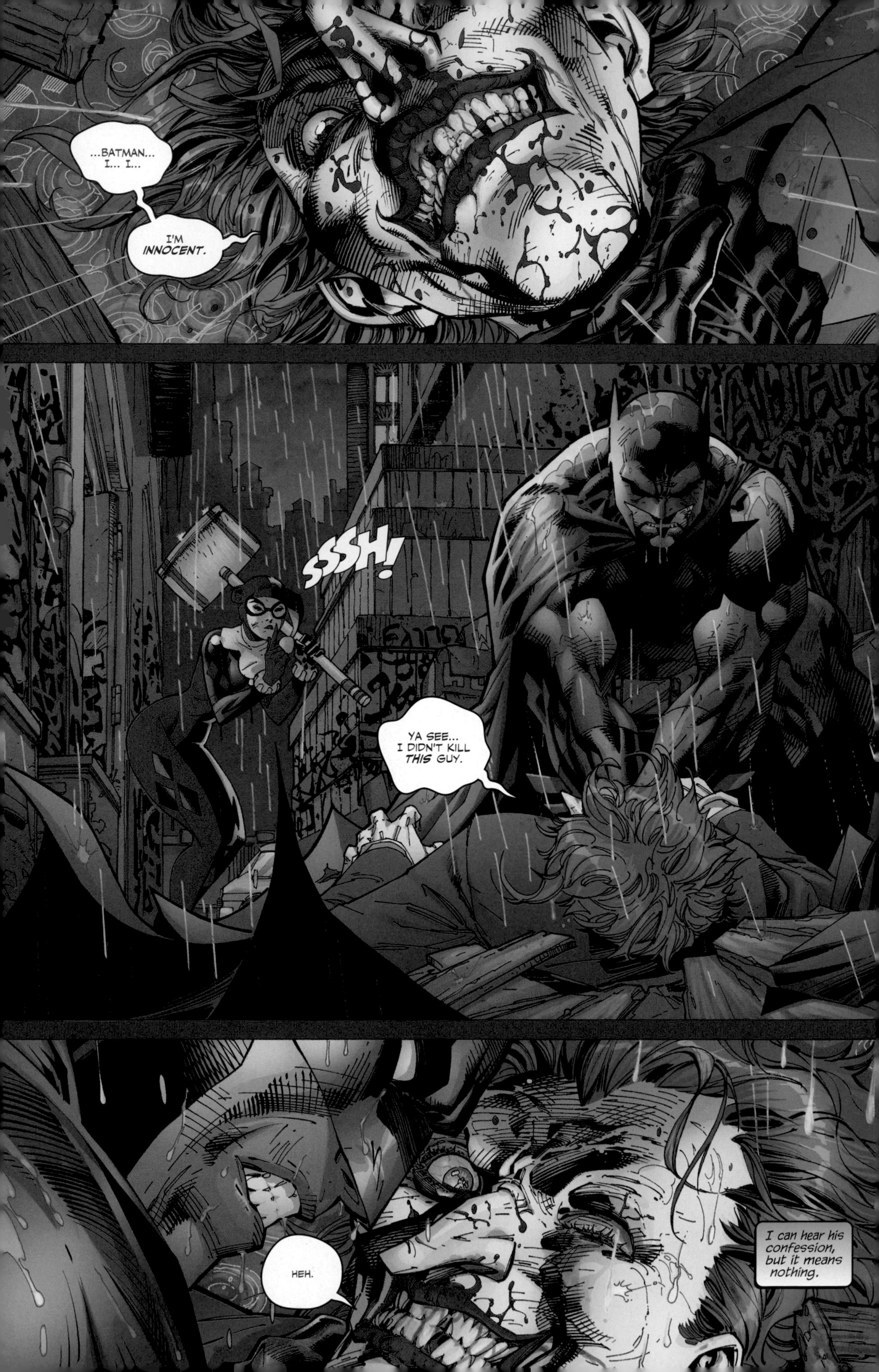
...BATMAN... I... I...
I'M INNOCENT.
SSSH!
YA SEE... I DIDN'T KILL THIS GUY.
HEH.
I can hear his confession, but it means nothing.

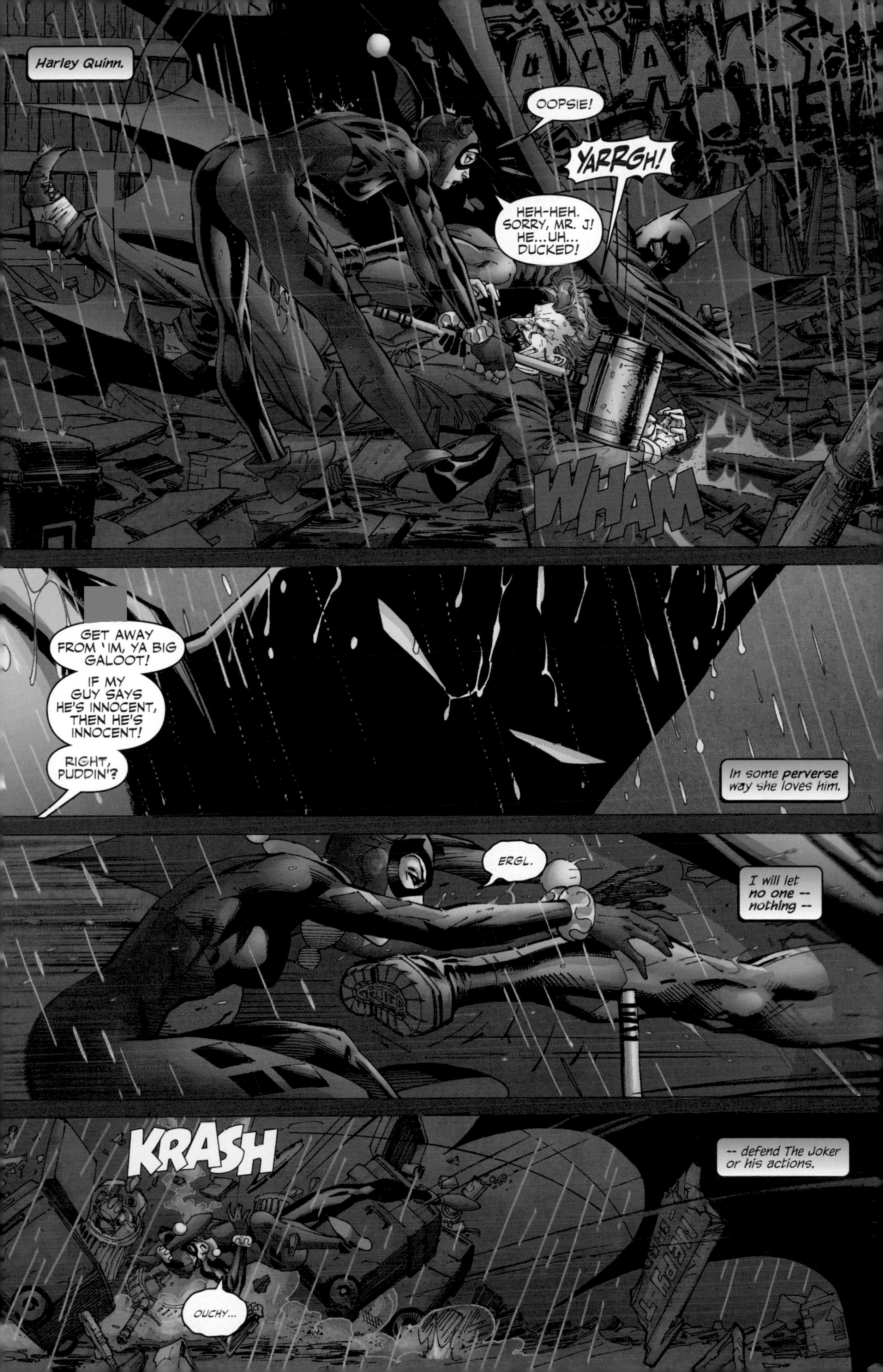
Harley Quinn.
OOPSIE!
YARRGH!
HEH-HEH. SORRY, MR. J! HE...UH... DUCKED!
WHAM
GET AWAY FROM 'IM, YA BIG GALOOT!
IF MY GUY SAYS HE'S INNOCENT, THEN HE'S INNOCENT!
RIGHT, PUDDIN'?
In some perverse way she loves him.
ERGL.
I will let no one -- nothing --
KRASH
-- defend The Joker or his actions.
OUCHY...

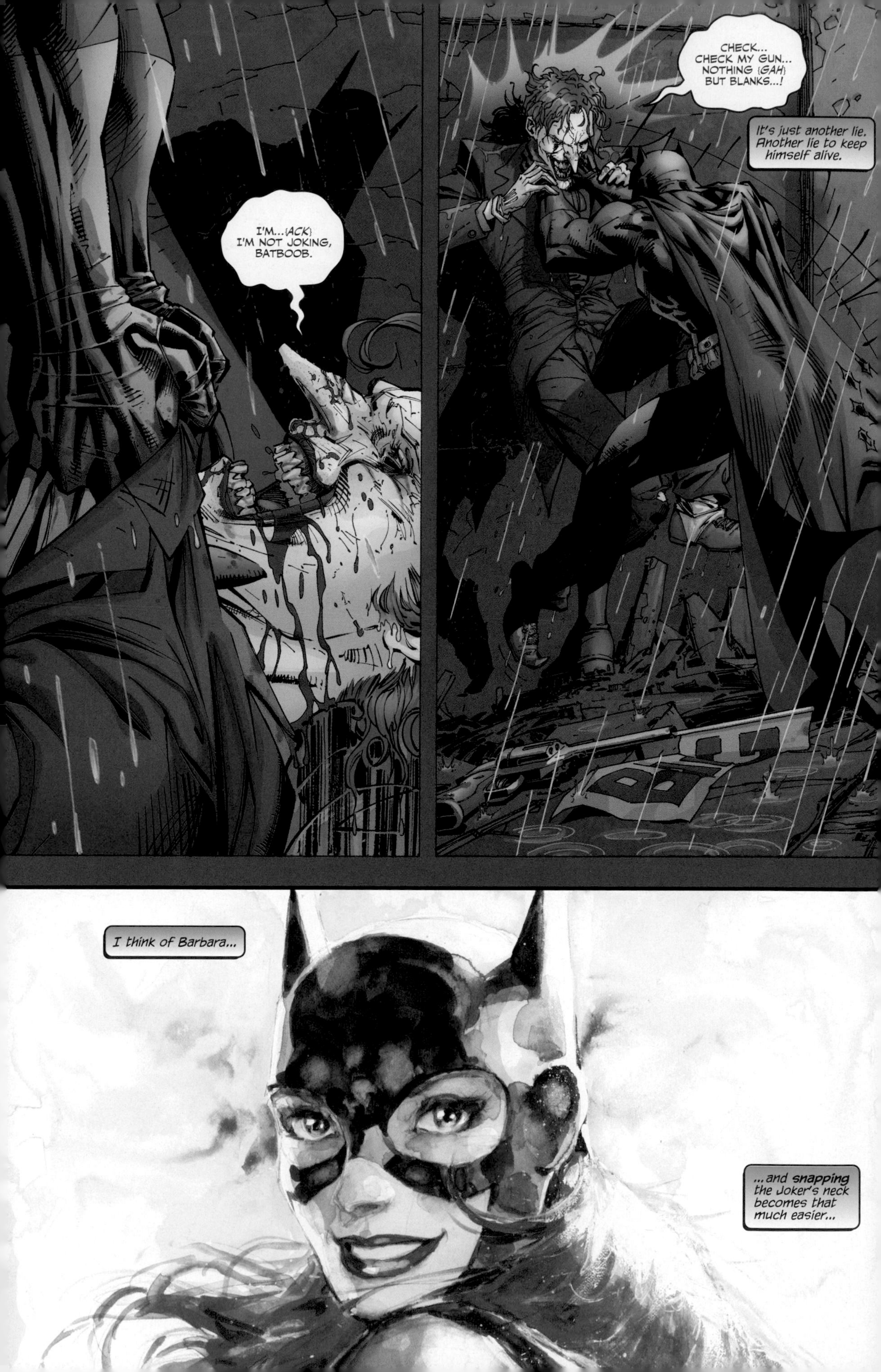
I'M...{ACK} I'M NOT JOKING, BATBOOB.
CHECK... CHECK MY GUN... NOTHING {GAH} BUT BLANKS...!
It's just another lie. Another lie to keep himself alive.
I think of Barbara...
...and snapping the Joker's neck becomes that much easier...

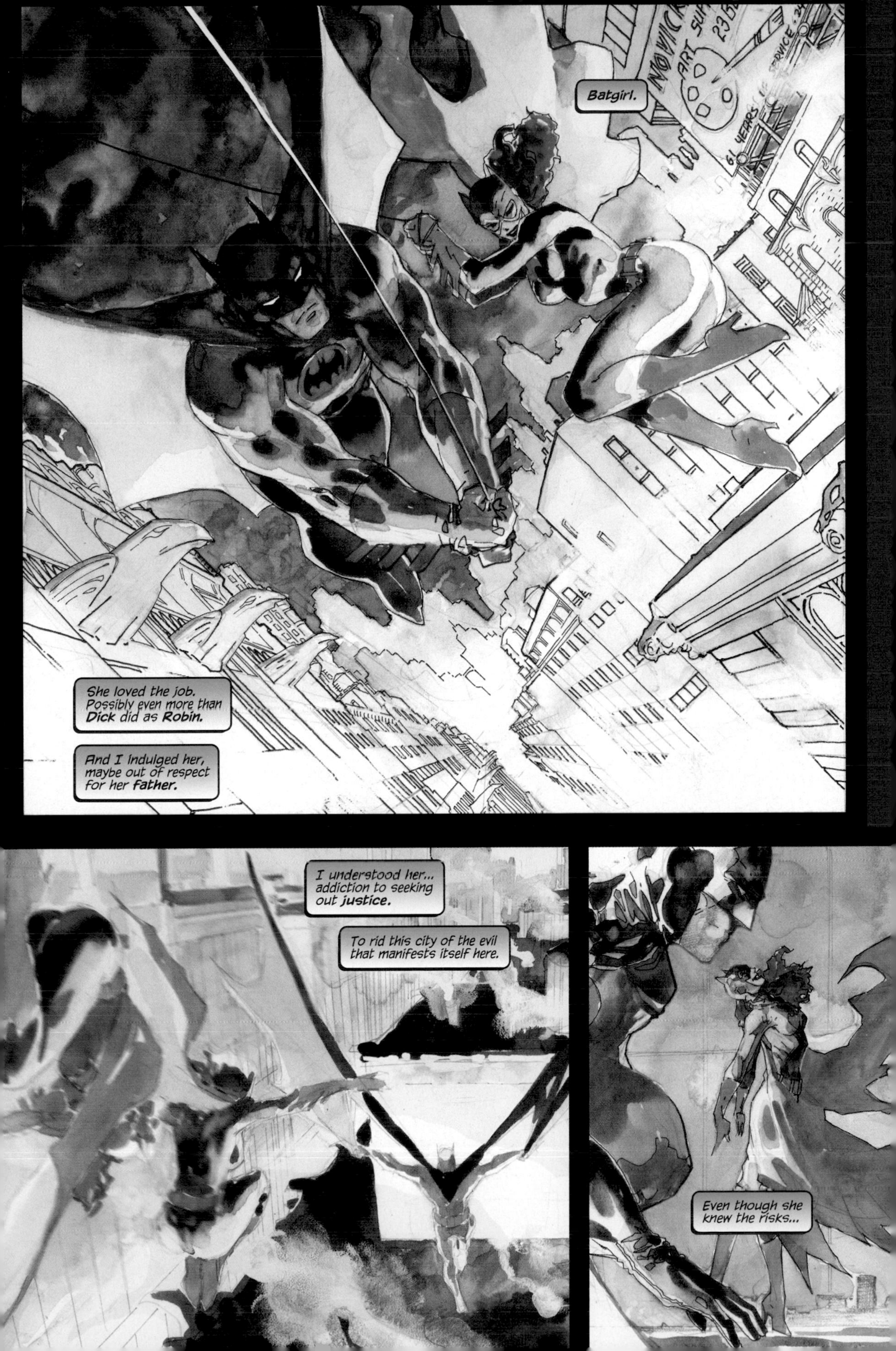
Batgirl.
She loved the job. Possibly even more than **Dick** did as **Robin.**
And I indulged her, maybe out of respect for her **father.**
I understood her... addiction to seeking out **justice.**
To rid this city of the evil that manifests itself here.
Even though she knew the risks...

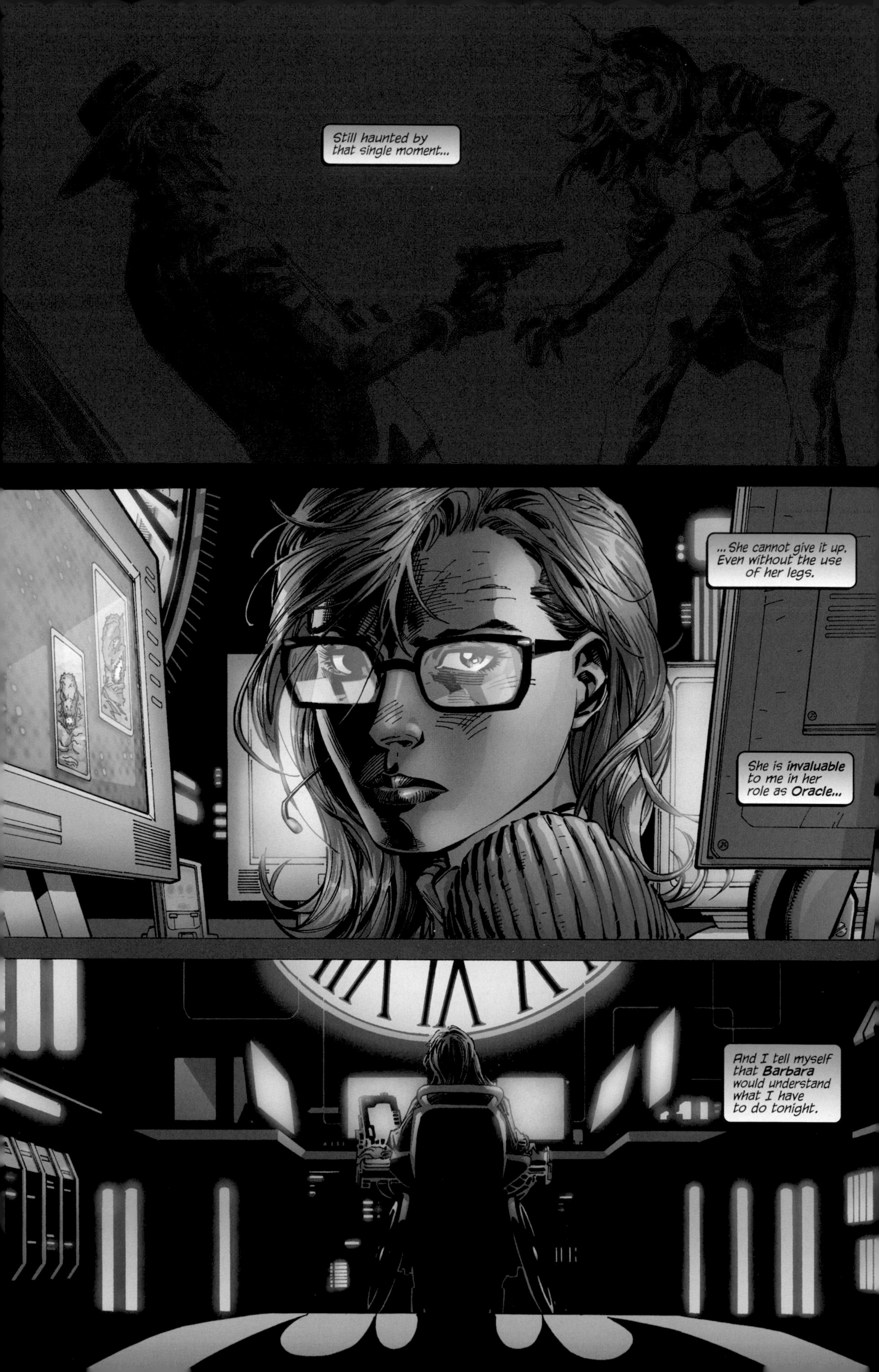

Still haunted by that single moment...
...She cannot give it up. Even without the use of her legs.
She is **invaluable** to me in her role as **Oracle**...
And I tell myself that **Barbara** would understand what I have to do tonight.

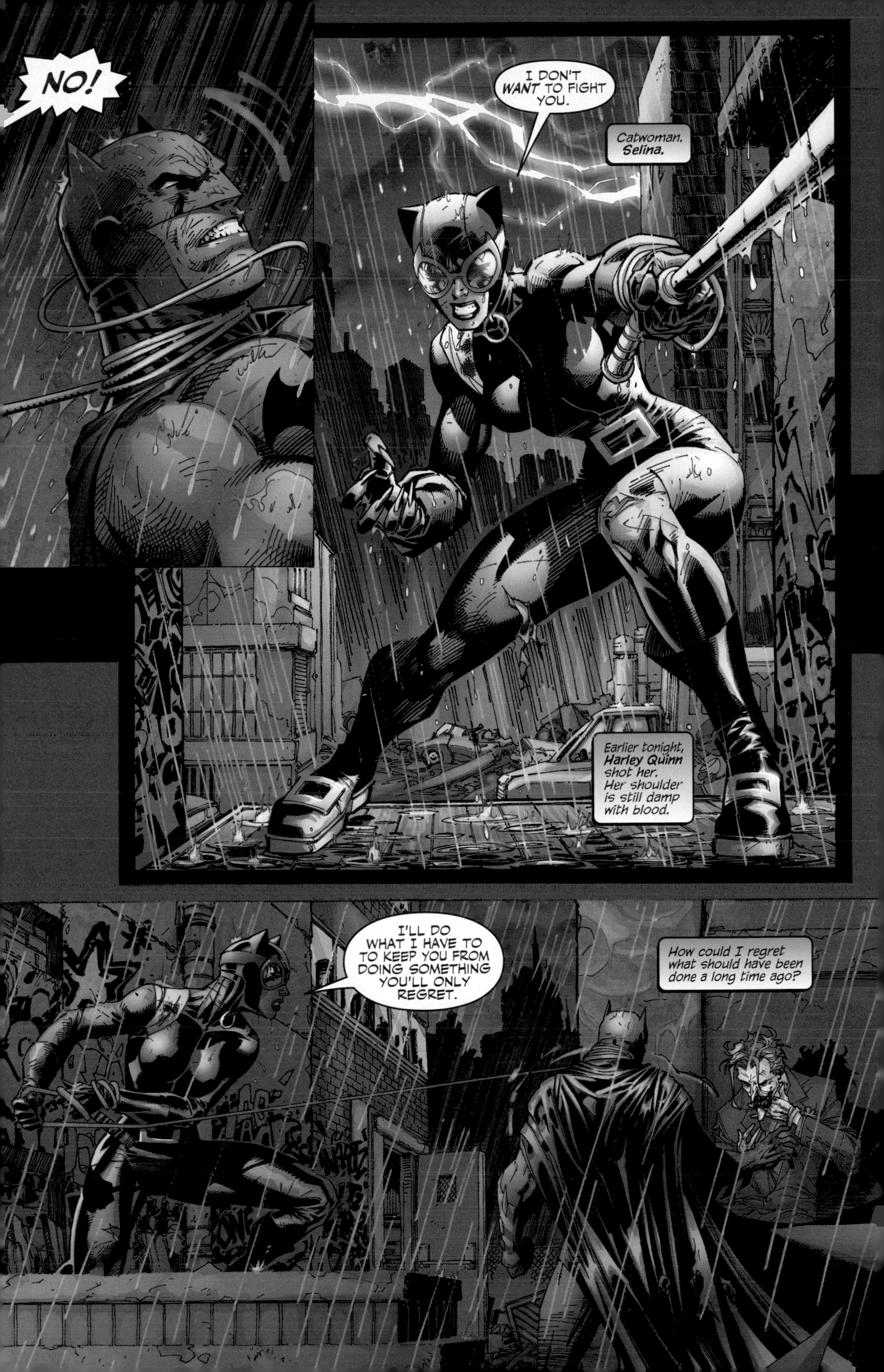
NO!
I DON'T WANT TO FIGHT YOU.
Catwoman. Selina.
Earlier tonight, Harley Quinn shot her. Her shoulder is still damp with blood.
I'LL DO WHAT I HAVE TO TO KEEP YOU FROM DOING SOMETHING YOU'LL ONLY REGRET.
How could I regret what should have been done a long time ago?

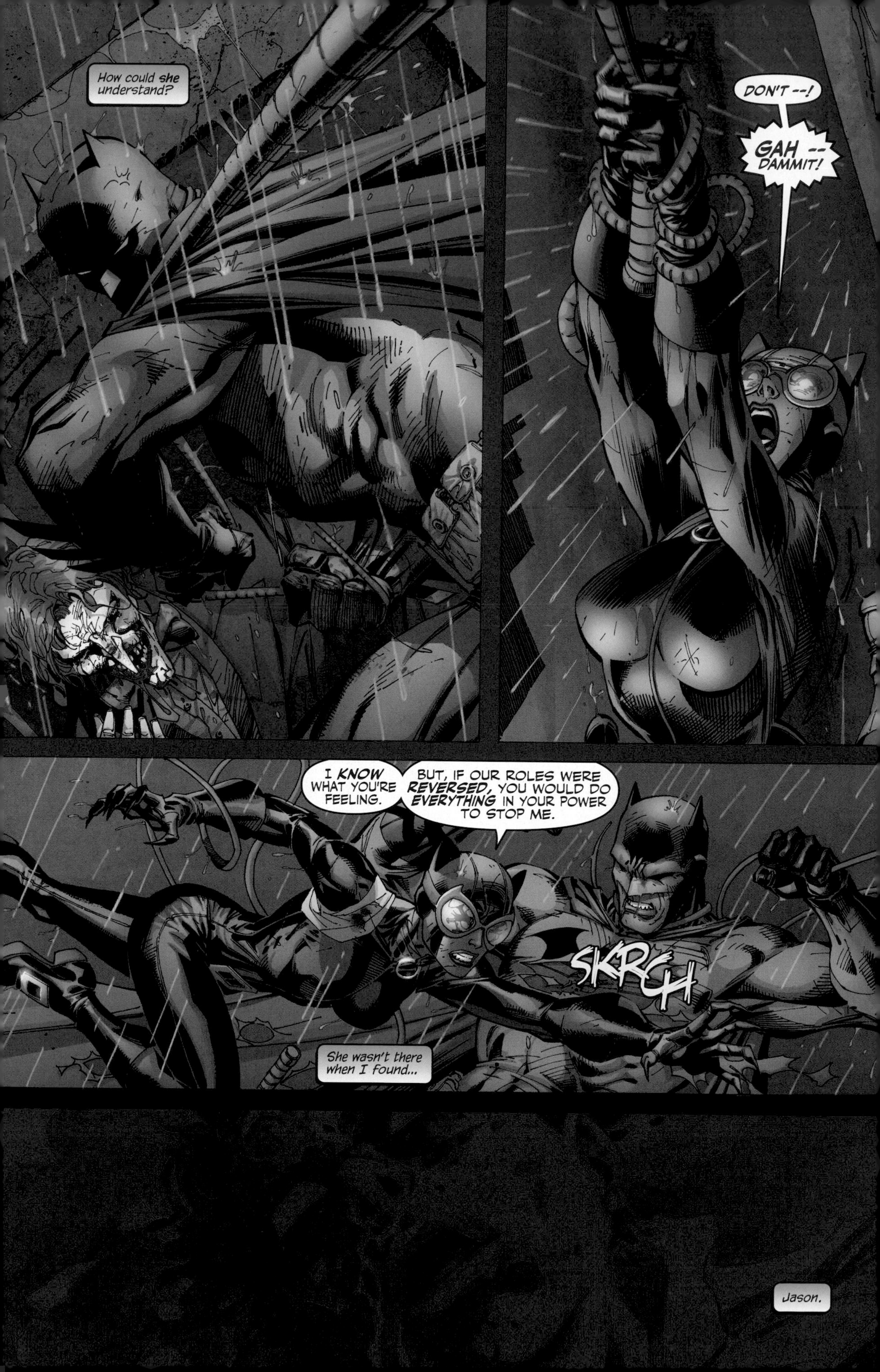
How could she understand?
DON'T --!
GAH -- DAMMIT!
I KNOW WHAT YOU'RE FEELING.
BUT, IF OUR ROLES WERE REVERSED, YOU WOULD DO EVERYTHING IN YOUR POWER TO STOP ME.
SKRCH
She wasn't there when I found...
Jason.

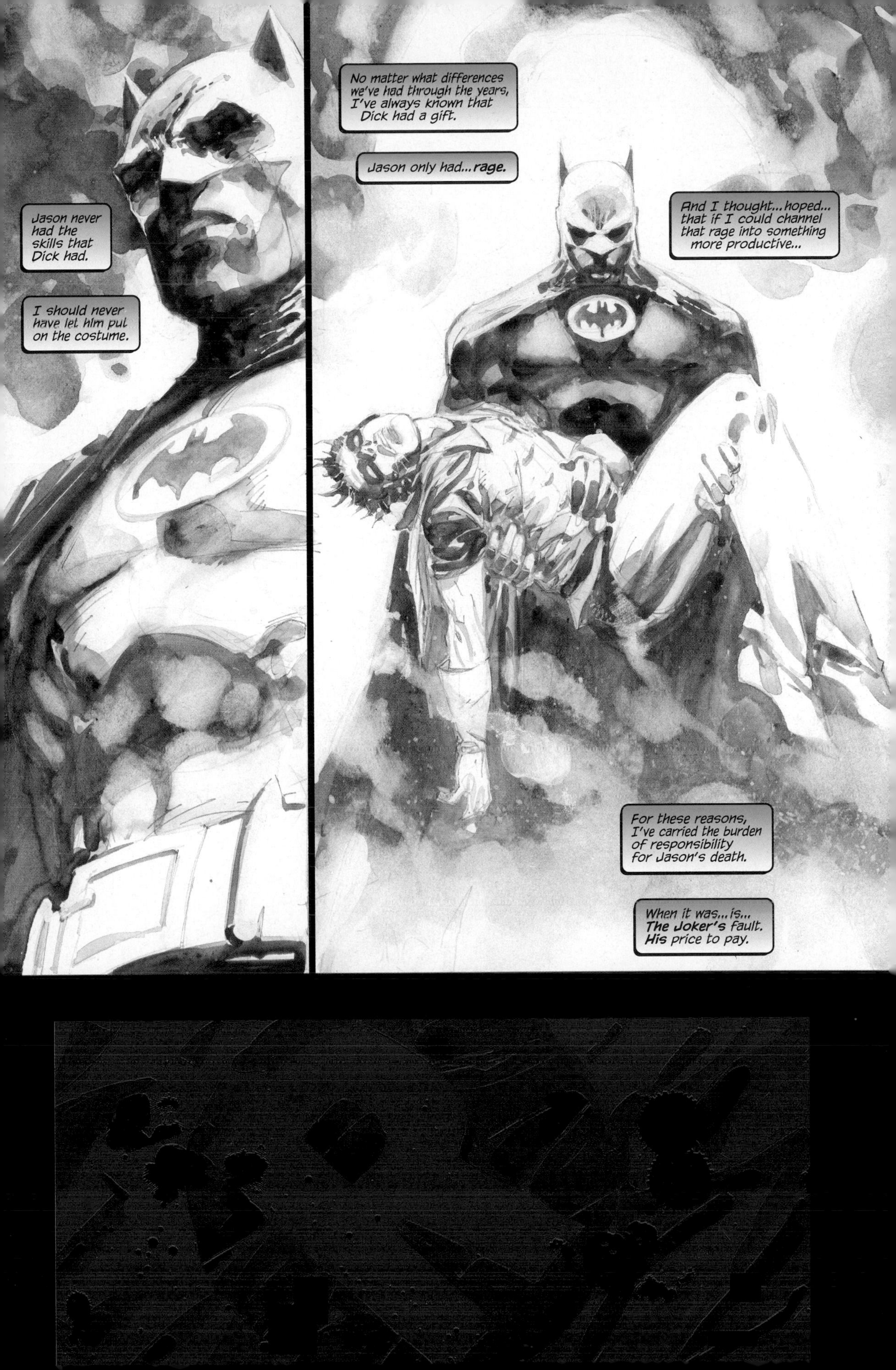
Jason never had the skills that Dick had.
I should never have let him put on the costume.
No matter what differences we've had through the years, I've always known that Dick had a gift.
Jason only had... **rage.**
And I thought... hoped... that if I could channel that rage into something more productive...
For these reasons, I've carried the burden of responsibility for Jason's death.
When it was... is... **The Joker's** fault. **His** price to pay.

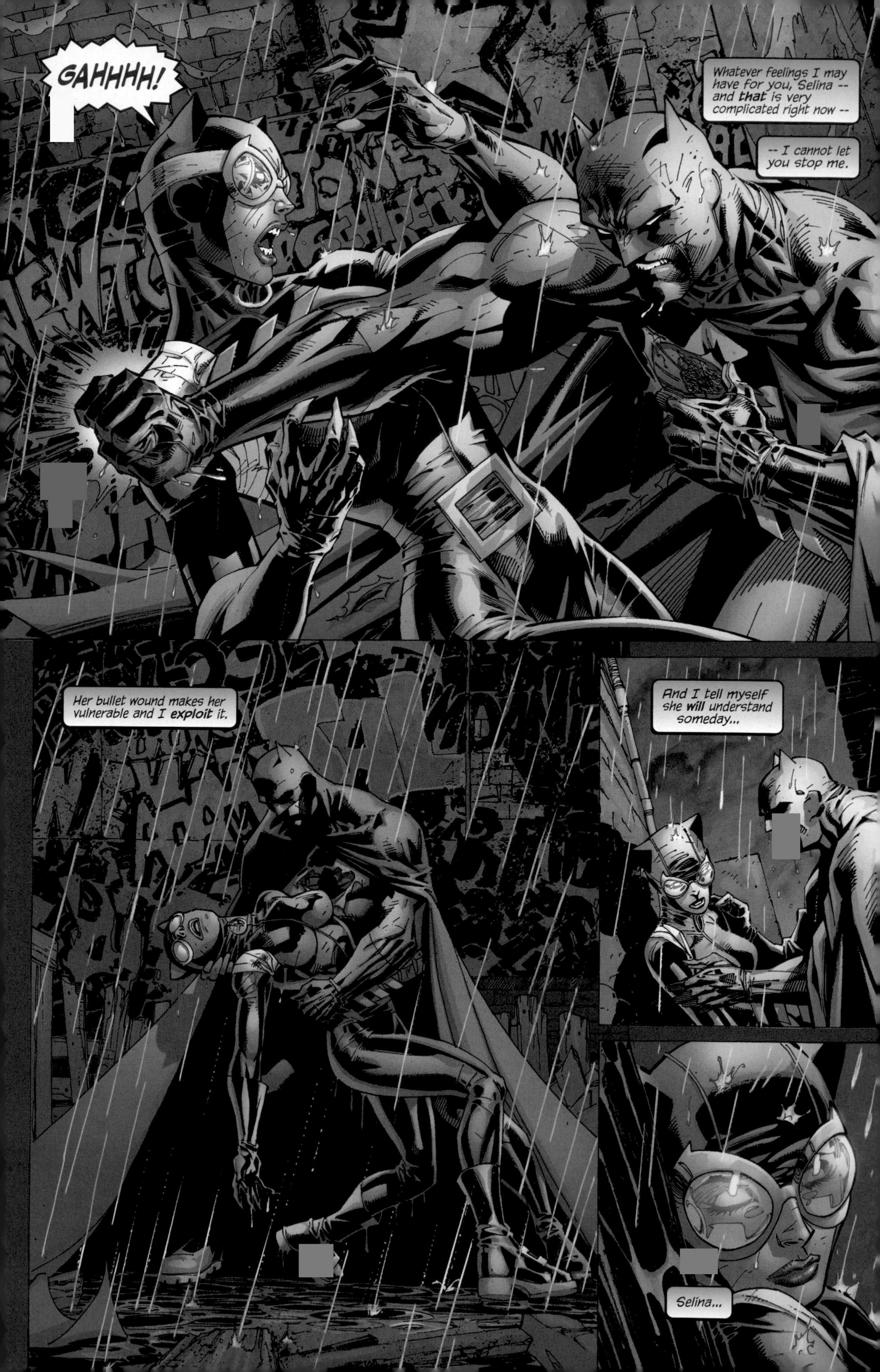
GAHHHH!
Whatever feelings I may have for you, Selina -- and **that** is very complicated right now --
-- I cannot let you stop me.
Her bullet wound makes her vulnerable and I **exploit** it.
And I tell myself she **will** understand someday...
Selina...

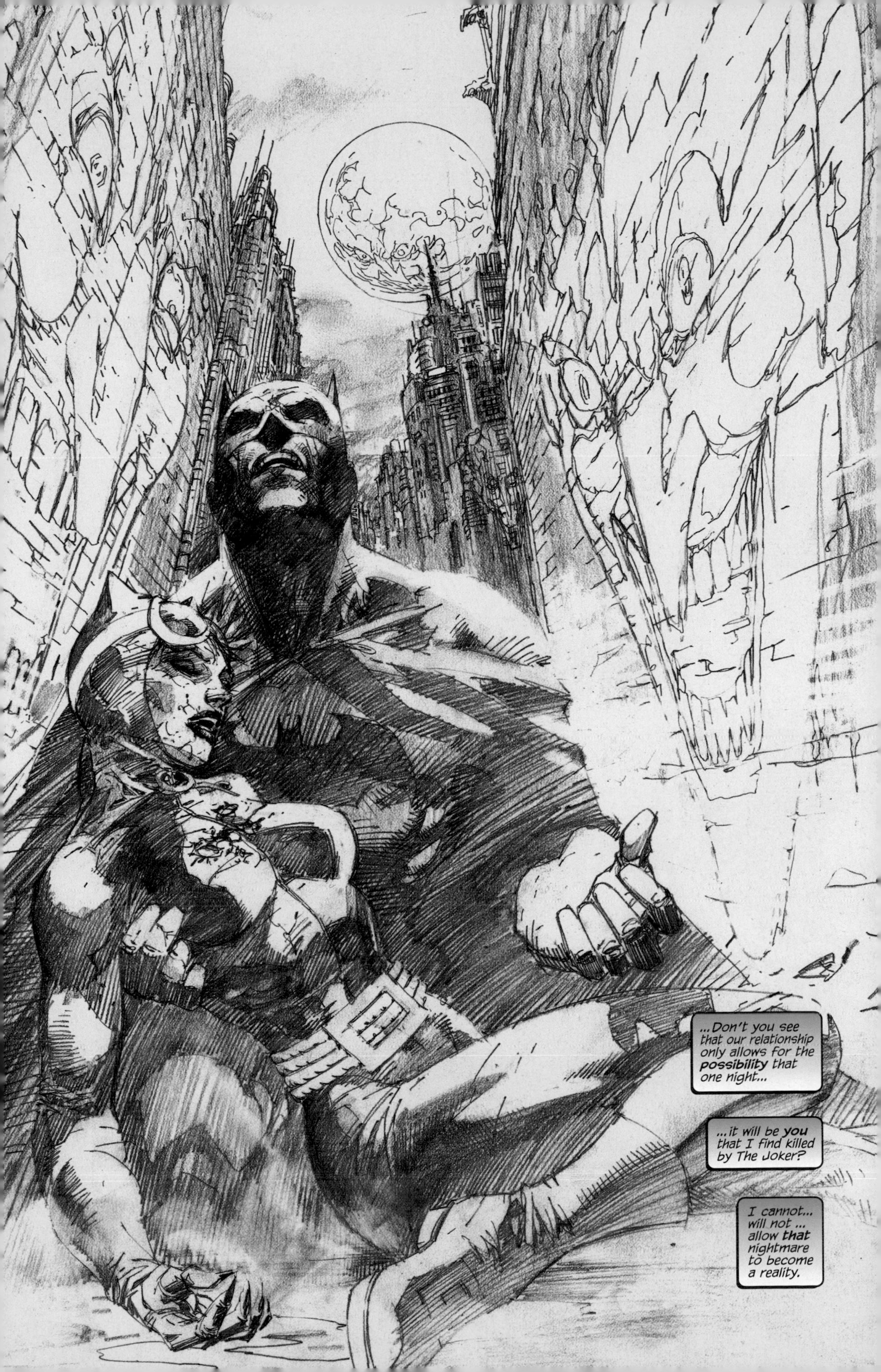
...Don't you see that our relationship only allows for the **possibility** that one night...
...it will be **you** that I find killed by The Joker?
I cannot... will not ... allow **that** nightmare to become a reality.

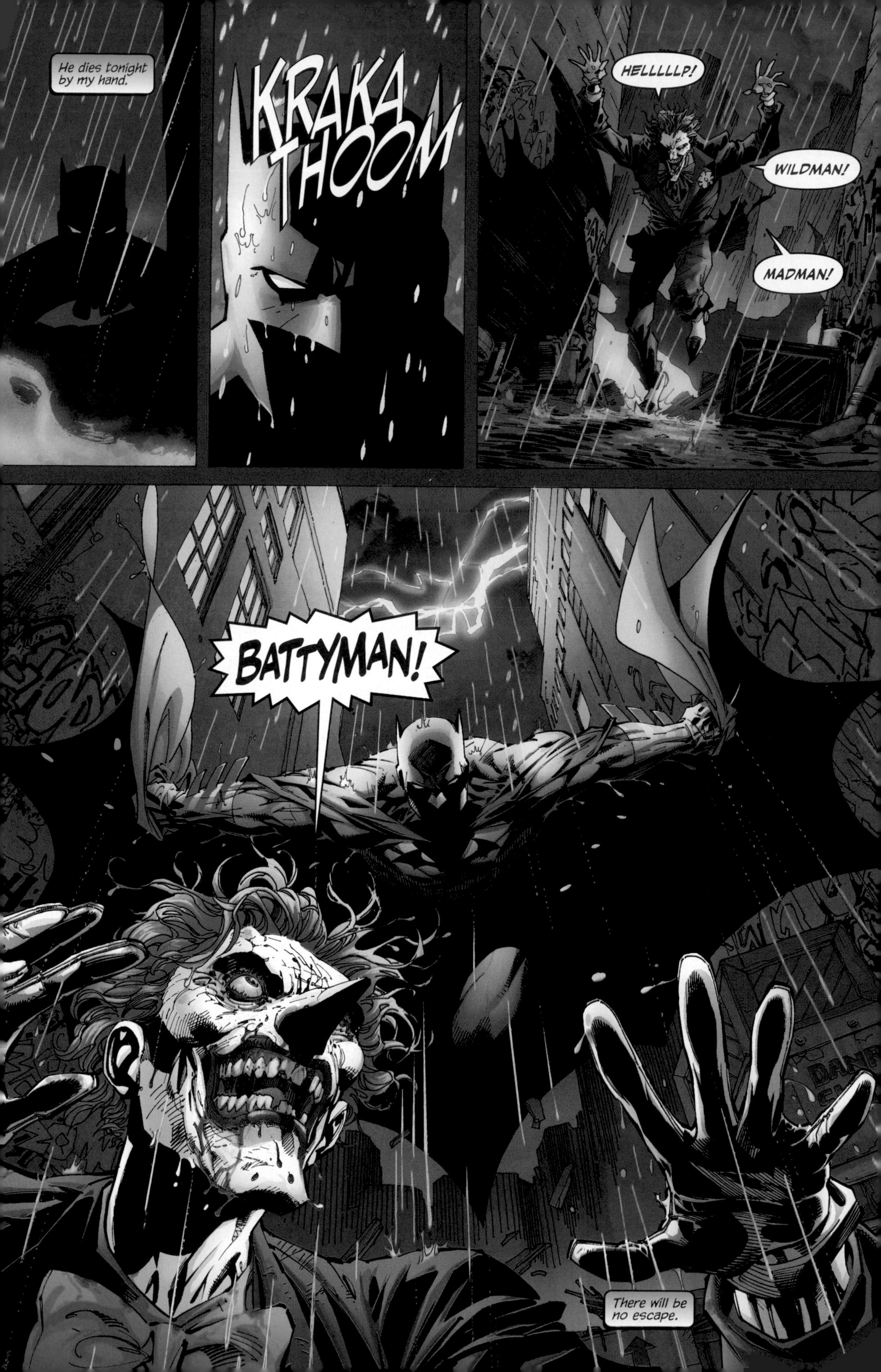
He dies tonight by my hand.
KRAKA THOOM
HELLLLLLP!
WILDMAN!
MADMAN!
BATTYMAN!
There will be no escape.

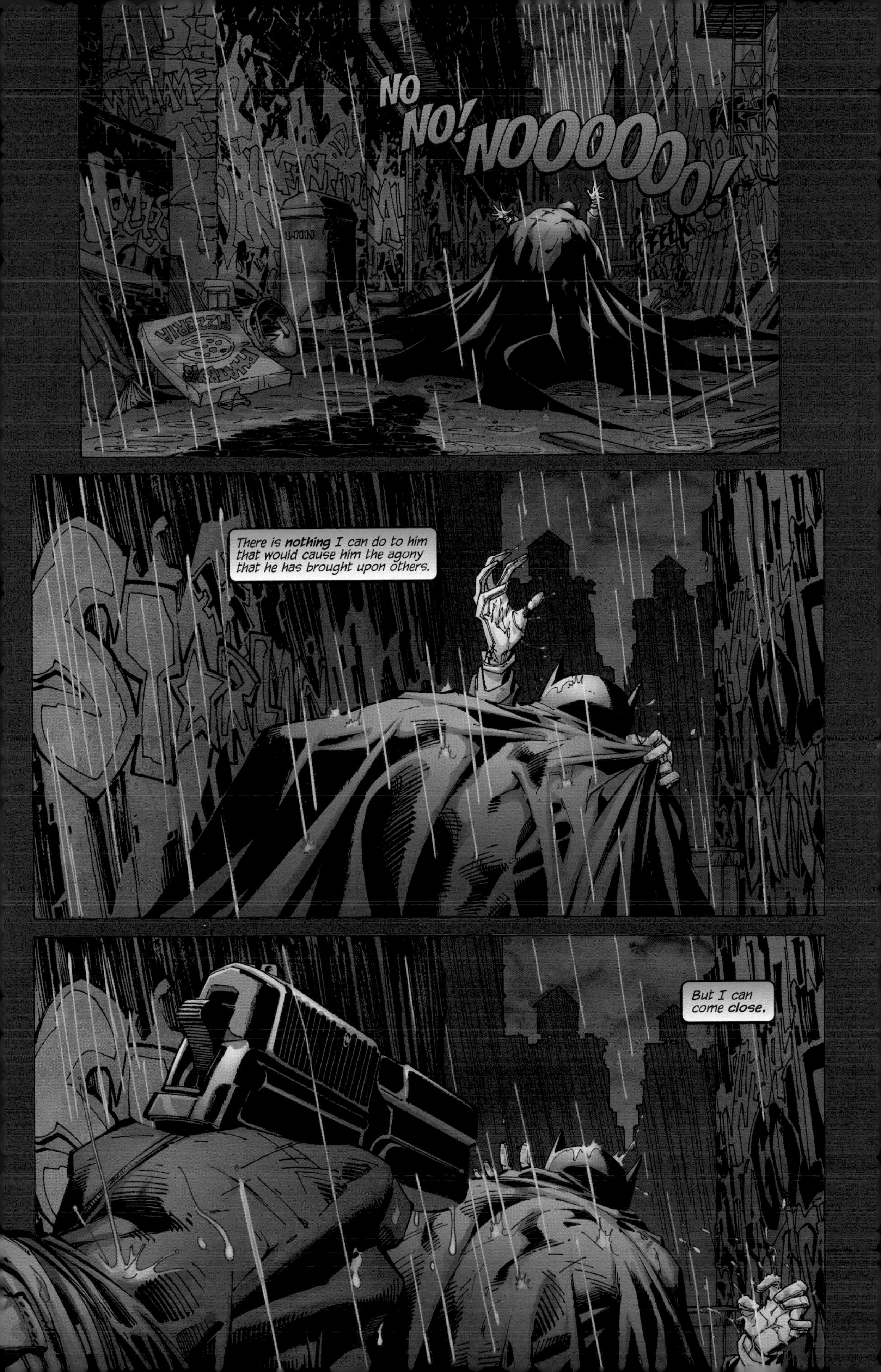
NO
NO! NOOOOOOO!
There is **nothing** I can do to him that would cause him the agony that he has brought upon others.
But I can come **close**.

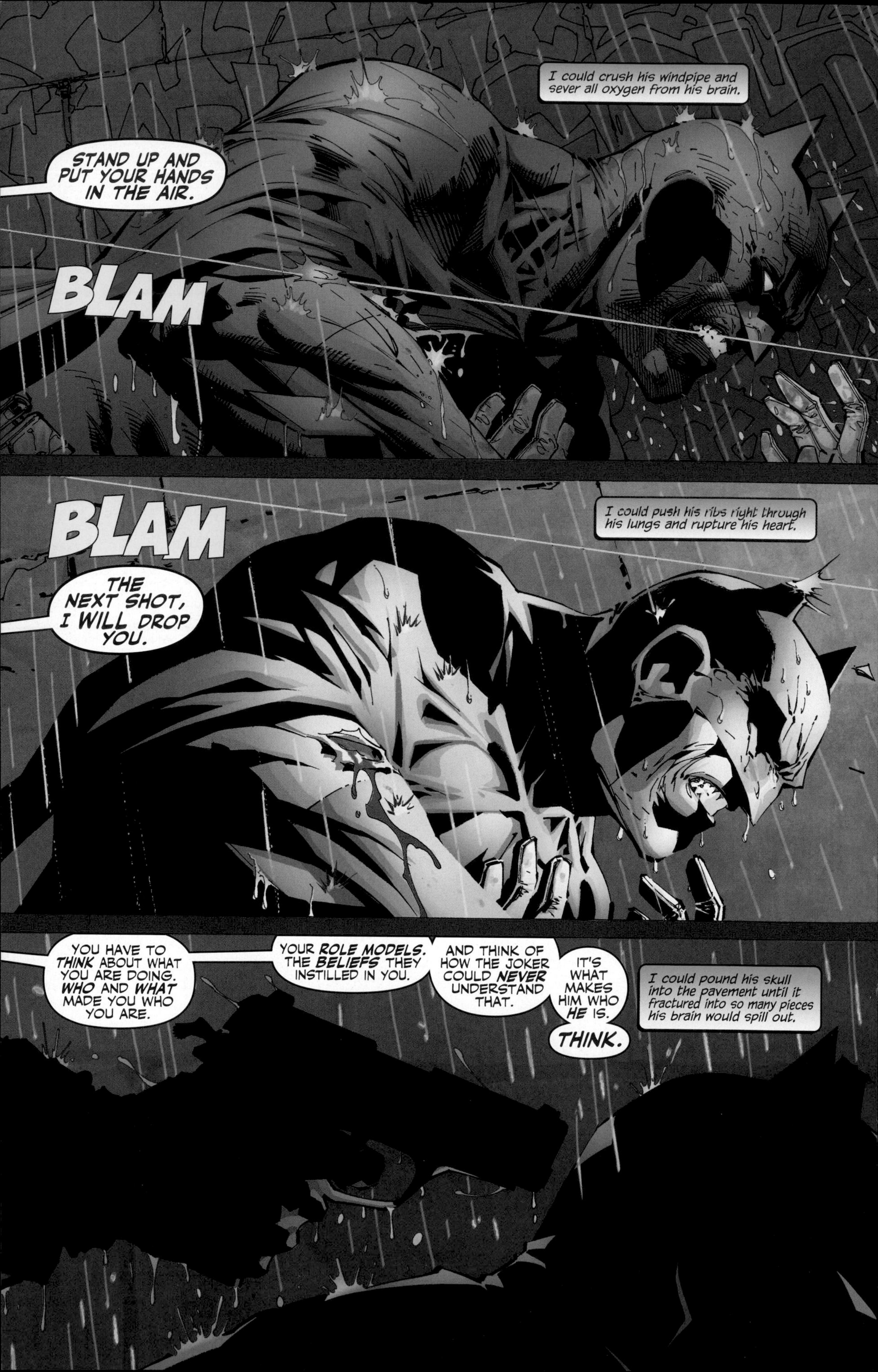

I could crush his windpipe and sever all oxygen from his brain.
STAND UP AND PUT YOUR HANDS IN THE AIR.
BLAM
I could push his ribs right through his lungs and rupture his heart.
BLAM
THE NEXT SHOT, I WILL DROP YOU.
YOU HAVE TO THINK ABOUT WHAT YOU ARE DOING. WHO AND WHAT MADE YOU WHO YOU ARE.
YOUR ROLE MODELS. THE BELIEFS THEY INSTILLED IN YOU.
AND THINK OF HOW THE JOKER COULD NEVER UNDERSTAND THAT.
IT'S WHAT MAKES HIM WHO HE IS.
THINK.
I could pound his skull into the pavement until it fractured into so many pieces his brain would spill out.

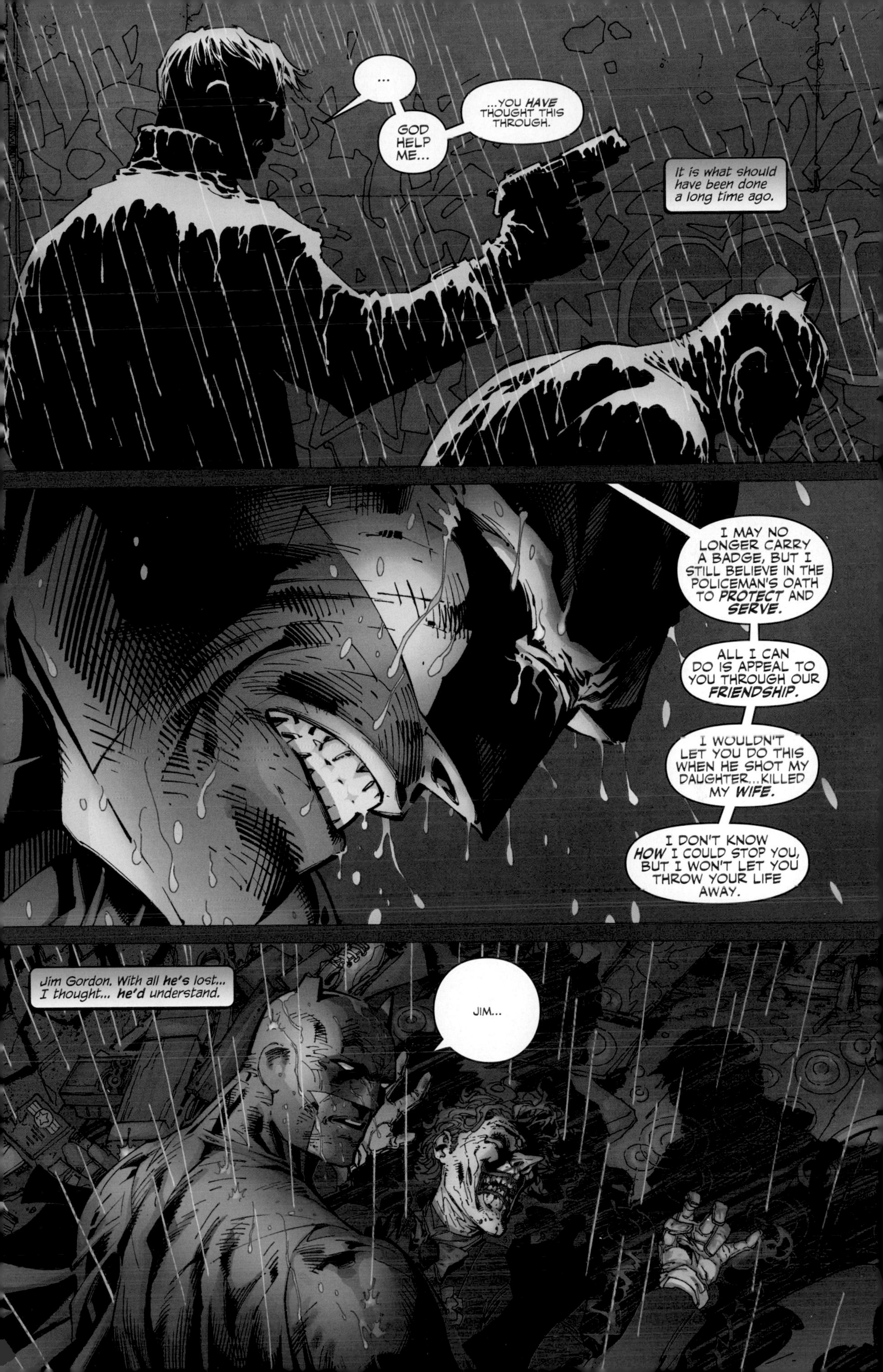
...
GOD HELP ME...
...YOU HAVE THOUGHT THIS THROUGH.
It is what should have been done a long time ago.
I MAY NO LONGER CARRY A BADGE, BUT I STILL BELIEVE IN THE POLICEMAN'S OATH TO PROTECT AND SERVE.
ALL I CAN DO IS APPEAL TO YOU THROUGH OUR FRIENDSHIP.
I WOULDN'T LET YOU DO THIS WHEN HE SHOT MY DAUGHTER...KILLED MY WIFE.
I DON'T KNOW HOW I COULD STOP YOU, BUT I WON'T LET YOU THROW YOUR LIFE AWAY.
Jim Gordon. With all he's lost... I thought... he'd understand.
JIM...

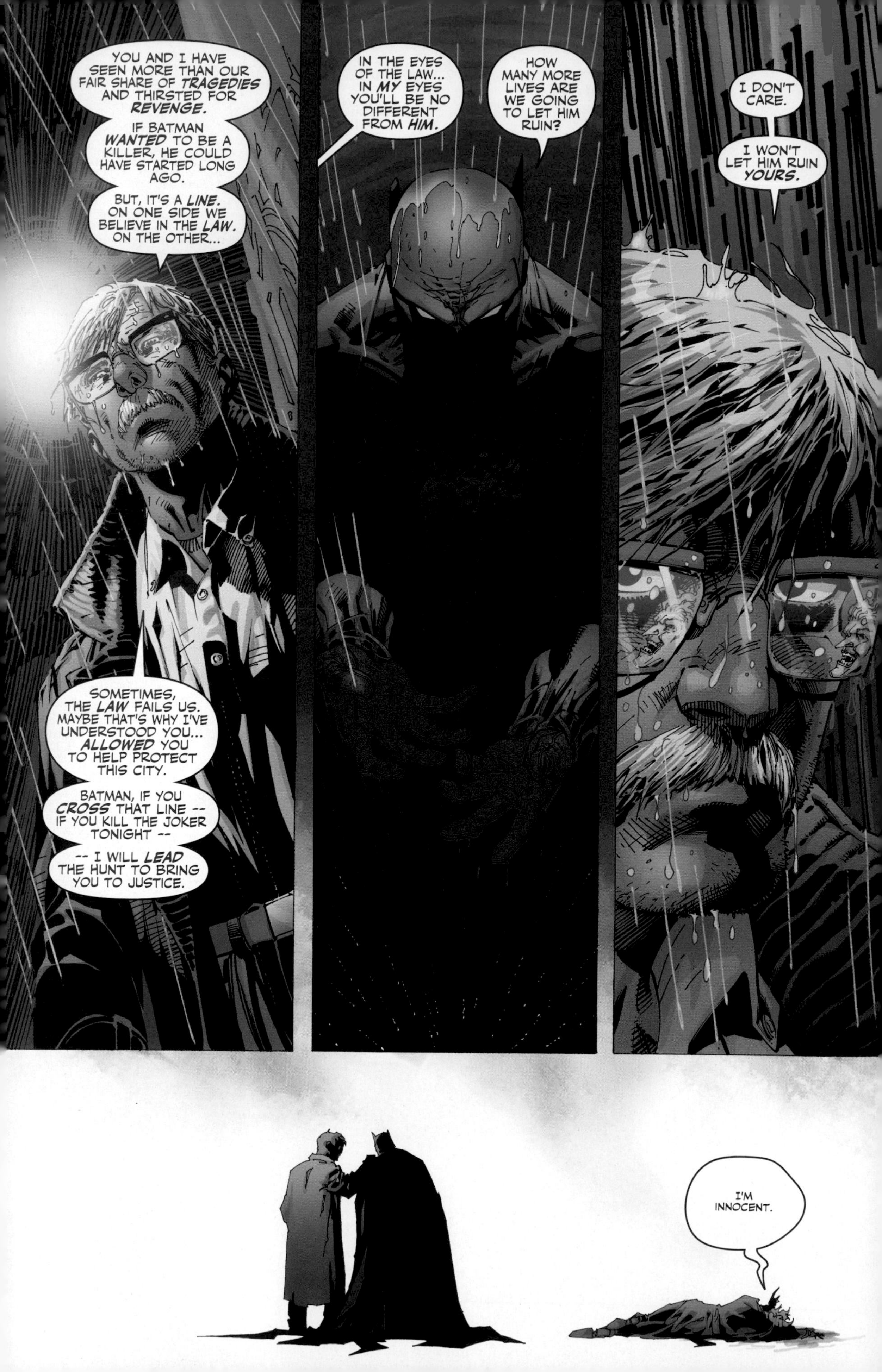
YOU AND I HAVE SEEN MORE THAN OUR FAIR SHARE OF TRAGEDIES AND THIRSTED FOR REVENGE.
IF BATMAN WANTED TO BE A KILLER, HE COULD HAVE STARTED LONG AGO.
BUT, IT'S A LINE. ON ONE SIDE WE BELIEVE IN THE LAW. ON THE OTHER...
SOMETIMES, THE LAW FAILS US. MAYBE THAT'S WHY I'VE UNDERSTOOD YOU... ALLOWED YOU TO HELP PROTECT THIS CITY.
BATMAN, IF YOU CROSS THAT LINE -- IF YOU KILL THE JOKER TONIGHT --
-- I WILL LEAD THE HUNT TO BRING YOU TO JUSTICE.
IN THE EYES OF THE LAW... IN MY EYES YOU'LL BE NO DIFFERENT FROM HIM.
HOW MANY MORE LIVES ARE WE GOING TO LET HIM RUIN?
I DON'T CARE.
I WON'T LET HIM RUIN YOURS.
I'M INNOCENT.

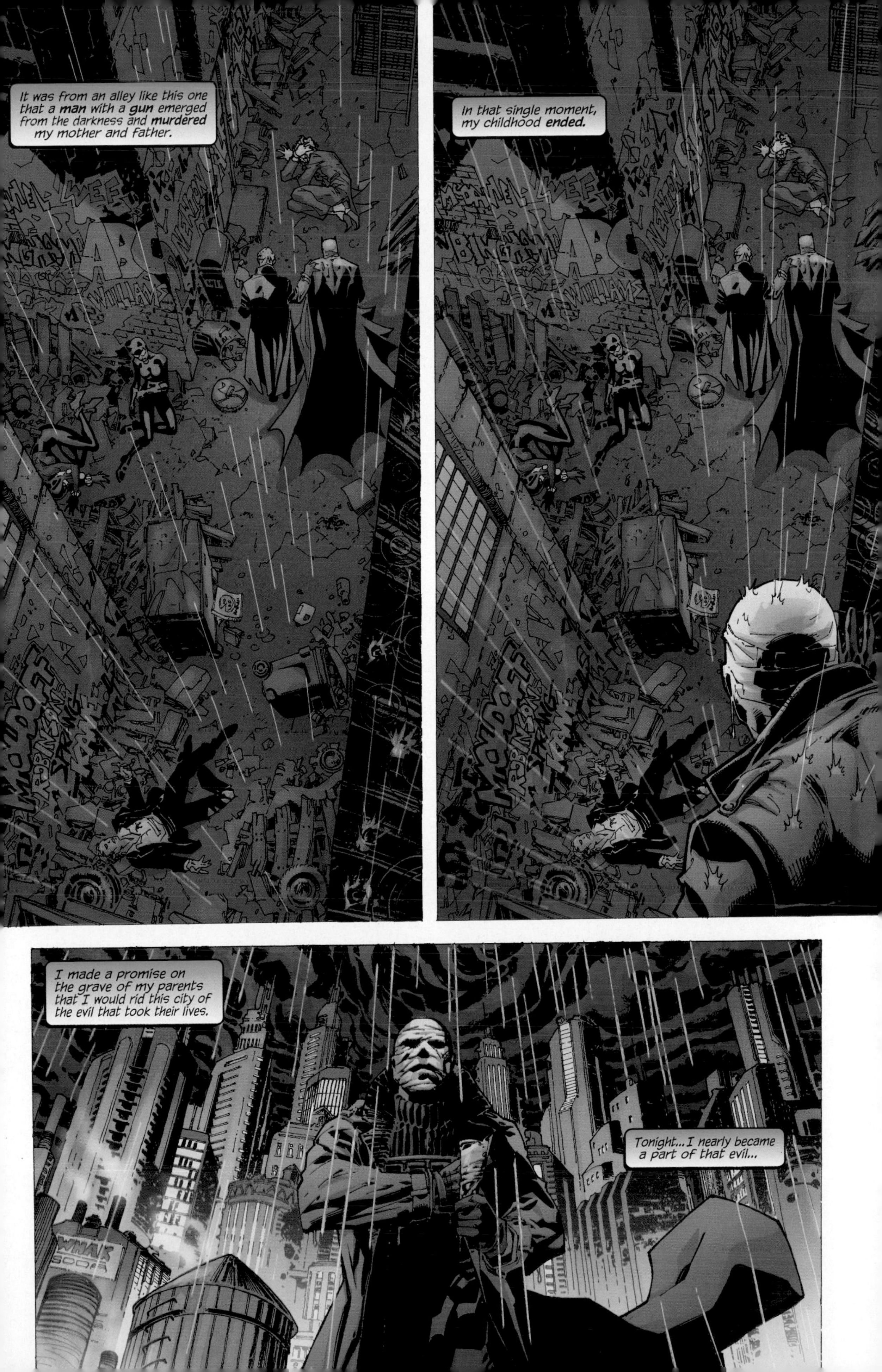
It was from an alley like this one that a **man** with a **gun** emerged from the darkness and **murdered** my mother and father.
In that single moment, my childhood **ended.**
I made a promise on the grave of my parents that I would rid this city of the evil that took their lives.
Tonight... I nearly became a part of that evil...

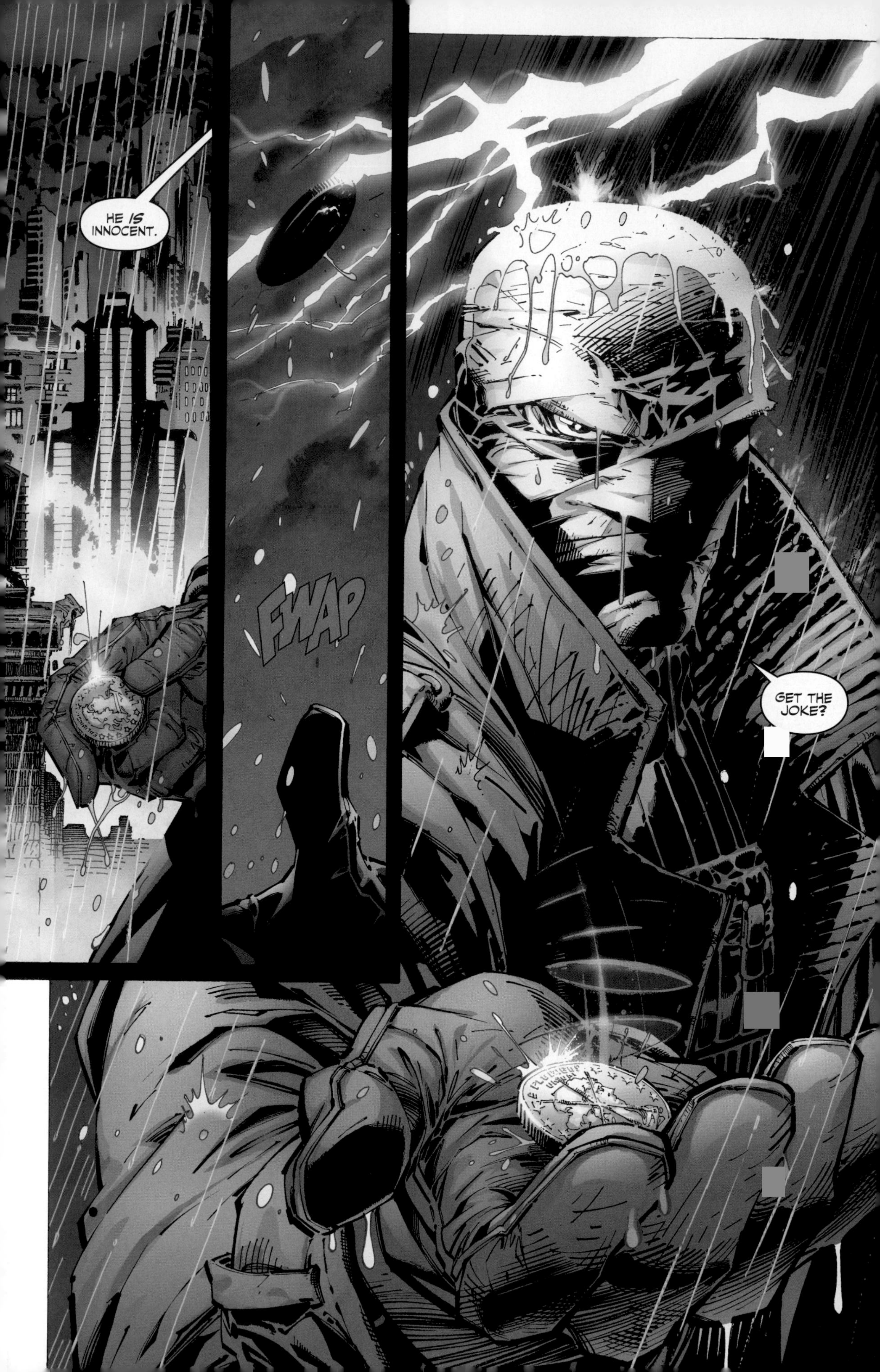
HE IS INNOCENT.
FWAP
GET THE JOKE?

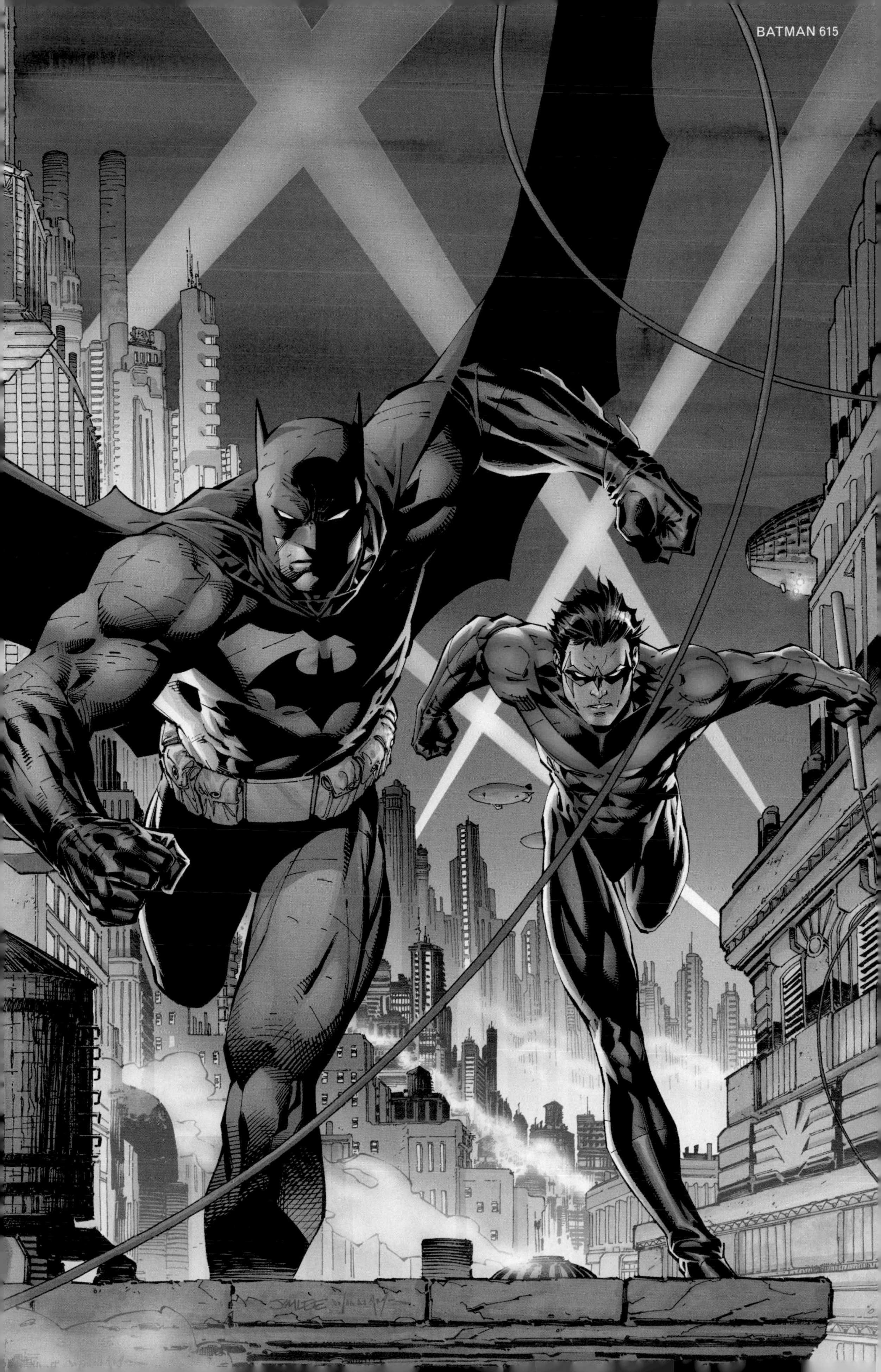

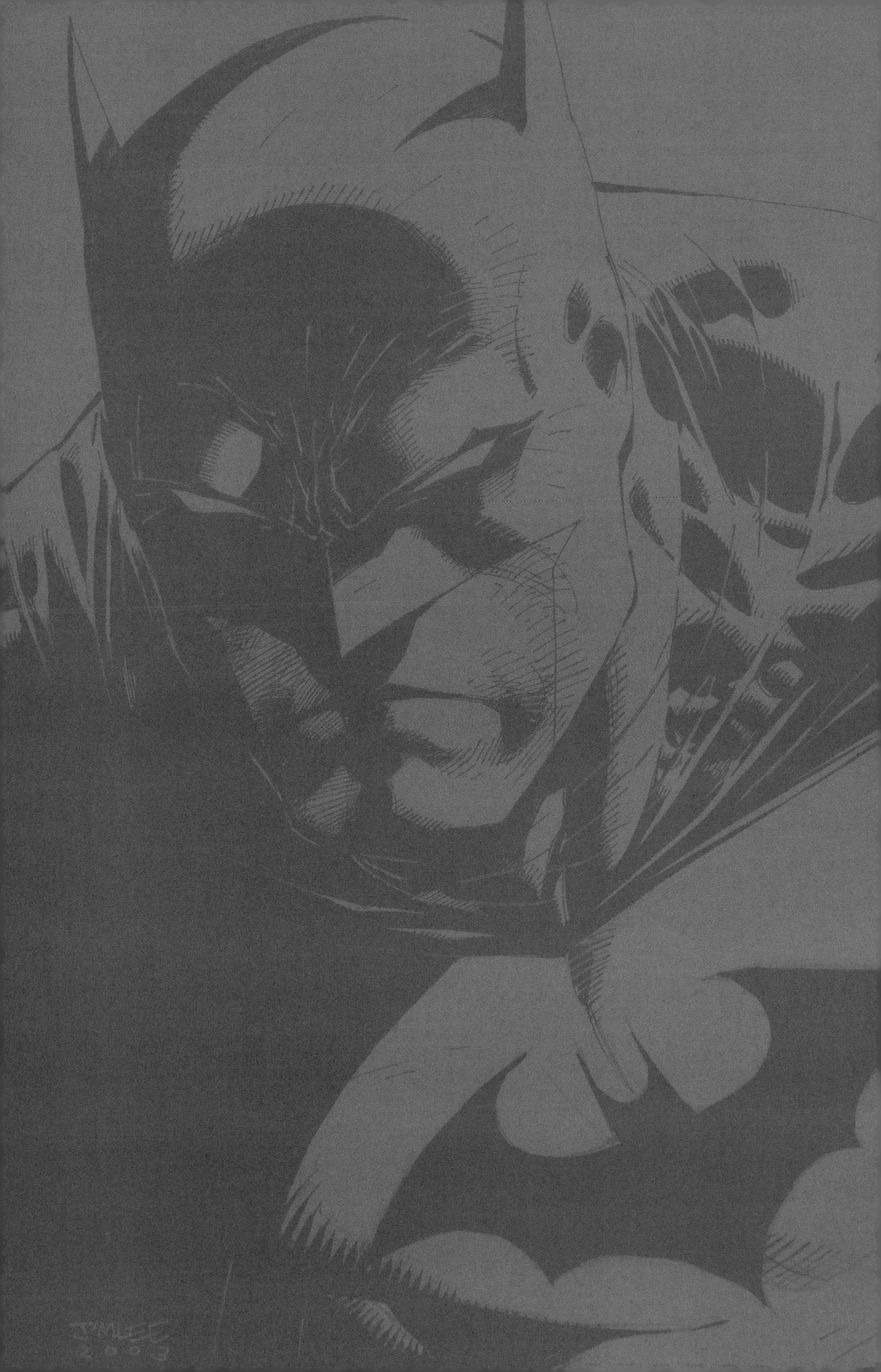
JIMLEE
2003

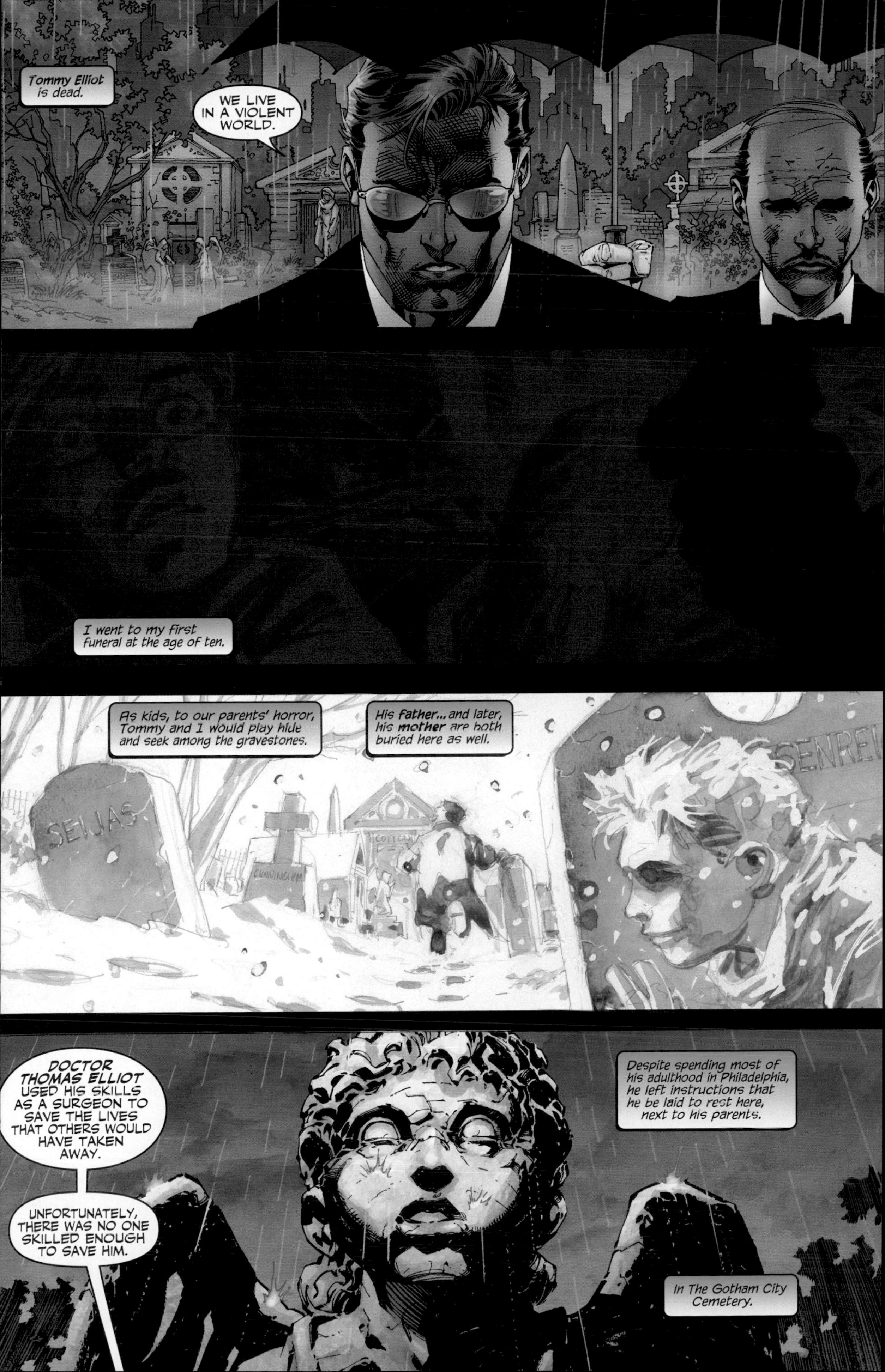
Tommy Elliot is dead.
WE LIVE IN A VIOLENT WORLD.
I went to my first funeral at the age of ten.
As kids, to our parents' horror, Tommy and I would play hide and seek among the gravestones.
His father... and later, his mother are both buried here as well.
DOCTOR THOMAS ELLIOT USED HIS SKILLS AS A SURGEON TO SAVE THE LIVES THAT OTHERS WOULD HAVE TAKEN AWAY.
UNFORTUNATELY, THERE WAS NO ONE SKILLED ENOUGH TO SAVE HIM.
Despite spending most of his adulthood in Philadelphia, he left instructions that he be laid to rest here, next to his parents.
In The Gotham City Cemetery.

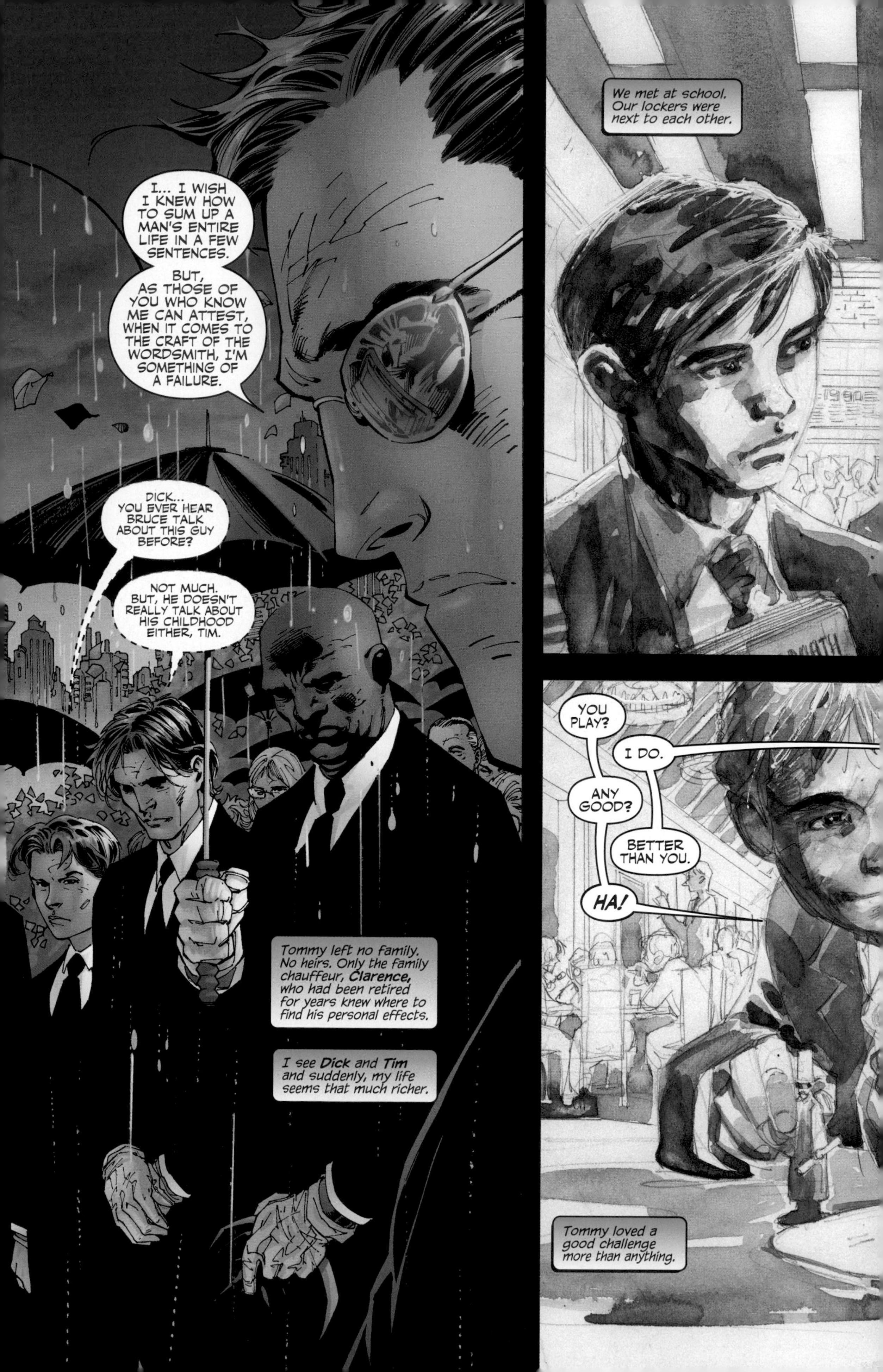
I... I WISH I KNEW HOW TO SUM UP A MAN'S ENTIRE LIFE IN A FEW SENTENCES.
BUT, AS THOSE OF YOU WHO KNOW ME CAN ATTEST, WHEN IT COMES TO THE CRAFT OF THE WORDSMITH, I'M SOMETHING OF A FAILURE.
DICK... YOU EVER HEAR BRUCE TALK ABOUT THIS GUY BEFORE?
NOT MUCH. BUT, HE DOESN'T REALLY TALK ABOUT HIS CHILDHOOD EITHER, TIM.
Tommy left no family. No heirs. Only the family chauffeur, Clarence, who had been retired for years knew where to find his personal effects.
I see Dick and Tim and suddenly, my life seems that much richer.
We met at school. Our lockers were next to each other.
YOU PLAY?
I DO.
ANY GOOD?
BETTER THAN YOU.
HA!
Tommy loved a good challenge more than anything.

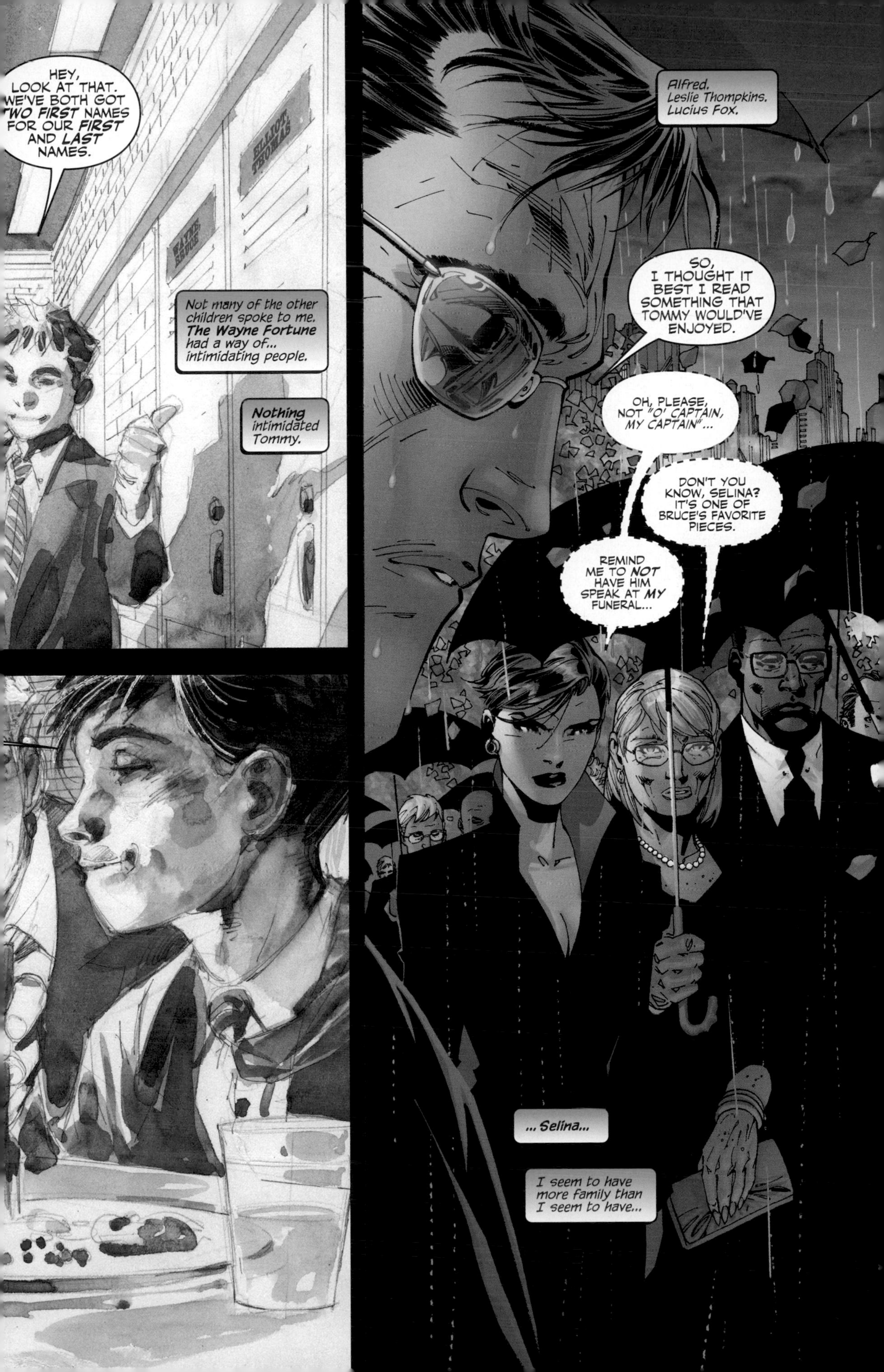
HEY, LOOK AT THAT. WE'VE BOTH GOT TWO FIRST NAMES FOR OUR FIRST AND LAST NAMES.
ELLIOT, THOMAS
WAYNE, BRUCE
Not many of the other children spoke to me. The Wayne Fortune had a way of... intimidating people.
Nothing intimidated Tommy.
Alfred. Leslie Thompkins. Lucius Fox.
SO, I THOUGHT IT BEST I READ SOMETHING THAT TOMMY WOULD'VE ENJOYED.
OH, PLEASE, NOT "O' CAPTAIN, MY CAPTAIN"...
DON'T YOU KNOW, SELINA? IT'S ONE OF BRUCE'S FAVORITE PIECES.
REMIND ME TO NOT HAVE HIM SPEAK AT MY FUNERAL...
...Selina...
I seem to have more family than I seem to have...

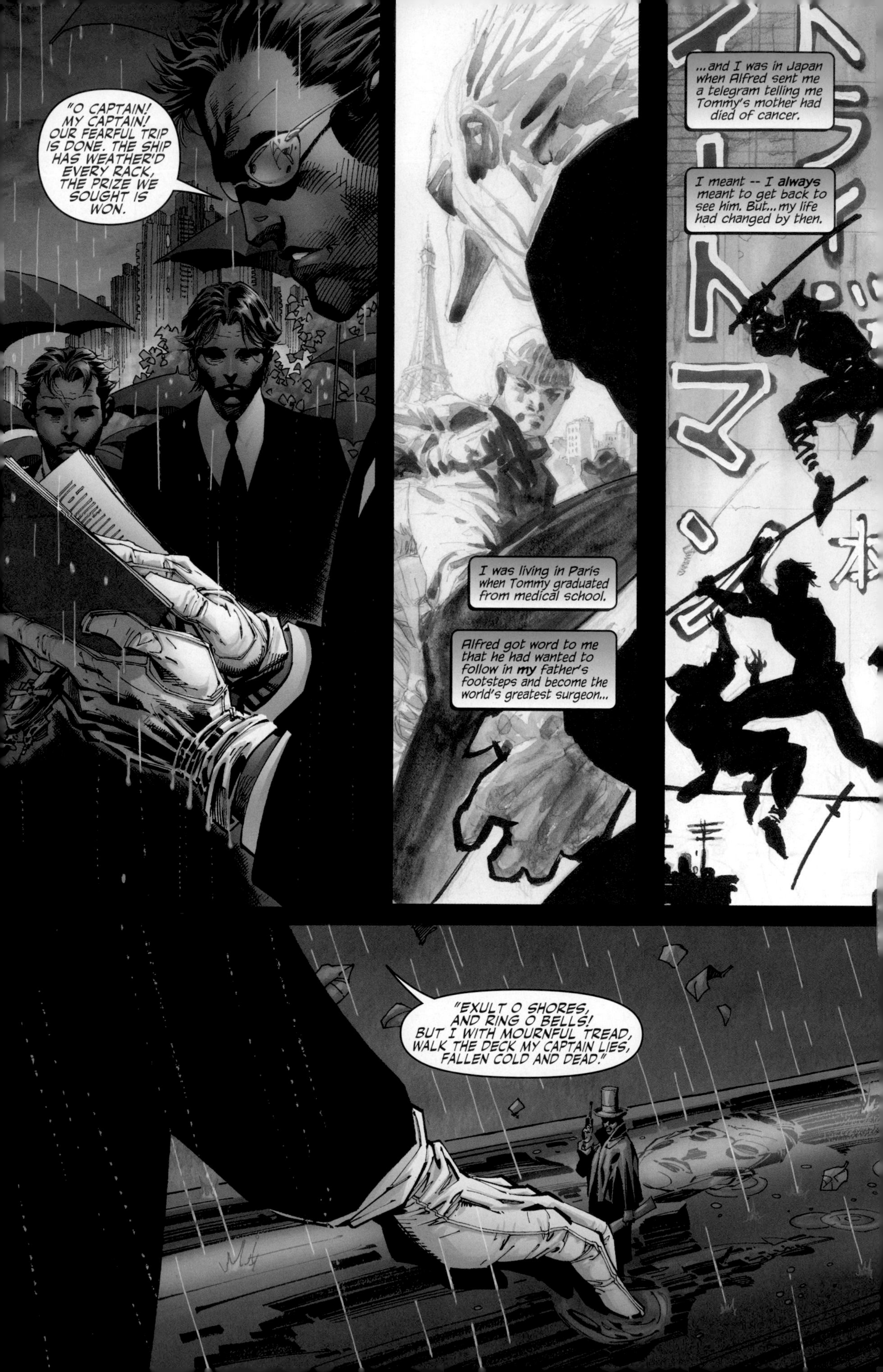
"O CAPTAIN! MY CAPTAIN! OUR FEARFUL TRIP IS DONE. THE SHIP HAS WEATHER'D EVERY RACK, THE PRIZE WE SOUGHT IS WON.
I was living in Paris when Tommy graduated from medical school.
Alfred got word to me that he had wanted to follow in my father's footsteps and become the world's greatest surgeon...
...and I was in Japan when Alfred sent me a telegram telling me Tommy's mother had died of cancer.
I meant -- I always meant to get back to see him. But...my life had changed by then.
"EXULT O SHORES, AND RING O BELLS! BUT I WITH MOURNFUL TREAD, WALK THE DECK MY CAPTAIN LIES, FALLEN COLD AND DEAD."

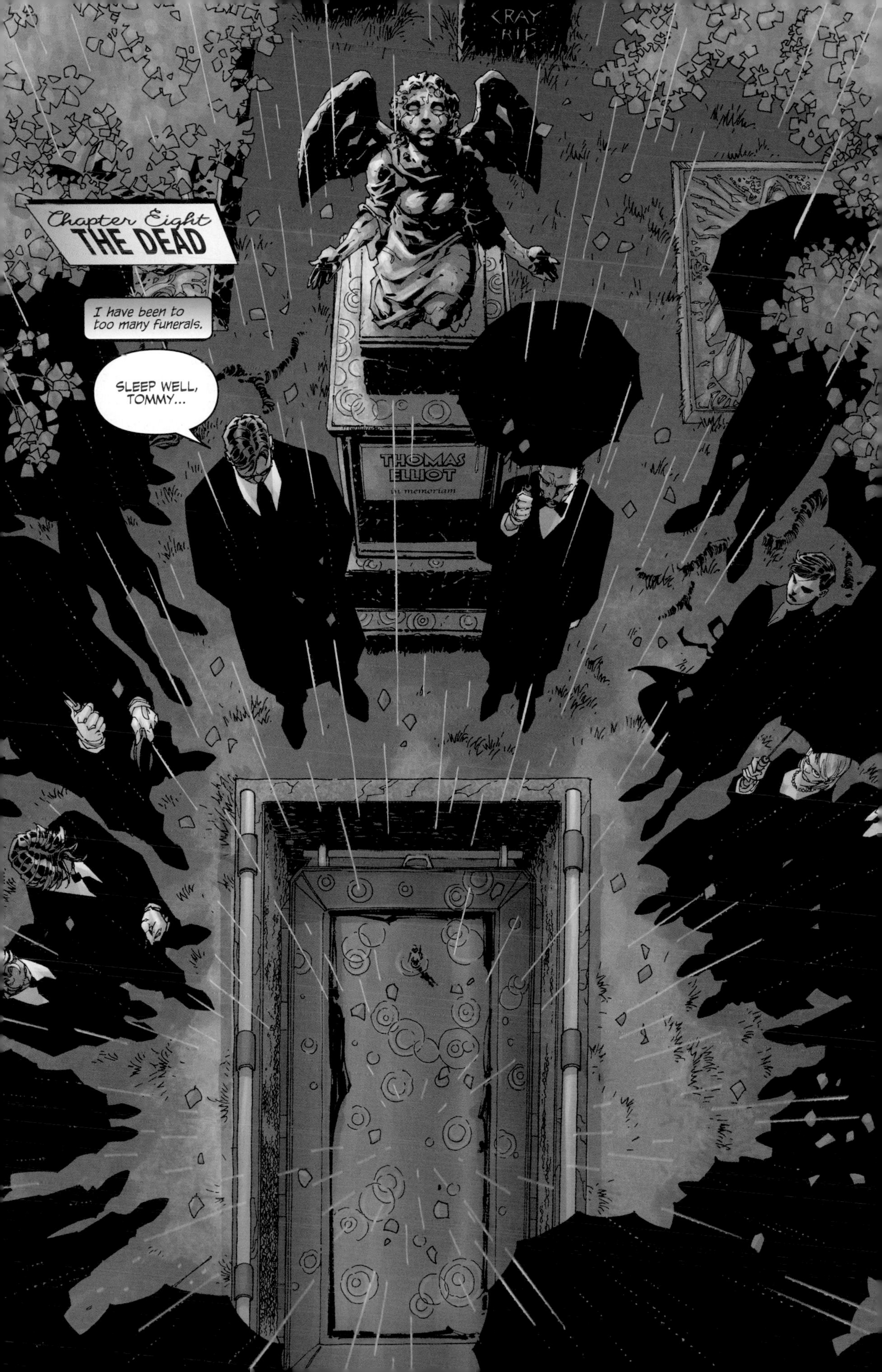

Chapter Eight
THE DEAD
I have been to too many funerals.
SLEEP WELL, TOMMY...
THOMAS ELLIOT
in memoriam

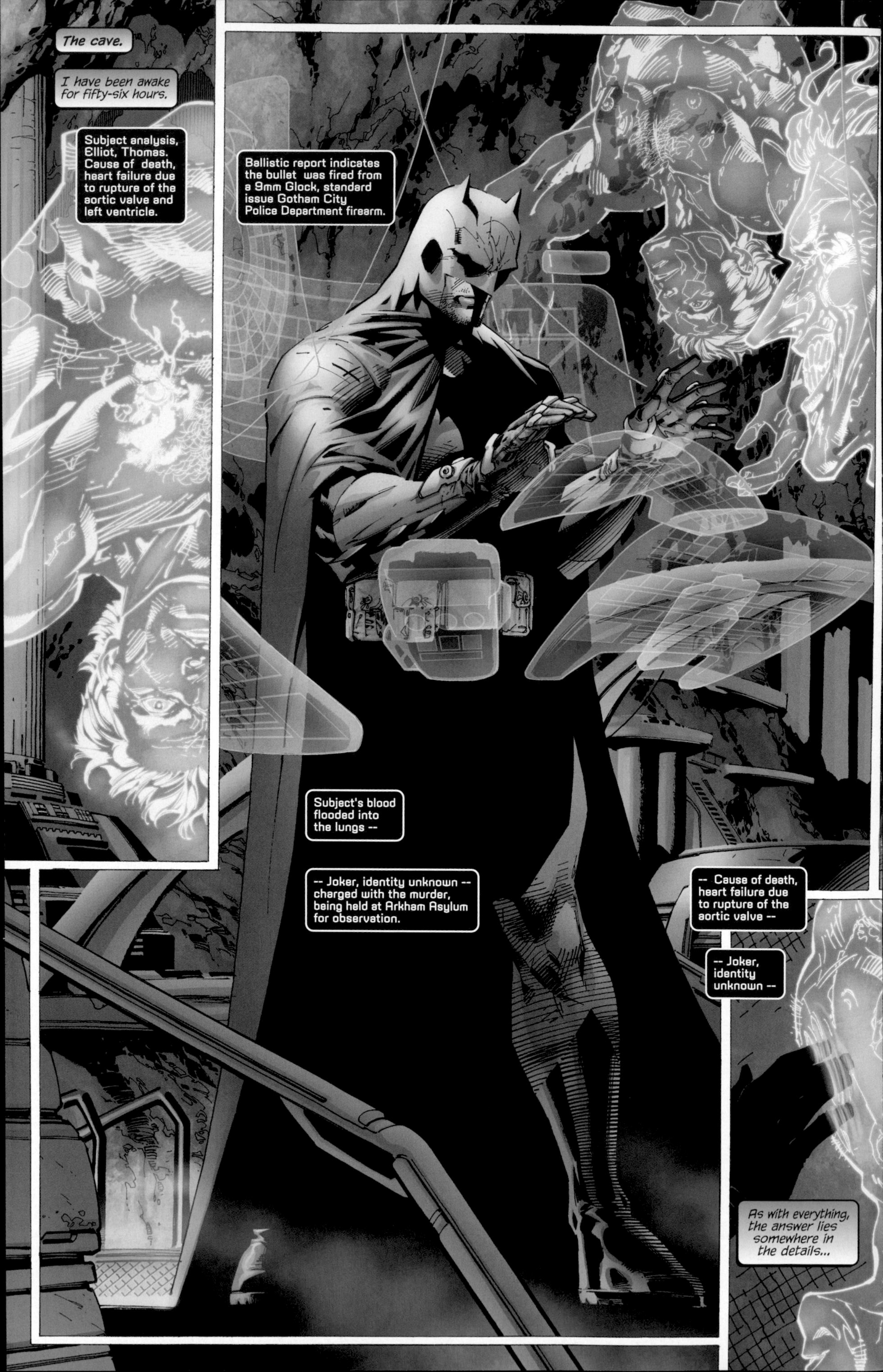
The cave.
I have been awake for fifty-six hours.
Subject analysis, Elliot, Thomas. Cause of death, heart failure due to rupture of the aortic valve and left ventricle.
Ballistic report indicates the bullet was fired from a 9mm Glock, standard issue Gotham City Police Department firearm.
Subject's blood flooded into the lungs --
-- Joker, identity unknown -- charged with the murder, being held at Arkham Asylum for observation.
-- Cause of death, heart failure due to rupture of the aortic valve --
-- Joker, identity unknown --
As with everything, the answer lies somewhere in the details...

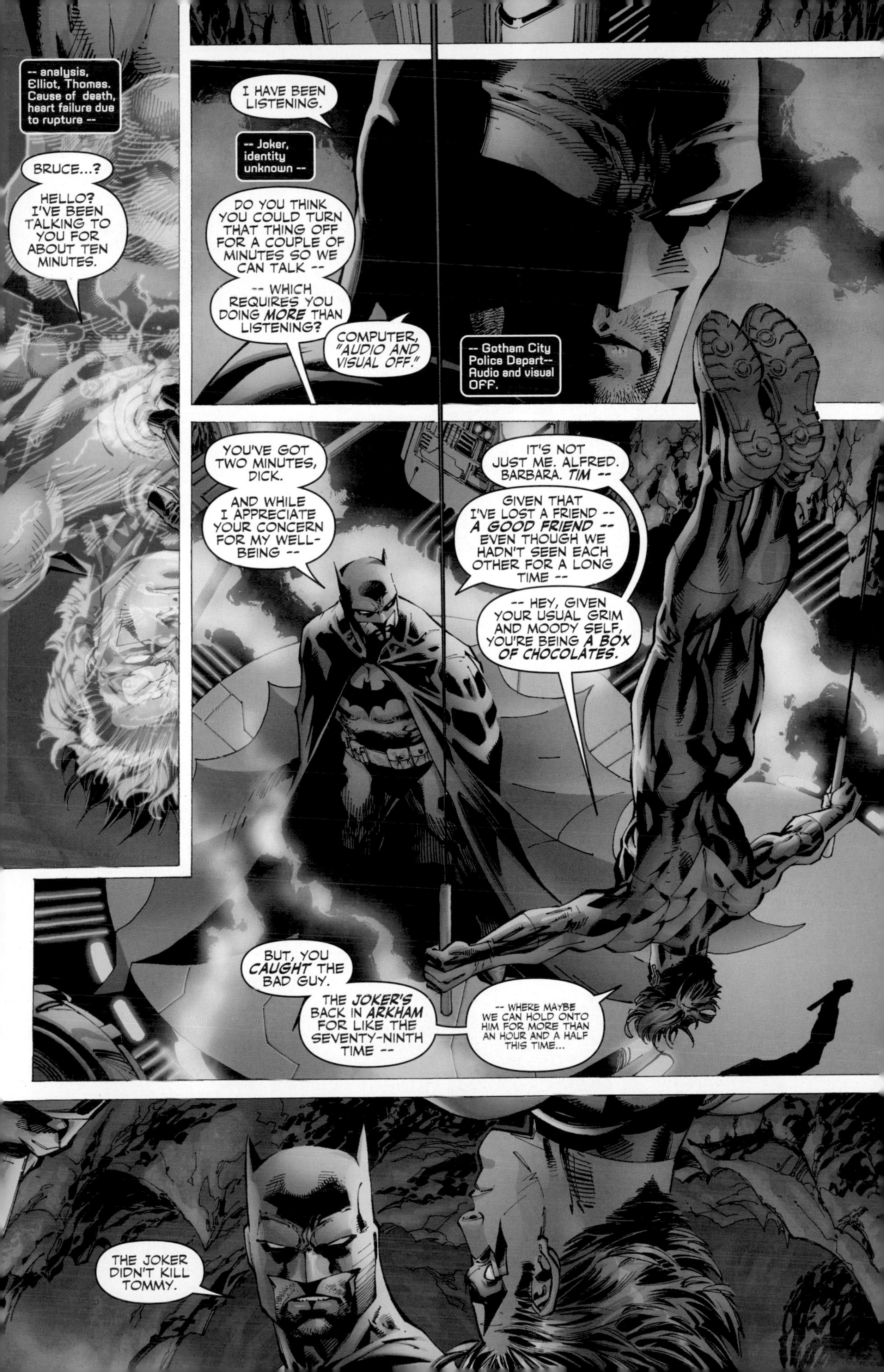
-- analysis, Elliot, Thomas. Cause of death, heart failure due to rupture --
BRUCE...?
HELLO? I'VE BEEN TALKING TO YOU FOR ABOUT TEN MINUTES.
I HAVE BEEN LISTENING.
-- Joker, identity unknown --
DO YOU THINK YOU COULD TURN THAT THING OFF FOR A COUPLE OF MINUTES SO WE CAN TALK --
-- WHICH REQUIRES YOU DOING MORE THAN LISTENING?
COMPUTER, "AUDIO AND VISUAL OFF."
-- Gotham City Police Depart-- Audio and visual OFF.
YOU'VE GOT TWO MINUTES, DICK.
AND WHILE I APPRECIATE YOUR CONCERN FOR MY WELL-BEING --
IT'S NOT JUST ME. ALFRED. BARBARA. TIM --
GIVEN THAT I'VE LOST A FRIEND -- A GOOD FRIEND -- EVEN THOUGH WE HADN'T SEEN EACH OTHER FOR A LONG TIME --
-- HEY, GIVEN YOUR USUAL GRIM AND MOODY SELF, YOU'RE BEING A BOX OF CHOCOLATES.
BUT, YOU CAUGHT THE BAD GUY.
THE JOKER'S BACK IN ARKHAM FOR LIKE THE SEVENTY-NINTH TIME --
-- WHERE MAYBE WE CAN HOLD ONTO HIM FOR MORE THAN AN HOUR AND A HALF THIS TIME...
THE JOKER DIDN'T KILL TOMMY.

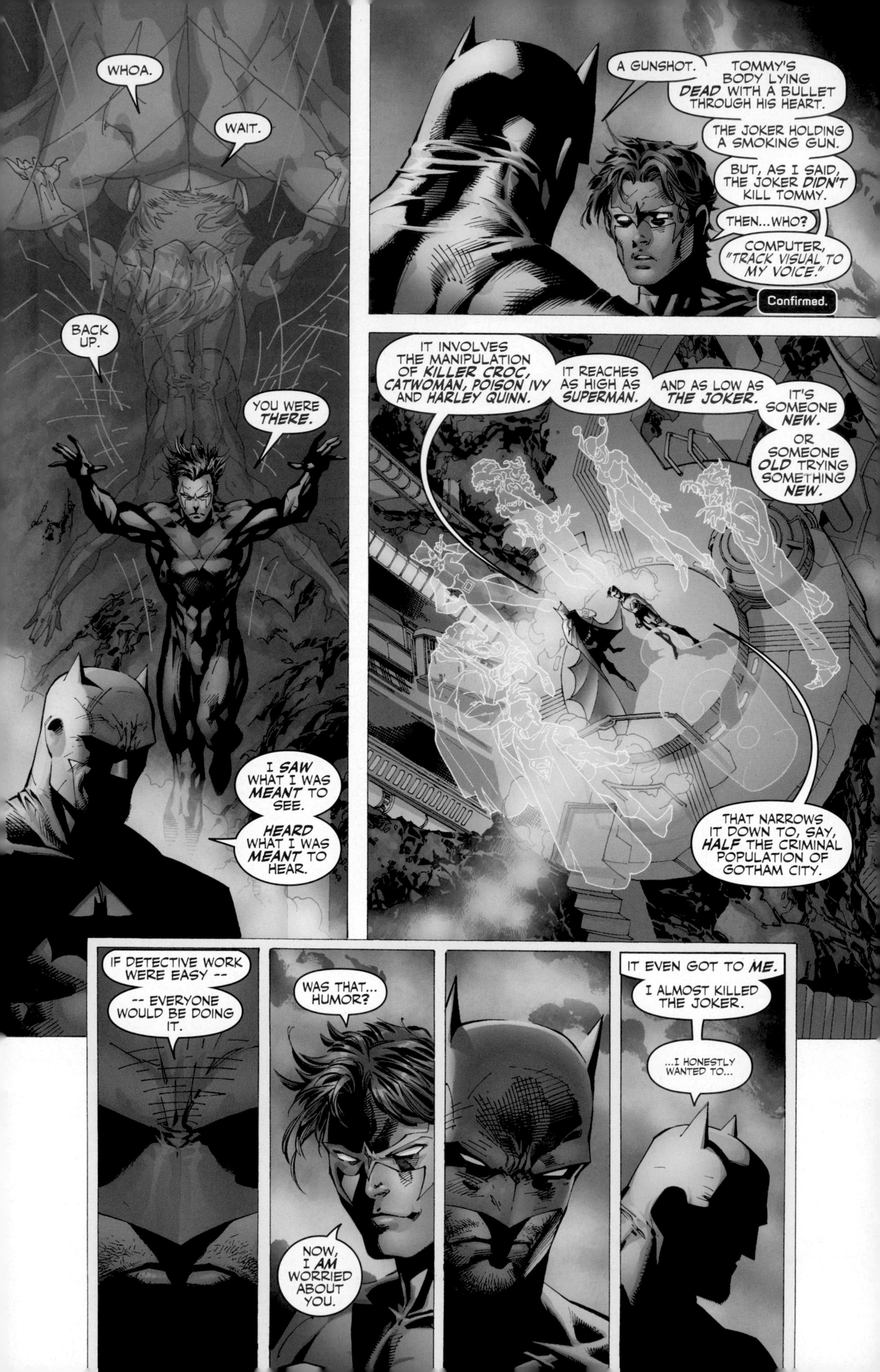
WHOA.
WAIT.
BACK UP.
YOU WERE THERE.
I SAW WHAT I WAS MEANT TO SEE.
HEARD WHAT I WAS MEANT TO HEAR.
A GUNSHOT.
TOMMY'S BODY LYING DEAD WITH A BULLET THROUGH HIS HEART.
THE JOKER HOLDING A SMOKING GUN.
BUT, AS I SAID, THE JOKER DIDN'T KILL TOMMY.
THEN...WHO?
COMPUTER, "TRACK VISUAL TO MY VOICE."
Confirmed.
IT INVOLVES THE MANIPULATION OF KILLER CROC, CATWOMAN, POISON IVY AND HARLEY QUINN.
IT REACHES AS HIGH AS SUPERMAN.
AND AS LOW AS THE JOKER.
IT'S SOMEONE NEW.
OR SOMEONE OLD TRYING SOMETHING NEW.
THAT NARROWS IT DOWN TO, SAY, HALF THE CRIMINAL POPULATION OF GOTHAM CITY.
IF DETECTIVE WORK WERE EASY --
-- EVERYONE WOULD BE DOING IT.
WAS THAT... HUMOR?
NOW, I AM WORRIED ABOUT YOU.
IT EVEN GOT TO ME.
I ALMOST KILLED THE JOKER.
...I HONESTLY WANTED TO...

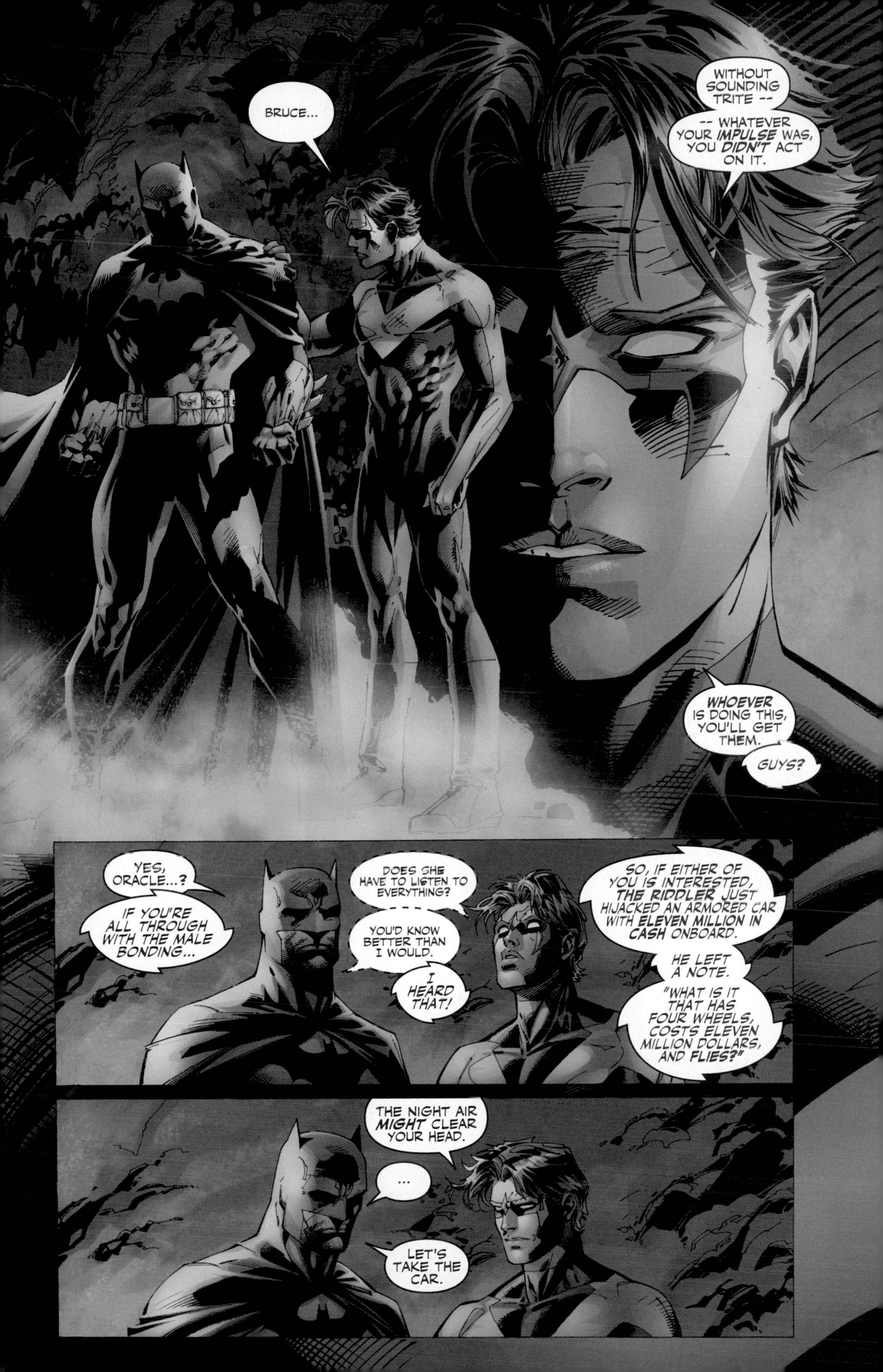
BRUCE...
WITHOUT SOUNDING TRITE --
-- WHATEVER YOUR IMPULSE WAS, YOU DIDN'T ACT ON IT.
WHOEVER IS DOING THIS, YOU'LL GET THEM.
GUYS?
YES, ORACLE...?
IF YOU'RE ALL THROUGH WITH THE MALE BONDING...
DOES SHE HAVE TO LISTEN TO EVERYTHING?
YOU'D KNOW BETTER THAN I WOULD.
I HEARD THAT!
SO, IF EITHER OF YOU IS INTERESTED, THE RIDDLER JUST HIJACKED AN ARMORED CAR WITH ELEVEN MILLION IN CASH ONBOARD.
HE LEFT A NOTE.
"WHAT IS IT THAT HAS FOUR WHEELS, COSTS ELEVEN MILLION DOLLARS, AND FLIES?"
THE NIGHT AIR MIGHT CLEAR YOUR HEAD.
...
LET'S TAKE THE CAR.

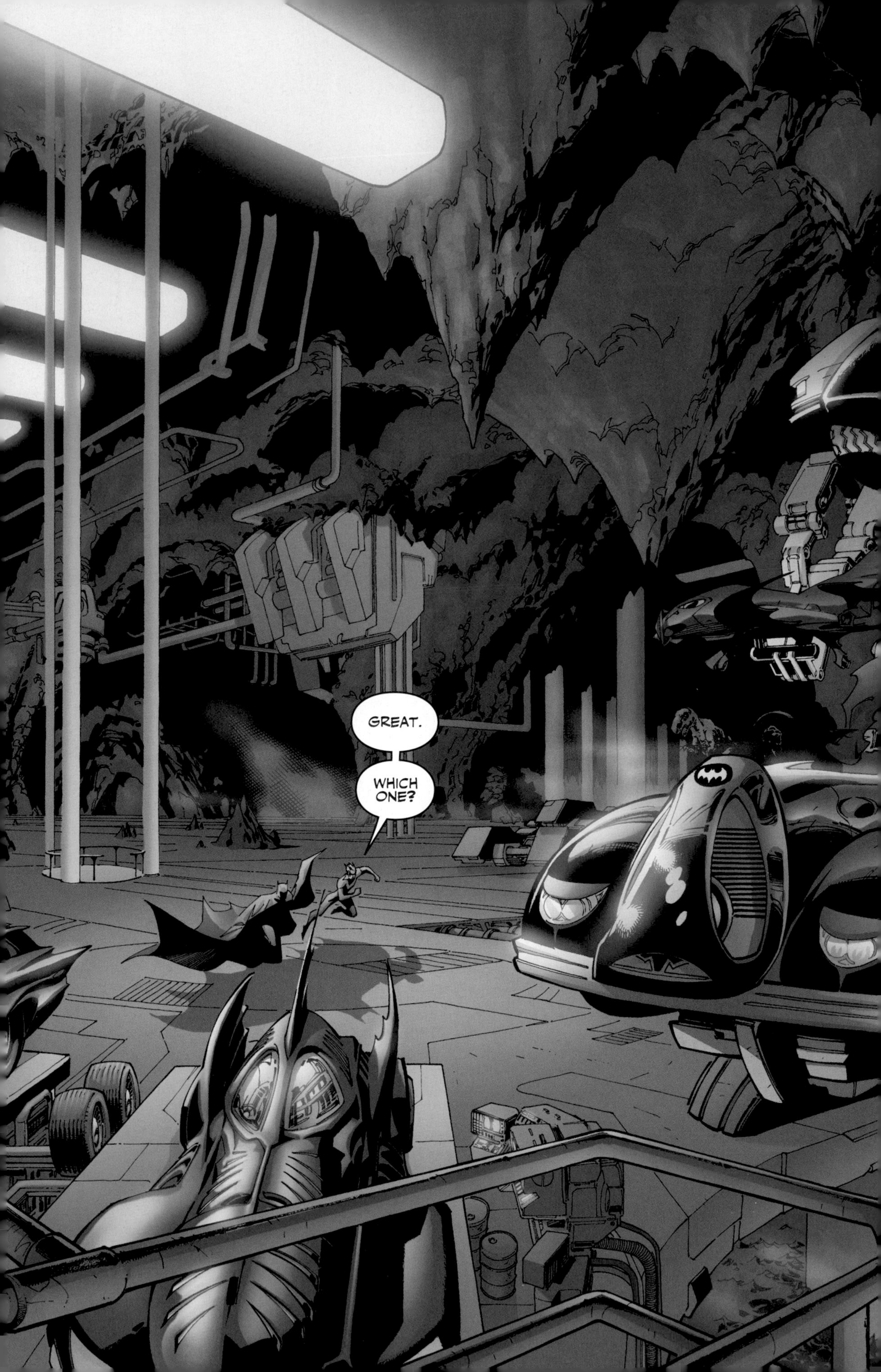
GREAT.
WHICH ONE?

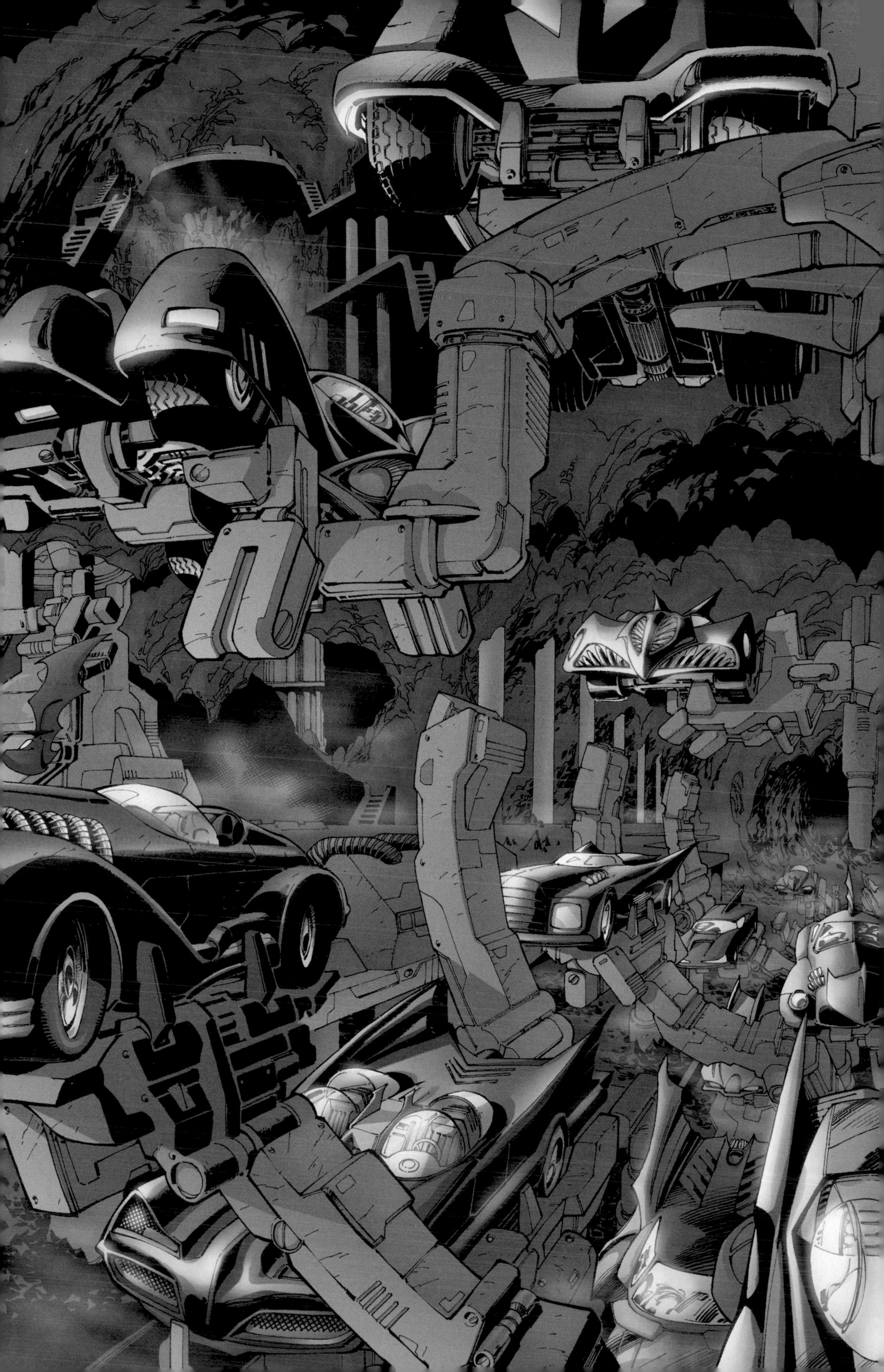

THROOOM

SO. WORD *UNDER* THE STREET IS YOU'RE SEEING CATWOMAN. ANY TRUTH IN THAT?

GOTHAM CITY
14 MILES

SKREEEEEE

HONK
HONK

SHELDON PARK EXIT A STREET
APARO EXPRESSWAY

WELCOME TO GOTHAM CITY

I TAKE IT BY YOUR SILENCE...

...IT *IS* TRUE!

*Dick always spoke to me without fear. No matter what else has happened to us through the years --*

*-- he has earned that right.*

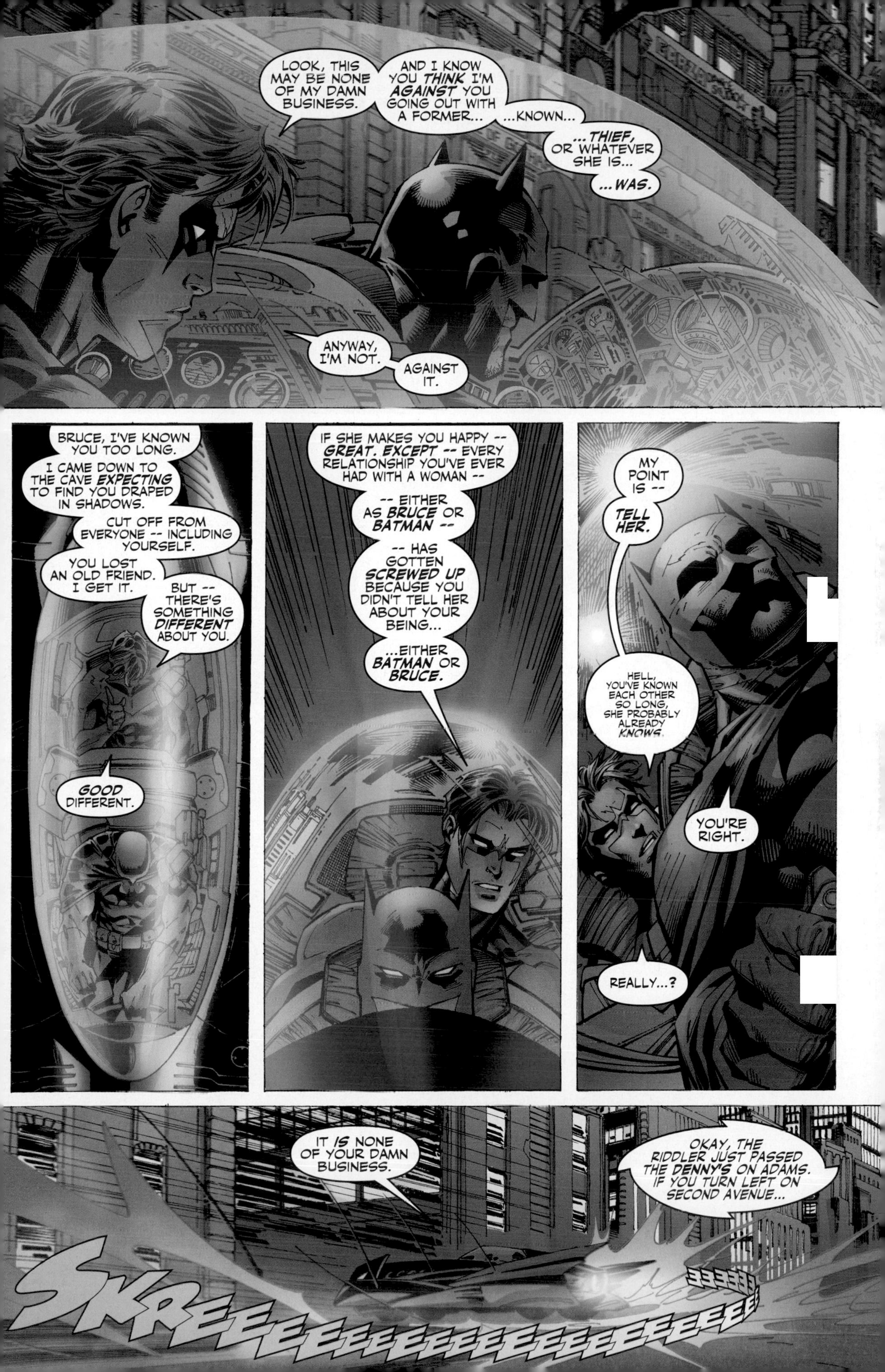
LOOK, THIS MAY BE NONE OF MY DAMN BUSINESS.
AND I KNOW YOU THINK I'M AGAINST YOU GOING OUT WITH A FORMER...
...KNOWN...
...THIEF, OR WHATEVER SHE IS...
...WAS.
ANYWAY, I'M NOT.
AGAINST IT.
BRUCE, I'VE KNOWN YOU TOO LONG.
I CAME DOWN TO THE CAVE EXPECTING TO FIND YOU DRAPED IN SHADOWS.
CUT OFF FROM EVERYONE -- INCLUDING YOURSELF.
YOU LOST AN OLD FRIEND. I GET IT.
BUT -- THERE'S SOMETHING DIFFERENT ABOUT YOU.
GOOD DIFFERENT.
IF SHE MAKES YOU HAPPY -- GREAT. EXCEPT -- EVERY RELATIONSHIP YOU'VE EVER HAD WITH A WOMAN --
-- EITHER AS BRUCE OR BATMAN --
-- HAS GOTTEN SCREWED UP BECAUSE YOU DIDN'T TELL HER ABOUT YOUR BEING...
...EITHER BATMAN OR BRUCE.
MY POINT IS --
TELL HER.
HELL, YOU'VE KNOWN EACH OTHER SO LONG, SHE PROBABLY ALREADY KNOWS.
YOU'RE RIGHT.
REALLY...?
IT IS NONE OF YOUR DAMN BUSINESS.
OKAY, THE RIDDLER JUST PASSED THE DENNY'S ON ADAMS. IF YOU TURN LEFT ON SECOND AVENUE...
SKREEEEEEEEEEEEEEEEEEEEEEEE

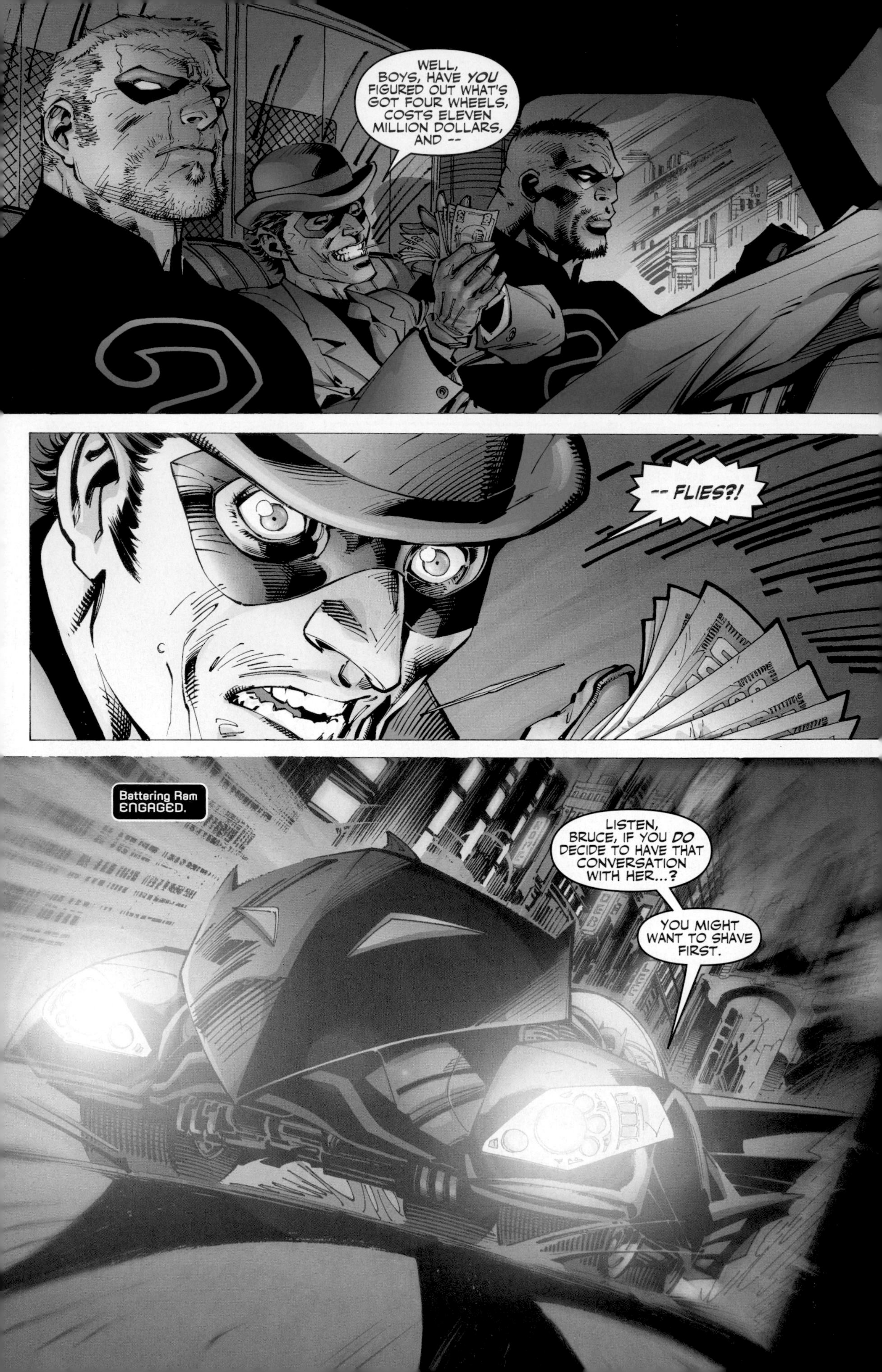
WELL, BOYS, HAVE *YOU* FIGURED OUT WHAT'S GOT FOUR WHEELS, COSTS ELEVEN MILLION DOLLARS, AND --
-- FLIES?!
Battering Ram ENGAGED.
LISTEN, BRUCE, IF YOU *DO* DECIDE TO HAVE THAT CONVERSATION WITH HER...?
YOU MIGHT WANT TO SHAVE FIRST.

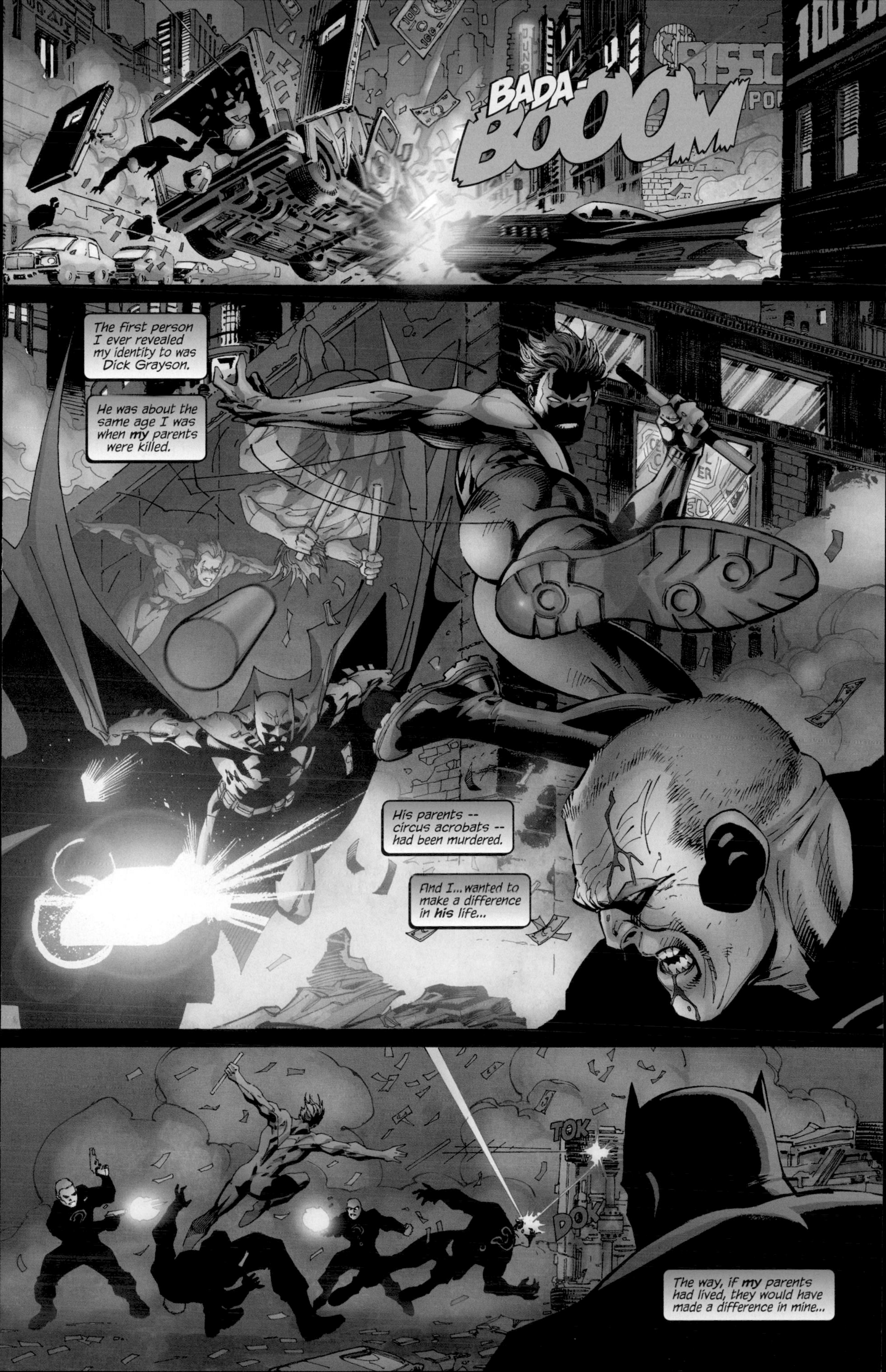

BADA-BOOOM
The first person I ever revealed my identity to was Dick Grayson.
He was about the same age I was when **my** parents were killed.
His parents -- circus acrobats -- had been murdered.
And I...wanted to make a difference in **his** life...
TOK
DOK
The way, if **my** parents had lived, they would have made a difference in mine...

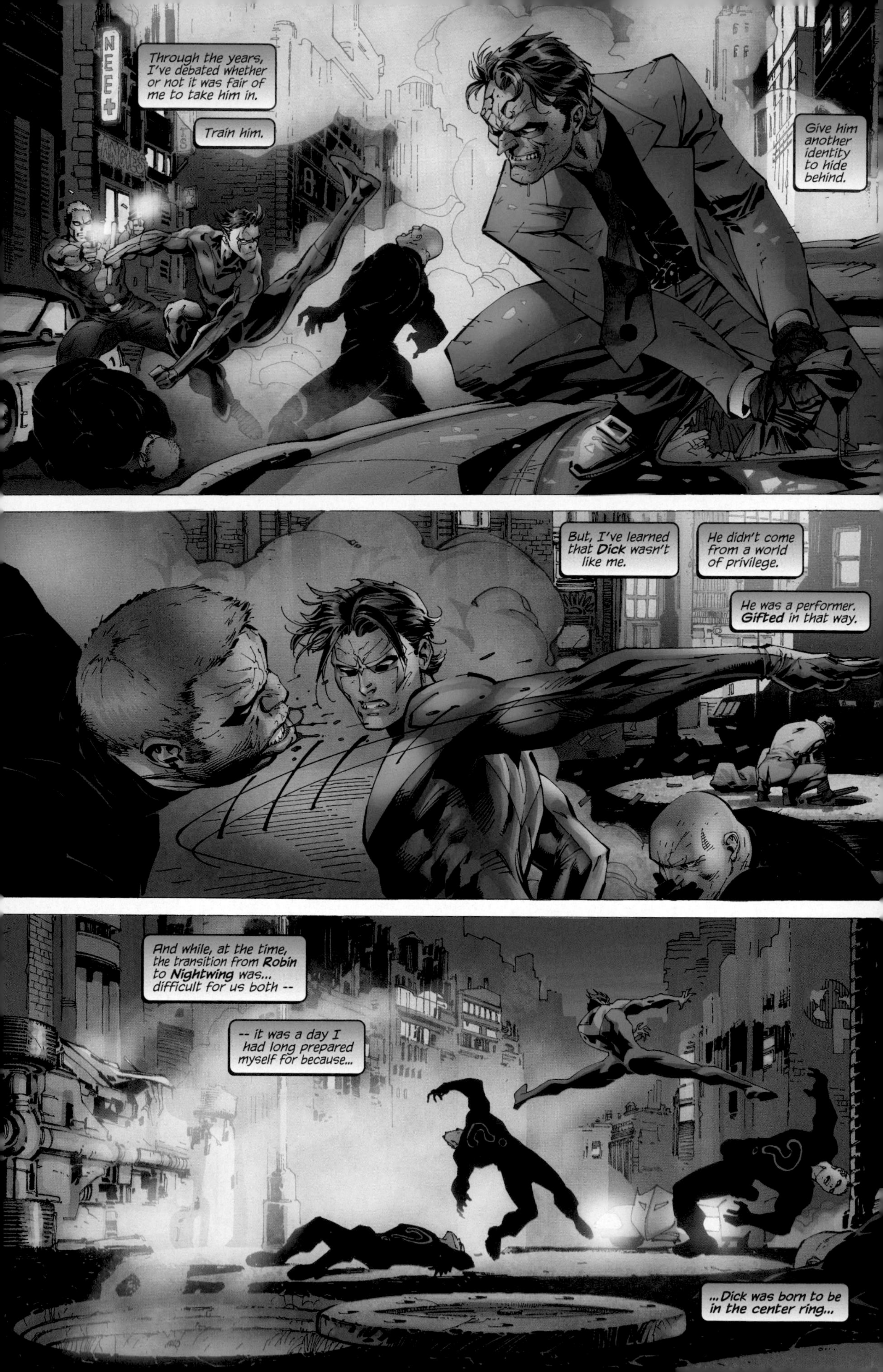
NEE
Through the years, I've debated whether or not it was fair of me to take him in.
Train him.
Give him another identity to hide behind.
But, I've learned that Dick wasn't like me.
He didn't come from a world of privilege.
He was a performer. Gifted in that way.
And while, at the time, the transition from Robin to Nightwing was... difficult for us both --
-- it was a day I had long prepared myself for because...
...Dick was born to be in the center ring...

HUFF
HUFF
HUFF

HUFF
HUFF
HUFF

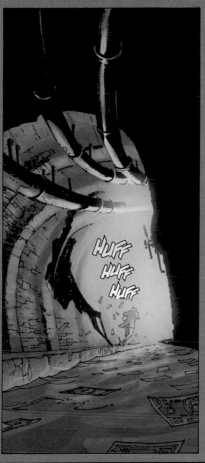

HUFF
HUFF
HUFF

HUFF
HUFF
HUFF

NNNGGGNNNN

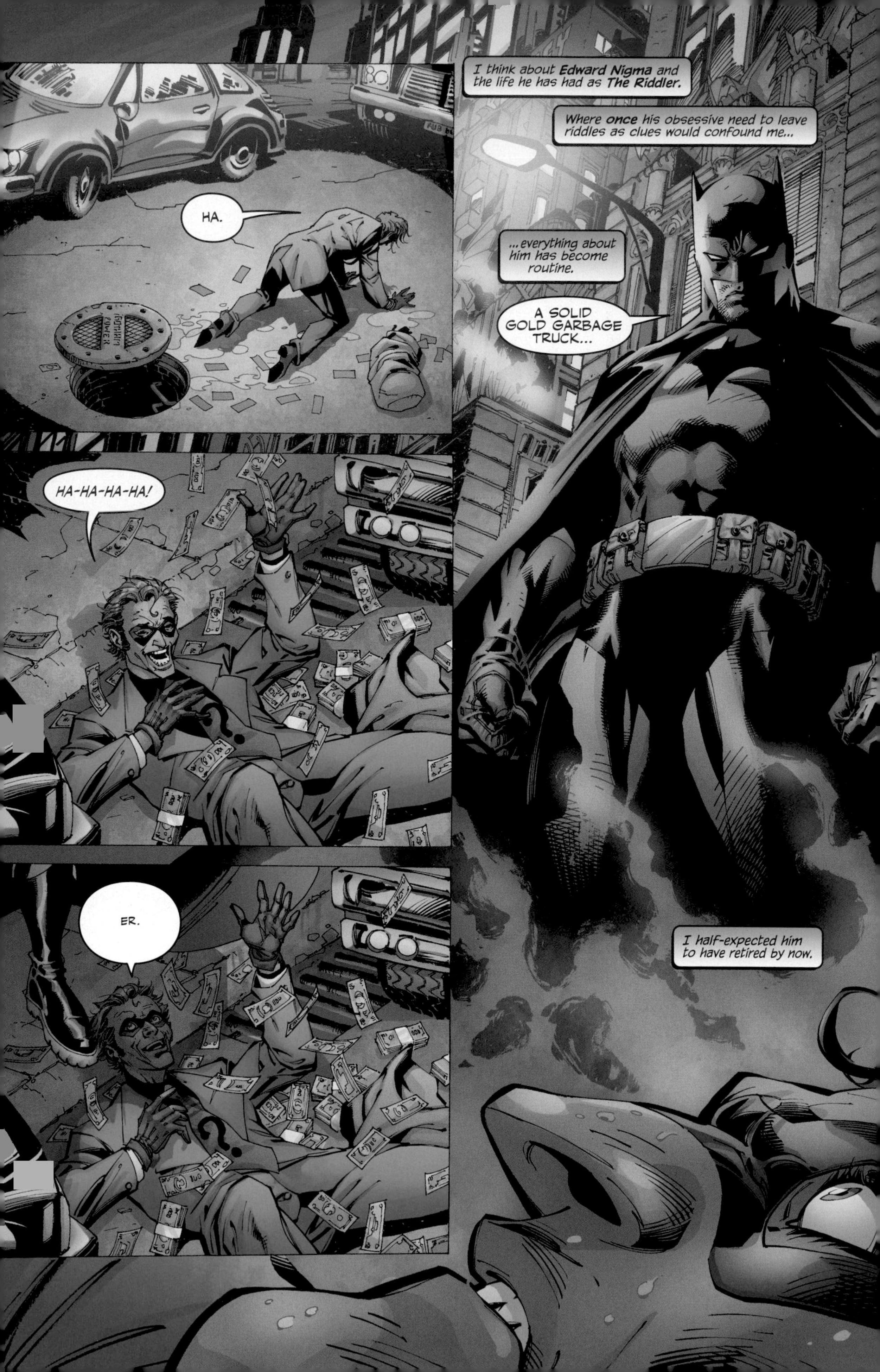
HA.
HA-HA-HA-HA!
ER.
I think about Edward Nigma and the life he has had as The Riddler.
Where once his obsessive need to leave riddles as clues would confound me...
...everything about him has become routine.
A SOLID GOLD GARBAGE TRUCK...
I half-expected him to have retired by now.

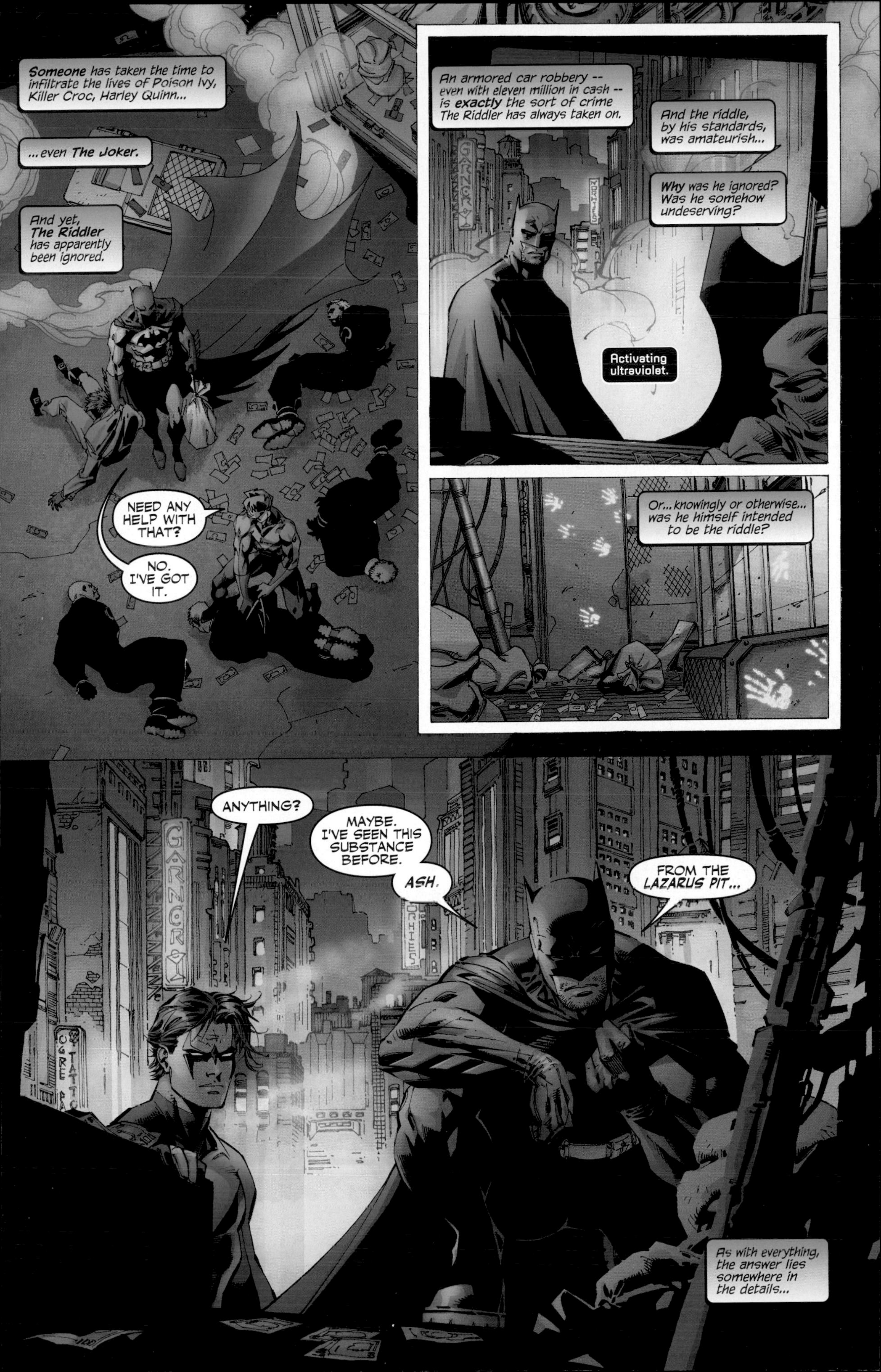

Someone has taken the time to infiltrate the lives of Poison Ivy, Killer Croc, Harley Quinn...
...even The Joker.
And yet, The Riddler has apparently been ignored.
NEED ANY HELP WITH THAT?
NO. I'VE GOT IT.
An armored car robbery -- even with eleven million in cash -- is exactly the sort of crime The Riddler has always taken on.
And the riddle, by his standards, was amateurish...
Why was he ignored? Was he somehow undeserving?
Activating ultraviolet.
Or... knowingly or otherwise... was he himself intended to be the riddle?
ANYTHING?
MAYBE. I'VE SEEN THIS SUBSTANCE BEFORE.
ASH.
FROM THE LAZARUS PIT...
As with everything, the answer lies somewhere in the details...

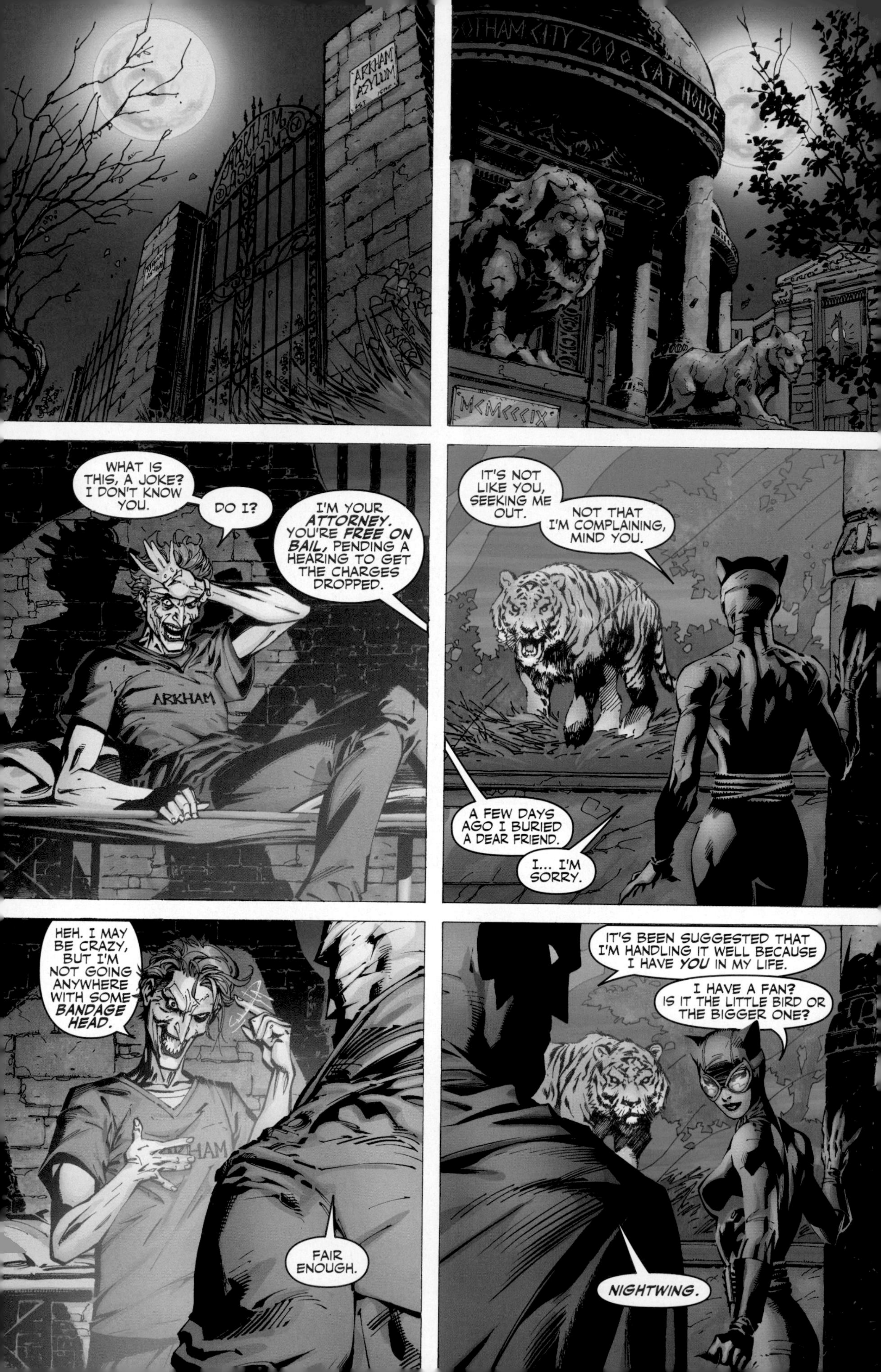
ARKHAM ASYLUM
GOTHAM CITY ZOO ◇ CAT HOUSE
MCMCCCIX
WHAT IS THIS, A JOKE? I DON'T KNOW YOU.
DO I?
I'M YOUR ATTORNEY. YOU'RE FREE ON BAIL, PENDING A HEARING TO GET THE CHARGES DROPPED.
ARKHAM
IT'S NOT LIKE YOU, SEEKING ME OUT.
NOT THAT I'M COMPLAINING, MIND YOU.
A FEW DAYS AGO I BURIED A DEAR FRIEND.
I... I'M SORRY.
HEH. I MAY BE CRAZY, BUT I'M NOT GOING ANYWHERE WITH SOME BANDAGE HEAD.
FAIR ENOUGH.
IT'S BEEN SUGGESTED THAT I'M HANDLING IT WELL BECAUSE I HAVE YOU IN MY LIFE.
I HAVE A FAN? IS IT THE LITTLE BIRD OR THE BIGGER ONE?
NIGHTWING.

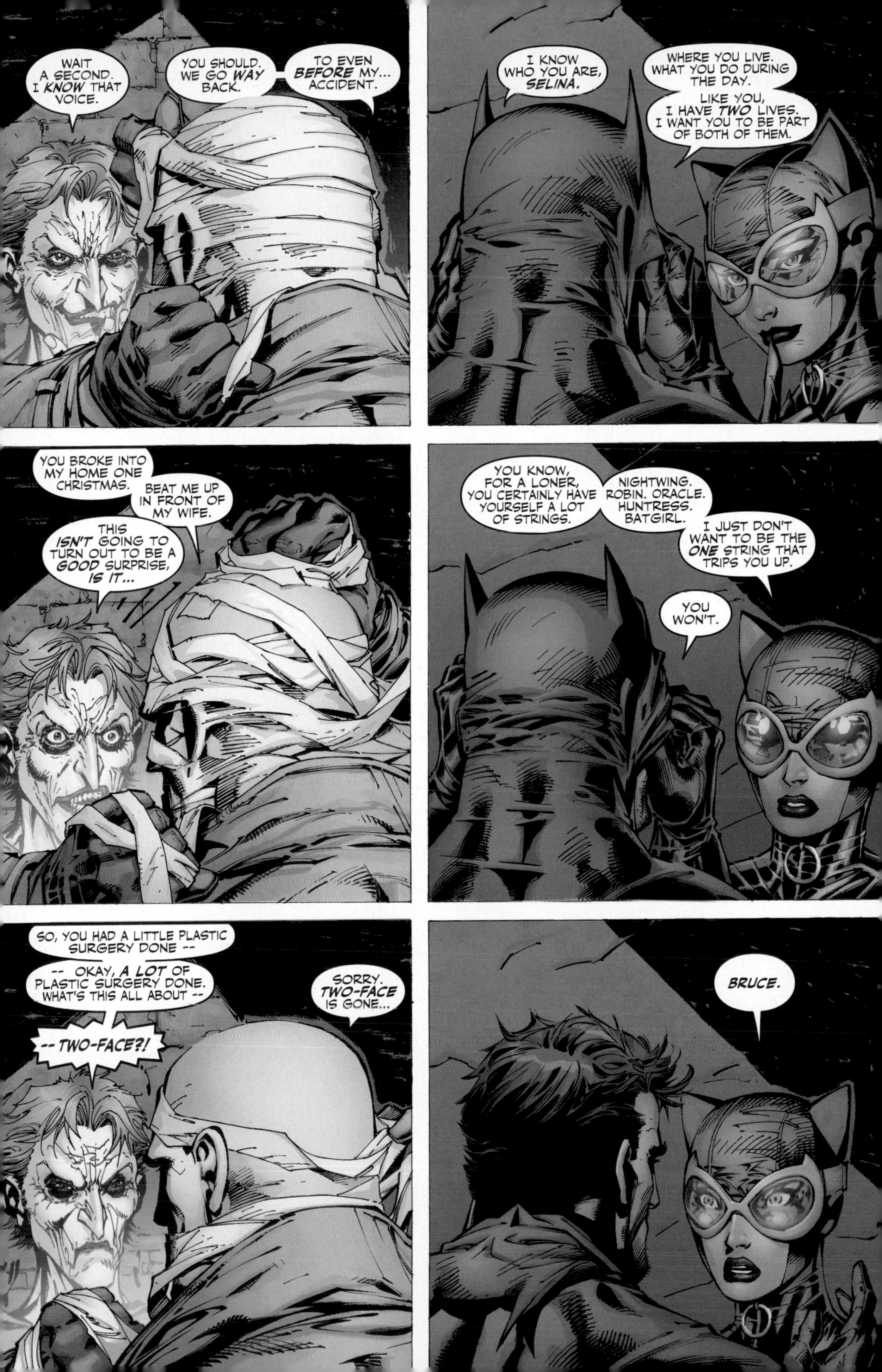
WAIT A SECOND. I KNOW THAT VOICE.
YOU SHOULD. WE GO WAY BACK.
TO EVEN BEFORE MY... ACCIDENT.
I KNOW WHO YOU ARE, SELINA.
WHERE YOU LIVE. WHAT YOU DO DURING THE DAY.
LIKE YOU, I HAVE TWO LIVES. I WANT YOU TO BE PART OF BOTH OF THEM.
YOU BROKE INTO MY HOME ONE CHRISTMAS.
BEAT ME UP IN FRONT OF MY WIFE.
THIS ISN'T GOING TO TURN OUT TO BE A GOOD SURPRISE, IS IT...
YOU KNOW, FOR A LONER, YOU CERTAINLY HAVE YOURSELF A LOT OF STRINGS.
NIGHTWING. ROBIN. ORACLE. HUNTRESS. BATGIRL.
I JUST DON'T WANT TO BE THE ONE STRING THAT TRIPS YOU UP.
YOU WON'T.
SO, YOU HAD A LITTLE PLASTIC SURGERY DONE --
-- OKAY, A LOT OF PLASTIC SURGERY DONE. WHAT'S THIS ALL ABOUT --
-- TWO-FACE?!
SORRY. TWO-FACE IS GONE...
BRUCE.

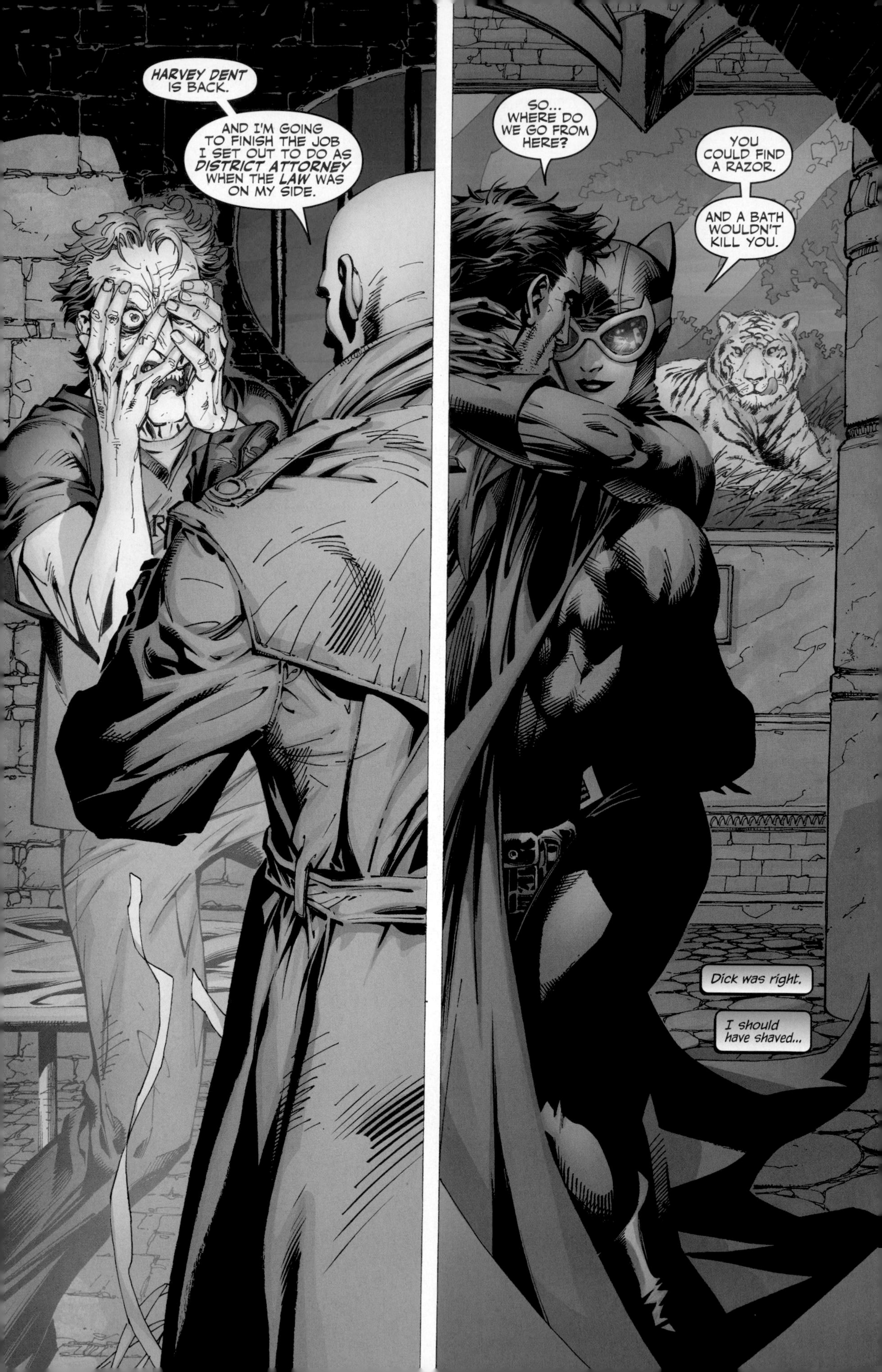
HARVEY DENT IS BACK.
AND I'M GOING TO FINISH THE JOB I SET OUT TO DO AS DISTRICT ATTORNEY WHEN THE LAW WAS ON MY SIDE.
SO... WHERE DO WE GO FROM HERE?
YOU COULD FIND A RAZOR.
AND A BATH WOULDN'T KILL YOU.
Dick was right.
I should have shaved...

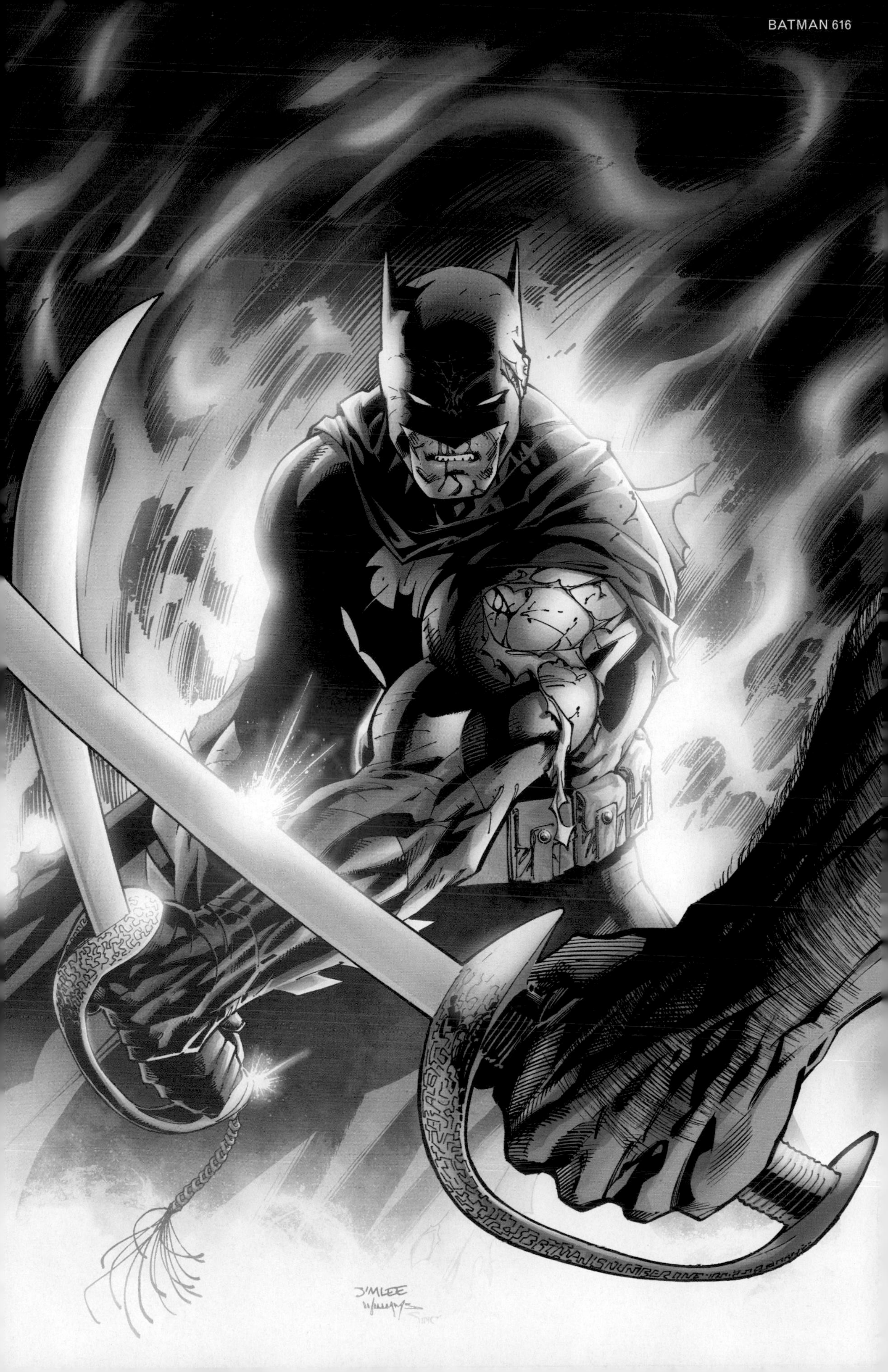
BATMAN IS NUMBER ONE
JIM LEE

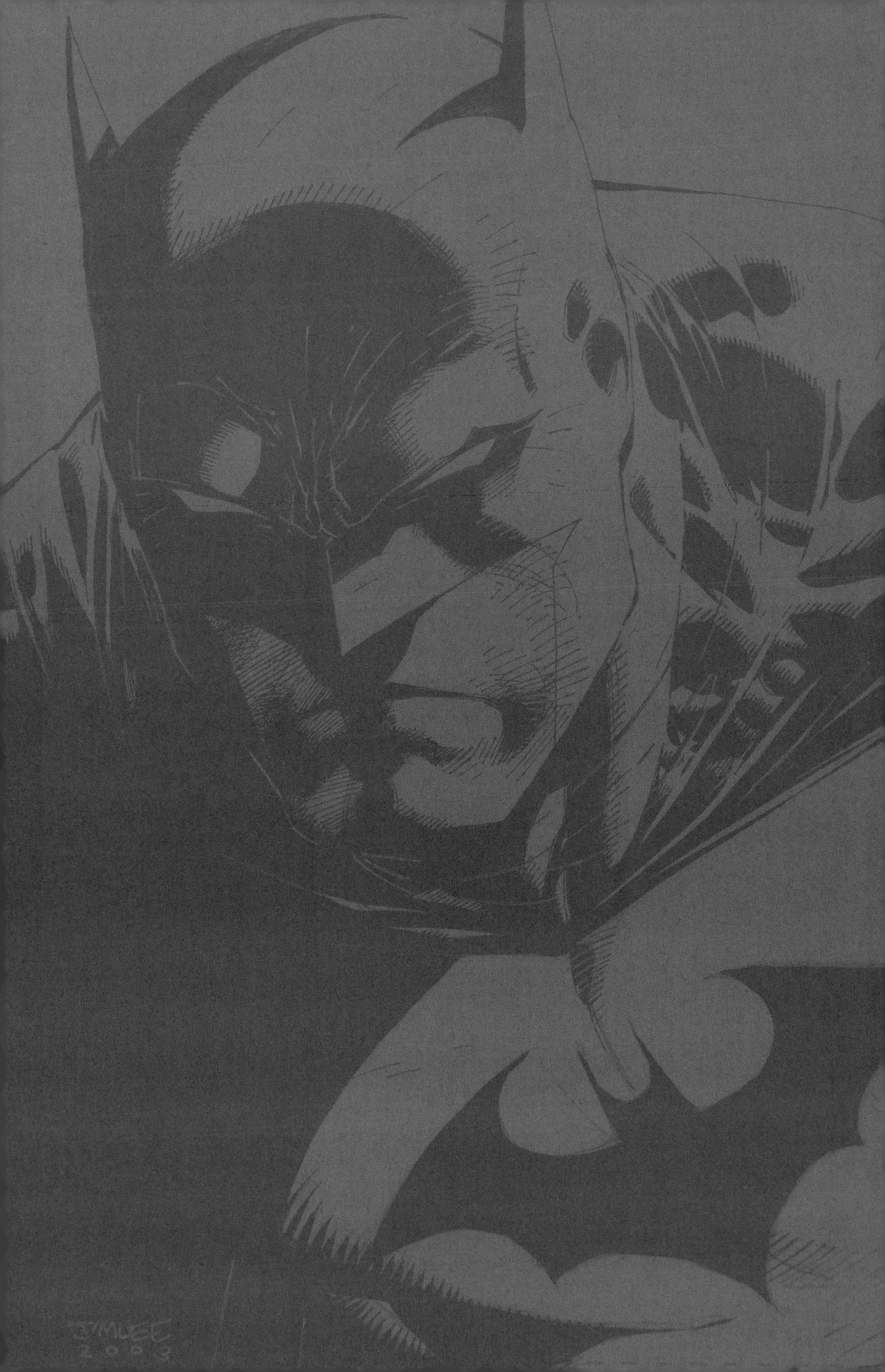
JIM LEE
2003

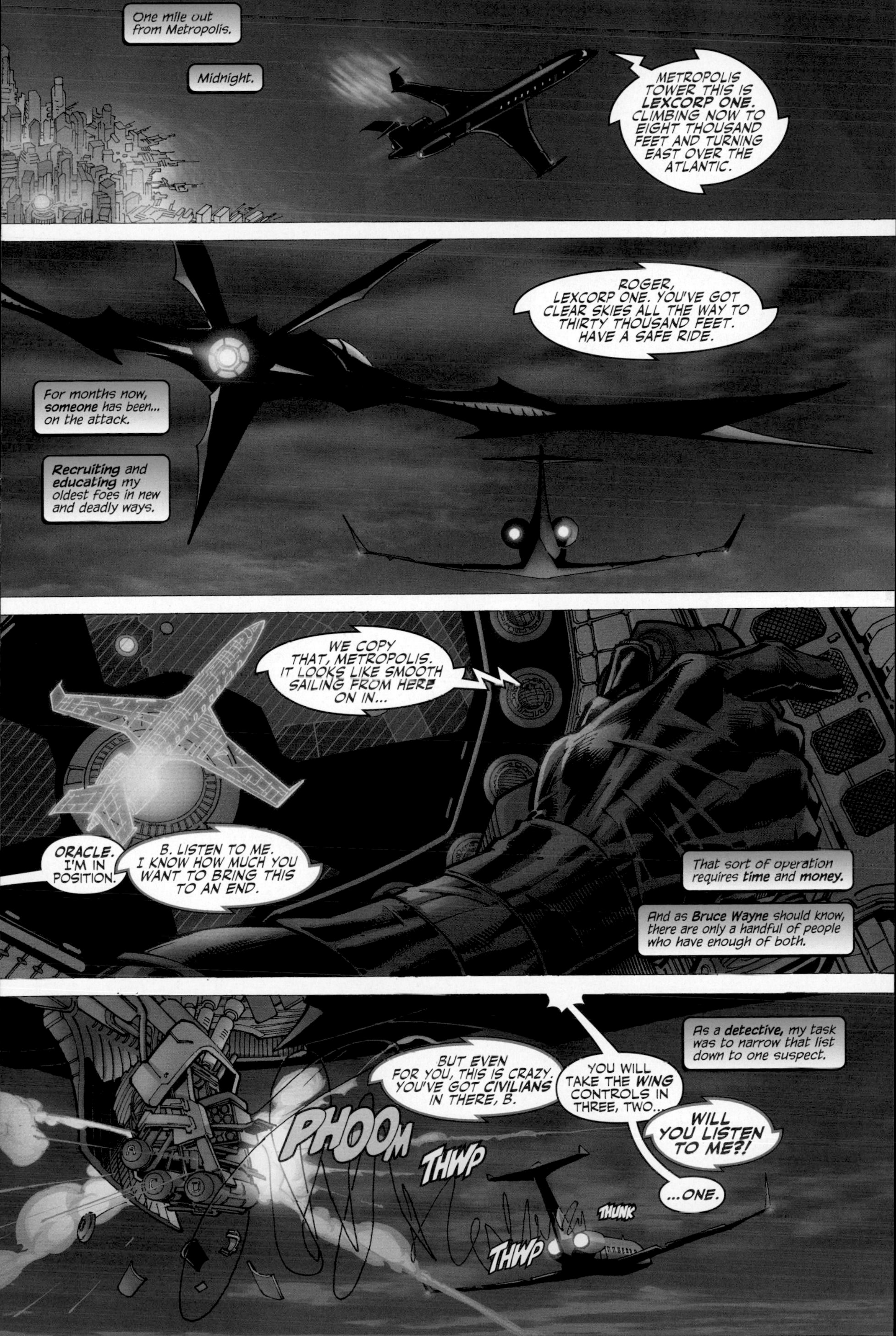

One mile out from Metropolis.
Midnight.
METROPOLIS TOWER THIS IS LEXCORP ONE. CLIMBING NOW TO EIGHT THOUSAND FEET AND TURNING EAST OVER THE ATLANTIC.
ROGER, LEXCORP ONE. YOU'VE GOT CLEAR SKIES ALL THE WAY TO THIRTY THOUSAND FEET. HAVE A SAFE RIDE.
For months now, someone has been... on the attack.
Recruiting and educating my oldest foes in new and deadly ways.
WE COPY THAT, METROPOLIS. IT LOOKS LIKE SMOOTH SAILING FROM HERE ON IN...
ORACLE. I'M IN POSITION.
B. LISTEN TO ME. I KNOW HOW MUCH YOU WANT TO BRING THIS TO AN END.
That sort of operation requires time and money.
And as Bruce Wayne should know, there are only a handful of people who have enough of both.
As a detective, my task was to narrow that list down to one suspect.
BUT EVEN FOR YOU, THIS IS CRAZY. YOU'VE GOT CIVILIANS IN THERE, B.
YOU WILL TAKE THE WING CONTROLS IN THREE, TWO...
WILL YOU LISTEN TO ME?!
...ONE.
PHOOM
THWP
THUNK
THWP

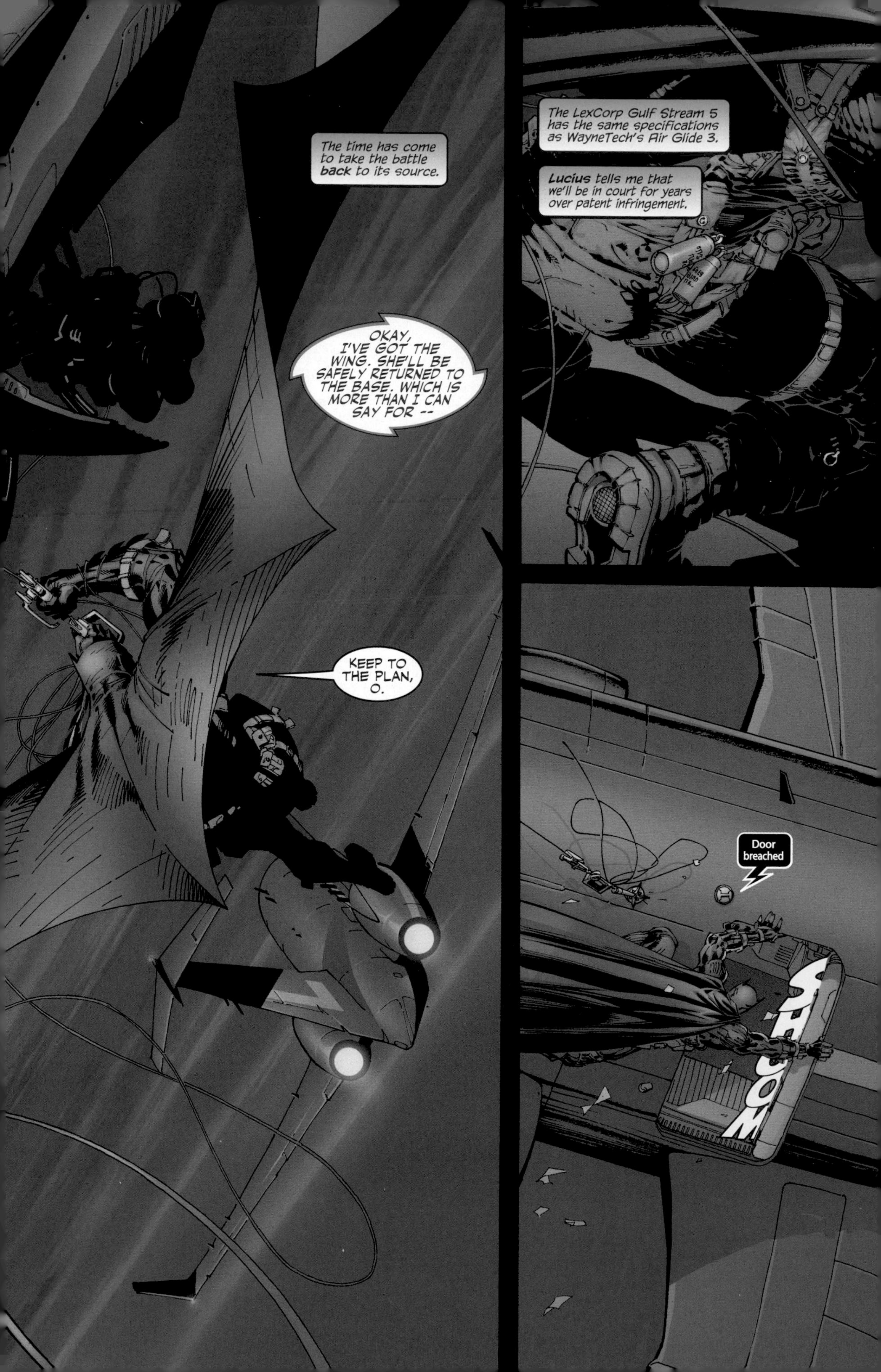
The time has come to take the battle back to its source.
OKAY, I'VE GOT THE WING. SHE'LL BE SAFELY RETURNED TO THE BASE. WHICH IS MORE THAN I CAN SAY FOR --
KEEP TO THE PLAN, O.
The LexCorp Gulf Stream 5 has the same specifications as WayneTech's Air Glide 3.
Lucius tells me that we'll be in court for years over patent infringement.
Door breached
SHOOM

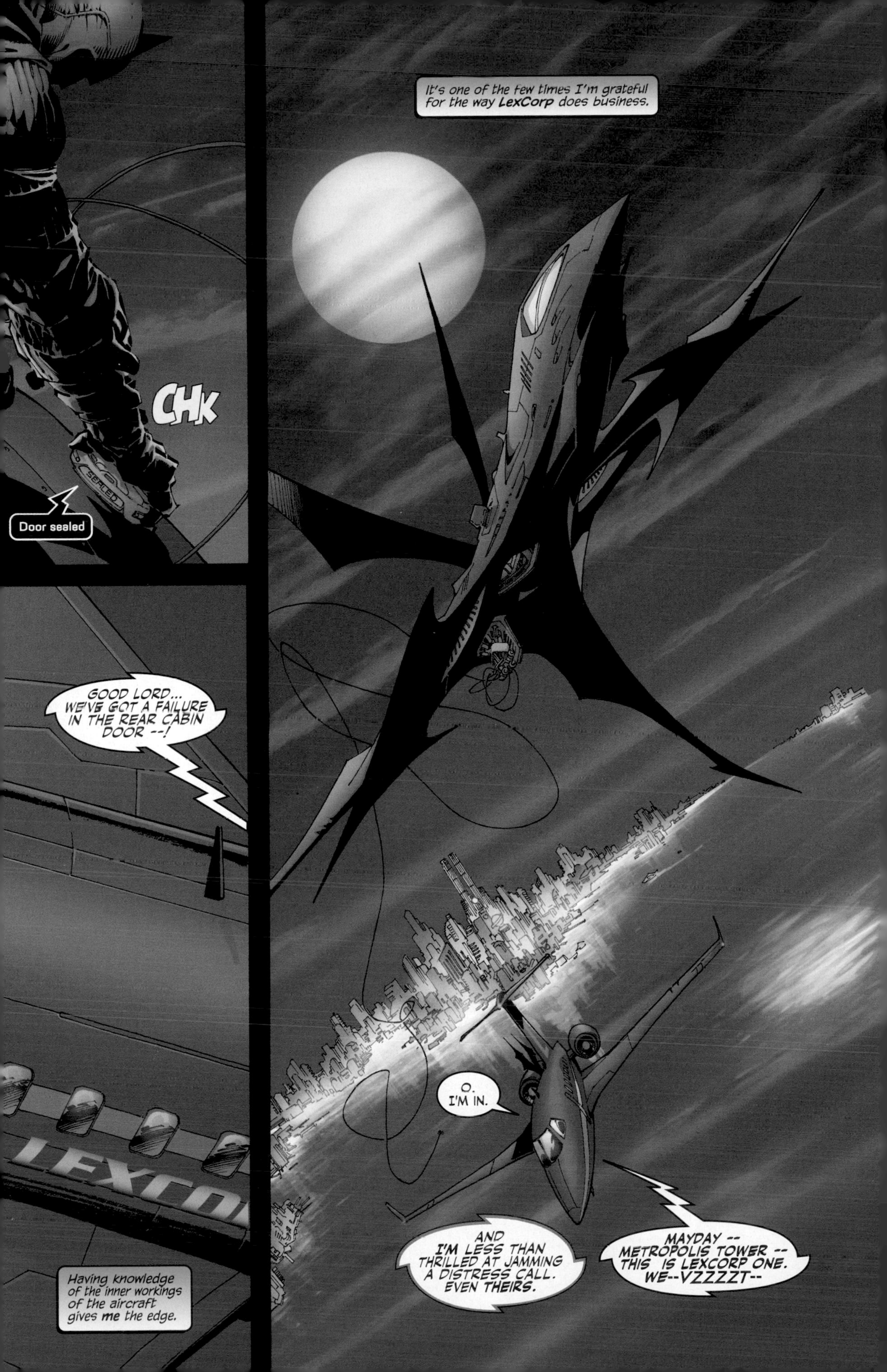
CHK
SEALED
Door sealed
It's one of the few times I'm grateful for the way LexCorp does business.
GOOD LORD... WE'VE GOT A FAILURE IN THE REAR CABIN DOOR --!
O. I'M IN.
LEXCO
Having knowledge of the inner workings of the aircraft gives me the edge.
AND I'M LESS THAN THRILLED AT JAMMING A DISTRESS CALL. EVEN THEIRS.
MAYDAY -- METROPOLIS TOWER -- THIS IS LEXCORP ONE. WE--VZZZZT--

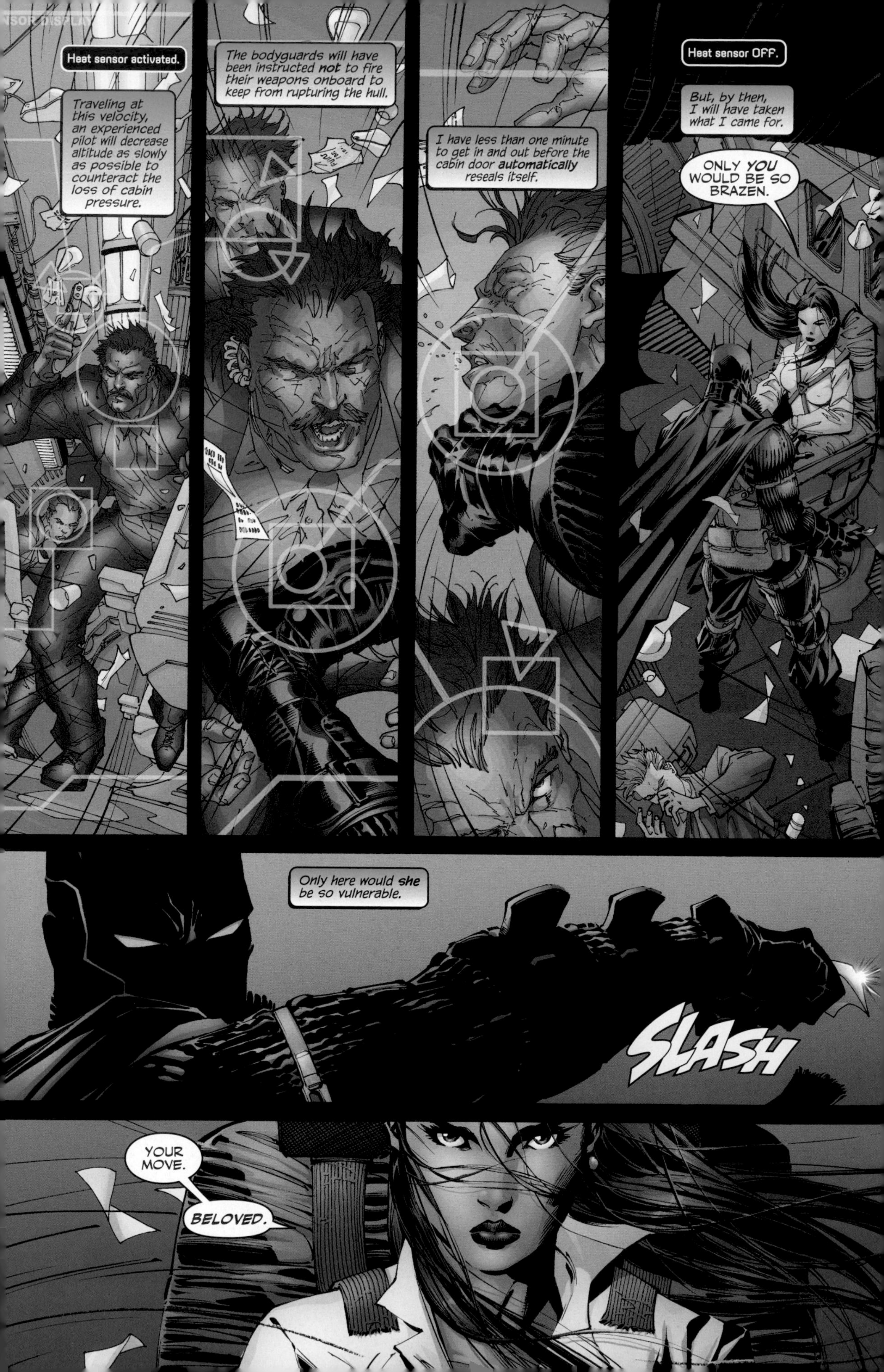
NSOR DISPLAY
Heat sensor activated.
Traveling at this velocity, an experienced pilot will decrease altitude as slowly as possible to counteract the loss of cabin pressure.
The bodyguards will have been instructed **not** to fire their weapons onboard to keep from rupturing the hull.
I have less than one minute to get in and out before the cabin door **automatically** reseals itself.
Heat sensor OFF.
But, by then, I will have taken what I came for.
ONLY *YOU* WOULD BE SO BRAZEN.
Only here would **she** be so vulnerable.
SLASH
YOUR MOVE.
BELOVED.

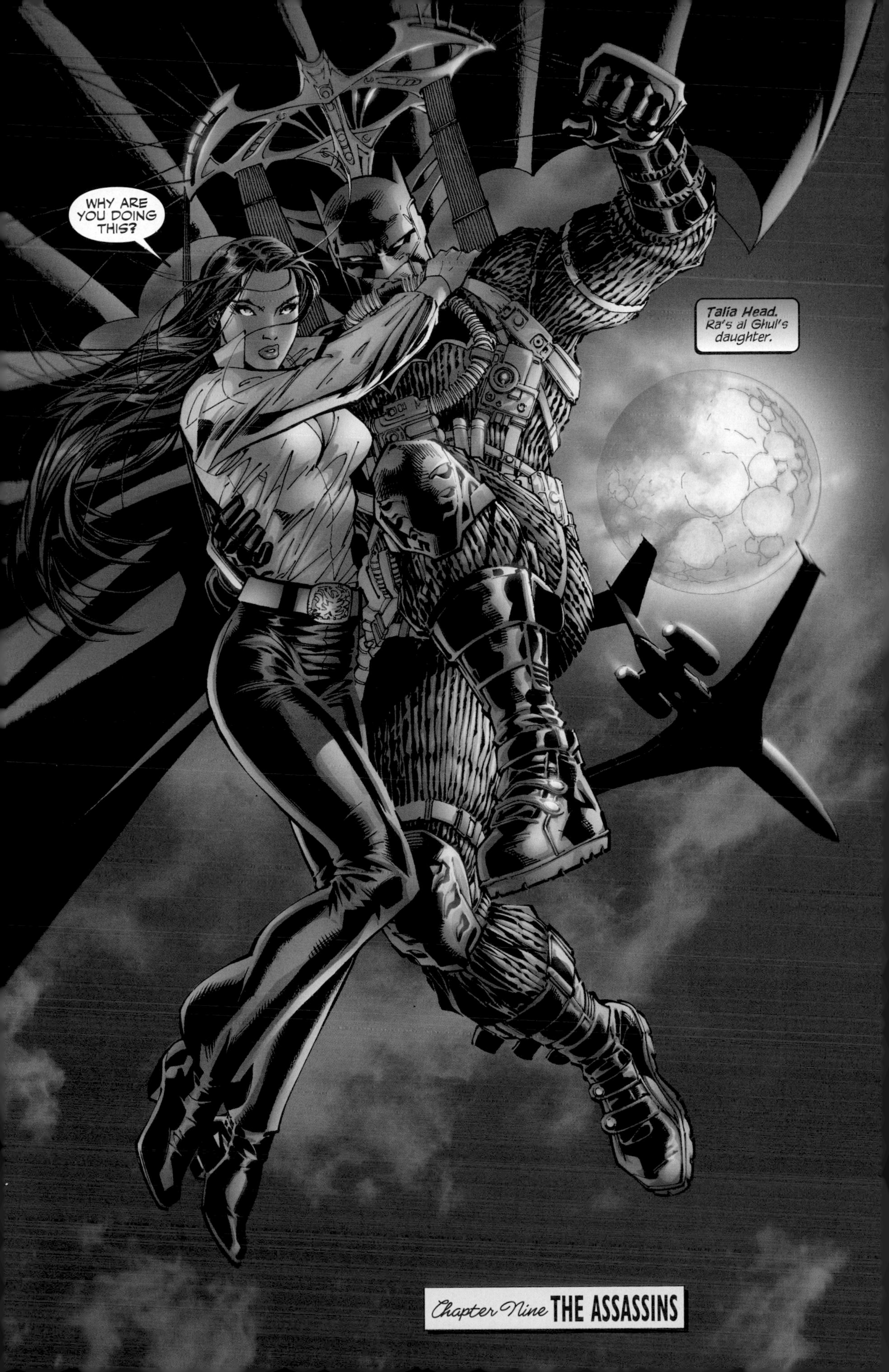

WHY ARE YOU DOING THIS?
Talia Head. Ra's al Ghul's daughter.
Chapter Nine THE ASSASSINS

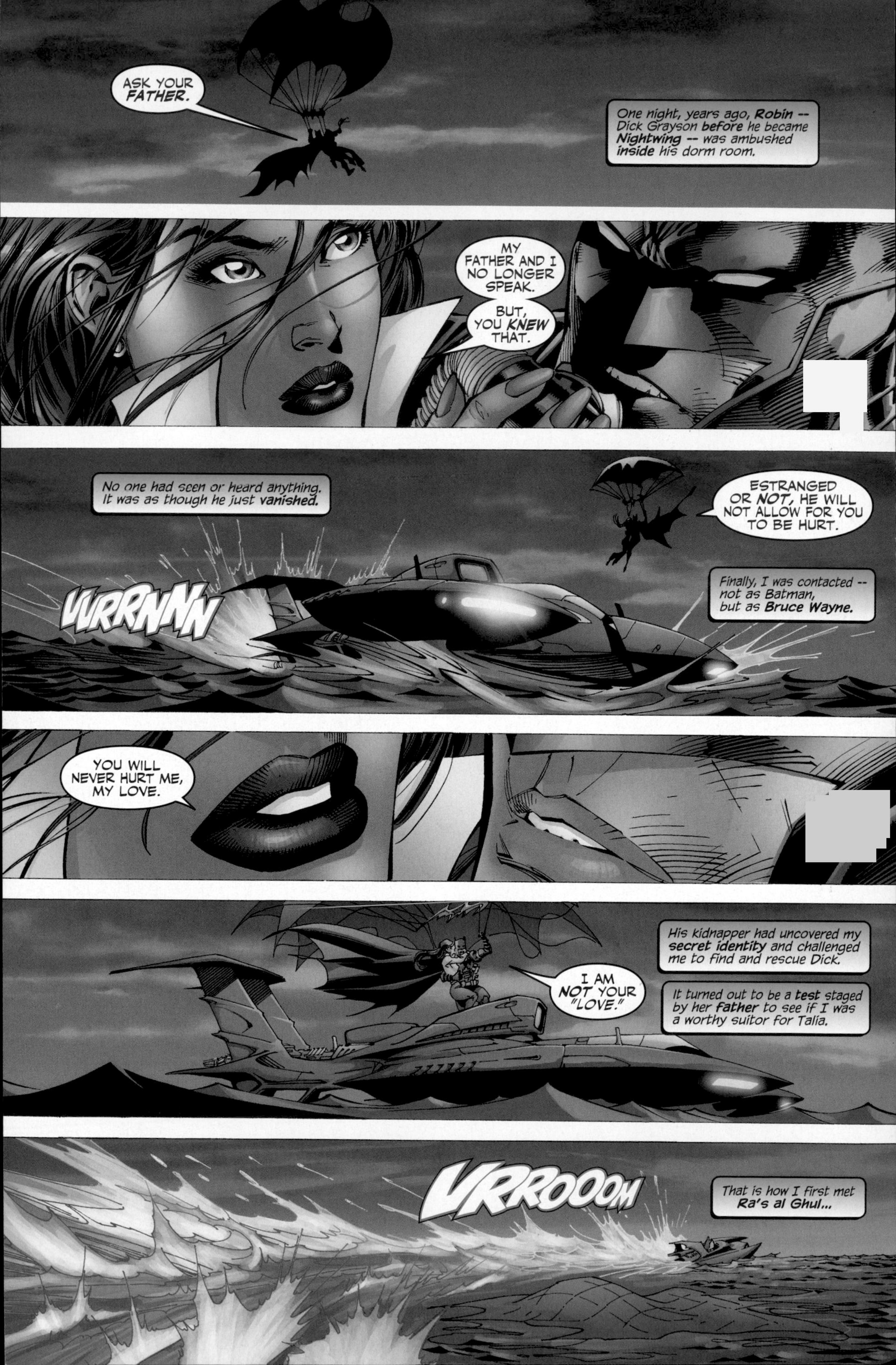
ASK YOUR FATHER.
One night, years ago, Robin -- Dick Grayson before he became Nightwing -- was ambushed inside his dorm room.
MY FATHER AND I NO LONGER SPEAK.
BUT, YOU KNEW THAT.
No one had seen or heard anything. It was as though he just vanished.
ESTRANGED OR NOT, HE WILL NOT ALLOW FOR YOU TO BE HURT.
VVRRNNN
Finally, I was contacted -- not as Batman, but as Bruce Wayne.
YOU WILL NEVER HURT ME, MY LOVE.
His kidnapper had uncovered my secret identity and challenged me to find and rescue Dick.
I AM NOT YOUR "LOVE."
It turned out to be a test staged by her father to see if I was a worthy suitor for Talia.
VRROOOM
That is how I first met Ra's al Ghul...

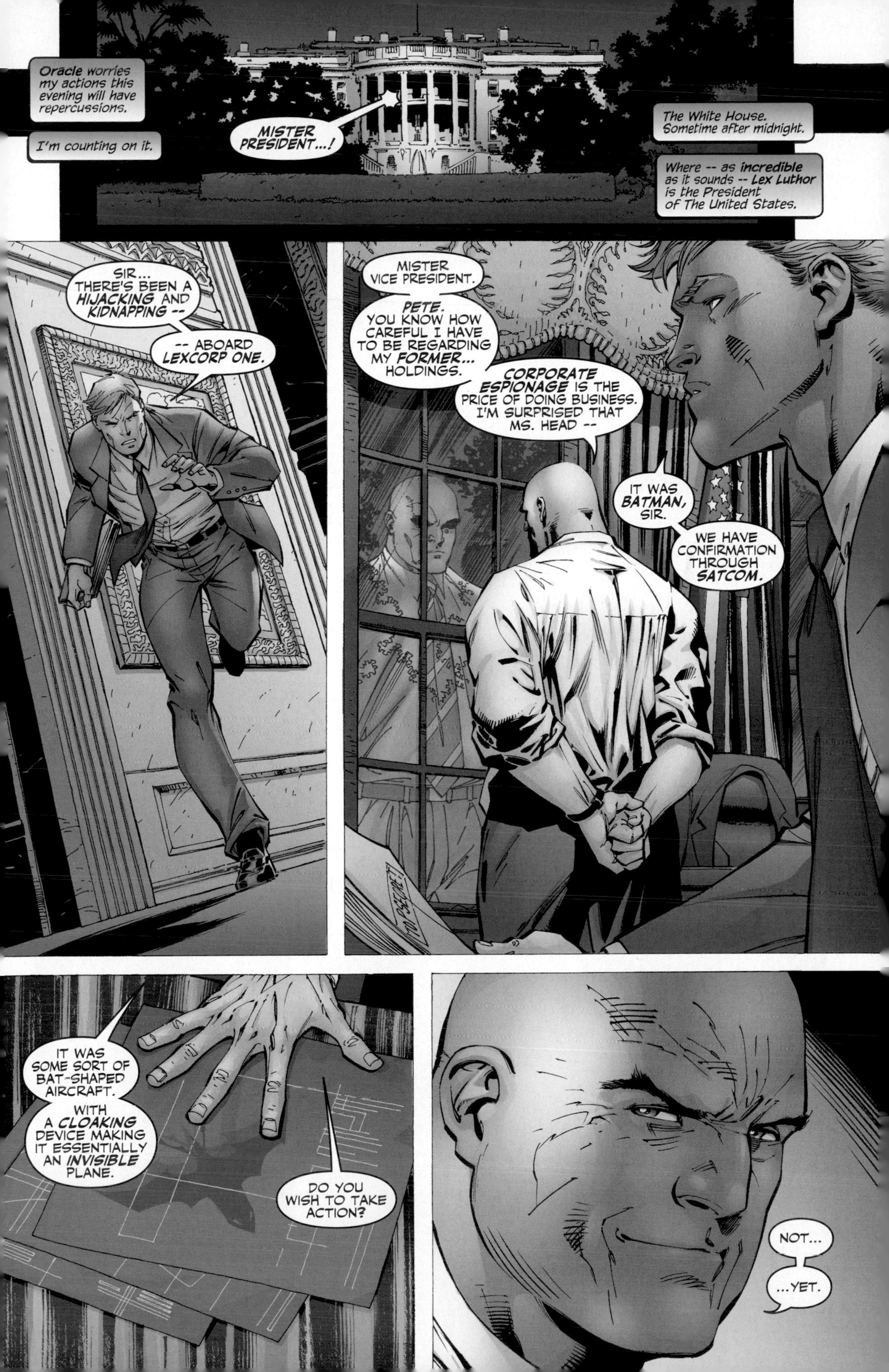
Oracle worries my actions this evening will have repercussions.
I'm counting on it.
MISTER PRESIDENT...!
The White House. Sometime after midnight.
Where -- as incredible as it sounds -- Lex Luthor is the President of The United States.
SIR... THERE'S BEEN A HIJACKING AND KIDNAPPING --
-- ABOARD LEXCORP ONE.
MISTER VICE PRESIDENT.
PETE. YOU KNOW HOW CAREFUL I HAVE TO BE REGARDING MY FORMER... HOLDINGS.
CORPORATE ESPIONAGE IS THE PRICE OF DOING BUSINESS. I'M SURPRISED THAT MS. HEAD --
IT WAS BATMAN, SIR.
WE HAVE CONFIRMATION THROUGH SATCOM.
IT WAS SOME SORT OF BAT-SHAPED AIRCRAFT.
WITH A CLOAKING DEVICE MAKING IT ESSENTIALLY AN INVISIBLE PLANE.
DO YOU WISH TO TAKE ACTION?
NOT...
...YET.

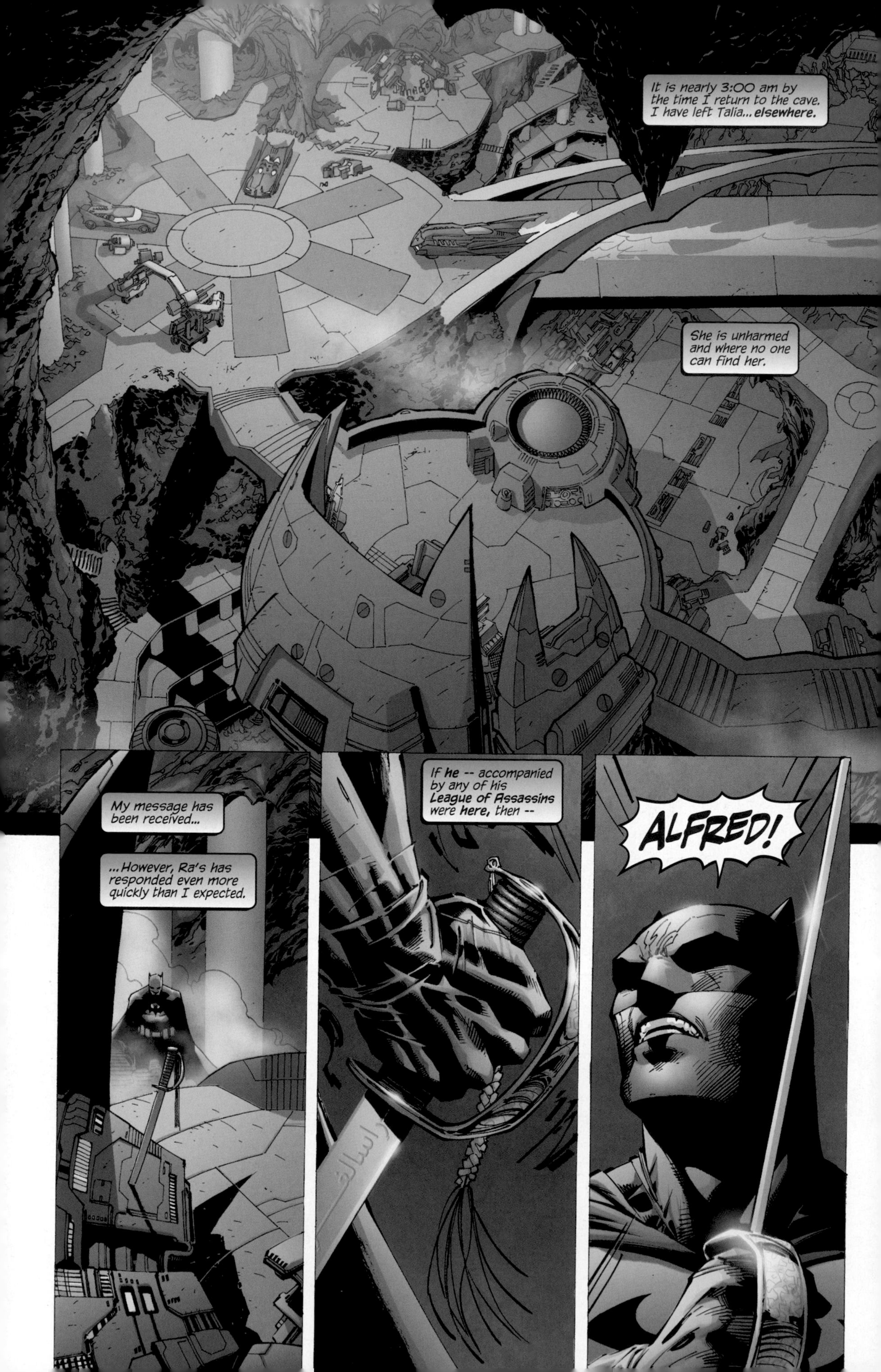
It is nearly 3:00 am by the time I return to the cave. I have left Talia... elsewhere.
She is unharmed and where no one can find her.
My message has been received...
...However, Ra's has responded even more quickly than I expected.
If he -- accompanied by any of his League of Assassins were here, then --
ALFRED!

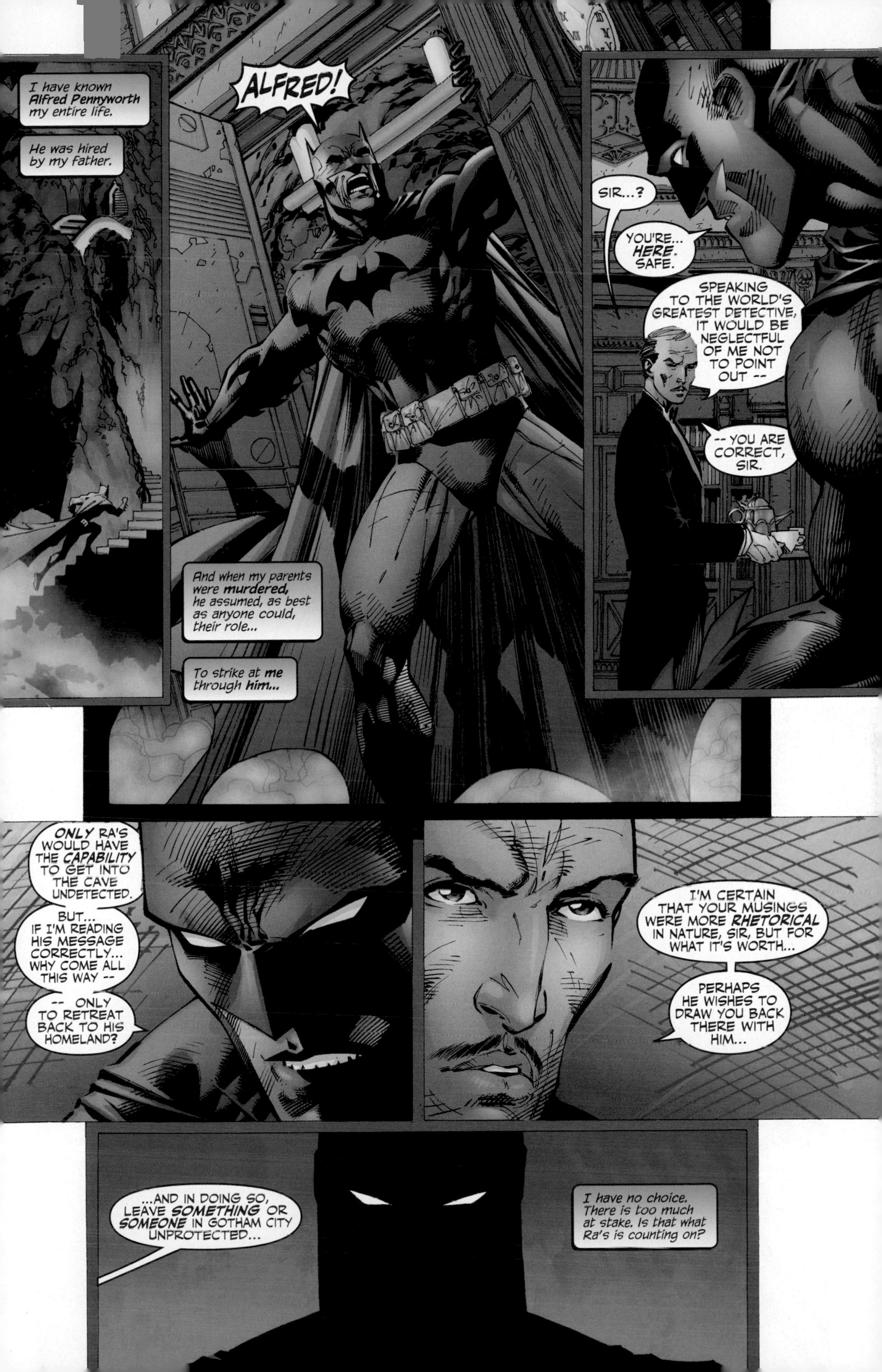

I have known Alfred Pennyworth my entire life.
He was hired by my father.
ALFRED!
And when my parents were murdered, he assumed, as best as anyone could, their role...
To strike at me through him...
SIR...?
YOU'RE... HERE. SAFE.
SPEAKING TO THE WORLD'S GREATEST DETECTIVE, IT WOULD BE NEGLECTFUL OF ME NOT TO POINT OUT --
-- YOU ARE CORRECT, SIR.
ONLY RA'S WOULD HAVE THE CAPABILITY TO GET INTO THE CAVE UNDETECTED.
BUT... IF I'M READING HIS MESSAGE CORRECTLY... WHY COME ALL THIS WAY --
-- ONLY TO RETREAT BACK TO HIS HOMELAND?
I'M CERTAIN THAT YOUR MUSINGS WERE MORE RHETORICAL IN NATURE, SIR, BUT FOR WHAT IT'S WORTH...
PERHAPS HE WISHES TO DRAW YOU BACK THERE WITH HIM...
...AND IN DOING SO, LEAVE SOMETHING OR SOMEONE IN GOTHAM CITY UNPROTECTED...
I have no choice. There is too much at stake. Is that what Ra's is counting on?

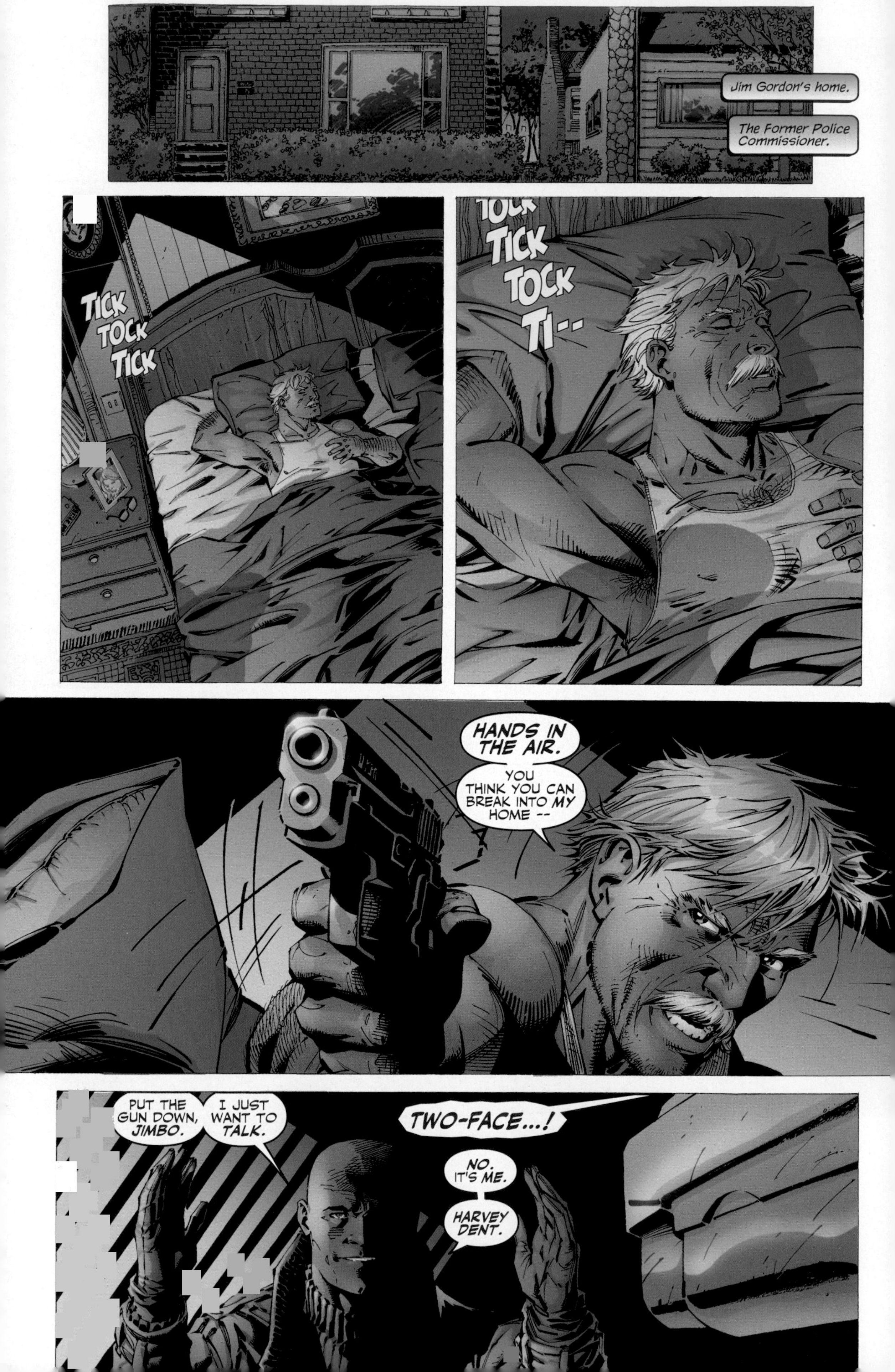

Jim Gordon's home.
The Former Police Commissioner.
TICK TOCK TICK
TOCK TICK TOCK TI--
HANDS IN THE AIR.
YOU THINK YOU CAN BREAK INTO MY HOME --
PUT THE GUN DOWN, JIMBO.
I JUST WANT TO TALK.
TWO-FACE...!
NO. IT'S ME.
HARVEY DENT.

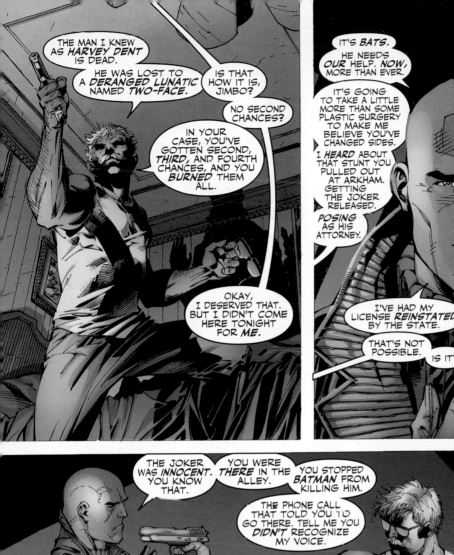

THE MAN I KNEW AS *HARVEY DENT* IS DEAD. HE WAS LOST TO A *DERANGED LUNATIC* NAMED *TWO-FACE.*

IS THAT HOW IT IS, JIMBO?

NO SECOND CHANCES?

IN YOUR CASE, YOU'VE GOTTEN SECOND, *THIRD,* AND FOURTH CHANCES, AND YOU *BURNED* THEM ALL.

OKAY, I DESERVED THAT. BUT I DIDN'T COME HERE TONIGHT FOR *ME.*

IT'S *BATS.* HE NEEDS *OUR* HELP. *NOW,* MORE THAN EVER.

IT'S GOING TO TAKE A LITTLE MORE THAN SOME PLASTIC SURGERY TO MAKE ME BELIEVE YOU'VE CHANGED SIDES. *I HEARD* ABOUT THAT STUNT YOU PULLED OUT AT ARKHAM. GETTING THE JOKER RELEASED. *POSING* AS HIS ATTORNEY.

I'VE HAD MY LICENSE *REINSTATED* BY THE STATE.

THAT'S NOT POSSIBLE.

IS IT?

THE JOKER WAS *INNOCENT.* YOU KNOW THAT.

YOU WERE *THERE* IN THE ALLEY.

YOU STOPPED *BATMAN* FROM KILLING HIM.

THE PHONE CALL THAT TOLD YOU TO GO THERE. TELL ME YOU *DIDN'T* RECOGNIZE MY VOICE.

...

WHAT THE HELL DO YOU WANT?

THE GUN THAT KILLED TOMMY ELLIOT.

WHEN ITS FOUND, IT WILL BE TRACED BACK TO *YOU.*

IT'S YOUR *SERVICE PISTOL.* THE ONE YOU *TURNED IN* WHEN YOU RETIRED.

HOW COULD YOU KNOW A THING LIKE THAT?

IT'S ALL PART OF A *GAME.*

...HOW MUCH LONGER DO YOU WANT TO PLAY?

LIKE IT NOT, WE'RE *TWO* OF THE PIECES.

THE QUESTION IS...

The camel's bridle on the **hilt** of the sword.

One of my **earliest** encounters with Ra's began with my finding one he had left behind.

It brought me here, to **North Africa**, as it has again.

WHERE IS MY DAUGHTER...

...DETECTIVE?

SAFE.

YOU **THINK** I AM RESPONSIBLE FOR YOUR RECENT...

...**MISFORTUNES.** THE DEATH OF YOUR FRIEND **THOMAS ELLIOT,** FOR EXAMPLE.

YOU ARE **MISTAKEN.**

YOU HAVE MEANS.

OPPORTUNITY.

AND **KNOWLEDGE** ONLY A **FEW** POSSESS...

...ABOUT MY PERSONAL LIFE.

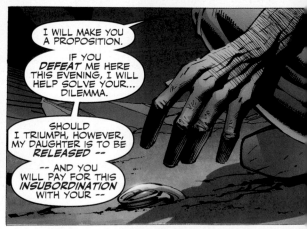

I WILL MAKE YOU A PROPOSITION.

IF YOU **DEFEAT** ME HERE THIS EVENING, I WILL HELP SOLVE YOUR... DILEMMA.

SHOULD I TRIUMPH, HOWEVER, MY DAUGHTER IS TO BE **RELEASED** --

-- AND YOU WILL PAY FOR THIS **INSUBORDINATION** WITH YOUR --

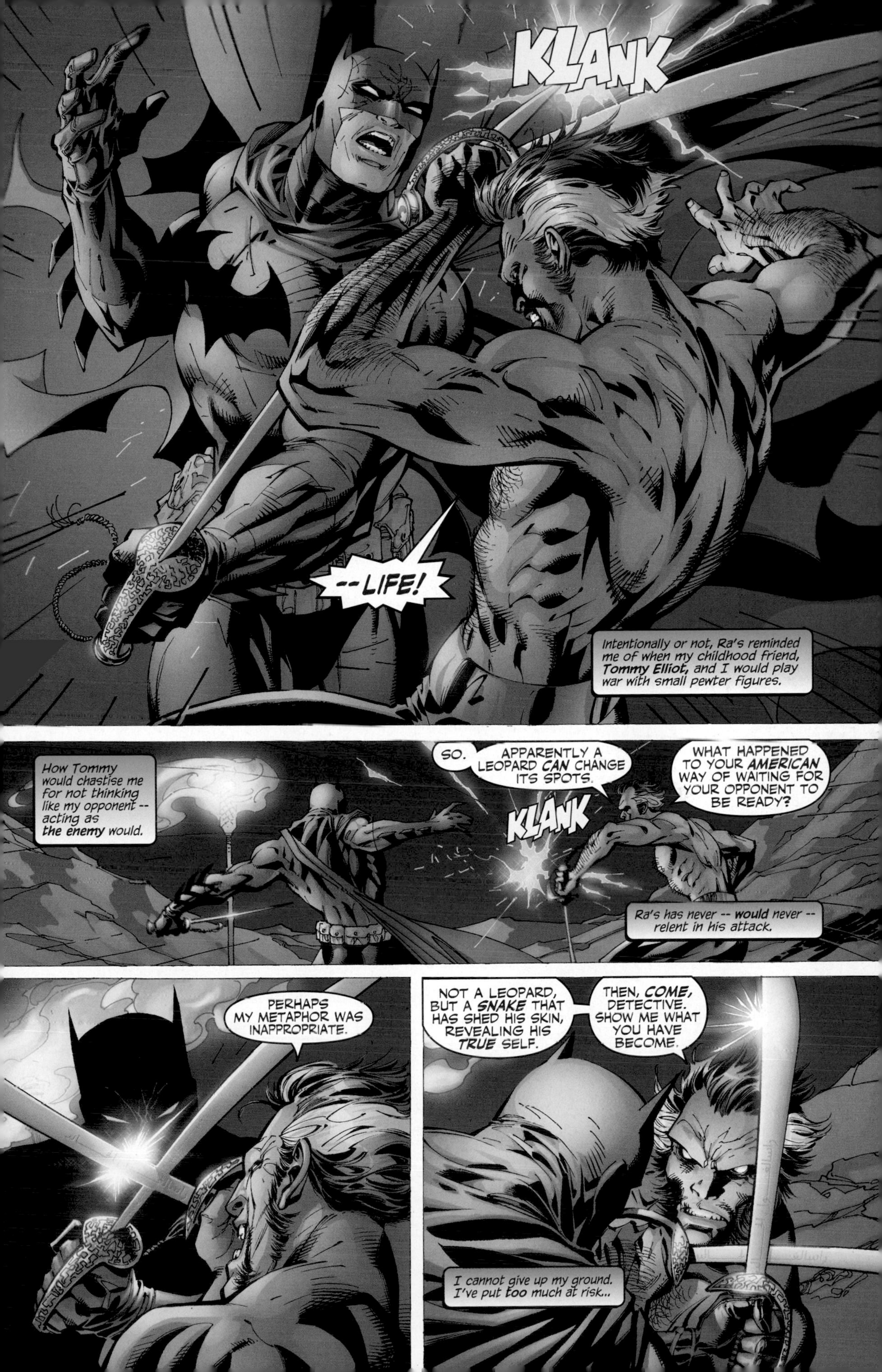
KLANK
--LIFE!
Intentionally or not, Ra's reminded me of when my childhood friend, Tommy Elliot, and I would play war with small pewter figures.
How Tommy would chastise me for not thinking like my opponent -- acting as the enemy would.
SO.
APPARENTLY A LEOPARD CAN CHANGE ITS SPOTS.
WHAT HAPPENED TO YOUR AMERICAN WAY OF WAITING FOR YOUR OPPONENT TO BE READY?
KLANK
Ra's has never -- would never -- relent in his attack.
PERHAPS MY METAPHOR WAS INAPPROPRIATE.
NOT A LEOPARD, BUT A SNAKE THAT HAS SHED HIS SKIN, REVEALING HIS TRUE SELF.
THEN, COME, DETECTIVE. SHOW ME WHAT YOU HAVE BECOME.
I cannot give up my ground. I've put too much at risk...

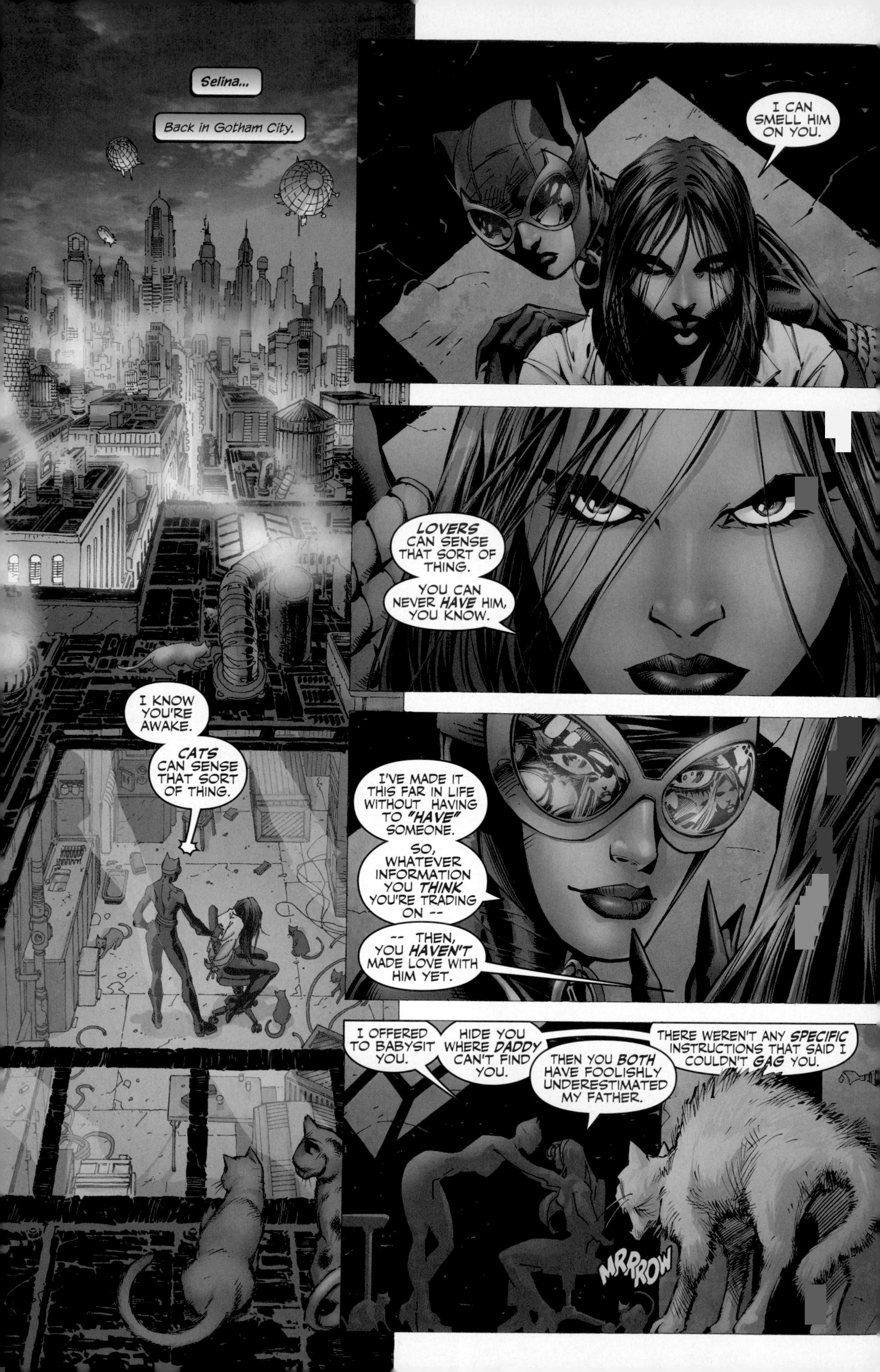
Selina...
Back in Gotham City.
I CAN SMELL HIM ON YOU.
LOVERS CAN SENSE THAT SORT OF THING.
YOU CAN NEVER HAVE HIM, YOU KNOW.
I KNOW YOU'RE AWAKE.
CATS CAN SENSE THAT SORT OF THING.
I'VE MADE IT THIS FAR IN LIFE WITHOUT HAVING TO "HAVE" SOMEONE.
SO, WHATEVER INFORMATION YOU THINK YOU'RE TRADING ON --
-- THEN, YOU HAVEN'T MADE LOVE WITH HIM YET.
I OFFERED TO BABYSIT YOU.
HIDE YOU WHERE DADDY CAN'T FIND YOU.
THEN YOU BOTH HAVE FOOLISHLY UNDERESTIMATED MY FATHER.
THERE WEREN'T ANY SPECIFIC INSTRUCTIONS THAT SAID I COULDN'T GAG YOU.
MRRROW

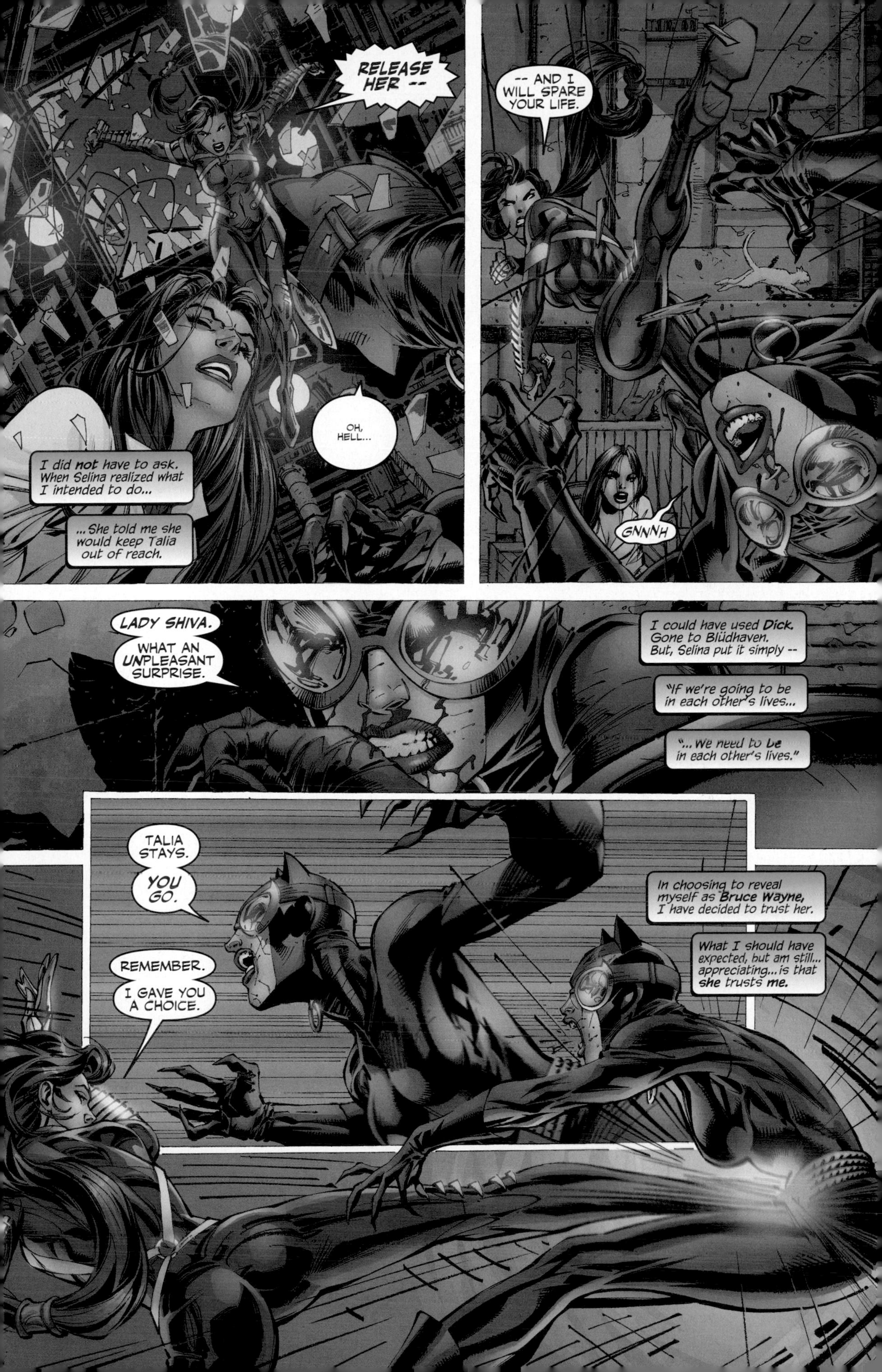
RELEASE HER --
-- AND I WILL SPARE YOUR LIFE.
OH, HELL...
I did **not** have to ask. When Selina realized what I intended to do...
...She told me she would keep Talia out of reach.
GNNNH
LADY SHIVA.
WHAT AN *UN*PLEASANT SURPRISE.
I could have used **Dick.** Gone to Blüdhaven. But, Selina put it simply --
"If we're going to be in each other's lives...
"...We need to **be** in each other's lives."
TALIA STAYS.
*YOU* GO.
REMEMBER.
I GAVE YOU A CHOICE.
In choosing to reveal myself as **Bruce Wayne,** I have decided to trust her.
What I should have expected, but am still... appreciating...is that **she** trusts **me.**

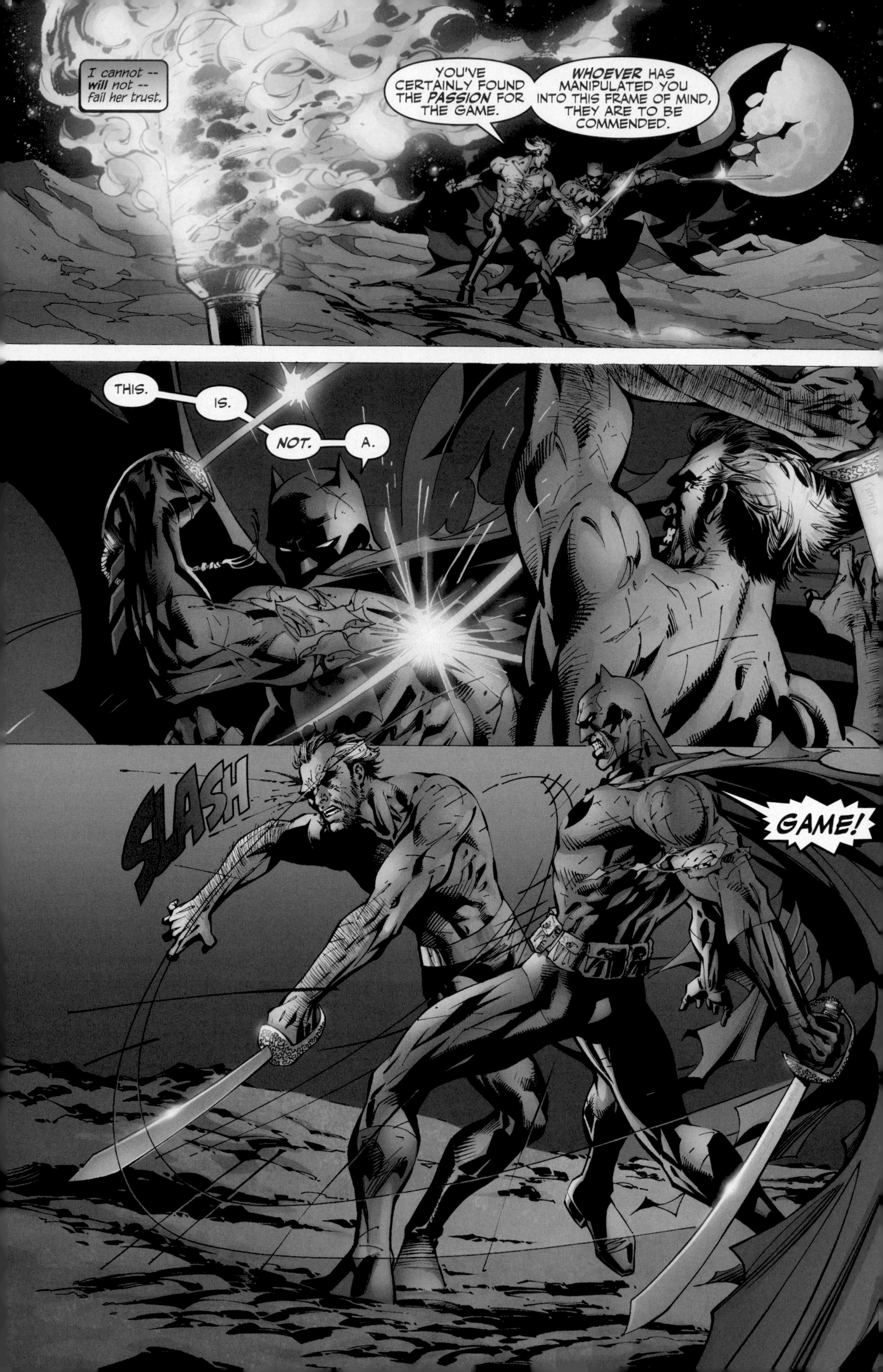
I cannot -- will not -- fail her trust.
YOU'VE CERTAINLY FOUND THE PASSION FOR THE GAME.
WHOEVER HAS MANIPULATED YOU INTO THIS FRAME OF MIND, THEY ARE TO BE COMMENDED.
THIS.
IS.
NOT.
A.
SLASH
GAME!

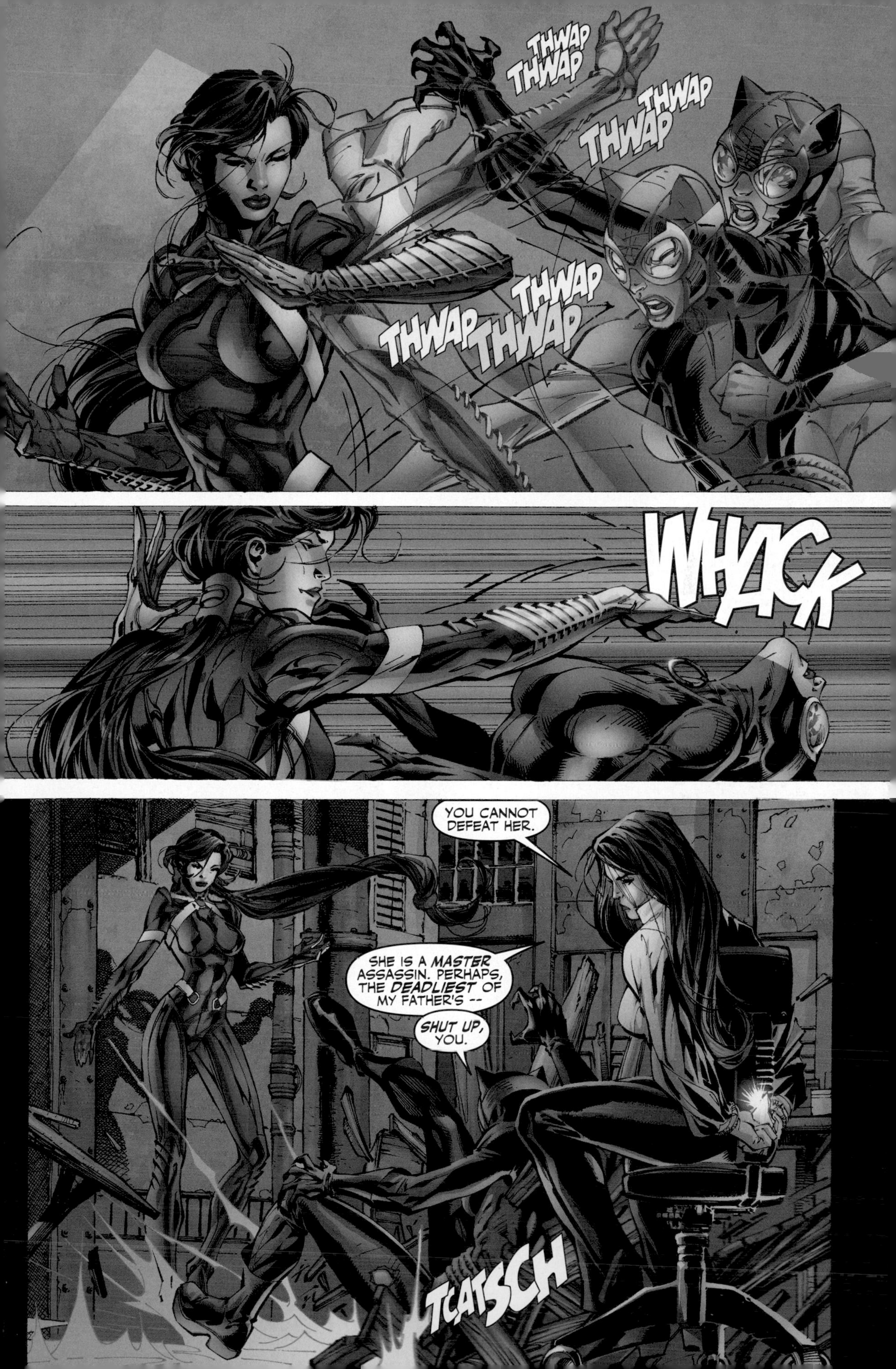
THWAP
THWAP
THWAP
THWAP
THWAP
THWAP
THWAP
WHACK
YOU CANNOT DEFEAT HER.
SHE IS A MASTER ASSASSIN. PERHAPS, THE DEADLIEST OF MY FATHER'S --
SHUT UP, YOU.
TCATSCH

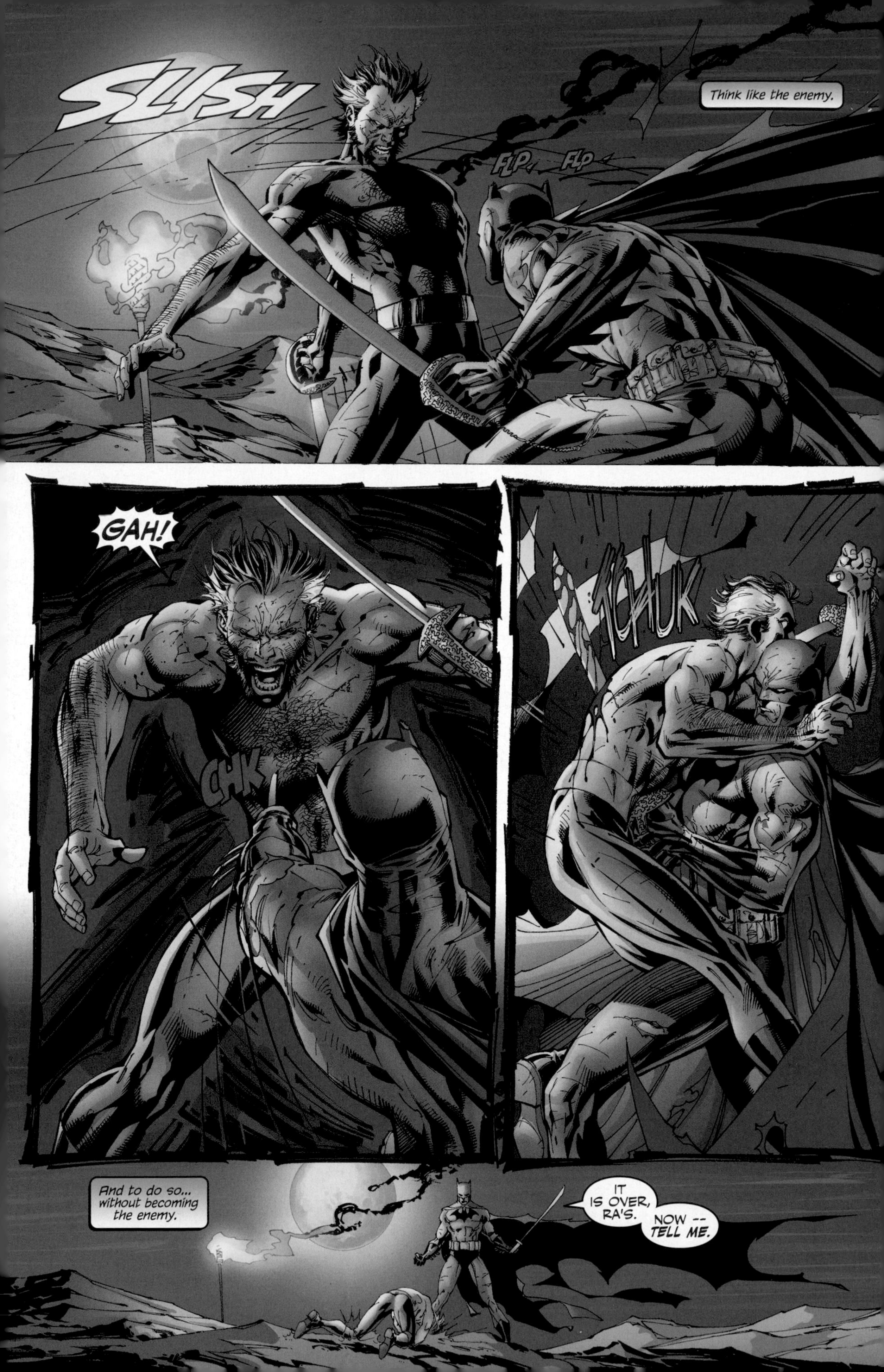
SLISH
Think like the enemy.
FLP
FLP
GAH!
CHK
KCHUK
And to do so... without becoming the enemy.
IT IS OVER, RA'S.
NOW -- TELL ME.

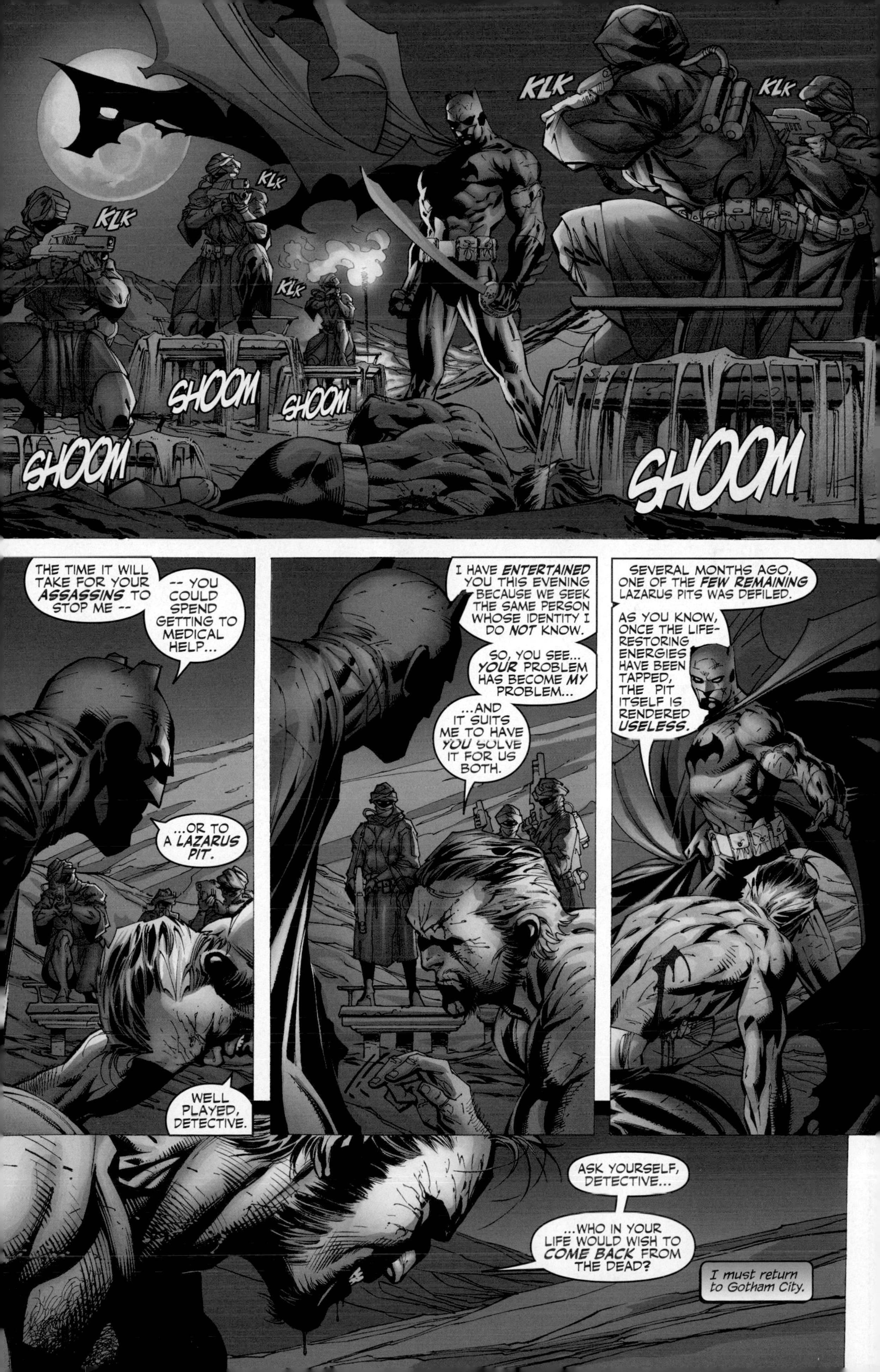
KLK
KLK
KLK
KLK
KLK
SHOOM
SHOOM
SHOOM
SHOOM
THE TIME IT WILL TAKE FOR YOUR ASSASSINS TO STOP ME --
-- YOU COULD SPEND GETTING TO MEDICAL HELP...
...OR TO A LAZARUS PIT.
WELL PLAYED, DETECTIVE.
I HAVE ENTERTAINED YOU THIS EVENING BECAUSE WE SEEK THE SAME PERSON WHOSE IDENTITY I DO NOT KNOW.
SO, YOU SEE... YOUR PROBLEM HAS BECOME MY PROBLEM...
...AND IT SUITS ME TO HAVE YOU SOLVE IT FOR US BOTH.
SEVERAL MONTHS AGO, ONE OF THE FEW REMAINING LAZARUS PITS WAS DEFILED.
AS YOU KNOW, ONCE THE LIFE-RESTORING ENERGIES HAVE BEEN TAPPED, THE PIT ITSELF IS RENDERED USELESS.
ASK YOURSELF, DETECTIVE...
...WHO IN YOUR LIFE WOULD WISH TO COME BACK FROM THE DEAD?
I must return to Gotham City.

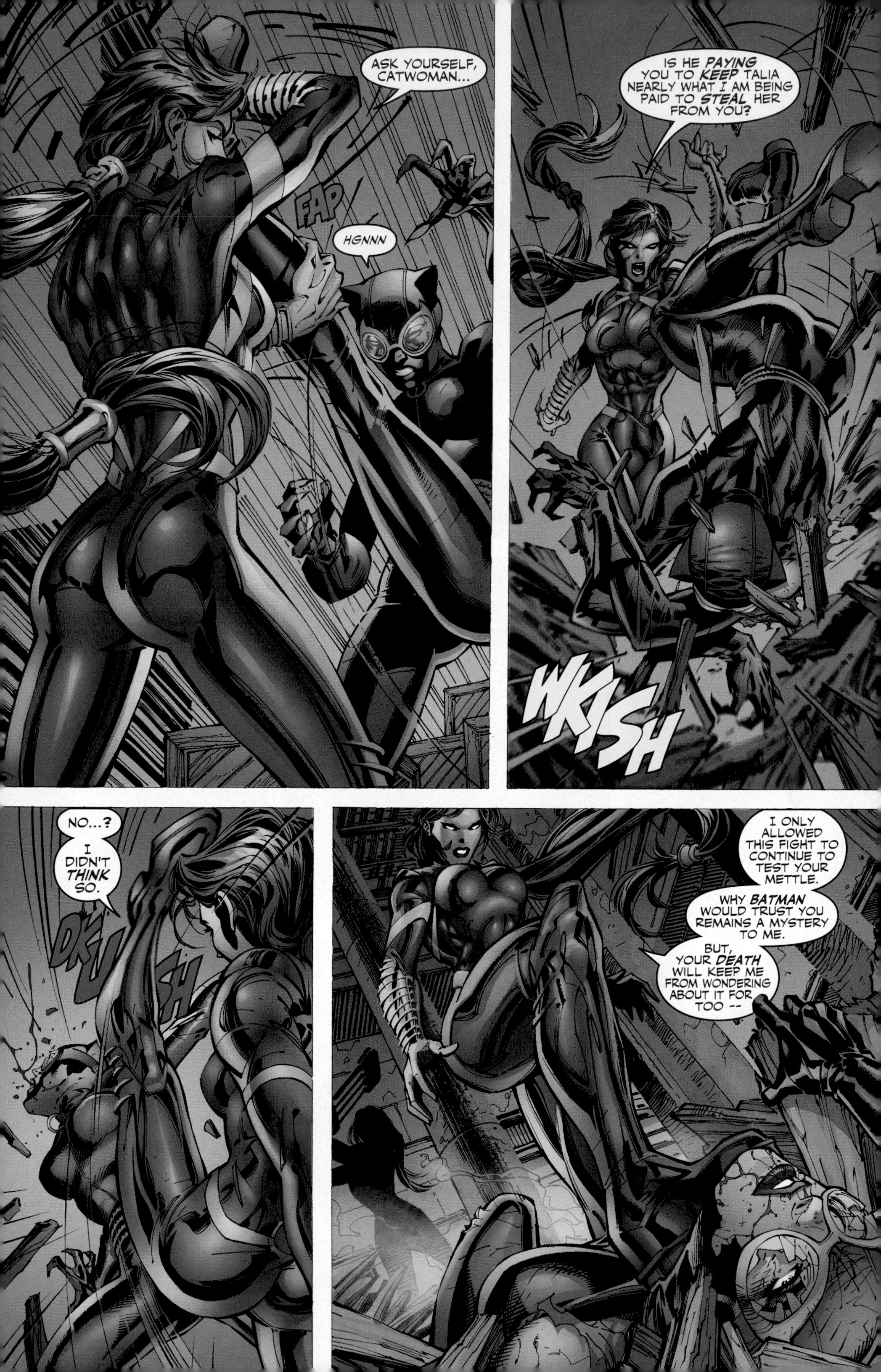
ASK YOURSELF, CATWOMAN...
FAP
HGNNN
IS HE *PAYING* YOU TO *KEEP* TALIA NEARLY WHAT *I* AM BEING PAID TO *STEAL* HER FROM YOU?
WKISH
NO...?
I DIDN'T *THINK* SO.
DKRUSH
I ONLY ALLOWED THIS FIGHT TO CONTINUE TO TEST YOUR METTLE.
WHY *BATMAN* WOULD TRUST YOU REMAINS A MYSTERY TO ME.
BUT, YOUR *DEATH* WILL KEEP ME FROM WONDERING ABOUT IT FOR TOO --

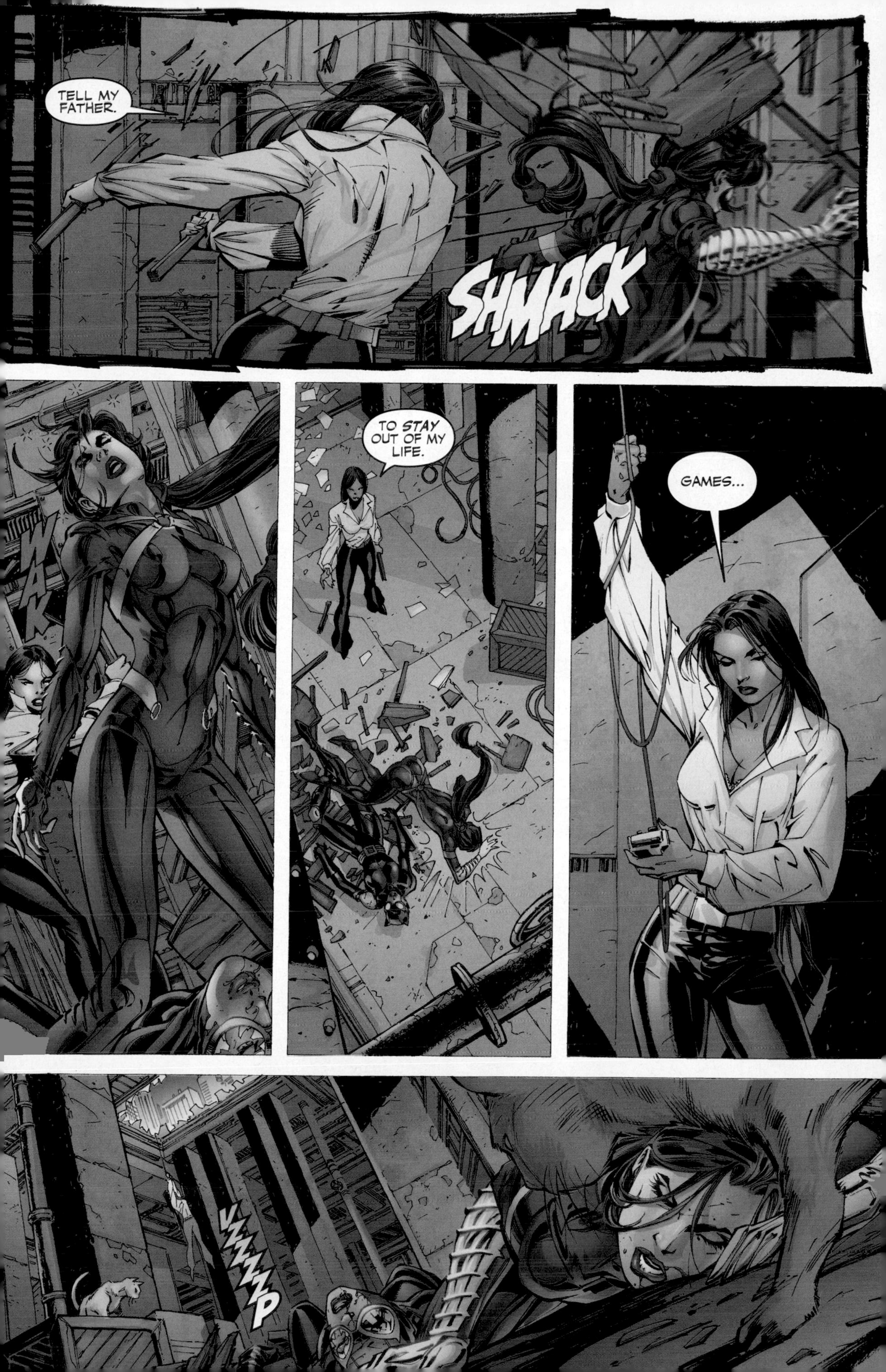
TELL MY FATHER.
SHMACK
WAK
TO STAY OUT OF MY LIFE.
GAMES...
VZZZZP

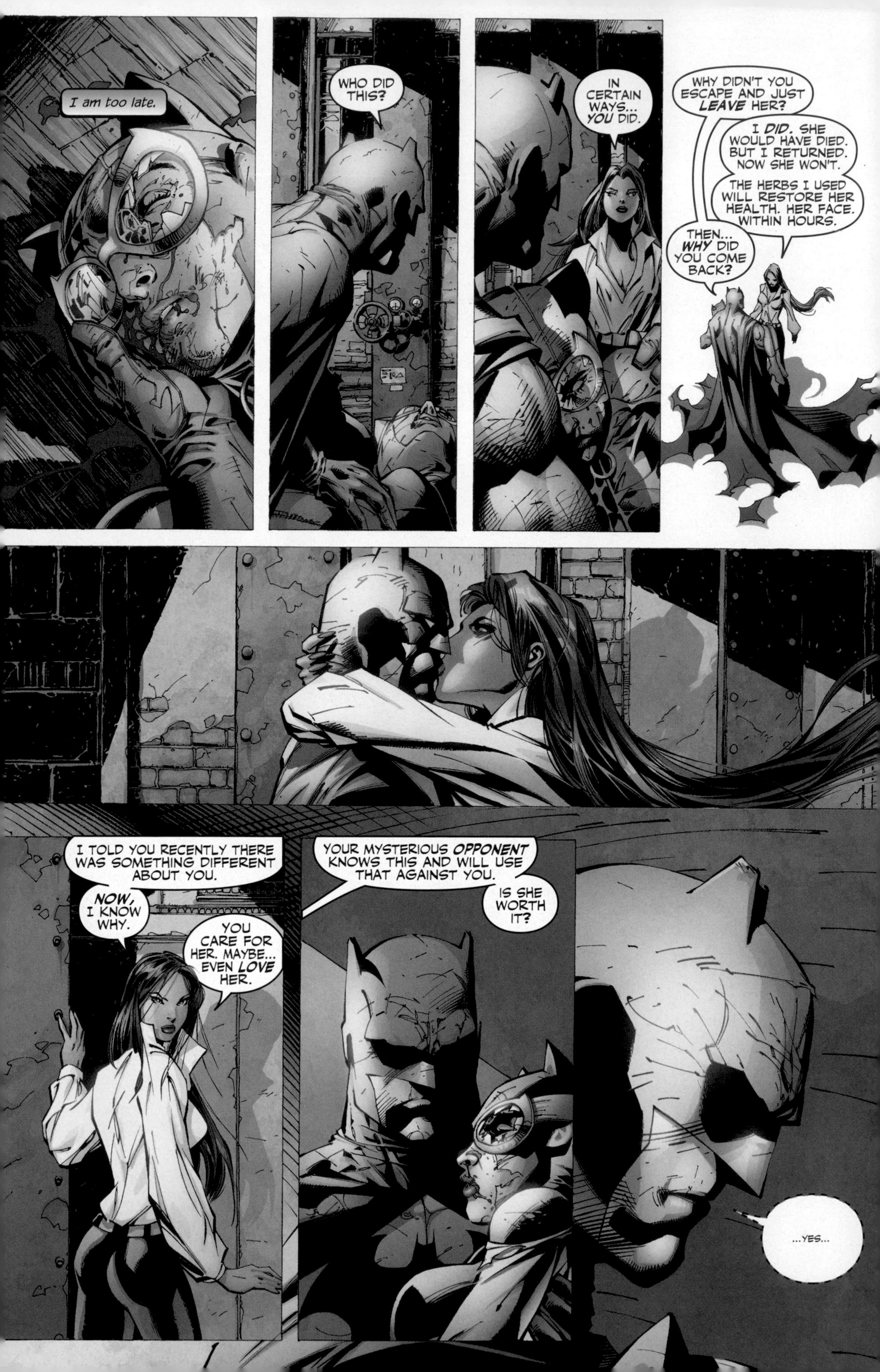
I am too late.
WHO DID THIS?
IN CERTAIN WAYS... YOU DID.
WHY DIDN'T YOU ESCAPE AND JUST LEAVE HER?
I DID. SHE WOULD HAVE DIED. BUT I RETURNED. NOW SHE WON'T.
THE HERBS I USED WILL RESTORE HER HEALTH. HER FACE. WITHIN HOURS.
THEN... WHY DID YOU COME BACK?
I TOLD YOU RECENTLY THERE WAS SOMETHING DIFFERENT ABOUT YOU.
NOW, I KNOW WHY.
YOU CARE FOR HER. MAYBE... EVEN LOVE HER.
YOUR MYSTERIOUS OPPONENT KNOWS THIS AND WILL USE THAT AGAINST YOU.
IS SHE WORTH IT?
...YES...

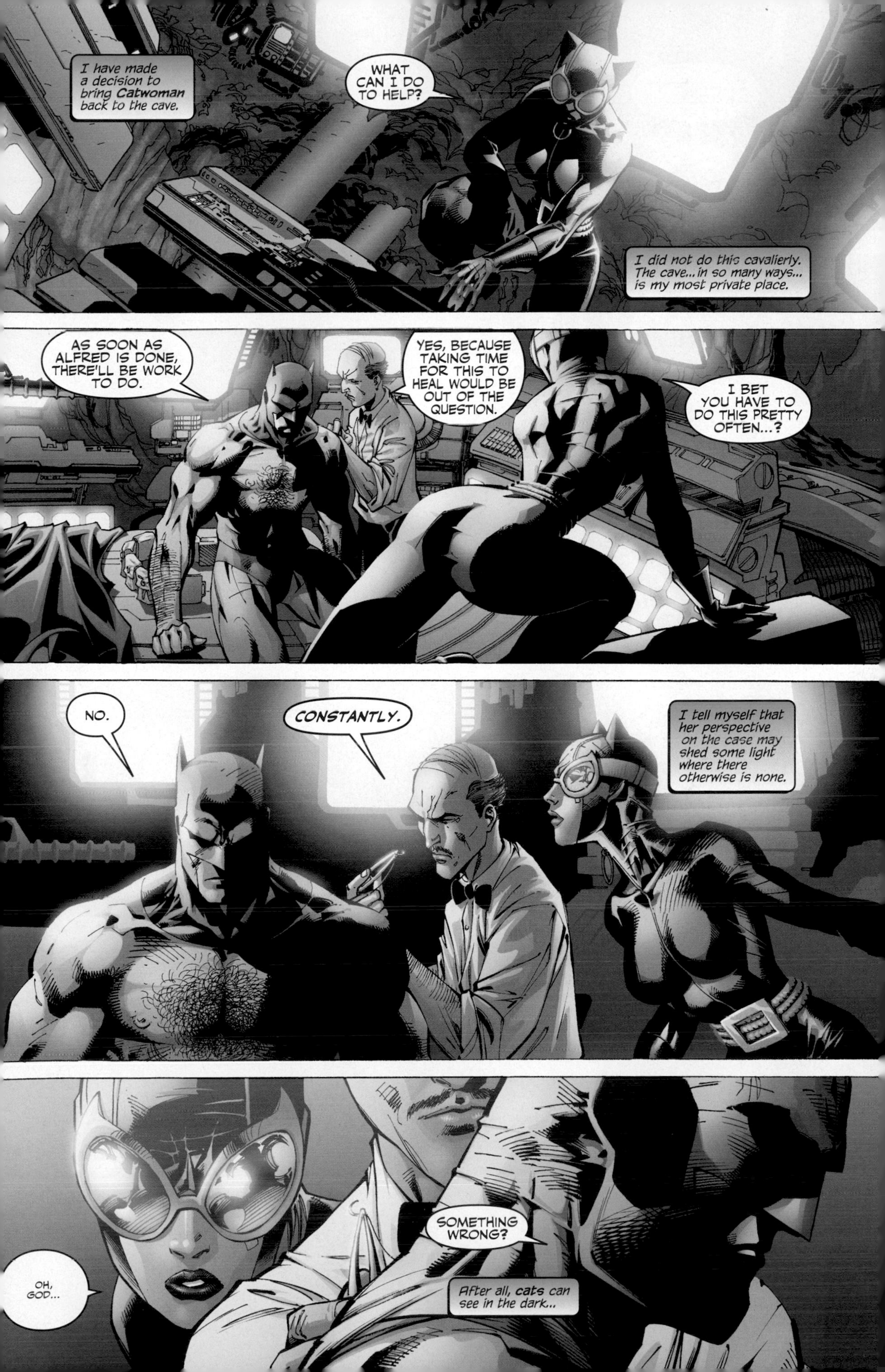
I have made a decision to bring Catwoman back to the cave.
WHAT CAN I DO TO HELP?
I did not do this cavalierly. The cave... in so many ways... is my most private place.
AS SOON AS ALFRED IS DONE, THERE'LL BE WORK TO DO.
YES, BECAUSE TAKING TIME FOR THIS TO HEAL WOULD BE OUT OF THE QUESTION.
I BET YOU HAVE TO DO THIS PRETTY OFTEN...?
NO.
CONSTANTLY.
I tell myself that her perspective on the case may shed some light where there otherwise is none.
SOMETHING WRONG?
OH, GOD...
After all, cats can see in the dark...

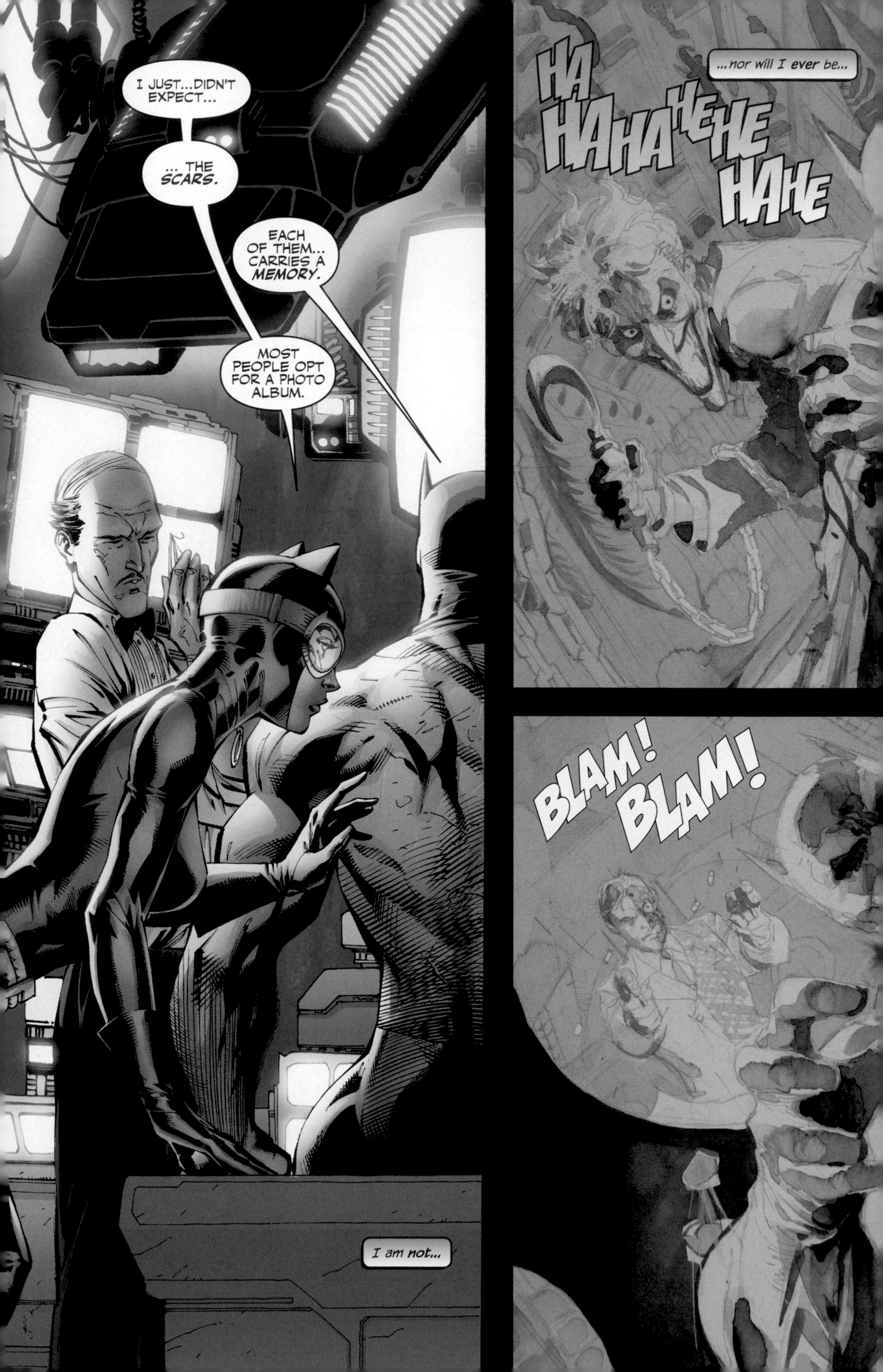

I JUST...DIDN'T EXPECT...
... THE SCARS.
EACH OF THEM... CARRIES A MEMORY.
MOST PEOPLE OPT FOR A PHOTO ALBUM.
I am not...
...nor will I ever be...
HA HAHAHEHE HAHE
BLAM! BLAM!

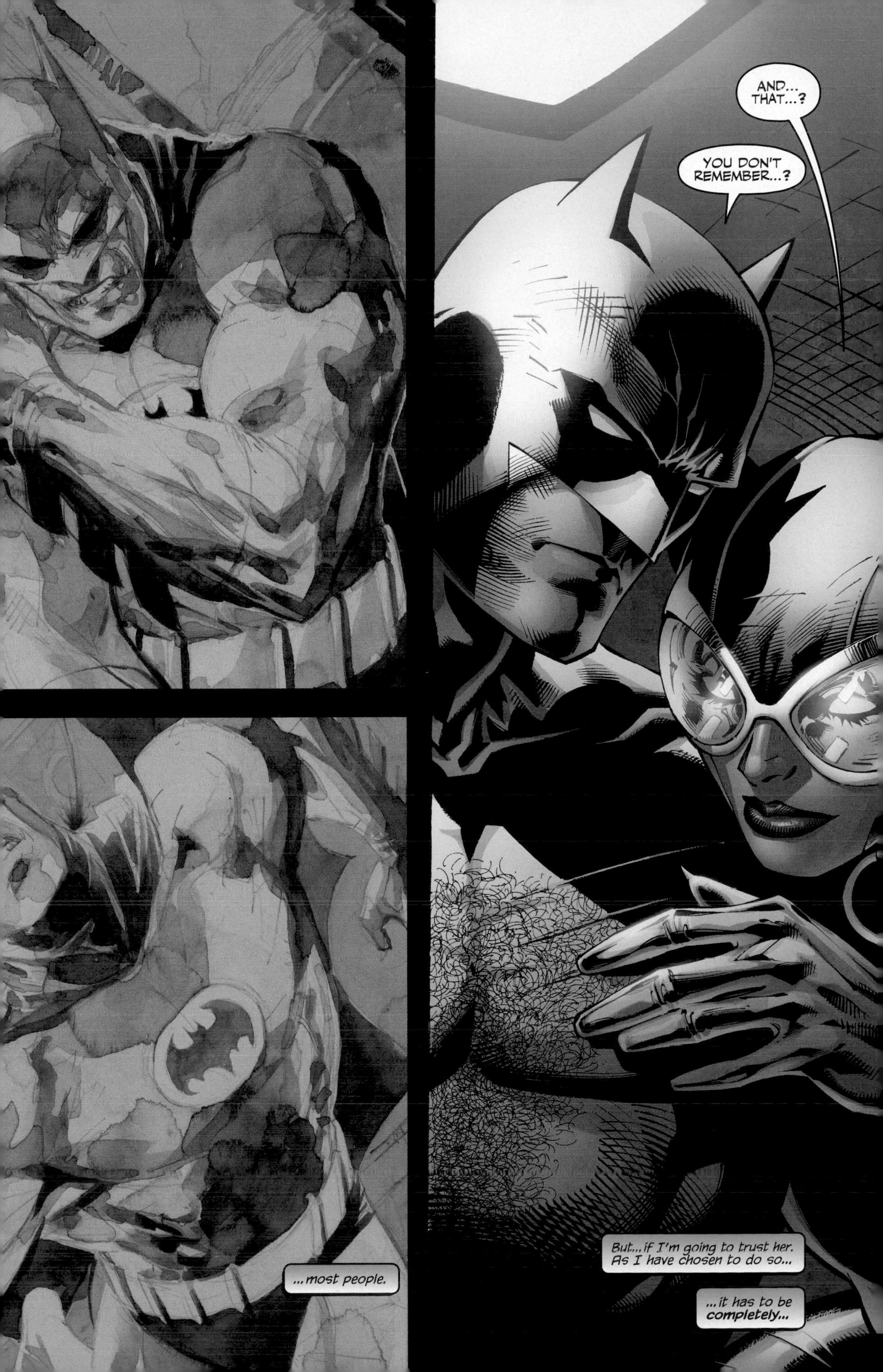
...most people.
AND... THAT...?
YOU DON'T REMEMBER...?
But...if I'm going to trust her. As I have chosen to do so...
...it has to be completely...

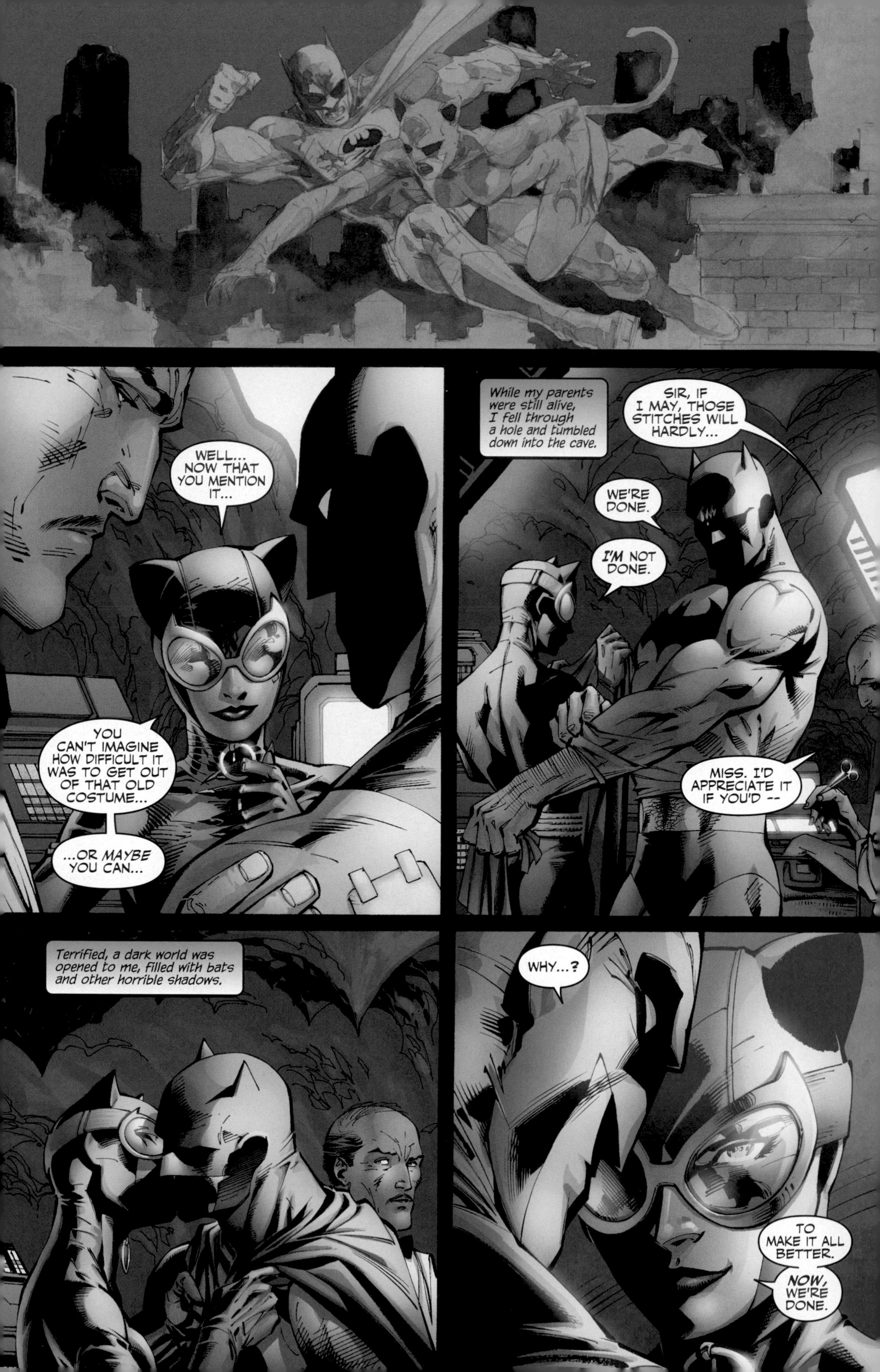
WELL... NOW THAT YOU MENTION IT...
YOU CAN'T IMAGINE HOW DIFFICULT IT WAS TO GET OUT OF THAT OLD COSTUME...
...OR MAYBE YOU CAN...
While my parents were still alive, I fell through a hole and tumbled down into the cave.
SIR, IF I MAY, THOSE STITCHES WILL HARDLY...
WE'RE DONE.
I'M NOT DONE.
MISS. I'D APPRECIATE IT IF YOU'D --
Terrified, a dark world was opened to me, filled with bats and other horrible shadows.
WHY...?
TO MAKE IT ALL BETTER.
NOW, WE'RE DONE.

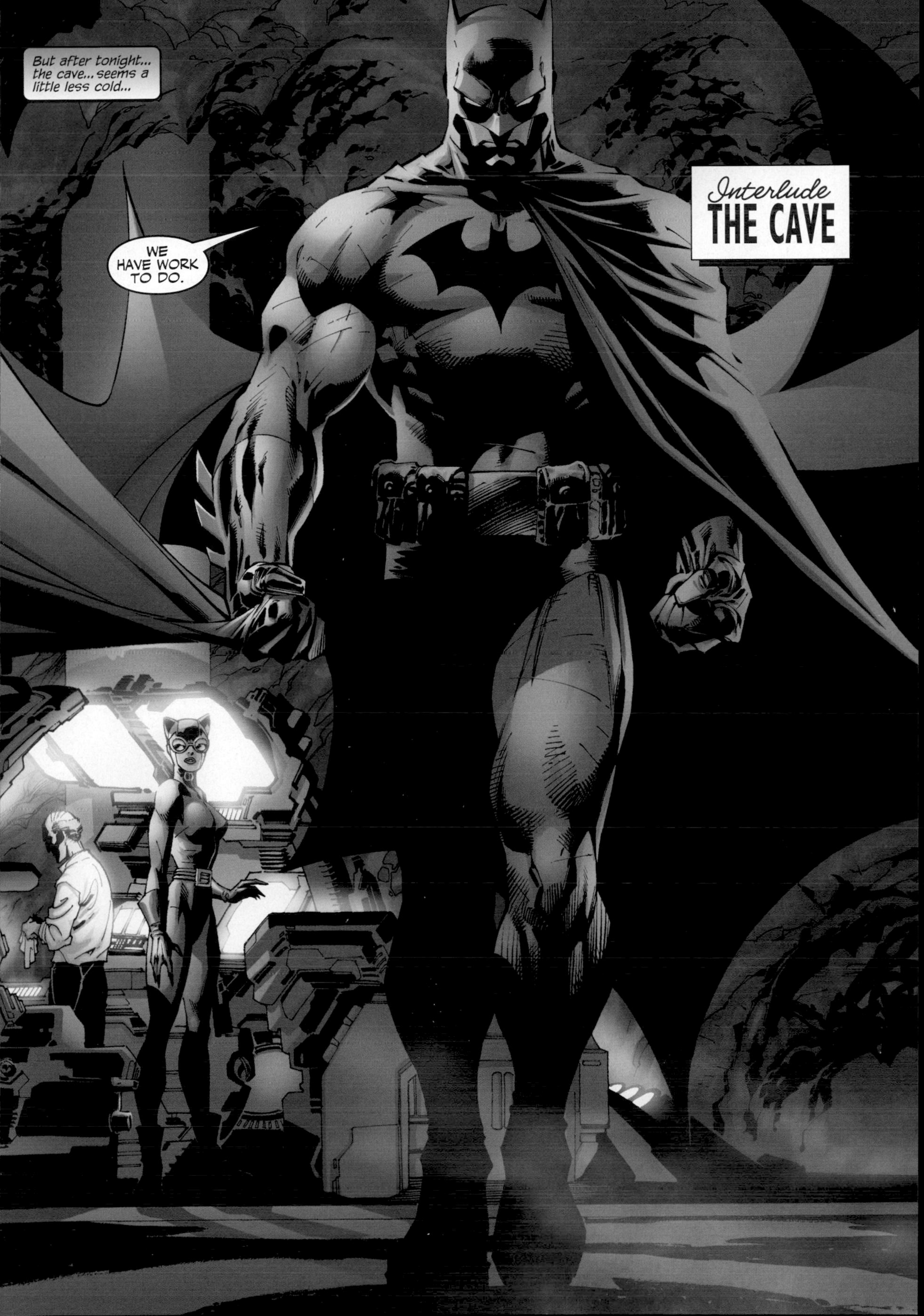
But after tonight... the cave... seems a little less cold...
WE HAVE WORK TO DO.
Interlude THE CAVE

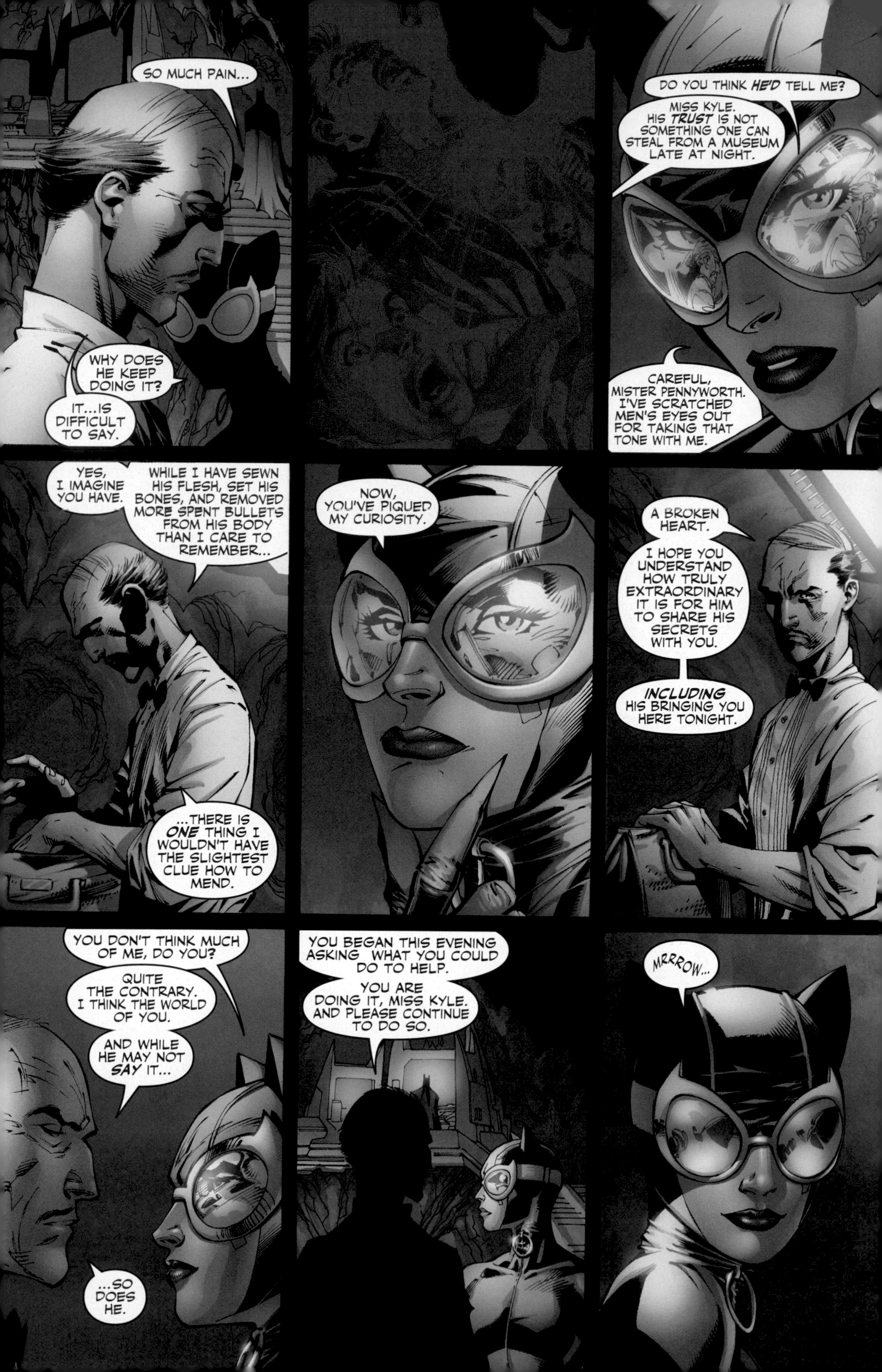
SO MUCH PAIN...
WHY DOES HE KEEP DOING IT?
IT...IS DIFFICULT TO SAY.
DO YOU THINK HE'D TELL ME?
MISS KYLE. HIS TRUST IS NOT SOMETHING ONE CAN STEAL FROM A MUSEUM LATE AT NIGHT.
CAREFUL, MISTER PENNYWORTH. I'VE SCRATCHED MEN'S EYES OUT FOR TAKING THAT TONE WITH ME.
YES, I IMAGINE YOU HAVE.
WHILE I HAVE SEWN HIS FLESH, SET HIS BONES, AND REMOVED MORE SPENT BULLETS FROM HIS BODY THAN I CARE TO REMEMBER...
...THERE IS ONE THING I WOULDN'T HAVE THE SLIGHTEST CLUE HOW TO MEND.
NOW, YOU'VE PIQUED MY CURIOSITY.
A BROKEN HEART.
I HOPE YOU UNDERSTAND HOW TRULY EXTRAORDINARY IT IS FOR HIM TO SHARE HIS SECRETS WITH YOU.
INCLUDING HIS BRINGING YOU HERE TONIGHT.
YOU DON'T THINK MUCH OF ME, DO YOU?
QUITE THE CONTRARY. I THINK THE WORLD OF YOU.
AND WHILE HE MAY NOT SAY IT...
...SO DOES HE.
YOU BEGAN THIS EVENING ASKING WHAT YOU COULD DO TO HELP.
YOU ARE DOING IT, MISS KYLE. AND PLEASE CONTINUE TO DO SO.
MRRROW...

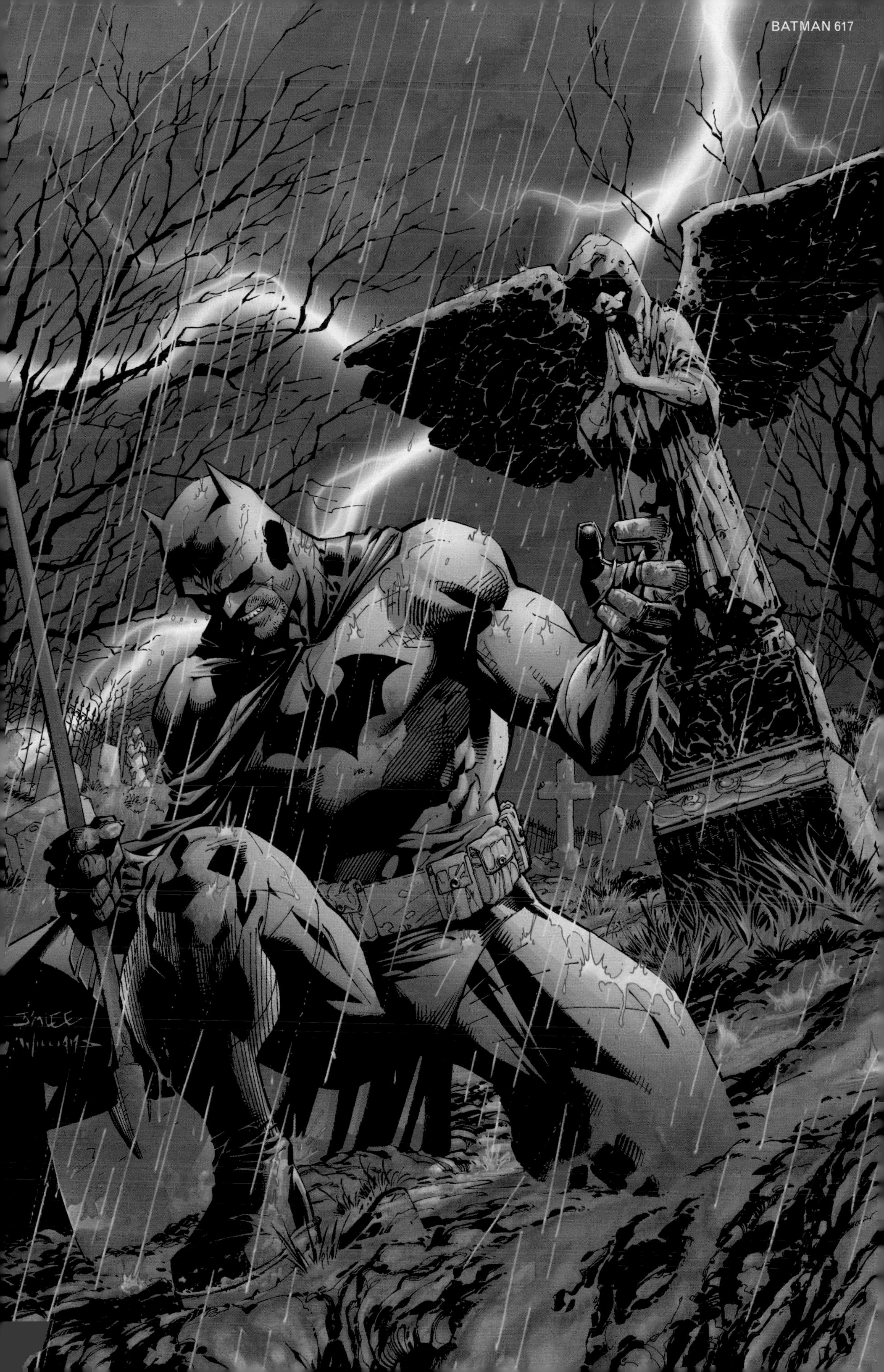

JIMLEE
2003

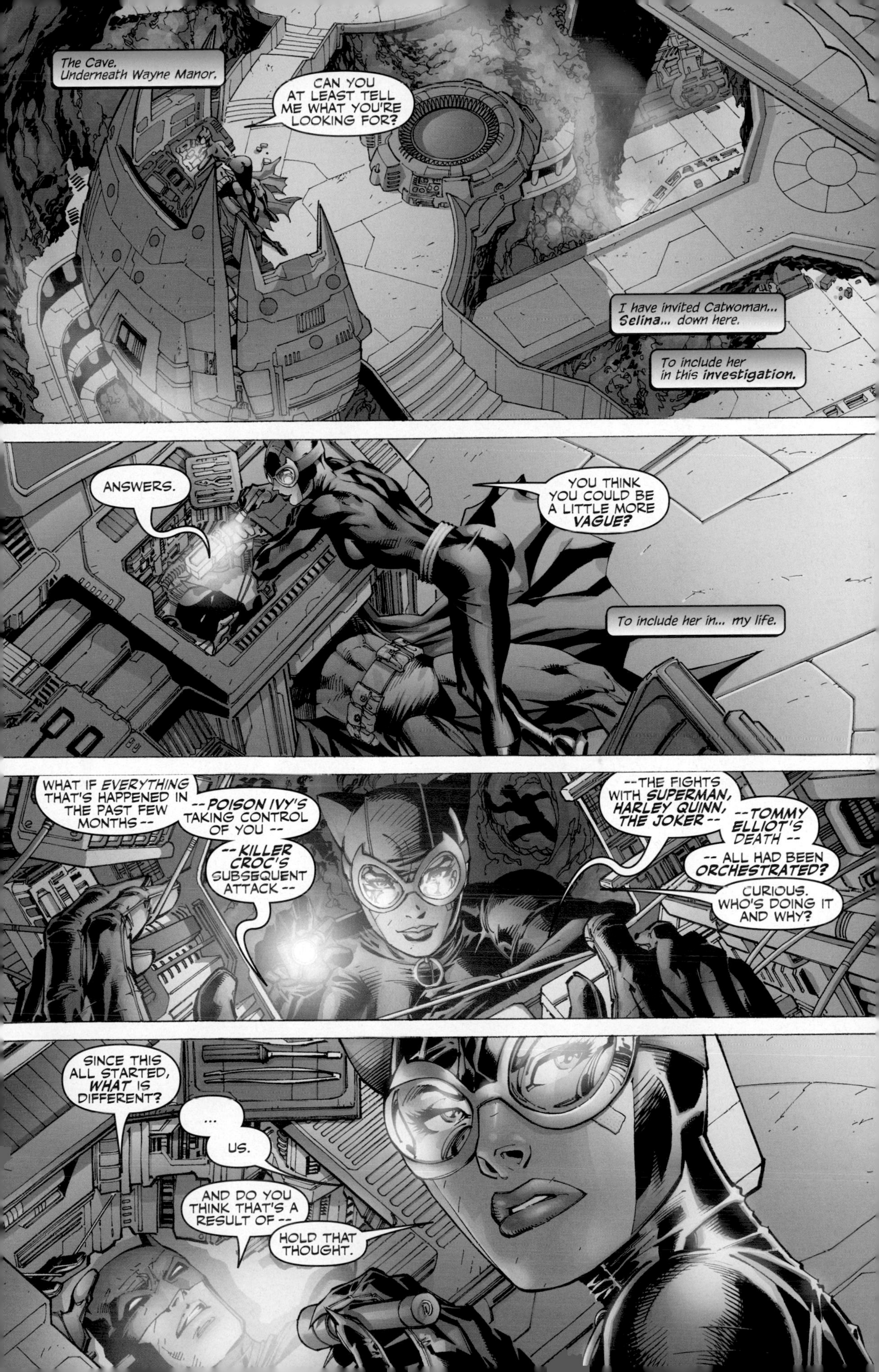
The Cave. Underneath Wayne Manor.
CAN YOU AT LEAST TELL ME WHAT YOU'RE LOOKING FOR?
I have invited Catwoman... Selina... down here.
To include her in this investigation.
ANSWERS.
YOU THINK YOU COULD BE A LITTLE MORE VAGUE?
To include her in... my life.
WHAT IF EVERYTHING THAT'S HAPPENED IN THE PAST FEW MONTHS --
--POISON IVY'S TAKING CONTROL OF YOU --
--KILLER CROC'S SUBSEQUENT ATTACK --
--THE FIGHTS WITH SUPERMAN, HARLEY QUINN, THE JOKER --
--TOMMY ELLIOT'S DEATH --
-- ALL HAD BEEN ORCHESTRATED?
CURIOUS. WHO'S DOING IT AND WHY?
SINCE THIS ALL STARTED, WHAT IS DIFFERENT?
...
US.
AND DO YOU THINK THAT'S A RESULT OF --
HOLD THAT THOUGHT.

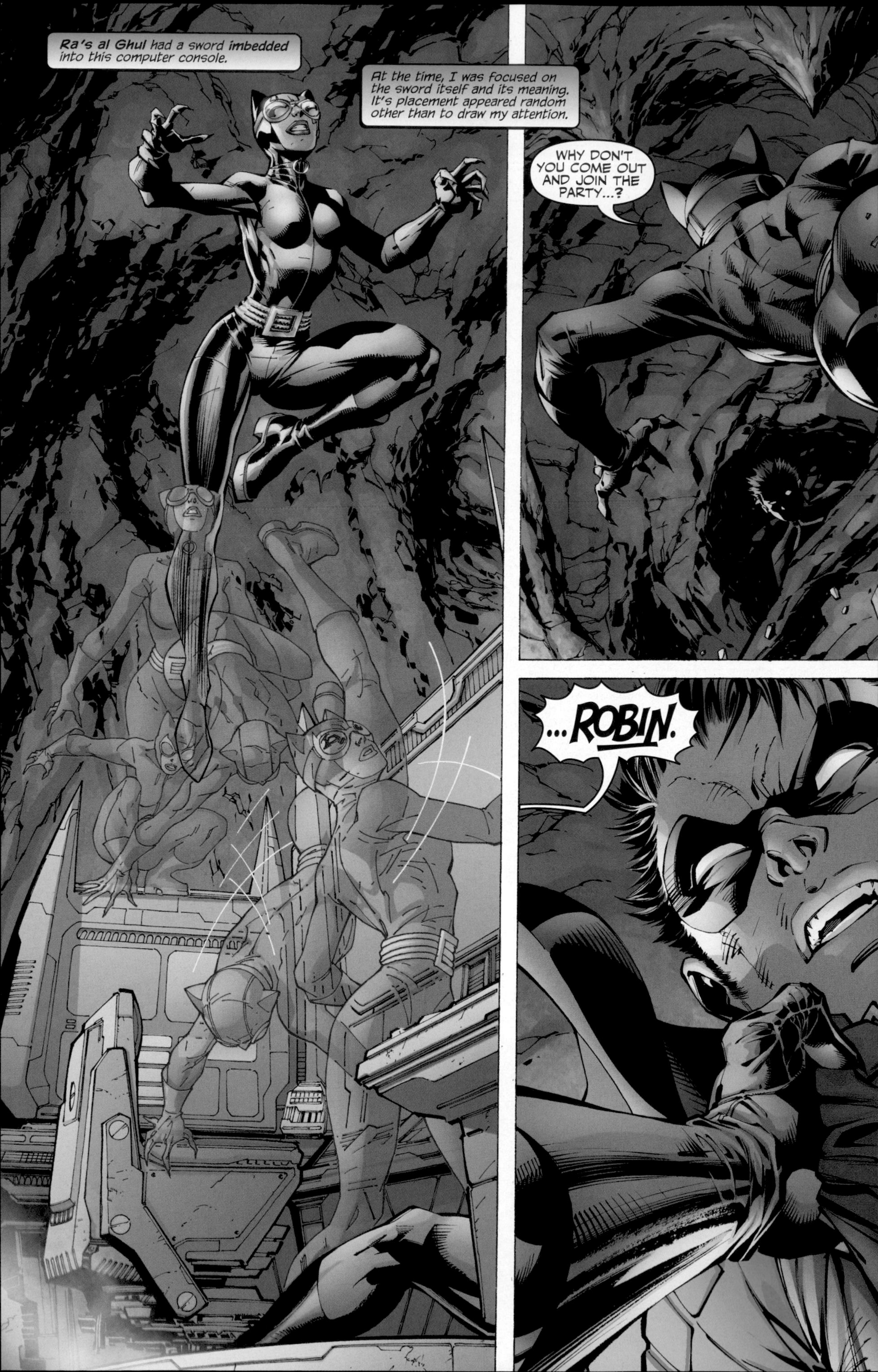
Ra's al Ghul had a sword imbedded into this computer console.
At the time, I was focused on the sword itself and its meaning. It's placement appeared random other than to draw my attention.
WHY DON'T YOU COME OUT AND JOIN THE PARTY...?
...ROBIN.

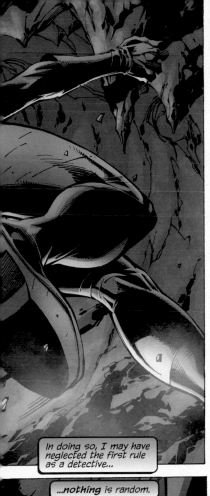

In doing so, I may have neglected the first rule as a detective...

...*nothing* is random.

SKEE

SKEE

SKEE

MAYBE BECAUSE I WASN'T ASKED.

BUT I'LL BE HAPPY TO *CRASH* IT.

WAP

Admittedly, Catwoman has been a... *distraction.*

Is that what my opponent intended?

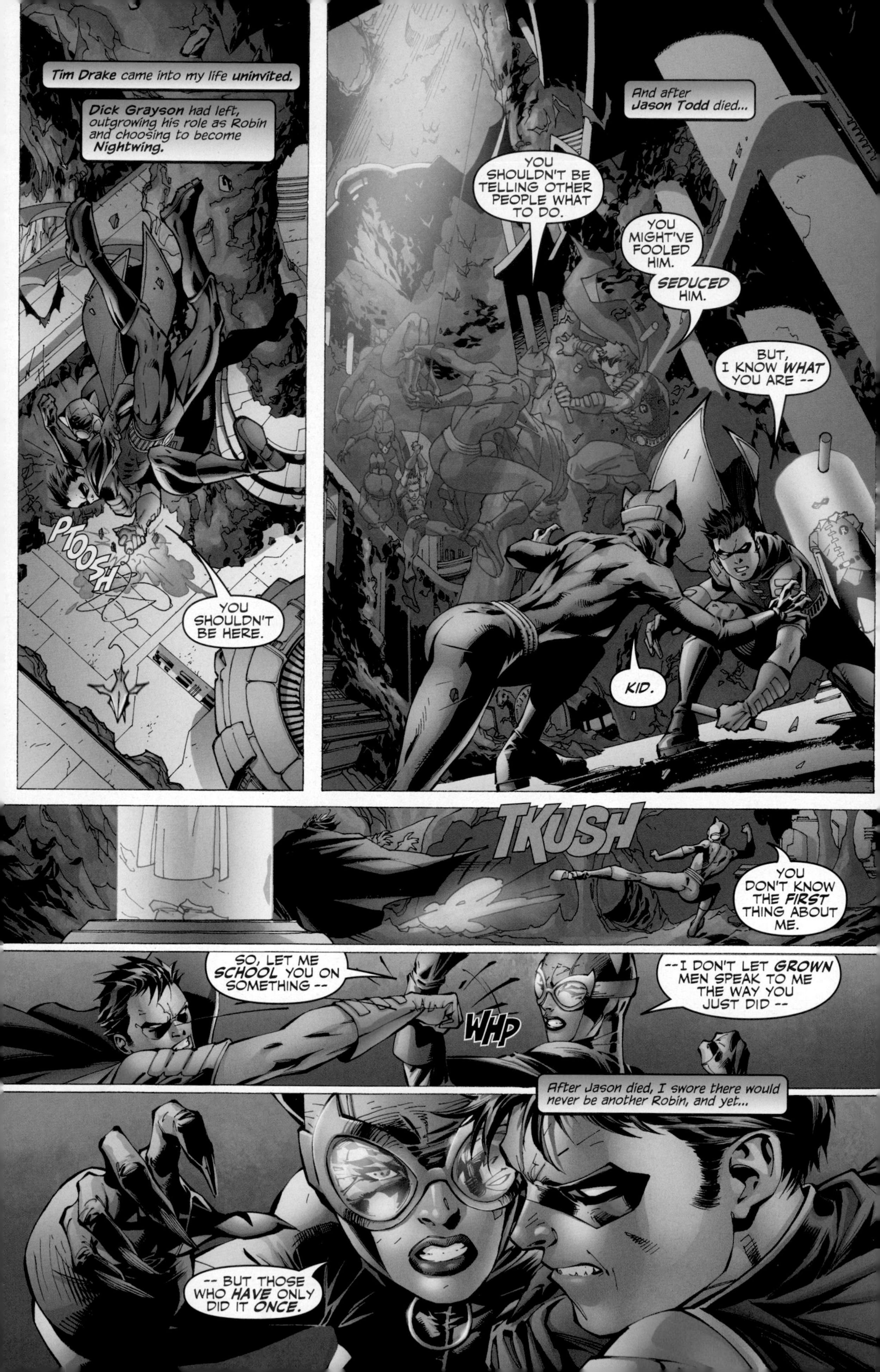
Tim Drake came into my life uninvited.
Dick Grayson had left, outgrowing his role as Robin and choosing to become Nightwing.
PTOOSH
YOU SHOULDN'T BE HERE.
And after Jason Todd died...
YOU SHOULDN'T BE TELLING OTHER PEOPLE WHAT TO DO.
YOU MIGHT'VE FOOLED HIM.
SEDUCED HIM.
BUT, I KNOW WHAT YOU ARE --
KID.
TKUSH
YOU DON'T KNOW THE FIRST THING ABOUT ME.
SO, LET ME SCHOOL YOU ON SOMETHING --
--I DON'T LET GROWN MEN SPEAK TO ME THE WAY YOU JUST DID --
WHP
After Jason died, I swore there would never be another Robin, and yet...
-- BUT THOSE WHO HAVE ONLY DID IT ONCE.

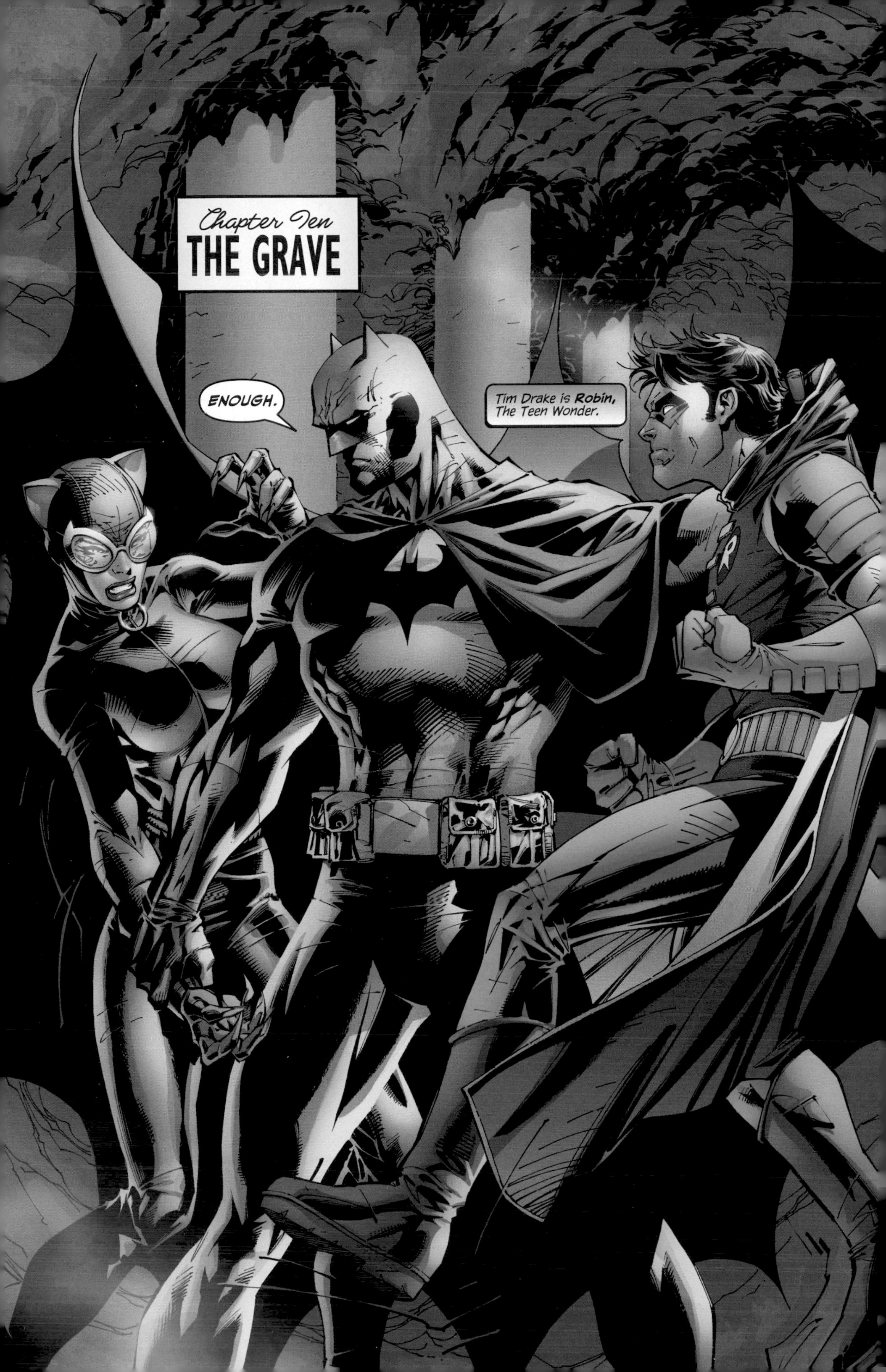
Chapter Ten
THE GRAVE
ENOUGH.
Tim Drake is Robin, The Teen Wonder.

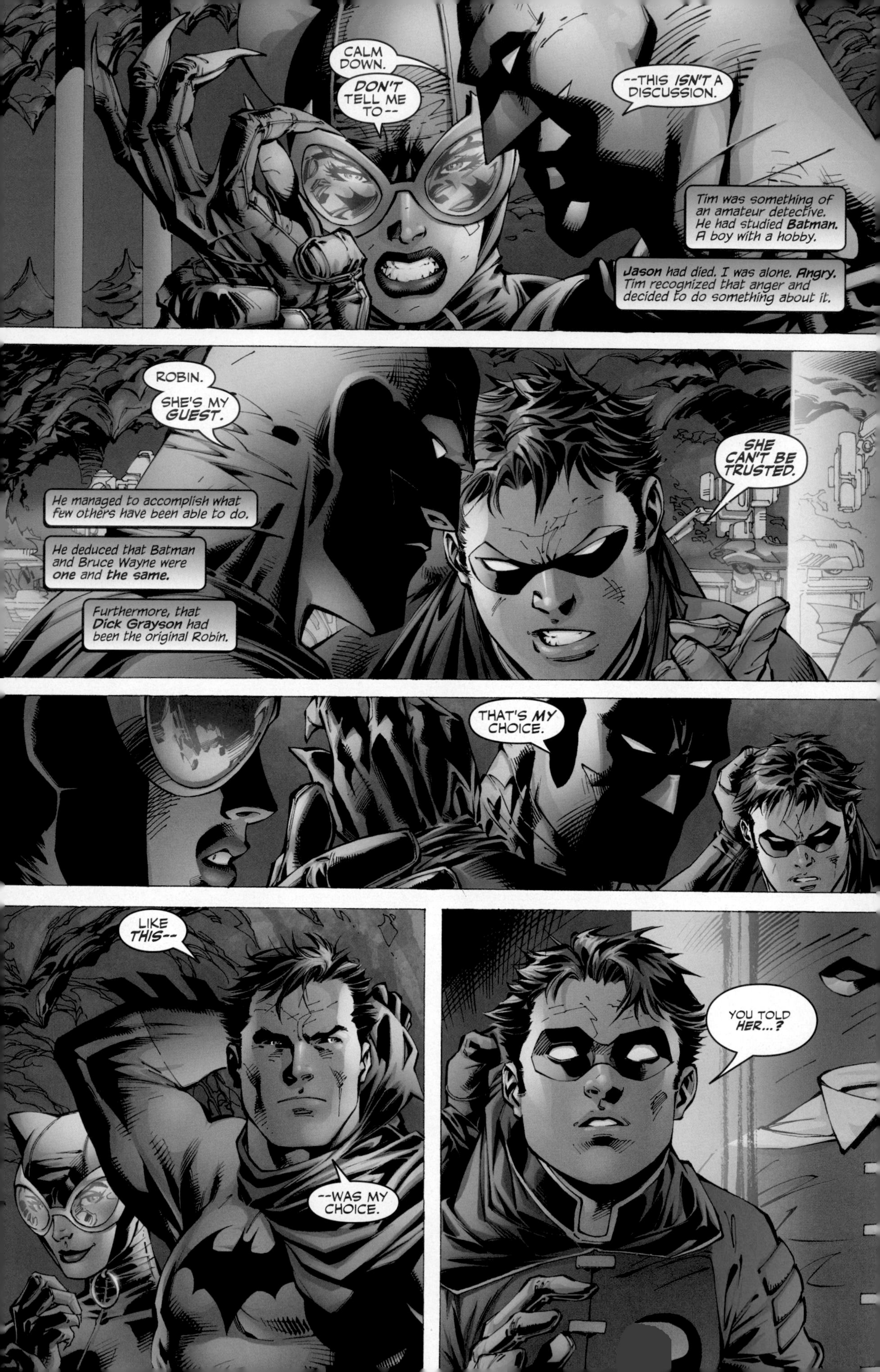
CALM DOWN.
DON'T TELL ME TO--
--THIS ISN'T A DISCUSSION.
Tim was something of an amateur detective. He had studied Batman. A boy with a hobby.
Jason had died. I was alone. Angry. Tim recognized that anger and decided to do something about it.
ROBIN.
SHE'S MY GUEST.
SHE CAN'T BE TRUSTED.
He managed to accomplish what few others have been able to do.
He deduced that Batman and Bruce Wayne were one and the same.
Furthermore, that Dick Grayson had been the original Robin.
THAT'S MY CHOICE.
LIKE THIS--
--WAS MY CHOICE.
YOU TOLD HER...?

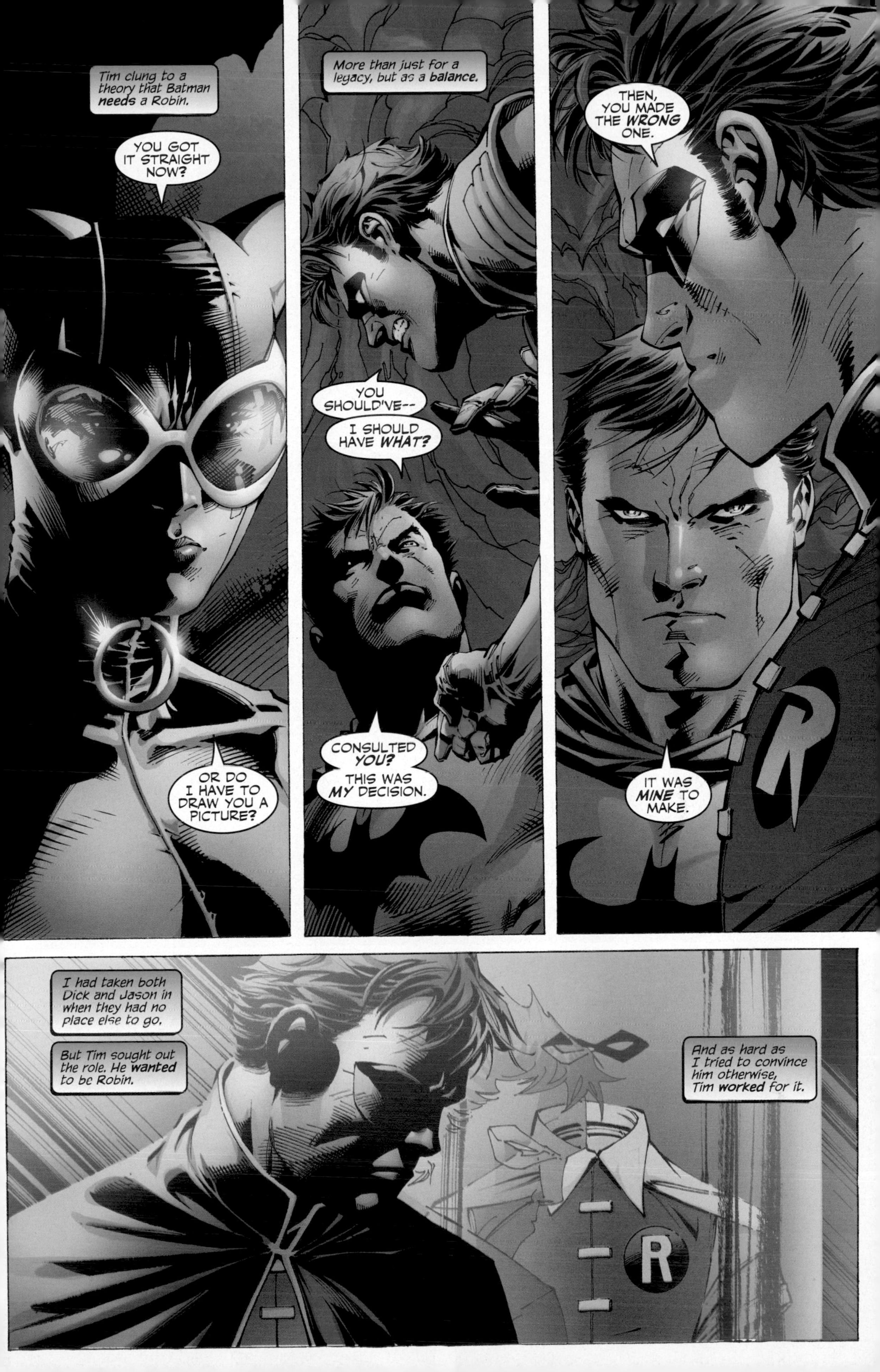
Tim clung to a theory that Batman needs a Robin.
YOU GOT IT STRAIGHT NOW?
OR DO I HAVE TO DRAW YOU A PICTURE?
More than just for a legacy, but as a balance.
YOU SHOULD'VE--
I SHOULD HAVE WHAT?
CONSULTED YOU? THIS WAS MY DECISION.
THEN, YOU MADE THE WRONG ONE.
IT WAS MINE TO MAKE.
I had taken both Dick and Jason in when they had no place else to go.
But Tim sought out the role. He wanted to be Robin.
And as hard as I tried to convince him otherwise, Tim worked for it.

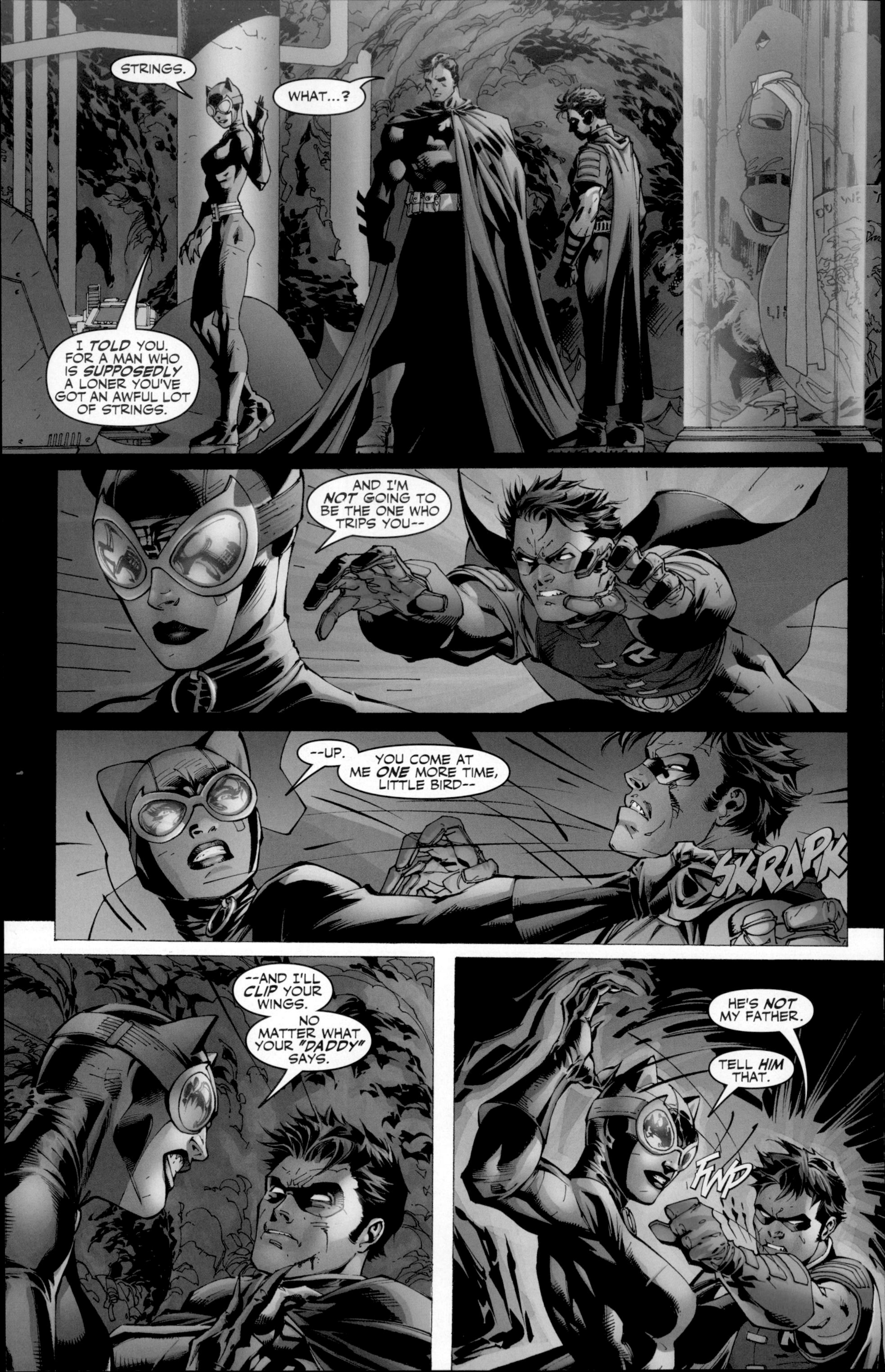
STRINGS.
WHAT...?
I TOLD YOU. FOR A MAN WHO IS SUPPOSEDLY A LONER YOU'VE GOT AN AWFUL LOT OF STRINGS.
AND I'M NOT GOING TO BE THE ONE WHO TRIPS YOU--
--UP.
YOU COME AT ME ONE MORE TIME, LITTLE BIRD--
SKRAPK
--AND I'LL CLIP YOUR WINGS.
NO MATTER WHAT YOUR "DADDY" SAYS.
HE'S NOT MY FATHER.
TELL HIM THAT.
FWP

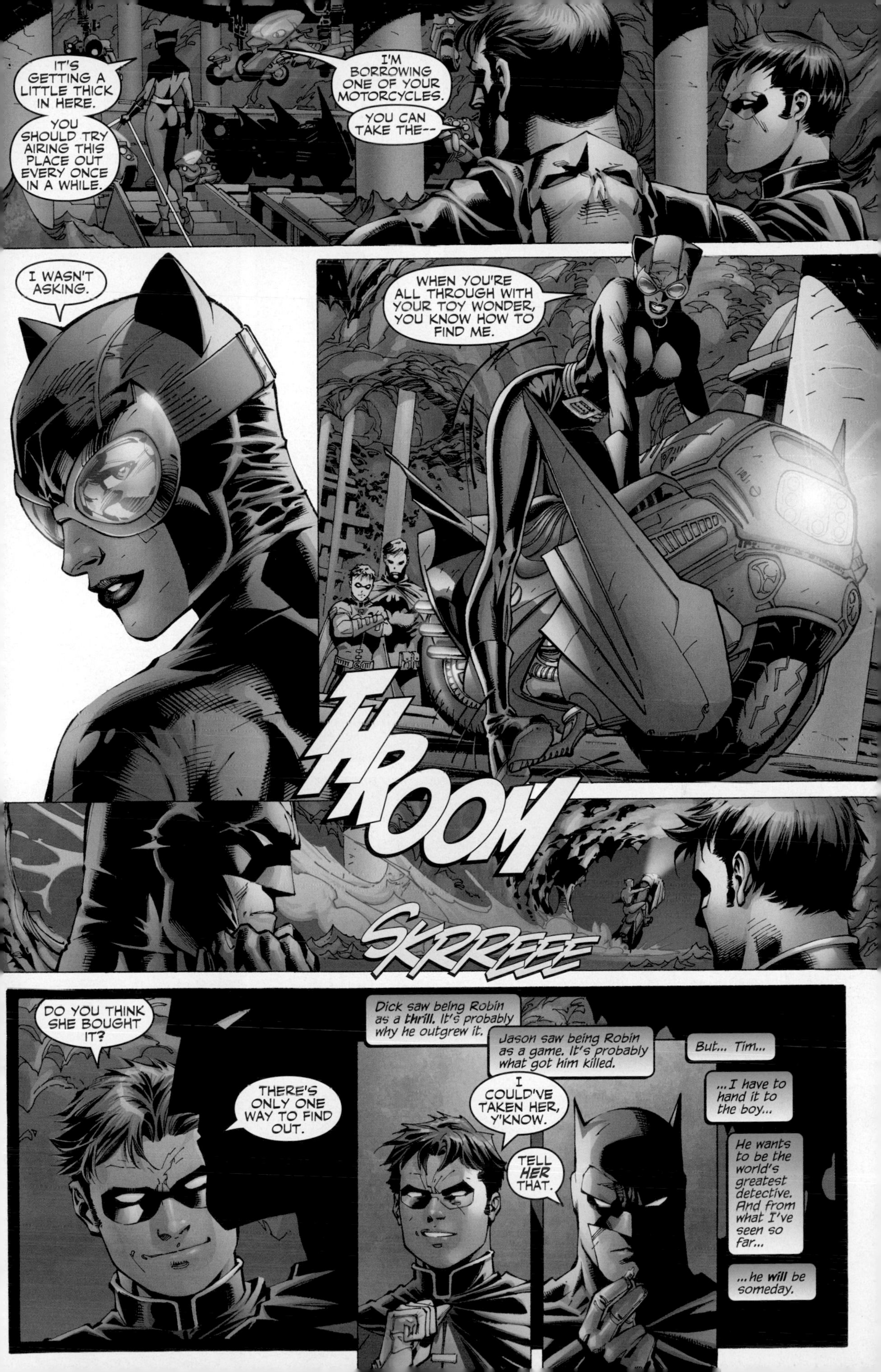
IT'S GETTING A LITTLE THICK IN HERE.
YOU SHOULD TRY AIRING THIS PLACE OUT EVERY ONCE IN A WHILE.
I'M BORROWING ONE OF YOUR MOTORCYCLES.
YOU CAN TAKE THE--
I WASN'T ASKING.
WHEN YOU'RE ALL THROUGH WITH YOUR TOY WONDER, YOU KNOW HOW TO FIND ME.
THROOM
SKRREEE
DO YOU THINK SHE BOUGHT IT?
THERE'S ONLY ONE WAY TO FIND OUT.
Dick saw being Robin as a thrill. It's probably why he outgrew it.
Jason saw being Robin as a game. It's probably what got him killed.
But... Tim...
I COULD'VE TAKEN HER, Y'KNOW.
TELL HER THAT.
...I have to hand it to the boy...
He wants to be the world's greatest detective. And from what I've seen so far...
...he will be someday.

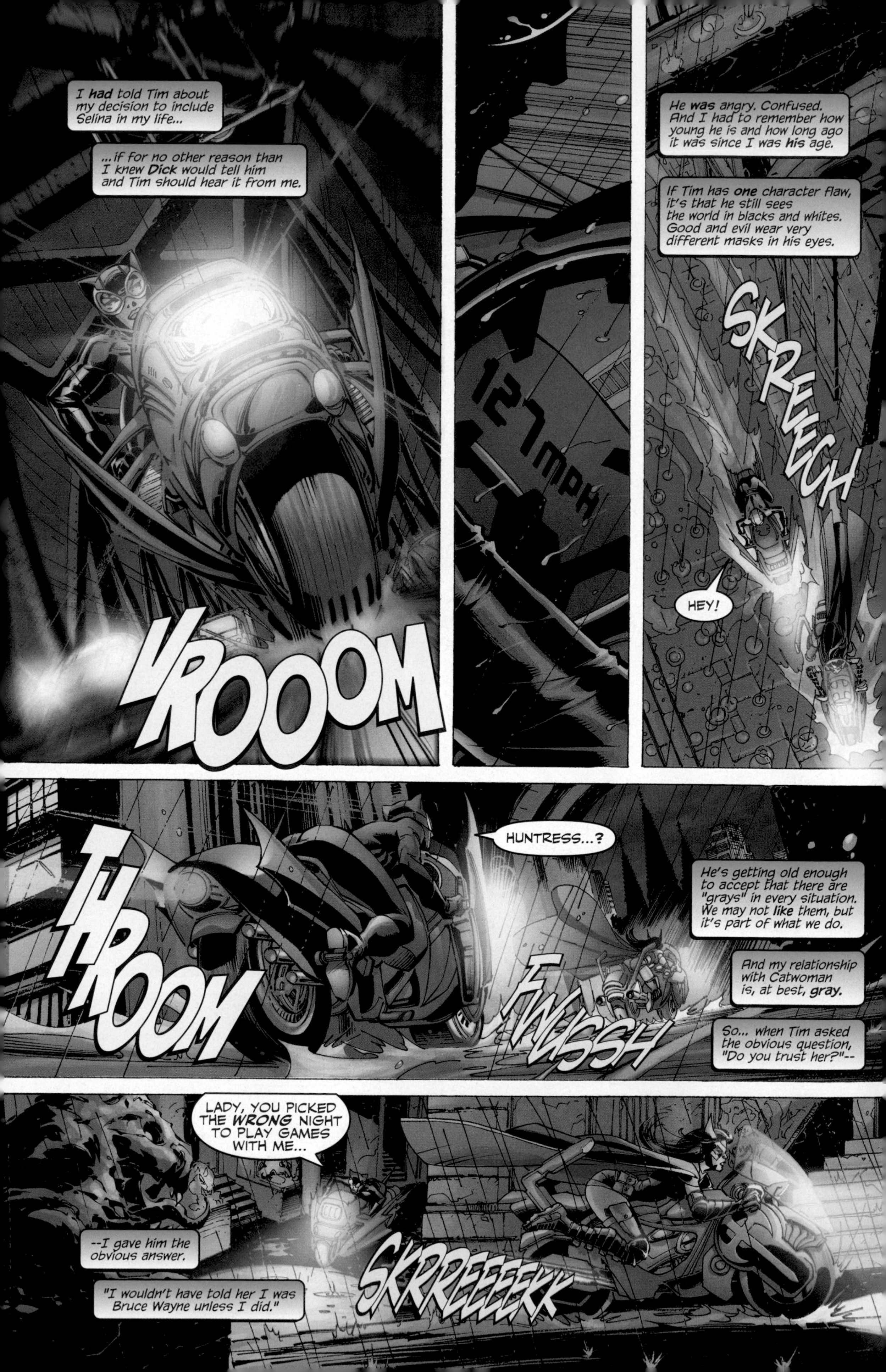

I **had** told Tim about my decision to include Selina in my life...
...if for no other reason than I knew **Dick** would tell him and Tim should hear it from me.
VROOOM
127mph
He **was** angry. Confused. And I had to remember how young he is and how long ago it was since I was **his** age.
If Tim has **one** character flaw, it's that he still sees the world in blacks and whites. Good and evil wear very different masks in his eyes.
SKREECH
HEY!
THROOM
HUNTRESS...?
He's getting old enough to accept that there are "grays" in every situation. We may not **like** them, but it's part of what we do.
FWUSSH
And my relationship with Catwoman is, at best, **gray.**
So... when Tim asked the obvious question, "Do you trust her?"--
LADY, YOU PICKED THE **WRONG** NIGHT TO PLAY GAMES WITH ME...
--I gave him the obvious answer.
SKRREEEEKK
"I wouldn't have told her I was Bruce Wayne unless I did."

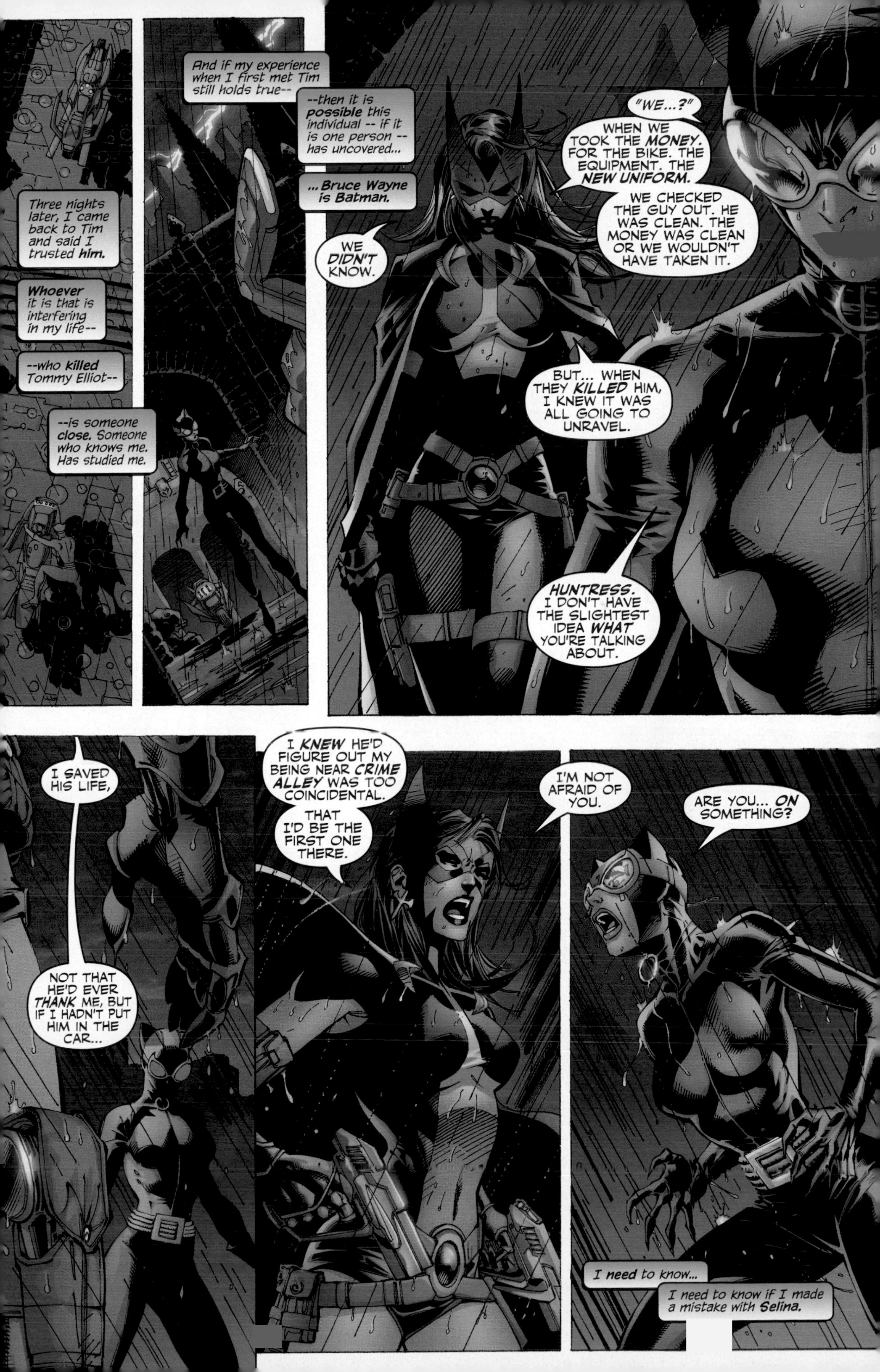

Three nights later, I came back to Tim and said I trusted **him.**
**Whoever** it is that is interfering in my life--
--who **killed** Tommy Elliot--
--is someone **close.** Someone who knows me. Has studied me.
And if my experience when I first met Tim still holds true--
--then it is **possible** this individual -- if it is one person -- has uncovered...
**...Bruce Wayne is Batman.**
WE ***DIDN'T*** KNOW.
"WE...?"
WHEN WE TOOK THE ***MONEY.*** FOR THE BIKE. THE EQUIPMENT. THE ***NEW UNIFORM.***
WE CHECKED THE GUY OUT. HE WAS CLEAN. THE MONEY WAS CLEAN OR WE WOULDN'T HAVE TAKEN IT.
BUT... WHEN THEY ***KILLED*** HIM, I KNEW IT WAS ALL GOING TO UNRAVEL.
***HUNTRESS.*** I DON'T HAVE THE SLIGHTEST IDEA ***WHAT*** YOU'RE TALKING ABOUT.
I SAVED HIS LIFE,
NOT THAT HE'D EVER ***THANK*** ME, BUT IF I HADN'T PUT HIM IN THE CAR...
I ***KNEW*** HE'D FIGURE OUT MY BEING NEAR ***CRIME ALLEY*** WAS TOO COINCIDENTAL.
THAT I'D BE THE FIRST ONE THERE.
I'M NOT AFRAID OF YOU.
ARE YOU... ***ON*** SOMETHING?
I **need** to know...
I need to know if I made a mistake with **Selina.**

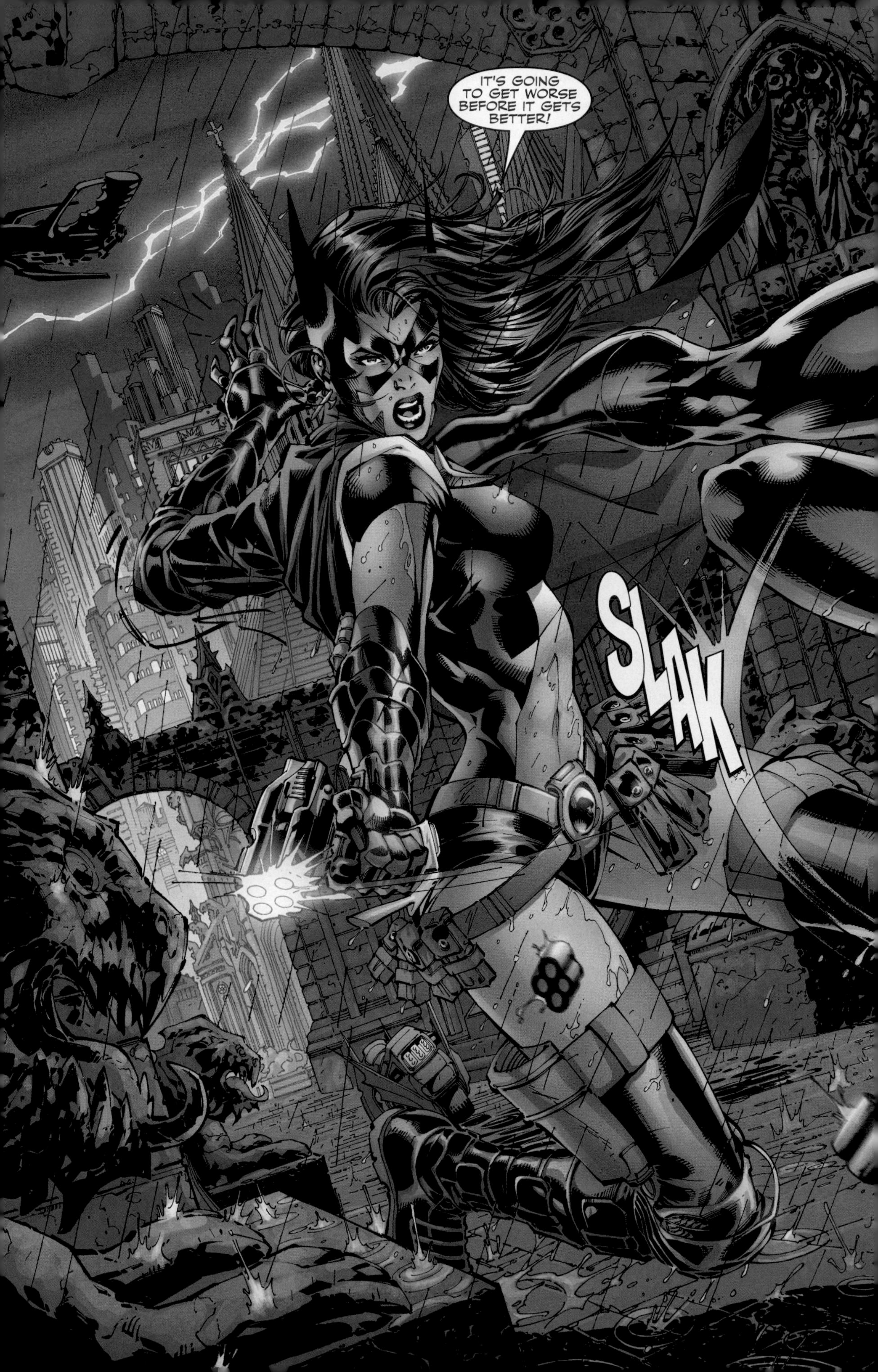
IT'S GOING TO GET WORSE BEFORE IT GETS BETTER!
SLAK

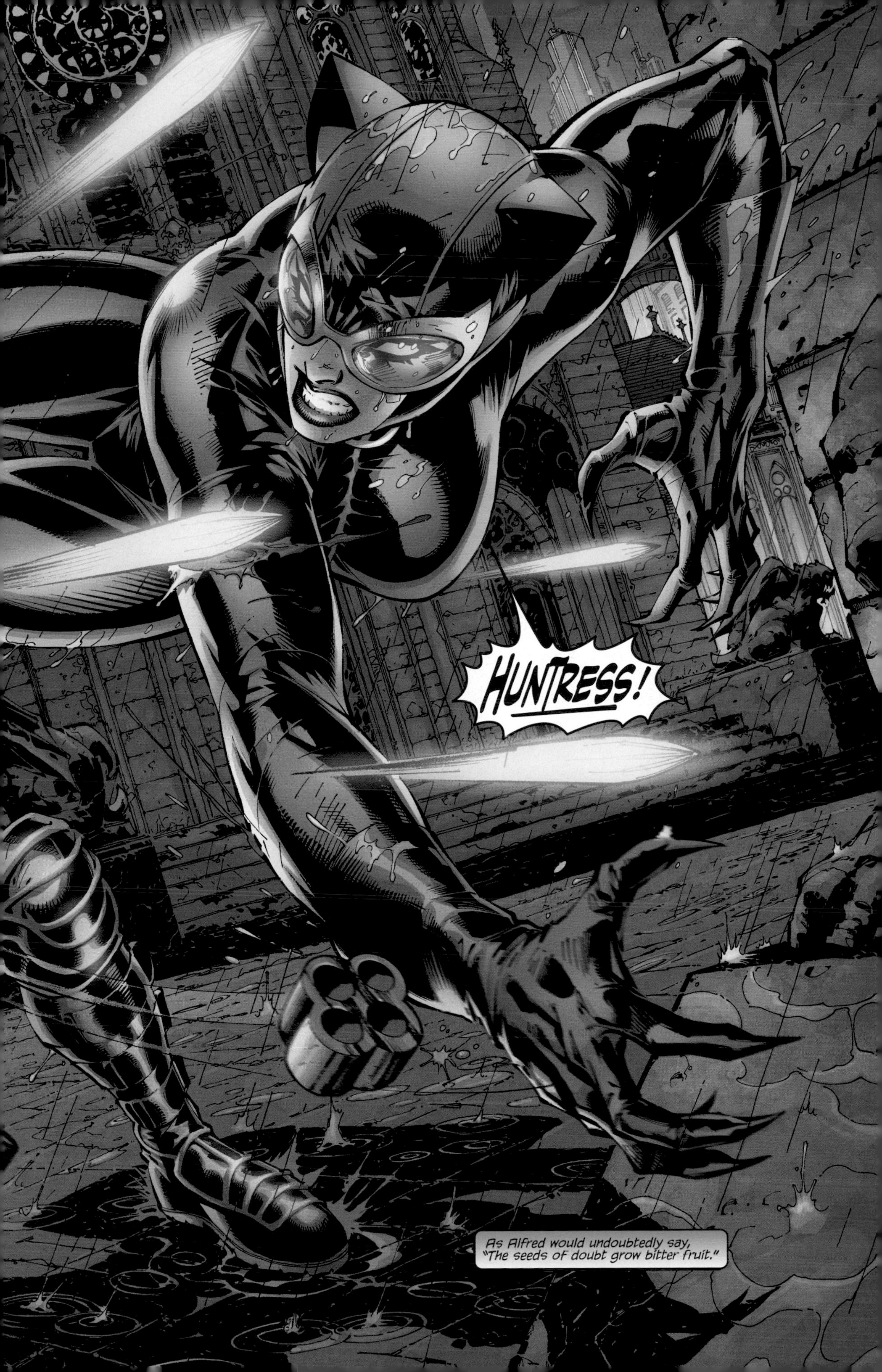
HUNTRESS!
As Alfred would undoubtedly say, "The seeds of doubt grow bitter fruit."

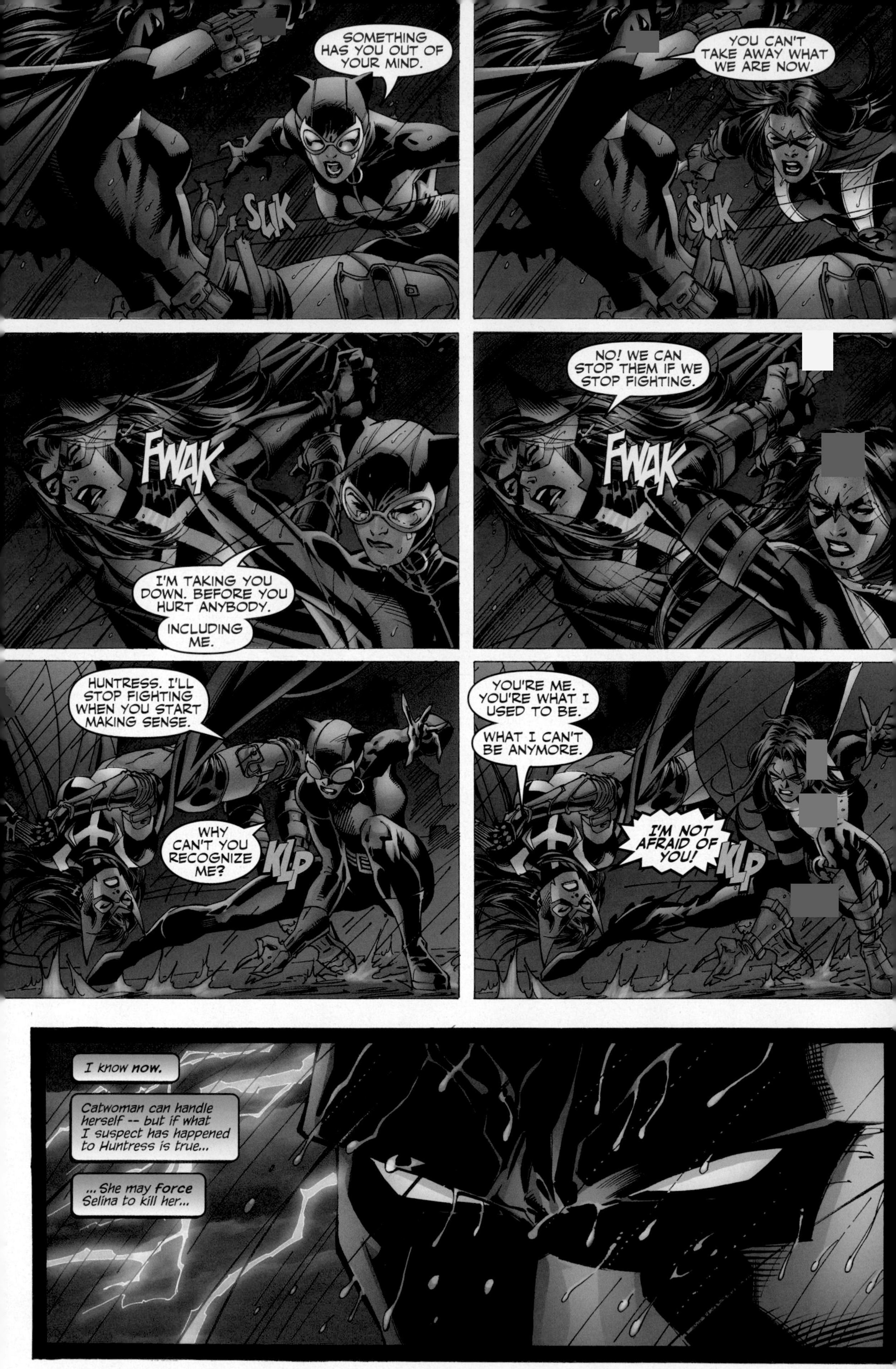
SOMETHING HAS YOU OUT OF YOUR MIND.
SLIK
YOU CAN'T TAKE AWAY WHAT WE ARE NOW.
SLIK
FWAK
I'M TAKING YOU DOWN. BEFORE YOU HURT ANYBODY.
INCLUDING ME.
NO! WE CAN STOP THEM IF WE STOP FIGHTING.
FWAK
HUNTRESS. I'LL STOP FIGHTING WHEN YOU START MAKING SENSE.
WHY CAN'T YOU RECOGNIZE ME?
KLP
YOU'RE ME. YOU'RE WHAT I USED TO BE.
WHAT I CAN'T BE ANYMORE.
I'M NOT AFRAID OF YOU!
KLP
I know now.
Catwoman can handle herself -- but if what I suspect has happened to Huntress is true...
...She may force Selina to kill her...

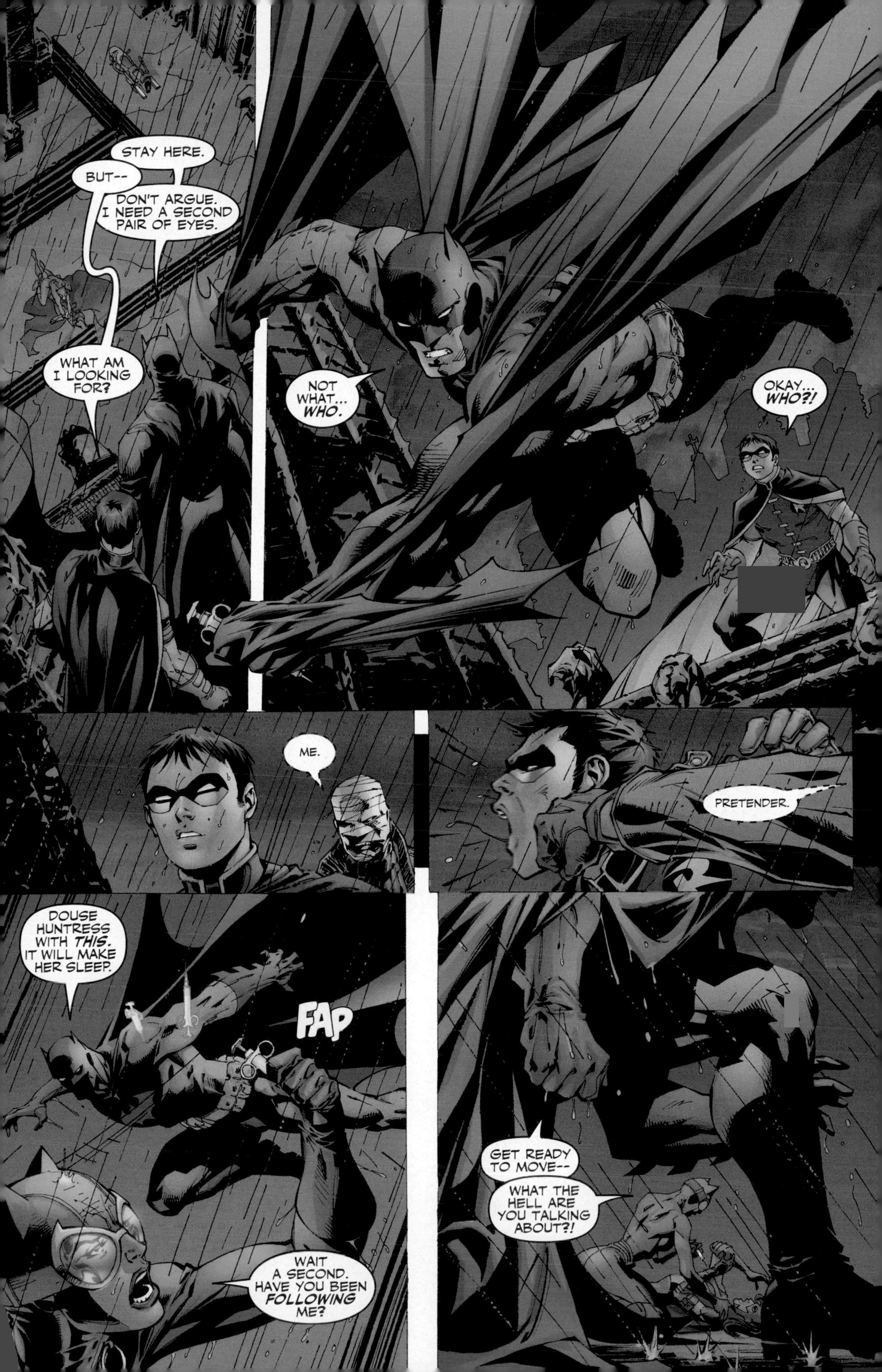
STAY HERE.
BUT--
DON'T ARGUE. I NEED A SECOND PAIR OF EYES.
WHAT AM I LOOKING FOR?
NOT WHAT... WHO.
OKAY... WHO?!
ME.
PRETENDER.
DOUSE HUNTRESS WITH THIS. IT WILL MAKE HER SLEEP.
FAP
WAIT A SECOND. HAVE YOU BEEN FOLLOWING ME?
GET READY TO MOVE--
WHAT THE HELL ARE YOU TALKING ABOUT?!

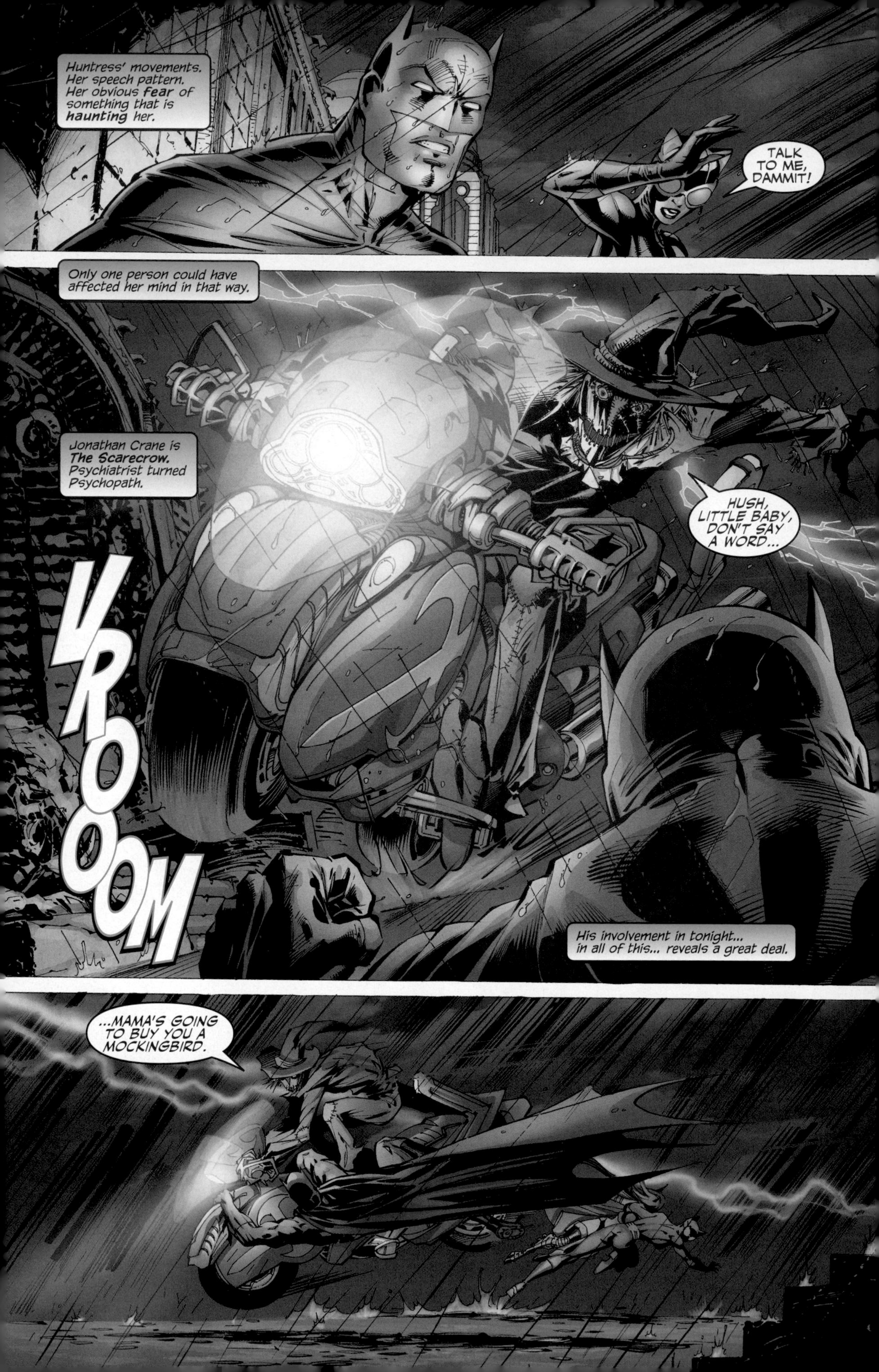
Huntress' movements. Her speech pattern. Her obvious fear of something that is haunting her.
TALK TO ME, DAMMIT!
Only one person could have affected her mind in that way.
Jonathan Crane is The Scarecrow. Psychiatrist turned Psychopath.
HUSH, LITTLE BABY, DON'T SAY A WORD...
VROOOOM
His involvement in tonight... in all of this... reveals a great deal.
...MAMA'S GOING TO BUY YOU A MOCKINGBIRD.

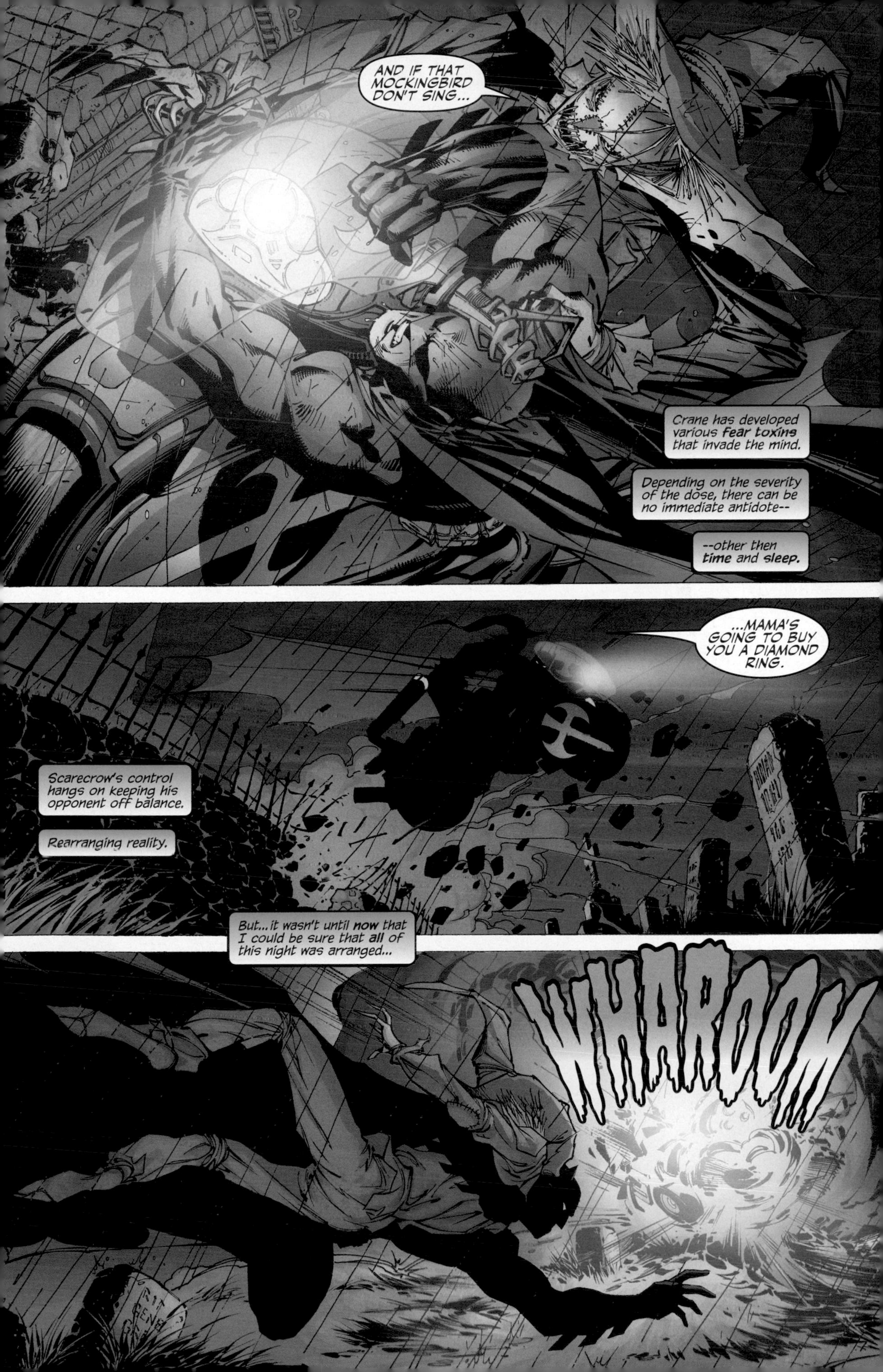
AND IF THAT MOCKINGBIRD DON'T SING...
Crane has developed various **fear toxins** that invade the mind.
Depending on the severity of the dose, there can be no immediate antidote--
--other then **time** and **sleep.**
...MAMA'S GOING TO BUY YOU A DIAMOND RING.
Scarecrow's control hangs on keeping his opponent off balance.
Rearranging reality.
But...it wasn't until **now** that I could be sure that **all** of this night was arranged...
WHAROOM

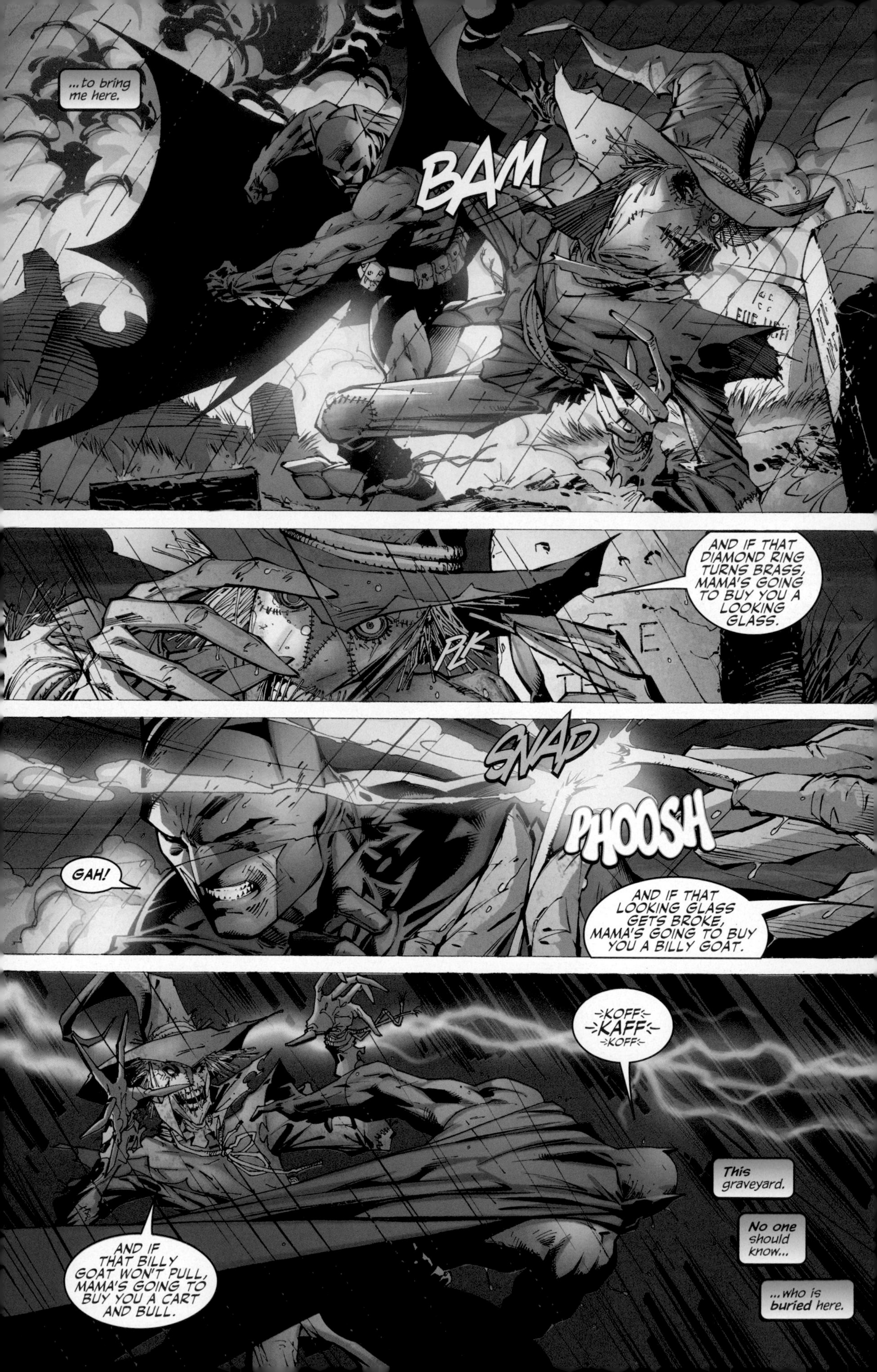
...to bring me here.
BAM
AND IF THAT DIAMOND RING TURNS BRASS, MAMA'S GOING TO BUY YOU A LOOKING GLASS.
PLK
SNAP
PHOOSH
GAH!
AND IF THAT LOOKING GLASS GETS BROKE, MAMA'S GOING TO BUY YOU A BILLY GOAT.
KOFF KAFF KOFF
AND IF THAT BILLY GOAT WON'T PULL, MAMA'S GOING TO BUY YOU A CART AND BULL.
This graveyard.
No one should know...
...who is buried here.

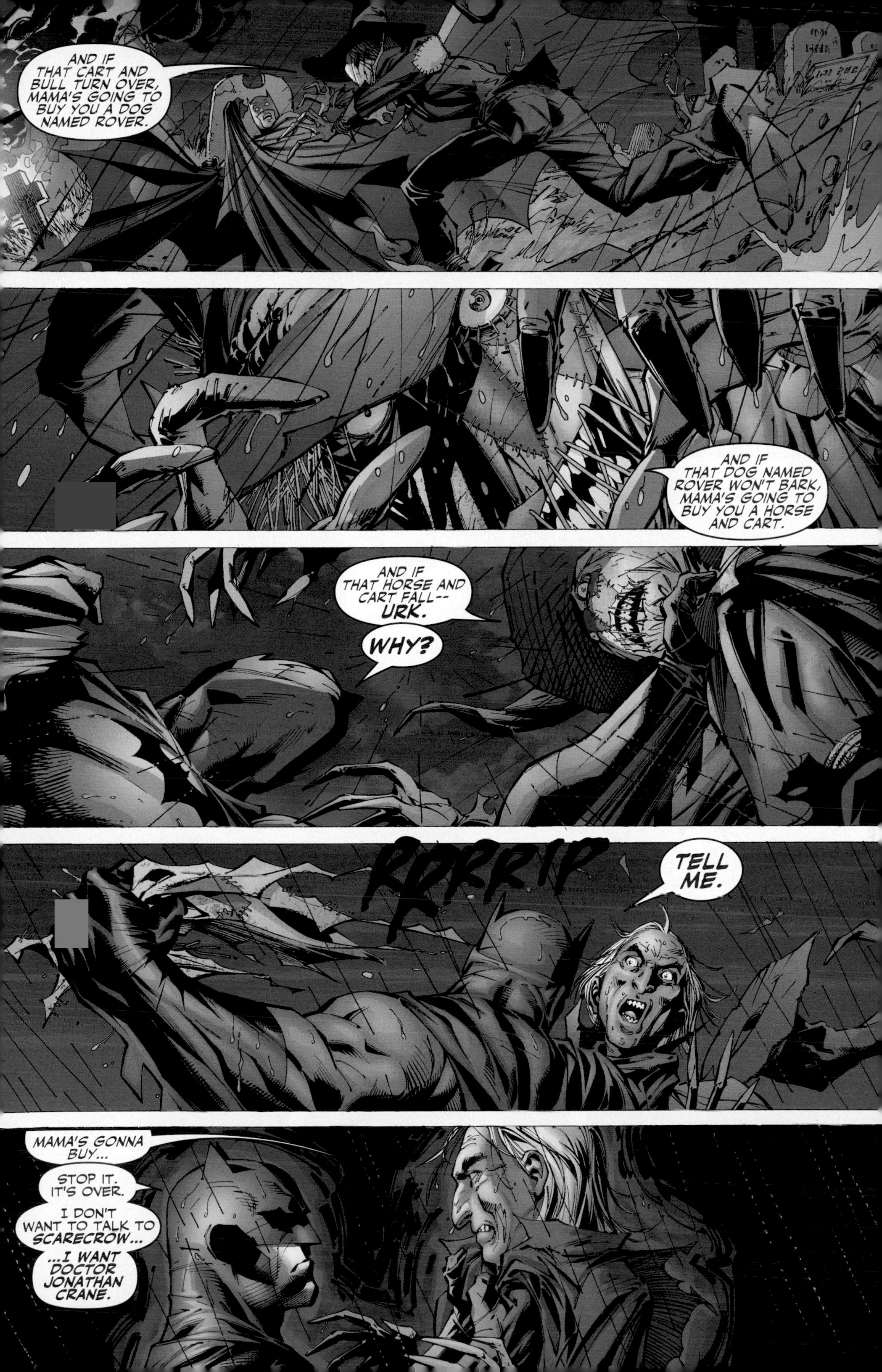
AND IF THAT CART AND BULL TURN OVER, MAMA'S GOING TO BUY YOU A DOG NAMED ROVER.
AND IF THAT DOG NAMED ROVER WON'T BARK, MAMA'S GOING TO BUY YOU A HORSE AND CART.
AND IF THAT HORSE AND CART FALL-- URK.
WHY?
RRRRIP
TELL ME.
MAMA'S GONNA BUY...
STOP IT. IT'S OVER.
I DON'T WANT TO TALK TO SCARECROW...
...I WANT DOCTOR JONATHAN CRANE.

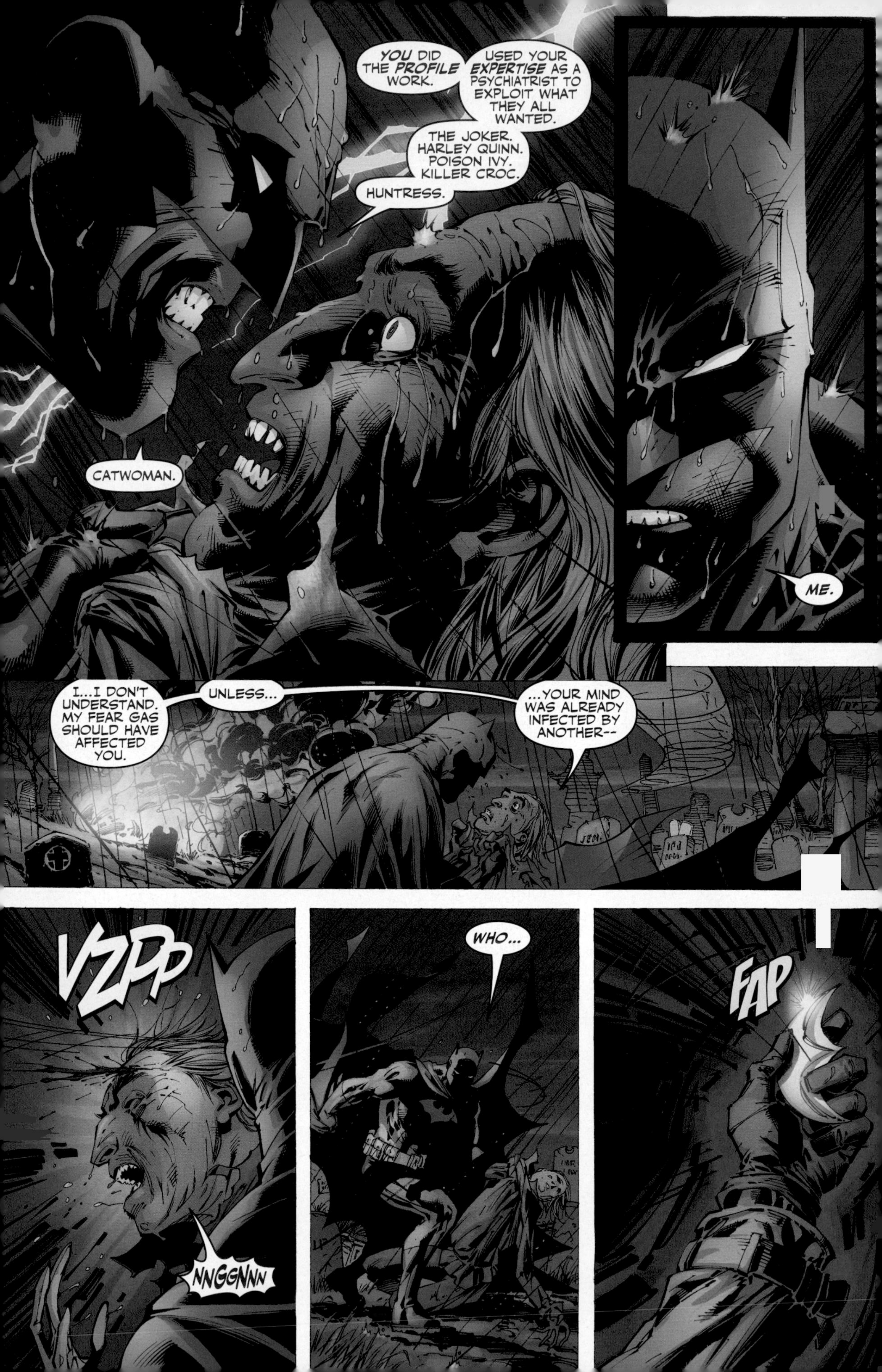
YOU DID THE PROFILE WORK.
USED YOUR EXPERTISE AS A PSYCHIATRIST TO EXPLOIT WHAT THEY ALL WANTED.
THE JOKER. HARLEY QUINN. POISON IVY. KILLER CROC.
HUNTRESS.
CATWOMAN.
ME.
I...I DON'T UNDERSTAND. MY FEAR GAS SHOULD HAVE AFFECTED YOU.
UNLESS...
...YOUR MIND WAS ALREADY INFECTED BY ANOTHER--
VZPP
NNGGNNN
WHO...
FAP

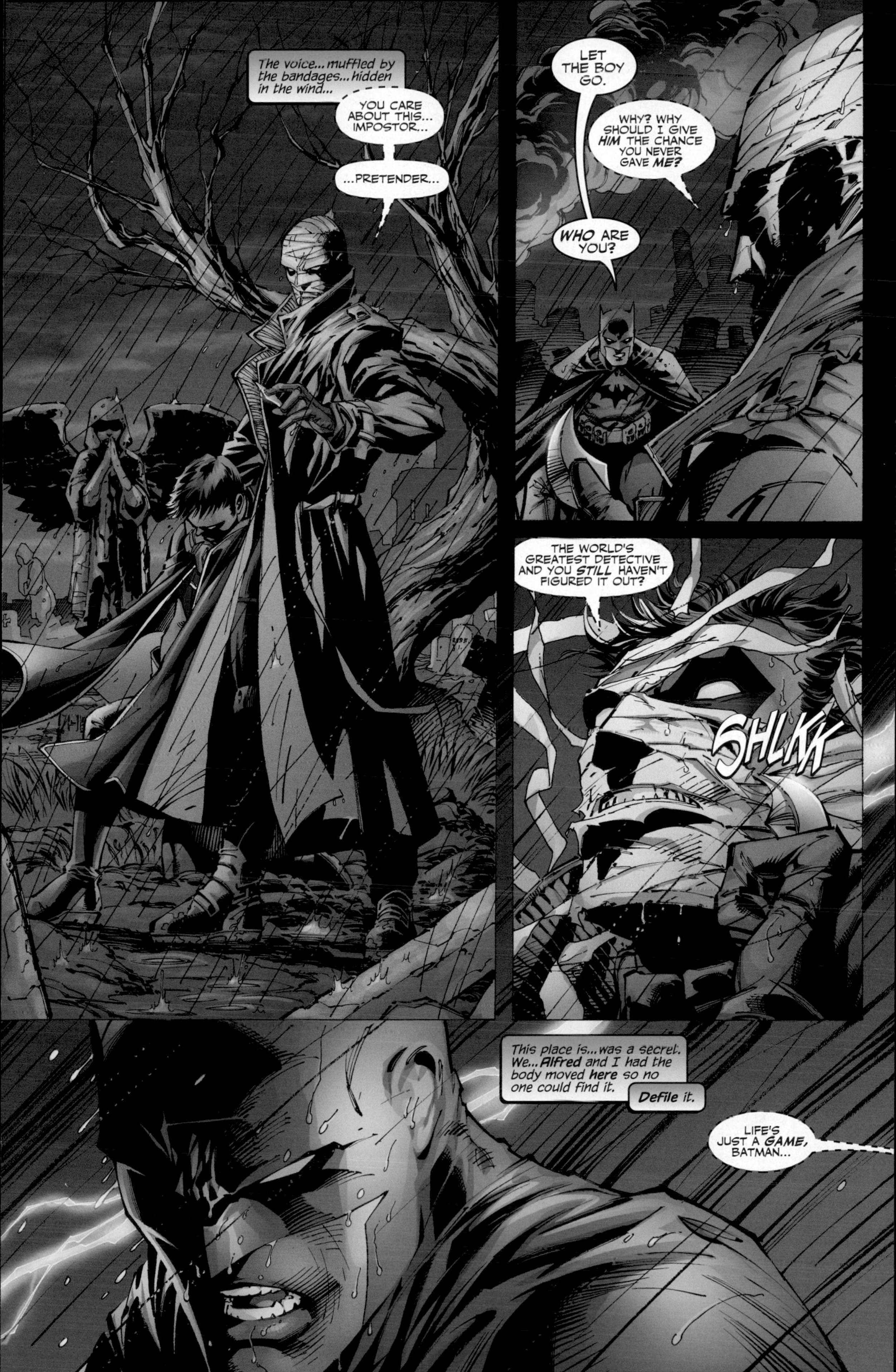
The voice... muffled by the bandages... hidden in the wind...
YOU CARE ABOUT THIS... IMPOSTOR...
...PRETENDER...
LET THE BOY GO.
WHY? WHY SHOULD I GIVE HIM THE CHANCE YOU NEVER GAVE ME?
WHO ARE YOU?
THE WORLD'S GREATEST DETECTIVE AND YOU STILL HAVEN'T FIGURED IT OUT?
SHLKK
This place is... was a secret. We... Alfred and I had the body moved here so no one could find it.
Defile it.
LIFE'S JUST A GAME, BATMAN...

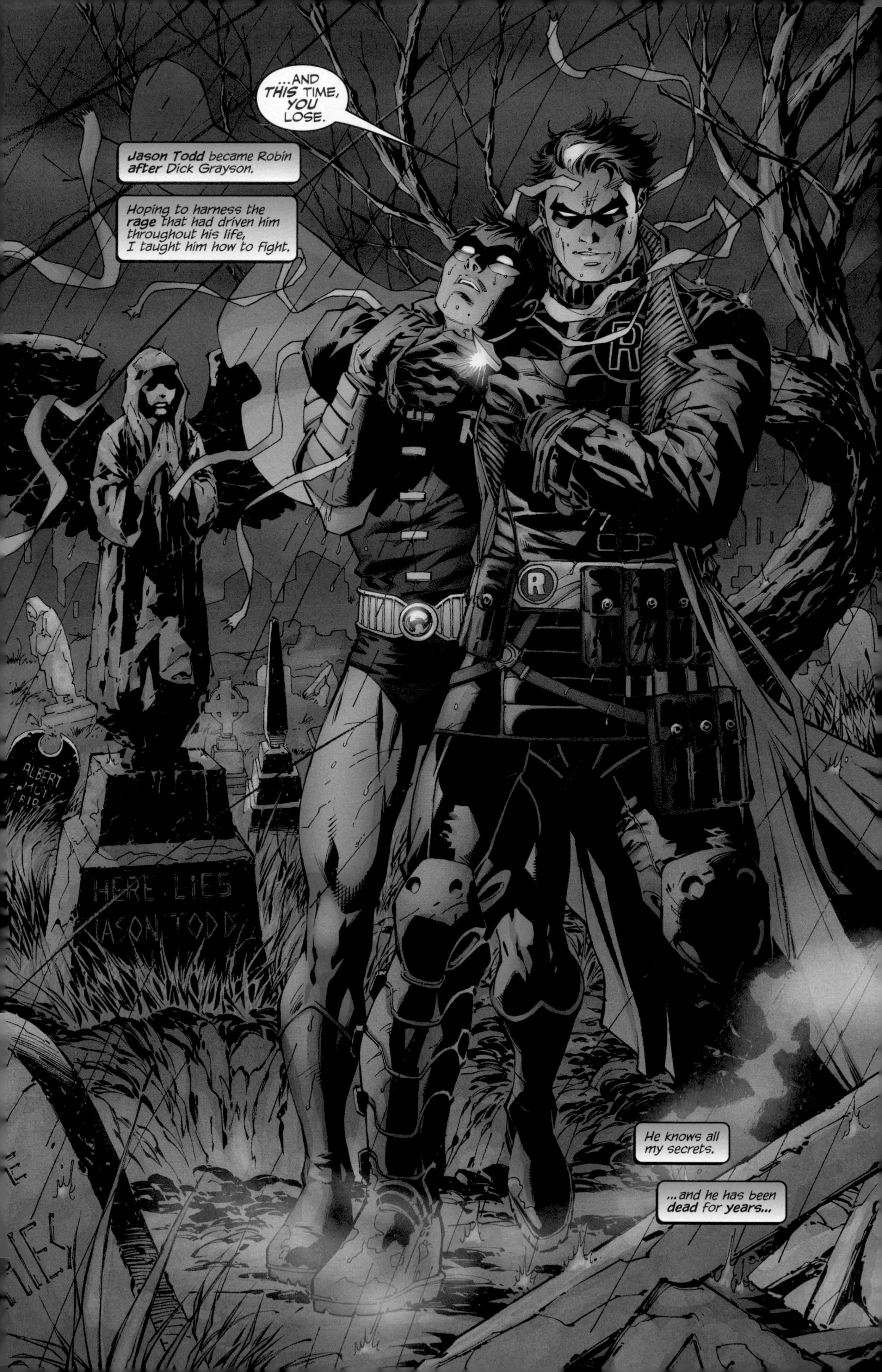

...AND *THIS* TIME, *YOU* LOSE.
*Jason Todd* became Robin **after** Dick Grayson.
Hoping to harness the **rage** that had driven him throughout his life, I taught him how to fight.
HERE LIES JASON TODD
ALBERT
He knows all my secrets.
...and he has been **dead** for **years...**

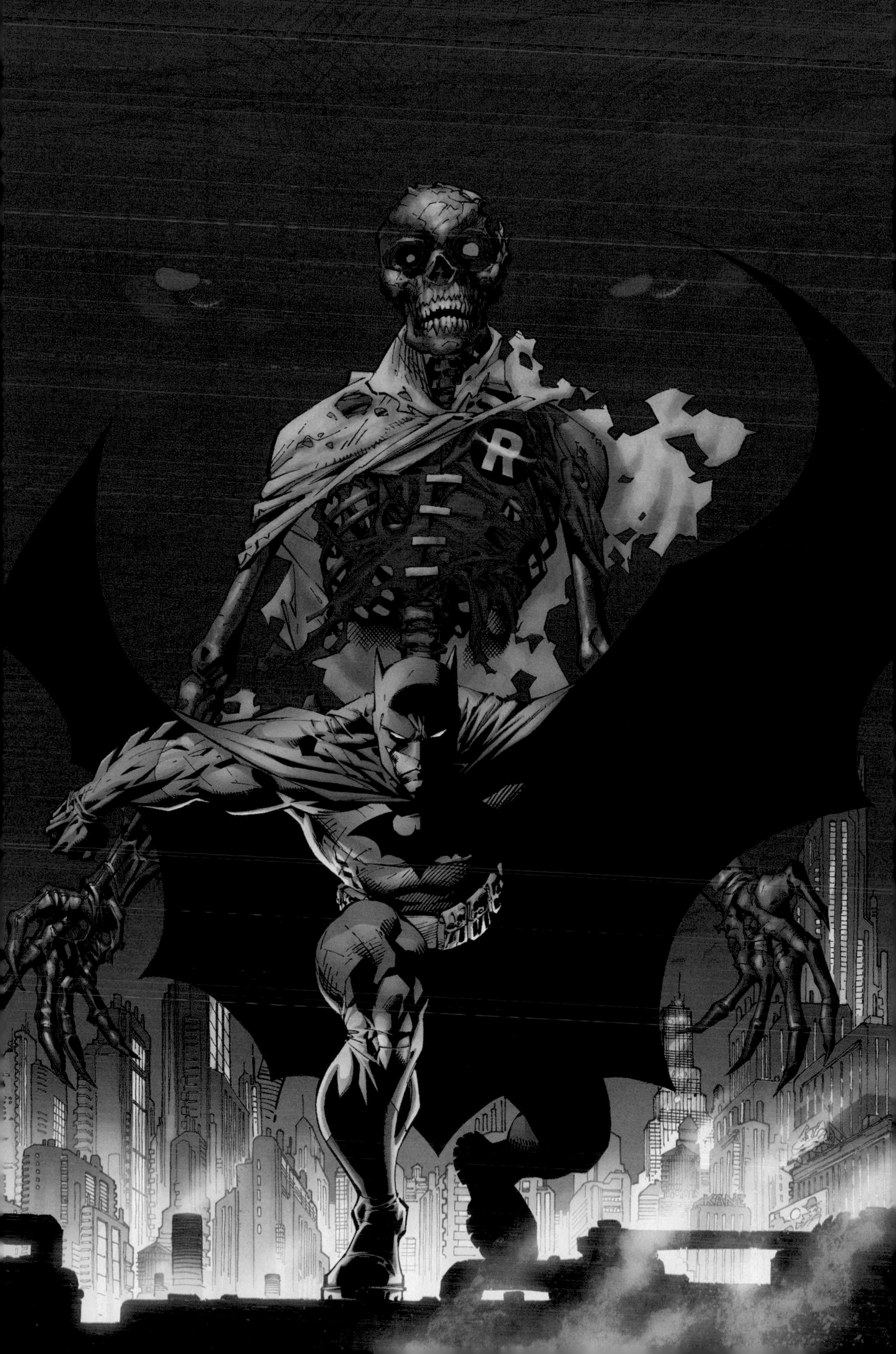

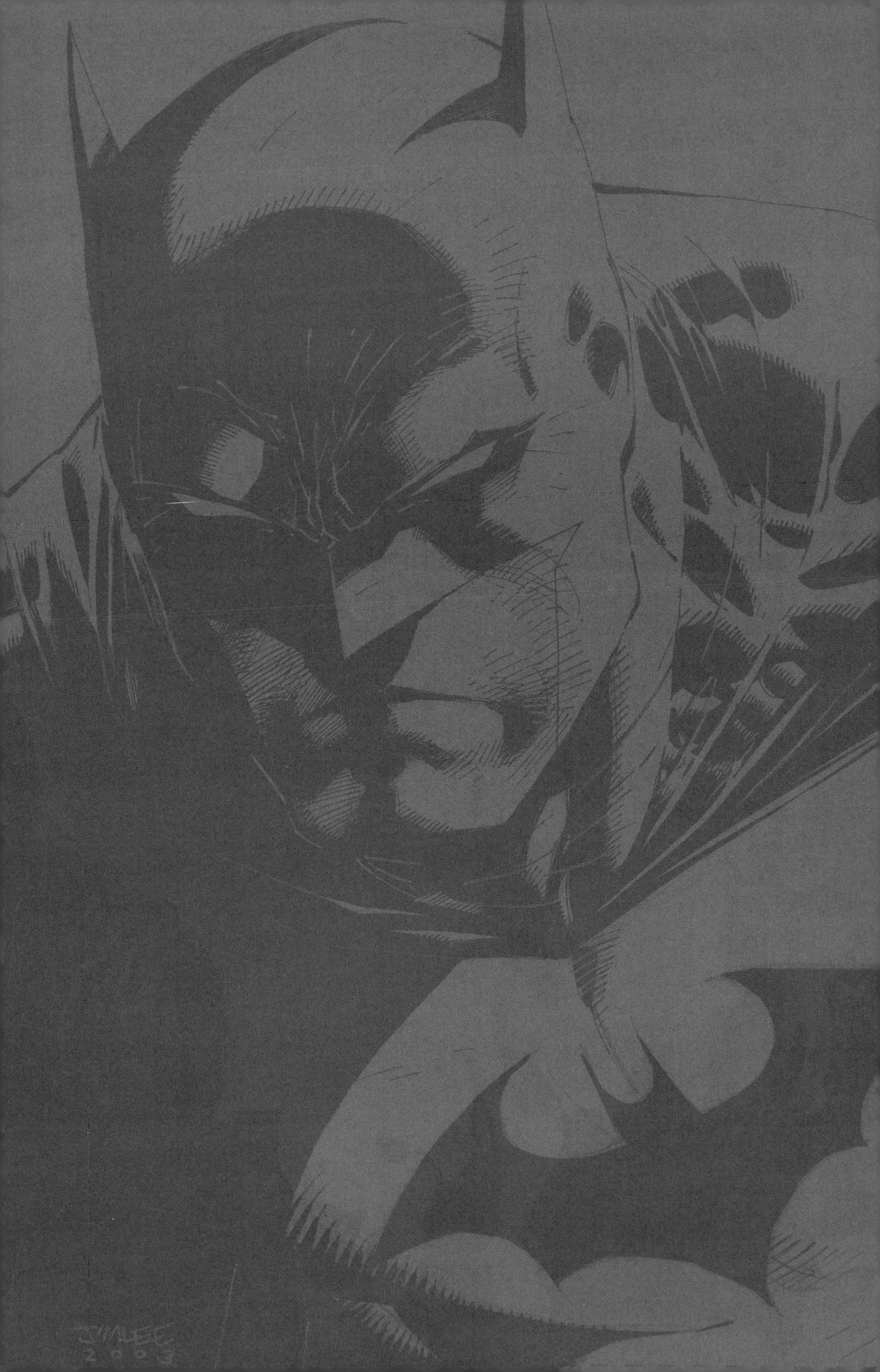

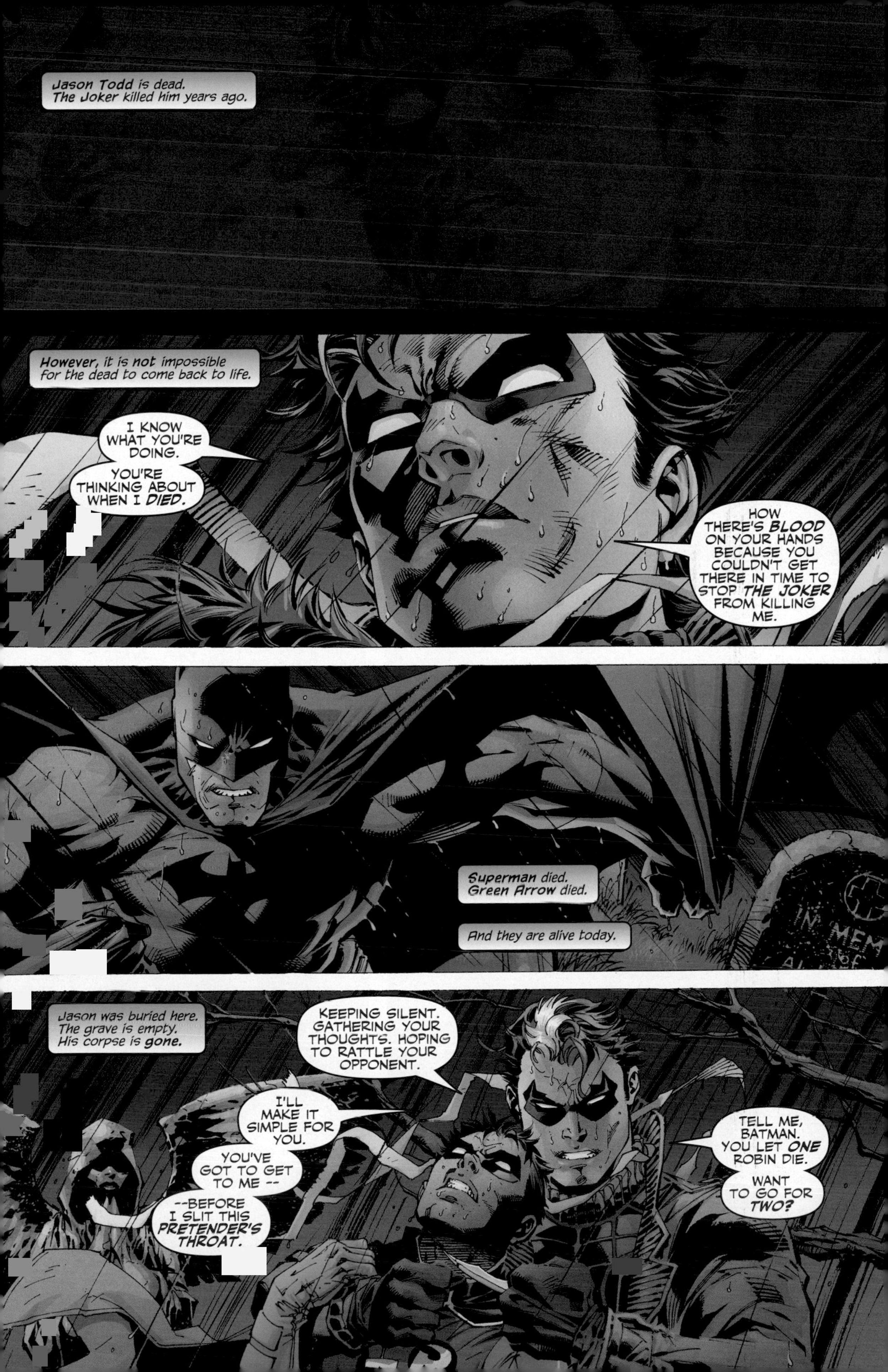
Jason Todd is dead.
The Joker killed him years ago.
However, it is not impossible for the dead to come back to life.
I KNOW WHAT YOU'RE DOING.
YOU'RE THINKING ABOUT WHEN I DIED.
HOW THERE'S BLOOD ON YOUR HANDS BECAUSE YOU COULDN'T GET THERE IN TIME TO STOP THE JOKER FROM KILLING ME.
Superman died.
Green Arrow died.
And they are alive today.
Jason was buried here.
The grave is empty.
His corpse is gone.
KEEPING SILENT. GATHERING YOUR THOUGHTS. HOPING TO RATTLE YOUR OPPONENT.
I'LL MAKE IT SIMPLE FOR YOU.
YOU'VE GOT TO GET TO ME --
--BEFORE I SLIT THIS PRETENDER'S THROAT.
TELL ME, BATMAN. YOU LET ONE ROBIN DIE.
WANT TO GO FOR TWO?

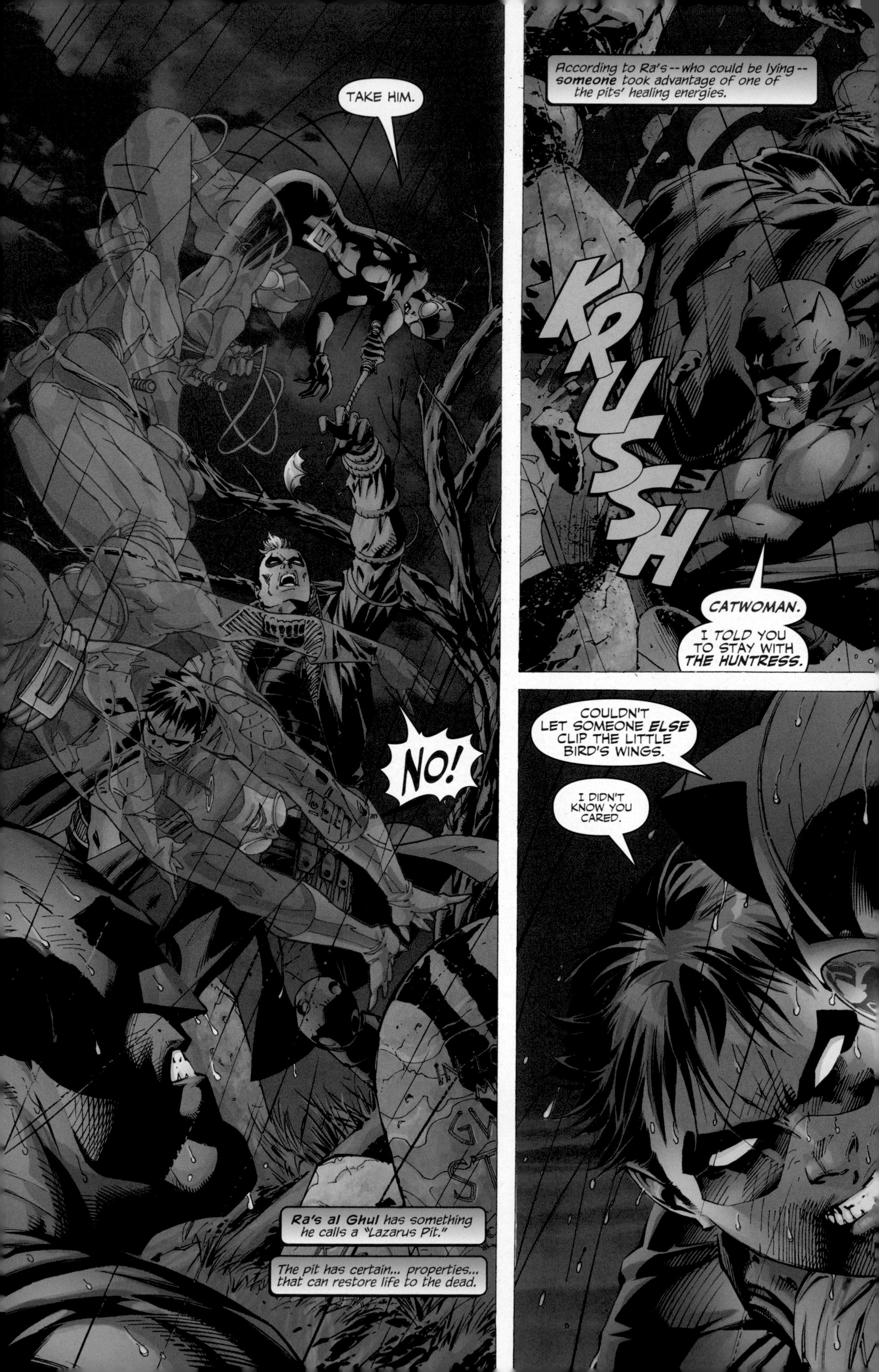
TAKE HIM.
NO!
Ra's al Ghul has something he calls a "Lazarus Pit."
The pit has certain... properties... that can restore life to the dead.
According to Ra's--who could be lying--someone took advantage of one of the pits' healing energies.
KRUSH
CATWOMAN.
I TOLD YOU TO STAY WITH THE HUNTRESS.
COULDN'T LET SOMEONE ELSE CLIP THE LITTLE BIRD'S WINGS.
I DIDN'T KNOW YOU CARED.

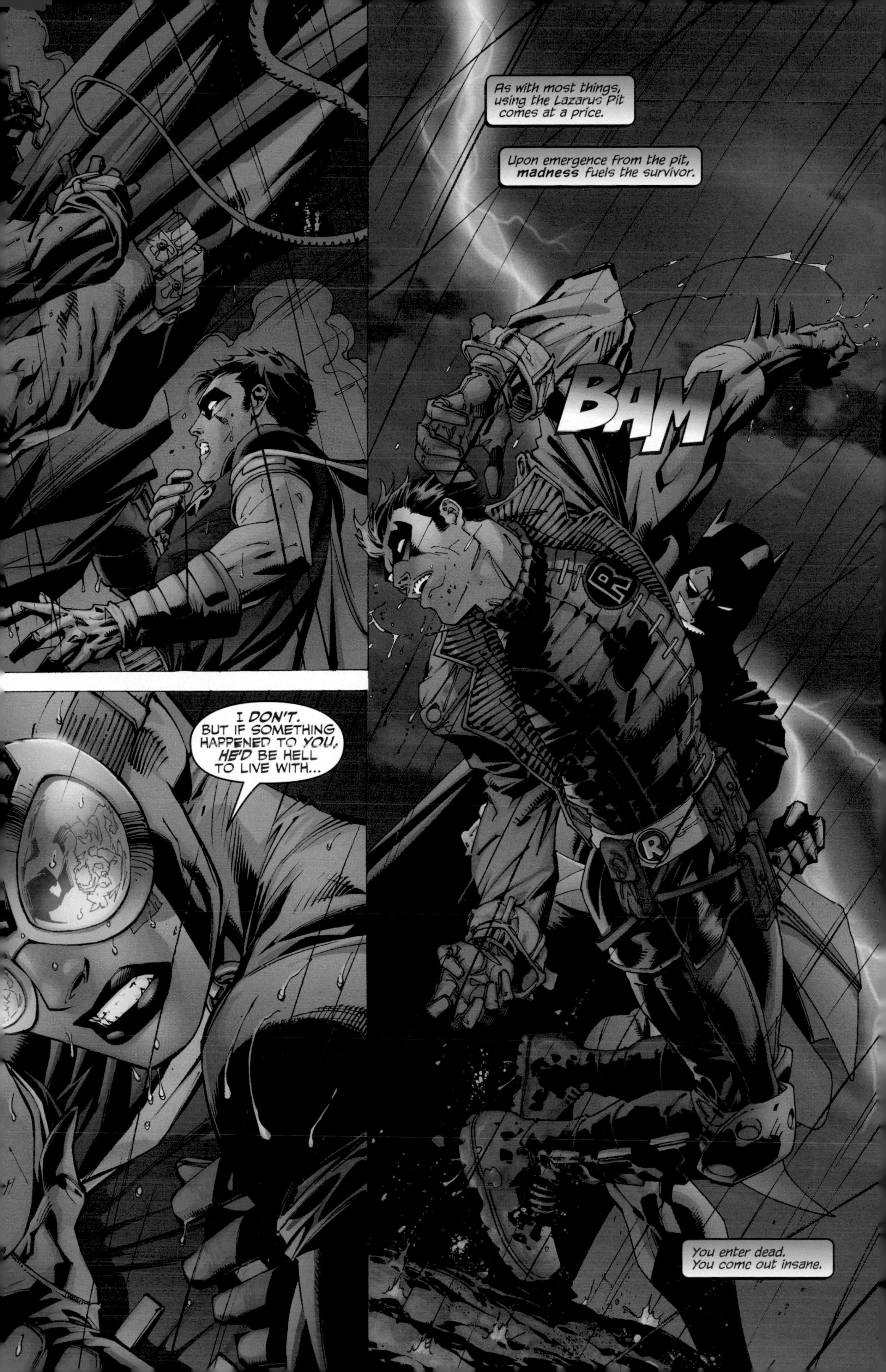
I DON'T. BUT IF SOMETHING HAPPENED TO YOU, HE'D BE HELL TO LIVE WITH...
As with most things, using the Lazarus Pit comes at a price.
Upon emergence from the pit, madness fuels the survivor.
BAM
You enter dead. You come out insane.

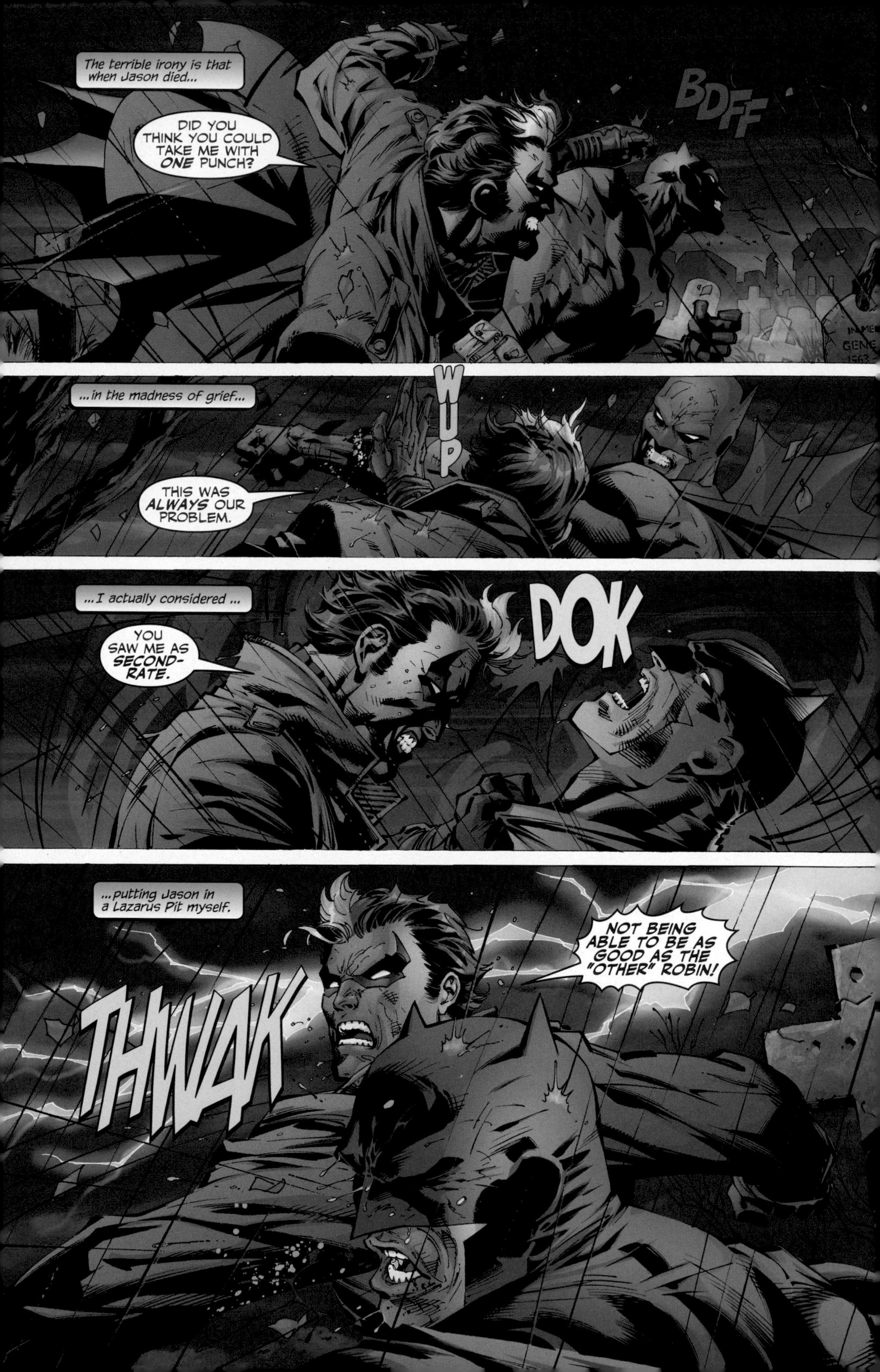
The terrible irony is that when Jason died...
DID YOU THINK YOU COULD TAKE ME WITH ONE PUNCH?
BDFF
...in the madness of grief...
WUP
THIS WAS ALWAYS OUR PROBLEM.
...I actually considered ...
YOU SAW ME AS SECOND-RATE.
DOK
...putting Jason in a Lazarus Pit myself.
NOT BEING ABLE TO BE AS GOOD AS THE "OTHER" ROBIN!
THWAK

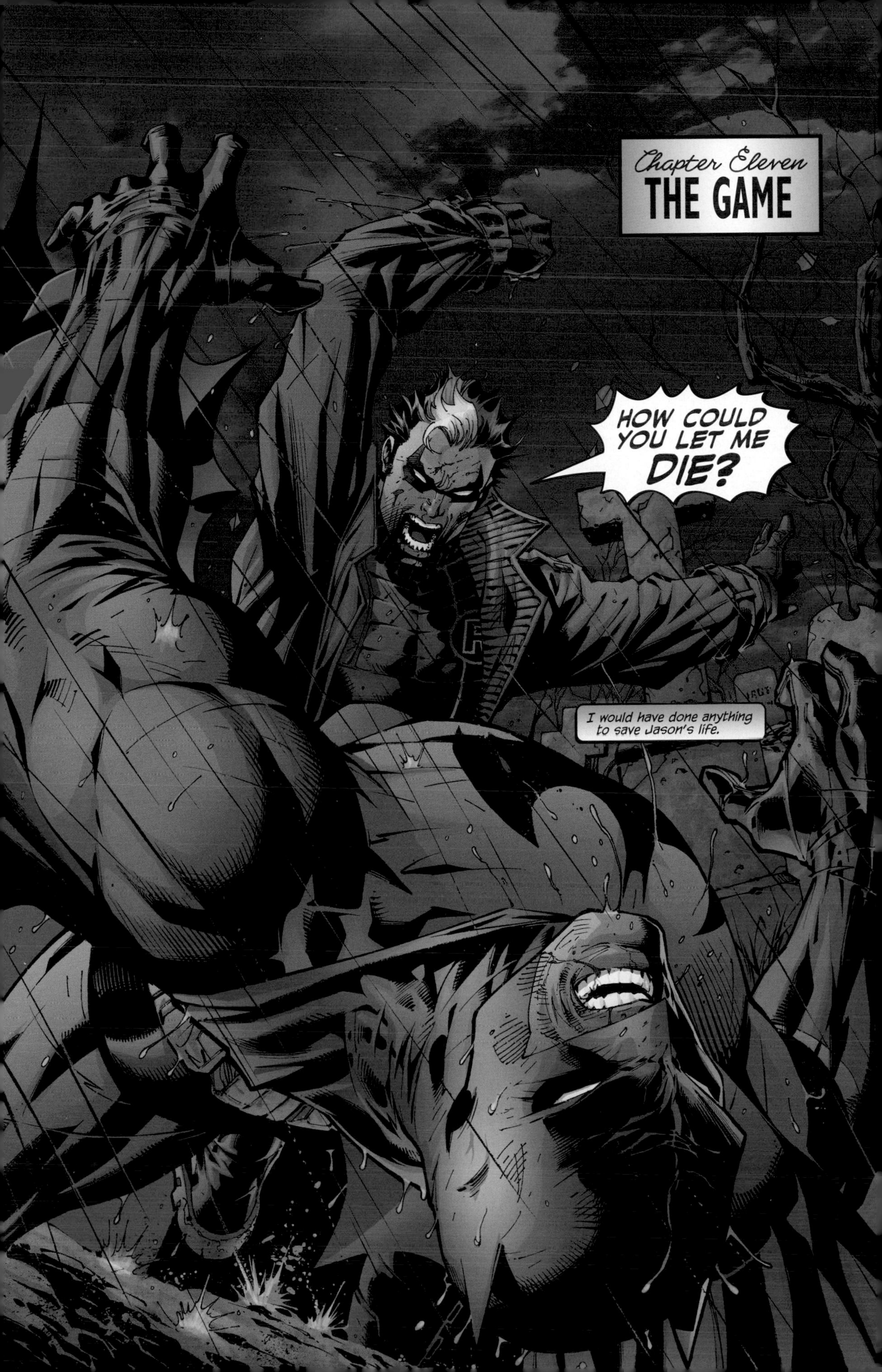
Chapter Eleven
THE GAME
HOW COULD YOU LET ME DIE?
I would have done anything to save Jason's life.

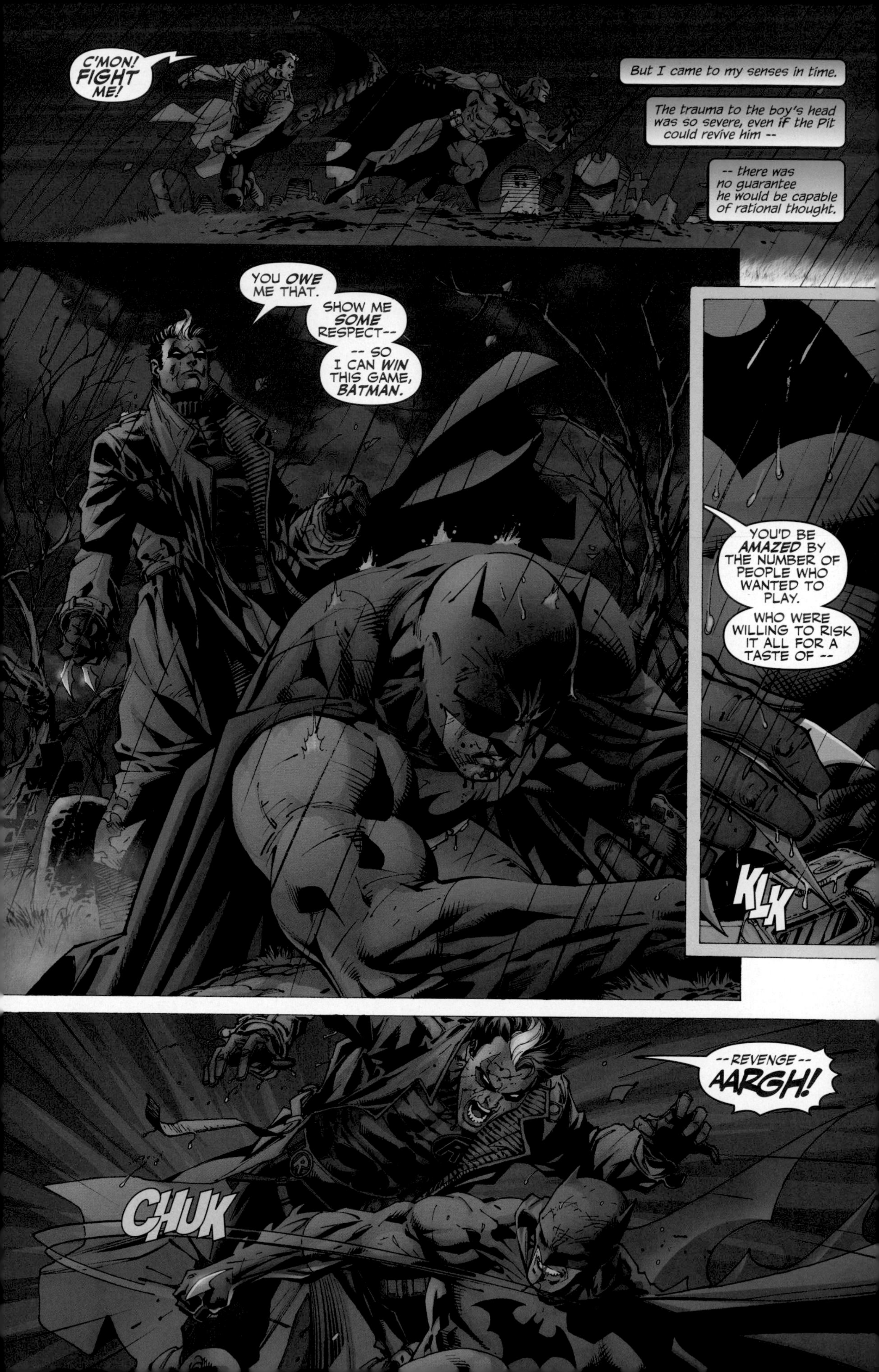
C'MON! FIGHT ME!
But I came to my senses in time.
The trauma to the boy's head was so severe, even if the Pit could revive him --
-- there was no guarantee he would be capable of rational thought.
YOU OWE ME THAT.
SHOW ME SOME RESPECT--
-- SO I CAN WIN THIS GAME, BATMAN.
YOU'D BE AMAZED BY THE NUMBER OF PEOPLE WHO WANTED TO PLAY.
WHO WERE WILLING TO RISK IT ALL FOR A TASTE OF --
KLIK
--REVENGE--
AARGH!
CHUK

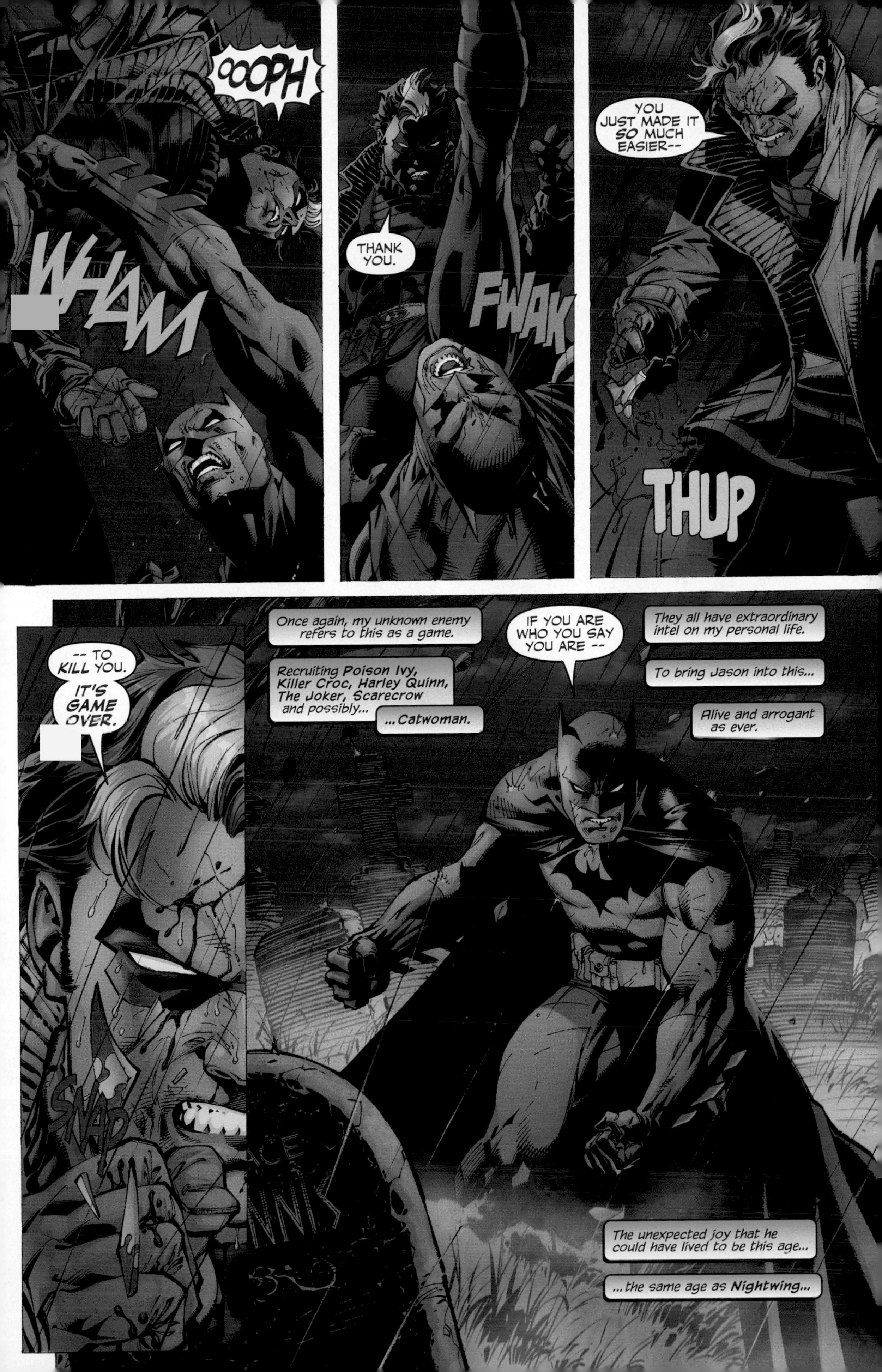
OOOPH
WHAM
THANK YOU.
FWAK
YOU JUST MADE IT SO MUCH EASIER--
THUP
-- TO KILL YOU. IT'S GAME OVER.
SNAP
Once again, my unknown enemy refers to this as a game.
Recruiting Poison Ivy, Killer Croc, Harley Quinn, The Joker, Scarecrow and possibly...
...Catwoman.
IF YOU ARE WHO YOU SAY YOU ARE --
They all have extraordinary intel on my personal life.
To bring Jason into this...
Alive and arrogant as ever.
The unexpected joy that he could have lived to be this age...
...the same age as Nightwing...

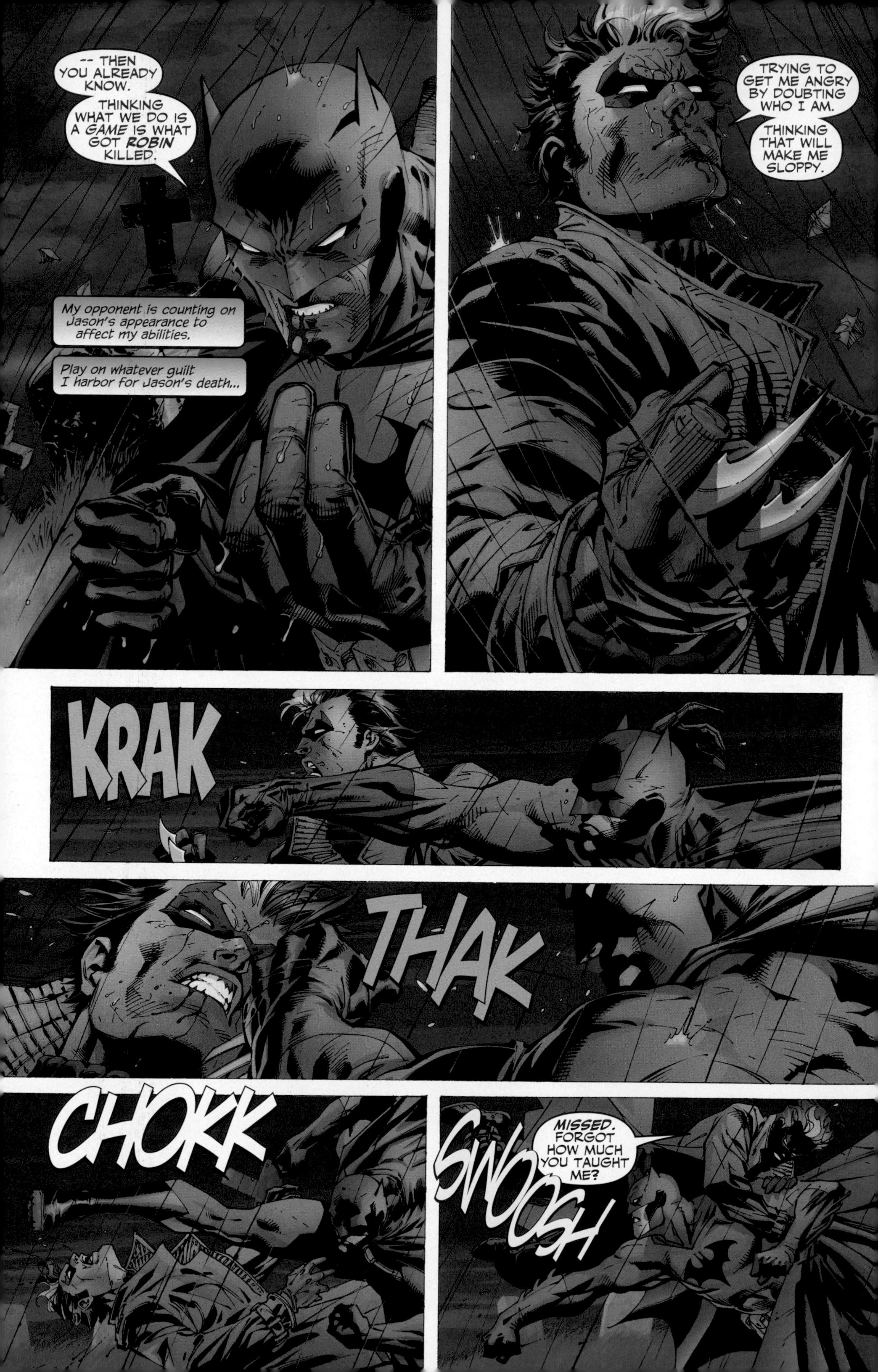
-- THEN YOU ALREADY KNOW. THINKING WHAT WE DO IS A *GAME* IS WHAT GOT *ROBIN* KILLED.
*My opponent is counting on Jason's appearance to affect my abilities.*
*Play on whatever guilt I harbor for Jason's death...*
TRYING TO GET ME ANGRY BY DOUBTING WHO I AM. THINKING THAT WILL MAKE ME SLOPPY.
KRAK
THAK
CHOKK
SWOOSH
*MISSED.* FORGOT HOW MUCH YOU TAUGHT ME?

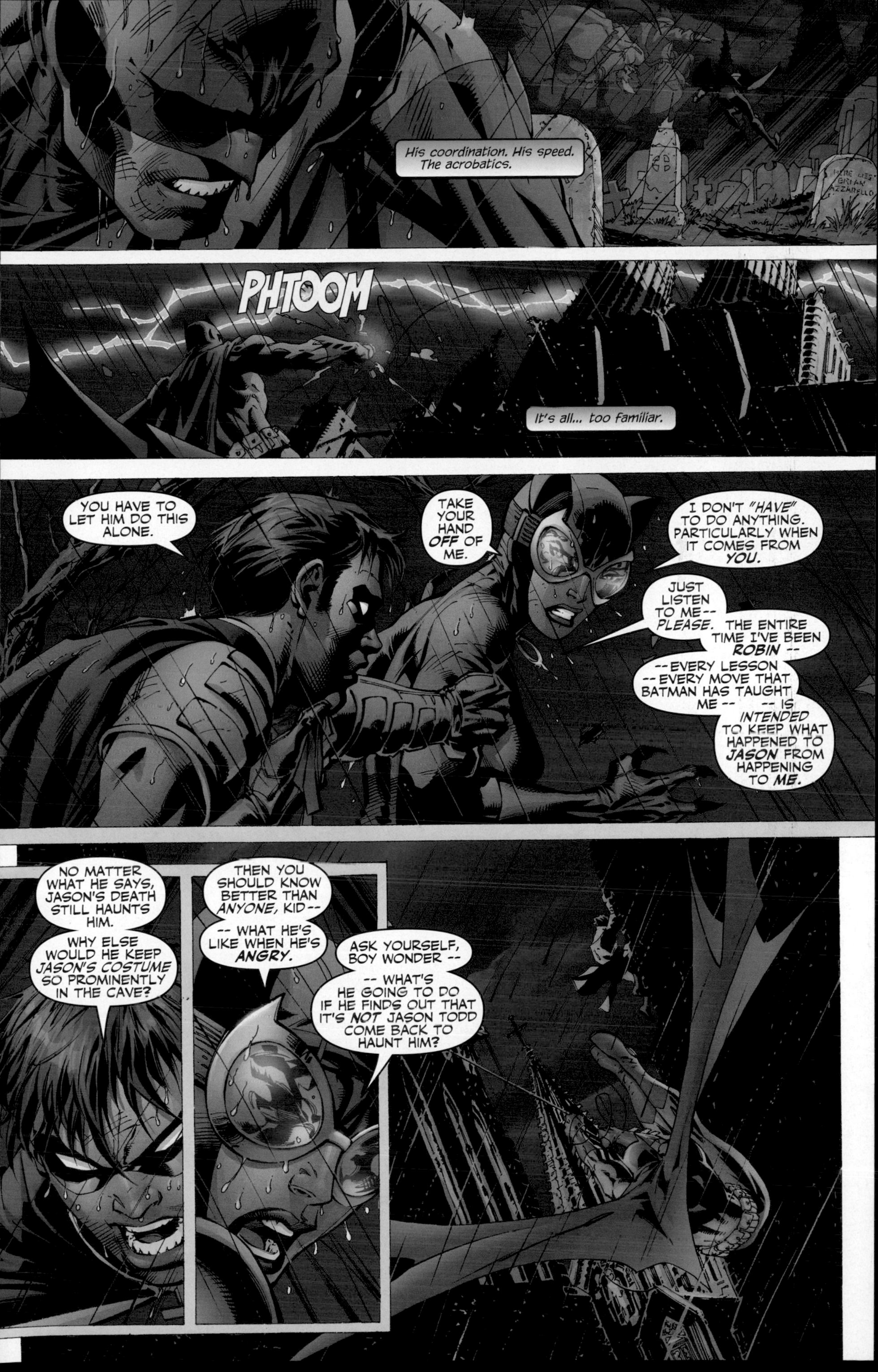
His coordination. His speed. The acrobatics.
PHTOOM
It's all... too familiar.
YOU HAVE TO LET HIM DO THIS ALONE.
TAKE YOUR HAND OFF OF ME.
I DON'T "HAVE" TO DO ANYTHING. PARTICULARLY WHEN IT COMES FROM YOU.
JUST LISTEN TO ME-- PLEASE. THE ENTIRE TIME I'VE BEEN ROBIN --
--EVERY LESSON --EVERY MOVE THAT BATMAN HAS TAUGHT ME -- --IS INTENDED TO KEEP WHAT HAPPENED TO JASON FROM HAPPENING TO ME.
NO MATTER WHAT HE SAYS, JASON'S DEATH STILL HAUNTS HIM.
WHY ELSE WOULD HE KEEP JASON'S COSTUME SO PROMINENTLY IN THE CAVE?
THEN YOU SHOULD KNOW BETTER THAN ANYONE, KID--
-- WHAT HE'S LIKE WHEN HE'S ANGRY.
ASK YOURSELF, BOY WONDER --
-- WHAT'S HE GOING TO DO IF HE FINDS OUT THAT IT'S NOT JASON TODD COME BACK TO HAUNT HIM?

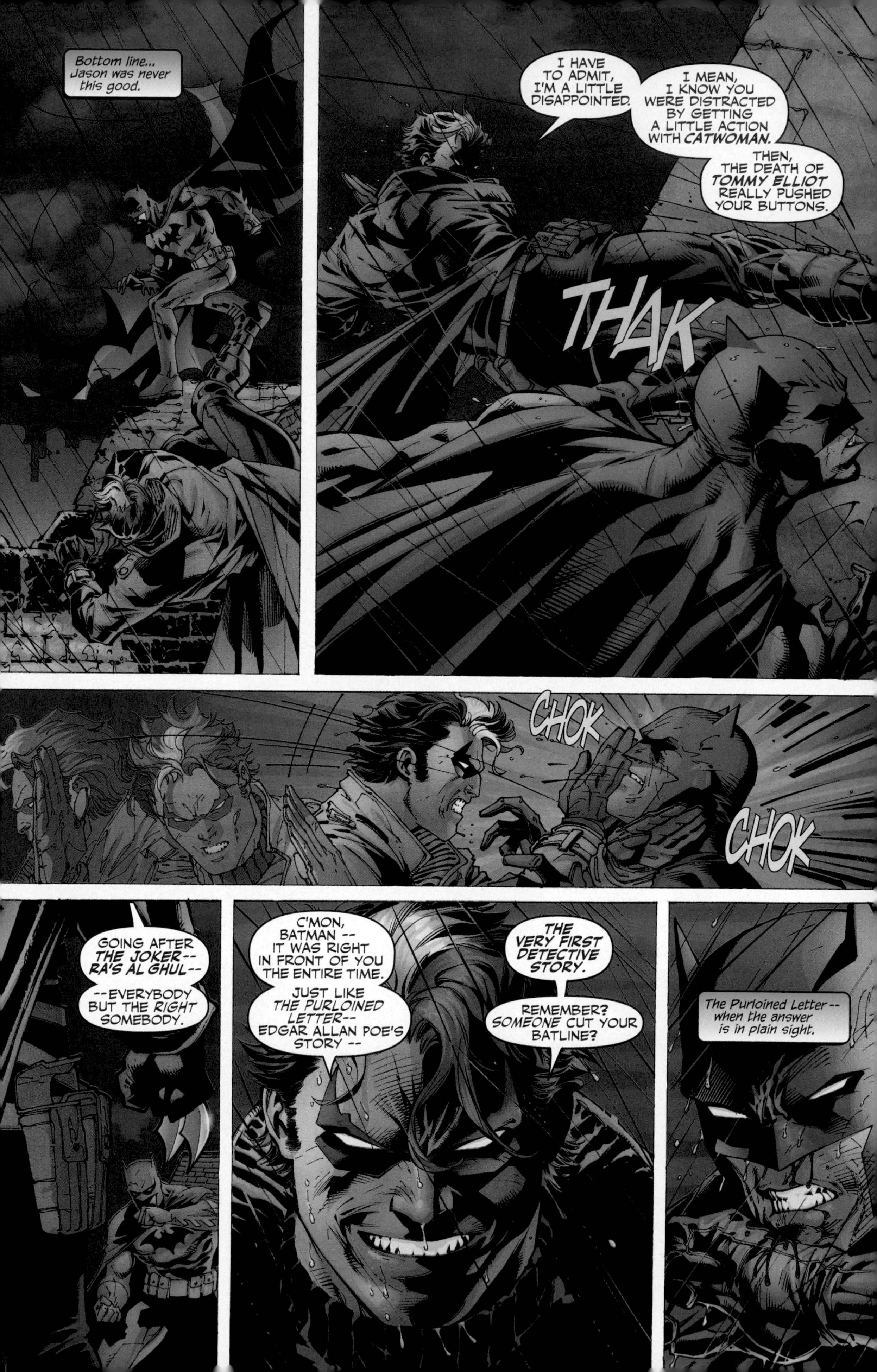
Bottom line... Jason was never this good.
I HAVE TO ADMIT, I'M A LITTLE DISAPPOINTED.
I MEAN, I KNOW YOU WERE DISTRACTED BY GETTING A LITTLE ACTION WITH CATWOMAN.
THEN, THE DEATH OF TOMMY ELLIOT REALLY PUSHED YOUR BUTTONS.
THAK
CHOK
CHOK
GOING AFTER THE JOKER-- RA'S AL GHUL--
--EVERYBODY BUT THE RIGHT SOMEBODY.
C'MON, BATMAN -- IT WAS RIGHT IN FRONT OF YOU THE ENTIRE TIME.
JUST LIKE THE PURLOINED LETTER-- EDGAR ALLAN POE'S STORY --
THE VERY FIRST DETECTIVE STORY.
REMEMBER? SOMEONE CUT YOUR BATLINE?
The Purloined Letter -- when the answer is in plain sight.

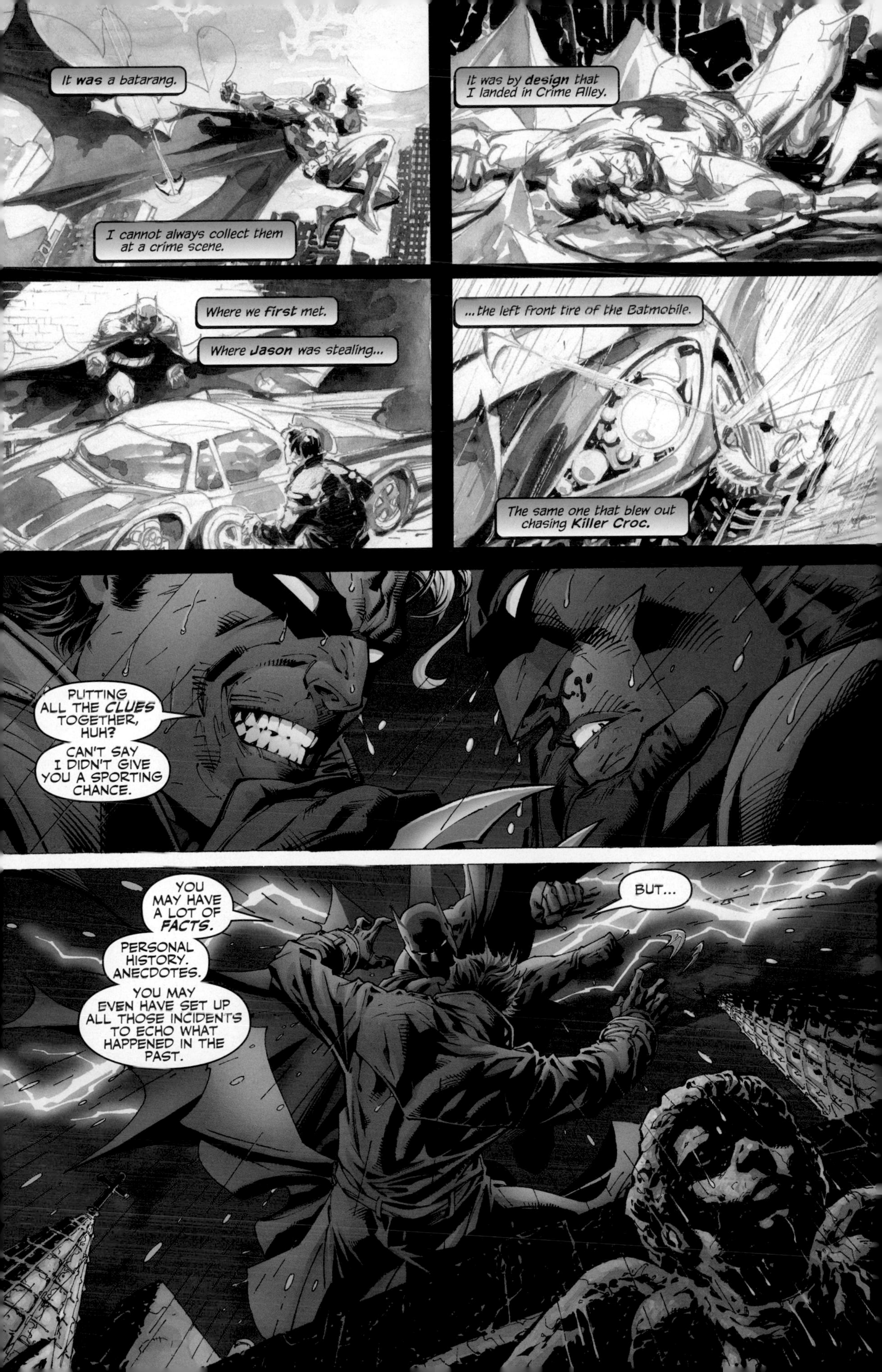
It was a batarang.
I cannot always collect them at a crime scene.
It was by design that I landed in Crime Alley.
Where we first met.
Where Jason was stealing...
...the left front tire of the Batmobile.
The same one that blew out chasing Killer Croc.
PUTTING ALL THE CLUES TOGETHER, HUH?
CAN'T SAY I DIDN'T GIVE YOU A SPORTING CHANCE.
YOU MAY HAVE A LOT OF FACTS.
PERSONAL HISTORY. ANECDOTES.
YOU MAY EVEN HAVE SET UP ALL THOSE INCIDENTS TO ECHO WHAT HAPPENED IN THE PAST.
BUT...

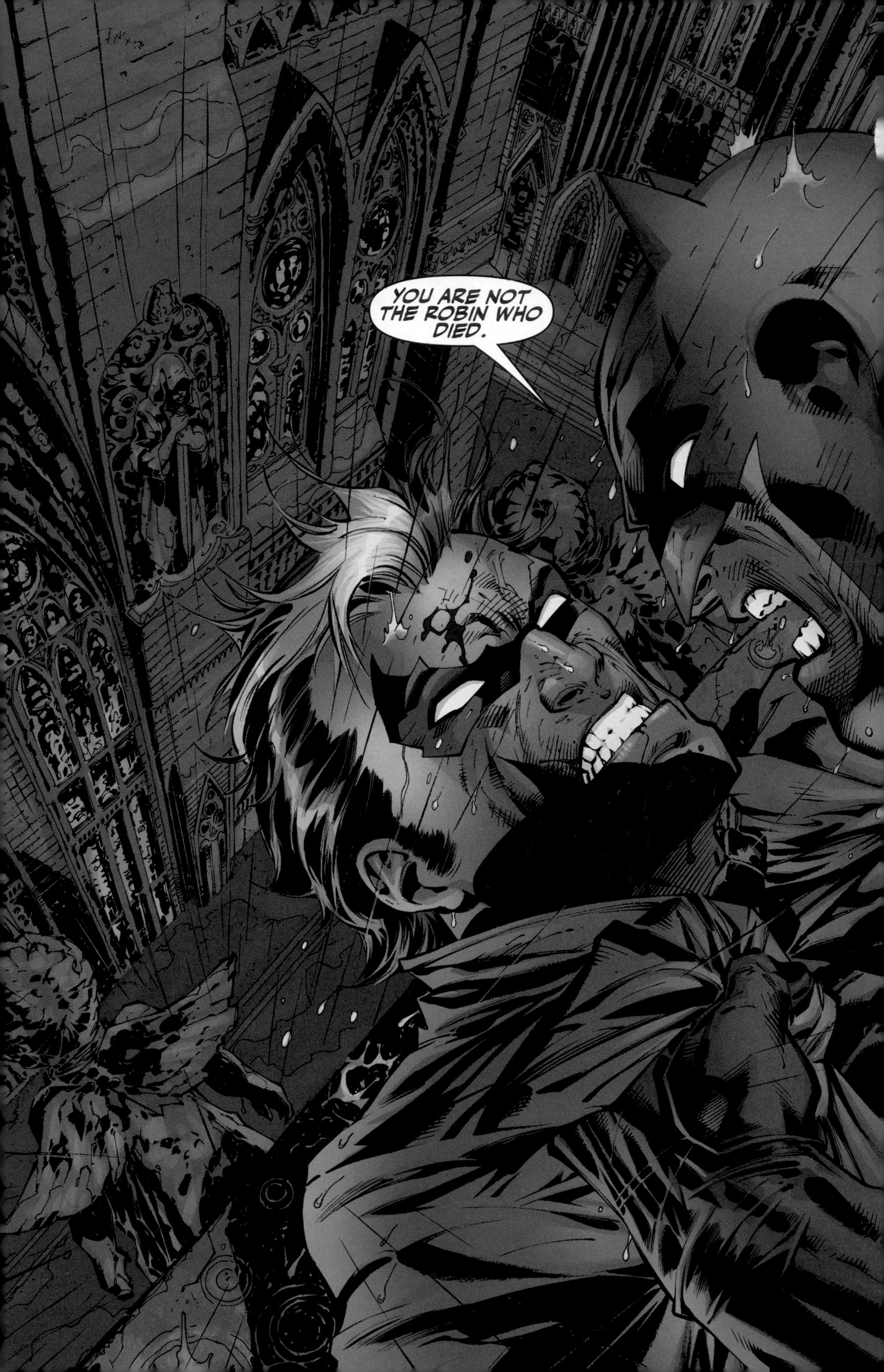
YOU ARE NOT THE ROBIN WHO DIED.

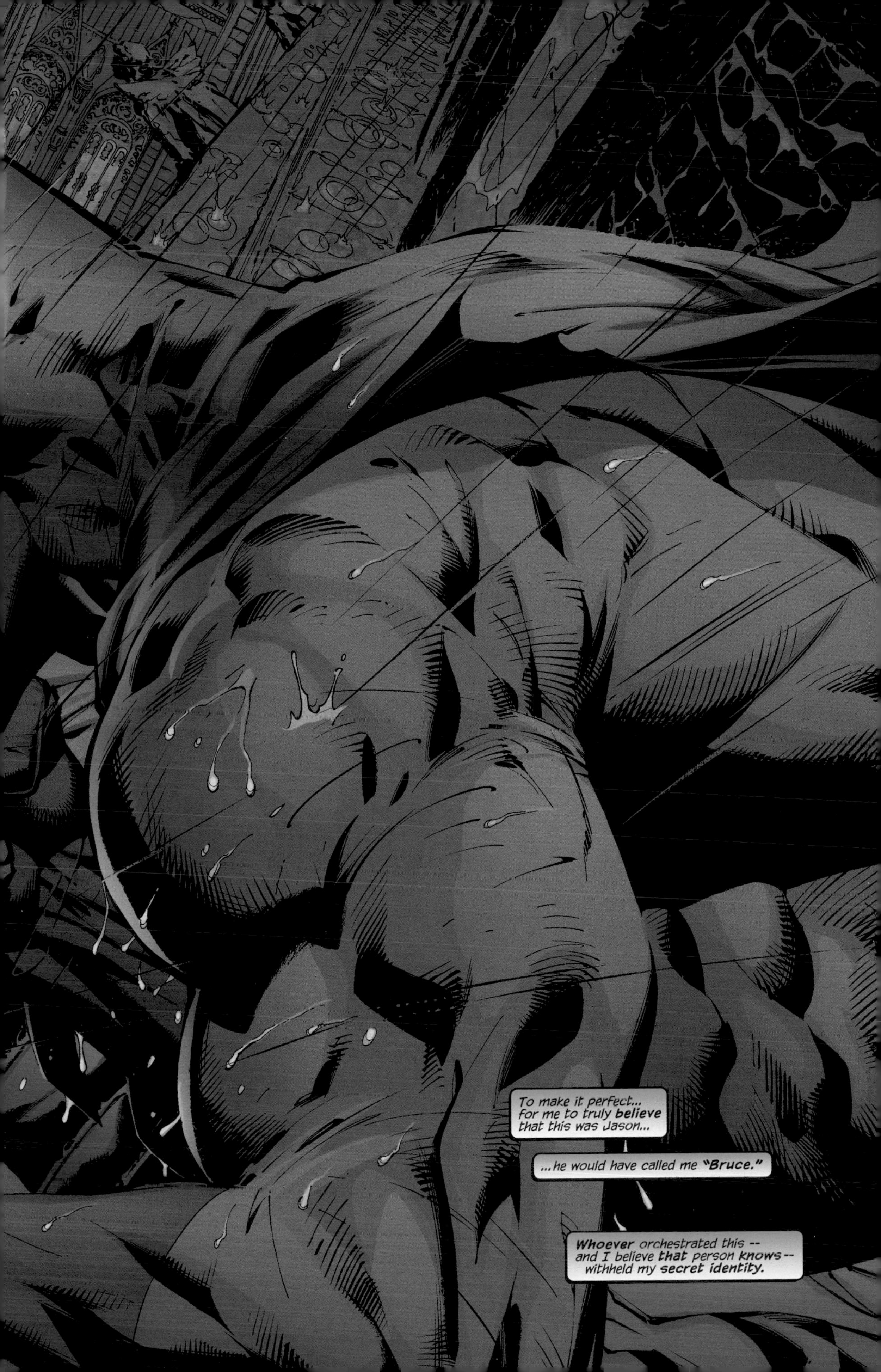
To make it perfect... for me to truly believe that this was Jason...
...he would have called me "Bruce."
Whoever orchestrated this -- and I believe that person knows -- withheld my secret identity.

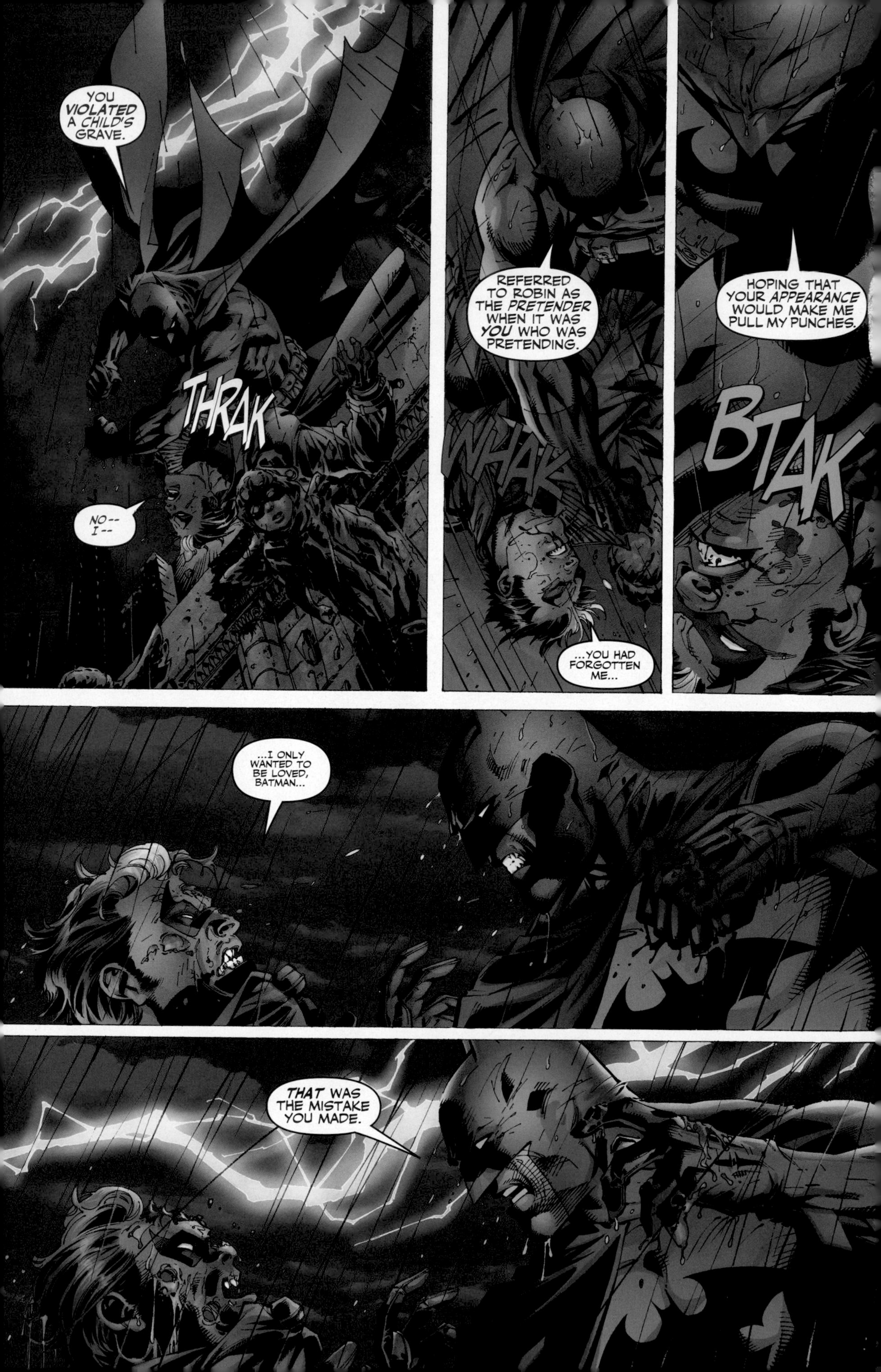
YOU VIOLATED A CHILD'S GRAVE.
THRAK
NO-- I--
REFERRED TO ROBIN AS THE PRETENDER WHEN IT WAS YOU WHO WAS PRETENDING.
WHAK
...YOU HAD FORGOTTEN ME...
HOPING THAT YOUR APPEARANCE WOULD MAKE ME PULL MY PUNCHES.
BTAK
...I ONLY WANTED TO BE LOVED, BATMAN...
THAT WAS THE MISTAKE YOU MADE.

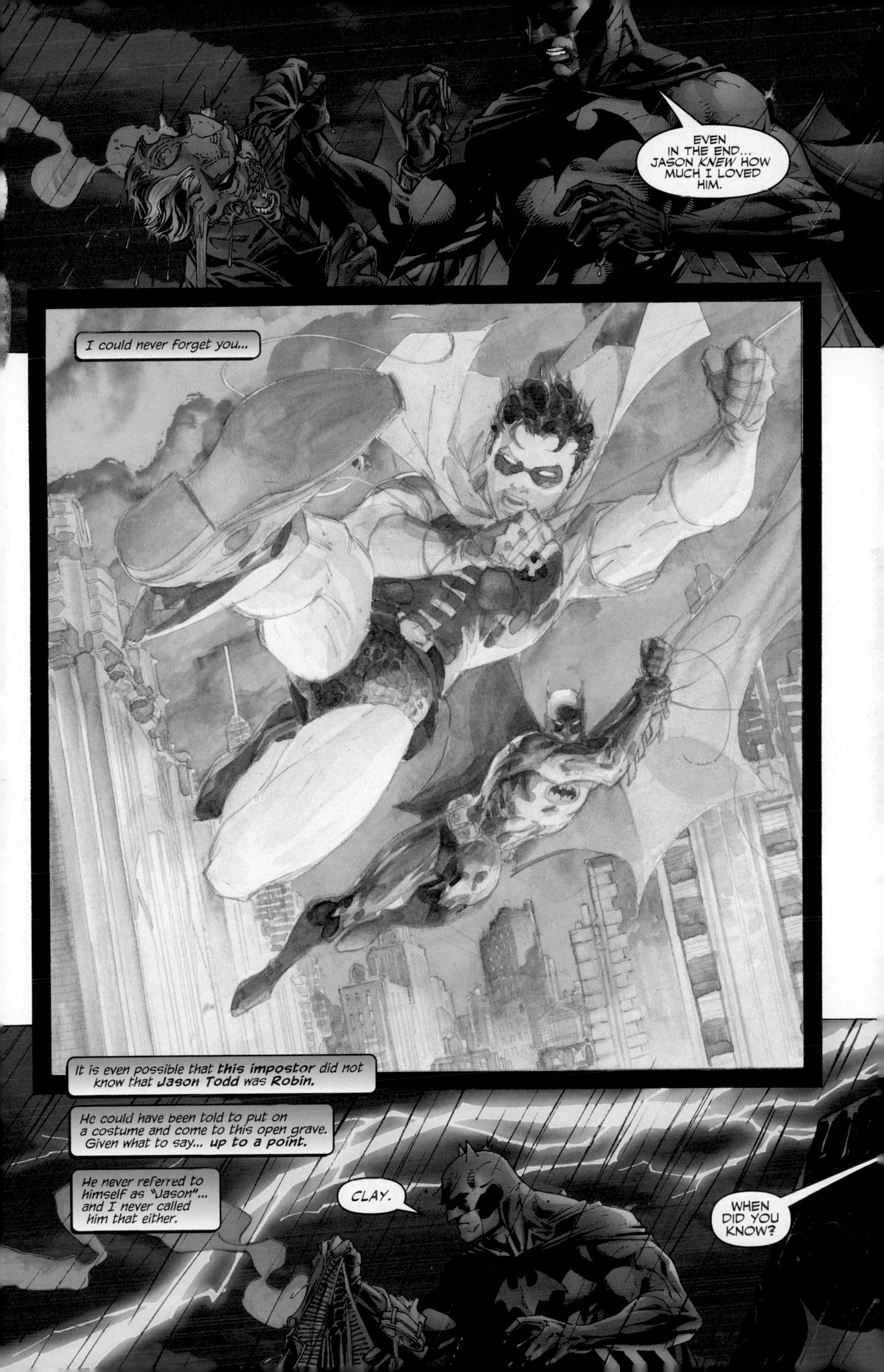
EVEN IN THE END... JASON KNEW HOW MUCH I LOVED HIM.
I could never forget you...
It is even possible that this impostor did not know that Jason Todd was Robin.
He could have been told to put on a costume and come to this open grave. Given what to say... up to a point.
He never referred to himself as "Jason"... and I never called him that either.
CLAY.
WHEN DID YOU KNOW?

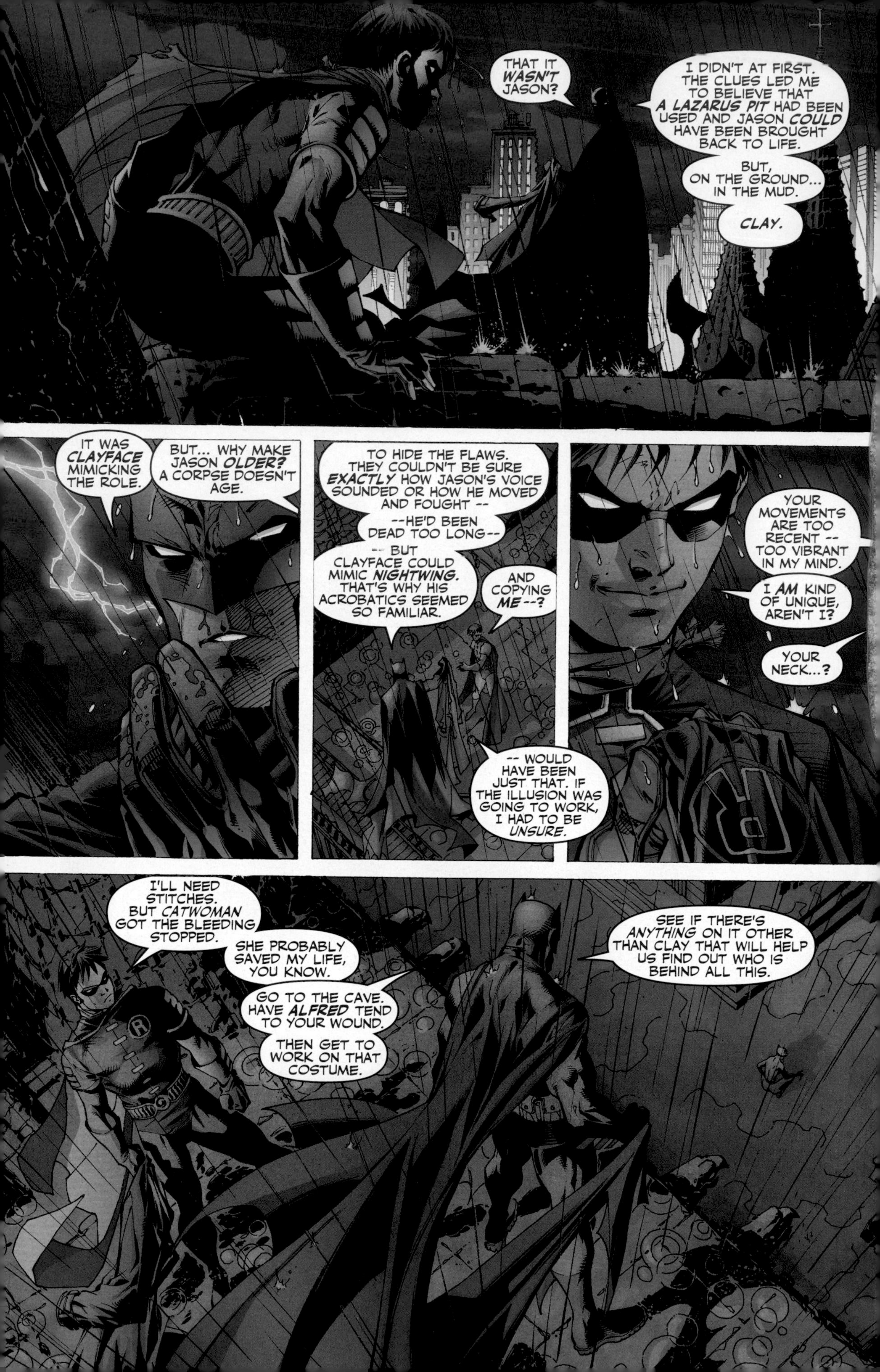
THAT IT WASN'T JASON?
I DIDN'T AT FIRST. THE CLUES LED ME TO BELIEVE THAT A LAZARUS PIT HAD BEEN USED AND JASON COULD HAVE BEEN BROUGHT BACK TO LIFE.
BUT, ON THE GROUND... IN THE MUD.
CLAY.
IT WAS CLAYFACE MIMICKING THE ROLE.
BUT... WHY MAKE JASON OLDER? A CORPSE DOESN'T AGE.
TO HIDE THE FLAWS. THEY COULDN'T BE SURE EXACTLY HOW JASON'S VOICE SOUNDED OR HOW HE MOVED AND FOUGHT --
--HE'D BEEN DEAD TOO LONG--
-- BUT CLAYFACE COULD MIMIC NIGHTWING. THAT'S WHY HIS ACROBATICS SEEMED SO FAMILIAR.
AND COPYING ME --?
-- WOULD HAVE BEEN JUST THAT. IF THE ILLUSION WAS GOING TO WORK, I HAD TO BE UNSURE.
YOUR MOVEMENTS ARE TOO RECENT -- TOO VIBRANT IN MY MIND.
I AM KIND OF UNIQUE, AREN'T I?
YOUR NECK...?
I'LL NEED STITCHES. BUT CATWOMAN GOT THE BLEEDING STOPPED.
SHE PROBABLY SAVED MY LIFE, YOU KNOW.
GO TO THE CAVE. HAVE ALFRED TEND TO YOUR WOUND.
THEN GET TO WORK ON THAT COSTUME.
SEE IF THERE'S ANYTHING ON IT OTHER THAN CLAY THAT WILL HELP US FIND OUT WHO IS BEHIND ALL THIS.

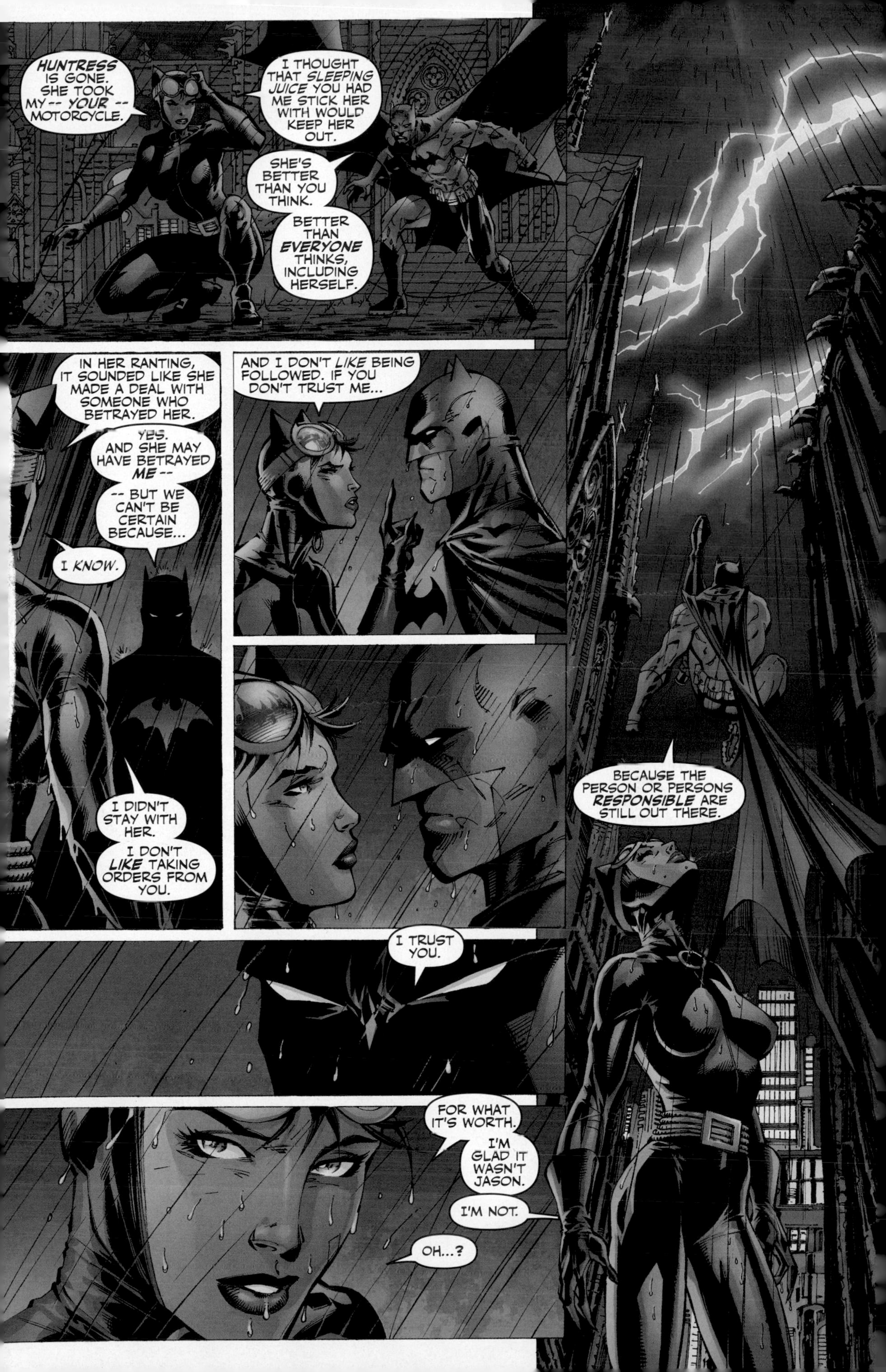
HUNTRESS IS GONE. SHE TOOK MY -- YOUR -- MOTORCYCLE.
I THOUGHT THAT SLEEPING JUICE YOU HAD ME STICK HER WITH WOULD KEEP HER OUT.
SHE'S BETTER THAN YOU THINK.
BETTER THAN EVERYONE THINKS, INCLUDING HERSELF.
IN HER RANTING, IT SOUNDED LIKE SHE MADE A DEAL WITH SOMEONE WHO BETRAYED HER.
YES. AND SHE MAY HAVE BETRAYED ME --
-- BUT WE CAN'T BE CERTAIN BECAUSE...
I KNOW.
I DIDN'T STAY WITH HER.
I DON'T LIKE TAKING ORDERS FROM YOU.
AND I DON'T LIKE BEING FOLLOWED. IF YOU DON'T TRUST ME...
BECAUSE THE PERSON OR PERSONS RESPONSIBLE ARE STILL OUT THERE.
I TRUST YOU.
FOR WHAT IT'S WORTH.
I'M GLAD IT WASN'T JASON.
I'M NOT.
OH...?

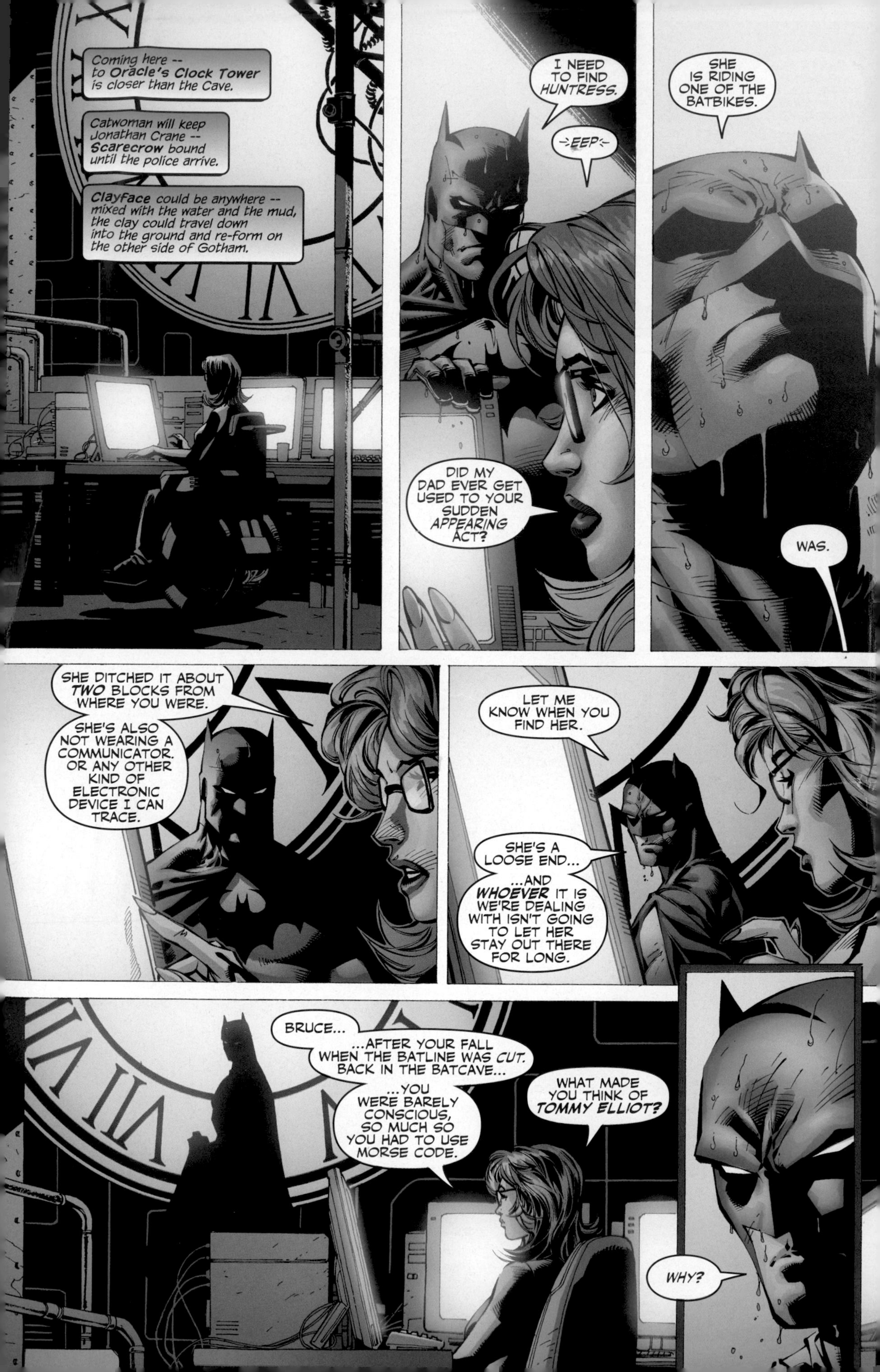
Coming here -- to Oracle's Clock Tower is closer than the Cave.
Catwoman will keep Jonathan Crane -- Scarecrow bound until the police arrive.
Clayface could be anywhere -- mixed with the water and the mud, the clay could travel down into the ground and re-form on the other side of Gotham.
I NEED TO FIND HUNTRESS.
EEP
DID MY DAD EVER GET USED TO YOUR SUDDEN APPEARING ACT?
SHE IS RIDING ONE OF THE BATBIKES.
WAS.
SHE DITCHED IT ABOUT TWO BLOCKS FROM WHERE YOU WERE.
SHE'S ALSO NOT WEARING A COMMUNICATOR. OR ANY OTHER KIND OF ELECTRONIC DEVICE I CAN TRACE.
LET ME KNOW WHEN YOU FIND HER.
SHE'S A LOOSE END...
...AND WHOEVER IT IS WE'RE DEALING WITH ISN'T GOING TO LET HER STAY OUT THERE FOR LONG.
BRUCE...
...AFTER YOUR FALL WHEN THE BATLINE WAS CUT. BACK IN THE BATCAVE...
...YOU WERE BARELY CONSCIOUS, SO MUCH SO YOU HAD TO USE MORSE CODE.
WHAT MADE YOU THINK OF TOMMY ELLIOT?
WHY?

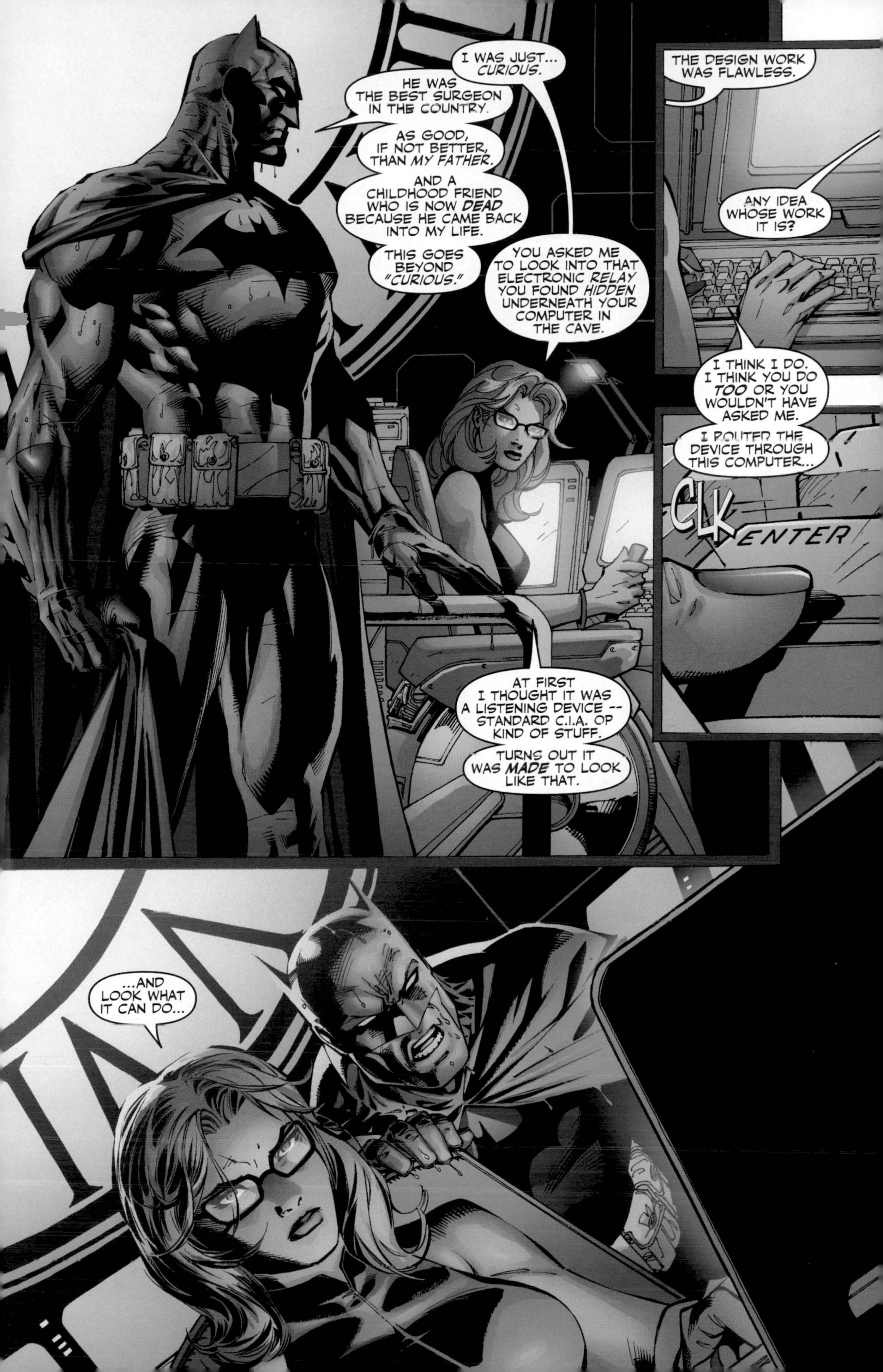
I WAS JUST... CURIOUS.
HE WAS THE BEST SURGEON IN THE COUNTRY.
AS GOOD, IF NOT BETTER, THAN MY FATHER.
AND A CHILDHOOD FRIEND WHO IS NOW DEAD BECAUSE HE CAME BACK INTO MY LIFE.
THIS GOES BEYOND "CURIOUS."
YOU ASKED ME TO LOOK INTO THAT ELECTRONIC RELAY YOU FOUND HIDDEN UNDERNEATH YOUR COMPUTER IN THE CAVE.
AT FIRST I THOUGHT IT WAS A LISTENING DEVICE -- STANDARD C.I.A. OP KIND OF STUFF.
TURNS OUT IT WAS MADE TO LOOK LIKE THAT.
THE DESIGN WORK WAS FLAWLESS.
ANY IDEA WHOSE WORK IT IS?
I THINK I DO. I THINK YOU DO TOO OR YOU WOULDN'T HAVE ASKED ME.
I ROUTED THE DEVICE THROUGH THIS COMPUTER...
CLK
ENTER
...AND LOOK WHAT IT CAN DO...

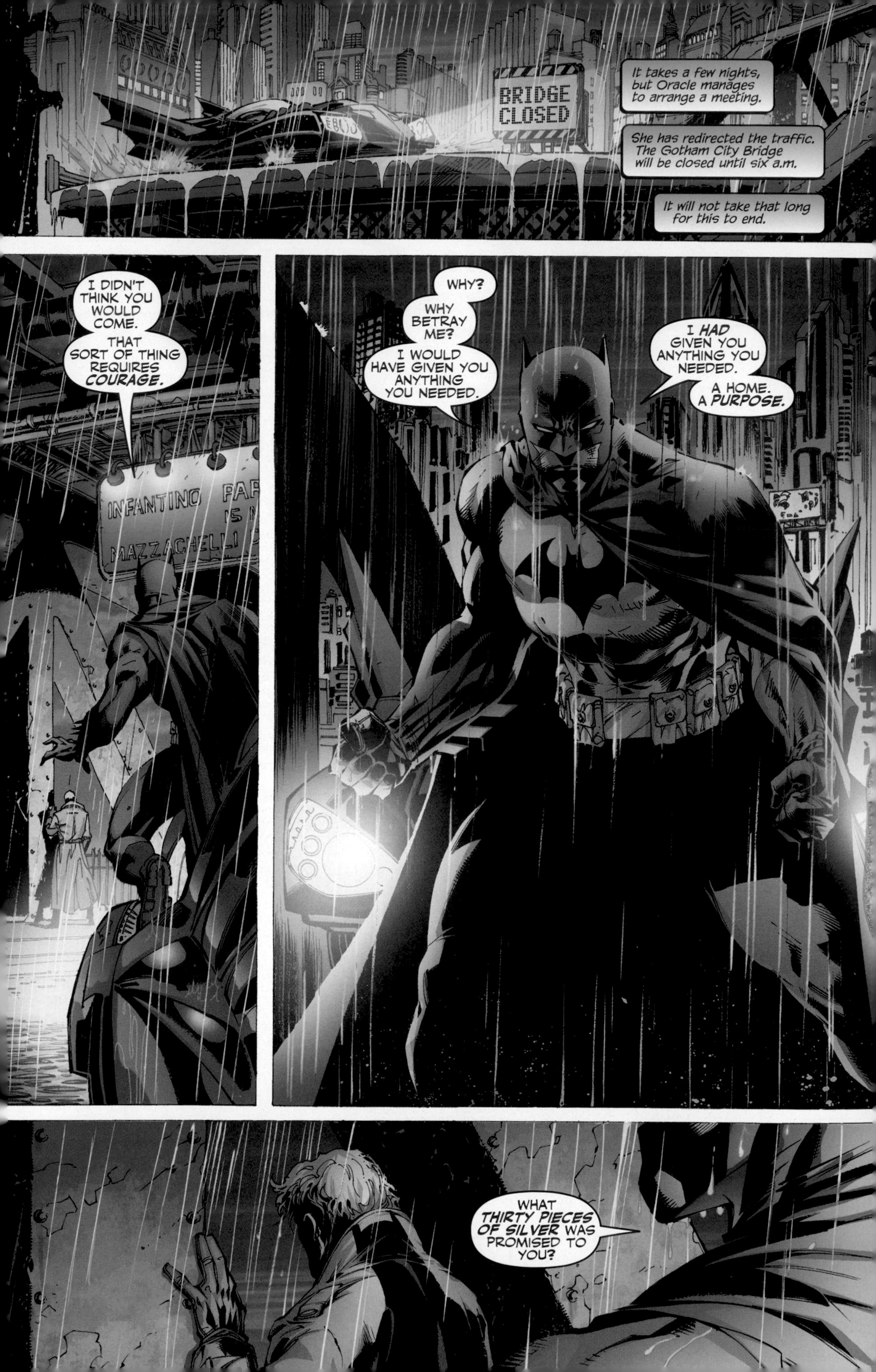
BRIDGE CLOSED
It takes a few nights, but Oracle manages to arrange a meeting.
She has redirected the traffic. The Gotham City Bridge will be closed until six a.m.
It will not take that long for this to end.
I DIDN'T THINK YOU WOULD COME.
THAT SORT OF THING REQUIRES COURAGE.
WHY?
WHY BETRAY ME?
I WOULD HAVE GIVEN YOU ANYTHING YOU NEEDED.
I HAD GIVEN YOU ANYTHING YOU NEEDED.
A HOME. A PURPOSE.
WHAT THIRTY PIECES OF SILVER WAS PROMISED TO YOU?

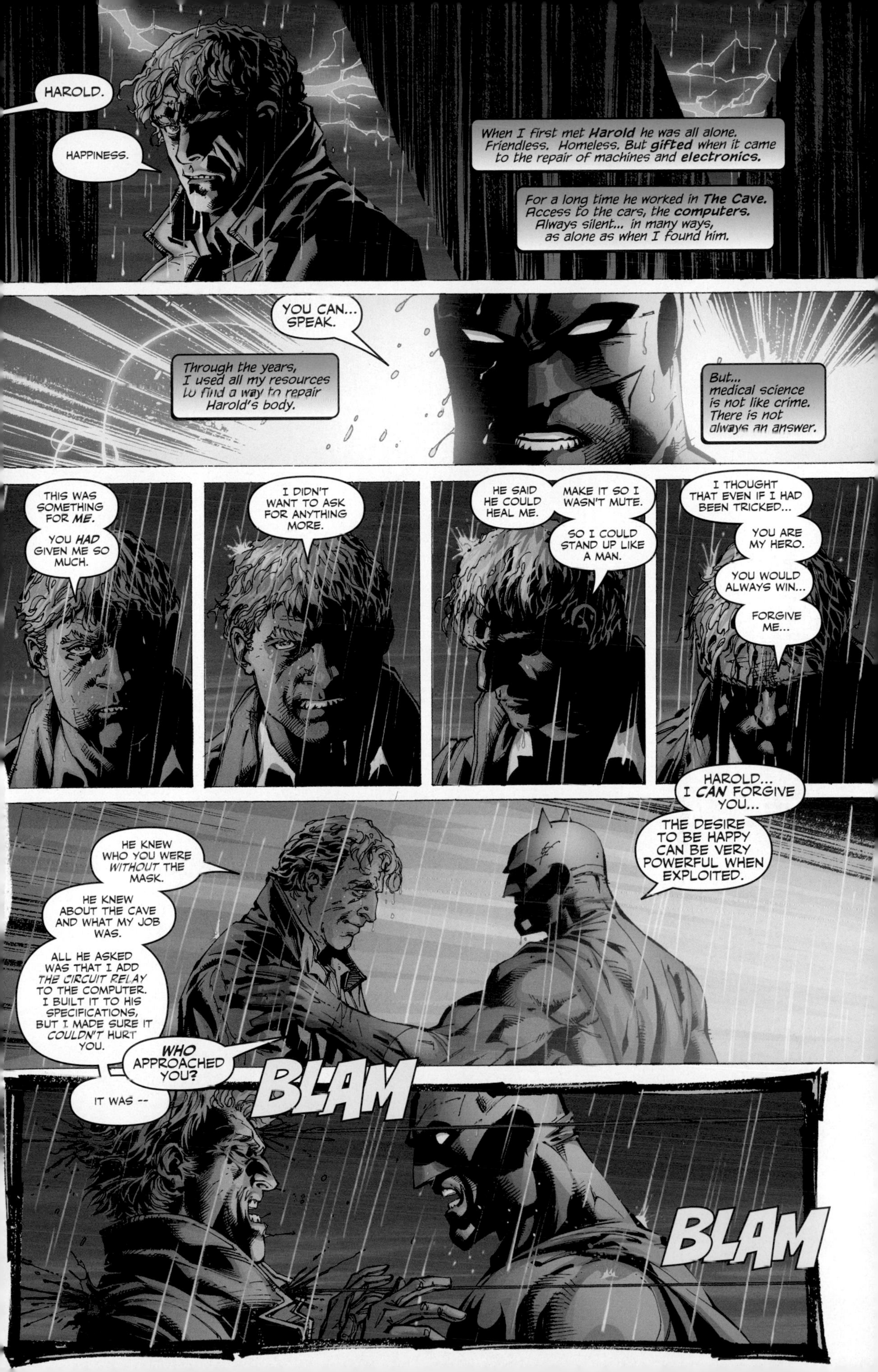
HAROLD.
HAPPINESS.
When I first met Harold he was all alone. Friendless. Homeless. But gifted when it came to the repair of machines and electronics.
For a long time he worked in The Cave. Access to the cars, the computers. Always silent... in many ways, as alone as when I found him.
YOU CAN... SPEAK.
Through the years, I used all my resources to find a way to repair Harold's body.
But... medical science is not like crime. There is not always an answer.
THIS WAS SOMETHING FOR ME.
YOU HAD GIVEN ME SO MUCH.
I DIDN'T WANT TO ASK FOR ANYTHING MORE.
HE SAID HE COULD HEAL ME.
MAKE IT SO I WASN'T MUTE.
SO I COULD STAND UP LIKE A MAN.
I THOUGHT THAT EVEN IF I HAD BEEN TRICKED...
YOU ARE MY HERO.
YOU WOULD ALWAYS WIN...
FORGIVE ME...
HAROLD... I CAN FORGIVE YOU...
THE DESIRE TO BE HAPPY CAN BE VERY POWERFUL WHEN EXPLOITED.
HE KNEW WHO YOU WERE WITHOUT THE MASK.
HE KNEW ABOUT THE CAVE AND WHAT MY JOB WAS.
ALL HE ASKED WAS THAT I ADD THE CIRCUIT RELAY TO THE COMPUTER. I BUILT IT TO HIS SPECIFICATIONS, BUT I MADE SURE IT COULDN'T HURT YOU.
WHO APPROACHED YOU?
IT WAS --
BLAM
BLAM

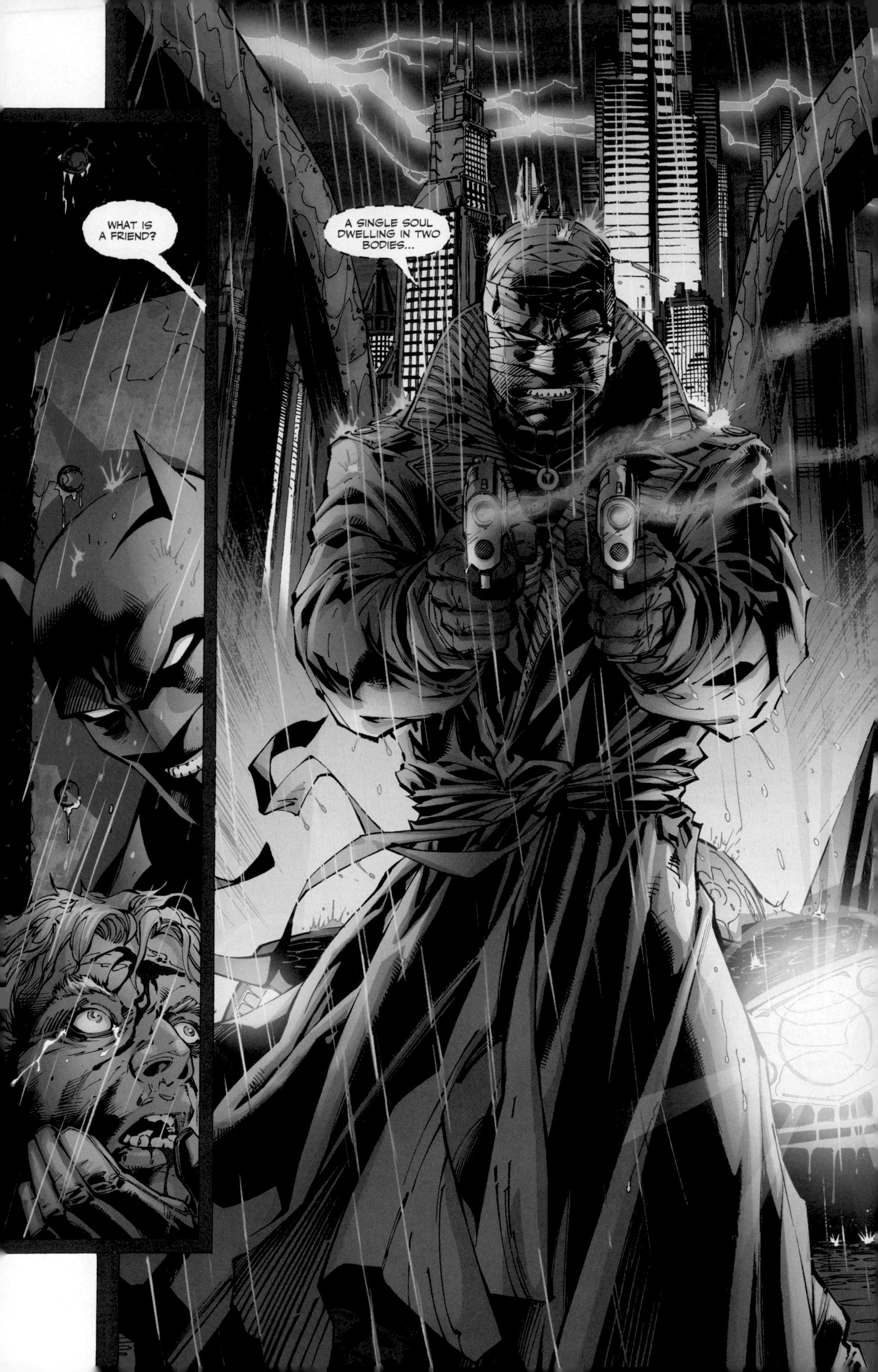
WHAT IS A FRIEND?
A SINGLE SOUL DWELLING IN TWO BODIES...

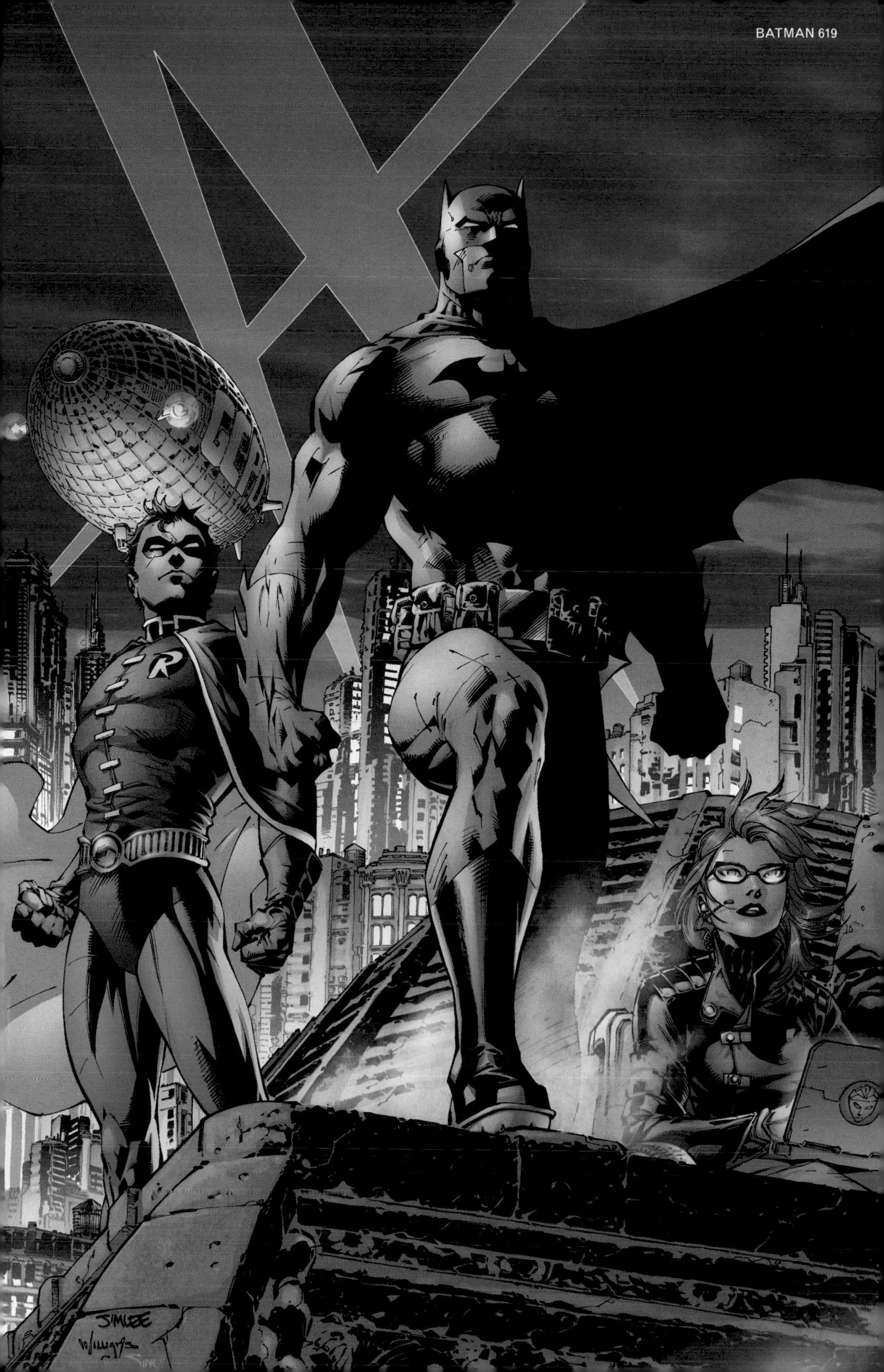

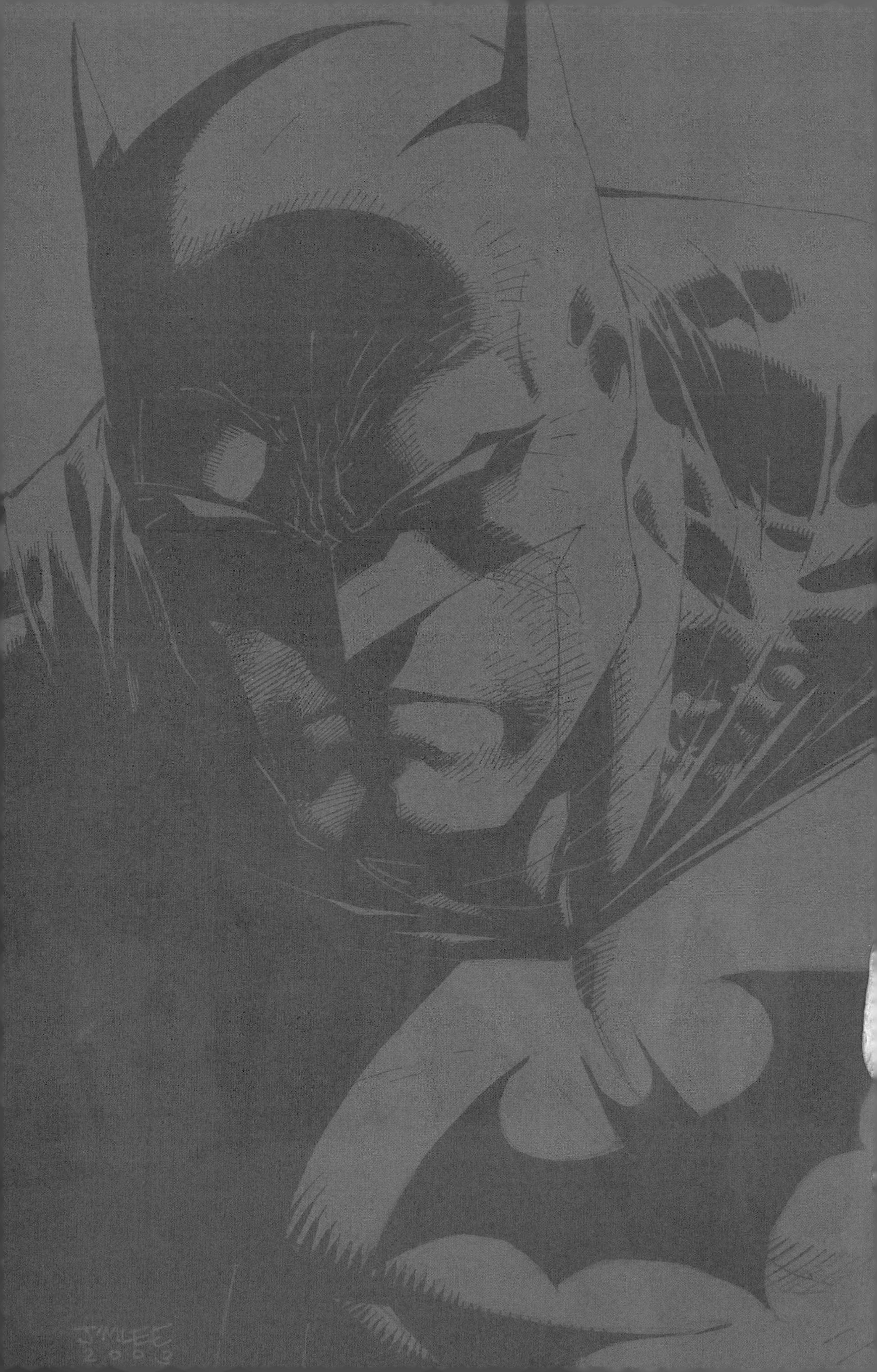

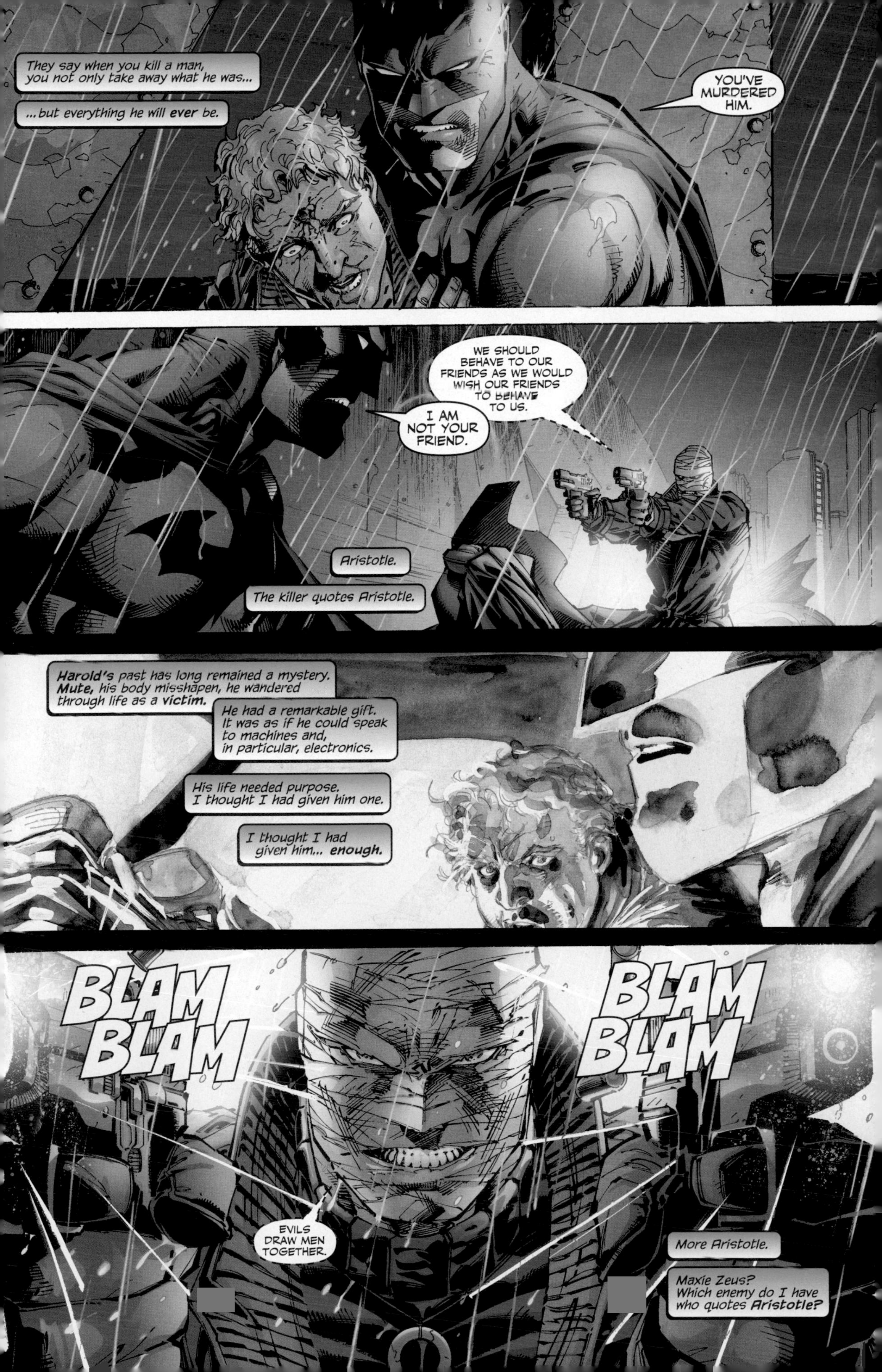

They say when you kill a man, you not only take away what he was...
...but everything he will ever be.
YOU'VE MURDERED HIM.
WE SHOULD BEHAVE TO OUR FRIENDS AS WE WOULD WISH OUR FRIENDS TO BEHAVE TO US.
I AM NOT YOUR FRIEND.
Aristotle.
The killer quotes Aristotle.
Harold's past has long remained a mystery. Mute, his body misshapen, he wandered through life as a victim.
He had a remarkable gift. It was as if he could speak to machines and, in particular, electronics.
His life needed purpose. I thought I had given him one.
I thought I had given him... enough.
BLAM BLAM
BLAM BLAM
EVILS DRAW MEN TOGETHER.
More Aristotle.
Maxie Zeus? Which enemy do I have who quotes Aristotle?

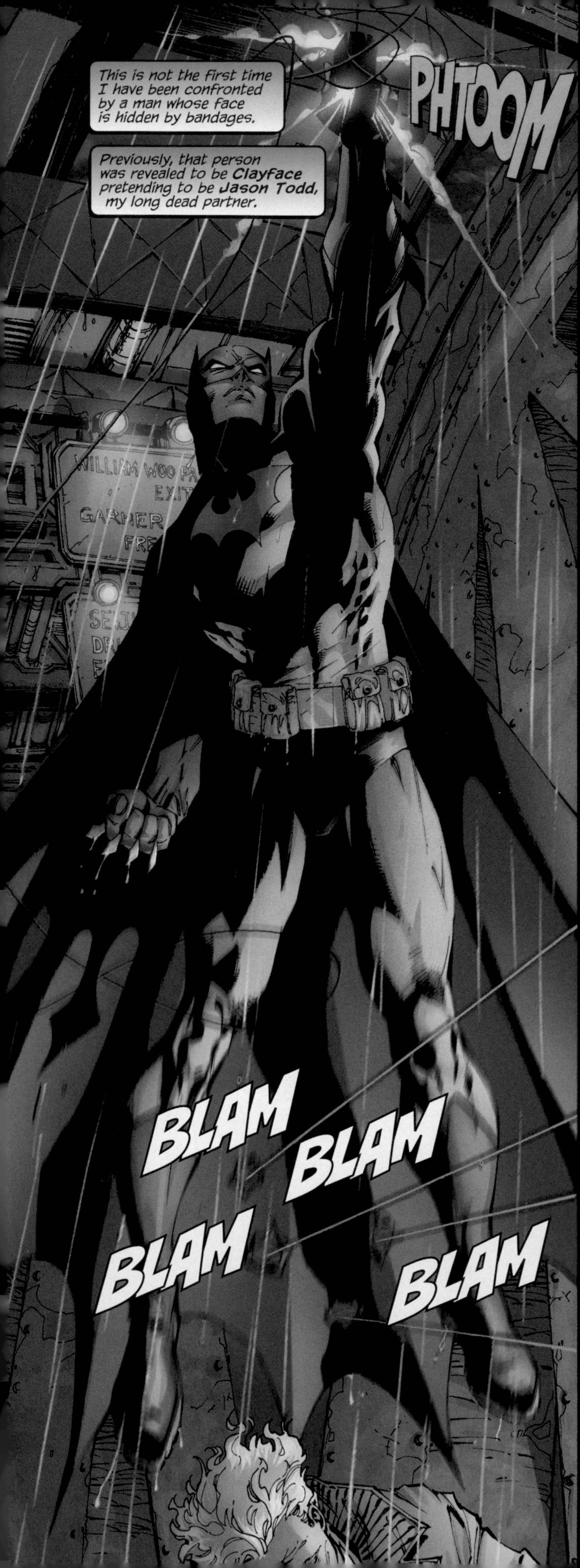

This is not the first time I have been confronted by a man whose face is hidden by bandages.
PHTOOM
Previously, that person was revealed to be **Clayface** pretending to be **Jason Todd**, my long dead partner.
BLAM
BLAM
BLAM
BLAM


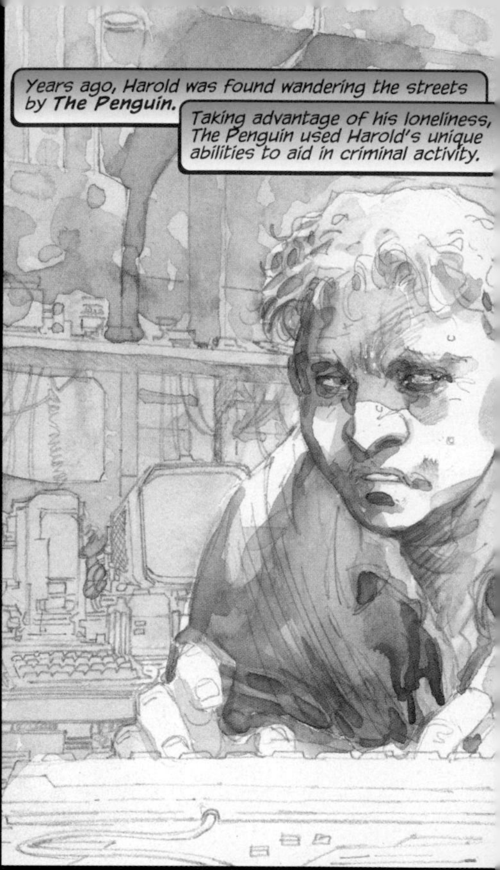

Years ago, Harold was found wandering the streets by **The Penguin.**
Taking advantage of his loneliness, The Penguin used Harold's unique abilities to aid in criminal activity.


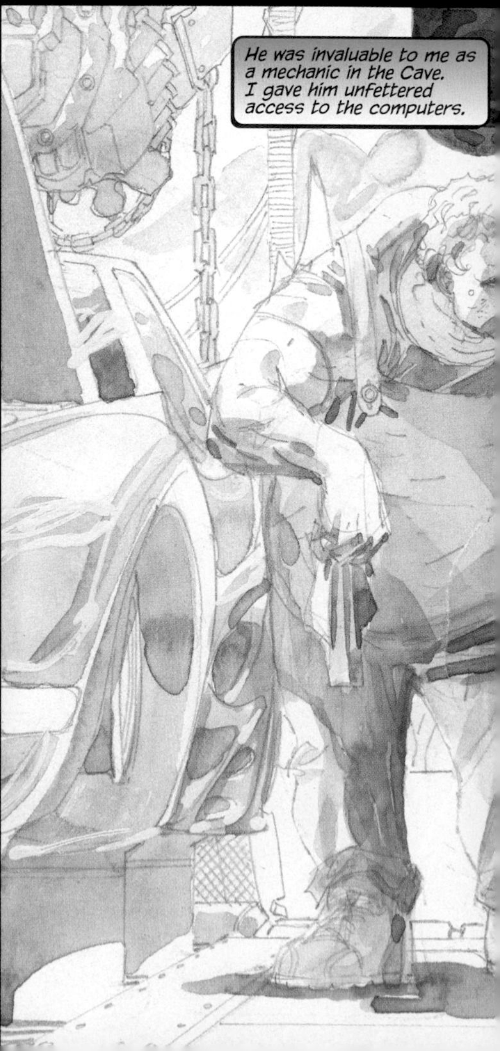

He was invaluable to me as a mechanic in the Cave. I gave him unfettered access to the computers.

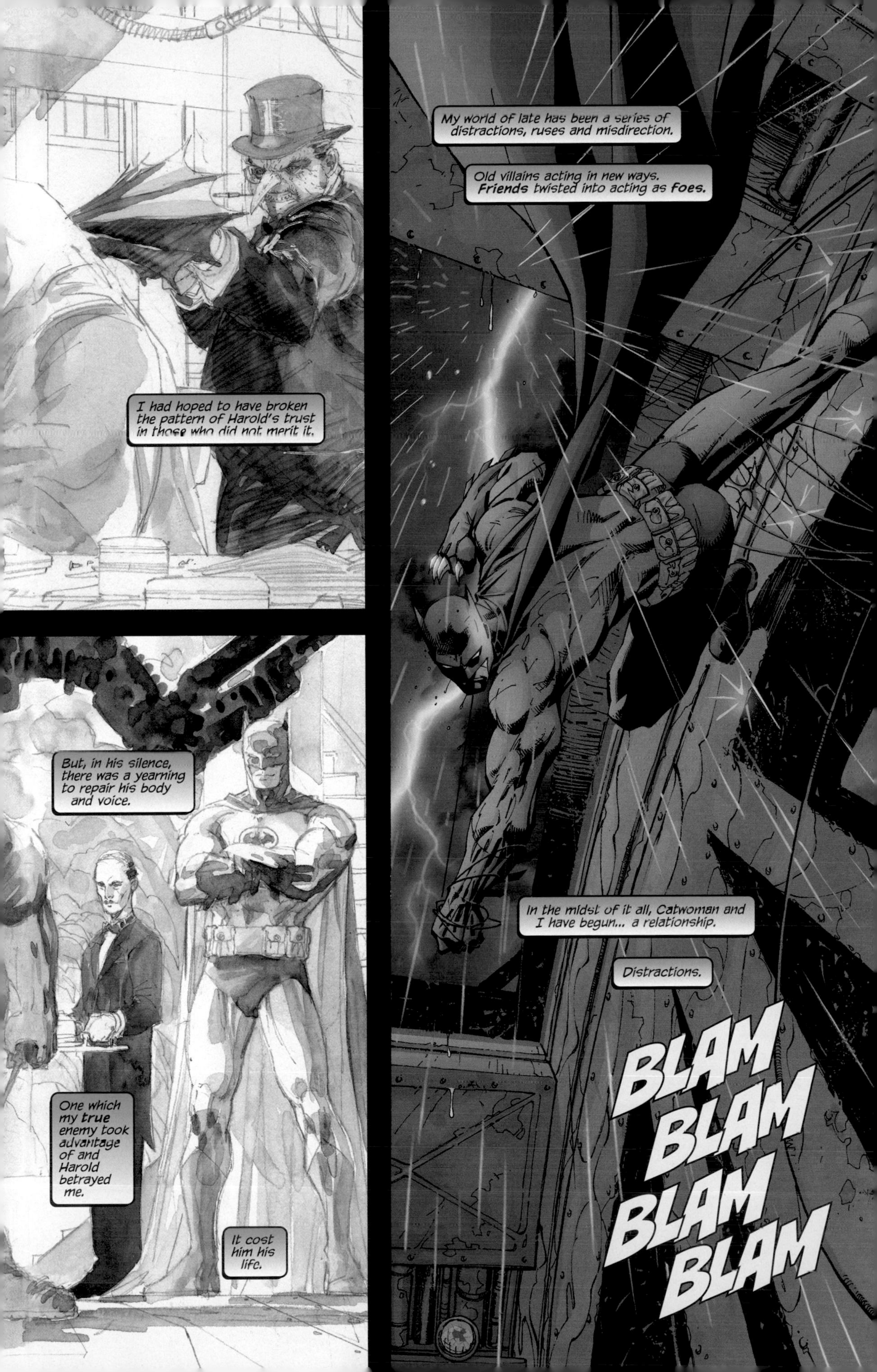
I had hoped to have broken the pattern of Harold's trust in those who did not merit it.
But, in his silence, there was a yearning to repair his body and voice.
One which my true enemy took advantage of and Harold betrayed me.
It cost him his life.
My world of late has been a series of distractions, ruses and misdirection.
Old villains acting in new ways. Friends twisted into acting as foes.
In the midst of it all, Catwoman and I have begun... a relationship.
Distractions.
BLAM
BLAM
BLAM
BLAM

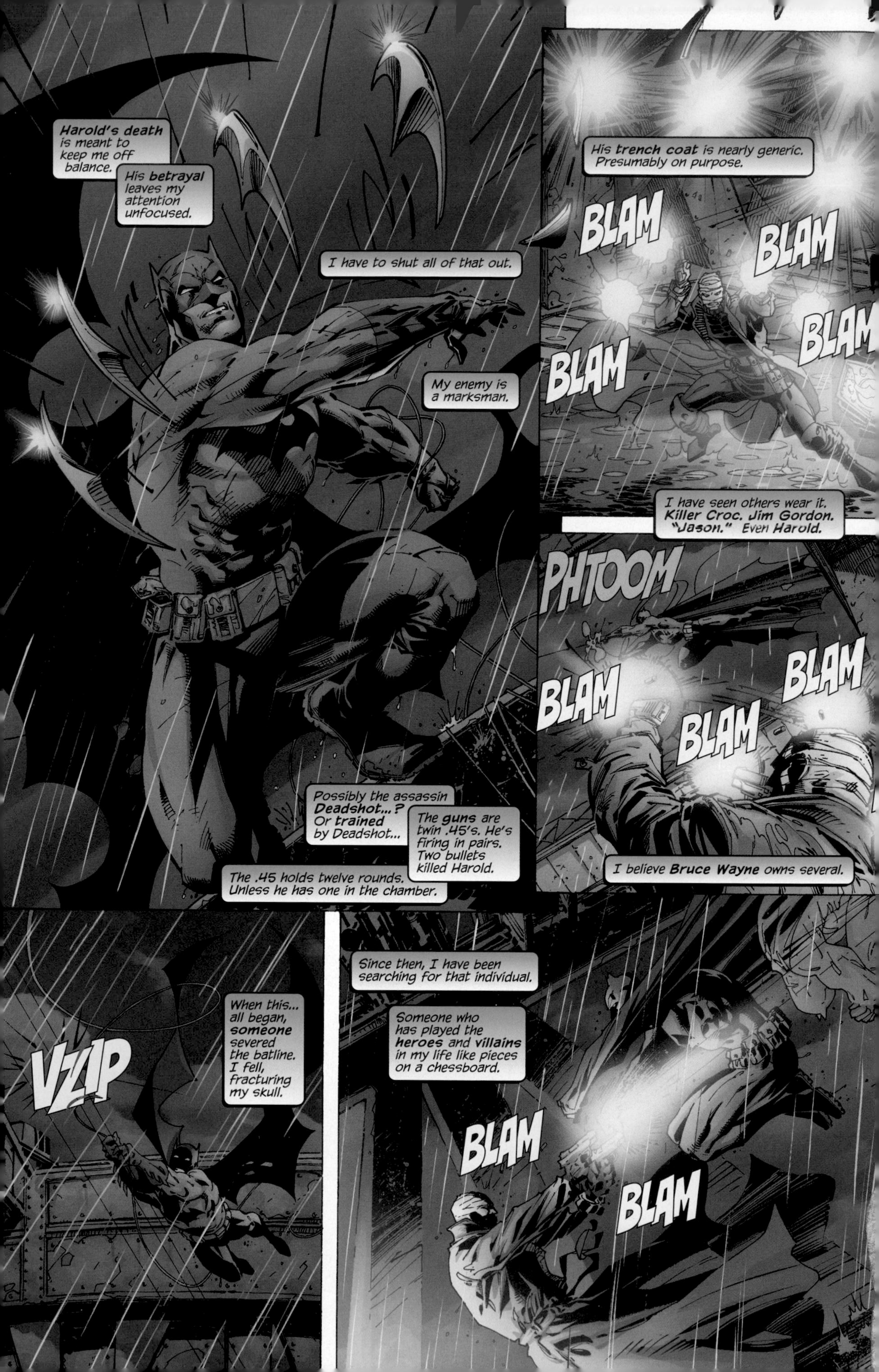

Harold's death is meant to keep me off balance.
His betrayal leaves my attention unfocused.
I have to shut all of that out.
My enemy is a marksman.
Possibly the assassin Deadshot...? Or trained by Deadshot...
The guns are twin .45's. He's firing in pairs. Two bullets killed Harold.
The .45 holds twelve rounds. Unless he has one in the chamber.
His trench coat is nearly generic. Presumably on purpose.
BLAM
BLAM
BLAM
BLAM
I have seen others wear it. Killer Croc. Jim Gordon. "Jason." Even Harold.
PHTOOM
BLAM
BLAM
BLAM
I believe Bruce Wayne owns several.
VZIP
When this... all began, someone severed the batline. I fell, fracturing my skull.
Since then, I have been searching for that individual.
Someone who has played the heroes and villains in my life like pieces on a chessboard.
BLAM
BLAM

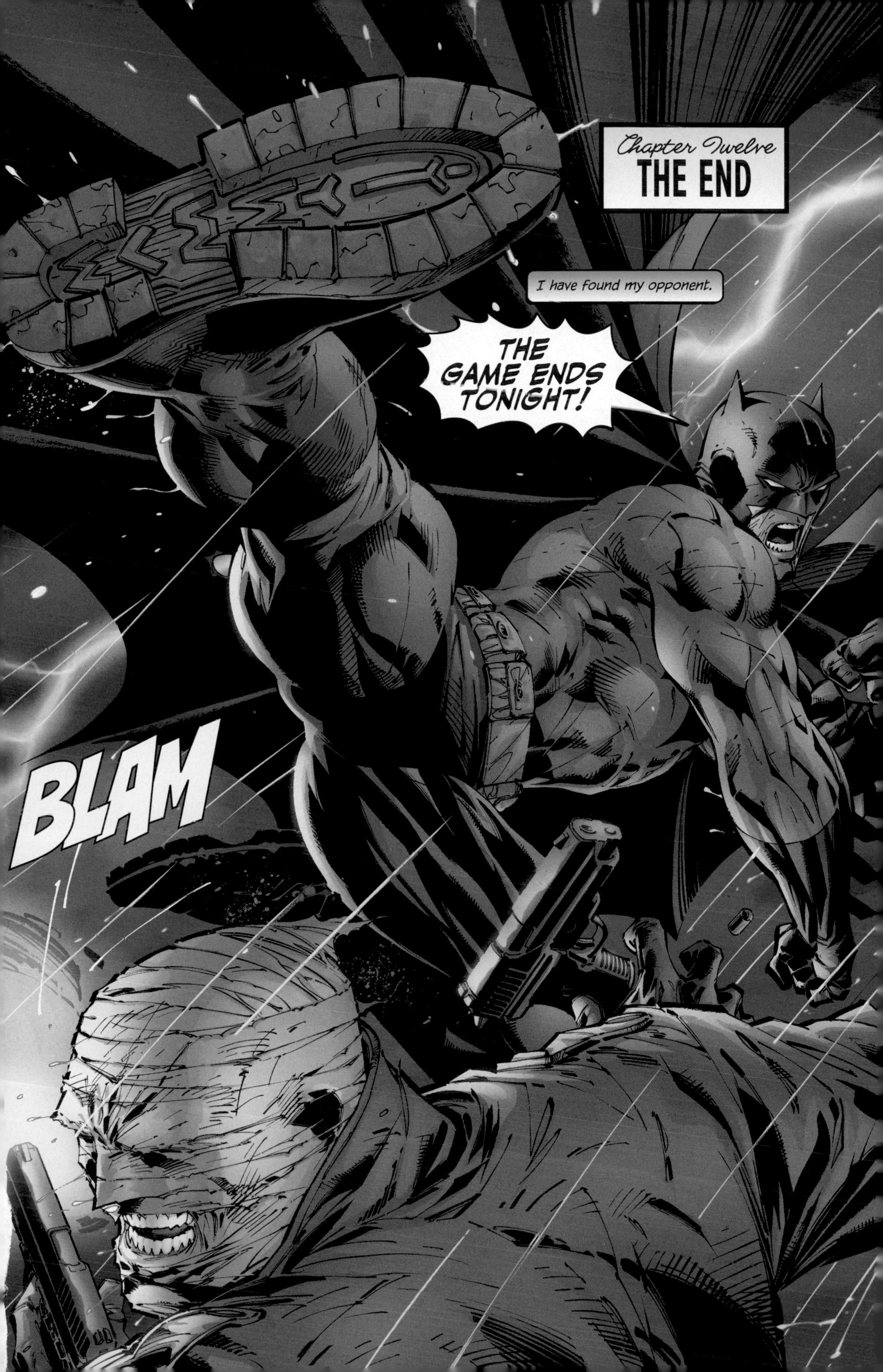
Chapter Twelve
THE END
I have found my opponent.
THE GAME ENDS TONIGHT!
BLAM

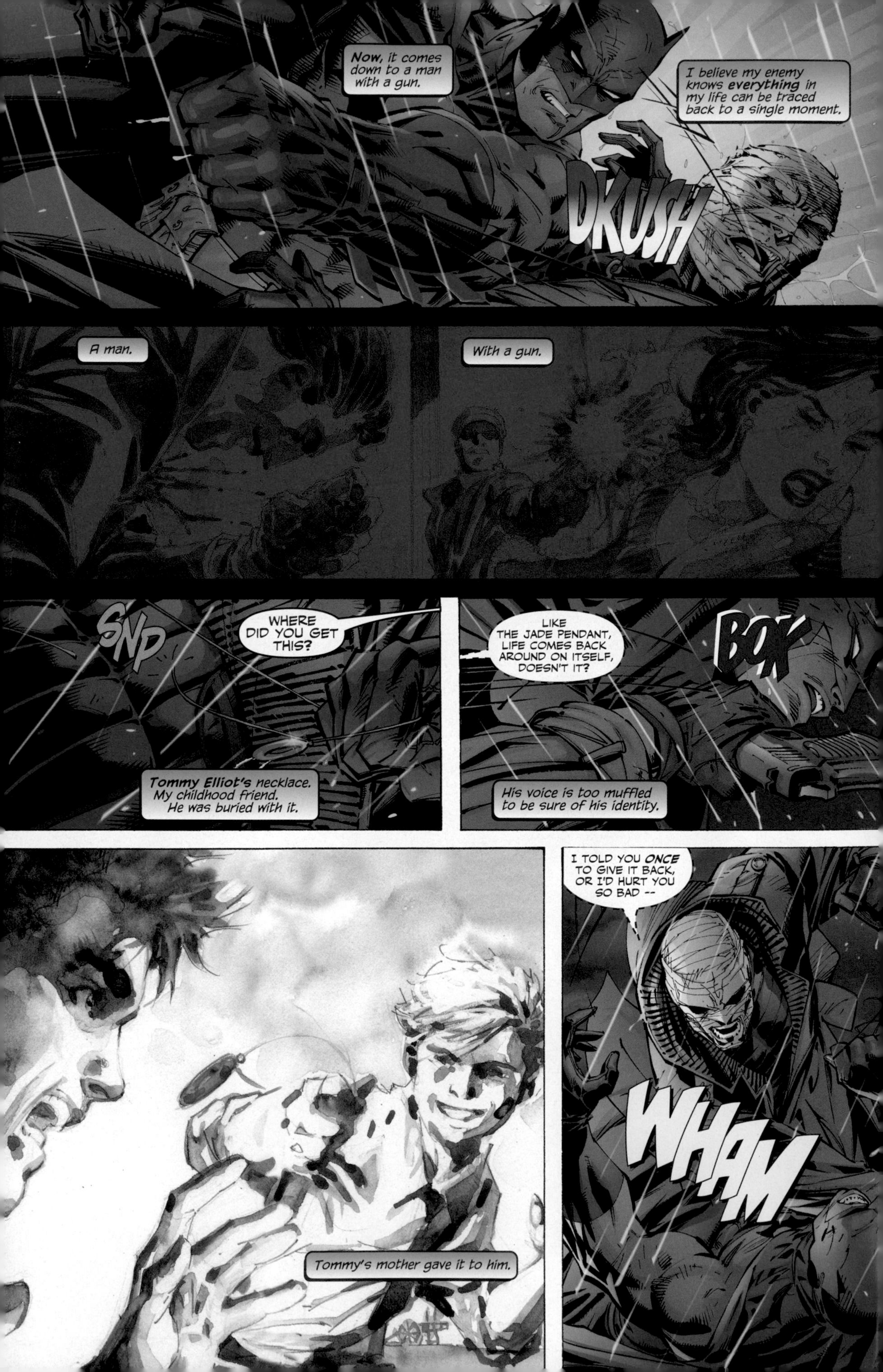
Now, it comes down to a man with a gun.
I believe my enemy knows everything in my life can be traced back to a single moment.
DKUSH
A man.
With a gun.
SNP
WHERE DID YOU GET THIS?
Tommy Elliot's necklace. My childhood friend. He was buried with it.
LIKE THE JADE PENDANT, LIFE COMES BACK AROUND ON ITSELF, DOESN'T IT?
BOK
His voice is too muffled to be sure of his identity.
Tommy's mother gave it to him.
I TOLD YOU ONCE TO GIVE IT BACK, OR I'D HURT YOU SO BAD --
WHAM

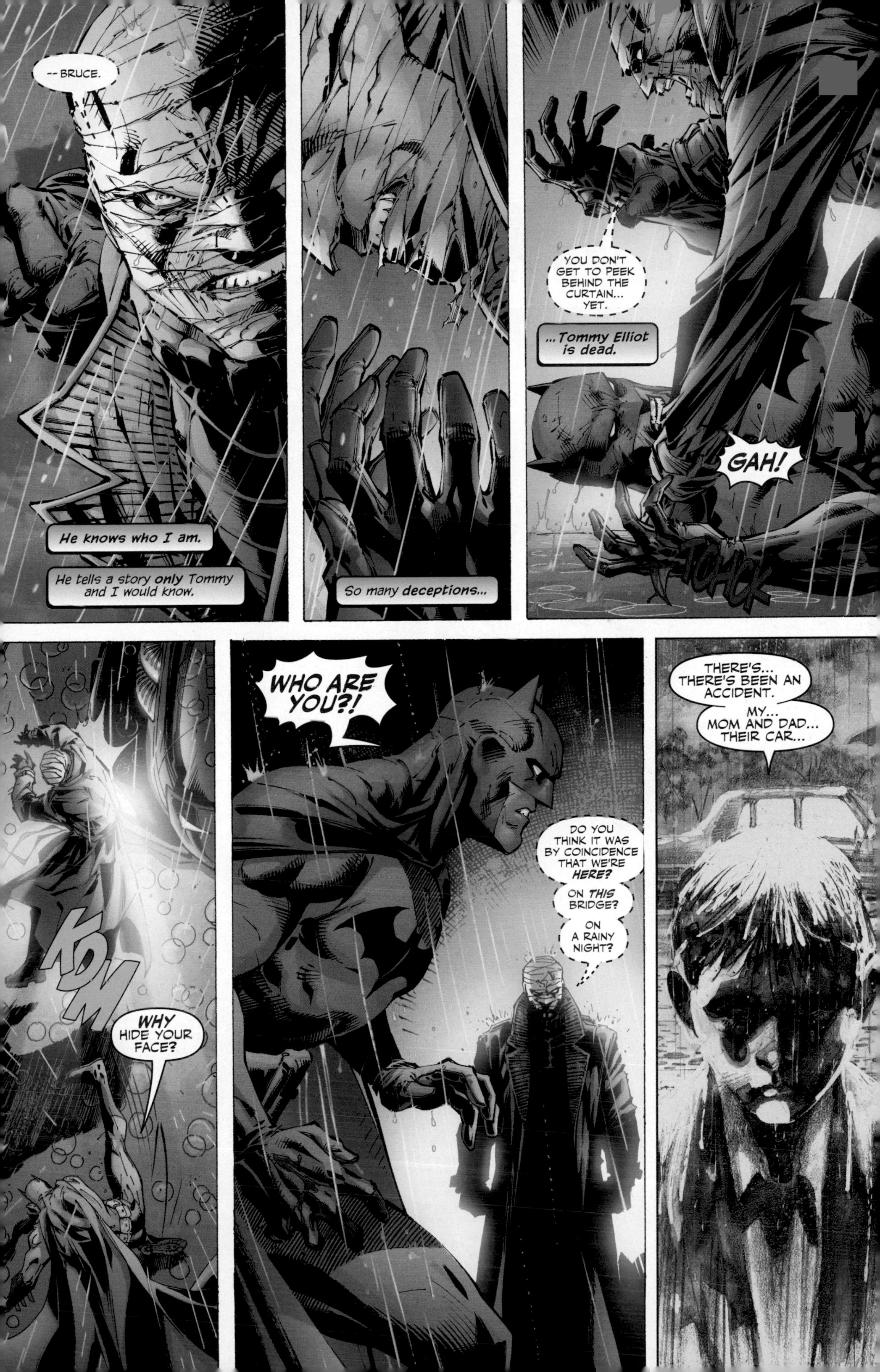
-- BRUCE.
He knows who I am.
He tells a story only Tommy and I would know.
So many deceptions...
YOU DON'T GET TO PEEK BEHIND THE CURTAIN... YET.
...Tommy Elliot is dead.
GAH!
TCHCK
KOM
WHY HIDE YOUR FACE?
WHO ARE YOU?!
DO YOU THINK IT WAS BY COINCIDENCE THAT WE'RE HERE?
ON THIS BRIDGE?
ON A RAINY NIGHT?
THERE'S... THERE'S BEEN AN ACCIDENT.
MY... MOM AND DAD... THEIR CAR...

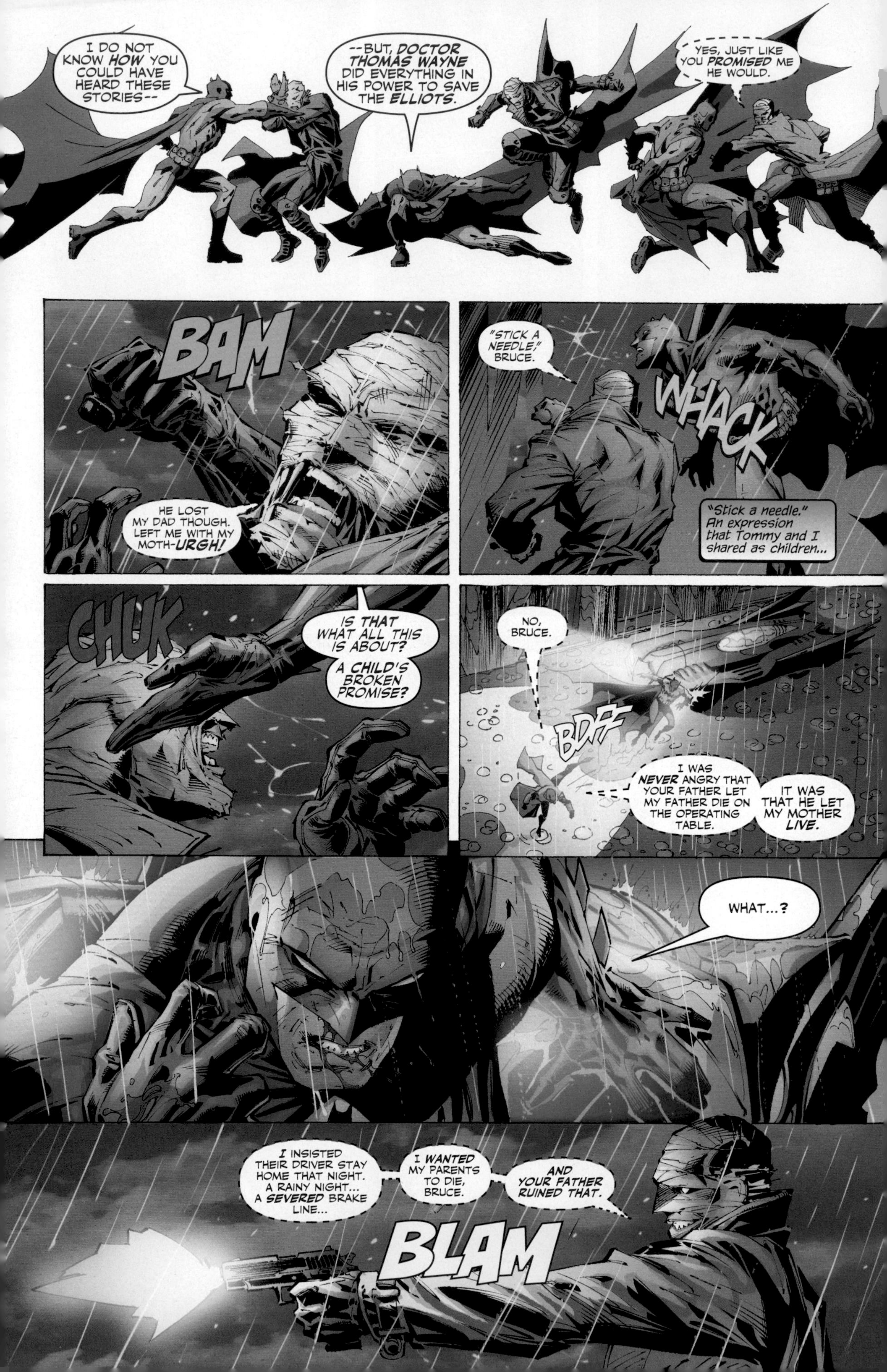
I DO NOT KNOW HOW YOU COULD HAVE HEARD THESE STORIES--
--BUT, DOCTOR THOMAS WAYNE DID EVERYTHING IN HIS POWER TO SAVE THE ELLIOTS.
YES, JUST LIKE YOU PROMISED ME HE WOULD.
BAM
HE LOST MY DAD THOUGH. LEFT ME WITH MY MOTH-URGH!
"STICK A NEEDLE," BRUCE.
WHACK
"Stick a needle." An expression that Tommy and I shared as children...
CHUK
IS THAT WHAT ALL THIS IS ABOUT?
A CHILD'S BROKEN PROMISE?
NO, BRUCE.
BDFF
I WAS NEVER ANGRY THAT YOUR FATHER LET MY FATHER DIE ON THE OPERATING TABLE.
IT WAS THAT HE LET MY MOTHER LIVE.
WHAT...?
I INSISTED THEIR DRIVER STAY HOME THAT NIGHT. A RAINY NIGHT... A SEVERED BRAKE LINE...
I WANTED MY PARENTS TO DIE, BRUCE.
AND YOUR FATHER RUINED THAT.
BLAM

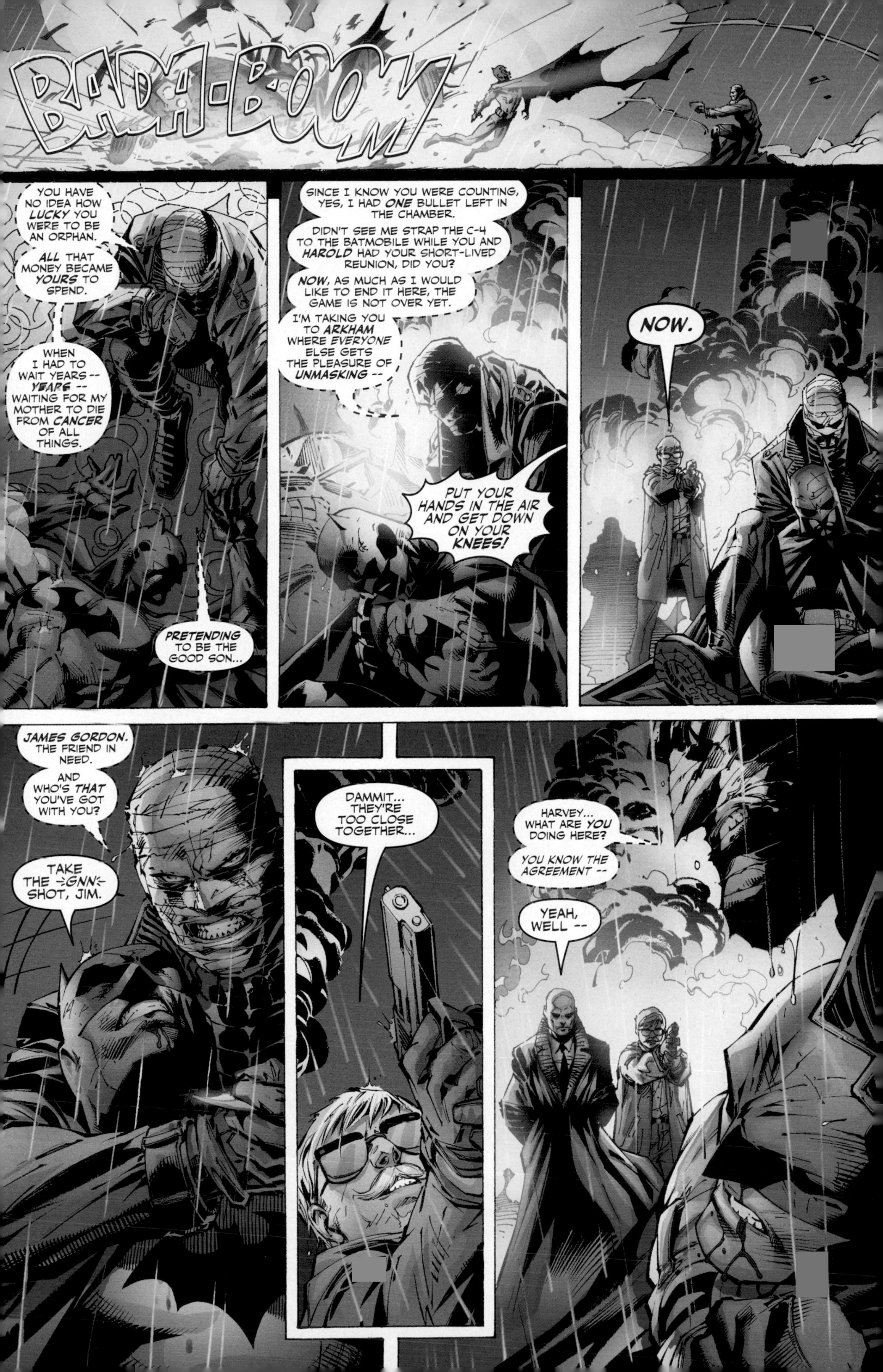
BADA-BOOM
YOU HAVE NO IDEA HOW LUCKY YOU WERE TO BE AN ORPHAN.
ALL THAT MONEY BECAME YOURS TO SPEND.
WHEN I HAD TO WAIT YEARS -- YEARS -- WAITING FOR MY MOTHER TO DIE FROM CANCER OF ALL THINGS.
PRETENDING TO BE THE GOOD SON...
SINCE I KNOW YOU WERE COUNTING, YES, I HAD ONE BULLET LEFT IN THE CHAMBER.
DIDN'T SEE ME STRAP THE C-4 TO THE BATMOBILE WHILE YOU AND HAROLD HAD YOUR SHORT-LIVED REUNION, DID YOU?
NOW, AS MUCH AS I WOULD LIKE TO END IT HERE, THE GAME IS NOT OVER YET.
I'M TAKING YOU TO ARKHAM WHERE EVERYONE ELSE GETS THE PLEASURE OF UNMASKING --
PUT YOUR HANDS IN THE AIR AND GET DOWN ON YOUR KNEES!
NOW.
JAMES GORDON. THE FRIEND IN NEED.
AND WHO'S THAT YOU'VE GOT WITH YOU?
TAKE THE -GNN- SHOT, JIM.
DAMMIT... THEY'RE TOO CLOSE TOGETHER...
HARVEY... WHAT ARE YOU DOING HERE?
YOU KNOW THE AGREEMENT --
YEAH, WELL --

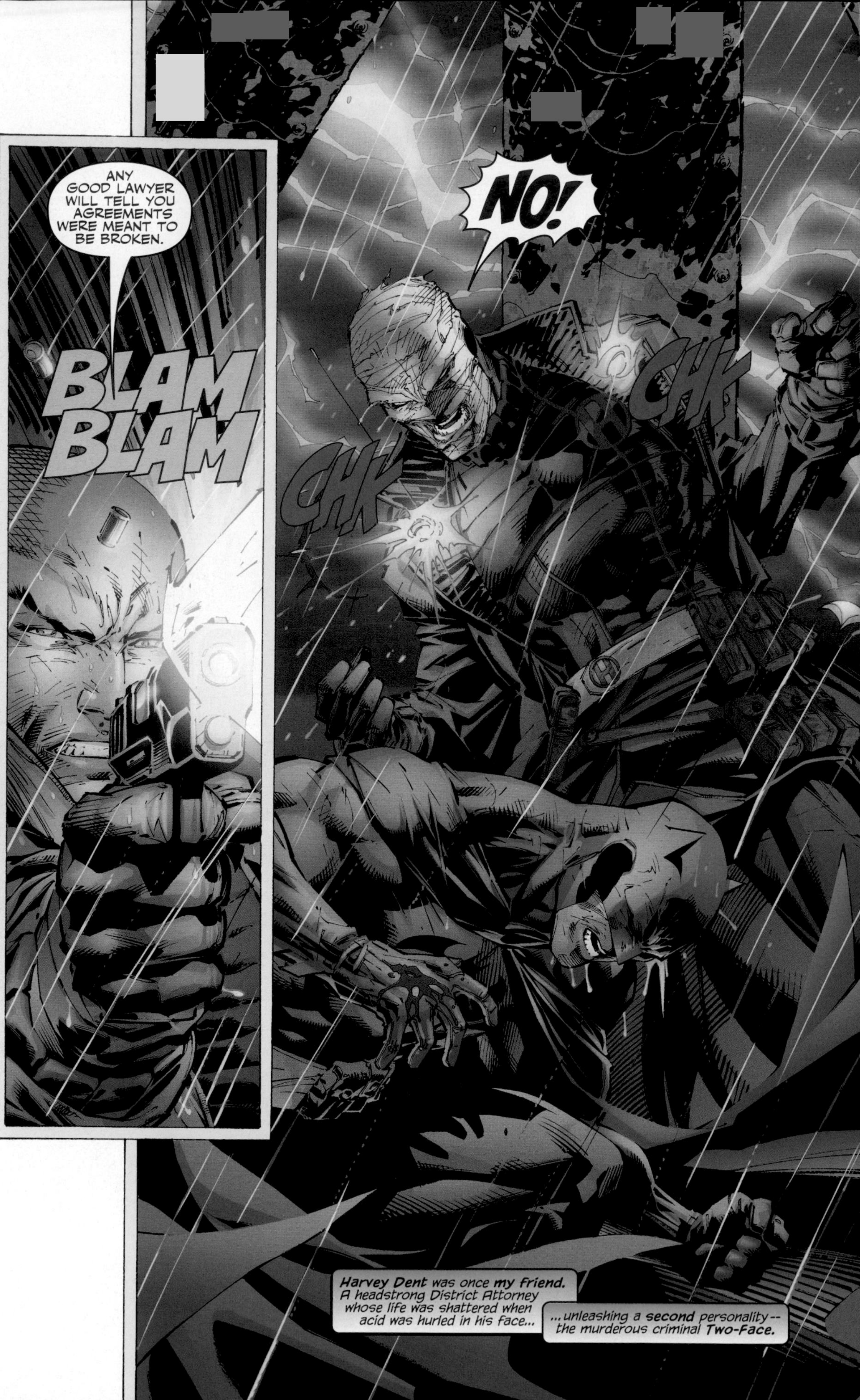
ANY GOOD LAWYER WILL TELL YOU AGREEMENTS WERE MEANT TO BE BROKEN.
BLAM
BLAM
NO!
CHK
CHK
Harvey Dent was once my friend. A headstrong District Attorney whose life was shattered when acid was hurled in his face...
...unleashing a second personality-- the murderous criminal Two-Face.

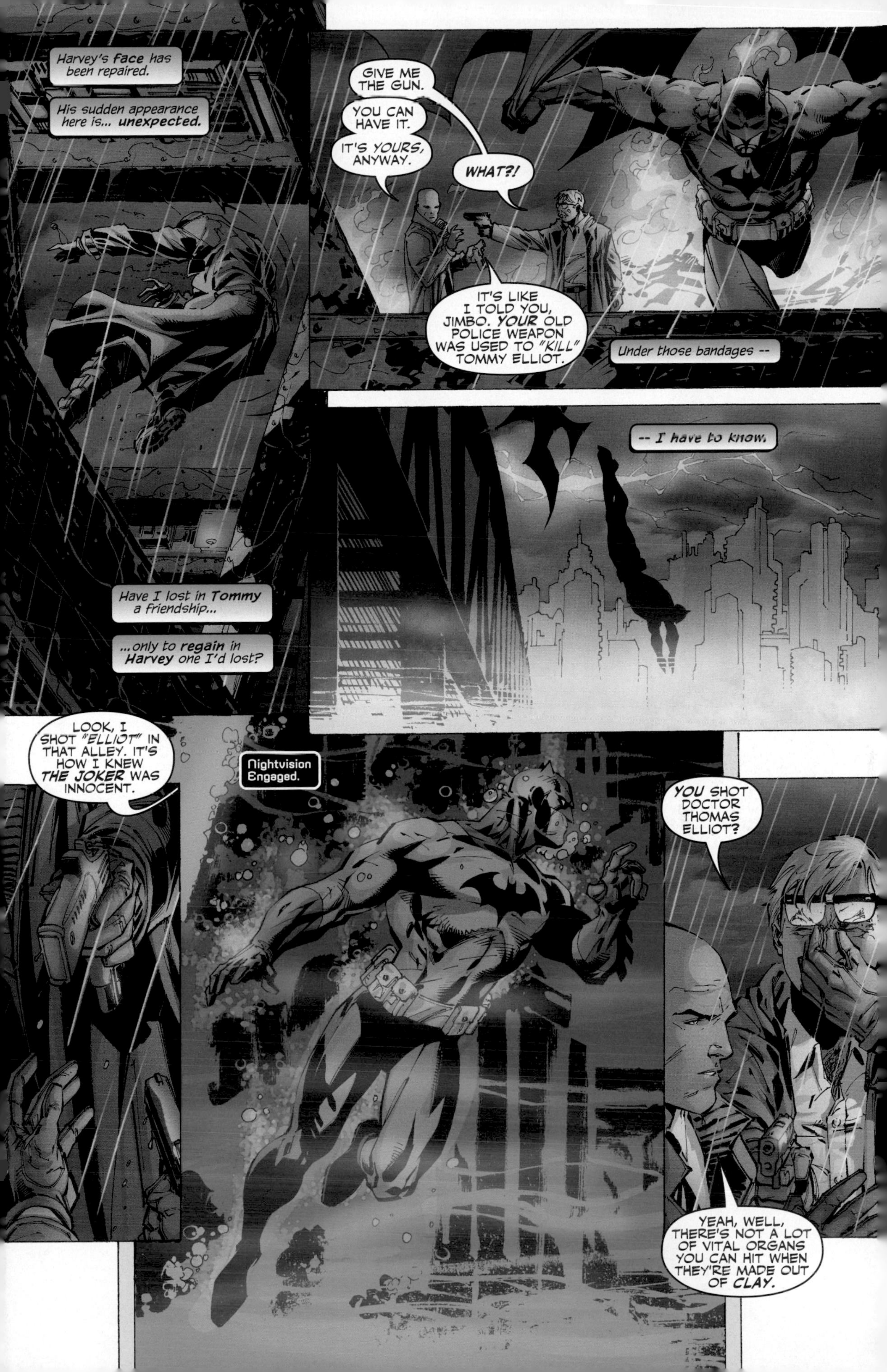
Harvey's face has been repaired.
His sudden appearance here is... unexpected.
GIVE ME THE GUN.
YOU CAN HAVE IT.
IT'S YOURS, ANYWAY.
WHAT?!
IT'S LIKE I TOLD YOU, JIMBO. YOUR OLD POLICE WEAPON WAS USED TO "KILL" TOMMY ELLIOT.
Under those bandages --
-- I have to know.
Have I lost in Tommy a friendship...
...only to regain in Harvey one I'd lost?
LOOK, I SHOT "ELLIOT" IN THAT ALLEY. IT'S HOW I KNEW THE JOKER WAS INNOCENT.
Nightvision Engaged.
YOU SHOT DOCTOR THOMAS ELLIOT?
YEAH, WELL, THERE'S NOT A LOT OF VITAL ORGANS YOU CAN HIT WHEN THEY'RE MADE OUT OF CLAY.

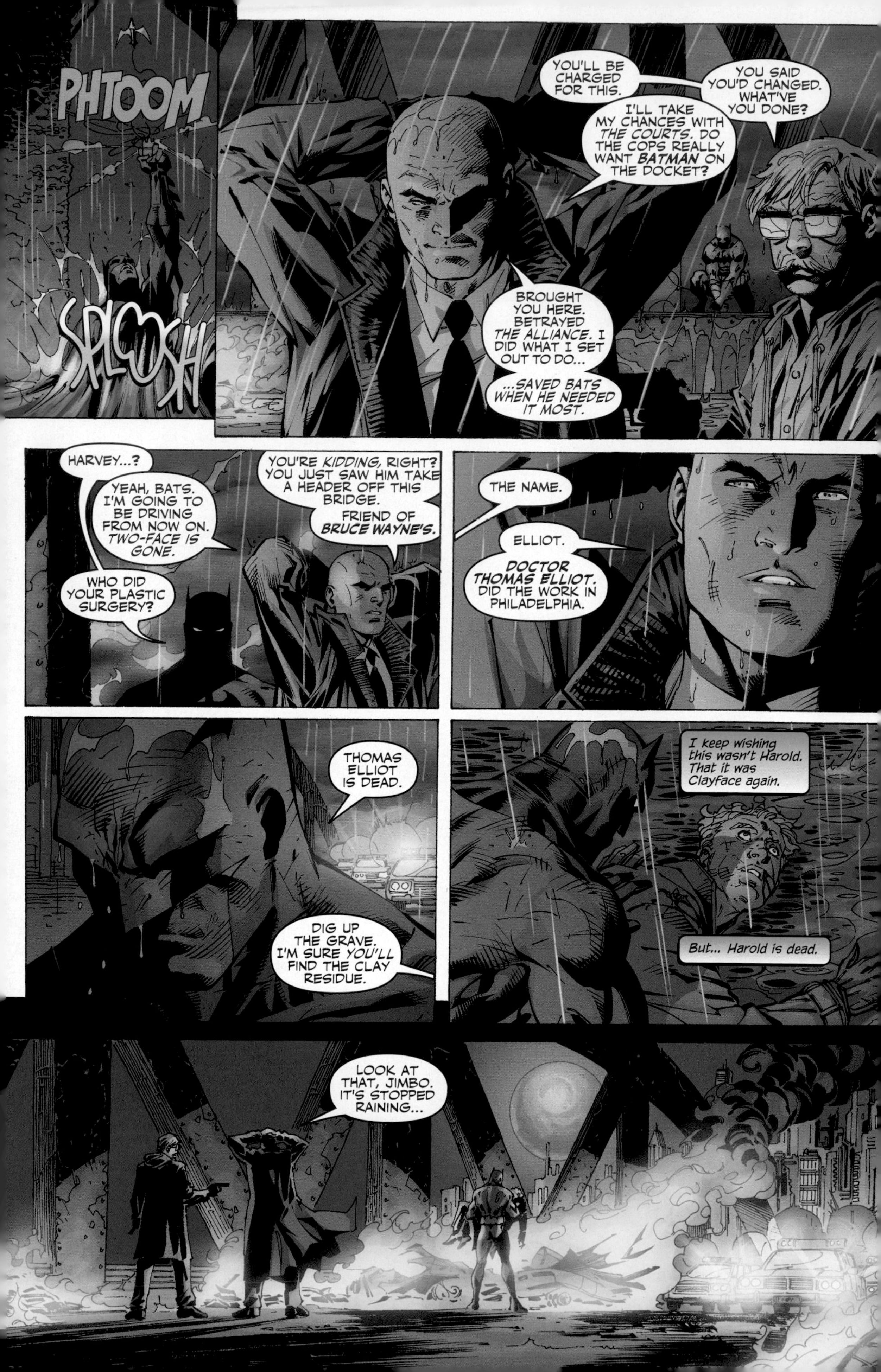
PHTOOM
SPLOOSH
YOU'LL BE CHARGED FOR THIS.
YOU SAID YOU'D CHANGED. WHAT'VE YOU DONE?
I'LL TAKE MY CHANCES WITH THE COURTS. DO THE COPS REALLY WANT BATMAN ON THE DOCKET?
BROUGHT YOU HERE. BETRAYED THE ALLIANCE. I DID WHAT I SET OUT TO DO...
...SAVED BATS WHEN HE NEEDED IT MOST.
HARVEY...?
YEAH, BATS. I'M GOING TO BE DRIVING FROM NOW ON. TWO-FACE IS GONE.
WHO DID YOUR PLASTIC SURGERY?
YOU'RE KIDDING, RIGHT? YOU JUST SAW HIM TAKE A HEADER OFF THIS BRIDGE.
FRIEND OF BRUCE WAYNE'S.
THE NAME.
ELLIOT.
DOCTOR THOMAS ELLIOT. DID THE WORK IN PHILADELPHIA.
THOMAS ELLIOT IS DEAD.
DIG UP THE GRAVE. I'M SURE YOU'LL FIND THE CLAY RESIDUE.
I keep wishing this wasn't Harold. That it was Clayface again.
But... Harold is dead.
LOOK AT THAT, JIMBO. IT'S STOPPED RAINING...

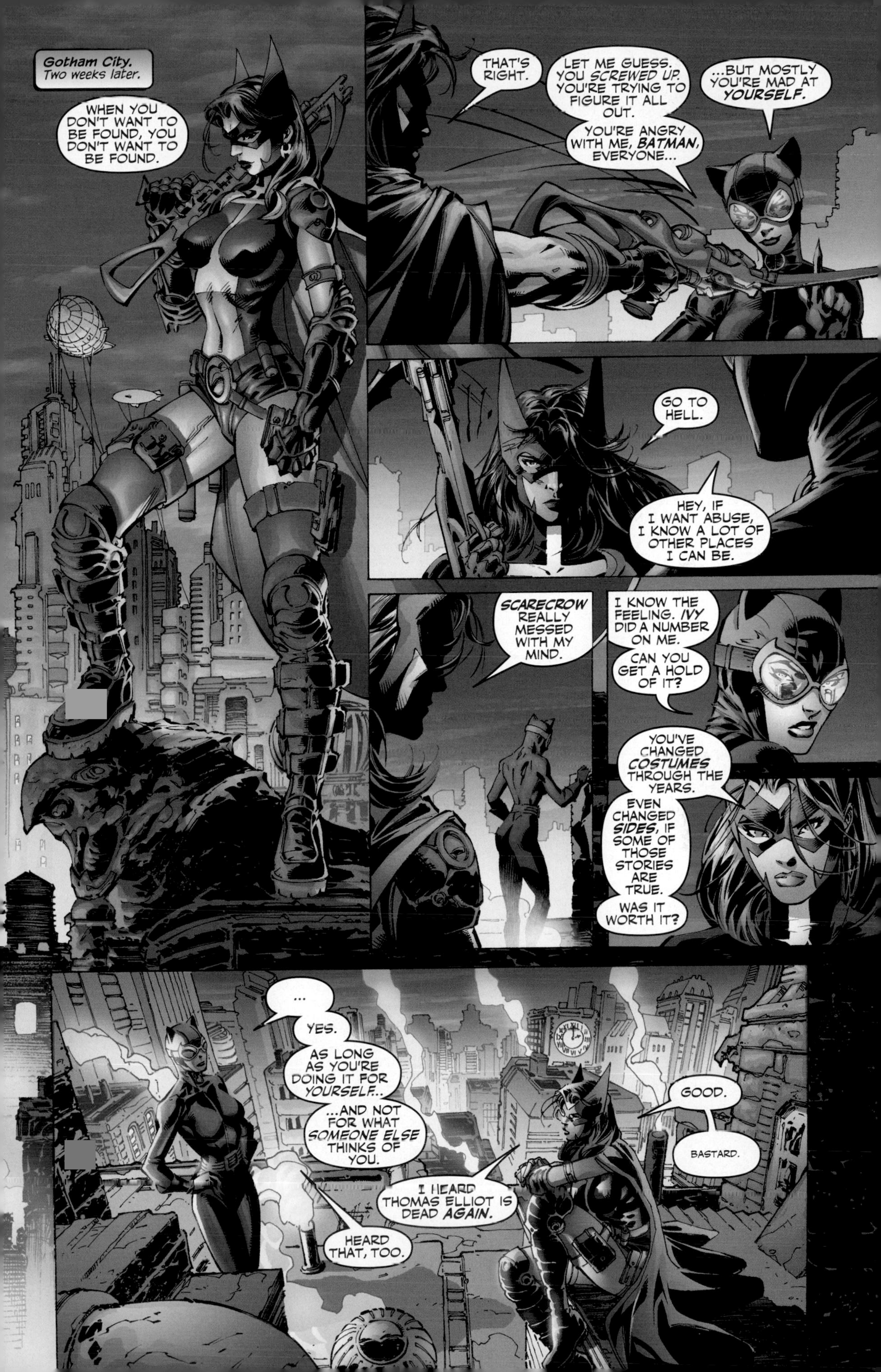

Gotham City. Two weeks later.
WHEN YOU DON'T WANT TO BE FOUND, YOU DON'T WANT TO BE FOUND.
THAT'S RIGHT.
LET ME GUESS. YOU SCREWED UP. YOU'RE TRYING TO FIGURE IT ALL OUT.
YOU'RE ANGRY WITH ME, BATMAN, EVERYONE...
...BUT MOSTLY YOU'RE MAD AT YOURSELF.
GO TO HELL.
HEY, IF I WANT ABUSE, I KNOW A LOT OF OTHER PLACES I CAN BE.
SCARECROW REALLY MESSED WITH MY MIND.
I KNOW THE FEELING. IVY DID A NUMBER ON ME.
CAN YOU GET A HOLD OF IT?
YOU'VE CHANGED COSTUMES THROUGH THE YEARS.
EVEN CHANGED SIDES, IF SOME OF THOSE STORIES ARE TRUE.
WAS IT WORTH IT?
...
YES.
AS LONG AS YOU'RE DOING IT FOR YOURSELF...
...AND NOT FOR WHAT SOMEONE ELSE THINKS OF YOU.
I HEARD THOMAS ELLIOT IS DEAD AGAIN.
HEARD THAT, TOO.
GOOD.
BASTARD.

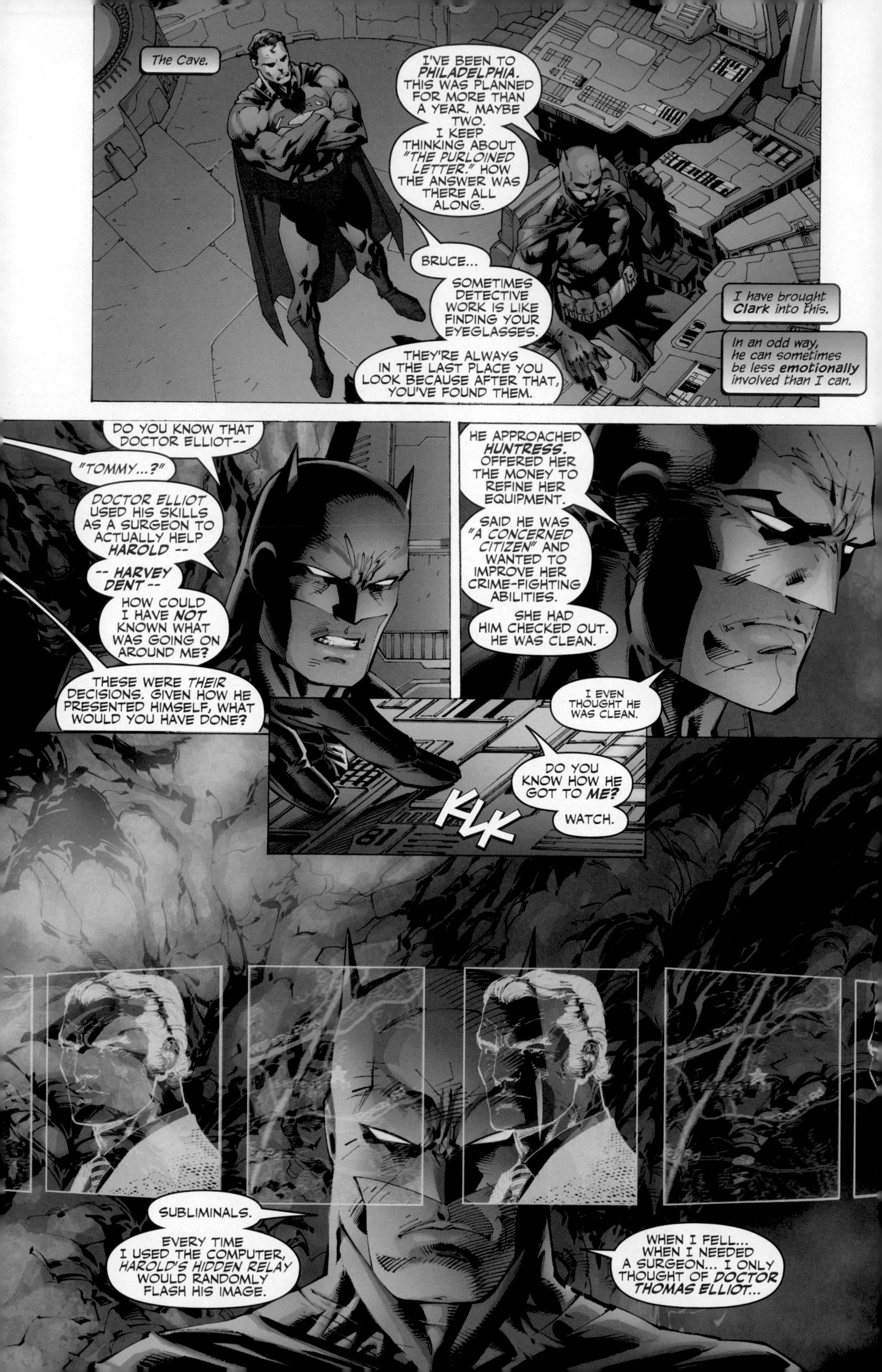

The Cave.
I'VE BEEN TO PHILADELPHIA. THIS WAS PLANNED FOR MORE THAN A YEAR. MAYBE TWO.
I KEEP THINKING ABOUT "THE PURLOINED LETTER." HOW THE ANSWER WAS THERE ALL ALONG.
BRUCE...
SOMETIMES DETECTIVE WORK IS LIKE FINDING YOUR EYEGLASSES.
THEY'RE ALWAYS IN THE LAST PLACE YOU LOOK BECAUSE AFTER THAT, YOU'VE FOUND THEM.
I have brought Clark into this.
In an odd way, he can sometimes be less emotionally involved than I can.
DO YOU KNOW THAT DOCTOR ELLIOT--
"TOMMY...?"
DOCTOR ELLIOT USED HIS SKILLS AS A SURGEON TO ACTUALLY HELP HAROLD --
-- HARVEY DENT --
HOW COULD I HAVE NOT KNOWN WHAT WAS GOING ON AROUND ME?
THESE WERE THEIR DECISIONS. GIVEN HOW HE PRESENTED HIMSELF, WHAT WOULD YOU HAVE DONE?
HE APPROACHED HUNTRESS. OFFERED HER THE MONEY TO REFINE HER EQUIPMENT.
SAID HE WAS "A CONCERNED CITIZEN" AND WANTED TO IMPROVE HER CRIME-FIGHTING ABILITIES.
SHE HAD HIM CHECKED OUT. HE WAS CLEAN.
I EVEN THOUGHT HE WAS CLEAN.
DO YOU KNOW HOW HE GOT TO ME?
WATCH.
KLIK
SUBLIMINALS.
EVERY TIME I USED THE COMPUTER, HAROLD'S HIDDEN RELAY WOULD RANDOMLY FLASH HIS IMAGE.
WHEN I FELL... WHEN I NEEDED A SURGEON... I ONLY THOUGHT OF DOCTOR THOMAS ELLIOT...

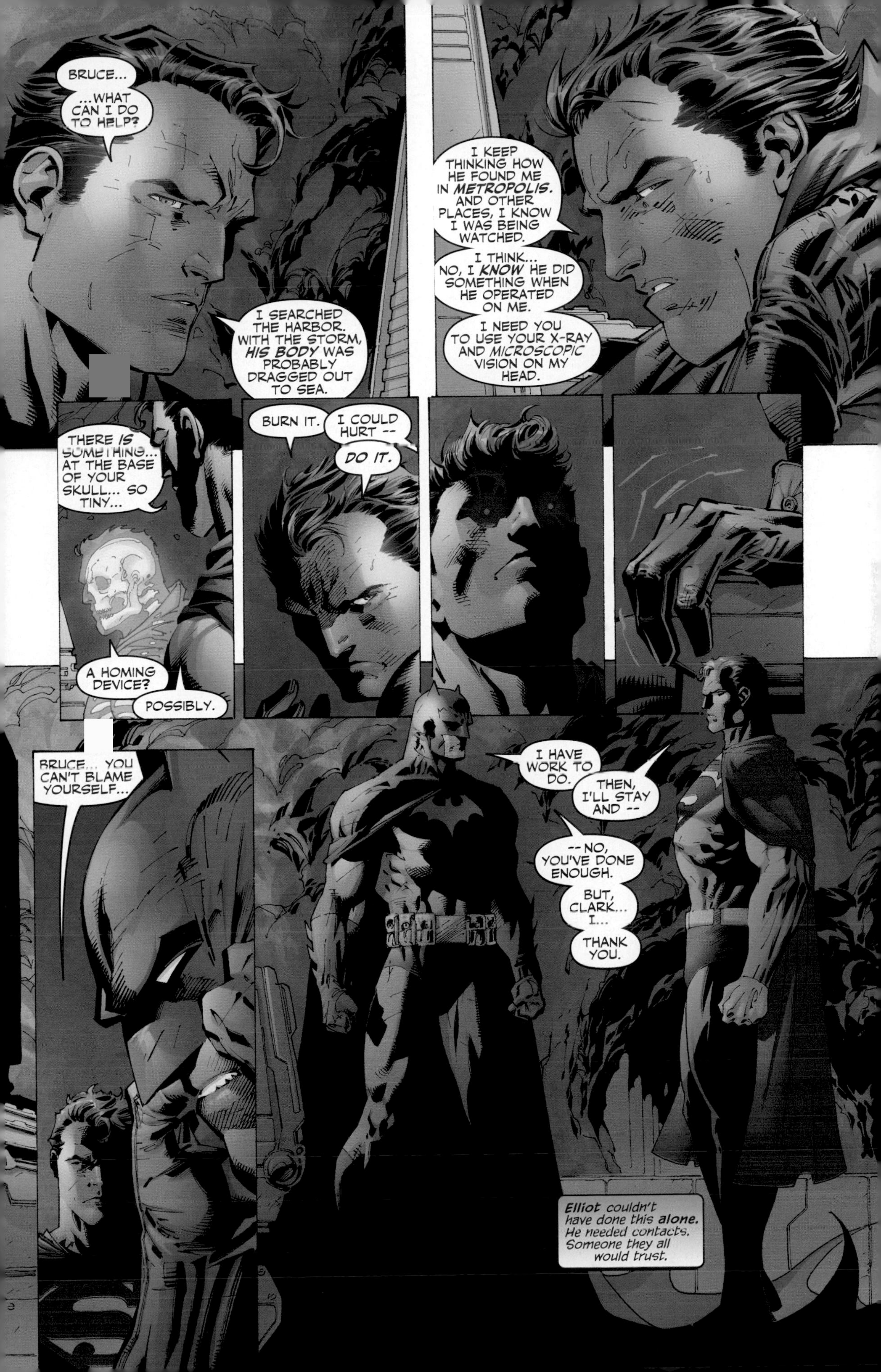
BRUCE... ...WHAT CAN I DO TO HELP?
I KEEP THINKING HOW HE FOUND ME IN *METROPOLIS*. AND OTHER PLACES, I KNOW I WAS BEING WATCHED.
I THINK... NO, I *KNOW* HE DID SOMETHING WHEN HE OPERATED ON ME.
I NEED YOU TO USE YOUR X-RAY AND *MICROSCOPIC* VISION ON MY HEAD.
I SEARCHED THE HARBOR. WITH THE STORM, *HIS BODY* WAS PROBABLY DRAGGED OUT TO SEA.
THERE *IS* SOMETHING... AT THE BASE OF YOUR SKULL... SO TINY...
A HOMING DEVICE?
POSSIBLY.
BURN IT.
I COULD HURT --
*DO IT.*
BRUCE... YOU CAN'T BLAME YOURSELF...
I HAVE WORK TO DO.
THEN, I'LL STAY AND --
-- NO, YOU'VE DONE ENOUGH.
BUT, CLARK... I...
THANK YOU.
*Elliot* couldn't have done this *alone*. He needed contacts. Someone they all would trust.

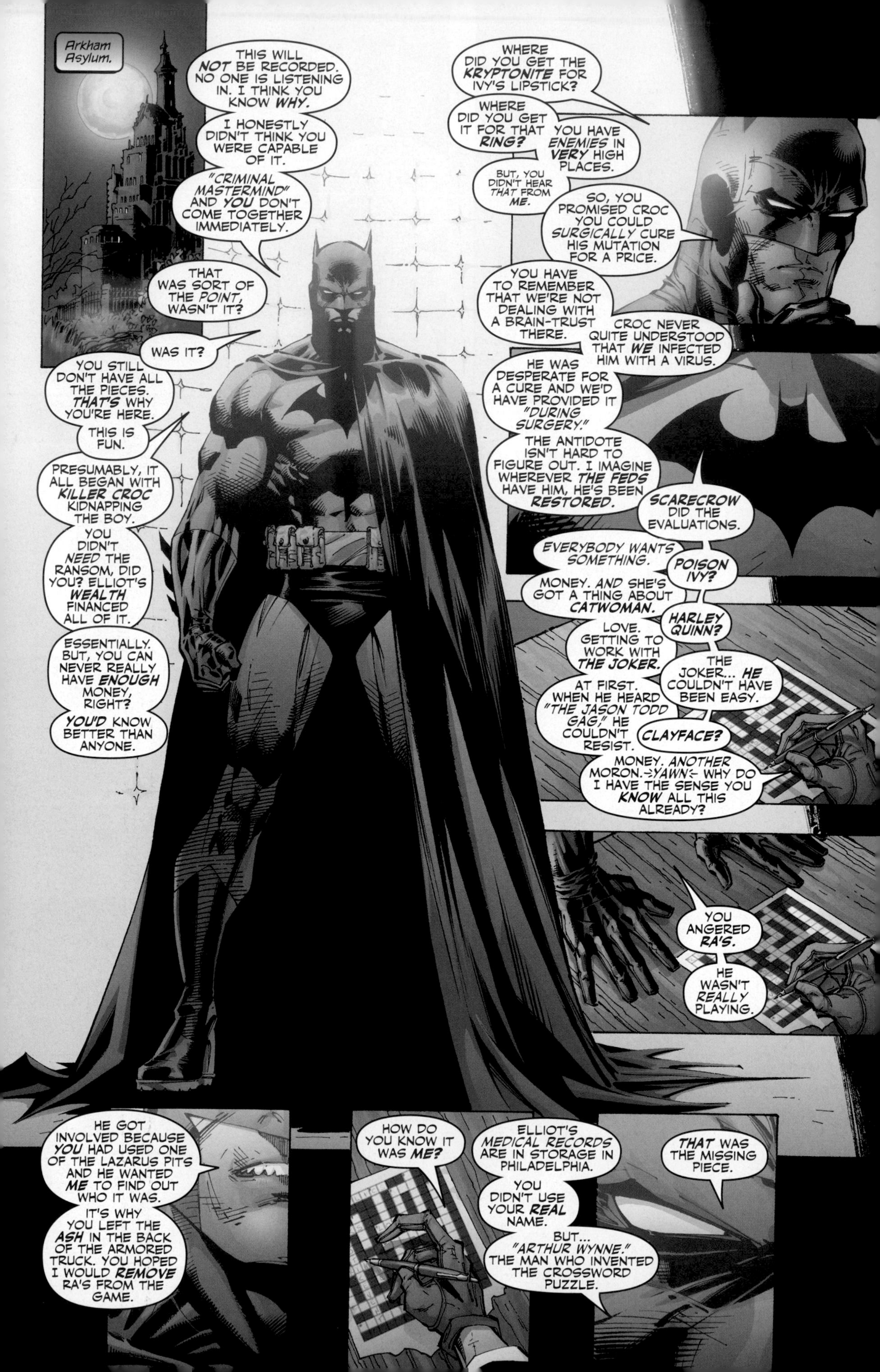
Arkham Asylum.
THIS WILL NOT BE RECORDED. NO ONE IS LISTENING IN. I THINK YOU KNOW WHY.
I HONESTLY DIDN'T THINK YOU WERE CAPABLE OF IT.
"CRIMINAL MASTERMIND" AND YOU DON'T COME TOGETHER IMMEDIATELY.
THAT WAS SORT OF THE POINT, WASN'T IT?
WAS IT?
YOU STILL DON'T HAVE ALL THE PIECES. THAT'S WHY YOU'RE HERE.
THIS IS FUN.
PRESUMABLY, IT ALL BEGAN WITH KILLER CROC KIDNAPPING THE BOY.
YOU DIDN'T NEED THE RANSOM, DID YOU? ELLIOT'S WEALTH FINANCED ALL OF IT.
ESSENTIALLY. BUT, YOU CAN NEVER REALLY HAVE ENOUGH MONEY, RIGHT?
YOU'D KNOW BETTER THAN ANYONE.
WHERE DID YOU GET THE KRYPTONITE FOR IVY'S LIPSTICK?
WHERE DID YOU GET IT FOR THAT RING?
YOU HAVE ENEMIES IN VERY HIGH PLACES.
BUT, YOU DIDN'T HEAR THAT FROM ME.
SO, YOU PROMISED CROC YOU COULD SURGICALLY CURE HIS MUTATION FOR A PRICE.
YOU HAVE TO REMEMBER THAT WE'RE NOT DEALING WITH A BRAIN-TRUST THERE.
CROC NEVER QUITE UNDERSTOOD THAT WE INFECTED HIM WITH A VIRUS.
HE WAS DESPERATE FOR A CURE AND WE'D HAVE PROVIDED IT "DURING SURGERY."
THE ANTIDOTE ISN'T HARD TO FIGURE OUT. I IMAGINE WHEREVER THE FEDS HAVE HIM, HE'S BEEN RESTORED.
SCARECROW DID THE EVALUATIONS.
EVERYBODY WANTS SOMETHING.
POISON IVY?
MONEY. AND SHE'S GOT A THING ABOUT CATWOMAN.
HARLEY QUINN?
LOVE. GETTING TO WORK WITH THE JOKER.
THE JOKER... HE COULDN'T HAVE BEEN EASY.
AT FIRST. WHEN HE HEARD "THE JASON TODD GAG," HE COULDN'T RESIST.
CLAYFACE?
MONEY. ANOTHER MORON. ›YAWN‹ WHY DO I HAVE THE SENSE YOU KNOW ALL THIS ALREADY?
YOU ANGERED RA'S.
HE WASN'T REALLY PLAYING.
HE GOT INVOLVED BECAUSE YOU HAD USED ONE OF THE LAZARUS PITS AND HE WANTED ME TO FIND OUT WHO IT WAS.
IT'S WHY YOU LEFT THE ASH IN THE BACK OF THE ARMORED TRUCK. YOU HOPED I WOULD REMOVE RA'S FROM THE GAME.
HOW DO YOU KNOW IT WAS ME?
ELLIOT'S MEDICAL RECORDS ARE IN STORAGE IN PHILADELPHIA.
YOU DIDN'T USE YOUR REAL NAME.
BUT... "ARTHUR WYNNE." THE MAN WHO INVENTED THE CROSSWORD PUZZLE.
THAT WAS THE MISSING PIECE.

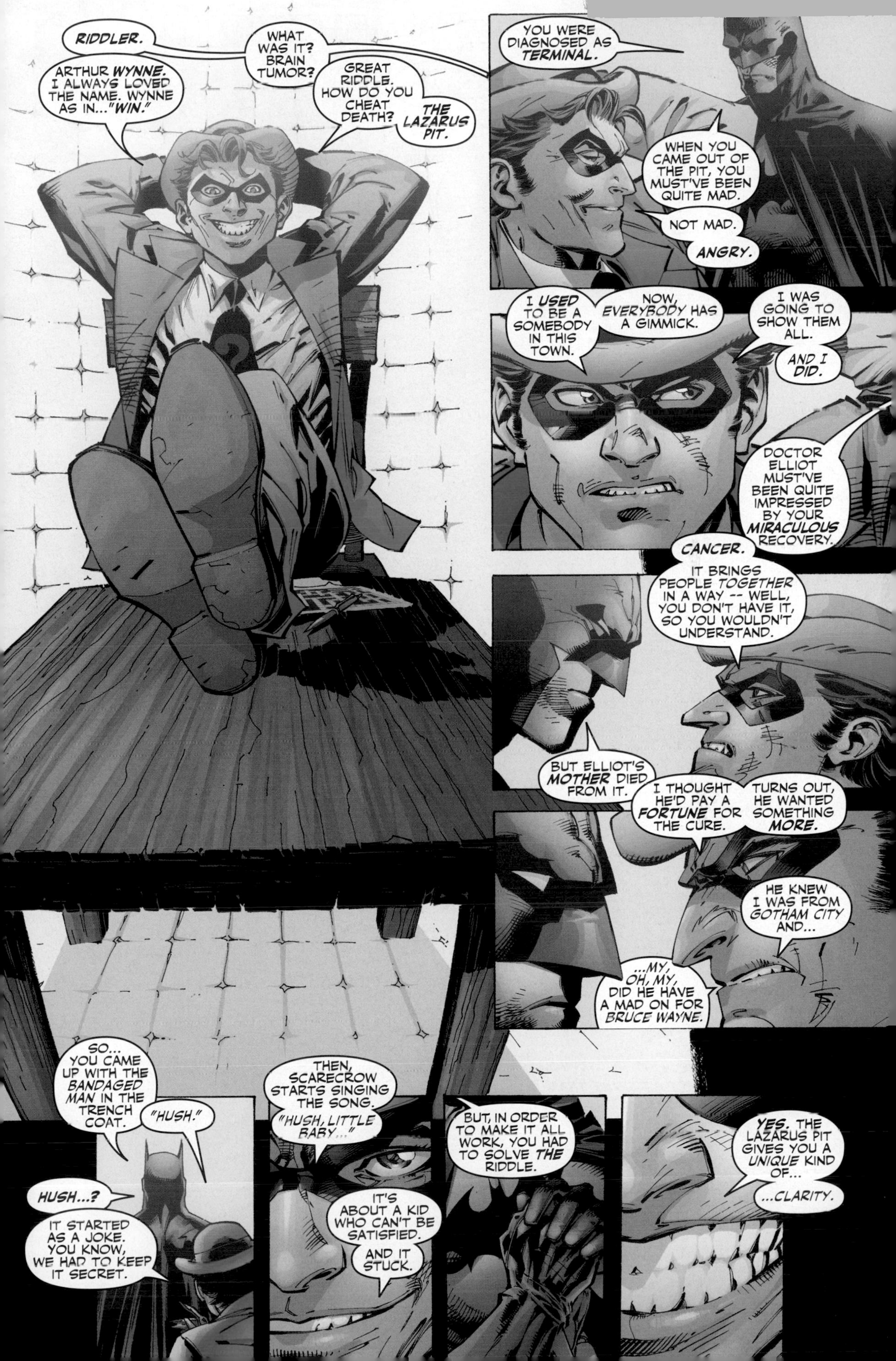
RIDDLER.
ARTHUR WYNNE. I ALWAYS LOVED THE NAME. WYNNE AS IN..."WIN."
WHAT WAS IT? BRAIN TUMOR?
GREAT RIDDLE. HOW DO YOU CHEAT DEATH?
THE LAZARUS PIT.
YOU WERE DIAGNOSED AS TERMINAL.
WHEN YOU CAME OUT OF THE PIT, YOU MUST'VE BEEN QUITE MAD.
NOT MAD.
ANGRY.
I USED TO BE A SOMEBODY IN THIS TOWN.
NOW, EVERYBODY HAS A GIMMICK.
I WAS GOING TO SHOW THEM ALL.
AND I DID.
DOCTOR ELLIOT MUST'VE BEEN QUITE IMPRESSED BY YOUR MIRACULOUS RECOVERY.
CANCER.
IT BRINGS PEOPLE TOGETHER IN A WAY -- WELL, YOU DON'T HAVE IT, SO YOU WOULDN'T UNDERSTAND.
BUT ELLIOT'S MOTHER DIED FROM IT.
I THOUGHT HE'D PAY A FORTUNE FOR THE CURE.
TURNS OUT, HE WANTED SOMETHING MORE.
HE KNEW I WAS FROM GOTHAM CITY AND...
...MY, OH, MY, DID HE HAVE A MAD ON FOR BRUCE WAYNE.
SO... YOU CAME UP WITH THE BANDAGED MAN IN THE TRENCH COAT.
"HUSH."
HUSH...?
IT STARTED AS A JOKE. YOU KNOW, WE HAD TO KEEP IT SECRET.
THEN, SCARECROW STARTS SINGING THE SONG.
"HUSH, LITTLE BABY..."
IT'S ABOUT A KID WHO CAN'T BE SATISFIED.
AND IT STUCK.
BUT, IN ORDER TO MAKE IT ALL WORK, YOU HAD TO SOLVE THE RIDDLE.
YES. THE LAZARUS PIT GIVES YOU A UNIQUE KIND OF...
...CLARITY.

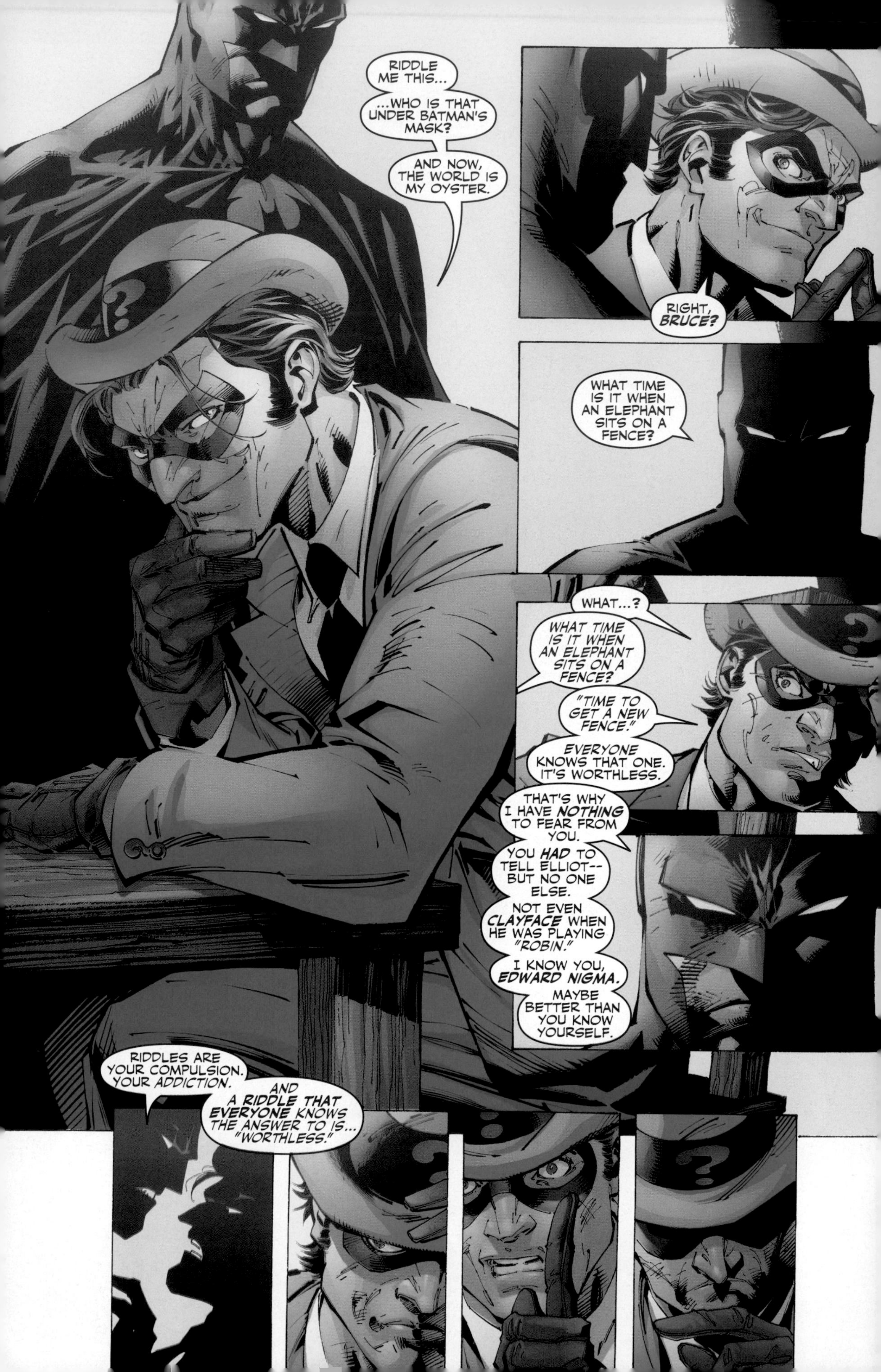
RIDDLE ME THIS...
...WHO IS THAT UNDER BATMAN'S MASK?
AND NOW, THE WORLD IS MY OYSTER.
RIGHT, *BRUCE?*
WHAT TIME IS IT WHEN AN ELEPHANT SITS ON A FENCE?
WHAT...?
*WHAT TIME IS IT WHEN AN ELEPHANT SITS ON A FENCE?*
*"TIME TO GET A NEW FENCE."*
*EVERYONE* KNOWS THAT ONE. IT'S WORTHLESS.
THAT'S WHY I HAVE *NOTHING* TO FEAR FROM YOU.
YOU *HAD* TO TELL ELLIOT-- BUT NO ONE ELSE.
NOT EVEN *CLAYFACE* WHEN HE WAS PLAYING *"ROBIN."*
I KNOW YOU, *EDWARD NIGMA.*
MAYBE BETTER THAN YOU KNOW YOURSELF.
RIDDLES ARE YOUR COMPULSION. YOUR *ADDICTION.*
AND A *RIDDLE THAT EVERYONE* KNOWS THE ANSWER TO IS... *"WORTHLESS."*

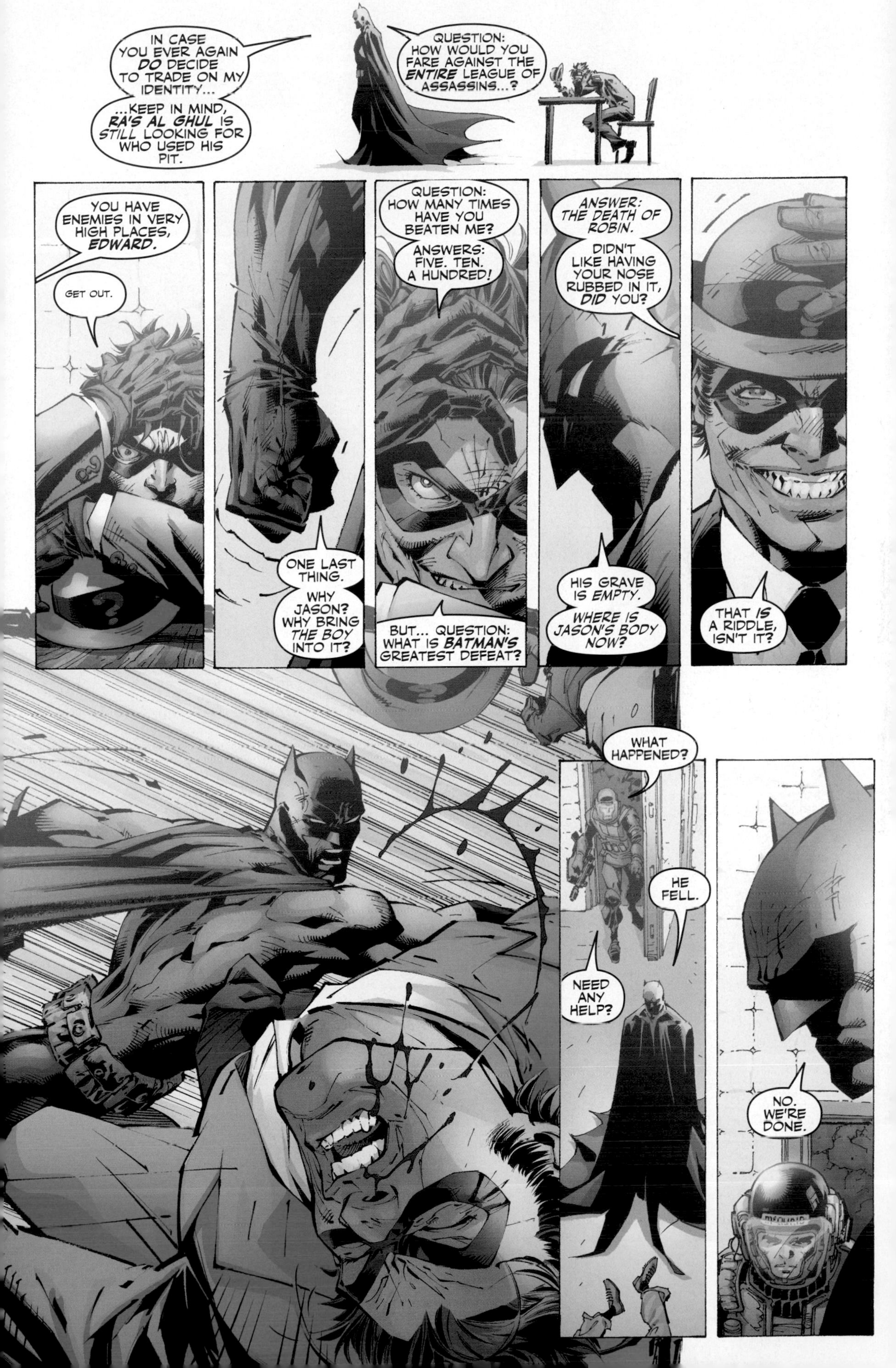

IN CASE YOU EVER AGAIN DO DECIDE TO TRADE ON MY IDENTITY...
...KEEP IN MIND, RA'S AL GHUL IS STILL LOOKING FOR WHO USED HIS PIT.
QUESTION: HOW WOULD YOU FARE AGAINST THE ENTIRE LEAGUE OF ASSASSINS...?
YOU HAVE ENEMIES IN VERY HIGH PLACES, EDWARD.
GET OUT.
ONE LAST THING.
WHY JASON? WHY BRING THE BOY INTO IT?
QUESTION: HOW MANY TIMES HAVE YOU BEATEN ME?
ANSWERS: FIVE. TEN. A HUNDRED!
BUT... QUESTION: WHAT IS BATMAN'S GREATEST DEFEAT?
ANSWER: THE DEATH OF ROBIN.
DIDN'T LIKE HAVING YOUR NOSE RUBBED IN IT, DID YOU?
HIS GRAVE IS EMPTY.
WHERE IS JASON'S BODY NOW?
THAT IS A RIDDLE, ISN'T IT?
WHAT HAPPENED?
HE FELL.
NEED ANY HELP?
NO. WE'RE DONE.

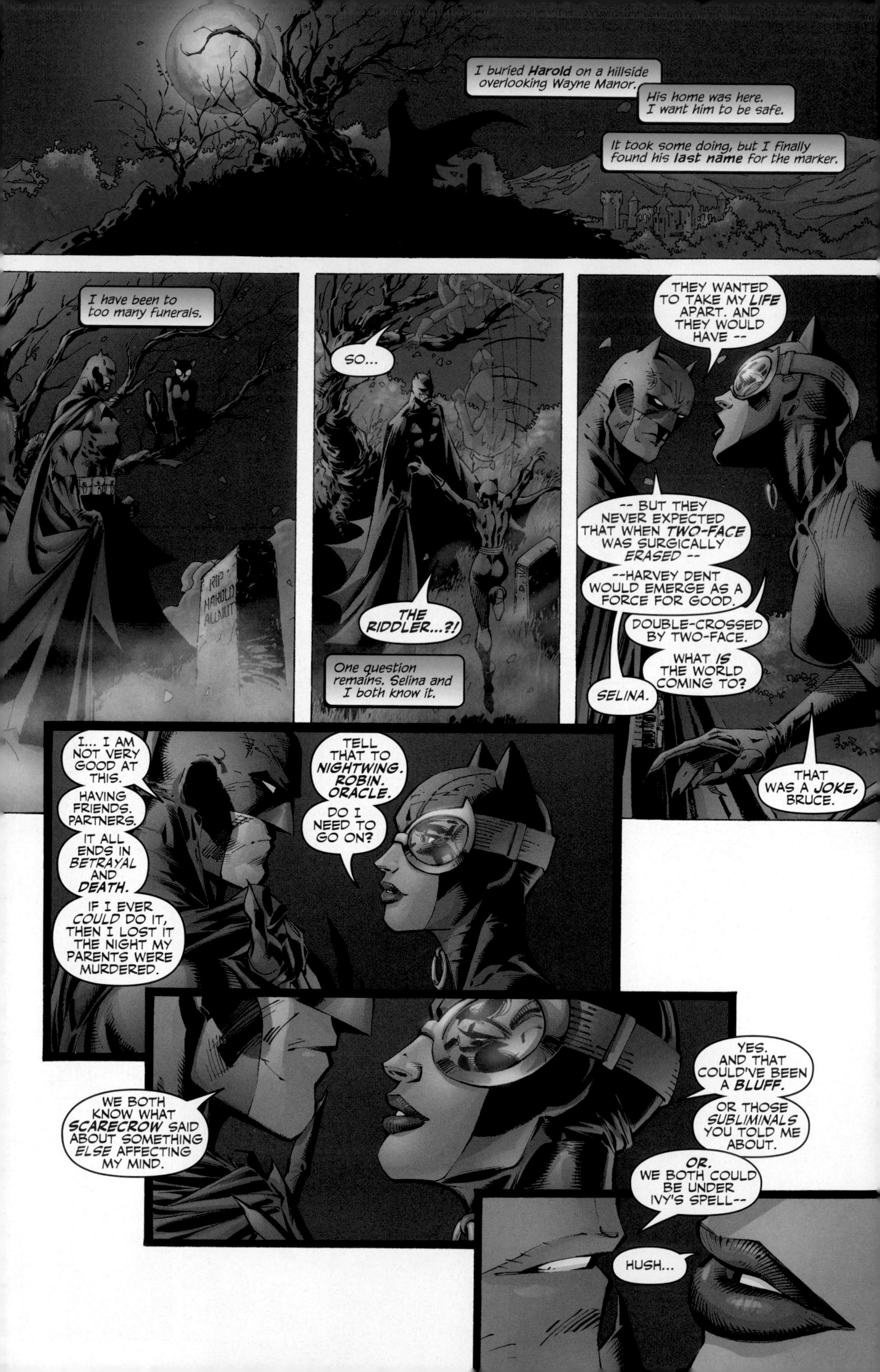
I buried Harold on a hillside overlooking Wayne Manor.
His home was here. I want him to be safe.
It took some doing, but I finally found his last name for the marker.
I have been to too many funerals.
RIP HAROLD ALLNUT
SO...
THE RIDDLER...?!
One question remains. Selina and I both know it.
THEY WANTED TO TAKE MY LIFE APART. AND THEY WOULD HAVE --
-- BUT THEY NEVER EXPECTED THAT WHEN TWO-FACE WAS SURGICALLY ERASED --
--HARVEY DENT WOULD EMERGE AS A FORCE FOR GOOD.
DOUBLE-CROSSED BY TWO-FACE.
WHAT IS THE WORLD COMING TO?
SELINA.
THAT WAS A JOKE, BRUCE.
I... I AM NOT VERY GOOD AT THIS.
HAVING FRIENDS. PARTNERS.
IT ALL ENDS IN BETRAYAL AND DEATH.
IF I EVER COULD DO IT, THEN I LOST IT THE NIGHT MY PARENTS WERE MURDERED.
TELL THAT TO NIGHTWING. ROBIN. ORACLE.
DO I NEED TO GO ON?
WE BOTH KNOW WHAT SCARECROW SAID ABOUT SOMETHING ELSE AFFECTING MY MIND.
YES. AND THAT COULD'VE BEEN A BLUFF.
OR THOSE SUBLIMINALS YOU TOLD ME ABOUT.
OR. WE BOTH COULD BE UNDER IVY'S SPELL--
HUSH...

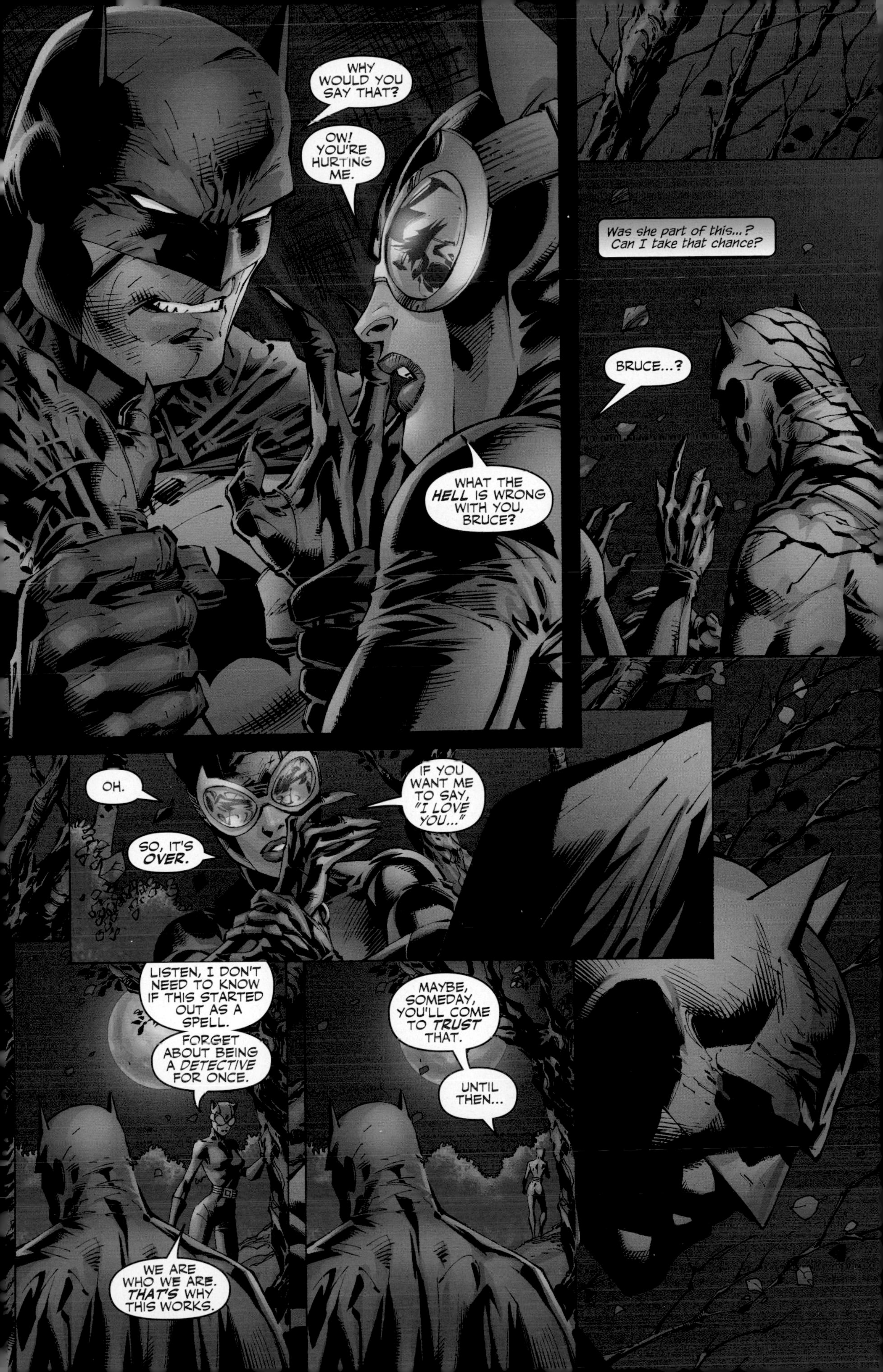
WHY WOULD YOU SAY THAT?
OW! YOU'RE HURTING ME.
WHAT THE *HELL* IS WRONG WITH YOU, BRUCE?
Was she part of this...? Can I take that chance?
BRUCE...?
OH.
SO, IT'S *OVER.*
IF YOU WANT ME TO SAY, *"I LOVE YOU..."*
LISTEN, I DON'T NEED TO KNOW IF THIS STARTED OUT AS A SPELL.
FORGET ABOUT BEING A *DETECTIVE* FOR ONCE.
WE ARE WHO WE ARE. *THAT'S* WHY THIS WORKS.
MAYBE, SOMEDAY, YOU'LL COME TO *TRUST* THAT.
UNTIL THEN...

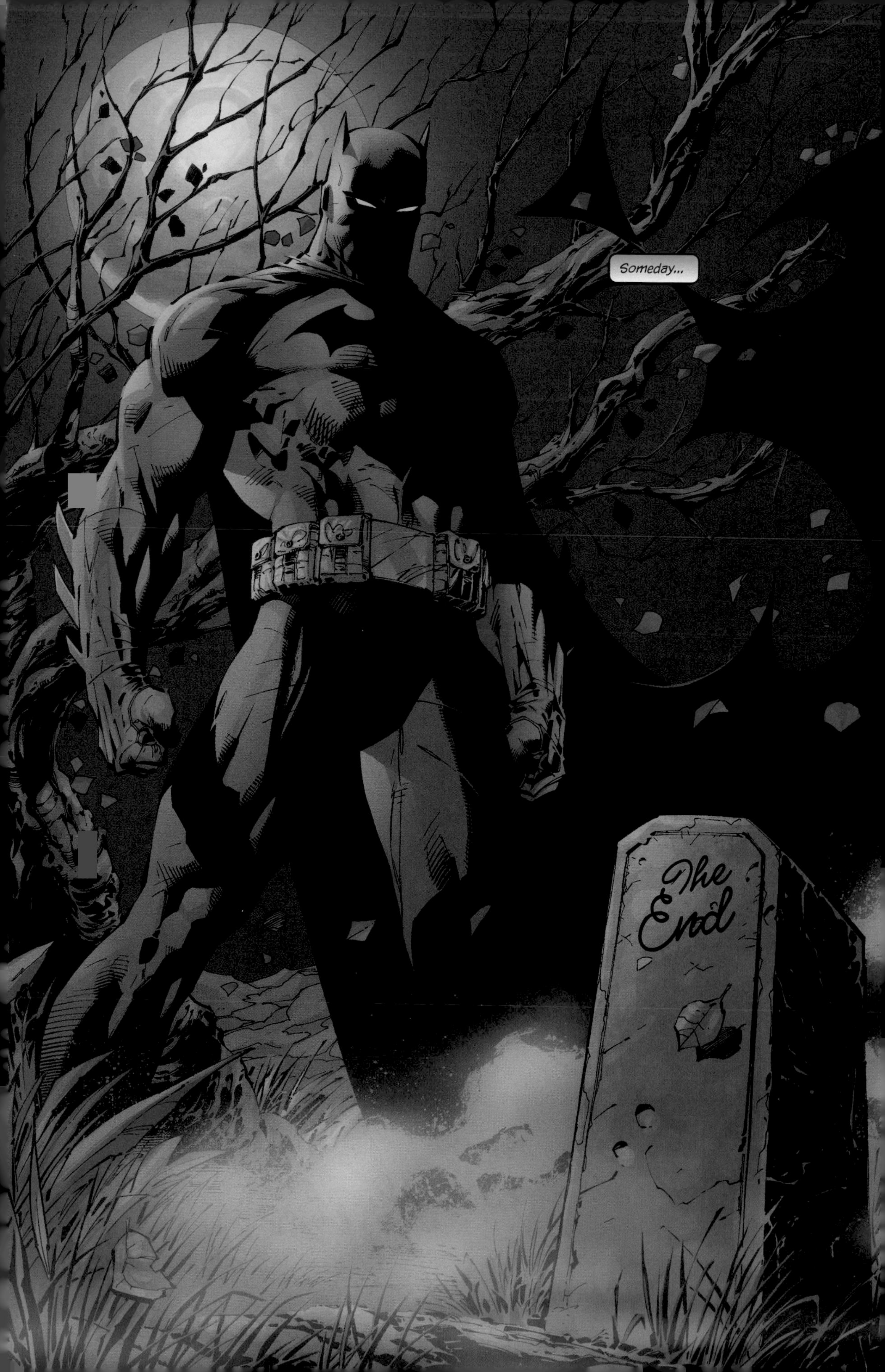
Someday...
The End

BATMAN 608 second printing

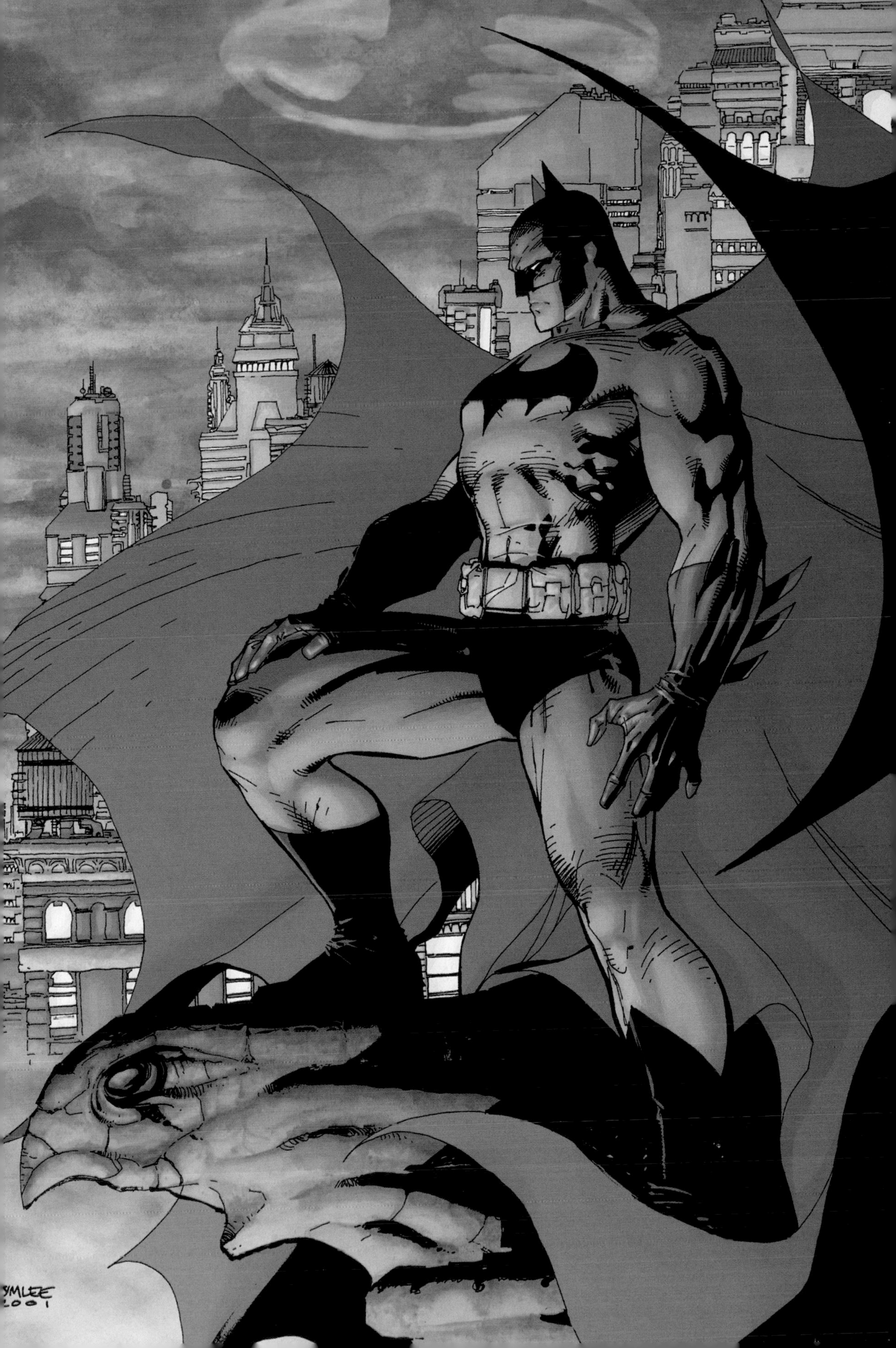

BATMAN 608 special promotional cover

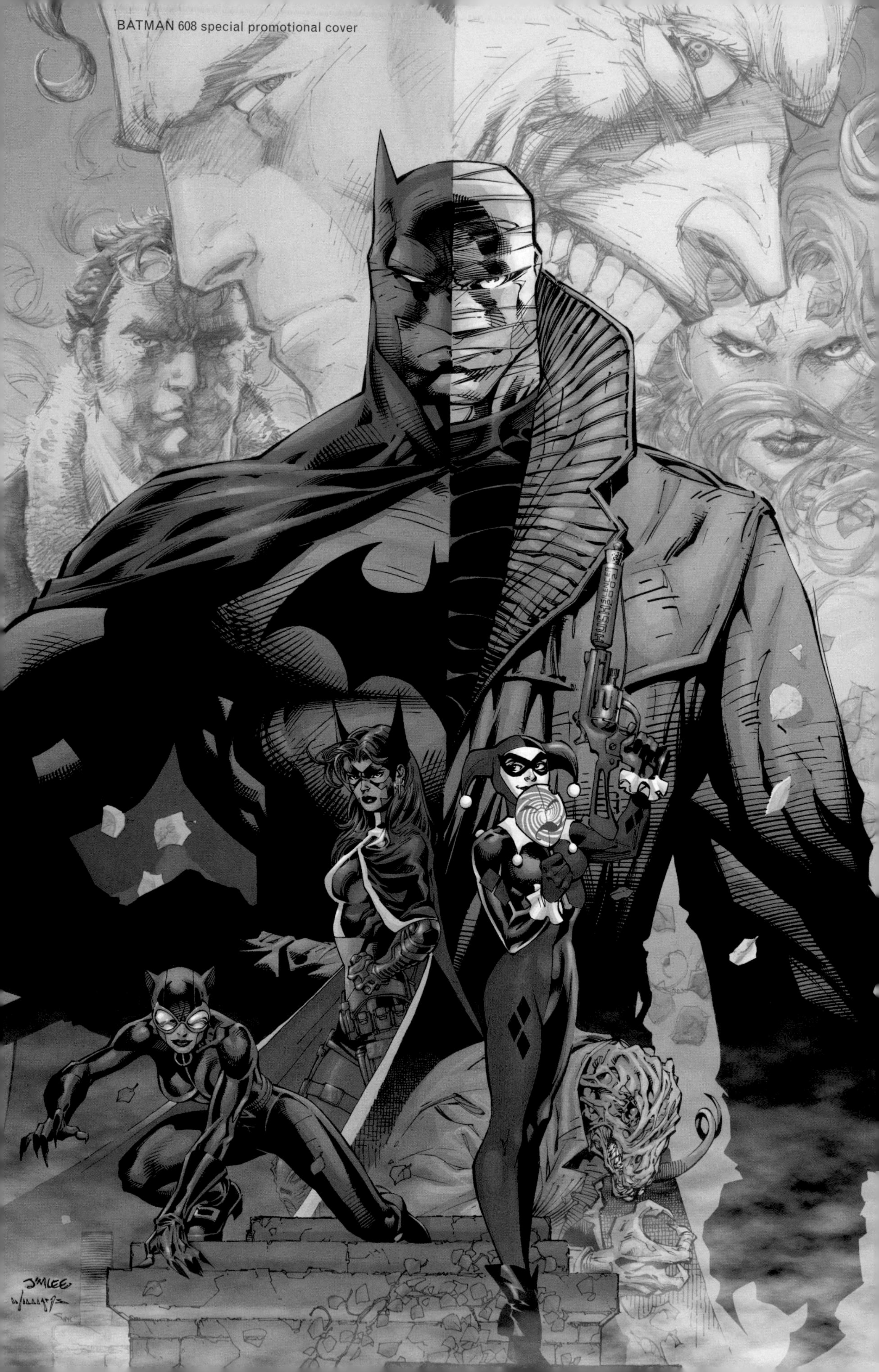

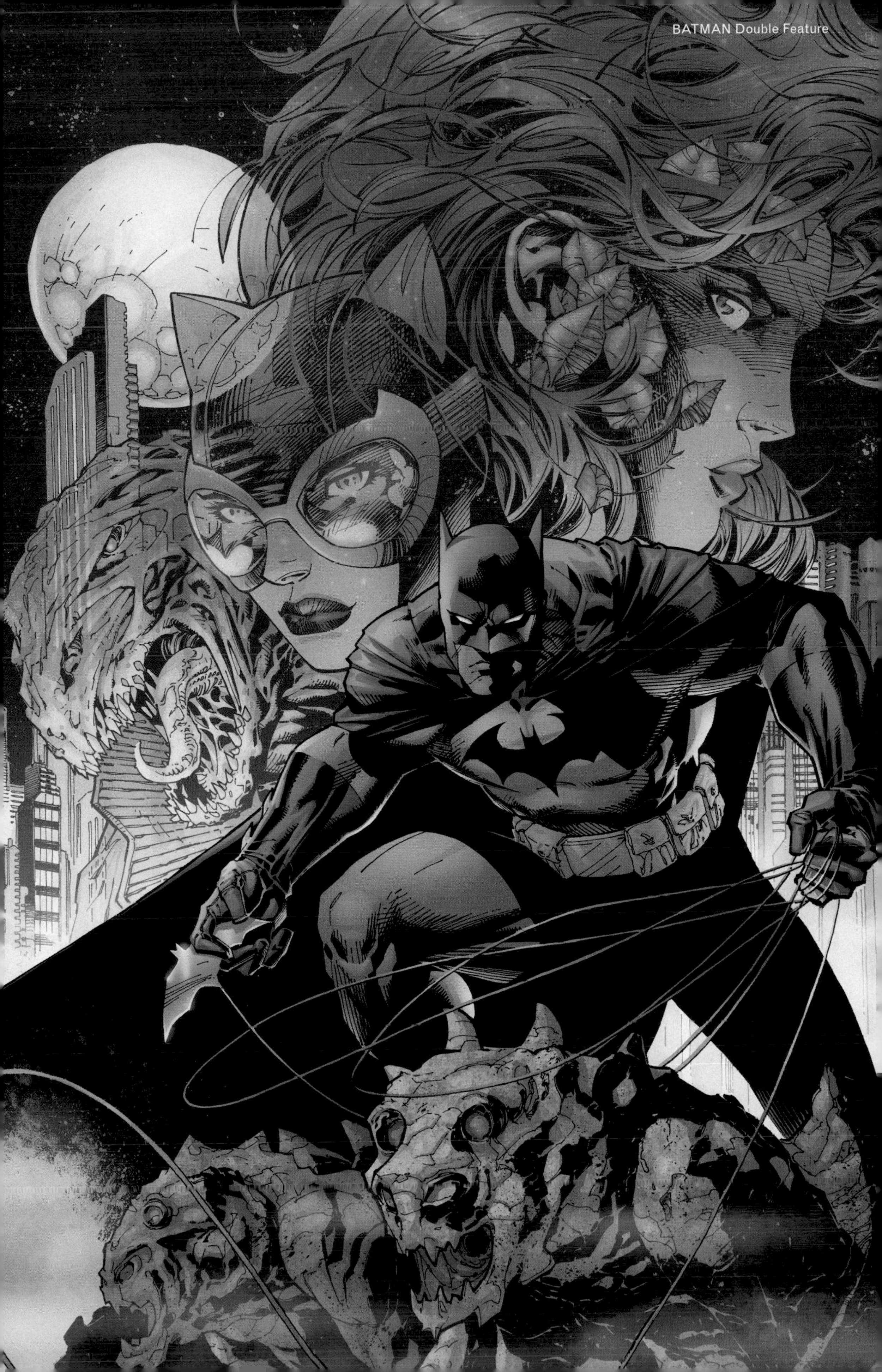

BATMAN 619 Heroes gatefold

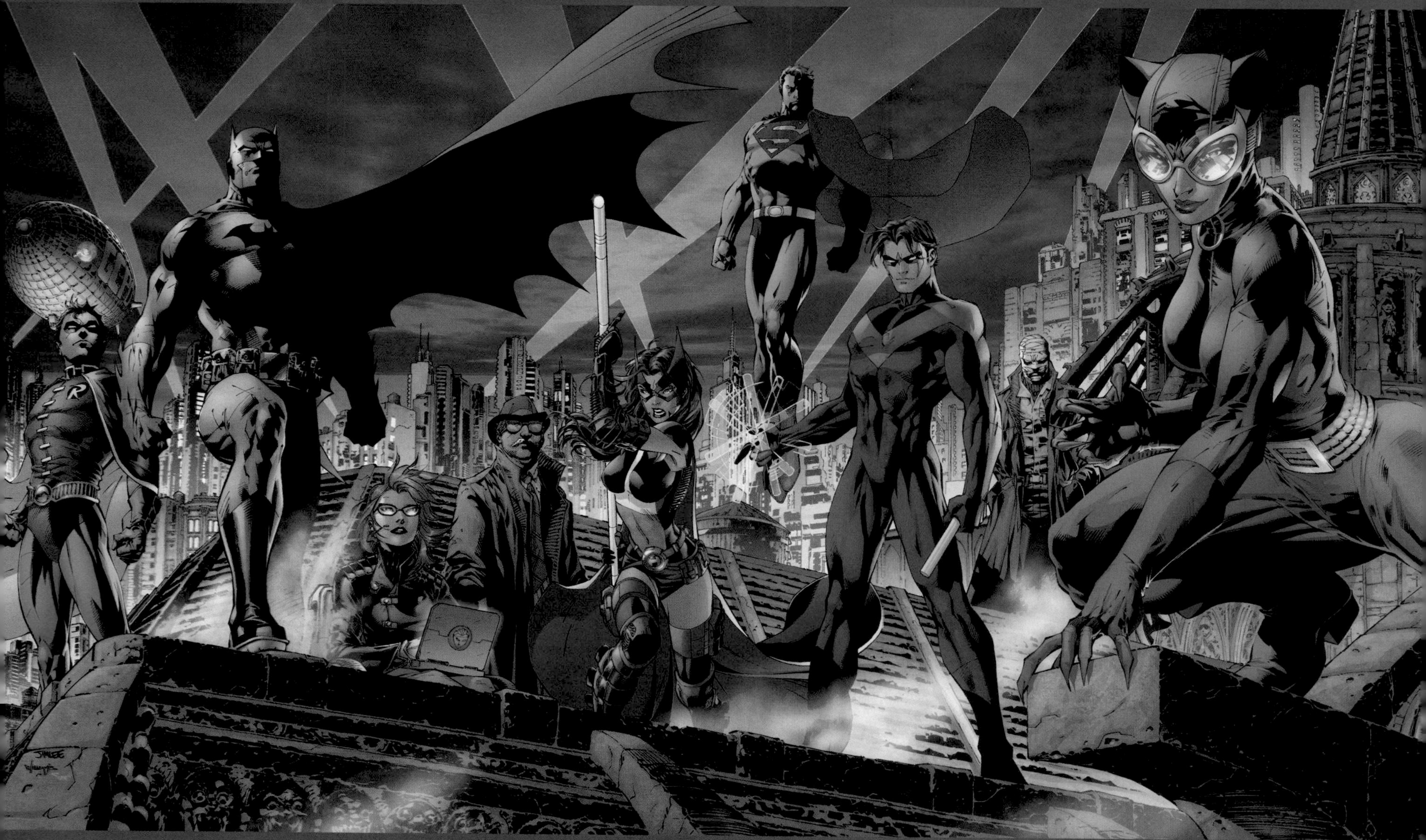

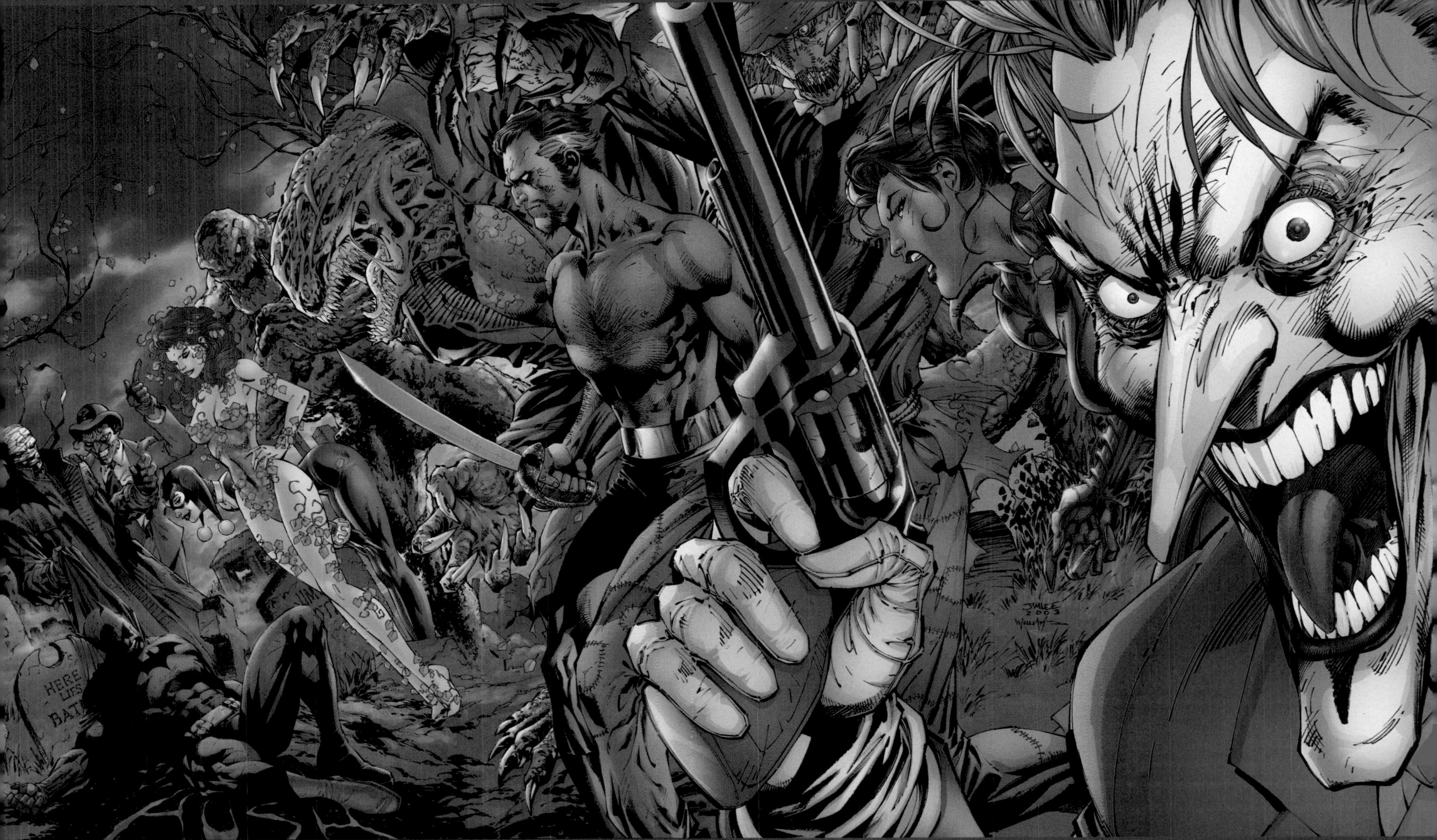
HERE
LIES
BAT

BATMAN 619 Villains gatefold

BATMAN 619 second printing

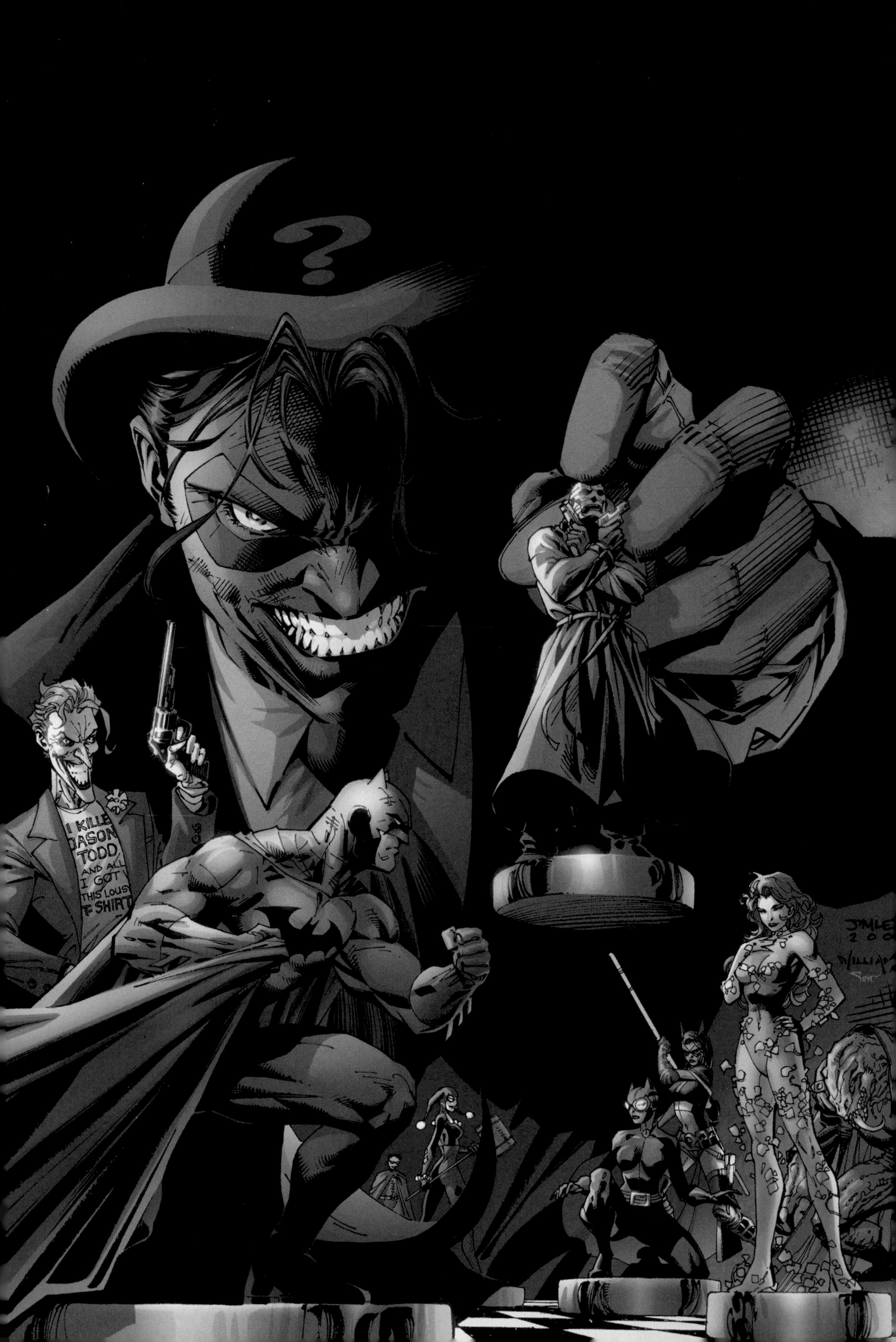
I KILLE
JASON
TODD
AND ALL
I GOT
THIS LOUS
T-SHIRT

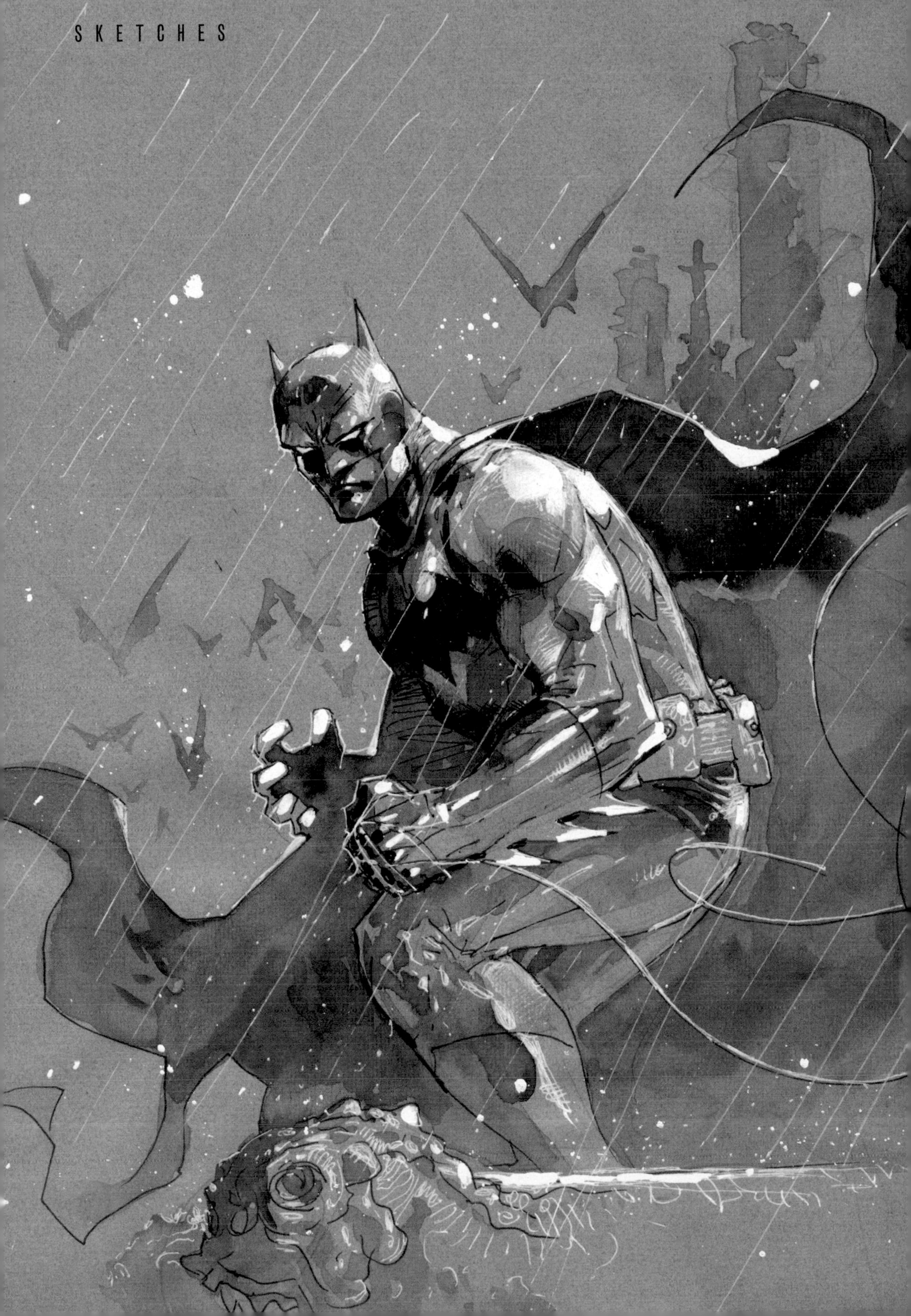

NUMERI

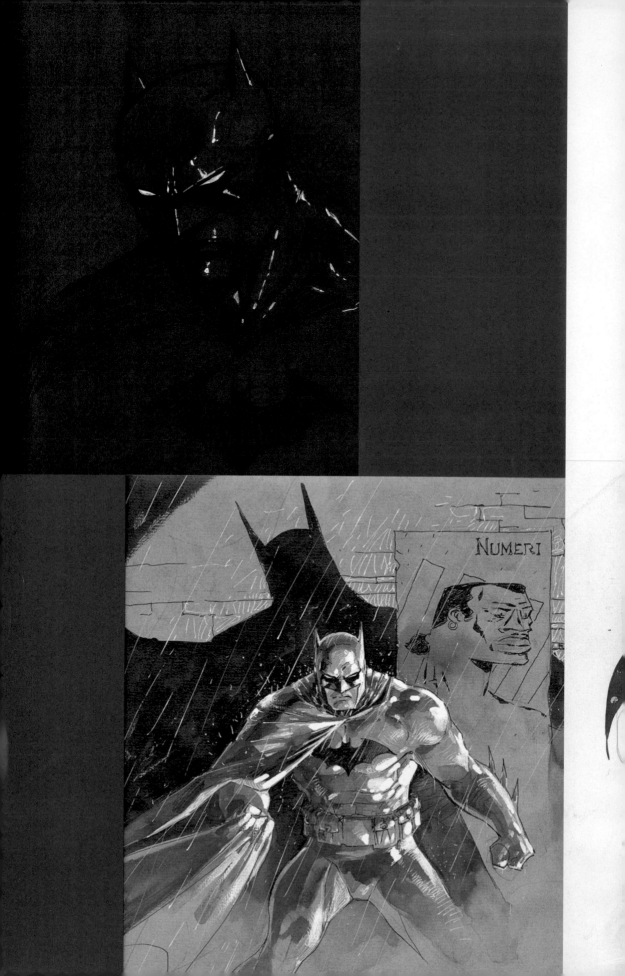

Hush.

It's true most comics are collaborations. All the creators have simple, clean titles under their names — writer, penciller, inker, letterer, colorist. But the truth is that we all are stepping on one another's toes, pitching in our two cents, sometimes — well, most times unsolicited. Sometimes we have to stop cc-ing those people. Sometimes they're right. So we have to fix and change things on the fly. Most times, the changes take all night.

It's also true the last man in the workflow gets stuck holding the bag. And Alex Sinclair, the colorist of the book, was the man most of those times on our run on Batman. And it was 4 a.m. and he was calling me out. In a nice way, of course, but essentially telling me not to call it a day (or night as the case may have been) and to stay up as long as it took to get the color proofs looking the way we wanted them to.

All artists have their own peculiar tastes vis-à-vis coloring, and I know I pressed Alex to make his own palette align more with mine. That took a lot of time and work and, most of all, patience on his part. And supreme dedication. But it went faster and easier as the issues passed by, not just because Alex was learning my tastes, but because I was learning his, and I know this run would look nowhere near as good without his tremendous coloring. Computer coloring has redefined the look of comics, and Alex was instrumental in redefining the look Scott and I were creating on Batman.

**"Very nice. If we make shipping, everyone gets a big, wet sloppy kiss from me…"**

Hush.

Editors have many hats to wear, many responsibilities to fulfill. Chief among them is to motivate the talent and to help focus and shape the creative process which BATMAN editor Bob Schreck did with aplomb. His honesty, wisdom and good humor were much appreciated as he and his assistant, Michael Wright, kept the motor running and the ship on course, making sure we focused on the important stuff and setting us straight when we frittered away time on the nonsensical. They plied us with reference and advised us on continuity so we looked like the experts we wish we were. You couldn't have asked for more.

**"Adam…I don't think I have any new ways of saying thanks to all the fans and retailers for their support. [laughter]"**

Hush.

When it first came out, it hit with a big splash, but then something strange happened: it just kept getting bigger and bigger, taking on a life of its own. Adam Philips of DC's marketing department was calling me every week (or so it seemed) for a new quote for press releases as BATMAN was tearing up the sales charts every issue. And it literally got to the point where I had run out of ways to rephrase my genuine excitement and astonishment at the phenomenon it had grown to be.

All I knew was that this was a special moment so I started to save and record bits and pieces of my memories from working on this book, some of which I have included here. Because I didn't do that before when I worked on the X-Men. Or WILDCATS. Or DIVINE RIGHT. Or any other series I had ever worked on. So that when I flip through these pages again in the future, I will see more than just the words and pictures, I will see and hear the people who made this book come alive.

## "Hush…the show is just starting."

— Jim Lee
San Diego, California
September 2003

Hush.

The name instantly created the air of mystery we wanted for the project, inciting readers all over the world to argue, fight, kick and claw one another on the message boards over the true identity of the bandaged man. It instantly created anticipation for the run, silencing the crowd before the performance began in earnest. It spoke of seriousness, of romance, of broken promises, and of old childhood secrets — themes that resonated throughout the storyline. But as secrets were exposed, new ones were created, further fueling fandom's fire.

It brought Jeph and me together on our very first collaboration. I had long admired his incredible work with artist extraordinaire Tim Sale on THE LONG HALLOWEEN, DARK VICTORY and SUPERMAN FOR ALL SEASONS. I will admit, I was initially worried about how we would work together. My sensibilities are nowhere near Tim's.

While he could create drama, mood and tension in a damn kitchen for God's sake with a confident, terse line, I would struggle. While he could make the rafters of Wayne Manor soar into the darkness, I would struggle. While he could make the black shadows of Batman's world seemingly come alive — I would struggle.

But my fears would be silenced — I was working with a professional; Jeph wrote to *my* strengths. I would joke on panels at conventions that that resulted in a book which needed no sense of storytelling — all sizzle with no steak. Only the humorless naysayers held onto this point of view.

Meanwhile, Jeph was pushing the fans' buttons, one at a time; slowly at first, but then at a manic pace, driving them back in droves to the world of Batman as they saw Batman's world literally turned upside down as he fell from the skies above Gotham, nearly to his death.

Jeph got into Batman's head like few other writers, exposing with deceptive simplicity the depths of the Dark Knight's sorrows, the frustrations of his mission, the love for his friends — unlocking the passions of one of the most stoic characters within comics.

And he could not have done it without the talents of letterer Richard Starkings. Superstarkingsman was only one of many nicknames Jeph coined for Richard, in tribute not only to his lettering skills but for his ability to make Jeph's writing look that much better on the page. Again, not only in appearance, but in tone. Unflinching in his feedback, Richard worked in tandem with Jeph and editor Bob Schreck to make the scripts sing.

**"Don't change it. I always thought it was cool when I was a fan when the art changed and evolved over the course of an artist's run on a book."**

**"Hmm...but it looks odd to me, Scott..."**

Hush.

Scott Williams was pulling Batman artwork from my hand, urging me to reconsider redrawing panels that I thought looked odd. Given the lead time on Batman, we, for the first time in our careers, had the luxury of going back and reconsidering the work we had done months ago. The pages weren't bad per se, but with the passage of time, I could see that the way I was drawing Batman had changed. The look we ended up with was very different from how we started. Batman had become leaner, his nose sharper, the shadows larger, the world darker. I was tempted to redraw some shots.

But Scott was right. Drawing comics is not about hitting the note every time the same way. It's not about making things look mechanical and as if they were processed by a cookie cutter.

*Especially* on Batman.

He would also decide to ink mostly with a brush and use technical pens for the details rather than his traditional, trusty crowquill nib — a first for him over my pencils. Again, those doubts. But Jeph and I were blown away by the results.

*Blown away.*

I always knew Scott was the best. Who knew he would be so versatile as well?

**"Dude."**

**"Let's get it done right. I can stay up longer."**

## "HUSH"

### "...the name of the villain is Hush."

I grinned ear to ear. Keeping projects secret in the world of comics is no mean feat — especially in a world of cell phones, IMs, message boards and online gossip hounds.

Yet writer Jeph Loeb and I had managed — for over a year — to keep our Batman project ultra top secret. Over a year!

But we hadn't come up with a name we were crazy about for the villain. And now, months into the project, Jeph had come through with the perfect one. A name not only for the villain, but also a name which completely captured the secrecy and spirit of the entire project.

Hush.

**"How about a nice miniseries with extra glossy covers..."**

**"Or how about doing a one-shot graphic novel; sure would look nice on a coffee table."**

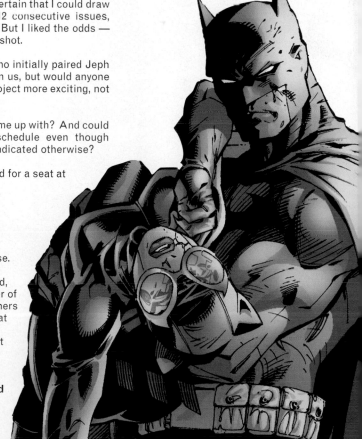

### AFTERWORD BY JIM LEE
# VOICES

Everyone had wanted me to do this run, not as a monthly but as a special project, and although I knew dead certain that I could draw every book and make my deadlines for 12 consecutive issues, virtually no one else seemed to believe it. But I liked the odds — the payoff — if we managed to hit the long shot.

DC editorial art director Mark Chiarello, who initially paired Jeph and me together on this project, believed in us, but would anyone else? The audacity of the idea made the project more exciting, not just to me but to the retailers and the fans.

What kind of story would these creators come up with? And could they meet the demands of a monthly schedule even though common sense and conventional wisdom indicated otherwise?

Stubbornly, we stood our ground and waited for a seat at the Big Boys' table.

We wanted a shot at *Batman*.

The regular *monthly* title.

One of *the* flagship titles of the DC Universe.

There would be no wiggle room. If we failed, we would have self-combusted at the center of a three-ring circus in plain view like few others had before us. But if we *succeeded* (and that would be the only real way of silencing the critics and naysayers)...who knew how *big* it would eventually get.

**"HAHAHA you loser! ! ! I told you that there was no way in hell XXXXXX could really be Hush!"**

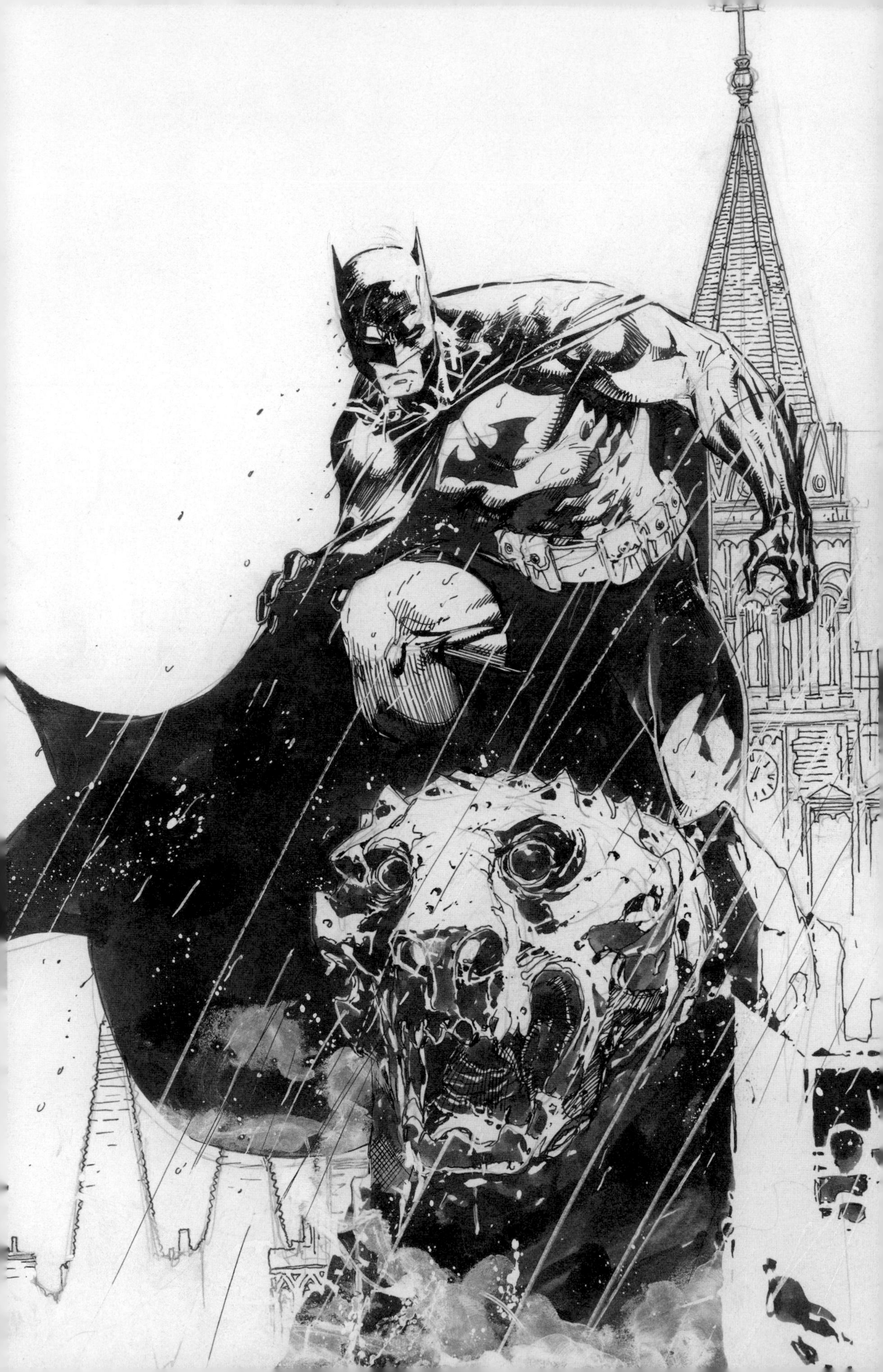

# BIOGRAPHIES

JEPH LOEB is the author of BATMAN: THE LONG HALLOWEEN, BATMAN: DARK VICTORY, SUPERMAN FOR ALL SEASONS, CATWOMAN: WHEN IN ROME, CHALLENGERS OF THE UNKNOWN MUST DIE!, *Spider-Man: Blue, Daredevil: Yellow* and *Hulk: Gray* — all of which are collaborations with artist Tim Sale. He has also written SUPERMAN/BATMAN, SUPERGIRL and THE WITCHING HOUR. A writer/producer living in Los Angeles, his television and movie credits include *Heroes, Lost, Smallville, Teen Wolf* and *Commando.*

JIM LEE was born in Seoul, South Korea in 1964 and made his debut at Marvel Comics in the late '80s. Lee gained the most notice as artist on *Uncanny X-Men.* Today Lee is the creative director of WildStorm Studios (which he founded in 1992) and the penciller for many of DC Comics' best-selling comic book and graphic novels, including ALL STAR BATMAN & ROBIN, THE BOY WONDER and SUPERMAN: FOR TOMORROW, as well as serving as Executive Creative Director for the DC Universe Online game.

SCOTT WILLIAMS is best known for his long-term partnership with artist Jim Lee. Williams was voted Favorite Inker for five years in a row (1990-1994) in the Comics Buyer's Guide Fan Awards. His inking work can be found in BATMAN: WHATEVER HAPPENED TO THE CAPED CRUSADER?, ALL STAR BATMAN & ROBIN, THE BOY WONDER, WILDC.A.T.s and *X-Men.*

ALEX SINCLAIR bought his first comic book — DETECTIVE COMICS #500 — with his brother, Celes, at the local convenience store. He immediately fell in love with comics and Batman. His other work includes FINAL CRISIS, 52: THE COVERS, JUSTICE LEAGUE OF AMERICA and KURT BUSIEK'S ASTRO CITY. He lives in San Diego with his wife Rebecca and four sidekicks Grace, Blythe, Meredith and Harley.

RICHARD STARKINGS is best known as the creator of the Comicraft studio, purveyors of unique design and fine lettering — and a copious catalogue of comic-book fonts — since 1992. He is less well known as the creator and publisher of Hip Flask and his semi-autobiographical cartoon strip, Hedge Backwards.

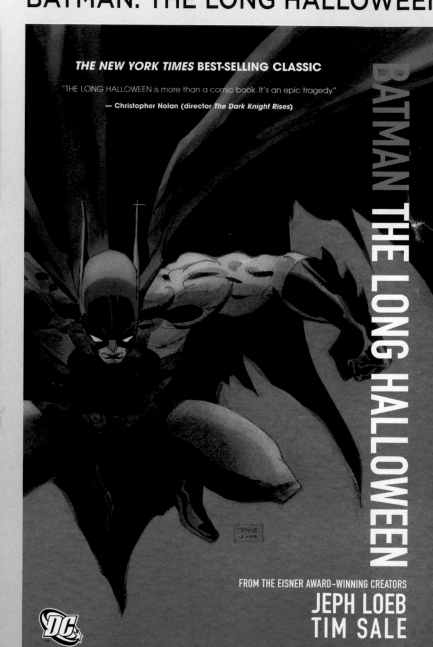